THE AFRICAN METHODIST EPISCOPAL CHURCH

In this book, Dennis C. Dickerson examines the long history of the African Methodist Episcopal (AME) Church and its intersection with major social movements over more than two centuries. Beginning as a religious movement in the late eighteenth century, the AME Church developed as a freedom advocate for blacks in the Atlantic World. Governance of a proud black ecclesia often clashed with its commitment to and resources for fighting slavery, segregation, and colonialism, thus limiting the full realization of the church's emancipationist ethos. Dickerson recounts how this black institution nonetheless weathered the inexorable demands produced by the Civil War, two world wars, the civil rights movement, African decolonization, and women's empowerment, resulting in its global prominence in the contemporary world. His book also integrates the history of African Methodism within the broader historical landscape of American and African American history.

Dennis C. Dickerson is James M. Lawson, Jr. Professor of History at Vanderbilt University. A scholar of American labor history, the American civil rights movement, and African-American religious history, he has received grants and fellowships from the American Academy in Berlin, the National Endowment for the Humanities, and the American Council of Learned Societies, among others. He is the author of *Out of the Crucible: Black Steelworkers in Western Pennsylvania, 1875–1980*, *African American Preachers and Politics: The Careys of Chicago*, and *Militant Mediator: Whitney M. Young, Jr.*, which was awarded the 1999 Distinguished Book from the National Conference of Black Political Scientists.

T0384612

The African Methodist Episcopal Church
A History

DENNIS C. DICKERSON
Vanderbilt University

CAMBRIDGE
UNIVERSITY PRESS

CAMBRIDGE
UNIVERSITY PRESS

University Printing House, Cambridge CB2 8BS, United Kingdom

One Liberty Plaza, 20th Floor, New York, NY 10006, USA

477 Williamstown Road, Port Melbourne, VIC 3207, Australia

314-321, 3rd Floor, Plot 3, Splendor Forum, Jasola District Centre, New Delhi - 110025, India

79 Anson Road, #06-04/06, Singapore 079906

Cambridge University Press is part of the University of Cambridge.

It furthers the University's mission by disseminating knowledge in the pursuit of education, learning and research at the highest international levels of excellence.

www.cambridge.org
Information on this title: www.cambridge.org/9780521153966
DOI: 10.1017/9781139017930

First published 2020
First paperback edition 2020

A catalogue record for this publication is available from the British Library

Library of Congress Cataloging in Publication data
NAMES: Dickerson, Dennis C., 1949– author.
TITLE: The African Methodist Episcopal Church : a history / Dennis Dickerson.
DESCRIPTION: Cambridge, United Kingdom ; New York, NY :
Cambridge University Press, 2020. | Includes bibliographical references and index.
IDENTIFIERS: LCCN 2019021511 | ISBN 9780521191524 (hardback) |
ISBN 9780521153966 (paperback)
SUBJECTS: LCSH: African Methodist Episcopal Church–History.
CLASSIFICATION: LCC BX8443 .D524 2020 | DDC 287/.83–dc23
LC record available at https://lccn.loc.gov/2019021511

ISBN 978-0-521-19152-4 Hardback
ISBN 978-0-521-15396-6 Paperback

To my grandchildren

Melanie Maria Rose Dickerson
Morgan Nicole Kinnard
Yordany William Cordero
Steven Anthony Cousin III
Dennis C. Dickerson III
Samuel Philip Allen Cousin
Yocelin Mariela Cordero
Devyn Kinnard
Tavian Kinnard
Yoandra Cordero
and those Unborn

Contents

Illustrations

Preface

This book is the product of a lifelong exploration of the history of the African Methodist Episcopal Church and a steady decades-long accumulation of primary materials collected from generous donors, including deceased family members, who encouraged my scholarly zeal to write the history of this historic religious body. Additionally, with financial assistance from Vanderbilt University through my endowed chair fund, I purchased a significant part of the large Charles S. Butcher Collection. In this collection belonging to a late AME minister and bibliophile was a copious aggregation of general and annual conference minutes consisting of several booklets from the antebellum and Civil War eras and several from the twentieth century. After the completion of this project, these many materials, some of them rare, will be donated to an appropriate and accessible repository for other scholars and students to explore. Without fellowships or grants, this manuscript was completed in response to a solicitation from the Cambridge University Press to submit a proposal for this present volume.

Several colleagues have read and critiqued individual chapters that immeasurably strengthened the manuscript, as did suggestions from the anonymous reviewers. They include Kenneth M. Hamilton of Southern Methodist University; John H. Wigger of the University of Missouri, Columbia; Reginald F. Hildebrand of the University of North Carolina, Chapel Hill; Bernard E. Powers, Jr. of the College of Charleston; Christina Dickerson Cousin of Quinnipiac University; and Richard J. M. Blackett of Vanderbilt University. Professor Blackett, a fellow member of our institution's Department of History, shared several documents pertaining to African Methodism from his own research in antebellum United States history and Caribbean history.

My wife, Mary A. E. Dickerson, and my children, Nicole Dickerson Kinnard, Valerie Dickerson Cordero, Christiana Dickerson Cousin, and Dennis C. Dickerson, Jr., have been ongoing reservoirs of support and endorsement. My grandchildren, to whom this volume is dedicated, are heirs to the liberationist tradition, however imperfectly pursued, outlined in this book. Whatever inadequacies that remain in narrating this history belong only to me.

Introduction

In 1903 W. E. B. Du Bois, hardly a denominational partisan, described "the great African Methodist Church" as "the greatest Negro organization in the world." Only the National Baptist Convention, recently organized in 1896, exceeded the half million membership that the African Methodist Episcopalians claimed. But the Baptists, an aggregation of autonomous state conventions and local congregations, lacked the hierarchal structure of this black Methodist body. The bishops, presiding elders, pastors, and many other officials of the African Methodist Episcopal (AME) Church forged a cohesive infrastructure that proved to doubtful whites that African Americans were fully capable of effective self-governance. In addition to Du Bois' praise for the institutional achievements of the AME Church, he was equally impressed with its longevity. Already a century old at the time of Du Bois' comments, African Methodism had become a venerable religious body with bishops who were "among the most powerful Negro rulers in the world." In 2004, Gayraud S. Wilmore, a Presbyterian and an African American religious intellectual, confirmed Du Bois' descriptions of the AME Church and called it "America's premier ... predominantly black denomination."[1]

Just as African Methodism drew Du Bois' and Wilmore's admiration, other scholars discovered crucial liberation themes in the AME narrative which explained, defined, and reflected the discourse and strategies that

---

[1] W. E. B. Du Bois, *The Souls of Black Folk* (New York, New American Library, 1903, 1969), 85, 215, 217; Gayraud S. Wilmore, "[A Review of] Dennis C. Dickerson, *A Liberated Past: Explorations in AME Church History* (Nashville, TN, AME Sunday School Union, 2003), in the *AME Church Review*, Vol. 119, No. 396, October–December 2004, 114.

Figure 0.1 Oil painting of Richard Allen by V. Yvonne Studevan, great-great-great-great-granddaughter of Richard Allen. The painting, titled *Under His Own Vine and Fig Tree*, was painted in 2016 for the Mother Bethel AME Church, Philadelphia, PA (Used with permission from the artist)

African Americans pursued to attain their freedom. Horace Mann Bond, for example, credited the Church with making "no compromise with the essential idea of human liberty" and for inspiring President Abraham Lincoln to insert this ideal into the Emancipation Proclamation. Eddie S. Glaude showed how the Exodus theme shaped black political discourse and viewed AME founder Richard Allen's exit from Philadelphia's St. George Church in 1787 as a reenactment of Moses and his followers' epic departure from slavery in Egypt. Allen's act defied the racism of Wesleyan whites and led to the rise of the AME Church and black congregations that either were independent or affiliated with white ecclesiastical bodies. Just as Moses led ancient Hebrews to their "promised land" in Canaan, the St. George incident was replicated in other episodes in the African American experience, and became a metaphor for ongoing efforts to find safe havens for the enslaved and oppressed.[2]

---

[2] Horace Mann Bond, "Richard Allen: His Contribution to the Sense of Human Liberty and to the Emancipation Proclamation," *AME Church Review*, Vol. 119, No. 389, January–March 2003, 101; Eddie S. Glaude, *Exodus: Religion, Race, and Nation in Early Nineteenth-Century Black America* (Chicago, University of Chicago Press, 2000), 58.

For denominational adherents the perspectives of Du Bois, Bond, and Glaude echoed their own view that African Methodism embodied an emancipatory ethos that blacks throughout the diaspora embraced and emulated. George A. Singleton, a prolific AME scholar, observed that "the very idea of former slaves resenting social injustice to the extent that they break away with the old organization is startling." In Allen's "philosophy," he declared, "there is no room for color discrimination or segregation," and that explained their separation from white Methodists. The AME founder, Singleton noted, rose "above caste and proscription" and sought liberation for the black population. Charles H. Wesley, an AME historian, added that "Richard Allen regarded the Negro people as an oppressed minority who needed an aggressive leadership to achieve its emancipation." The AME Church, Wesley declared, was Allen's vehicle to realize this objective. Hence, as the denomination grew and the organization was strengthened, the march toward black liberation gained momentum. When planning expansion in Maryland, a slave state, Allen hoped "that the example of free Negroes who had their own preachers and churches would have the effect of keeping slaves dissatisfied with their condition." That was precisely the point that Allen aimed to articulate. He clearly envisaged African Methodism as a part of a freedom movement to liberate slaves and secure black freedom throughout the Atlantic World.[3]

Just as the liberation of black Atlantic defined the mission and ministry of African Methodism, its anchoring in Wesleyan theology also reinforced its emancipationist ethos. As a freedom church, AMEs developed as a different denomination from what whites in the Methodist Episcopal (ME) Church established at the 1784 "Christmas" Conference. Far more than their Caucasian counterparts, African Methodists adhered to John Wesley's unyielding opposition to slavery and found within his "practical theology" a moral warrant to challenge sinful societal structures that sustained and perpetuated racial oppression. AMEs understood that personal renewal or scriptural holiness experienced through the salvific process of sanctification and perfectionism extended into and required replication into all of creation. Hence, saved and sanctified Methodists should practice social holiness and serve as a leaven to perfect society away from slavery and other forms of human subjugation. Commitments to these theological tenets spurred Richard Allen, Daniel Coker, and other AME founders, during the lifetime of John

---

[3] George A. Singleton, *The Romance of African Methodism: A Study of the African Methodist Episcopal Church* (Boston, MA, Exposition Press, 1952), 18; Charles H. Wesley, *Richard Allen: Apostle of Freedom*, (Washington DC, Associated Publishers, Inc., 1935), 7; 180.

Wesley, to develop an alternative version of American-based Methodism that was truer to the founder's intentions than what Wesleyan whites envisaged.[4]

The origins of the AME Church lay in the Atlantic World context in which diverse African peoples populated the ministry and membership of this emerging Wesleyan body. African Methodism, developing in Philadelphia out of the Free African Society in 1787, through Bethel Church in 1794, and as a denominational body in 1816, exemplified black self-determination, which shaped its identity and praxis as a freedom church. The denomination pursued liberationist activities on both sides of the Atlantic for marginalized peoples through church expansion into racially hostile settings and in strong opposition to slavery, segregation, and colonialism. This emancipationist ethos, however, matured through succeeding centuries in dynamic tension with the necessities and requirements of institutionalization. Though formal structures strengthened AME capacities to protect and protest on behalf of its black diaspora constituency, these same systems and their insatiable but justifiable appetite for institutional growth and preservation rivaled, and at times undermined, the church's ingrained insurgent impulses.

Daniel A. Payne (1811–1893), an early bishop, viewed these competing tendencies as complementary facets of his denomination's emancipationist ethos. At the same time, he thought that the fight against oppression, while dangerous, drew far more applause than founding churches and schools and expanding them into unfriendly territories. He fervently believed that his institutional activities fulfilled liberationist objectives that would sustain African Americans in their hard won freedoms. Carol V. R. George, in her assessment of antebellum black clergy, who selected institution-building over abolitionist activity, acknowledged the tensions between these two vocational paths and concluded that both choices involved emancipationist objectives.[5]

Earlier in his ministry, however, Payne faced the choice of building a denominational aegis for blacks or joining the abolitionist movement to achieve their release from slavery. Lewis Tappan and other colleagues in the American and Foreign Anti-slavery Society, after hearing Payne preach in

[4] See Dennis C. Dickerson, *African Methodism and Its Wesleyan Heritage: Reflections on AME Church History*, (Nashville, TN, AME Sunday School Union, 2009), 40–42.

[5] Daniel A. Payne, *Recollections of Seventy Years* (New York, Arno Press and the *New York Times*, 1888, 1969), 67; Carol V. R. George, "Widening the Circle: The Black Church and the Abolitionist Crusade," in Timothy E. Fulop and Albert Raboteau (eds.), *African American Religion: Interpretive Essays in History and Culture* (New York, Routledge, 1996), 157–173.

1837, asked him to become a full-time lecturer at a generous annual salary of $300. "Here was an inducement," Payne said, to "an inviting field, yet [one] as laborious and dangerous as it was flattering to the pride and ambition of a young man," like himself. He added that "heroism and consequent fame offered their laurels to any young man of talent and intelligence who might be willing to become the fearless and successful opponent of American slavery and the eloquent defender of liberty and human rights." After a few years as a Presbyterian pastor, Payne transferred to the AME Church in 1841, was elected historiographer in 1848, and was consecrated as a bishop in 1852. Already a crusader for an educated ministry, the impecunious bishop purchased Wilberforce University in 1863, on a pledge of $10,000, and then launched the mission to newly freed slaves in the former Confederacy in 1865. The development of African Methodism and its infrastructure, rather than abolitionist and civil rights activism, claimed the entirety of Payne's energies. Though each endeavor was aimed at black liberation, Payne believed that his AME activities were foundational to other freedom initiatives in education, moral reform, and equal rights. African Methodism was itself a bulwark against the degradation of blacks. Therefore, he declared that "when the institution of Slavery was striking its root deep into the American State and the spirit of caste building its nest in the bosom of the American Church, the origin of the African ME Church was necessitated."[6]

Payne offered an apologia for his vocational decision by comparing himself to his contemporary, Frederick Douglass (1818–1895), the celebrated abolitionist and black equal rights champion. Douglass, who had been affiliated with Baltimore's Bethel AME Church, escaped from slavery in 1838 and became an AME Zion exhorter in New Bedford, Massachusetts. Like Payne, white abolitionists heard him speak and immediately drafted the eloquent ex-slave into organized abolitionism. Payne believed, however, that he and Douglass were divinely assigned to their respective roles in the black freedom struggle. "Frederick Douglass," he declared, "was fitted for his specialty; Daniel Alexander Payne for his. Frederick Douglass could not do the work that was assigned to Daniel Alexander Payne, nor Daniel Alexander Payne the work assigned to Frederick Douglass." Du Bois agreed that Douglass and Payne, though different, both embodied a liberationist

---

[6] Ibid., 67–68; Dennis C. Dickerson, *Religion, Race, and Region: Research Notes on AME Church History* (Nashville, TN, AME Sunday School Union, 1995), 35–48; Daniel A. Payne, "The African M.E. Church in Its Relations to the Freedmen," *Bishop Payne's Address before the College Aid Society* (Xenia, OH, Torchlight Company, 1868), 3–4 (copy in Bridwell Library, Perkins School of Theology, Southern Methodist University, Dallas, Texas).

persona. Douglass, Du Bois said, was "the greatest of American Negro leaders," but Payne was "less conspicuous but of greater social significance."[7]

Henry M. Turner (1834–1915), himself a leading black spokesman, Reconstruction politician, and AME bishop, recognized the dual spheres in which Payne and Douglass operated. When Douglass visited the 1884 General Conference in Baltimore, Turner declared "that as Frederick Douglass was the greatest colored statesman in the world, and as Bishop Payne is the greatest colored theologian, he would ask Bishop Payne" to present Douglass to the AME audience. Payne "in a very able and graceful manner introduced Mr. Douglass as the great statesman and advocate of freedom." Douglass, in turn, acknowledged the influence and significance of the church. "Great is the press [and] great is the ballot," he declared, "but still greater is the pulpit." This nod to Payne validated the bishop's institutional labors as integral to African American advancement as much as his own involvements in politics and protest. Payne and Douglass, in different but complementary arenas, authenticated each other as frontline leaders in the black freedom struggle.[8]

Payne envisaged the expansion of African Methodism as an affront to slavery and as a blow for freedom. Hence, those who undertook institutional tasks were obliged to relate them to emancipationist objectives. During Reconstruction several AME preachers did just that and became clergy/politicians. In this regard, Richard H. Cain (1825–1887) and others like him exposed Payne to both the lofty goals and the unpleasant practices of politics. On one hand, the bishop believed that "when a Christian approaches the poll he is morally bound to cast his vote for no one, but an open and fearless advocate of liberty, justice and all righteousness." Therefore, "in all the reconstructed [southern] States, our Church is proportionately represented" by AME ministers in various legislatures and other public offices. For these reasons Payne endorsed their efforts to safeguard black civil rights and implement the freedom ethos of African Methodism. But Payne, on the other hand, criticized Cain and some others for bringing secular political methods into AME elections. He said these activities compromised their "usefulness" and integrity. Payne was loath to admit that Cain and other clergy/politicians like him legitimately embodied the denomination's liberationist legacy even as they practiced the sometimes unsavory methods

---

[7] Payne, *Recollections*, 68; Du Bois, *The Souls of Black Folk*, 86.
[8] *Journal of the 18th Session and 17th Quadrennial Session of the General Conference of the African Methodist Episcopal Church in the World* held in Bethel Church, Baltimore, MD, May 5–26, 1884 (Philadelphia, Rev. James C. Embry, General Business Manager, 1884), 59–60.

of politics. Historian Reginald F. Hildebrand has described Cain as a proponent of the "gospel of freedom."[9] He built Emanuel AME Church in Charleston, South Carolina, into a congregation of 3,000 and parlayed his pastoral popularity into votes for public office. As a local official and later as a member of the US House of Representatives, Cain believed that his congregation and community were well served through his dual roles in the pulpit and in the public square. Payne, though recognizing the value of Cain's public role, retreated from his earlier approval and disparaged him as a mere political operative. Despite this intended slur, Cain, who also became a bishop, included himself in the same AME liberationist tradition that Payne extolled.[10]

Hence, we discover that the crucial issue facing AMEs, including Allen, Payne, Cain, and their posterity, was how the liberationist rhetoric and praxis of the denomination met the inexorable and multiple challenges of history: the abolitionist movement, the Civil War, Reconstruction, industrialization, urbanization, gender equity, colonialism, globalization, and other transformative events and phenomena. Despite a tightly organized structure, a disciplined polity, and a prominent institutional profile, the AME Church was neither uniformly influential nor determinative on many challenges that confronted the communicants and communities it served. Additionally, members of the AME Church, notwithstanding an ironclad commitment to its mission for freedom, constantly had to rethink and rearticulate their Wesleyan theology and reassess their grounding in African and African-American folk religion. Each contained theological tenets and liberationist principles, which required a vigorous social witness and incubated cultural idioms that affirmed the humanity of blacks. African Methodists blended these theological traditions and drew from them resources to critique and resist the powerful social, economic, and political forces that had enslaved and subordinated them.

Serious successors to Richard Allen, who explicitly linked their activism to the AME founder, especially in the twentieth century, included A. Philip Randolph, the pioneer labor leader and advocate of nonviolent grassroots

---

[9] Reginald F. Hildebrand, "Richard Harvey Cain, African Methodism, & the Gospel of Freedom," AME Church Review, Vol. 117, No. 381, January–March 2001, 42-44, and Reginald F. Hildebrand, "The Times Were Strange and Stirring," Methodist Preachers and the Crisis of Emancipation (Durham, Duke University Press, 1995), 33, 120.

[10] Daniel A. Payne, "The African M. E. Church in Its Relations to the Freedmen," Bishop Payne's Address, 5-6; cited in Dickerson, Religion, Race and Region, 78; Reginald F. Hildebrand, "Richard Harvey Cain, African Methodism, & the Gospel of Freedom," 42-44.

mobilization, Rosa Parks, the progenitor of the Montgomery bus boycott, and J. A. De Laine, the sponsor of a foundational case in South Carolina that led to the Supreme Court's landmark public school desegregation decision in 1954. These individuals, both clergy and lay, emulated Allen's emancipation-ist efforts even as denominational leaders, more concerned with institutional affairs, focused their support of liberationist objectives mainly through celebratory and hagiographical rhetoric. Though institutional development and preservation, themselves acts of black self-determination, increasingly preoccupied the AME hierarchy over two centuries, Allenite activism attracted the commitment of other rank and file ministers and members. Embedded within these phenomena were tensions between those who emphasized organizational governance and those who argued for a greater focus on social insurgency (often at the expense of governance). Hence Randolph, Parks, and De Laine, more than their denominational superiors, became energetic and authentic carriers of their church's emancipationist ethos.

Sustaining the balance between denominational involvement and liber-ationist activities existed in AME institutional life and within the hearts and minds of individuals. There were many ministers and members who embodied these "warring selves." And the battleground on which these tensions were addressed and resolved lay in the realm of lived religion. Hymnody, especially in the familiar lyrics of Wesleyan compositions and black spirituals, showed the direct link between the pursuit of spiritual and temporal freedom. Did the search for salvation culminate in personal piety and perfectionism, or did it also extend to "practical divinity" and the pursuit of "the new creation" embedded within Wesleyan theology? How did lived religion as informed by black folk practices in culture, worship, music, Biblical hermeneutics, and ecstatic expressions of spirituality steer the clergy and laity toward the sacred task of institutional maintenance and the sacred duty of spearheading societal transformation? How did AMEs under-stand and define ecclesiology, and in what ways did it influence how their faith was lived out in devotional practices, denominational engagement, and social activism? And what emancipationist themes, already intrinsic to black folk religion, spurred AME activism?

Did these tendencies in the lived religion of African Methodists over two centuries cause the clergy and laity to draw from their black religious experience blended commitments to liberationist practice and personal piety? Here the contributions of Cecil W. Cone, a theologian of AME heritage, in *The Identity Crisis in Black Theology*, and Dale P. Andrews, a scholar in the AME Zion tradition, in *Practical Theology for Black Churches*, are especially suggestive. Cone contended that black theologians and other scholars should historicize and construct "Black Theology upon the foundations of the black religious tradition." Black theology for Cone was inauthentic unless black religion defined it. That included idioms drawn from the indigenous African/African American background and adopted Euro-American doctrine and discipline. Emancipationist efforts are a part of black religion and are, therefore, the salient concern in black religion and theology. In a similar vein Andrews was concerned with theological tasks that emancipationist scholars undertake and how they often misconstrue issues of faith, worship, and spirituality, important practices to pastors and parishioners, as tangential to liberationist objectives. Instead, "the self-image of black churches," he argued, "involves a caring community that cultivates both spiritual and social liberation." Scholars sometimes fail to appreciate these dualities of discourse within black religious communities, especially in historical context. Andrews observed that "faith identity" is core to African American religion. He asserted that "the domain of faith identity nurtures black personhood and embraces a sense of people hood in God. In turn, shaping black ecclesiology in the paradigm of "faith identity" offers a platform for readdressing black theology to black churches." This gulf between black liberationist scholars and black church ministers and members can be bridged if black folk religion and its concerns with preaching, pastoral care, and spirituality inform how "liberation is functioning in black religious folk life" and how it can sustain emancipationist activities.[11]

Historian Douglas Brinkley, in his biography of Rosa Parks, confirms the observations of Cone and Andrews. Parks, he contends, embodied social holiness and linked it to her devotional life at St. Paul AME Church in Montgomery, Alabama. Moreover, Parks's defiance of sinful segregationist practices on local city buses reflected devotional practices that developed out of her experiences in private and public worship and her understanding of herself as a twentieth-century heir to Richard Allen. Parks, a stewardess who helped to prepare the Eucharist at her Montgomery church, also believed that memorializing Jesus' sacrifice to conquer sin required the same demonstration of selflessness against the injustice of racism. Beyond her historical act in inspiring the Montgomery bus boycott, Brinkley challenged historians

---

[11] Cecil W. Cone, *The Identity Crisis in Black Theology* (Nashville, TN, AME Sunday School Union, Revised Edition), 1975, 2003, 15, 59–61, 67–68, Dale P. Andrews, *Practical Theology and African American Folk Religion* (Louisville, KY, Westminster John Knox Press, 2002), 8, 49, 130.

to probe the interior of Parks's lived religion as an AME and uncover how it connected to her social activism.[12]

Brinkley explored Parks' piety, spirituality, and devotional practices with insight, and tied them to social holiness. Robert Thomas, Jr., an activist AME pastor in Chicago and later Parks's bishop in Detroit, anticipated Brinkley's scholarship when he petitioned the 2000 AME General Conference to "beautify" this civil rights pioneer. Hence, Thomas petitioned the denominational body to insert in *The Doctrine and Discipline of the African Methodist Episcopal Church* the name of "Sister Rosa Parks" in the consecration collect for church deaconesses, an office reserved for "holy women" within African Methodism. Hence, Parks's name appears on the roster of Christian matriarchs along with Deborah, "Mary, the Holy Mother," Phoebe, [and] Lydia" as among those (who) give themselves . . . entirely to the ministrations of the Church and to suffering humanity." Parks therefore exemplified personal renewal, experienced through the Eucharist and holy living, as culminating in societal transformation through her fight against segregation.[13]

Although Parks and other AME women embodied the denomination's freedom rhetoric and praxis, they still experienced gender discrimination especially in the matter of female ordination. From Richard Allen's reluctance to authorize Jarena Lee to preach in 1809 to the overdue election of the first female bishop, Vashti Murphy McKenzie, in 2000, AMEs seldom saw gender inequality as a serious flaw in their liberationist identity. Despite a mostly male monopoly on influential leadership positions, women established themselves as productive pastors and parishioners who aided AME development. Sometimes through derivative authority flowing from their marriage to bishops and other high officials and at other times through female auxiliaries, AME women pursued liberationist objectives through their activities in education and missions and through womanist interpretations of scripture. As a result, they became crucial carriers of the church's emancipationist ethos, often exceeding the majority of males who were mainly involved in governance. Hence, Jarena Lee married the AME emphasis on Wesleyan piety and perfectionism with support for the abolitionist movement; Sarah Allen, a participant in the Underground Railroad, sustained fugitive slaves as they escaped from bondage; Charlotte Manye and

[12] See Douglas Brinkley, *Rosa Parks* (New York, Lipper/Viking, 2000); Dennis C. Dickerson, "Review" of Douglas Brinkley, *Rosa Parks* (2000), in the *AME Church Review*, Vol. 117, No. 383, July–September 2001, 96–97. Also see Dennis C. Dickerson, "Theologizing Rosa Parks," *AME Church Review*, Vol. 124, No. 411, July–September 2008, 29–37.

[13] "The Consecration of Deaconesses," in *The Doctrine and Discipline of African Methodist Episcopal Church, 2004-2008* (Nashville, TN, AME Sunday School Union, 2005), 516.

Europa Randall spearheaded AME expansion in Africa; Sadie T. M. Alexander vigorously pressed for civil rights as a presidential appointee during the Truman administration; and Gloria White-Hammond recovered the denomination's abolitionist legacy and aimed it against twenty-first century slavery and genocide in Darfur, Sudan. These and countless other women routinely drew from insurgent impulses ingrained in the AME ethos. Notwithstanding the barriers of gender, they cited as models such Biblical women as Deborah, Esther, and Mary Magdalene, and adopted as their own narrative the rhetoric and celebration of the autonomy that Allen's exit from St. George Church symbolized. These influential examples established them as authoritative interpreters and practitioners of the AME liberationist heritage.

Ethnicity inserted into African Methodism a diversity of languages, rituals, and idioms drawn from the broad geographical span of the Atlantic World. Despite these differences, AMEs remained committed to the emancipation of diverse black populations whether in the slave and segregated American South, in the colonial Caribbean, or in apartheid South Africa. African Methodism during the Civil War, for example, negotiated its dual obligations to prospective new members among recently freed slaves and fulfilling transatlantic aspirations in Africa. This recurring debate roiled the 1862 Baltimore Annual Conference, when the breadth of these tasks compelled delegates both to acknowledge and to prioritize these objectives. Alexander Crummell, an African American Episcopal priest and educator serving in Liberia and a fellow Liberian traveler, reminded the assembly "about Africa and our duty to her." In response, the delegates resolved that "we will do our duty to our fatherland, as soon as and as fast as God in his Providence shall give us the means." Additionally, they saluted the United States Senate "in passing a law recognizing the independence of Hayti and Liberia," an act "which is ominous of good to our race." The conferees also observed that "the advocates of Africa, Hayti . . . and San Domingo have been pointed out as suitable places for our people to emigrate to, and aid in building up a nationality of the black and colored races of the United States." To that end AMEs pledged their "imperative duty to follow our race into whatever clime thay may go."[14]

At the same time, during the Civil War, AMEs viewed evangelistic opportunities generally within the diaspora and specifically in the American

---

[14] *Minutes of the Baltimore Annual Conference of the African M. E. Church* held in Washington, City, DC, April 17–May 2, 1862 (Baltimore, MD, Bull & Tuttle, Clipper Office, 1862), 12, 21.

South as "gathering upon us so rapidly, looking to our final enfranchise-ment." Beyond their gestures toward engagement with Africa and emigra-tion outside the United States, the Baltimore Conference resolved that the bishop should appoint "a missionary to our brethren who may be set free by the operations of the war." Moreover, at the conference's 1864 session a delegation of AME clergy was authorized to meet Secretary of War Edwin M. Stanton "to procure from him an order granting to the ministers of the AME Church power to take possession of all churches and other church property now held by persons of African descent of the Methodist persua-sion, and all places formerly built for the use of the same within the geographical limits of the seceded States."[15]

As AMEs gestured toward transatlantic engagement while pursuing ini-tiatives to evangelize freedmen in the American South, they affirmed their black Atlantic consciousness despite dissent within their ranks. A cantankerous Henry M. Turner, the first black chaplain in the Union Army and later an African emigrationist, scolded fellow clergy at the 1864 Baltimore Annual Conference saying that "African" in their denomin-ational title "was merely to distinguish it from the M. E. Church, composed to the exclusion of black men." Turner expressed these views during a debate about deleting "African" as their denominational marker. "We are doing nothing for Africa," Turner declared, "and we are not Africans." His col-leagues, however, rebuked this perspective by voting near unanimously to overturn Turner's singular objection "to use their efforts to prevent the word "African" being stricken from the Discipline." Turner's minority stand showed that the majority of AMEs, while institutionally impecunious, con-nected themselves to the black Atlantic though focused more immediately on evangelizing newly freed slaves in the American South.[16]

This ambitious pan-Africanism, however, did not remove the tensions between forces compelling church officials to focus on institutional business and the countervailing challenge to confront hegemonic structures that subordinated peoples of African descent. As AMEs pushed expansion out-side the United States, these divergent tendencies coalesced and were pur-sued with a liberationist thrust. When the denomination, for example, organized its Canadian congregations in 1856 as the British Methodist Episcopal Church, the new religious body pledged to protect the freedoms

[15] Ibid., 12; *Proceedings of the Forty-Seventh Session of the Baltimore Annual Conference of the African M. E. Church* held in Washington, DC, April 1864 (Washington DC, Gibson Brothers, 1864), 20.
[16] *Proceedings of the Forty-Seventh . . . Baltimore Annual Conference, 1864*, 9–10.

of blacks throughout the British Empire and to provide a haven for fugitive slaves escaping bondage in the United States. Similarly, when the AME Church merged in 1896 with South Africa's Ethiopian Church, their embrace of black self-determination attracted followers opposed to white dominance in both political and ecclesiastical spheres. However, as the denomination stabilized, conflicts between institutional maintenance and insurgent activities reemerged. After the Nationalist Party won control in 1948, for example, apartheid policies were rapidly enacted and enforced. When the AME General Conference of 1948 assigned an Alabama-born bishop to preside in the region, he promised noninterference with the government's segregationist goals. In return for this acquiescence the bishop was allowed into the country to supervise AME annual conferences and schools. Presiding elders in South Africa in 1949 assured authorities that "the Bishop's work" was ecclesiastical and not political.[17] Unlike Allen and Payne, who, while tending to denominational duties, continued forthright opposition to racism, several twentieth-century bishops seemed compelled to choose between institutional and insurgent activities. Hence, the AME liberationist posture, though at times pursued surreptitiously, generally lost its edge against an openly racist South African regime. The denomination's liberationist legacy, though still acknowledged and celebrated, was deprived, at least for a time, of an effective praxis to fight apartheid. Once the momentum of a broader grassroots movement against apartheid reached fruition in the 1980s and early 1990s, AMEs ultimately, and perhaps belatedly, stood with black South Africans in their successful effort to destroy state-sponsored racial oppression.

Conflicts about Western cultural influences also lessened the denomination's emancipationist energies. These disagreements mostly focused on the ecstatic and exuberant religious practices of ex-slave Southerners or the religious idioms of indigenous Africans. Educated clergy and missionaries, however, emphasized dignified worship, orthodox Christian beliefs, and the elimination of egregious traces of the African religious background. The exercise of these preferences, especially in areas outside the United States, motivated AME expansionists, at least initially, to identify with Creole populations, particularly in Africa. Hence, the AMEs had their earliest success in the 1890s among descendants of repatriated settlers in Sierra

---

[17] Letter to The Minister of the Interior, December 14, 1949, Korresp: 1949–1978; Leer NR 16; I. H. Bonner to Fellow Worker in Christ, n.d.; Korresp: 1948–1977; Leer NR 55; *Easter M. Gordon Collection*, Institute for Historical Research, University of the Western Cape, Bellville, Cape Province, Republic of South Africa.

Leone and Liberia and within the Cape colored population in South Africa. In Liberia, for example, these Creole settlers, known as Americo-Liberians, denigrated indigenous peoples and eschewed power sharing with them in both church and civic arenas. Though the church's emancipationist ethos resonated within these populations, their sense of cultural superiority over indigenous peoples made them less enthusiastic about equal ecclesiastical treatment toward their social inferiors. Therefore, Western cultural attitudes and actions sometimes undermined the cohesion of AME ministers and members, and often prevented their freedom rhetoric from transcending these differences.

AMEs easily interacted with Westernized Africans who like themselves exhibited the blended attributes of Christianity and civilization. AME clergyman William H. Heard, Minister Resident and Consul General of the United States to Liberia and later a bishop, wrote in his 1898 book *The Bright Side of African Life* that he found these characteristics within the ruling elite of this West African nation. He lavishly praised Liberia, established as a republic in 1847, for emulating the government structure of its patron, the United States of America, and having as its officialdom exemplary officers of African American free and slave descent. "Liberia," he said, "is struggling to maintain its existence and to hold up the light of Christianity to its own people." The Americo-Liberians, he added, influenced "thousands of the aborigines" to adopt Christianity and civilization, "and today they are clothed and in their right minds and enjoying Christianity." Moreover, Liberia, a model "black Republic," reflected how Heard envisaged AME pan-Africanism and its emphasis on black self-determination. Like Liberia, the AME Church, present in the country since the 1880s, was "a race church" and "it is the composition of the church that makes it take in Africa." Not only "at its head are Negroes," but they were Christian and civilized peoples who wanted the same for the indigenous population.[18]

Alfred L. Ridgel, an Arkansas native whom Heard commended for his ministry "in advancing African Methodism" in Liberia, offered a similar definition for AME pan-Africanism and its special role in developing the "mother continent." He regretted that AMEs and other black religious bodies "have not as a whole realized our heaven-imposed duties to Africa" and should, therefore, welcome white denominations to share with them responsibilities "for the christianization and civilization of Africa." Nonetheless, "the people of Africa prefer our church government to that of other

[18] William H. Heard, *The Bright Side of African Life* (Philadelphia, PA, AME Publishing House, 1898), 9, 91.

churches here. They regard our polity more in keeping with genuine Christianity and better suited for a people just emerging from heathenism."
Africans, he said in his 1896 publication, *Africa and African Methodism*,
"like the Methodist fire," which provides "consolation to the soul" and "can
be touched by gospel magnetism." Therefore, the African "approves of
African Methodism." Lifting Africans from primitivism through AME evangelism was a consensus that Heard, Ridgel, and other denominational
leaders espoused.[19]

These stubborn prejudices, which informed AME pan-Africanism, were
foundational to AME interactions with indigenou peoples in Africa. African
Methodism, based in the United States, functioned as a conduit for African
modernization done through Christianity and the adoption of Western
education. This version of AME pan-Africanism that African Americans
defined yielded to independence movements after World War II that
asserted and achieved African self-determination in state matters and in
formerly white-led missionary and ecclesiastical bodies. Though AMEs
embraced the anticolonialism of African ministers and members, the
denomination was slow to apply this same advocacy to their denominational
governance. Not until Africans redefined pan-Africanism as denoting full
access to the episcopacy did indigenization become integral to AME
operations.

Historian Laurie Maffly-Kipp correctly contends that black religious
bodies, despite a shared racial heritage, possessed "a sharply defined denominational consciousness." The AME Church, in its history, hagiography, and
celebration of itself, embodied a particular "consciousness" whose core
characteristic lay in its freedom rhetoric and praxis. Because the very
existence of the AME Church symbolized racial autonomy and self-
determination, its maintenance and preservation became a liberationist
enterprise. Additionally, those who developed the denomination had an
equal obligation to mobilize its resources to fight societal structures that
subordinated black peoples. These emancipationist efforts, while creating a
distinctive AME culture, also placed organizational and insurgent objectives
in constant tension with each other.[20]

[19] Ibid., 91; Alfred Lee Ridgel, *Africa and African Methodism* (Atlanta, GA, Franklin Printing
and Publishing Company, 1896), 58, 61.
[20] Laurie Maffly-Kipp, "Denominationalism and the Black Church," in Robert Bruce Mullin
and Russell E. Richey (eds.), *Reimaging Denominationalism: Interpretive Essays* (New York,
Oxford University Press,1994), 65.

Though other black churches fought for black freedom, none had embedded in their history an exodus narrative reenacted as powerfully as Richard Allen's dramatic departure from a white-dominated church determined to segregate its black members. Additionally, AMEs expressed their emancipationist ethos through scriptural interpretations often sung in slave spirituals and black hymnody, and freedom objectives embedded in Wesleyan social holiness. These intellectual resources provided AMEs with a cogent liberationist theology and praxis and a keen awareness of their insurgent identity. These characteristics also distinguished the AMEs from the ME Church and other white Wesleyan bodies for whom maintenance of racial hegemony mattered more than black emancipationist objectives. Lastly, the AME Church, an intricate institutional entity, unlike other black religious bodies, possessed a geographical reach during its early decades that spanned the Atlantic World. A connectional presence in several areas within the Northeast and Midwest and parts of the slave South; in Haiti and Canada; and influence in Sierra Leone, exclusively owing to AME cofounder Daniel Coker, extended and exposed the denomination to diverse black populations. Tensions between liberationist objectives, institution building, and spiritual faith practices similarly appeared in other black religious bodies. The longevity and territorial breadth of African Methodism, however, magnified these competing characteristics often above those in other African American churches.

The AME Church, located throughout its history within the Atlantic World, faced the forces of subjugation, which fixed the status of its large colored constituencies. Though AME ministers and members were themselves vulnerable peoples, they focused on the dual tasks of developing and maintaining an independent religious body and confronting powerful national, political, and economic structures aimed at black subordination. While institutional governance was itself a liberationist activity, it competed and, at times, undermined equally important efforts to defeat oppressive systems of slavery, segregation, colonialism, and apartheid. The history of the AME Church is a narrative about these tensions. Such significant historical figures as the slave insurrectionist Denmark Vesey, the pioneering preacher Jarena Lee, African church founder M. M. Mokone, the Little Rock school segregation fighter Daisy Bates, and the anticolonial nation builder Hendrik Witbooi became articulate and conscious carriers of their denomination's liberationist legacy. They demonstrated how pervasive and enduring was the insurgent impulse of African Methodism.

❦

1

Richard Allen and the Rise of African Methodism in the Atlantic World, 1760–1831

THE FIRST AFRICAN METHODISTS

Historian David Hempton correctly describes Methodism as a "transatlantic/transnational religious movement" that rapidly spread from Great Britain to its colonies in the Americas in the mid-eighteenth century. As the British consolidated their hegemony across the globe, particularly among various vulnerable populations, "mobile" Methodist preachers connected with "cultural outsiders" in both British and American society. Their emotional, extemporaneous preaching, their plain appeals to sinners to be saved, and their ecstatic expressions of "enthusiasm" resonated with non-elites in both Britain and the Americas.[1] Hence, Scipio Africanus, one of a few hundred blacks in London, regularly attended evangelical services in about 1739 and became, according to one scholar, "the first black Methodist." The receptivity that Africans experienced among British Methodists continued into the early nineteenth century. For example, Samuel Barber (1786–1828), the mulatto son of a Jamaican-born father and valet to the remarkable Dr. Samuel Johnson, converted to Christianity in 1805 in a "great revival of religion among the Methodists." Later, he connected with the Burslem Sunday School and regularly ministered to the poor in a local workhouse "endeavouring to instruct and feed" these neglected persons. In 1809 he

---

[1] David Hempton, *Methodism: Empire of the Spirit* (New Haven, CT, Yale University Press, 2005), Vol. 2, 30–31, 33–35. Hempton wrote that "Methodist expansion was the result not of an evangelistic strategy concocted by elites, but was carried primarily by a mobile laity." I have adopted Hempton's terminology of "mobile laity" through the book to characterize how AME expansion was similarly driven by clergy following the migratory patterns of their black Atlantic constituents.

became a local preacher in the Primitive Methodist Church, and "there are now good (Methodist) societies" in existence because of Barber.[2] Hence, in Britain these and other black followers of John Wesley became a foundational presence in his maturing Methodist movement.

Moreover, increasing numbers of slaves on the North American mainland and in the Caribbean provided unprecedented opportunities for Methodism to grow within an untapped African population. The trauma of enslavement and separation from their tribes in Africa, the need to negotiate their adjustment to an alien culture, and exposure to the liberty language embedded in the Bible gained eager listeners for the Methodist message. That these pioneer British evangelists targeted blacks and drew Betty, a slave in New York City, as their first American convert, showed Methodists that Africans in the Atlantic world would readily embrace them. Joseph Pilmore, whom John Wesley himself dispatched to British North America, preached to blacks and noted in 1769 that "many of the poor Africans are obedient to the faith." He made a similar observation in 1770 in Philadelphia, where he said that "ever the poor Negroes came forth and bore a testimony for God our Saviour."[3] Similarly, Francis Asbury noted in Baltimore in 1773 that "poor Negroes have been deeply affected with the power of God" and that one particular convert "will be fit to send to England soon, to preach." That the number of black Methodists in the United States grew from 1,500 in 1784 to 12,215 in 1797 testified to why Asbury was so greatly enamored with African-American converts. The same could have been said about Methodists in Antigua where, in 1758, John Wesley baptized two slaves whom he said were "the first African Methodists I have known." Thomas Coke in 1786 converted Antiguan Frances Clearkley and her two granddaughters, Anne and Elizabeth Hart. Later, the two sisters, though their mulatto father was a slave owner, became abolitionists. Because they believed that bondage encouraged vice among slaves, they preached Methodism to them and urged their education. Because of such efforts, black Methodists who numbered 2,379 in 1797 vastly outnumbered Antigua's tiny group of Wesleyan whites.

---

[2] Gareth Lloyd, "Scipio Africanus: The First Black Methodist," *Wesley and Methodist Studies*, Vol. 3 (2011), 87–95; Kathleen Chater, *Untold Stories: Black People in England and Wales during the Period of the British Slave Trade, c. 1660–1807* (Manchester, Manchester University Press, 2009), 26; Cedric Barber (ed.), *A Memoir of Samuel Barber: A Black "Ranter" from the Mother Town* (Stoke-on-Trent, Tentmaker Publications, 2007), 9–10, 14, 23.

[3] John Lenton, "The Attitudes towards Black Methodists in America and the West Indies of Some of Wesley's Preachers, 1770–1810," *Wesley and Methodist Studies*, Vol. 3 (2011), 98–99.

In 1820 there were 25,500 black Methodists in the Caribbean, nearly all of whom were black.[4]

These black Methodists comprised a subset of a larger population of Atlantic Creoles. Historian Jane G. Landers described them as "a diverse group, born in the West Indies, in Haut du Cap [in Haiti], in Jamaica, in Havana, or in the Indian nations of Florida." She could have added both British North America and New France. Landers added that:

> Some were born enslaved; others were always free. Some were literate, urban, and propertied, while others rose out of more degraded circumstances. What united them was not only their time and place, but a determined quest for freedom. Refusing to be "bound in shallows and miseries," they took tide, and while few went on to gain fortunes, many achieved liberty.[5]

These Atlantic World peoples, through maroons, armed rebellion, and other liberationist strategies, fought bondage and racial restrictions through whatever means that were available to them. For black Methodists a religious route to freedom, both physically and spiritually, also seemed to promise success.

Egalitarian tendencies were deeply anchored in Methodist evangelism in British North America. The revivals and camp meetings, which regularly attracted large crowds, provided equal access to all. Open-air venues in both urban and rural settings drew persons of all classes and colors. Even when services were held in churches and other places indoors, the lack of restrictions ensured the presence of diverse attendees on a nonsegregated basis. Moreover, sermons and invitations to accept Christ gave deference neither to elitism nor to racial hierarchy. All were sinners and needed to make their peace with God. Because there was no favoritism in Zion, everyone stood in need of salvation and equality was established among the saved. Moreover,

---

[4] Harry V. Richardson, *Dark Salvation: The Story of Methodism as It Developed among Blacks in America* (Garden City, NY, Anchor Press, 1976), 35; quoted in John Lenton, "The Attitudes towards Black Methodists in America and the West Indies of Some of Wesley's Preachers, 1770–1810" (2011), 98–99, 105; quoted in Warren Thomas Smith, *Harry Hosier: Circuit Rider* (Nashville, TN, Upper Room, 1981), 21; cited in Dennis C. Dickerson, *Religion, Race, and Region: Research Notes on AME Church History* (Nashville, TN, AME Sunday School Union, 1995), 14; cited in *Journal of the Twentieth Quadrennial Session of the General Conference of the African Methodist Episcopal Church* held in St. Stephen AME Church, Wilmington, NC, May 4–22, 1896 (Philadelphia, AME Publishing House, 1896), 89; John Saillant, "Antiguan Methodism and Anti-slavery Activity: Anne and Elizabeth Hart in the Eighteenth Century Atlantic," *Church History*, Vol. 69, No. 1 (March 2000), 86–89; Hempton, *Methodism*, 24.

[5] Jane G. Landers, *Atlantic Creoles in the Age of Revolutions* (Cambridge, MA, Harvard University Press, 2010), 14.

Methodists, like their Baptist counterparts, routinely licensed blacks to preach and again demonstrated their commitment to a color-blind Christianity. Their openness to black preachers facilitated evangelism among African-Americans and accounted for the greater success of Methodists compared with what the Anglicans, Presbyterians, and several other sects had achieved.

Though no census of black Methodist preachers exists for the late eighteenth century, the few for whom records survived significantly affected the Wesleyan movement in the Atlantic world. They achieved manumission from slavery and adopted the rights rhetoric of the revolutionary eras in the British North American colonies, France, and Haiti. The language of human equality found in Methodist evangelism and pervasive democratic discourse clothed them in clerical authority in front of the interracial audiences that they often addressed. John Marrant (1755–1791), though born free in New York, settled with his sister in Charleston in 1766. The famed revivalist George Whitfield converted Marrant to Christianity and challenged him to preach to the Cherokee. At various times the Cherokee befriended him, held him as a captive, and later received him as an evangelist. After he was compelled to serve in the British navy during the American Revolution, Marrant lived in Britain where in 1785 he was ordained as a minister in Whitfield's Calvinist Methodist sect. Marrant preached broadly within the Atlantic world, namely in Britain, the United States, and in Canada. One of his African-American converts was Cato Perkins, who was ordained in Nova Scotia in 1786 as a Huntingdonian Methodist. Perkins, a former Charleston slave, had left for Canada with the British after their defeat in the American Revolution. Perkins headed a Methodist group in Nova Scotia, and later migrated with them to Sierra Leone. He continued in the clergy and preached to indigenous Africans until his death in 1805. Boston King (1760–1802), another Charleston slave, fled with defeated British soldiers in 1783 to New York City and then to Burch Town in Shelburne County, Nova Scotia. Freeborn Garrettson, the well-known Methodist evangelist, drew him to Christianity in 1784, and in 1785 he became an exhorter. After he and others in 1792 settled in Sierra Leone, King enhanced his preaching with study in Britain, where local Methodists financed his schooling.[6]

---

[6] "The Rev. John Marrant 1755–1791," www.wallbuilders.com/LIBprinterfriendly.asp?id=136; "Cato Perkins," www.blackloyalistlist.com/canadiandigitalcollection/peoplereligious/per kins.htm; Simon Schama, *Rough Crossings: Britain, the Slaves and the American Revolution* (New York, Ecco/Harper Collins, 2006), 375–376; Ruth Holmes Whitehead and Carmelita A. M. Robertson (eds.), *The Life of Boston King* (Halifax, NS, Nimbus Publishing and Nova Scotia Museum, 2003), 8–9, 23–25, 29, 31.

The transatlantic mobility of Marrant, Perkins, and King paralleled the less expansive itinerancy of other black Methodist preachers in the former British North American colonies. Though they confined their travels to specific areas on the eastern seaboard, their evangelistic efforts attracted innumerable audiences of black and white listeners. Henry Evans (c.1740–1810) was probably born free, converted to Christianity, and licensed as a Methodist preacher all in Virginia. He settled in Fayetteville, North Carolina in around 1780 where his effective evangelism among blacks and whites yielded a biracial congregation.[7] Harry Hosier (c.1750–1806), manumitted from slavery in North Carolina, met Asbury in 1780 and agreed to accompany him on a preaching mission to slaves in Virginia and the Carolinas. In 1781 in Falls Church, Virginia, he preached to a largely white gathering who fixed their "attention" on the talented black preacher. Apparently, Hosier, though illiterate, developed exemplary preaching skills and spoke with a "voice [that] was pure music." Benjamin Franklin called him "the greatest orator in America." Despite his closeness to Asbury, Hosier also associated with other white Methodist preachers including Freeborn Garrettson. In 1790, for example, Hosier and Garrettson traveled throughout New England preaching to large crowds including some who were intrigued to see and hear "Black Harry." Hosier was never ordained despite Methodist legislation in 1800 that granted ministerial orders to black preachers. In 1805 a roster of nineteen members of St. George Church in Philadelphia petitioned Bishop Asbury and their annual conference for the services of "Harry Hosine [sic], an African," whom they believed "wanted to be very useful." The endorsement of Hosier came with a caveat, however, saying that his assignment should occur "without establishing a bad precedent," probably pertaining either to ordination or appointment as pastor.[8]

THE RISE OF RICHARD ALLEN

The formation of the ME Church in 1784 drew Harry Hosier and another black Methodist preacher, Richard Allen, to the historic Baltimore meeting of the first General Conference of the Methodist Episcopal Church in America. Though the Christmas Conference took place because of the

---

[7] Richardson, *Dark Salvation*, 176–178; Smith, *Harry Hosier*, 18.

[8] Smith, *Harry Hosier*, 18–22, 24–25, 36–37, 41, 49; Petition from the Members of St. George Church to the Bishop and Conference of the Methodist Episcopal Church, May 1, 1805 (re. Harry Hosine[sic], Conference Letters, St. George United Methodist Church Archives, Philadelphia, Pennsylvania – Reverend Alfred T. Day III, General Secretary of the General Commission on Archives and History of the United Methodist Church shared this document with the author October 21, 2015).

remarkable success of the Methodist mission to America, Francis Asbury, who, with Thomas Coke, was consecrated a bishop, declared in 1796 that Methodism would have been better off "if we had entered here to preach only to the Africans."[9] Hosier and Allen's deep spirituality and profound understanding of Methodist belief and practice greatly impressed the bishop. Moreover, their reputation as talented and productive preachers also validated Asbury's sentiments. Hosier, however, was content to be known as a well-traveled evangelist, but Allen developed as an ecclesiastical leader whose stature surpassed that of Garrettson and rivaled that of Asbury. Additionally, in founding a black Wesleyan body, Allen institutionalized African Methodism and built it into an energetic ecclesiastical presence within the Atlantic world. Marrant, Perkins, and King became noted black Methodists within particular enclaves in Atlantic Methodism, and Evans and Hosier, though focused in their American context, attained similar recognition for their evangelistic achievements. Allen emerged, however, as a seminal figure whose religious, organizational, and public persona drew disciples and imitators in other black Wesleyan groups.

Allen rose from slavery to found the African Methodist Episcopal (AME) Church, whose growth and influence followed the geographical spread of African peoples within the Atlantic world. Allen's association with "mobile" Methodists, who traveled across the Atlantic into the settled and frontier areas of British North America and within the new United States, familiarized him with the dynamic development of this expanding religious sect. The ships that brought British Methodists to preach in America and the horses, saddlebags, and other tropes of Methodist material culture introduced Allen to networks of circuit riders anxious to address audiences regardless of color or class. He also witnessed revivals, camp meetings, bands, and classes where the unsaved were converted and believers were sustained in the faith. Allen, however, pressed Methodism onto a new religious frontier. Though he had preached mostly to whites, he thought that blacks had been neglected and deserved his best evangelical energies. His focus on this subordinate population compelled Methodists to acknowledge their grounding among non-elites in both Britain and America. He specifically praised the Methodists because they "were the first people that brought glad tidings to the colored people." Moreover, Allen's embrace of the emancipationist ethos embedded

---

[9] Cited in Dickerson, *Religion, Race, and Region*, 13. John Wigger has written the definitive *American Saint: Francis Asbury and the Methodists* (New York, Oxford University Press, 2009).

in the rights rhetoric of the American Revolution, themes of universal freedom found in the British and American anti-slavery movements, and social holiness tenets derived from Wesleyan theology energized his reinvention of Methodism and spearheaded its advance among prospective black members.[10]

Allen should not be viewed, however, through an exclusively racial prism. He was a thoroughly Methodist man whose understanding of Wesleyan theology affirmed the humanity of all peoples and required that all should be physically and spiritually freed from the bondage of both slavery and sin. Methodism, as a vehicle to achieve these objectives, mandated an energized spiritual holiness and an aggressive social holiness aimed at addressing both personal and social iniquity. These Wesleyan impulses also committed the saved to draw upon their spiritual energies to reconstruct societal structures to conform to what God intended for creation. Hence, for Allen the practice of prejudice against blacks, to which Methodists increasingly succumbed, was evidence of a spiritual declension that was manifested in raw racism. Methodists in the United States, in distancing themselves from their non-elite origins in Britain and colonial America, were becoming, by the end of the eighteenth century, an established church, which eschewed identification with the poor and the slave. Allen experienced this development in the 1780s and 1790s as former egalitarian Methodist ministers became callous and cavalier toward him when he sought black religious autonomy. Asbury in 1796 affirmed Allen's observations when he declared that too much of Methodist spirituality had become "superficial" and that Wesleyan whites should emulate the piety of black Methodists.[11]

Richard Allen, like other black Methodist preachers, consciously shaped his ministry into an Atlantic World project. For this reason, he, unlike his peers, established an ecclesiastical entity to bring collective purpose to their disparate evangelical and emancipationist efforts. He realized that geographical mobility back and forth across the Atlantic connected diverse African populations and placed them in complicated interactions with each other. These encounters joined them in indefatigable opposition to slavery and

---

[10] *Emancipation: The Abolition of Slavery in the North* (Chicago, University of Chicago Press, 1967); Christopher L. Brown, *Moral Capital: Foundations of British Abolitionism* (Chapel Hill, University of North Carolina Press, 2006); Dennis C. Dickerson, "Liberation, Wesleyan Theology, and Early African Methodism, 1760–1840," *Wesley and Methodist Studies*, Vol. 3 (2011), 109–121.

[11] Dickerson, *Religion, Race and Region*, 13.

other forms of racial subjugation. At different times and in various venues they searched for ideas and methodologies to affirm their humanity and worth as spiritual beings. Available to them were multiple intellectual and tactical resources, which lay in the rights rhetoric of the American, French, and Haitian revolutions, transatlantic anti-slavery thought and action, and liberty themes grounded in Methodist belief and praxis. Moreover, one theologian has argued that Methodism encouraged among its adherents ongoing theological inquiry about the integrity of the human spirit and posed fresh questions about how to nurture and sustain it.[12] Toward this end, Methodism energized Christians to tackle new issues pertaining to the human condition and to discern God's purpose and direction for human-kind. Therefore, Allen, beyond the assurance he received from his conver-sion, may have drawn from this facet of Methodism an impetus to understand his world of slavery and to challenge inhuman practices that violated the sanctity of the soul and person whom God created.

Allen, in reinventing Methodism through the AME Church, created an institution that advocated and facilitated the furtherance of black freedom despite the forces of empire that promoted the slave trade and slavery. He designed African Methodism to connect with the emancipationist forces stirring in the Atlantic World to end slavery and validate the personhood of blacks. Though entrenched hegemonic structures in Europe and in the Americas profited from slavery, the rise of abolitionism and the presence of evangelical and Quaker insurgency against bondage pushed Allen to found a "freedom church" to encourage and sustain these emancipationist initiatives. These factors became intrinsic to the institutional fabric of the AME Church. They influenced the theology and ethos of this emerging black sect and spread their territorial and transatlantic impact to blacks within the Atlantic World.

Richard Allen, from birth to manhood, was shaped by slavery and molded in Methodism. These forces intersected, perhaps, at a point of personal crisis, and clarified for Allen the meaning of freedom in each sphere of his being. Christianity, as expressed in Wesleyan belief and practice, played a crucial role in increasing Allen's dissatisfaction with his slave condition and valid-ating his strong sense of self-worth. Moreover, Methodism taught him that ultimate freedom for the body and soul was divinely ordained and that fellowship within a religious community committed to the emancipation

---

[12] Kenneth Wilson, *Methodist Theology* (New York, T & T Clark International, 2011), vii–viii.

of slaves was available to him. Surely, his Wesleyan awakening reinforced his motivation to seek manumission from slavery.[13]

Originally, the Allen family was probably connected to slave owner William Allen, whose daughter, Elizabeth, married the Philadelphia attorney Benjamin Chew. When William Allen departed for Great Britain in 1774, Chew succeeded him as Chief Justice of the Pennsylvania Supreme Court. It seems likely that the Allen surname, rather than the last name, Chew, drew from these origins. Herbert G. Gutman in his classic *The Black Family in Slavery and Freedom* recounted the practice among slaves to adopt surnames from early slave owners in order to establish intergenerational lineage in the event of sale and the splitting of black families. The transfer of the Allens to Chew and the later sale of some of them, including Richard Allen, to another slave owner in Delaware, validates the Gutman argument. In any case, Chew, a Quaker, was one of over 500 slave owners in Philadelphia, 17 percent of whom were Quakers. In addition to his well-appointed residence in the Germantown section of the city, Chew also owned a plantation in Kent County, Delaware, which spanned 1,000 acres. Because his large number of slaves worked at both of his estates, the Allen family probably experienced bondage in both urban and rural settings. Since Chew often bought and sold slaves, it was not strange that he allowed his Delaware neighbor, Stokeley Sturgis, to purchase the Allens in 1768. In this way, Richard Allen, though born on February 14, 1760, in Philadelphia, became the property of Sturgis and grew up primarily in the rural environs of Dover, Delaware.[14]

Though Allen described Sturgis as a kind man with a fatherly mien, neither he nor his family was spared the cruelties of slavery. Sturgis, an impecunious farmer, separated the Allen family by selling away the mother and three of her children to another slaveholder. Allen, though a brother and a sister remained with him, was profoundly hurt by this trauma of permanent family separation and declared that slavery was "a bitter pill." Moreover, in later years, Allen wrote about these cruelties in slavery and noted "the heartrending distress, when the husband is separated from the wife, and the

[13] Hempton, *Methodism*, 63; Allen, *The Life Experience and Gospel Labors*, 15–16.
[14] Gary B. Nash, "Slaves and Slaveowners in Colonial Philadelphia," *The William and Mary Quarterly*, Third Series, Vol. 30, No. 2 (April 1973), 237, 246–247, 253; Charles L. Blockson, C. R. Cole, and Marion T. Lane, "Richard Allen Memorandum," National Society of the Daughters of the American Revolution 8-9 (Courtesy of Yvonne Studevan, Athens, GA); Herbert G. Gutman, *The Black Family in Slavery and Freedom, 1750-1925* (New York, Vintage, 1976), 232, 240–241, 244–245; Gary B. Nash, "New Light on Richard Allen: The Early Years of Freedom," *The William and Mary Quarterly*, Third Series, Vol. 46, No. 2 (April 1989), 333–334.

parents from the children, who are never more to meet in this world." No doubt, he was thinking about his own family circumstances. Allen's conversion to Christianity in 1777 occurred at some unspecified time after the sale of his family. Becoming a Christian, perhaps, aided him in surmounting these sorrows and his powerless position as another man's chattel. Allen, in resolving to become his own master, drew upon psychic and religious resources that a timely introduction to Methodism provided. Wesleyan adherents were especially active in that part of the Delmarva Peninsula where Allen lived. Because they preached enthusiastically and evangelized without regard to race, Allen and his two siblings were pulled into the Methodist fold.[15]

Allen's conversion brought him enormous satisfaction, which he enthusiastically shared with others. He beckoned to "old companions," Allen said, "to seek the Lord." He noted, however, that "many, old experienced Christians" doubted the authenticity of his conversion. Therefore, he sought "the Lord afresh" through intense prayers and appeals to God for deliverance. Then, "all of a sudden," he exclaimed, "my dungeon shook, my chains flew off, and glory to God I cried," acknowledged Jesus Christ as his Savior, and received forgiveness for his sins.[16]

Allen, who remembered his conversion years later, used terminology found in scripture and in Methodist hymnody. Perhaps some Methodist whom he heard readily recalled Peter's release from prison in Acts 12:7, which said:

And the angel of the Lord came upon him, and a light shined in the prison; and smite Peter on the side, and raised him up, saying, Arise up quickly. And his chains fell off from his hands.

Most Methodists, however, knew Charles Wesley's widely sung hymn, "And Can It Be That I Should Gain." A crucial stanza declared:

Long my imprisoned spirit lay,
Fast bound in sin and nature's night:
Thine eye diffused a quickening ray-
I woke; the dungeon flames with light;
My chains fell off, my heart was free,
I rose, went forth, and followed thee.[17]

[15] Allen, *The Life Experience and Gospel Labors*, 13–14, 75.   [16] Ibid., 13.
[17] Dennis C. Dickerson, *African Methodism and Its Wesleyan Heritage: Reflections on AME Church History* (Nashville, TN, AME Sunday School Union, 2009), 15.

Allen may have been familiar with Acts 12:7, but he surely knew Wesley's hymn. Both passages had become standard phraseology in Methodist conversion narratives long before Allen repeated them in his own religious awakening.[18] That these words flowed from Allen's pen testified to a deep Methodist consciousness. Moreover, the metaphors pertaining to chains and imprisonment aptly mirrored the bondage that both slavery and sin represented. Liberation from both oppressive circumstances linked in Allen's mind a dual determination to be free. He acted on each through painstaking labor and effort to become emancipated both physically and spiritually.

Strategically, Allen introduced various Methodist preachers to Sturgis and his wife, ostensibly to save the souls of these unconverted slaveholders. The Sturgis couple, "being old and infirm," allowed these clergy, at Allen's suggestion, "to preach at (their) home." After several services, Freeborn Garrettson, the well-known itinerant, came to the Sturgis household and delivered a poignant sermon from Daniel 5:27: "Thou are weighed in the balance, and art found wanting." Garrettson, who declared that this scripture applied to slave owners, steered Sturgis to a renunciation of slavery. He therefore decided "he could not be satisfied to hold slaves, believing it to be wrong." Hence, Allen's evangelical objective transposed easily toward an emancipationist result for him and his brother. Sturgis permitted the Allens to work to earn $2,000 in Continental money to buy their freedom.[19]

Methodism provided the means through which Sturgis was saved and Allen was freed. Sturgis was influenced as much by the Methodist ministers who preached in his home as by Allen's own example of worship and work. Fellow slave owners, for example, taunted him for permitting the Allens to attend biweekly Methodist services. "Stokeley's Negroes would soon ruin him," they said, because the Allen brothers allegedly neglected their chores in order to go to class meetings. They resolved, therefore, to prove the naysayers wrong. "We would work night and day," Allen recalled, "to get our crops forward." Sometimes they refused to go to religious gatherings if they were behind in their work. They were determined to disprove the fiction that "religion made us worse servants." Even Sturgis noticed that the Allens were so serious about their labor that he admonished them to resume their regular attendance at Methodist services.[20]

Allen deployed a Methodist methodology to buy his freedom and to establish a reputation of trust, integrity, and reliability. These characteristics,

---

[18] Ibid.; M. Bruce Hindmarsh, "'My chains fell off, my heart was free: Early Methodist Conversion Narrative in England," *Church History*, Vol. 68, No. 4 (December 1999), 910.
[19] Allen, *The Life Experience and Gospel Labors*, 15.   [20] Ibid., 14–15.

all visibly displayed and affirmed by observers, showed the depth of his Methodist identity. Sturgis already knew about Allen's industry and resourcefulness in finding extra work to pay for his emancipation. He cut wood, worked in a brickyard, and hauled salt from Sussex County, Delaware, during "the Continental war." For bringing this needed commodity to Valley Forge, the military camp that General George Washington used in the winter of 1777–1778, validates Allen's awareness of the Revolutionary War and its freedom prospects for African Americans. Allen, like the 5,000 blacks who fought in the Continental Army as their route to emancipation, sided with American whites who fought for independence from Great Britain. Similarly, other blacks, in response to British promises of manumission, supported the Redcoats and left with them after their defeat in 1781. With his earnings Allen, who chose his own pathway out of slavery, paid Sturgis in 1783 and became a free man. He acknowledged Sturgis as "a kind, affectionate and tender-hearted master." Nonetheless, he was aware that Sturgis, despite his supposed decency, would still sell him if his precarious financial condition mandated this inhumane transaction. In 1779, for example, Sturgis owed to Benjamin Chew a bond of £340. These and other debts showed Allen that he had no security in slavery. Allen, of course, preferred to be his own master. His work ethic and honesty reflected ascetic habits for which Methodists were known and which he greatly exemplified. Hence, he emerged out of slavery with a Methodist persona, which had already drawn the respect of those who knew him as a slave and now as a free man. God, he believed, created him as a free agent bound only to the moral guideposts that he learned from Methodism. As he doggedly labored to purchase his freedom, Allen internalized the Wesleyan tenet of spiritual/scriptural holiness, which required adherents to practice integrity in all of their religious and vocational dealings. For Allen, the urgency to be free and the necessity of being a moral man owed to his fateful encounters with the Wesleyan movement.[21]

Between 1783 and 1786, Allen's interactions, mainly with whites, introduced him as a fervent Methodist preacher and a conscientious practitioner of piety and moral living. Like many ministers, Allen simultaneously preached and worked as a manual laborer to support himself. These dual

---

[21] Ibid., 14–16; Stokeley Sturgis Debt, "Amount of Principal and Interest due on Stokeley Sturgis' bond, 1779" (Courtesy of Yvonne Studevan, Genealogist and 7th Generation Descendant of Richard Allen, Athens, Georgia); Blockson et al., "Richard Allen Memorandum," 14–15, NSDAR; see Benjamin Quarles, *The Negro in the American Revolution* (Chapel Hill, University of North Carolina Press, 1961).

activities demonstrated his seriousness about evangelizing and depending on none but himself to provide funds to advance his ministry. Even before Sturgis manumitted him, Allen preached while he worked to buy his freedom. He continued this routine after liberty allowed him a broader sphere of travel throughout New Jersey, Pennsylvania, and Maryland. Wherever he preached, he connected with networks of fellow Christians who gave him lodging and helped him find work. In nearly every instance Allen remained with his hosts for days and weeks, and reported a harvest of saved souls because of his ministrations. At one location in New Jersey, for example, Allen "was employed cutting wood, although (he) preached the Gospel at night and on Sundays." God "blessed my labors," he declared, and he also found other jobs. At Radnor, Pennsylvania, where he remained for "several weeks," Allen recalled, "many souls were awakened and cried aloud to the Lord to have mercy upon them."[22]

Allen's spirituality and moral discipline resonated through his secular dealings. In Delaware, for example, he found a trunk containing cash and other valuables. He placed a newspaper advertisement inviting the rightful owner to claim the lost property. When the owner appeared, Allen declined the monetary reward, but was convinced to receive an unpretentious suit befitting "a plain Methodist." This and other examples of Allen's self-deprecating conduct stirred various observers to attest publicly about his integrity. Thomas Attmore, a Quaker, commented that Allen was known as a man of "Christian Temper" full of charity toward the sick and poor. He echoed Sturgis and others in testifying to Allen's impeccable character and how he embodied basic Methodist attributes.[23]

Allen developed relationships with widening circles of Methodists as he encountered them in expanding venues between New York and the Carolinas. He met the legendary Francis Asbury who came to America from England in 1771, traveled thousands of miles as a preacher and bishop, and emerged as the undisputed leader of American Methodism. Asbury asked Allen to accompany him on an evangelical journey to the American South. Because Asbury could not guarantee equal treatment and accommodations, Allen declined the invitation. Perhaps Asbury did not fully appreciate that Allen had experienced a color-blind Christianity with various Methodists and had preached and brought to salvation countless Caucasians in the Middle Atlantic.[24] Though

[22] Allen, *The Life Experience and Gospel Labors*, 20.
[23] Nash, "New Light on Richard Allen," 337, 339–340.
[24] Charles H. Wesley, *Richard Allen: Apostle of Freedom* (Washington DC, Associated Publishers, 1935), 33.

Harry Hosier acquiesced to such requests from Asbury, these differences created no fissures between him and Allen. Both attended in Baltimore in December 1784 the "Christmas" Conference, which formally organized the Methodist denomination in the United States. Hosier and Allen, who witnessed the consecration of Asbury and Coke as bishops, joined them as members of the founding generation of the Methodist Church in America.

ENVISAGING AFRICAN METHODISM

While Richard Allen believed in a color-blind Christianity, he also embraced a heightened black consciousness. The former facilitated an easy interaction with Wesleyan whites while the latter drove his desire to evangelize African Americans. During his preaching tour of the Middle Atlantic, he observed that "most of my congregation was white" and that "there were but few colored people in the neighborhood." As a Methodist preacher committed to the salvation of all, this was a problem. After a prominent elder among Philadelphia Methodists invited him to preach in the city, he "saw a large field open in seeking and instructing my African brethren, who had been a long forgotten people." Allen arrived in February 1786 and accepted early morning preaching assignments at St. George Church and in other venues in the metropolis. The success of his preaching resulted in a "society" of forty-two black people who endorsed Allen's proposal to start an African American congregation. Opposition, however, came from leading black Philadelphians and from white Methodists who "used very degrading and insulting language to us, to try to prevent us from going on." But Allen was grateful for the steadfast support of three fellow blacks, including Absalom Jones, who shared his desire for a black church.[25]

There was an odd congruence of experiences that convinced Allen to recover for Methodism the depth of spirituality and racial egalitarianism that he saw in this fledgling sect in the 1770s. He surmised that superficial religiosity and formalism were becoming the unhappy consequences of rapid Methodist maturation in the 1780s. Though the "Christmas" Conference reflected the growth of Methodism toward an establishment status, its zeal for lost souls regardless of color and class increasingly yielded to slavery and other hegemonic structures. In his reflection on the first General Conference Allen described it as "the beginning of the Episcopal Church amongst the Methodists. Many of the ministers were set apart in holy orders and were

---

[25] Allen, *The Life Experience and Gospel Labors*, 19, 21–22.

said to be entitled to the gown." He firmly rejected this formalism and pretension and concluded that "religion has been declining in the church ever since." What followed was a steady retreat in Methodist opposition to slavery, especially as the denomination expanded into the American South. Allen most poignantly saw concrete evidence of this spiritual declension in racist attitudes exhibited at St. George Church.[26]

Though Allen continued to hold separate worship services, white Methodists remained opposed to a black church. Nonetheless, "a number of us usually attended St. George ... and when the colored people began to get numerous ... they moved us from the seats we usually sat on, and placed us around the wall." On a Sunday morning in November 1787, however, "we went to church and the sexton stood at the door, and told us to go in the gallery." Allen, Absalom Jones, and others in their group sat in the place they normally occupied. As prayers began, a trustee pulled Jones from his knees. As he resisted, another trustee was summoned to enforce the new seating arrangements. After William White was similarly accosted, Allen observed that "prayer was over, and we all went out of the church in a body, and they were no more plagued with us." This racial incident, which derived from diminished Methodist spirituality, "filled" Allen and his followers "with fresh vigor" to build their own church.[27]

Some scholars dispute when Allen dated this crucial event. Allen, Daniel Coker, and James Champion, in an 1817 historical account about the origin of the AME Church, declared the following:

In November 1787, the colored people belonging to the Methodist Society in Philadelphia, convened together, in order to take into consideration the evils under which they labored, arising from the unkind testament of their white brethren, who considered them a nuisance in the house of worship, and even pulled them off their knees while in the act of prayer, and ordered them to the back seats.[28]

Allen's major biographers, Charles H. Wesley in 1935 and Carol V. R. George in 1972, validate the testimony about the racial conflict at St. George found in the first *AME Doctrine and Discipline*. Milton C. Sernett in 1975,

[26] Ibid., 20; Russell E. Richey, Kenneth E. Rowe, and Jean Miller Schmidt, *The Methodist Experience in America: A History*, Volume I (Nashville, TN, Abingdon Press, 2010), 58–60.
[27] Allen, *The Life Experience and Gospel Labors*, 22–24.
[28] Richard Allen, Daniel Coker, and James Champion, "To the Members of the African Methodist Episcopal Church in the United States of America," in *The Doctrine and Discipline of the African Methodist Episcopal Church*, first edition, Philadelphia, Published by Richard Allen and Jacob Tapsico for the African Methodist Connection in the United States (1817, Nashville, TN, AME Sunday School Union, reprint 1985), 11.

however, contended that the gallery to which Allen referred in his autobiography was not built until the early 1790s. Hence, the St. George incident probably occurred in 1792 or 1793, and not in 1787. Other historians, including Gary B. Nash, Albert J. Raboteau, and John Wigger, believe Sernett and doubt the written account of Allen, Coker, and Champion. Richard S. Newman's biography, published in 2008, leaves open the possibility that either Allen's account that claims 1787 or Sernett's research in St. George's records that argues for 1792 or 1793 may be correct. Since Allen's overall recollections about his life and the origin of African Methodism have generally proven reliable, and were not disputed by any of his contemporaries, it is hard to challenge his chronology of the centerpiece event in his life and ministry.[29]

Fortunately, Allen and his followers had already organized on April 12, 1787 the Free African Society (FAS), which focused on mutual aid. Members paid dues out of which funds were disbursed to assist the needy. These FAS activities attached to Allen as a legacy of economic self-help that remained for subsequent centuries in African Methodism and that complemented his other emancipationist initiatives. The FAS, after the St. George incident, also became a venue through which Allen could start a church. Disagreements arose about whether the affiliation would be Methodist or Anglican. Only Allen and Jones favored Methodism, but "a large majority [voted] in favor of the Church of England." The African Episcopal Church of St. Thomas emerged out of the FAS and dedicated its edifice in 1794. Allen, increasingly uncomfortable with the FAS's Quaker practices, declined an invitation to become the rector but endorsed the congregation's second choice, Absalom Jones. He and Jones, however, stayed as close friends. They jointly led a municipally sponsored effort in 1793 to bring relief to victims of the yellow fever epidemic. Even though Allen had been afflicted himself, the two ministers perfected their bleeding techniques through instructions from

[29] Wesley, *Richard Allen: Apostle of Freedom*, 52–53; Carol V. R. George, *Segregated Sabbaths: Richard Allen and the Emergence of Independent Black Churches, 1760–1840* (New York, Oxford University Press, 1972), 56–57; Milton C. Sernett, *Black Religion and American Evangelicalism: White Protestants, Plantation Missions and the Flowering of Negro Christianity, 1787–1865* (Metuchen, NJ, Scarecrow Press, 1975), 117–118, 219–220; Gary B. Nash, *Forging Freedom: The Formation of Philadelphia's Black Community, 1720–1840* (Cambridge, MA, Harvard University Press, 1988), 118–119; Albert J. Raboteau, "Richard Allen and the African Church Movement," in Leon Litwack and August Meier (eds.), *Black Leaders of the Nineteenth Century* (Urbana, University of Illinois Press, 1988), 1; John Wigger, *American Saint: Francis Asbury and the Methodists* (New York, Oxford University Press, 2009), 247–248; Richard S. Newman, *Freedom's Prophet: Bishop Richard Allen the AME Church, and Black Founding Fathers* (New York, New York University Press, 2008), 63–68.

Dr. Benjamin Rush and administered this treatment to patients. They also buried the dead and executed other public health measures. Except for their different denominational decisions, Allen and Jones became an inseparable leadership duo among Philadelphia blacks until the latter's death in 1818.[30]

Nevertheless, Allen remained a Methodist. "I could not be anything but a Methodist," he said, "as I was born and awakened under them." He was "thankful that ever I heard a Methodist preach." Their presence among African Americans, Allen believed, was unambiguously "beneficial." He declared that "we are beholden to the Methodists under God for the light of the Gospel we enjoy." Allen's sentiments, however, did not apply to Methodism in institutional form. He lamented, for example, that the church had abandoned "the simplicity of the Gospel." He regretted "that they conform more to the world and the fashions thereof" and hoped that Methodists "would ask for the good old way, and desire to walk therein." He wanted a return to the Methodism that he experienced in Delaware at the time of his conversion.[31]

The task of recovering this lost Methodism, Allen concluded, belonged to blacks. They surely had a rightful claim to be the saviors of Methodism. When the Methodists came to Delaware, for example, Allen said, "the colored people were their greatest support." He recalled that "slaves would toil in their little patches [and gardens] many a night" and sell the produce to contribute to Methodist preachers. Such actions showed that blacks had a stake in the Methodist enterprise. Therefore, when the Wesleyan mission in America went awry, blacks had both the standing and authority to critique it and redirect it to its evangelical/egalitarian beginnings. For Allen, African Methodism became a vehicle to achieve these objectives. The opposition of white Methodists toward his effort to start a black Methodist parish and their racist conduct at St. George Church validated Allen's analysis about America's wayward Wesleyan movement. Hence, he constructed a different version of Wesleyan Christianity that was closer to what the still living John Wesley envisaged for the Methodist movement than the church that white American practitioners were developing. The founder's steadfast opposition to slavery was resurrected in African Methodism at a time when the ME Church was retreating from this commitment. A theology grounded in religious and racial egalitarianism became a distinguishing characteristic of

---

[30] Allen, *The Life Experience and Gospel Labors*, 27–28; Gary B. Nash, *Forging Freedom*, 111–128; Absalom Jones and Richard Allen, "A Narrative of the Proceedings of the Colored People during the Awful Calamity in Philadelphia, in the Year 1793; And A Refutation of Some Censures Thrown upon Them in Some Publications," in Allen, *The Life Experience and Gospel Labors*, 47–49; Newman, *Freedom's Prophet*, 85–86.

[31] Allen, *The Life Experience and Gospel Labors*, 28.

Allen's AME movement. Moreover, Allen and his followers, according to a black British theologian, Anthony G. Reddie, differed from white Christians, who emphasized "believing in Jesus" while black Christians put stress on "following him." In this latter emphasis, says Reddie, lay Allen's "praxis of spiritual and social liberation."[32]

Perhaps Allen's energetic application of Wesleyan social holiness lay in his larger role in bringing aid to victims of the 1793 yellow fever epidemic. When affluent Philadelphians fled the city, the poor and middling classes, both white and black, remained behind to confront the ravages of the disease. Because the viral cause of yellow fever, incubated in putrid water puddles and transmitted through mosquitoes, was then unknown, the recommended treatment, though ineffectual, was bleeding. This ancient remedy drawn from the humoral theory had no effect upon the fever, the hemorrhaging, and the jaundice that afflicted the sufferers. Such public health measures as quarantine, immediate removal of corpses, and the disposal of mattresses and other items associated with the deceased, however, helped to reduce the spread of the plague. In response to pleas from physician Benjamin Rush, who taught Richard Allen and Absalom Jones how to bleed, and Phila-delphia Mayor Matthew Clarkson, Allen and Jones volunteered to take care of the sick and bury the dead.[33]

Allen, who contracted the disease along with Jones, during the four months of the epidemic and amid 5,000 deaths, bled and comforted patients, hired nurses, purchased coffins, and employed laborers to aid in mortuary duties. Notwithstanding, unsubstantiated and anti-black charges of extortion and theft against black Philadelphians, including Allen and Jones, they encountered unusual danger and exhibited special empathy for yellow fever victims. For Allen, who was impressed with the abolitionism of the early Methodists, through his own frontline fight against the Philadelphia plague,

[32] Ibid., 27; See John Wesley, *Thoughts upon Slavery*, fifth edition (London, G. Paramore, and Methodist Publishing House, 1792); also see Anthony G. Reddie, "A Black Theological Approach to Reconciliation: Responding to the 200th Anniversary of the Abolition of the Slave Trade in Britain," *Black Theology: An International Journal*, Vol. 5, No. 2, 2007, 184–202.

[33] See J. Worth Estes and Billy G. Smith (eds.), *A Melancholy Scene of Devastation: The Public Response to the 1793 Philadelphia Yellow Fever Epidemic* (Canton, MA, Science History Publications, 1997); Absalom Jones and Richard Allen, "A Narrative of the Proceedings of the Colored People during the Awful Calamity in Philadelphia, in the Year 1793; And A Refutation of Some Censures Thrown upon Them in Some Publications," in Richard Allen, *The Life Experience and Gospel Labors of the Rt. Rev. Richard Allen* (reprint 1990), 48–49.

broadened the scope of Wesleyan social holiness and implanted it into his vision of African Methodism.[34]

While envisaging his own version of the Wesleyan movement, Allen invited Asbury in 1794 to dedicate Bethel AME Church, originally a blacksmith's shop. The preachers, however, were developing a different understanding of the congregation's relationship to American Methodism. Asbury, though opposed to preachers who exercised too much independence, did not want to alienate Allen and the Methodist mission to blacks. Since Allen agreed to submit to Methodist doctrine and discipline, Asbury accepted Bethel's separate status. While he and Allen believed that Methodist evangelicalism had not reached its fullest potential among whites and blacks, they differed on how this objective would be accomplished. Asbury, unlike Allen, did not understand that another version of the Wesleyan movement in America was emerging within African Methodism. Allen's infant organization, though still within the American Methodist fold, was developing at its core a vigorous emancipationist ethos. American Methodism was becoming complicit in a religious status quo anchored in diminished advocacy for black freedom. Allen, however, was positioning African Methodism as an insurgent force within the Atlantic World, aimed at saving blacks from slavery and sin. John Wigger, Asbury's definitive biographer, correctly contends that "race clearly separated Allen and Asbury" and that the bishop "would never fully comprehend the realities of slavery and racism." Hence, these two clergymen developed different expectations for the Wesleyan movement in response to these challenges. Though Asbury's racial liberalism convinced him to ordain Allen a deacon in 1799 and to license other black preachers, he could not see beyond these men and their followers as segregated entities within American Methodism. Allen, however, envisaged broader possibilities for Wesleyan blacks in the Atlantic World.[35]

The dictatorial behavior of a succession of ministers associated with St. George ratified Allen's decision to found Bethel Church. Despite his respect for regular order in the ME Church, Allen built boundaries to guard Bethel's autonomy and to provide a refuge for fugitive slaves and freed black people. Moreover, between 1794 and 1816, Allen slowly but steadily constructed canonical and civic foundations for Bethel's independence as a legal

---

[34] Newman. *Freedom's Prophet*, 85–86; Jones and Allen, "A Narrative of the Proceedings of the Colored People," 47, 49–50, 54–55, 61.

[35] Wigger, *American Saint*, 247–248, 250–251, 294.

Wesleyan entity. Moreover, he became in Philadelphia a widely known practitioner of the spiritual and social disciplines of Wesleyan holiness.

Though Allen faced opposition to starting a black church, he also gained some allies. For example, John McClaskey, the area presiding elder, admonished him to cease the solicitation of funds to build an edifice else he would be expelled from the Methodist connection. Allen, however, drew relief from the appointment of an old acquaintance, Freeborn Garrettson, as McClaskey's successor. John Dickens was also supportive and called a halt to any harassment of Allen. Instead, he joined Bishop Asbury at the church's dedication and even suggested the name, Bethel, to launch the new congregation.[36]

After Bethel became an institutional reality, various Methodist clergy commenced efforts to control the church. Since the annual conference usually owned all congregational properties, Bethel, they argued, had no claim to autonomy. Hence, a succession of ministers considered Bethel to be an entity existing within St. George, the parent congregation, and subject to its authority. However, in 1796 Ezekiel Cooper, a ministerial associate at St. George, deceived Allen with an incorporation document that invalidated Bethel's autonomy. After unwittingly signing it, the AME founder resorted to the Pennsylvania Supreme Court to correct the error. Allen sought the guidance of an attorney who advised him to add an African Supplement to Bethel's incorporation. This addendum stated that Bethel's trustees, rather than the Methodist Conference, controlled the church's property. Furthermore, the trustees, if the pastor at St. George was neglectful in fulfilling various preaching and sacramental duties, would engage someone else. Of course, that person was Richard Allen. Therefore, the African Supplement codified through court action Bethel's right to self-determination.[37]

Though Allen outflanked white Methodists in civil rather than church courts, St. George ministers continued their bold assertion of authority based on Methodist disciplinary rules. Some of them tried to persuade Allen and his congregation to submit to them. But, John Emory, Robert R. Roberts, and Robert Burch published letters declaring that Bethel was a renegade congregation. Roberts, for example, invited himself to the Bethel pulpit, but was rebuffed – with Bethel members on one occasion blocking him from entering the pulpit to oust a black exhorter already at the lectern. These and other incidents precipitated a final break between Bethel and white Methodists. On January 1, 1816, Burch challenged the validity of Allen's

[36] George, *Segregated Sabbaths*, 64–65; Wigger, *American Saint*, 250.   [37] Ibid., 65–71.

BETHEL AFRICAN METHODIST EPISCOPAL CHURCH, PHILAD†

Figure 1.1 [Mother] Bethel AME Church, Philadelphia, 1805 (Used with permission from The Library Company of Philadelphia)

African Supplement in the Pennsylvania Supreme Court. The court, however, denied Burch's claim that he had a right to preach over the objection of Bethel members. The ruling was Bethel's official and long overdue declaration of independence.[38]

This formal break occurred long after African Methodism had developed a distinctive theological thrust that distinguished it from American Methodism. Ostensibly, the Bethel battle was a demonstration of successful black resistance to white ecclesiastical power. Examined at a deeper level, however, the quest for black religious autonomy incubated the rise of African Methodism and its emphasis on emancipationist themes embedded in both Wesleyan theology and in American civic culture.[39] These ideas showed how blacks expected Methodism to speak to their experiences in slavery and address their encounter with racial subjugation. The freedom ethos,

---

[38] Ibid., 81–84.
[39] Dennis C. Dickerson, "Liberation, Wesleyan Theology, and Early African Methodism, 1760–1840," *Wesley and Methodist Studies*, 2011, Vol. 3, 109–120.

which drew from their understanding of Methodism, made their liberation-ist objectives a matter of scriptural and societal urgency. Moreover, Meth-odism mandated that personal renewal realized in salvation, sanctification, and perfectionism led to the renewal of society, pursued through the destruction of slavery and other forms of human exploitation.

Hence, African Methodism, even before it coalesced into a denomination, engaged survival issues that affected both enslaved and emancipated blacks in the Atlantic World. Richard Allen, Flora Allen, Daniel Coker, and other founders envisaged a "freedom church" that articulated their claims to full humanity and stood as an institutional challenge against slavery and black degradation. So influential was the walkout of Allen and his followers in 1787 from St. George Church that it "became the symbol and substance of their rebellion" against white hegemony and a precedent for "black self-determination."[40] This reenactment of the Exodus story in the Hebrew Bible, according to such scholars as Eddie S. Glaude and Richard S. Newman, became a powerful symbol for other religious and emancipationist movements in the United States and beyond. That Richard Allen stood in juxtaposition to Toussaint L'Ouverture, the leader of the successful 1791 Haitian slave insur-rection, showed the importance of the emancipationist energies that African Methodism mirrored for blacks in the Atlantic World.[41]

ESTABLISHING AFRICAN METHODISM

Throughout his ministry Richard Allen recognized that blacks densely inhabited the Americas, lived in modest numbers in Europe, and over-whelmingly populated Africa. He also realized that their well-being, despite these disparate locations, intricately connected them to each other. In 1795, for example, the welfare of twenty-five Jamaicans, manumitted by an Eng-lishman, was entrusted to a Philadelphia abolitionist who soon sent them to Allen and the Bethel congregation. The AMEs welcomed them to worship services at Bethel Church and they received commendations for their assist-ance to these expatriate blacks. Similarly, in 1808 Allen celebrated the end of the African slave trade to the United States and marked it as a milestone for the broader effort to free all blacks from this terrible traffic in human cargo. Additionally, Allen's extensive correspondence and cooperation with Paul Cuffee, a black ship owner in New Bedford, Massachusetts, became another

---

[40] Eddie Glaude, *Exodus: Religion, Race, and Nation in Early Nineteenth Century Black America* (Chicago, University of Chicago Press, 2000), 57–58; Newman, *Freedom's Prophet*, 112–113, 239.
[41] Ibid.

example of his pan-African consciousness. Cuffee dreamed of establishing a lucrative commerce between African Americans and Africans, hoping to spearhead the economic development of the "mother" continent. In this effort Allen pledged his support in persuading selected African Americans to immigrate to Africa. For racist reasons, the American Colonization Society (ACS), founded in 1817, the same year that Cuffee died, also encouraged free blacks to leave the United States in hopes of ending their abolitionist appeals. At first, Allen, who conflated the objectives of Cuffee and the ACS, eventually realized that the two were pursuing different objectives. Cuffee and Allen promoted African emigration to facilitate black economic self-sufficiency through transatlantic commerce. Some colonizationists, however, wanted to strengthen slavery while others envisaged American society without any blacks at all. These activities illustrate Allen's familiarity with pressing issues facing blacks on both sides of the Atlantic. These extensive involvements also suggest his expansive view about the potential reach of African Methodism and the need for its protective presence wherever black freedom required advocacy.[42]

Allen believed that an autonomous African institution was foundational to any effort to advance the interests of blacks in the Atlantic World. Therefore, Bethel's victory in the Pennsylvania Supreme Court in 1816 affirming its independence from Wesleyan white domination drew encomiums from black Methodists elsewhere in the Middle Atlantic. Hence, James Champion, a minister at Bethel Church, and Daniel Coker, a leader of black Methodists in Baltimore, joined Allen as coauthors of an apologia about the rise of African Methodism. The treatise recounted the long roster of conflicts with St. George pastors over attempts to control Bethel's spiritual and temporal affairs. Though the authors said "we experienced grievances too numerous to mention," they praised their deliverance from white ecclesial abuse. Bethel's ordeal in Philadelphia also paralleled the experiences of black Methodists in other locales. Allen and Champion recognized, for example, that Baltimore blacks "were treated in a similar manner by white preachers and trustees." Daniel Coker, who had been monitoring Allen's activities, led his Baltimore parishioners in finding "a place of worship for themselves." Coker hailed the court victory for the Philadelphia group, and at the same time as Allen urged their congregations to form a denomination. The AME body could institutionalize their independence across broad geographical areas and promote emancipationist objectives for blacks in

---

[42] Newman, *Freedom's Prophet*, 154–155, 157, 182–207.

the Atlantic World. Coker's role in Baltimore, the same as Allen's leadership in Philadelphia, galvanized the city's Free African Society, founded in 1785, into an organized black Methodist body. Coker, like Allen, had grown restless under the jurisdiction of whites who were derisive of his ministerial authority. A minority of 200 of Sharp Street ME Church's 1,400 black members joined the Coker-led Bethel Church in Baltimore.[43]

Richard Allen encountered in Daniel Coker a compelling and vigorous contender for AME Church leadership. Though Allen was twenty years older, he shared with Coker a background in slavery, a similar fight to establish an autonomous black church, and an Atlantic World consciousness. For these reasons Coker's role in the founding of African Methodism suggests that his episcopacy in the AME Church, had it occurred, would have linked the AME Church to its Atlantic World environment as much as Allen's bishopric. Like Allen, Coker would also have maintained an emancipationist ethos toward blacks in the diaspora. Born as a slave in about 1780 as Isaac Wright in Frederick County, Maryland, Coker's mother, Susan Coker, was a white indentured servant, and his father, Edward Wright, was an African American slave. Though both parents labored for the same "master," Coker was schooled with the son of the owner. Sometime in the 1790s Coker, who looked Caucasian, escaped to New York City where he joined a fledgling black Methodist congregation that would later develop as an AME Zion church. Francis Asbury, whom he met, ordained Coker as deacon in the Methodist Episcopal Church. He returned in 1801 to Maryland, settling in Baltimore where he taught at the abolitionist-sponsored African Academy. Because he was still technically a slave, a Quaker friend bought his freedom, Coker also became more visible as an educator, founded in 1806 his own Daniel Coker School, and became the minister to an emergent group of black Methodists.[44]

Just as Allen wrote such anti-slavery tracts as "An Address To Those Who Keep Slaves and Approve the Practice," in 1810 Coker published "A Dialogue Between a Virginian and an African Minister." Coker, like Allen, had

---

[43] Allen, Coker, and Champion, "To the Members," 13–14; George, *Segregated Sabbaths*, 56; Nina Honemond Clarke, *History of the Nineteenth Century Black Churches in Maryland and Washington, D.C.* (New York, Vantage Press, 1983), 19; J. Gordon Melton, *A Will to Choose: The Origins of African American Methodism* (Lanham, MD, Rowman & Littlefield Publishers, Inc., 2007), 69.

[44] Betty Thomas, "Daniel Coker," in Rayford W. Logan and Michael R. Winston (eds.), *Dictionary of American Negro Biography* (New York, W. W. Norton & Co., 1982), 119; Mary F. Corey, "Daniel Coker," in Henry Louis Gates, Jr. and Evelyn Brooks Higginbotham (eds.), *African American National Biography*, Vol. 2 (New York, Oxford University Press, 2008), 348; Melton, *A Will to Choose*, 65.

become impatient with white Methodists who countenanced black slavery and others who denigrated the humanity of African Americans. Mindful of Allen's struggles to assert African Methodist independence, in 1814 Coker led Baltimore's black Methodists in parting with Wesleyan whites and establishing a separate congregation. When the Allenites won their final court victory, Coker preached on January 21, 1816, a commemorative sermon in tribute to Allen's judicial triumph. In their coauthored publication, it was probably Coker who inserted that "many of the coloured people, in other places, were in a situation nearly like those of Philadelphia and Baltimore." Therefore, "delegates from Baltimore, and other places met those of Philadelphia, and taking into consideration their grievances, and in order to secure their privileges [and] promote union and harmony among themselves" formed the AME Church. Though representatives also came from Attleborough, Pennsylvania, and Salem, New Jersey, Allen and Coker knew that the necessity for African Methodism extended beyond the Middle Atlantic region. By including "Episcopal" in the denominational title of the new Wesleyan body, the two leaders signaled that an aggregation of African Methodist churches and African Methodist meetinghouses coalesced into a formally established ecclesia with a duly elected prelate. Allen, who in the 1807 African Supplement described his congregation as an AME Church "known by the name of Bethel Church," deployed "Episcopal" in his terminology. In showing Bethel's autonomy, his nomenclature charted a course for his African Methodist movement toward an eventual break with the ME Church and the founding of an independent AME connection.[45]

Allen and Coker called black Methodists to meet in Philadelphia on April 9, 1816. On that day Coker was elected the first bishop of this new Wesleyan body. On April 10, however, Coker either declined the episcopacy or resigned in favor of Allen. Accounts about the switch vary widely from Coker's Caucasian features as a barrier to leading a black denomination to Allen's insistence that a compromise making both of them bishops would tax the resources of the infant body. A later AME historian, however, insisted that Coker should be described as the "First bishop-elect" in the new denomination. In any case, Allen, who emerged as the undisputed head of the AMEs, was elected and consecrated a bishop "by the prayer and imposition of the hands of five regularly ordained ministers," including Absalom Jones, now an ordained Episcopal priest. Initially, the AME

---

[45] Ibid., 348–349; Allen, Coker, and Champion, "To the Members," 11, 13–14; *Poulson's American Daily Advertiser*, March 14, 1801; Allen, *The Life Experience and Gospel Labors of the Rt. Rev. Richard Allen*, 35–39.

Church's four congregations in the Middle Atlantic hardly dwarfed the innumerable emergent black Methodist churches that remained in the ME Church. Throughout the antebellum period, however, black preachers and parishioners, who experienced their own encounters with racial discrimination from Wesleyan whites, withdrew to affiliate with independent African Methodists.[46]

Hagiographical accounts and some histories, in correctly emphasizing Allen's large presence and major contributions to African Methodism, have unnecessarily elevated him too far above his younger, but equally talented peers. Daniel Coker of Baltimore and Peter Spencer of Wilmington, Delaware, like the other representatives from Attleborough and Salem, were persons of heightened black consciousness. They, as much as Allen, surmounted white Methodist opposition to their assertions of religious independence. Coker was the undisputed leader of the Baltimore group and Spencer, who founded an independent black Methodist church in Wilmington in 1805, drew four other congregations together in 1813 to form the Union Church of Africans. Historian Lewis V. Baldwin noted that Spencer attended the organizational meeting of the AME Church, but decided against joining it. "Spencer," Baldwin observed, "may have felt that it was more incumbent upon Richard Allen and other black Methodists to join his movement." The Union Church of Africans, Baldwin argued, "already settled upon a Discipline" and had become a connectional institution. John M. Brown, later an AME bishop, noted that Spencer "should be elected" a bishop over Coker or Allen. The Union Church of Africans, Spencer and his associate claimed, "had existed longer than Bethel"; this "gave them 'priority of birth,' and therefore Rev. Peter Spencer should be the man elevated." Nonetheless, Spencer's sect had only a regional reach and Coker, like Allen, saw greater geographical possibilities for African Methodism in the Atlantic World than the smaller Union Church of Africans. Nonetheless, Coker and Spencer, born respectively in 1780 and 1782 and young enough to be Allen's sons, deferred to their older colleague, despite their rivalry with him, and acknowledged his unprecedented episcopacy. AME development, however, would have been steered toward the Atlantic World whether "Bishop" Coker or Bishop Allen stood at the helm of the new denomination. The trajectory

[46] James Handy, *Scraps of AME Church History* (Philadelphia, AME Book Concern, n.d.), 14, 32–33; Wesley, *Richard Allen*, 90, 152–155; Robert H. Reid, Jr., *Irony of Afro-American History: An Overview of AME History and Related Developments* (Nashville, TN, AME Sunday School Union, 1984), 66; Melton, *A Will to Choose*, 102–104, 107–108, 139, 214–216.

of Coker and Allen activities, after they established the AME body, showed
the extent of their pan-African ambitions.[47]

Word about the founding of the AME denomination spread to free black
communities in numerous sections of the United States and abroad.
Between 1817 and 1819, for example, local black bodies in Charleston,
Pittsburgh, and Brooklyn sought affiliation with the AME movement.
Morris Brown, a free mulatto shoemaker, organized a black congregation
in Charleston, which grew from 1,000 in 1817 to 3,000 in 1822. These black
Methodists, upon learning about the AME Church, sent Brown to Philadelphia to connect the group with the newly founded denomination.
Brown, fully ordained in 1818, led the congregation until white authorities
closed it in 1822 because of its connection to a planned slave insurrection.
Though he fled to Philadelphia, members of Emanuel AME Church,
formally organized in 1865, claimed descent from the underground congregation that survived after Brown's pastorate. In Pittsburgh, members of an
African church, in existence since 1808, asked Bishop Allen and the
1818 Baltimore Annual Conference to supply them with a minister. Hence,
David Smith came to western Pennsylvania, officially organized what
would become Wylie Avenue AME Church, and planted additional congre-
gations in Uniontown and Washington, Pennsylvania. Additionally, the
Pittsburgh congregation became the nucleus for a Western/Ohio district,
which joined in 1830 the Philadelphia, Baltimore, and New York Annual
Conferences as one of four jurisdictions within the expanding AME
Church. Elsewhere in the Middle Atlantic, Bishop Allen in 1819 assigned
a missionary to organize a church in Manhattan in New York City.
Members in an existing congregation in Brooklyn, the African Wesleyan
ME Church, learned about this development and also affiliated with the
AME Church. The African Wesleyan ME parish derived from a congregation that a British evangelist had established in 1766. This interracial
group of Methodists worshipped together until whites wanted the growing
black membership to pay a quarterly assessment to occupy the gallery. The
blacks therefore withdrew, raised funds to found their own church, and
later visited Bishop Allen to ask him to supply them with a pastor. Hence,

---

[47] Lewis V. Baldwin, *"Invisible" Strands of African Methodism: A History of the African Union
Methodist Protestant Church and Union American Methodist Episcopal Church*, 1805–1980
(Metuchen, NJ, American Theological Library/Scarecrow Press, 1983), 44–47, 51–55; John
M. Brown, "Biographical Sketches of Bishop Allen and His Coadjutors," *AME Church
Review*, Vol. LIX, No. 171, January–March 1952, 14.

their AME affiliation began in 1818 and the congregation, the Bridge Street Church, became a permanent part of the denomination.[48]

As the AME Church spread westward to Cincinnati, northward to Albany, and southward from Baltimore to Washington DC, Allen and Coker also envisaged expansion possibilities in the Caribbean and Africa. Coker, in the interim of his suspension from the Baltimore Annual Conference on an unspecified charge and his restoration in 1819, deepened his interest in Africa. In learning about Cuffee's African voyages and interacting with the ACS, Coker became acquainted with British efforts to settle emancipated blacks from Britain and America in Sierra Leone. When the ACS transported African Americans to this West African destination, Coker and about ninety others accepted the offer and set sail on the *Elizabeth*. He landed and lived at Campellar and later settled at Hastings. Though he associated with the Wesleyan Methodists, disagreements among black expatriate members led Coker to organize a west African Methodist group. Because his AME credentials allowed him to ordain at least two ministers, it seemed that he functioned, until his death in 1846, as a bishop in this independent black Methodist body.[49]

Coker, who lived more than a decade after Allen died, became an African Methodist leader of bicontinental significance. The sect that he led, though organically separate from the AME Church, derived at least in part from the black Methodist movement that Coker helped to launch. Coker, however deplored the separate development in Baltimore of Bethel AME and Sharp Street Church, where blacks remained loyal to the Methodist Episcopal Church. But, in Africa, he said, "we wish to know nothing of Bethel and of Sharp Street." So that Africans can be evangelized "by a united effort," he added, "the Sharp-Street brethren will be to me as the Bethel brethren; all will be alike." At the same time Coker's transatlantic church involvements reflected the same pan-African vision that Allen, his rival, also envisaged. A few years after Coker left Baltimore for Sierra Leone, Allen contacted President Jean-Pierre Boyer of Haiti in 1824 about emigration to the black republic, "where they might enjoy liberty and equality." Allen, after meeting a Haitian emissary in Philadelphia and sponsoring a meeting at Bethel

---

[48] Daniel A. Payne, *History of the African Methodist Episcopal Church* (Nashville, TN, AME Sunday School Union, 1891), 26, 45; Wesley, *Richard Allen*, 185; also see Amos Jordan, Christine A. Powell, and Andy M. Smith, *The African Wesleyan Methodist Episcopal Church* (1980); Taylor T. Thompson (ed.), *The Legacy of African Methodism in the Third Episcopal District* (Nashville, TN, AME Sunday School Union, 1988), 74.

[49] Payne, *History of the African Methodist Episcopal Church*, 15, 28; Matei Markwei, "The Rev. Daniel Coker of Sierra Leone," *Sierra Leone Bulletin of Religion*, Vol. 7, No. 2 (1965), 43–47.

Church, received the names of 500 possible émigrés. He also harnessed AME expansion to the emigration project. He told Boyer about two persons "who I have authorized to preach." In 1827 the Reverend Scipio Beanes went out from the Baltimore Annual Conference to Haiti as an AME missionary. Additionally, Allen's son, John, emigrated to the island and resided there for a time. Besides Haiti, there were numerous connections that tied AME congregations to Africa. St. Paul AME Church in Columbus, Ohio, for example, during Allen's episcopacy affiliated in 1824 with the denomination. The original organization, however, started in 1814 with "a charter member" who was "a manumitted Negro from Africa." Hence, Allen and Coker, despite their rivalry for the AME episcopacy, created a transatlantic Methodist initiative, which boldly encountered European hegemony with brave assertions of black institutional independence.[50]

Just as Coker's black Wesleyan experiences influenced his derivative denomination in Sierra Leone, James Varick, Christopher Rush, and other founders of the AME Zion Church, based in New York City, chose ecclesiastical autonomy because of the example set by AME leaders. Moreover, the Zionites, though they had a separate origin from the AME Church, considered a possible affiliation with this expanding black Methodist body. Hence, the Zionites and Coker's West African Methodist body shared a nonorganic linkage to the black Wesleyan organization that both Coker and Allen had been elected to lead. Like their counterparts, who started separate African American Methodist congregations elsewhere in Middle Atlantic, aggrieved blacks at John Street Church in New York City withdrew in 1796 and legally established in 1801 their own African chapel. Ultimately, they and other black Methodists formed their own independent religious body. They wanted Bishop Allen to ordain their clergy, but the shortsighted prelate offered affiliation with his denomination as a precondition for his ecclesiastical services. Since the bishop had already attracted a Brooklyn congregation into the AME organization, he may have thought that the Zionites would follow them into the Allenite group. But the bishop miscalculated. Instead, the Zionites, along with black Methodists on Long Island, in New Haven, and a dissident group that had bolted from Allen's Philadelphia

[50] Julius H. Bailey, "'Too Light to Lead': Daniel Coker and Racial Hybridity in the Early African Methodist Episcopal Church," *AME Church Review*, Vol. CXXVI, No. 417, January–March 2010, 52; Newman, *Freedom's Prophet*, 238–239; Wesley, *Richard Allen*, 214–215, 262; Richard Allen to Jean-Pierre Boyer, August 22, 1824, reprinted in the *AME Church Review*, Vol. LXXVI, No. 203, January–March 1960, 30; *Minutes and Reports of the Ninth Quadrennial Convention of the African Methodist Episcopal Church* held in St. Paul AME Church, Columbus, OH, October 4–11, 1927, 7.

congregation, formed in 1821 the AME Zion Church. Despite Zion's friction with the AME denomination, they, like the West African Methodists, pursued institutional independence because of the precedent that Allen and Coker had set in Philadelphia in 1816. These "freedom" churches, in spite of the disagreements and distances that separated them, blended into a composite African Methodist movement. Their emancipationist energies poured into building free black communities, invigorating the abolitionist movement, and resisting Euro-American hegemony throughout the Atlantic World.[51]

AN EMANCIPATION ETHOS

The establishment of an autonomous African Methodism signified an insurgency against racial hierarchy in the Americas and Africa, where enslaved and colonized peoples yielded labor and land to white settlers. These institutional initiatives also stirred individual activities, which aimed at black emancipationist objectives. Hence, Allen, through his writings, abolitionist associations, and organizational efforts, personally pursued the same freedom agenda that his founding of the AME Church represented. Because he was born into slavery, Allen understood his chattel status and the destructive separation it imposed upon him and his family. While laboring for Stokeley Sturgis by day and toiling to purchase his freedom whenever spare time was available, Allen also knew that the value of his labor accrued to his slave master and not to himself. Moreover, Flora Allen, his Virginia born wife whom he married in 1794, remained a slave until her manumission in 1795. Though freed by the Pennsylvania Abolition Society, Flora, like her husband, had fresh memories of bondage and the uncertainties of a chattel existence. Hence, the Allens, though flourishing as free blacks in Philadelphia, identified with those still in slavery. Historian Erica Armstrong Dunbar has plausibly argued that Ona Judge, a slave to Martha and George Washington may have conferred with Allen about her escape from the presidential household in Philadelphia. Washington, a customer to Allen's chimney sweep service, may have met Judge while discharging his sanitation duties. Judge, already aware of Allen's stature among Philadelphia blacks, could have furtively solicited his counsel about the possibilities of fleeing slavery. Notwithstanding this likely encounter, Allen connected the injustices of slavery to his own experiences. Moreover, his familiarity with Afrocentric

---

[51] David H. Bradley, Sr., *A History of the AME Zion Church*, 1796–1872, 2 vols. (Nashville, TN, Parthenon, 1956), 48–54, 80–81, 83.

scriptural references validated his view that human bondage violated Biblical teachings. From Deuteronomy 23:7, for example, he admonished slave owners that "thou shalt not abhor an Egyptian, because thou wast a stranger in his land." Allen, in one of his anti-slavery pamphlets, also beckoned to slave owners "to consider how hateful slavery is in the sight of that God who hath destroyed kings and princes for their oppression of the poor slaves." God, Allen said, was both "the protector and avenger of slaves" and "the first pleader of the cause of slaves." Hence, "if you love your children, if you love your country, (and) if love the God of love, clear your hands from slaves; burden not your children or your country with them."[52]

As Allen's visibility increased as an opponent of slavery, he also commended others who denounced this "mighty evil." He lauded those "who have engaged in the cause of the African race" because they "have wrought deliverance from more than Egyptian bondage." Abolitionists, he observed, had worked to bring blacks "complete redemption from the cruel subjection they are in." He referred to efforts to provide education for blacks and "to call the most abject of our race brethren, children of one God." Allen also warned slave owners that in keeping slaves "under the grievous yoke," those in bondage turned to "dreadful insurrections" as an unpleasing alternative. Though he may have thought about Toussaint L'Ouverture's successful Haitian slave rebellion in 1791, he was certainly pondering his tangential tie to Denmark Vesey and his aborted plans for a slave insurrection in South Carolina.[53]

Morris Brown's AME congregation in Charleston included Vesey, a former slave, as a member and class leader. He was born probably in St. Thomas in the Virgin Islands, but his slave owner, Joseph Vesey, sold him into Haiti. Later, he reclaimed Vesey and settled in South Carolina in 1783, where his slave learned carpentry. In 1800 Denmark Vesey won the lottery, purchased his freedom, but never succeeded in buying the freedom of his wife and children. In connecting with Brown's AME Church in Hampstead, Vesey, as he became familiar with the denomination's insurgent origins, also gained proficiency in Biblical scriptures related to the ancient Hebrews and

---

[52] Earl K. Johnson, Jr., "Flora Allen: Founding Mother of African Methodism," *AME Church Review*, Vol. CXIX, No. 389, January–March 2003, 50; Erica Armstrong Dunbar, *Never Caught: The Washingtons' Relentless Pursuit of Their Runaway Slave, Ona Judge* (New York, Atria, 2017), 107–108; Allen, "An Address to Those Who Keep Slaves and Approve the Practice," in *The Life Experience and Gospel Labors*, 69–71.

[53] Allen, "A Short Address to the Friends of Him Who Hath No Helper;" Allen in "An Address to Those Who Keep Slaves and Approve the Practice," in *The Life Experience and Gospel Labors*, 71, 75.

how they resembled enslaved African Americans. Hence Vesey proposed in 1822 a slave insurrection in which blacks would seize a Charleston arsenal and use its weapons to fight to free themselves.[54]

Vesey's slave revolt was developed under the cloak of AME class meetings. White authorities noted that these nocturnal gatherings, "avowedly for religious instruction," stirred in parishioners an "inflammatory and insurrectionary doctrine." Vesey, according to his accusers, tried to "kindle in (his) hearers" a "perverted religion and fanaticism." In reality, white officials fully understood that his Biblical exegesis placed scripture on the side of revolt and that his allegiance to an independent black denomination signified resistance to white domination. Moreover, his closest allies, Gullah Jack, an Angolan and reputed sorcerer, Monday Gell, Ned Bennett, and Peter Poyas, were fellow members of the AME Church.[55]

Brown, their pastor, according to one slave, "swore on the Bible never to divulge the secret" concerning the proposed slave rebellion. Two others suggested that Brown knew about the plot, but declared that "I am going to the North, but if you can get men (to support the effort then) you can try this business, but don't call my name." Since the key persons planning the insurrection were Brown's parishioners it is likely that he gave them his tacit approval. The failed recruitment of Peter Prioleau, however, led the slave to tell his owner about the plot. Charleston officials, therefore, arrested 131 blacks and convicted sixty-seven. Thirty-five, including Vesey, were hanged. Richard Allen beckoned Brown to Philadelphia where the bishop gave him refuge, received him as his associate minister at Bethel Church, and consecrated him in 1828 as the second AME bishop.[56]

Allen probably knew nothing about the proposed plot until it was uncovered. Once he learned about the details, he knowingly involved himself with a major suspect, Morris Brown. Though Brown was exonerated, the congregation, which he founded and led, was banned and burned in South Carolina. Hence, the first three elected bishops of the AME Church, Coker, Allen, and Brown, were associated either with policies, persons, or plots to overthrow slavery. Moreover, the ecclesiastical body that they established steadily expanded its insurgency against black subjugation in the Americas

---

[54] *The Trial Record of Denmark Vesey* [Introduction by John Oliver Killens] (Boston, MA, Beacon Press, 1970), x, 11; Bernard E. Powers, Jr., "Seeking the Promised Land: Afro-Carolinians and the Quest for Religious Freedom to 1830," in James Lowell Underwood and W. Lewis Burke (eds.), *The Dawn of Religious Freedom in South Carolina* (Columbia, University of South Carolina Press, 2006), 139.

[55] *The Trial Record of Denmark Vesey*, 13–15.   [56] Ibid., xvi, xviii–xix, 94–96, 131.

and Africa. The institutional energies of African Methodism, which these leaders unleashed, were harnessed to these emancipationist ends.

Allen's affiliation with various black betterment organizations enhanced his emancipationist efforts. His singular distinction as the only black bishop of any ecclesiastical body in the Atlantic World conferred on Allen a stature that few of his contemporaries could match. Hence, the first National Convention of Colored Persons, which Allen helped to organize in 1830, was held at Bethel Church with the venerable prelate in the chair as presiding officer. The convention, the earliest gathering of black leaders, met in Philadelphia to debate the best strategies to advance the black population. The delegates were especially focused on emigration to Canada to allow the escape of blacks from "a land of barbarians." Others, like Allen, had held eclectic views about how to attain black progress, including the promotion of exodus movements to Africa and Haiti, insistence on black citizenship rights in the United States, and emphasis on economic self-sufficiency. Allen's multiple business and property holdings served as an example. Allen also tried a direct attack on slavery through his support of the Free Produce movement, which aimed at the boycott of goods derived from slave labor. He belonged to the Colored Free Produce Society, which he hosted at Bethel Church with an attendance of some 500 supporters. The organization drew a broad constituency of anti-slavery advocates and ratified Allen as a "dedicated abolitionist worthy of emulation."[57]

The liberationist thrust that invigorated Vesey's planned slave revolt and Allen's affiliation with anti-slavery activities were replicated in less dramatic, but significant assertions of black autonomy in other areas of the Atlantic World. Hence, as the denomination expanded to innumerable communities, especially in the Northeast and Midwest, African Methodism was inescapably associated with blacks who pursued institutional independence from white churches and opposed slavery and racial inequality. In 1810, for example, a congregation of whites, blacks, and Indians in Flushing, New York, formed the Macedonia Methodist Episcopal Society. Though white clergy regularly ministered to them, they refused preaching privileges to blacks. Therefore, Macedonia members in 1822 broke with the ME Church and shifted their allegiance to the AME Church. Similarly, the Religious Society of Free Africans was organized in Trenton, New Jersey, in 1811. After they learned in 1816 about the founding of the AME Church, Bishop Allen met with the renamed Mount Zion African Church and brought the

---

[57] Newman, *Freedom's Prophet*, 264, 266–268, 271.

congregation into the denomination. Another group of "free persons of colour," including thirty families, in Rahway, New Jersey, also sought an AME affiliation. Additionally, denominational growth moved westward from Philadelphia toward western Pennsylvania and Ohio. Initially, black and white Methodists in Chillicothe, Ohio, worshipped together, perhaps as early as 1796. As the numbers of African Americans increased, they were assigned to a gallery and told to receive the communion after whites had finished. In 1821 they departed to organize their own congregation with guidance from the Reverend William Paul Quinn. Blacks in Steubenville, Ohio, also with assistance from Quinn, started their AME congregation in 1823. Former slaves founded a congregation in 1830 in West Bridgewater, Pennsylvania, several miles northwest of Pittsburgh. These and other churches, whether in the Northeast or the Midwest, became a part of Allen's growing roster of churches serving blacks recently manumitted from slavery and anxious to establish themselves as communities of free people.[58]

Allen attempted the difficult task of integrating into AME polity liberationist themes expressed in the discipline, hymnody, and culture of African Methodism. He believed, for example, that Methodism was beneficial to blacks because it possessed a "plain doctrine" and "a good discipline." Though mostly adopted from Wesleyan whites, the AME *Discipline*, published in 1817, followed Methodist "Rules" on governance and "creeds." Despite similarities in polity and belief with the MEC, an apologia, which Allen coauthored with Coker and Champion, was inserted in the volume. The book framed the distinctive identity of the denomination and articulated its raison d'être in insurgent language. Allen and his followers were a religious people whose humanity had been devalued and their worship desecrated in sacrilegious acts of racial arrogance. As supporting members of St. George, they rejected this treatment and instead founded two other congregations, including one that was authentically Methodist. They developed for their African Methodist denomination a *Discipline* with codes of conduct for Methodist ministers and members and guidelines for the operation of conferences, classes, and bands. Buried in the subtext of familiar passages were mandates to develop AMEs into a moral people faithful to the tenets of Methodism. In following these disciplinary precepts, AMEs constructed themselves as a free people, whether in the Americas or Africa, and demonstrated their capacity for self-sufficiency and exemplary moral

---

[58] *The African Methodist Episcopal Church: One-Hundred Eighty-Eight Years of Progress* (1976), n.p.; Thompson (ed.), *The Legacy of African Methodism in the Third Episcopal District* (1988), 77, 109, 132.

character. Allen, a serial purchaser of property and practitioner of thrift, said one of his biographers, secured for himself "an irrefutable place in American civic and social culture" through self-help. If Methodism could instill the values of personal discipline, integrity, and autonomy in the founder, it could do the same for blacks throughout the Atlantic World. In these ways blacks would be truly free. Such subtexts spoke to liberationist objectives, which lay behind Allen's adoption of the Methodist Discipline. The section on slavery, however, was an explicit expression on how Allen linked the AME polity to the attainment of black freedom. "We will not receive any person into our society as a member," the *Discipline* said, "who is a slave-holder." Moreover, "any who are now members, that have slaves, and refuse to emancipate them" could not belong to an AME congregation. To Allen tying the terms AME and slaveholder constituted an oxymoron. Though white Methodists in the late eighteenth century held this same position, their later retreat from these principles convinced Allen to reemphasize them and insert them in the *AME Doctrine and Discipline*.[59]

Hymnody, a major Methodist medium, communicated the gospel, ener-gized the faith, and enhanced worship. The Wesley brothers, for example, published thirty hymnals, which showed the centrality of these "sacred songs" to Methodist identity and practice. John Wesley said hymns embraced "all the important truths of our most holy religion" and served as their "handmaid of piety." Charles Wesley, who alone wrote thousands of hymns, often articulated the nomenclature of freedom in his many compos-itions: "Come, thou long expected Jesus, born to set Thy people free." The liberation to which Wesley referred often involved the Savior breaking the power of sin and the chains of iniquity. But when black listeners heard "born thy people to deliver," such phrases implied that Jesus would release those in bondage to both sin and slavery. Allen, like the Wesleys, viewed hymnody as integral to AME worship and as a primer to show the way to salvation. Hence, in the AME Discipline there was the exhortation that the minister should interrupt singing to inquire if parishioners knew what they were saying, and that they should "speak no more than" what they felt and perhaps understood. Moreover, Allen and cofounder Coker, again like Charles Wesley, in his poetry transposed into hymnody, articulated emanci-pationist themes derived from the assurance of divine protection. In reflec-tions on Bethel Church and its battle with white Methodists, Coker declared, "Bethel surrounded by her foes, but not yet in despair, Christ heard her

---

[59] Allen, *The Life Experience and Gospel Labors*, 27; Newman, *Freedom's Prophet*, 178, 197; *The Doctrine and Discipline of the African Methodist Episcopal Church* (1817), 105.

supplicating cries; the God of Bethel heard." This testimony to God's superiority to temporal and ecclesiastical power invigorated AME audacity in
declaring independence from "the proud oppressor's frown." Allen published Coker's poem in his autobiography and showed they were of one
mind about AME hymnody. Though Allen's vision for AME music, displayed in three published collections, adhered to standard Wesleyan, camp
meeting, and folk sections, it also acknowledged the black religious culture of
his AME followers. One scholar identified the pioneering second hymnal for
its emphasis on "revival songs" or "gospel hymns" signifying a "merged
tradition of revival orality and evangelical literacy that fed his congregation's
worship experience." His hymnals also created idiomatic space for musical
expressions drawn from the black Atlantic and accommodated multiple
forms of religious expression. Therefore, he attached to various hymns
"wandering choruses" that could be randomly appended to sundry selections
depending on the spiritual direction that worshippers discerned. This practice offered a framework for AME expansion to untapped areas in the
Atlantic World where new and African derived expressions of religiosity
could be absorbed.[60]

Allen's aggregate experiences as a fighter against slavery, ecclesiastical
abuse, and racial inequality facilitated the founding of the AME Church.
Hence, he aligned the denomination's discipline and infrastructure to black
emancipationist objectives. Denial of membership to slave owners and
efforts to embed in AME hymnody a liberationist ethos and openness to
black cultural idioms showed his attempt to create a freedom church in both
structure and practice. Order and governance, however, did not prevent
tensions between required institutional activities and demands to accommodate critiques and claims from dissident AMEs. Allen encountered such
conflicts in his awkward dealings with Jonathan Tudas and Jarena Lee. In
both instances Allen, the freedom fighter, yielded to Allen, the institutional
administrator who viewed himself as a protector of AME sectarian interests,
despite the legitimate grievances of individual ministers and members.

Tudas's grievances focused on Allen's alleged fiscal improprieties. Allen,
of course, defended his integrity by noting documentary evidence and

---

[60] Hempton, *Methodism*, 69; *The Doctrine and Discipline of the African Methodist Episcopal Church* (1817), 56; Allen, *The Life Experience and Gospel Labors*, 34; Christopher N. Phillips, "Versifying African Methodism: Or What Did Early African-American Hymnbooks Do?" *The Papers of the Bibliographical Society of America*, Vol. 107, No. 3, September 2013, 326; J. Roland Braithwaite (ed.), *Richard Allen, A Collection of Hymns and Spiritual Songs* (Nashville, TN, AME Sunday School Union, 1987), xiii–xiv; Wesley, *Richard Allen: Apostle of Freedom*, 146.

testimonials that unequivocally exonerated him. Allen, even after his election as bishop, served as Bethel's treasurer up until 1820, but never relinquished his pastorate of the "mother" congregation. Although he took no salary from the congregation, except when the trustees compelled him, he was officially both bishop and pastor. The conflation of these ecclesiastical functions stoked Tudas's animosity toward Allen. As an influential figure in black religious life, both locally and internationally, he tried to portray the bishop as hungry for financial and ecclesiastical control. Tudas, according to Allen biographer Richard S. Newman, may have resented Allen's higher class position. His attacks on Allen failed because members at both Bethel and the derivative Wesley AME Zion Church distrusted Tudas and remembered him as a dissident influence within both congregations. The narrative emerging from this insular conflict, however, was scarcely liberationist, but an exercise in raw institutional power by Allen aimed at defeating Tudas. Whenever African Methodism plunged into such battles, its emancipationist emphasis receded and its institutional activities focused on denominational preservation. This dilemma plagued the AME Church throughout its existence and created tension between its liberationist mission and its legitimate quest for institutional continuance. In fact, denominational defenders argued that keeping African Methodism alive, notwithstanding accusations against it, was itself a liberationist act. Nonetheless, Allen's reputation remained intact because of a forceful rebuttal against Tudas in a widely disseminated pamphlet, *The Sword of Truth*. Allen's honor and that of his episcopacy were protected and the esteem of the AME Church was maintained. These objectives, however, were achieved because Allen played "hardball" and defeated his weaker, but daring, detractor.[61]

Unlike the Tudas case, Jarena Lee's confrontation with the bishop inadvertently strengthened the liberationist thrust of the denomination. Though slavery was unambiguously denounced, there was no such clarity on the status of women. Lee, a member of Allen's Bethel Church, told her pastor in 1809 that she had been called to preach. "Our Discipline knew nothing at all about it," Allen said, "it did not call for women preachers." Despite this rebuff, Lee, while worshipping at Bethel eight years later, spontaneously stood and completed the sermon of a spiritually exhausted exhorter. Allen, now a bishop, witnessed what had happened and was immediately convinced that Lee had been inspired by the Holy Spirit. Bishop Allen then admitted that he had been wrong to deny her call to preach and authorized

---

[61] *The Sword of Truth: Or a Reply to Facts Relative to the Government of the African Methodist Episcopal Church Called Bethel* (1823), 4, 6, 10–11; Newman, *Freedom's Prophet*, 223.

her to proclaim the gospel. He wrote testimonials attesting to her legitimacy as a preacher throughout the Northeast and invited her to exhort in AME annual conferences. She "was called to that work," Allen observed, "as any of the (other) preachers (whom he) sent." Lee contended that when a denominational discipline conflicted with "the word of life," the church risked opposition to divine authority. Because "nothing is impossible with God," she declared, then "why should it be thought impossible, heterodox, or improper for a woman to preach?" Bishop Allen, despite his ecclesiastical standing, was pushed by Lee into uncharted disciplinary terrain. Few established churches had unequivocally declared women eligible to preach. But, Allen, the head of an upstart denomination, because of Lee's persistence, enlarged the liberationist reach of his black religious body. Though it was not Allen's original design, the AME Church in the Atlantic World gestured toward making gender equity as important as pan-Africanist inclusion as a part of the mission of African Methodism. Though the full ordination of women eluded Lee and several generations of AME women, the definition of full freedom for persons of African descent belatedly included gender as a component of the church's liberationist ethos.[62]

Embedded in Allen's vision for African Methodism was an Atlantic consciousness that he channeled into the AME movement. This awareness, present in Allen's early ministry, showed that his perspectives and activities operated within this intellectual framework. Allen revealed his knowledge about the black Atlantic in the narrative that he coauthored with Absalom Jones about Philadelphia's 1793 yellow fever epidemic. "The public," they wrote, "was informed that in the West Indies and other places, where this terrible malady had been, it was observed that the blacks were not affected." That conventional wisdom, based on the observations of Allen and Jones, was demonstrably incorrect. "When the people of color had the sickness and died," they noted, "we were imposed upon, and told it was not with the prevailing sickness, until it became too notorious to be denied; then were told some few died." Antagonists, though trying to discredit the on-the-ground experiences of Allen and Jones and accuse them of fabricating their expenses for performing vital public health services for their city, did no harm to their published testimony. Whites in Philadelphia, a major port for international trade, were familiar with the Caribbean. But so were Allen and Jones. That Allen understood the racial and health characteristics of the West Indies equipped him to assess and compare how blacks lived in

---

[62] Jarena Lee, *The Religious Experiences and Journal of Mrs. Jarena Lee* (Nashville, TN, AME Sunday School Union, 1991), 13, 22, 41, 44.

different areas within the Atlantic World. He increasingly deployed this information to facilitate AME expansion in the years after Jones's death.[63]

When Richard Allen died on March 26, 1831, the AME Church stretched outward from Philadelphia to several states and to Haiti and Canada. He had envisaged the denomination for slave and free, African and Creole, and indigenous and expatriate populations in various territories across the Atlantic World. Because Euro-American hegemony compelled these "unsettled" peoples into forced migrations, Allen spearheaded a transatlantic religious movement to offer a stable institutional presence in their otherwise uncertain existence. Because AME belief and praxis included an emancipationist ethos, Allen developed African Methodism as a liberationist project. The church's ecclesiastical interests, however, increasingly focused on policies and activities, which lay in the realm of institutional preservation. Therefore, tensions between the denomination's liberationist heritage and the need for organizational maintenance emerged during the Allen era and persisted after his death. The continued growth of the denomination within settled and migrant communities obliged ministers and members to pursue potentially conflicting tasks. Even as they tended to institutional affairs, their adherence to African Methodism required a commitment to both organizational and emancipationist objectives. Whether AMEs would prioritize the fight against slavery and black inequality over narrow efforts to protect their sectarian interests would determine if the heirs of Allen could reconcile these dualities within an increasingly complex institution.

---

[63] Jones and Allen, "A Narrative of the Proceedings of the Colored People," 59.

2

☙

The Freedom Church, 1831–1861

RECONCILING INSTITUTION BUILDING AND INSURGENCY

The African Methodist Episcopal (AME) Church emerged out of the age of democratic revolution in the late eighteenth century. The fledgling religious body drew moral and intellectual energy from anti-slavery and anti-slave trade initiatives that grew out of the American, French, and Haitian revolutions and from British abolitionism. Within this Atlantic context African Methodism defended the rights and freedom of African and Creole peoples in Africa and the Americas as these mobile populations identified shifting areas of safety where they could realize their autonomy and pursue self-determination. The AME Church, itself an African and Creole institution, linked its development to this "mobile laity" of expatriates, ex-slaves, and emigrationists who were pursuing freedom objectives in varying locations within the Atlantic World. This mobility stirred debates within African Methodism about the transnational identities of their constituents and about how they could achieve the full emancipation of the broader black population. Hence, AME authenticity derived from its commitment to the emancipationist objectives of its diverse and mobile membership. The denomination, in constructing the necessary structures and operations to sustain itself as an expanding ecclesiastical body, however, experienced tensions between these legitimate institutional activities and espousing its emancipationist ethos. These conflicts at times resulted in less rigorous attention to the full freedom of the denomination's multiple constituencies. Holding together an ambitious agenda of securing freedom for a large and varied population of black peoples and building a strong institutional structure became an insuperable task for this vital, but vulnerable, denomination.

Sarah Allen and Morris Brown, Richard Allen's closest confidantes, lived out different facets of the liberationist legacy and diasporic ethos of the AME founder. Mrs. Allen, who married the Philadelphia pastor in August 1801, a few months after Flora's death, bore their six children. Two of them emulated the wanderlust that had characterized their father's early itinerancy as a Methodist preacher. John, who learned both French and Spanish, lived for a few years in Haiti during the 1820s, studied to be a missionary to Africa, and validated Allen's vision for denominational expansion within the Atlantic World. After he returned to Philadelphia, he left again and settled near Flesherton, Ontario. He married Ann Gowland and died in 1859 in Canada. Another son, Peter Allen, departed Philadelphia in 1835, settled in Huntsville, Alabama, and married a slave woman named Mary. He volunteered to serve in the military as a flutist and saw action in Texas against the Mexicans at the Battle of Coleto Creek. He was killed in 1836 with others in his regiment. At some point before his death, he purchased land in Texas, which stirred a dispute between his siblings and his widow. Mary Allen, who prevailed in the Texas Supreme Court, probably knew little about her father-in-law and how her husband imitated his zeal to acquire property. Economic self-sufficiency and identification with those in slavery were identifiable traits within the Allen family. These characteristics, replicated in John and Peter, drew as much from the AME founder as from their mother, Sarah, a Virginia migrant and longtime resident in Philadelphia.[1]

Mrs. Allen is usually portrayed in hagiographical accounts as a supportive spouse and as an AME stalwart with a motherly mien. Perhaps she deliberately cultivated this persona of herself as Allen's "consort" and as a "mother in Israel." This one-dimensional view of Sarah Allen, however, conceals the emancipationist temperament that she, as much as her husband, modeled for their sons, John and Peter. Born in the Isle of Wight, Virginia, in 1764, it is unclear whether or not she was a slave, and if so whether or not she was manumitted after coming to Philadelphia at the age of eight. Her eulogists hinted at a slave background when they wrote, maybe in reference to her early life in Virginia, "she was first seen to glide from the stormy element of

[1] Richard S. Newman, *Freedom's Prophet: Bishop Richard Allen the AME Church, and Black Founding Fathers* (New York, New York University Press, 2008), 207–208, 262; Katharine B. Dockens and Yvonne Y. B. Studevan, "In the Shadow of Their Ancestors: The Descendants of Richard and Sarah Allen," *AME Church Review*, Vol. 117, No. 381, January–March, 2001, 14–15; John Allen Cemetery headstone, Flesherton (Ontario) Cemetery, Ward B, Lot 81 (Document, Allen Family Tree-Courtesy of Yvonne Studevan, Athens, Georgia, seventh generation descendant of Richard and Sarah Allen); Stephen Taylor, "Peter Allen: A Son of the AME Founder," *AME Church Review*, Vol. 127, No. 421, January–March 2011, 33–35.

oppression." Known as Sarah Bass, she was previously married and was the widow whom Allen and Absalom Jones hired as a nurse during Philadelphia's 1793 yellow fever epidemic. They commended her and other black nurses because they endangered themselves while helping victims of the deadly plague. Additionally, she assisted "several families" without compensation, and when offered money she left the decision to "those she served." Sarah Allen, now the widow to the AME founder, no less than well-known abolitionists hid and aided fugitive slaves by giving them shelter and funds. Like her husband, who sheltered slave runaways, Allen's association with the Underground Railroad elicited from those who mourned her death in 1849 regrets that "the poor, flying slave, trembling and panting in his flight, [had] lost a friend not easily replaced." Furthermore, "her purse" was no longer available to those whom she "would bid God speed to the land of liberty, where the slave is free from his master, and the voice of the oppressor is no longer heard."[2]

Hence, Sarah Allen joined a cadre of black female abolitionists who undermined slavery in both public and private acts of insurgency. Some were motivated by the same Wesleyan social holiness that shaped Allen's spirituality while others remembered their own manumission from slavery and determined to help free those who were still in bondage. Sojourner Truth and Harriet Tubman, both with ties to the AME Zion Church, became conspicuous anti-slavery activists, one on the abolitionist lecture circuit and the other as a conductor and guide on the Underground Railroad. Sarah Allen, more than a generation older than both women, labored, however, in the shadow and memory of her venerable husband. Nevertheless, her material assistance to an unknown number of fugitive slaves drew from an emancipationist ethos that she and the first generation of AMEs inserted into the theology and lived religion of their denomination.[3]

Jarena Lee, like Allen, highlighted how AME women were aligned with the abolitionist movement. Through her presence at anti-slavery events in Buffalo and New York City in 1834 and 1840, and in speaking in Philadelphia in 1853 at the national meeting of the American Anti-slavery Society, she

[2] Daniel A. Payne, *History of the African Methodist Episcopal Church* (Nashville, TN, AME Sunday School Union, 1891), 86–88; Absalom Jones and Richard Allen, "A Narrative of the Proceedings of the Black People during the Late Awful Calamity in Philadelphia in the Year 1793 and a Refutation of the Censures, Thrown upon Them in Some Late Publications," in *Richard Allen, The Life Experience and Gospel Labor of the Rt. Rev. Richard Allen* (Reprint 1990), 55.
[3] Shirley J. Yee, *Black Women Abolitionists: A Study in Activism, 1828–1860* (Knoxville, University of Tennessee Press,1992), 3.

blended her evangelistic travels with abolitionist activity. When the colonization issue was debated at the Philadelphia meeting, Lee joined other women, including Sojourner Truth, in opposing it. After preaching in Burlington, New Jersey, Lee left for an anti-slavery meeting in New York City. She joined a female comrade "who was ever zealous in the good cause of liberty and the rights of all." Lee testified that a particular speech strongly affected her, in which the speaker had said since "[we] are all children of one parent, no one is justified in holding slaves." As a result, Lee "felt that the Spirit of God was in the work" of abolitionism, so she decided to join an anti-slavery society. "The cause is good," she said, "and I pray God to forward on the work of abolition until it fills the world, and then the Gospel will have free course to every nation, and in every clime." Both Allen and Lee, unsung abolitionists, embodied the impact of this movement in the early development of African Methodism.[4]

Less dramatic, but no less important, however, was the protective presence of African Methodism as an institutional aegis for blacks in hostile locales throughout the Northeast and Midwest. Morris Brown, Vesey's pastor and Allen's episcopal successor, presided over denominational growth during this period. Brown understood that AME churches were places where black self-determination was promoted, and functioned as venues where preaching and concrete opposition to slavery were normative activities. Moreover, he sustained Allen's view of African Methodism as a church for the black Atlantic. In 1840, for example, he formally organized the Canada Annual Conference. This jurisdiction, the first outside the United States, consisted of congregations primarily in Ontario. The members were slave escapees and expatriates from embattled black communities in Philadelphia, Cincinnati, and other cities where racial violence threatened their physical well-being. They filled the church in Toronto with 250 members and populated congregations on the St. Catherine, London, and Brantford circuits. Alexander Helmsley, for example, a slave born in Maryland, escaped to New Jersey. Though he was arrested and faced extradition, the New Jersey Supreme Court manumitted him. To remain safe from slave catchers, Helmsley and his family migrated to St. Catharine, where he served until 1854 as a pastor among Canada AMEs. John W. Lindsay, born free in Washington DC, was kidnapped and enslaved in Tennessee. He ran away to Pennsylvania in 1835 and passed as white. He too

---

[4] Frederick Knight, "The Many Names for Jarena Lee," *Pennsylvania Magazine of History and Biography*, Vol. 141, No. 1, January 2017, 61; Jarena Lee, *The Religious Experiences and Journal of Mrs. Jarena Lee* (Nashville, TN, AME Sunday School Union, 1991), 134–135.

settled in St. Catharine and joined the AME congregation. Bishop Brown's ministers and members, living in regions west of the Alleghenies, were advocates for fugitives such as Helmsley and Lindsay. In 1840 they denounced slavery and established African Methodism as an insurgent force against it. "It is the duty of all Christians," they said, "to use their influence and energies against all systems that rudely trample under foot the claims of justice." Therefore, every effort would be mobilized to break "every fetter" until "all men enjoy the liberty that the Gospel proclaims."[5]

Hence, Brown faced a twofold task as the second AME bishop. He realized that AMEs tied themselves to the abolition of slavery and to advocacy for free and fugitive blacks. The organization of new congregations and annual conferences facilitated the attainment of these objectives. Therefore, AME churches became places where abolitionists hid fugitive slaves and where free blacks constructed their communities and asserted their social and economic autonomy. These developments correlated with steady AME expansion throughout the North and Canada and into the border slave states. Church growth, however, required Brown to tend to denominational governance and other institutional duties, which, at times, deflected his focus from the frontline fight for black freedom. Ecclesiastical responsibilities, when they drew Brown's full attention, challenged the church's reputation for militancy and slowed its expansion into the broader Atlantic World. Furthermore, in managing these tensions AME leaders were wrongly perceived as more interested in their own insular interests than with major matters confronting the black population.

When the 1840 New York Annual Conference convened in New York City, Charles B. Ray, the editor of the *Colored American*, compared the AME jurisdiction unfavorably to the AME Zion conference in both size and involvement in black causes. AME clergy in New York and elsewhere, Ray observed, "while they are men of worth and piety . . . exhibit, perhaps, less of liberality and public spirit, and of interest in the great questions of the day, than ministers" in the Zion group. Ray's assessment drew from his misconception that AME preachers "are mostly from the south and west," which explained their lack of militancy. The AMEs, of course, vehemently objected and Brown sent a delegation to tell him personally. Their rebuttal, however, focused on minor factual errors rather than the poignant charge of laxity in

[5] Payne, *History of the African Methodist Episcopal Church*, 128–130; Report by Samuel Ringgold, March 24, 1853, in C. Peter Ripley (ed.), *The Black Abolitionist Papers*, Volume II, Canada, 1830–1865 (Chapel Hill, University of North Carolina Press, 1986), 260–261, fn. 7, fn. 8.

pursuing the fight for black freedom. They did not criticize Ray for omitting Brown's Vesey connection and that the slave insurrectionist himself was an AME exhorter. He knew nothing about Sarah Allen's furtive efforts in behalf of fugitive slaves. He had heard about Edward Waters, whom the AMEs had elected to the episcopacy in 1836 to assist Bishop Brown. But Ray was unaware that he was one of a circle of AMEs who had influenced Frederick Douglass, a young adult slave in Baltimore and a future abolitionist.[6]

Ray surely knew that Brown and other AME leaders blended these hidden activities with other secret strides in building churches in hostile locations both for a brief time in South Carolina in the late 1810s and throughout the slave areas of Maryland and the District of Columbia in the 1830s. As an expansive African Methodism pushed into multiple places where no AME Zion congregations existed, ministers and members discharged numerous emancipationist and institutional commitments through public and private means. At times, it meant direct aid to fugitive slaves even as they avoided contact with slave authorities. After the adjournment of the 1840 General Conference in the slave city of Baltimore, for example, AME leaders decided against wide dissemination of their proceedings. "The terror of slave-holders," said one observer, probably persuaded Brown to abbreviate the record of their transactions. In this way seemingly innocent information could neither be learned nor used against the church or the slave members whom they served.[7]

Ray and his ministerial colleagues in black Congregational and Presbyterian circles were conspicuous in the abolitionist movement as journalists, lecturers, and organizers. Ray, Theodore S. Wright, Samuel E. Cornish, Henry Highland Garnet, and others, though they served black Calvinist congregations, were unlike Morris Brown. The AME prelate was constructing a connectional religious body with a transatlantic reach while his

[6] "Minutes of the New York Annual Conference, June 13–22, 1840," in *Minutes of the General and Annual Conferences of the African Methodist Episcopal Church*, comprising Four Districts for A.D. 1836–1840 (Brooklyn, George Hogarth, 1840), 33–34, 40–43; also cited in Dennis C. Dickerson, *A Liberated Past: Explorations in A.M.E. Church History* (Nashville, TN, AME Sunday School Union, 2003), 30.

[7] Payne, *History of the African Methodist Episcopal Church*, 131. Contrary to what Payne declared in his history, the proceedings were published, but seemingly in an abbreviated form. See "The Seventh General Conference of the African Methodist Episcopal Church, Baltimore, Maryland, May 4, 1840, and continued in session ten days successively," in *Minutes of the General and Annual Conferences of the African Methodist Episcopal Church*, comprising Four Districts for A.D. 1836–1840 (Brooklyn, New York, George Hogarth, 1840), 1–5.

Figure 2.1 The presentation of a gold snuff box, Bethel AME Church, Baltimore, 1845, from Pastor Darius Stokes to the Reverend R. J. Breckenridge in gratitude for his efforts to prevent legislation to restrict the manumission of slaves. (Used with permission from the Maryland Historical Society)

Congregational and Presbyterian counterparts, though at times discharging their pastoral duties, labored as full-time abolitionists. Since Brown was shouldering both emancipationist and institutional obligations, he had less visibility in the abolitionist cause than Ray deemed desirable. In fact, one scholar, Gayraud S. Wilmore, has noted that "the pressures of ecclesiastical affairs in the burgeoning new (black) denominations distracted many of their ministers from a fuller involvement in secular affairs." Hence, Wilmore argued that after "the 1830s black ministers in the predominantly white denominations began to play an important role in reform work and anti-slavery agitation." Neither Ray in the nineteenth century nor Wilmore, a black Presbyterian historian in the twentieth century, emphasized that building the AME denomination was as much an act of African American insurgency and crucial to the freedom of slave and nonslave blacks as were formal anti-slavery activities, a position consistent with that expressed by historian Carol V. R. George. They scarcely recognized that AME membership in 1837, for example, stood at 7,288, which was twice the size of the AME Zion Church whose membership was 2,884 and five times bigger than the 1,263 members in the Union Church of Africans. AMEs also exceeded the less than 1,000 black Presbyterians and Congregationalists scattered in fourteen congregations exclusively in the Northeast.[8]

Ray's charge resonated, however, in various church and civic venues. While still a slave in Maryland, Frederick Douglass, who attended Baltimore's Bethel AME Church, received intimate spiritual nurturing from two members, one of them a local preacher. In later years he attended the 1884 General Conference and said that in the "old" Bethel Church he "sat under the quiet teaching of Bishop (Edward) Waters" who became the denomination's third bishop. Though he attributed to his Bethel religious experience his lasting faith formation, Douglass had grown disenchanted with the congregation because some officers showed hostility to the abolitionist movement. Five trustees in 1835 criticized anti-slavery publications as "vile" and "incendiary." Though these Bethelites might have feared for the safety of their church and its continued existence in a slave city, their vilification of bold abolitionist voices was judged inexcusable and cowardly by Douglass. In Columbus, Ohio, at the 1849 all black Mass State Convention, a Cleveland delegate accused the AME Church as being "proslavery" and another speaker made a similar denunciation about black Baptists. Standing in the sanctuary of Bethel AME Church, the convention site, the delegate disparagingly declared that "the Methodist denomination, as such, was opposed to us as a people. 'Why sir, the brethren in whose house we now sit, dare not come and defend their position.'" Bethel's pastor and the

[8] See David E. Swift, *Black Prophets of Justice: Activist Clergy before the Civil War* (Baton Rouge, Louisiana State University Press,1989); Gayraud S. Wilmore, *Black Religion and Black Radicalism: An Interpretation of the Religious History of Afro-American People* (Garden City, New York, Doubleday, 1973), 91–92; Carol V. R. George, "Widening the Circle: The Black Church and the Abolitionist Crusade," reprinted in Timothy E. Fulop and Albert J. Raboteau (eds.), *African American Religion: Interpretive Essays in History and Culture* (New York, Routledge, 1996), 165–169; cited in Lewis V. Baldwin, *"Invisible" Strands of African Methodism: A History of the African Union Methodist Protestant Church and Union American Methodist Episcopal Church, 1805–1980* (Metuchen, NJ, American Theological Library/Scarecrow Press, 1983), 60; *The Minutes and Sermon of the Second Presbyterian and Congregational Convention* held in The Central Presbyterian Church, Philadelphia, 28 October, 1858 (1858), 20.

convention chaplain, John Mifflin Brown, whose compelling Underground Railroad activities refuted the AME censure, rose to challenge his Cleveland colleague. He declared that "the minutes of the last Conference of the AME Church" surely showed denominational opposition to slavery and a bar to fellowship with slaveholders.[9]

What AME detractors misunderstood was that emancipationist energies within African Methodism drew from the contested terrain of worship, belief, and culture. What clergy preached, how believers expressed their religiosity, and what adherents espoused in theological and cultural idioms shaped African Methodism into a distinctively black religious body. Moreover, Wesleyan "practical divinity" articulated through an AME understanding of spiritual and social holiness interacted with liberationist principles and praxis derived from their enslaved and marginalized experiences. These factors that focused AMEs on the fight to emancipate slaves in the United States and to evangelize blacks in the broader Atlantic World were sustained through their own peculiar practices in faith formation and communicated through distinctive hermeneutical approaches to scripture, sermons, and songs. Hence, a blend of the Wesleyan, African, and African American religious background integrated black religiosity into black freedom objectives for AMEs in the Americas and Africa.

Attaining and protecting the physical freedom of blacks, however, addressed only one facet of the denomination's emancipationist ethos. Liberation also meant the personal reconstruction of enslaved and marginalized peoples and developing them into free but moral beings equal to whites in both the civic and cultural spheres. Hence, temperance, moral reform, and education became as much the business of African Methodism as its anti-slavery and emigrationist initiatives. All of these factors influenced AME discourse surrounding the meaning of freedom. Ending the bondage of slavery and ignorance became the twin goals of the AME mission and ministry.

[9] Dickson J. Preston, *Young Frederick Douglass: The Maryland Years* (Baltimore, MD, Johns Hopkins University Press, 1980), 97, 149–150; *Journal of the 18th Session and 17th Quadrennial Session of the General Conference of the African Methodist Episcopal Church in the World* held in Bethel Church, Baltimore, MD, May 5–26, 1884, 60; "Minutes of the Mass State Convention, Ohio, 1849," in Philip S. Foner and George E. Walker (eds.), *Proceedings of the Black State Conventions, 1840–1865*, Vol. 1 (Philadelphia, PA, Temple University Press, 1979), 220–221, 224; Richard R. Wright, Jr., *The Bishops of the African Methodist Episcopal Church* (Nashville, TN, AME Sunday School Union, 1963), 111–112; Randolph Paul Runyon, *Delia Webster and the Underground Railroad* (Lexington, University Press of Kentucky, 2015), 33.

ITINERANT MINISTERS AND A "MOBILE LAITY"

AME clergy served a mobile black population and became the glue that held their denomination together. Their constituents constantly crossed the boundaries between slavery and freedom and between settled and unsettled areas across innumerable borders within the Atlantic World. They preached Wesleyan doctrine and discipline, integrated black idioms into Methodist religious practice, explained the benefits of belonging to an autonomous religious body, and offered it as a reliable presence within destabilized and besieged black communities. They drew inspiration from the hagiographies of Richard and Sarah Allen, Daniel Coker, Morris Brown, and others in the founding generation of African Methodism. Whether they were converted in majority white religious settings or among fellow black worshippers, these preachers envisaged their faith formation as reaching optimal authenticity in a black religious body. For them the raison d'être of African Methodism lay in realizing emancipationist objectives by attaining and protecting the physical freedom of blacks and achieving their moral reformation. Though scriptural and social holiness were hardly familiar terms, these attributes of Wesleyan practical theology guided their understanding of African Methodism. These factors drew them to a variety of anti-slavery and moral reform organizations. Through African Methodism, clergy were developing a new people who would be physically free from slavery and morally emancipated from sin and ignorance.

These male ministers handled the hard work of establishing, expanding, and maintaining congregations, schools, and other AME infrastructure. These tasks, relating to institution building, also had liberationist implications. AMEs, whether in hostile northern communities, oppressive southern settings, or in emerging enclaves in Canada and other areas outside the United States, depended on their congregations to function as their protectors and advocates. The churches were venues where fugitive slaves were assisted, where slavery itself was denounced, and where blacks organized to defend their rights. Clergy led, supported, and facilitated these functions. Like the griots of West Africa, these preachers acted as guardians of black religious practices and traditions. This required knowledge and respect for the music, worship styles, and other idioms derived from the black religious background. Moreover, they and their parishioners created cultural space within Wesleyan worship and belief to accommodate black religion and constitute African Methodism as an historic black denomination.

Most preachers fulfilled only some of these functions. Many emphasized evangelism, others preached religious and racial independence, and a visible few were devoted fully to abolitionism and black equal rights. All of them, in interaction with their parishioners, encouraged black cultural autonomy and self-determination. These indispensable characteristics helped to establish blacks as a free people within their diverse Atlantic communities. This solidarity, incubated within African Methodism, drew from the black theology and black folk religion that clergy espoused and encouraged among their members. Cecil W. Cone contends that "black theology" was rooted in the black religious experience and in black "testimonies" about encounters with "the Almighty Sovereign God." They received "a new life of freedom in the Spirit" that transcended slavery and racial oppression and allowed blacks to function as autonomous human beings. AME theology drew from these sacred sensibilities and shaped the institutional ethos of the denomination. Black folk religion, performed in sermon, song, and worship, reflected these theological perspectives and became, as Dale P. Andrews argues, "a rallying call to unite in radical fervor for the sociopolitical and economic liberation of black Americans."[10]

Hence, black theology and black folk religion derived from experiences rooted in slavery and other facets of unfreedom. This condition influenced the content of black belief and faith identity. Embedded in their doctrine and practices were hermeneutical approaches to scripture and sermons that yielded liberationist themes and the singing of hymns and spirituals whose lyrics required their manumission from sin and bondage. Belief and worship, when performed through ecstatic spirituality and through rituals drawn from the African heritage, showed the energy behind black folk practices. When merged into Wesleyan doctrine and discipline, grassroots black religion produced a distinctive African Methodism sharply different from what whites espoused. Their assertions of cultural autonomy energized AMEs to fight against racial subjugation and the societal structures that facilitated their oppression. Therefore, the black religious experience and Wesleyan scriptural and social holiness developed within African Methodism an emancipationist thrust that ministers preached to their parishioners. Some explicitly blended their evangelical and emancipationist perspectives as intrinsic to their ministries. Thomas Woodson, an Ohio pastor until his death in 1846, consciously articulated these twin objectives. Therefore, in a scriptural allusion about himself Woodson observed that "all I desire is, the Lord's will be done, and our cause to go forward, until the millions who are

[10] Cecil W. Cone, *The Identity Crisis in Black Theology* (Nashville, TN, AME Sunday School Union, Revised Edition), 1975, 2003, 68; Dale P. Andrews, *Practical Theology and African American Folk Religion* (Louisville, KY, Westminster John Knox Press, 2002), 5.

now groaning under the iron hand of oppression shall be free! And the kingdom of God prevail over all the earth!" In their diverse activities Woodson and other clergy, through evangelism, education, moral reform, and abolitionism, made black freedom their frontline concern.[11]

Typically, antebellum clergy served churches across a wide expanse of territory and laid foundations for several fledgling circuits and congregations. Despite their purely religious pursuits, local whites interpreted their efforts to organize and develop black churches as racial insurgency deserving of stiff opposition and hostility. Since many of these early clergy had been affiliated with the Methodist Episcopal (ME) Church, these encounters deepened their commitment to African Methodism as an autonomous religious body and justified their departure from among Wesleyan whites. David Smith, Dandridge F. Davis, and Richard Robinson exemplified this first generation of AME ministers.

Smith vied with William Paul Quinn for the designation of "first itinerant preacher in the AME Church." Perhaps Quinn had the better claim because he traveled more speedily by horseback; Smith, who lacked equestrian skills, walked to his distant assignments. Born into slavery in Maryland in 1782, Smith became a ministerial understudy to Daniel Coker and learned from his mentor the circumstances that brought the AME Church into being. As the chattel to a Catholic slave owner, his conversion to Christianity by the Methodists led his master to sell him to a Georgia buyer. The intervention of a sympathetic family member saved him from the sale and effected his manumission from slavery. "Now, I am free," he said, "both soul and body." Smith then joined in Baltimore the Sharp Street Church, a black ME congregation whose exhorters were under white control. Their mistreatment persuaded him to support Daniel Coker in establishing a separate African Methodist congregation and witness his partnership with Richard Allen in building an independent denomination. He credited Coker for showing him that the AME Church "could do more good among my people than the ME Church."[12]

Smith's ministry started in the environs of Baltimore where he preached to blacks in slavery. They "became better servants," he noted, but more importantly "obtained their [physical] freedom." As an AME pastor Smith

---

[11] *Proceedings of the Seventeenth (Ohio) Annual Conference of the African M. E. Church* held in the City of Zanesville, October 16, 1847, and continued in Session eleven days, 1847 (Cincinnati, *Herald of Truth*, 1847), 9.

[12] David Smith, *Biography of Rev. David Smith of the AME Church* (Xenia, OH, Xenia Gazette Office, 1881), 9–21, 25–31, 41–42, 134.

served congregations in central Pennsylvania on the Harrisburg Circuit, in Maryland, and in Washington DC. Churches in western Pennsylvania also drew him away from his native Baltimore. A pastoral interlude in the AME Zion Church preceded his return to AME congregations in Ohio in 1831, and later in New Orleans, Louisville, southern Indiana, and back again to Ohio. In these sundry sites, where he either organized or pastored AME congregations, Smith often encountered hostile whites. In the slave city of Washington DC, for example, "a great many colored men" guarded him "from the violence" of white vigilantes. Moreover, "three constables" appeared, he said, "to prevent me from preaching," but permission from other municipal authorities allowed him to proceed. Smith then preached and informed potential members about the AME Church and received forty-three persons to join "our connection."[13]

These experiences affirmed Smith's conviction that "a connection being controlled entirely by colored people" advanced African American freedom. He recalled preaching in Washington, Pennsylvania where the "galleries of the ME Churches were the auditoriums for the Ethiopian brethren and sisters." When Smith preached, he invited local blacks to resist this degradation. Hence, he reported that "forty-eight persons came forward" and became AME members. He believed that his denomination had a "sweeping field" to develop "Christian manhood" and showcase a religious body that allowed black men to attain high ecclesiastical offices without the barrier of color.[14]

Dandridge F. Davis, like Smith, entered the itinerancy and ministered to mostly upstart congregations on the expanding frontier west of the Alleghenies. Despite discouragement from white ME ministers, Davis viewed African Methodism as integral to the black freedom movement. So, for Davis, building churches and promoting spiritual discipline became implicitly tied to black self-determination as an interactive component of his ministry. He was born in Virginia in 1807 to free parents and moved with them to Kentucky. He was converted and became, like his mother, a member of the ME Church. Davis "was authorized to lead prayer-meetings and exhort," and later was licensed to preach. Hence, as an ME preacher "he was solicited to take a tour through Kentucky, Virginia, North and South Carolina, and Georgia" to evangelize among the "white and colored, and

[13] Ibid., 21–24, 49–51, 55–62, 66–67, 69–96.   [14] Ibid., 58–59, 135.

even to the red man." While enrolled in Augusta College in Kentucky during 1834, Davis continued to preach in Kentucky and Ohio.[15]

Around this time Davis felt "directed by the Spirit to seek his oppressed brethren." Though he was "entirely ignorant" about the AME Church, he had a dream in which he imagined a denomination consisting of "an army of colored soldiers, officers, and all the sable sons of Africa." He asked one of his teachers at Augusta College if he "knew of such a thing as congregations being established and conducted by colored men?" Yes, was the reply: in "Ohio and other free States, the colored people had large Churches and Circuits as the whites had." Davis, who now determined to find the African Methodists, learned in 1835 that a camp meeting in southern Ohio would be "conducted entirely by their own ministers, and their Bishop would be present also!" He found the site and met Morris Brown and William Paul Quinn. The preaching, singing, and participation of various AME clergy and converts convinced Davis that "here is the place, and this is the people that I will unite with." He told Brown about his decision and then shared the news with his ME colleagues. They discouraged him because "such a course would prove deleterious to his brethren in the South." His departure from the ME Church would set a bad precedent, "harm" blacks, and create "dissatisfaction amongst the slaves." Some might "follow his example" of black insurgency and gravely aggravate the white population. Davis dismissed their comments and affirmed his decision by going to southern Ohio to begin preaching to the AMEs on the Chillicothe Circuit. After his ordination as a deacon in 1835, Davis was assigned to Ohio's Columbus Circuit. In 1836, Brown ordained him an Elder and assigned him to other churches in Ohio, Indiana, and western Pennsylvania until his death in 1847. Like Smith, Davis was convinced "about the great advantages the AME Connexion was destined to prove to the colored race." AME clergy also benefited from this affiliation because it gave them opportunities "for improving their minds and talents to the glory of God and the good of the race." Davis, observed one contemporary, "was wholly absorbed in the advancement of the African cause" and believed that African Methodism would bring blacks out of the "thraldom" of racial oppression. John Stewart, an ME missionary to Wyandott Indians in Ohio, drew a similar conclusion. After he "was visited by some colored preachers belonging to the Allenites,"

[15] A. R. Green, *The Life of the Rev. Dandridge F. Davis of the African M. E. Church* (Pittsburgh, PA, Benjamin F. Peterson, 1850), 6–7, 20–23, 25–26.

Stewart left the ME Church, "believing he could be more useful among his own people than among the whites."[16]

Richard Robinson, said one scholar, typified in his ministry the "multidimensional, transnational quest for freedom during an era when the most virulent forms of oppression seemed to have the upper hand." Born in Maryland in around 1796, Robinson was converted in Bucks County, Pennsylvania, in what appeared to be a revival in around 1823 at which William Paul Quinn was preaching. After ordination in the Philadelphia Annual Conference, Robinson connected to the AME mission in Haiti, becoming an émigré to the black republic in around 1830. Scipio Beanes, whom Bishop Allen dispatched to the island to serve between 1826 and 1829, returned, after a struggle with tuberculosis, in 1832, but died in 1835. Robinson arrived in Haiti during this interregnum period as Beanes' likely successor. He ministered to a small congregation in Port-au-Prince that worshiped in an edifice erected to seat 200 people. Some time after his return to the United States in 1834, the mission was absorbed into a larger Methodist operation in Haiti. Robinson was later assigned to congregations in New York City, Boston, and Baltimore, where he urged a continued AME commitment to the black-ruled island.[17]

Though hardly learned and barely literate, Robinson embodied and deeply understood the AME ethos as both diasporic and emancipationist. Allen and L'Ouverture, whose recent revolts against the perpetrators of black subjugation grounded Robinson's introduction to African Methodism in the Atlantic World. Hence, he weighed, throughout his ministry, the institutional insurgency that Allen pioneered and the daring defeat of French racial hegemony in Haiti that L'Ouverture achieved. In balancing these influences, Robinson accepted as axiomatic that the ontological reality of African Methodism represented a prima facie rebuke to black slavery and subordination. Notwithstanding the denomination's African American advocacy and Robinson's view that "every colored man is an abolitionist and slaveholders know it," there was no escaping that a minuscule minority of slave masters trespassed upon AME sacred space. Though they were blacks who purchased slaves in order to free them, a few, under this humanitarian guise, pursued

---

[16] Ibid., 26–30, 33, 35, 39, 46, 49, 55, 63–64; James B. Finley, *History of the Wyandott Mission at Upper Sandusky, Ohio under the Direction of the Methodist Episcopal Church* (Cincinnati, OH, Cincinnati Publishing, 1840), 214–215. (Many thanks to Professor Christina Dickerson-Cousin of Quinnipiac University for bringing the Finley volume to my attention.)

[17] Stephen W. Angell, "'The Shadows of the Evening Stretched Out': Richard Robinson and the Shaping of African Methodist Identity, 1823–1862," *Journal of Africana Religions*, Vol. 3, No. 3, 2015, 228–229, 231–233.

selfish pecuniary benefits. Moreover, "inflammatory language" denouncing slavery subjected congregations, especially in border and southern cities, to harassment from white authorities that Robinson himself had experienced in Baltimore. Unequivocal abolitionist statements, Robinson believed, might threaten African Methodism where it could least defend itself. Robinson, unapologetically anti-slavery like other African Methodists, argued that the denomination's Atlantic and liberationist activities, as much as condemnations of slavery, revealed what was essential to AME identity.[18]

Some clergy, though active as pastors, preferred visibility as anti-slavery and equal rights advocates. Tending to their parishioners, while important to them, became ancillary to their frontline association with full-time abolitionists and equal rights advocates. William T. Catto, despite a busy schedule as a pastor to churches in Philadelphia and in central and southern New Jersey, and as an AME book agent, constructed himself primarily as an activist preacher. Catto was a mulatto born in around 1810 in Charleston, South Carolina, to a manumitted mother and an unknown father. He became a millwright and taught in a short-lived black-operated Sabbath school. Catto, though he had worshipped with status-conscious mulattoes at the white-controlled Trinity ME Church, supported the elevation of blacks in the Americas and Africa. Hence, he joined Second Presbyterian Church and persuaded Calvinist leaders to sponsor him as a missionary to Haiti or Liberia. After seminary training in Columbia, South Carolina, Catto and his family in 1848 headed to Baltimore to secure passage to Liberia. Now that he had been won over to the colonizationist cause, Catto attracted support from the Presbyterian Board of Foreign Missions and became an employee of the Maryland Colonization Society. However, a mysterious letter, which said that he "would excite discontent and insurrection among slaves," overturned these plans. Word of this seeming duplicity reached his Presbyterian sponsors in South Carolina. After they revoked his preacher's license and state authorities issued a warrant to arrest and extradite him, the Cattos fled to Philadelphia.[19]

Since Catto had joined the AME Church's Baltimore Annual Conference, he was accepted into the Philadelphia jurisdiction as a fully credentialed minister. Catto invited black abolitionists to his churches to denounce slavery and defend black civil rights. Though his pastoral peers quickly

---

[18] Ibid., 234–237.
[19] Daniel R. Biddle and Murray Dubin, *Tasting Freedom: Octavius Catto and the Battle for Equality in Civil War America* (Philadelphia, PA, Temple University Press, 2010), 9–10, 15, 17, 22–25, 59–60, 66–72, 74, 155.

learned that Catto was a vocal opponent of slavery, he also knew that some of them demurred for fear of inciting whites who had "torched or stoned" churches suspected of anti-slavery activities. Catto, however, never sanitized the evils of slavery, but depicted the harsh realities that he had seen "with his own eyes." While serving at the Brick Wesley Church in Philadelphia, he called a meeting to demand that Pennsylvania blacks regain the right to vote. He did the same during a pastorate in New Jersey to get black suffrage in that state.[20]

Catto frequently interacted with Frederick Douglass, Charles Lenox Remond, William Still, and Henry Highland Garnet. Douglass in his *North Star* commended Catto's pastorate at Brick Wesley Church as one of the few places "where the cause of the slave could be freely pleaded." Still and Catto called a meeting in 1850 at this same church to protest the passage of the Fugitive Slave Act. Garnet, well known for his call to slaves to adopt as their motto "resistance, resistance, resistance," attended the dedication of Catto's rebuilt Macedonia AME Church in Camden, New Jersey.[21]

Catto exhibited a "boldness," Douglass said, that AME leaders "lacked." Perhaps Douglass was unaware of Catto's AME colleague, J. J. G. Bias, an ex-slave whose wife joined him in helping other slaves to escape from Maryland. Furthermore, he may have been unfamiliar with the AME affiliation of Stephen Smith, a native Pennsylvanian and the mulatto son of a slave mother, who purchased his indenture from a Revolutionary War veteran. Smith, a wealthy businessman and AME preacher, was a benefactor to congregations in Columbia, Chester, and Philadelphia, Pennsylvania, and to another AME church in Cape May, New Jersey. He supported the Underground Railroad, the Pennsylvania Anti-slavery Society, and the Pennsylvania State Convention of Colored Citizens. Catto, Bias, and Smith coauthored a resolution at the 1851 Philadelphia Annual Conference, which denounced colonization as a threat to black freedom. "Spurn the advice," they said, of anyone, "white or coloured," who tried to undermine "the permanence of our people in their native land." Douglass, who agreed with all three AME preachers in their views on colonization, already described it as an alliance between "slaveholders in the South and Negro haters of the North." Douglass, echoing an earlier error by Charles B. Ray, mistakenly

---

[20] *Minutes of the Thirty-Fourth Annual Conference of the African Methodist E. Church for the Baltimore District*, April 18, 1851 (Baltimore, MD, Sherwood & Co., 1851), 3; *Minutes of the Philadelphia District Annual Conference*, 1851 (n.p., 1851), 2; *Minutes of the Philadelphia District Annual Conference*, 1853 (n.p., 1853), 12; Biddle and Dubin, *Tasting Freedom*, 90, 93, 105, 139.
[21] Biddle and Dubin, *Tasting Freedom*, 77, 88–89, 111, 146, 154.

thought that Catto stood alone among AMEs as a conspicuous opponent of slavery and as a visible proponent for black equal rights. Douglass may have likened most AME clergy to M. M. Clark, a former Presbyterian turned African Methodist whose interaction with the Free Church of Scotland drew his derision. While representing the AME Church in London in 1846 at the convention of the Evangelical Alliance, Clark, a black rights proponent, abolitionist, and later editor of the *Christian Recorder*, as he raised money for the AME Church, developed contacts among Scottish clergy who were weak in their opposition to black slavery. Douglass, despite his disdain for Clark, knew about the courageous Catto, but seemed unaware that the militant Bias and Smith were his AME colleagues.[22]

Ultimately, the breadth of Catto's clerical and abolitionist interactions with leaders such as Garnet, a Presbyterian pastor, eased his exit from the AME Church in 1854 back into the Calvinist fold. His appointment to the Allentown Circuit, whose congregations stretched over 40 miles in southern New Jersey, interfered with plans to enroll his son, Octavius, in Philadelphia's Institute for Colored Youth. Since the solution lay in locating closer to the city, Catto accepted the pastorate of the First African Presbyterian Church. Some part of Catto, however, stayed connected to his former denomination. He praised it in 1857, for example, as an "independent organization, governed and controlled by black men." He remained impressed with its commitment to black self-determination and thought that his activist associations with Bias, Smith, and others affirmed the AME commitment to racial insurgency.[23]

Morris Brown, Vesey, and Gullah Jack, AMEs of varied Atlantic experiences, viewed black emancipation from these complicated perspectives. For them, black culture and folk belief blended with insurgent interpretations of Biblical scripture and the boldness of AME institutional independence. Gullah Jack, known as a sorcerer and "feared by the natives of Africa, who

[22] Ibid., 79; *Minutes of the Philadelphia District Annual Conference*, 1851, 9; Richard P. McCormick, "Stephen Smith," in Rayford W. Logan and Michael R. Winston (eds.), *Dictionary of American Negro Biography* (New York, W. W. Norton & Co., 1982), 566; Frederick Douglass, "Slavery, The Slumbering Volcano: An Address Delivered in New York, New York, on 23 April 1849," in John W. Blasingame (ed.), *The Frederick Douglass Papers, Volume 2: 1847–54* (New Haven, CT, Yale University Press, 1982), 149; Frederick Douglass, "Slavery, the Evangelical Alliance, and the Free Church: An Address Delivered in Glasgow, Scotland, on 30 September 1846," in John Blasingame (ed.), *The Frederick Douglass Papers, Volume 1: 1841–46* (New Haven, CT, Yale University Press, 1979), 441, 444, 447, 447 fn. 9.

[23] Biddle and Dubin, *Tasting Freedom*, 154, 158; William T. Catto, *A Semi-centenary Discourse, Delivered in the First African Presbyterian Church, Philadelphia, May 4, 1857, with a History of the Church from Its First Organization* (Philadelphia, PA, J. M. Wilson, 1857), 82.

believed in witchcraft," especially reminded AMEs about their link to their African religious background. Fellow South Carolinian Daniel A. Payne, however, eschewed these African survivals and stressed the construction of African Methodism into an orthodox Christian denomination. Though periodically involved in abolitionism, Payne focused more on building an ecclesiastical culture aimed at ministerial education, moral reformation, established dogma, and distance from the African religious background. His steely determination to attain these objectives benefited from his election as a bishop in 1852. His lasting impact upon the AME Church influenced three areas. First, his insistence upon an educated clergy, starting in 1844, though resisted throughout his long clerical career, inspired the founding of innumerable schools to achieve this objective. Secondly, his daring purchase of Wilberforce University (see Chapter 3) in 1863 provided the denomination with an educational center and locus of power, which helped to establish it as an influential religious body. Finally, his disdain for most expressions of vernacular black culture, especially when they reflected African retentions, contrasted with his prolific production of poetry, hymns, and prose about orthodox Christian beliefs and rituals.[24]

In each area Payne's proposals were contested by others who envisaged AME ecclesiology differently than the bishop. Euro-American education and culture, whether required for ministerial ordination or diffused to unlettered AME members, de-emphasized the African American experience as a primary source for shaping black religiosity and identity.[25] Even Payne's zeal for Wilberforce as the national university for AMEs collided with the desire of southern ministers and members for their own institutions that better reflected their local and regional mores and identities. Though Payne won many of these battles and greatly influenced AME development, his views about the status of African Americans, both civilly and culturally, stirred denominational debate and discourse about what constituted black freedom.

Payne, as much as any other minister, advanced his own definition of his church's emancipationist ethos. Despite frontline support of abolitionism and black equal rights, he believed that if blacks embraced pietistic and abstemious religious beliefs and practices, attained literacy, and adopted the cultural tastes of elite whites, they would become autonomous moral beings. Payne was born to free parents, London and Martha Payne, in Charleston in

---

[24] *The Trial Record of Denmark Vesey* [Introduction by John Oliver Killens] (Boston, MA, Beacon Press, 1970), 11, 14–16.

[25] Cone, *Identity Crisis in Black Theology*, 9 makes the opposite point. Cone contends that the black experience is the principal source for doing black theology.

1811, but his father, a Virginia freedman, had been kidnapped and sold into slavery. Later, he purchased his freedom. The Paynes were Methodists and sent their son to be educated at the Minor Moralist Society. Though equipped as a teacher to black youth Payne encountered "the exercise of slaveholding power" in 1835 when a racist state law forced him to close his school. Hence, Payne was hardly unfamiliar with racial oppression inherent to a slave society and that free blacks were themselves vulnerable to reenslavement or sharp restrictions. He realized that the degradation of blacks required resistance and strategies to undermine racial hegemony in order to nullify its effects. Thinking through these challenges lay ahead of Payne as he migrated from South Carolina to the Northeast and contemplated how he would connect to efforts to emancipate the black population.[26]

Payne, during a brief sojourn in New York City in 1835, interacted extensively with abolitionists. He met clergymen Charles B. Ray and Samuel E. Cornish, and became a friend to Theodore S. Wright. Abolitionist Lewis Tappan persuaded Payne to advocate the immediate emancipation of slaves despite their lack of an education. Payne, however, was not convinced to become either an abolitionist lecturer or a missionary to Africa, which several white clergy advised him to consider. Instead, he accepted an offer to study at the Lutheran-sponsored Gettysburg Seminary in Pennsylvania. The school's missions society had committed to educate an African American devoted to "the intellectual, moral, and social elevation" of free blacks. After two years in the seminary, a Lutheran ordination in the anti-slavery Frankean Synod, and a Presbyterian pastorate in Troy, New York, in 1841 Payne joined the AME Church.[27]

Immediately after Bishop Brown appointed him to Israel Church in Washington DC in 1843, Payne commenced his crusade for an educated clergy, writing a series of "Epistles on the Education of the Ministry" in a denominational periodical. A supportive Bishop Brown urged him to attend the 1844 General Conference to press his cause. As chairman of the Committee on Education, Payne proposed a ministerial course of study that was defeated, then resurrected, and ultimately adopted. A delegate from Pittsburgh was credited with saving the resolution by telling delegates that younger clergy needed to be prepared for the awesome task of ministry. Separate tracks for exhorters and preachers were established. The broader curriculum for traveling clergy required English grammar, biblical studies,

---

[26] Daniel A. Payne, *Recollections of Seventy Years* (New York, Arno Press and the *New York Times*, 1888, 1969), 11–12, 15, 17, 19, 31.
[27] Ibid., 48, 50–58.

theology, philosophy, church history, and other subjects spread over four years. As a bishop, Payne continued his advocacy for ministerial education. He declared to clergy at the inaugural session of the 1852 New England Annual Conference that "ignorance and Christianity are antagonistic principles" and that "the Christian minister cannot be content with ignorance."[28]

Payne described opponents of clergy education as "enemies of Christian culture." Ministerial training, he believed, was foundational to an AME grounding in orthodox belief and practice. These developments would produce a religious body that resembled all other Christian churches. That is why he disdained worship practices at his Baltimore pastorate where "I would not let them sing their 'spiritual' songs." He tried "to modify some of the extravagances in worship" that these "Corn-field ditties" inspired. He recoiled at the expressions of African spirituality that probably resonated through the vernacular music that his members enjoyed. To Payne's dismay the music sounded nothing like the Euro-American hymns that he preferred the congregation to sing.[29]

Perhaps Payne's boldest move to establish an AME orthodoxy lay in the motto he developed in 1856 at the request of his two episcopal colleagues. Within an episcopal seal he inserted God Our Father, Christ Our Redeemer, Man Our Brother. He broke theological convention through an explicit and audacious assertion that God was creator of all humankind, including black slaves, and that Christ was the savior, even of those classified as chattels. Moreover, all were included within a human family and were eligible for salvation. Despite these daring freedom declarations, Payne merely referenced the Holy Ghost as "the Eternal Spirit, in the form of a dove, hovering over" the seal. Explicit mention of the Holy Ghost, the third person in the Godhead, might provide license to unorthodox worship practices and doctrinal beliefs. Though emancipationist themes are embedded in Christian pneumatology, as Richard Allen's conversion narrative shows, Payne downplayed this theological tenet in the AME seal because of his opposition to ecstatic expressions of black religiosity. Otherwise, spiritual excesses could be encouraged and sanctioned. Though AME ministers and members never abandoned exuberant worship services, Payne articulated an official doctrine

---

[28] Ibid., 74–77; Josephus R. Coan, *Daniel Alexander Payne: Christian Educator* (Philadelphia, PA, AME Book Concern, 1935), 67–69; *Minutes of the New England Annual Conference of the African Methodist Episcopal Church* held in the City of New Bedford, MA, June 10–21, 1852 (New Bedford, MA, Press of Benjamin Lindsey, 1852), 5.

[29] Payne, *Recollections*, 76, 93–94; James H. Cone, "God Our Father, Christ Our Redeemer, Man Our Brother: A Theological Interpretation of the AME Church," *AME Church Review*, Vol. 106, No. 341, January–March 1991, 25–33.

and discipline that discouraged vernacular religious rituals and practices. Educated clergy and restrained worship signified for Payne a church and a people who were prepared for freedom and prepared to become a sect indistinguishable from other Christian bodies.[30]

Creating a concrete infrastructure within African Methodism provided Payne with the means to realize his religious and cultural objectives. In 1837 AMEs in Ohio had already founded the Union Seminary near Columbus. Focused on practical and agricultural subjects, the school, still in operation in 1852, included sixty-nine students and a rented farm. The curriculum aimed at preparing graduates for economic self-sufficiency. Payne, in envisaging a broader project, saw possibilities in another institution, which white Methodists founded in 1856 near Xenia, Ohio, at Tawawa Springs. Originally, Wilberforce University was designed to supply well-trained teachers and preachers to serve blacks in the Old Northwest Territory. Some AMEs were suspicious of the ME Church because, they, according to the *Christian Recorder* editor, M. M. Clark, were "proslavery and colonizationist." That Tawawa Springs reputedly became a site to educate the mulatto offspring of southern slaveholders gave credence to Clark's criticism. Payne, however, thought the venture could be turned to other objectives. He viewed the school as a vehicle for black cultural uplift, where "the best moral and religious influences" would be available to black youth. Since the Wilberforce purchase in 1863 gave AMEs the means to morally construct a free black population, Ohio AMEs liquidated the assets of Union Seminary and used them to fund the new Tawawa venture. Payne praised the prospect for "the Christian education" of an "enslaved and ostracized" people. He echoed the Ohio Annual Conference, which declared that the education of black youth would "adorn their minds with that jewel that will elevate, ennoble, and rescue the bodies of our long injured race from the shackles of bondage, and their minds from [the] trammels of ignorance and vice." As a crusader for ministerial training and as a member of the National Moral Reform Association, which emphasized temperance and other healthy habits, Payne chose educational and religious reconstruction as his preferred instruments to prepare leaders and build freedom within the African American population.[31]

---

[30] Dennis C. Dickerson, *African Methodism and Its Wesleyan Heritage* (Nashville, TN, AME Sunday School Union, 2009), 53–54; Payne, *History of the African Methodist Episcopal Church*, 359.

[31] *Minutes of the Ohio Annual Conference of the African M. E. Church* held in Cincinnati, OH, August 6–18, 1852 (Pittsburgh, PA, *Christian Herald* [A. R. Green], 1852), 16–19; Payne, *Recollections*, 67, 149–153; Payne, *History of the African Methodist Episcopal Church*, 357, 399–401, 404.

How ministry was envisaged in the AME Church and how clergy defined and defended freedom for their members evolved as male responsibilities. Women, however, contested men for the right to preach. Although ordination remained forbidden, the periodic presence of women in the pulpit expanded their gender advancement. Nonetheless, male clergy, whenever they articulated emancipationist themes, generally excluded women. Richard Allen, despite his initial rebuff to Jarena Lee, licensed her to exhort and evangelize. She traveled throughout the Northeast, often with the known endorsement of the bishop, and sometimes accompanied him to speak at annual conferences. Lee's example, and perhaps that of other females, persuaded some men to support their official inclusion in the ministry. Delegates to the 1848 General Conference authorized annual conferences and pastors in their local churches and circuits to license women to preach. A strong dissent from Daniel A. Payne and fifteen other male clergy, however, vehemently opposed this action. They said that "such a course as this is calculated to break up the sacred relations which women bear to their husbands and children by sending them forth as itinerant preachers, wandering from place to place, to the utter neglect of their household duties and obligations." Moreover, "such a course is unwarranted by the word of God" and "the whole History of the Church does not furnish a single instance where the legislative body of a Church has ever licensed women to preach." Hence, these ministers presented their "solemn protest in the presence of the Church, against this movement of the majority of the General Conference, as a measure [which is] Anti-scriptural, anti-domestic, and revolutionary." These perspectives, so vigorously advanced, apparently capsized support for women preachers. At the 1852 General Conference the measure that women should be licensed to preach was reintroduced. An Ohio delegate moved the motion, "but after a spirited discussion the resolution was lost." Therefore "the sister preachers were again rejected."[32]

Male clergy preferred that women should be supportive of their ministerial efforts rather than pursue their own calling. Hence, such organizations as the Daughters of the Conference were developed to provide supplemental funds for the itinerancy. At the 1836 New York Annual Conference, for example, the group donated money "for the aid of the traveling preachers."

[32] Lee, *Religious Experiences and Journal of Mrs. Jarena Lee*, 12–14, 22–23, 39, 41, 44, 48, 55, 64, 70–71; *Proceedings of the Eighth General Conference of the African M. E. Church* held in the City of Philadelphia, PA, May 1, 1848, and continued in Session twenty-one days (Pittsburgh, PA, *Christian Herald*, 1848), 30; *Minutes of the Tenth General Conference of the African Methodist Episcopal Church* held in the City of New York, May 3–20, inclusive (Philadelphia, PA, Wm. S. Young, Printer, 1852), 3, 5.

The Daughters of the Conference at Bethel Church in Baltimore commended their pastor for organizing them to give money to clergy to bring "the glad tidings of salvation to our downtrodden and oppressed race." In 1851 they raised $100 to "cheerfully divide" among eligible Baltimore ministers. Similarly, at the 1853 New York Annual Conference the United Daughters in Binghampton, New York, "feeling as we do [about] the importance of missionary labor, and also of the itinerant system belonging to our government," contributed $10 "to be divided among the brethren of the Conference." Other AME women, in eschewing the Daughters' role and ignoring both license and ordination, pursued their spiritual gifts within all female prayer and praise assemblies. Their ecstatic expressions aroused the suspicions of Bishop Morris Brown, once a supporter of Lee, and other male clergy who, at times, invaded their meetings. Rebecca Cox Jackson, respectively a sister and a spouse to two AME preachers in Philadelphia, experienced such deep spirituality that she exercised her religiosity in trance-like episodes of worship and fellowship with like-minded women. Though she became a Shaker and renounced her carnal desires, other women remained in the denomination, but developed underground female networks to nurture their spiritual and preaching gifts. As for Lee, Brown's death in 1849 deprived her of what little support she had from the episcopacy. Even while the bishop lived, AMEs refused to underwrite the printing of a longer edition of her autobiography or save her from poverty before she died in 1864.[33]

Despite Lee's visibility as an evangelist, many male ministers could not imagine women as traveling preachers. They would be abandoning the "domestic sphere" where the supervision of their households was their required responsibilities. Surely, the church could neither encourage nor facilitate such a subversion of gender roles as to license or ordain women to preach. Others did not envisage their emancipationist rhetoric about race as applying to gender. Though increased discourse about women's suffrage gained traction, especially after the Seneca Falls convention of 1848, few AME males adjusted their freedom pursuits to accommodate AME women. As AMEs engaged African and Creole peoples in the Atlantic World, the

---

[33] *Minutes of the New York Annual Conference* (1836), 58; *Minutes of the Thirty-Fourth Annual Conference . . . For the Baltimore District* (1851), 13–14; *Minutes of the Annual Conference for the New York District, African Methodist Epis. Church* held in Bethel Church, Second Street, New York, 1853 (New York, D. Mitchell, 1853), 19; Lee, *Religious Experiences and Journal of Mrs. Jarena Lee*, 41, 130; Jean McMahon Humez (ed.), *Gifts of Power: The Writings of Rebecca Cox Jackson, Black Visionary, Shaker Eldress* (Amherst, University of Massachusetts Press, 1981), 8, 17–20, 22, 24–26; Knight, "The Many Names for Jarena Lee," 61, 63, 67.

denomination's expansive emancipationist ethos remained restricted to race and indifferent to the potent spirituality of female members. AME elders scarcely recognized that the male eulogists of Sarah Allen acknowledged that she opened her home to attend the needs of "weary and worn" preachers and at the same time aided slaves as a station conductor on the Underground Railroad. Her lived religion, while gesturing toward domestic chores that accommodated male preferences, embodied concrete activities that sustained AME insurgency against slavery. Julia Ann Steward Shorter, the spouse of the Reverend (later Bishop) James A. Shorter, emulated Allen and became her activist heir. During her husband's pastorate in Columbia, Pennsylvania, a fugitive slave from Maryland arrived in their town and was "dragged off to Philadelphia." Just as his slave owner was laying claim to his chattel, Shorter "raised money and bought him" and prevented his return to bondage. Allen and Shorter, in ways that would have pleased the AME founder, promoted a praxis beyond their domestic sphere that sought freedom for the enslaved and affirmed their rights as American citizens.[34]

EVANGELISM AND EMANCIPATION

Because no other black religious body possessed the geographical reach of African Methodism, AMEs believed African and Creole peoples, wherever they lived within the Atlantic World, were potential adherents. Realizing an Atlantic World vision, however, became a difficult objective for the denomination to attain. During the 1841 New York Annual Conference, for example, Morris Brown referred to an invitation to send a representative to a pan-Methodist meeting in Haiti designed to form a federated Wesleyan organization. The Reverend Charles Spicer, whom Brown planned to appoint, reneged and shifted his attention elsewhere. One observer blamed Spicer for hindering AME "ascendancy" and squandering "the labors of three missionaries" who had previously evangelized in Haiti. Daniel A. Payne, the AME's first historiographer, recalled that "Bishop Brown had neither the men nor the money" to build African Methodism on the island. Though the Union Methodist Church was formed, it too failed because of a "lack of competent leaders." These personnel problems, however, never meant that AME leaders abandoned their geographical ambitions, but certainly their Haiti mission had been hampered. Therefore, the Atlantic World vision of African Methodism focused on emigration into the

[34] Payne, *History of the African Methodist Episcopal Church*, 87; Alexander W. Wayman, *The Life of Rev. James Alexander Shorter* (Baltimore, MD, J. Lanahan, Publisher, 1890), 14, 39–40.

American West, escape and expansion to Canada and other British territories, and penetration into the Gulf region. Haiti and Liberia periodically appeared as desirable destinations, depending on resources and AME attitudes toward colonizationist influences.[35]

Throughout the antebellum period, Brown and other leaders managed the expansion of African Methodism as a routine activity. They understood that denominational growth was inextricably linked to freedom issues that constantly confronted both slave and nonslave African Americans. AMEs regularly encountered raw white hegemony through such state measures as Ohio's discriminatory "Black Laws" of 1807 or the federal fugitive slave proviso in the United States Constitution. They believed, therefore, that being AME required involvement with the civic and physical welfare of black people. David Smith reported that on the Hamilton Circuit in Ohio "whites were very much opposed to the prosperity of the colored people." Blacks and abolitionists, he said, "were persecuted and driven from their little homes which they had accumulated by hard labor. Their churches and houses were stoned and many were compelled to sell out and go to Canada." Additionally, "the fugitive slave law was in full force and this hellish instrument made the low class of whites companions of blood hounds and Negro hunters. In search for fleeing slaves, they would come in our houses at night and maltreat our wives and daughters, and we had no appeal." At the Shawneetown Circuit in Illinois the pastor reported on a "cruel mob" that caused the near "annihilation of one of our most flourishing circuits." "The mob," he said, "is the result of a cruel prejudice which manifests itself more in some free States than (was) found in Southern States." Hence, in settled communities outside the South AME churches were under assault because they affirmed the racial identity of African Americans, provided venues to oppose antiblack activities, and established cohesion within their embattled enclaves. Migrant African Americans, whether fleeing slavery in the South or victimized by racial rioting in northern cities, relied on AME churches to receive them into the new communities that they reconstituted in various areas of the United States and Canada. Itinerant AME preachers and a mobile laity harnessed these exodus experiences to the dynamic expansion of new congregations into numerous territorial asylums.[36]

[35] Payne, *History of the African Methodist Episcopal Church*, 131–132, 478.
[36] Smith, *Biography of Rev. David Smith of the AME Church*, 74–75; *Journal of Proceedings of the Third Annual Conference of the African M. E. Church for the District of Missouri held at Louisville, KY, September 5, 1857* (Louisville, KY, Rev. John M. Brown, Secretary, 1857), 8–9.

Figure 2.2 Priscilla Baltimore, who aided the Reverend William Paul Quinn in founding antebellum AME congregations in Brooklyn, Illinois, and St. Louis, Missouri. Reprinted from Sarah J. W. Early, *The Life and Labors of Rev. Jordan W. Early* (Nashville, TN, AME Sunday School Union, 1894)

Often, enterprising itinerant clergy spearheaded AME growth in virgin locales. Richard Williams, for example, reported to the 1836 New York Annual Conference on "his mission" to western New York and Canada. He planted a congregation of twenty-six members at Rochester, another church with thirty-one members at Buffalo, and licensed preachers at both cities. Next, he traveled to Toronto, where British "authorities" gave him "every encouragement" for evangelizing black settlers. Hence, Williams started new congregations in Niagara, St. David's, and St. Catherine. His yield of 148 members and two preachers showed the relationship between black community development and the spread of African Methodism.[37]

These congregations established cohesion among free, ex-slave, and fugitive blacks. Sometimes they founded separate settlements and at other times they cooperated with abolitionist whites in operating the Underground Railroad. In these varied circumstances, AME congregations anchored black communities and became venues where advocacy for free and fugitive blacks was pursued. Brooklyn, "a freedom village on the Illinois frontier," for

[37] *(Minutes) of the New York Annual Conference of the African Methodist Episcopal Church, New York, New York, June 4 –June 14, 1836*, 61.

example, began in 1829 with AMEs among its most active progenitors. These "freedpeople and fugitives" from Missouri included John and Priscilla Baltimore and eleven others who left a slave state to build a "home on free soil." Hence, they started "clearing land, erecting shelters, providing for their subsistence, and constructing social institutions," and with guidance from William Paul Quinn, established an AME congregation between 1829 and 1837. John and Priscilla Baltimore, the key persons in launching the town and church, had been born in 1798 and 1805 in Virginia and Kentucky respectively. John's status was unclear, but Priscilla had been a slave sold to a Methodist preacher in Missouri. As an exhorter, perhaps before she left Kentucky, Baltimore reputably preached with "spiritual power," and may have taken some Missouri slaves to a religious gathering in Illinois. During her sojourn she may have spotted land on which the Brooklyn settlement could be built. Before moving to Illinois, Baltimore, who purchased her freedom, met Quinn and his associate, Ezekiel Pines. She smuggled them into St. Louis to preach to slaves, organize St. Paul Church in 1841, and aid escaping fugitives. Baltimore and other AME members also offered their church as a station on the Underground Railroad. African Methodism in Brooklyn created bonds between free and fugitive blacks, and established freedom for both segments of the African American population. Moreover, such churches, though founded by black émigrés, also beckoned succeeding groups of migrants to settle in these safe havens.[38]

Churches in other locales also operated as stations on the Underground Railroad and functioned as enclaves of autonomy and self-determination for free blacks. In Cincinnati, Ohio, the AME Church, later called Allen Temple, became an Underground Railroad center and "helped refugees for decades." Throughout Pennsylvania, AME congregations promoted racial solidarity within small but diverse constituencies of freed and fugitive blacks. St. Paul Church in Bellefonte was founded in 1836 and was an Underground Railroad station. In Delaware County, the AME congregation in Marple Township offered sustenance, shelter, and travel information to fugitives. The Honeycomb Church in Lima included members who were slave escapees, and they in turn helped others to flee bondage. Similarly, members at Bethel Church in Wilkes-Barre hid slaves and supported local abolitionists. Backing for the Underground Railroad also came from Bethel Church in Gettysburg.[39]

[38] Sundiata Keita Cha-Jua, *America's First Black Town: Brooklyn, Illinois, 1839–1915* (Urbana, University of Illinois Press, 2000), 18, 32, 36–40.
[39] J. Blaine Hudson, *Fugitive Slaves and the Underground Railroad in the Kentucky Borderlands* (Jefferson, NC, McFarland & Co., 2011), 120; "Voices of Central Pennsylvania," February

Particular parishes became more than way stations on the Underground Railroad. Some of these congregations, primarily in the Northeast, mirrored the maroons in the Caribbean and in South America where escaped slaves were defended against slave hunters seeking to retrieve them for their slave owners. "In the days of slavery," recalled one AME minister familiar with the history of Montrose, Pennsylvania, a town nestled in the mountains near the New York state line, described it as "the city of refuge for slaves." One early AME evangelist, Thomas Myers Decatur Ward, had preached among some of the runaways. Perhaps he was attracted to Montrose because it reminded him of his parents who fled in 1823 from the slave state of Maryland, 5 miles across the Mason-Dixon line to Hanover, Pennsylvania, a few months before Ward was born. A retrospective account in an AME publication noted that "no slave-holder or slave-seeker could ever take a slave from Montrose." Fugitive blacks, "once reaching the highest point of the Allegheny mountains in Montrose," reached freedom and were safe. Slave catchers, when navigating "through a deep ravine" and climbing "to the summit of the mountain" to capture slave escapees, "never returned alive." The AME congregation, an aegis for fugitive slaves, existed in these surroundings "where our people from the south followed it and stayed there until the death of slavery."[40]

William Paul Quinn, born in 1784 either in the Caribbean or in Central America, and Thomas M. D. Ward, before their election to the episcopacy became pivotal to AME growth into the expanding western frontier. As they planted churches in the broad territories between the Midwest and the Pacific Coast, Quinn and Ward knew that slavery, while barred in these areas, included laws that discouraged black migration and required African Americans to post bonds against potential vagrancy. Moreover, in some areas, the franchise was either withheld from them or was severely restricted. Hence, the communities in which they founded congregations existed in unwelcome locations where whites preferred that no blacks should live. Nonetheless, the 1840 General Conference authorized Quinn to travel into the Old Northwest Territory as a missionary to "unexplored regions beyond the bounds of any of our districts." Quinn, though he had been in the Midwest in the 1830s, surveyed the 18,000 blacks living in Indiana and Illinois, and noted that "many of them, within the last ten or fifteen years,

2006, voicesweb.org/archive/february06/Page 06.pdf; Charles L. Blockson, *The Underground Railroad in Pennsylvania* (Jacksonville, NC, Flame International, 1981), 64, 133, 146.

[40] *Minutes of the Twenty-Seventh Session of the Pittsburg[h] Annual Conference of the African Methodist Episcopal Church held at Wayman's Chapel AME Church, Wheeling, West Virginia, October 3 to 7, 1894* (Altoona, PA, H. & W. H. Slep, 1894), 33–34; Wright, *The Bishops of the African Methodist Episcopal Church*, 350.

broke away from the fetters of slavery and settled with their families in these states." Their occupations as farmers and artisans enabled them to sustain families, churches, and schools "in a manner (that was) truly surprising." Hence, he boasted success in the slave city of St. Louis, where St. Paul Church grew into "a very prosperous state" with 150 members.[41]

Moreover, the Louisville church, later known as Quinn Chapel, was reported "in a flourishing condition" when Quinn gave his report to the 1844 General Conference. Because its membership of free blacks oriented the congregation to oppose slavery, Bethel, its original name, became known as "an abolition church." It also became a lynchpin for Underground Railroad activity among AMEs in the tristate area of north central Kentucky and southern Indiana and Ohio together with their Quaker allies. Because local slaveholders were never comfortable with independent black churches, Quinn was arrested when he first met the Louisville congregation in 1838. Though Louisville slave owners prohibited their chattels from visiting the AME Church, the congregation still flourished and relocated to a better site in 1854. Along with a derivative congregation, Asbury Chapel AME Church, these churches served both free and fugitive blacks in the Louisville area. Quinn, therefore, broadened the boundaries of African Methodism and strengthened the cohesion of innumerable black communities in both free and slave states. To sustain these efforts he was elected in 1844 as the fourth AME bishop, and the Paul Quinn Missionary Society was organized to respond to "where our people are calling for our aid."[42]

Quinn's broad missionary jurisdiction of free and neighboring slave states reflected AME alignments with abolitionism and aiding slave runaways. It was rumored, for example, that Quinn helped fugitive slaves arriving in Indianapolis and elsewhere in Indiana. Through Quinn's successor as an AME superintendent in Indiana and collaborator on the Underground Railroad, Byrd Parker, a nexus between the Louisville church and a congregation in New Albany, Indiana, became a fulcrum for visible black advocacy. Parker, born in North Carolina, headed the Louisville congregation in

---

[41] Eugene H. Berwanger, *The Frontier against Slavery: Western Anti-Negro Prejudice and the Slavery Extension Controversy* (Urbana, University of Illinois Press, 1967); *Minutes of the Seventh General Conference*, 1840, 4; Payne, *History of the African Methodist Episcopal Church*, 170–171; *Journal of Proceedings of the Fifteenth Annual Conference of the African Methodist Episcopal Church for the District of Indiana held at Indianapolis, September 6, 1854* (Indianapolis, IN, Rawson Vaile,1854), 22.

[42] Hudson, *Fugitive Slaves and the Underground Railroad in the Kentucky Borderland*, 109; J. Blaine Hudson, "African American Religion in Ante Bellum Louisville, Kentucky," *The Griot*, Vol. 17, No. 2, Fall 1998, 45–47.

around 1850 and simultaneously served Bethel Church in New Albany, where he also resided. Founded in 1841, the building of the Indiana church was set on fire in that same year. Arsonists probably suspected abolitionism within the congregation or opposed Bethel's uplift efforts for the local black population. During his tenure at both churches, which ended in 1853, Parker emerged as a well-known African American spokesman. In 1853 in Rochester, New York, he attended Frederick Douglass's National Convention of Colored People. After Parker relocated to Chicago, which was included in Quinn's jurisdiction as a bishop, he became an agent for *Frederick Douglass' Paper* and cooperated with local Underground Railroad activists.[43]

Despite the abolitionist reputation of Quinn Chapel, Louisville and its connection to an insurgent African Methodist parish in New Albany, the other AME congregation in Louisville, Asbury Chapel, consisting mainly of slaves, had a history of mixed Methodist affiliations. In a setting of property disputes and a seemingly unscrupulous pastor, Asbury Chapel, notwithstanding the abolitionist advocacy of one of its ministers, maintained a pliant posture that was nonthreatening to white authorities. When the ME Church split in 1844 and yielded the pro-slavery ME Church, South, the affiliated black congregation, despite its automatic transfer from one white controlled denomination to another, boldly affiliated with the black-run AME Church. By 1852 Pastor J. Harper, who had bolted from the AMEs, assumed possession of the church property and rejoined the ME Church, South, but later formed an independent church. Neither the northern nor southern branches of white Methodism advanced any property claims against Asbury Chapel, now a part of the AME Church. Perhaps, to mollify whites, both the dissident Harper and his slave followers and the slave members of Asbury Chapel "repudiated Northern influence" and defined the disputes as property matters. A local white newspaper that reported on Harper's seeming character flaws noted that he came to Louisville "from Cincinnati, Ohio, where abolitionism is luxuriant and remained here (in the city) contrary to law." Harper was also blamed for unrest in Asbury Chapel according to the newspaper, which claimed that "the African churches were then at peace, and [at the time] satisfied with the control of their white brethren" until the minister interfered. Moreover, the police hit Harper "for being found at an unlawful gathering which was not for the purpose of religious worship." Notwithstanding his advocacy for black freedom, the

---

[43] Pamela R. Peters, *The Underground Railroad in Floyd County, Indiana* (Jacksonville, NC, McFarland & Co., 2001), 69, 71–72; Payne, *History of the African Methodist Episcopal Church*, 287.

local newspaper said, "it is not true that Harper was induced to abandon the African Church on the score of abolitionism" and "it is not true that the African Church is an abolition foreign corporation." Even the AMEs had expelled Harper "for rebellion and sowing dissension." These experiences illustrated the convergence of two types of subversive activities. Both a minister, overt in his "abolitionist" attitudes and actions, and a congregation, though compelled to obey the protocols of a slave society, insisted on an insurgent association with the AME Church.[44]

The establishment of the St. Louis and Louisville churches became indispensable lynchpins for potential AME expansion into slave and peripherally slave territories. Though originally in the Indiana Annual Conference, these churches formed the nucleus out of which the Missouri Annual Conference emerged in 1855. Not only were additional congregations established in the vicinity of these parishes, but African Methodism also spread to the slave state of Louisiana. A New Orleans church, St. James, founded in 1844 and incorporated in 1848, and other congregations both in the city and a neighboring parish became a part of the Missouri jurisdiction. Bishop Payne recalled a visit to "the Covington Mission, on Lake Pontchartrain, which was planted by Rev. Niles in 1854, under great opposition from certain whites." Churches in these slave settings in Louisiana and other southern locations faced difficulties that congregations in the free states largely avoided. Accounting for slave members and their whereabouts, for example, posed special challenges. "The condition of our people in the Southern States who become members of our church, many of whom are bondsmen, [are] liable to sudden removal owing to their peculiar condition," said a poignant declaration at the 1857 Missouri Annual Conference. This situation put "the pastors of our Southern work in an awkward position in making out annual reports." They recognized that these slave members were a mobile people, either because of their potential sale as chattels or from their status as runaways. Therefore, pastors were advised to retain slave members on their rolls unless for some reason they had been expelled. These ministers needed discretion in these matters because only they knew "the situation of our people." Slave members "are placed out on plantations-go traveling [and] neither pastor nor leader know anything of their absence or whereabouts." Some "are brought back after an absence for months from the place where they joined church," conferees were told, and they "exemplified an amount of thankfulness which is not found in other persons in more favored

<hr />

[44] *Louisville Daily Courier*, April 22, 1852, April 28, 1852 (courtesy of Professor Richard J. M. Blackett, Vanderbilt University).

circumstances." Delegates were also mindful that their meeting at Asbury AME Church in the slave city of Louisville meant that they could not call undue attention to their proceedings lest they divulge information about their slave constituency. Hence, they complimented municipal officials for their "kind protection" while still debating strategies to maintain their presence among the slaves and aid their efforts to escape bondage.[45]

Thomas M. D. Ward extended Quinn's western mission by focusing on the Pacific Coast. Born in Pennsylvania in 1823, Ward accepted from the 1856 General Conference an appointment as missionary superintendent for the Far West. At the 1864 General Conference he reported on four newly established churches in the San Francisco area and in Virginia City in the Nevada Territory. He either spearheaded or supervised a total of twelve churches in northern California. To achieve these hard-won results, Ward recalled "riding over mountains for three hundred miles, sometimes by stage, sometimes footing it [and] sometimes taking a blanket and lying out under the trees." Though he did not tire from "pleading the cause of a broken and suffering people, who are identified with me in race, blood, complexion and destiny," he requested relief from the rigors of travel. Now a bishop for California was needed to oversee the denomination's growing presence in the Far West. Already, one bishop boasted that "poor, ignorant, [and] despised, we have gradually advanced from state to state, until now our connection unfurls the blood-stained banners of the cross from the mountainous regions of Maine to the low-lands of Louisiana, and from the blue waves of the Atlantic to the majestic billows of the Pacific Ocean." The AME Church had become a national denomination![46]

AME Zion history paralleled the AME experience. The involvement of clergy in abolitionism, in the Underground Railroad, and in educational initiatives was as embedded in the Zion body as in the AME. The denomination's dense growth in New York and New England exposed clergy to organized abolitionism and drew some into the movement. Thomas James, the AME Zion pastor in New Bedford, Massachusetts, introduced his

[45] *Journal of Proceedings of the Third Annual Conference of the African Methodist Episcopal Church for the District of Missouri, 1857* (Louisville, KY, Rev. John M. Brown, 1857), 1, 10–12, 17, 32: Payne, *Recollections*, 129–130.
[46] Wright, *The Bishops of the African Methodist Episcopal Church*, 350; *Thirteenth General Conference of the African Methodist Episcopal Church* held in Philadelphia, PA, May 2, 1864 (1864), 44–45; *Minutes of the New England Annual Conference of the African Methodist Episcopal Church* held in the City of New Bedford, June 10–21, 1852 (1852), 5; *Minutes of the Sixty-Ninth Session of the Baltimore Annual Conference of the African Methodist Episcopal Church in the United States of America* held in Mount Moriah AME Church, Annapolis, MD, April 28–May 5, 1886 (Baltimore, MD, Hoffman & Co., 1886), 20.

parishioner, Frederick Douglass, into New England anti-slavery circles. James himself had been born a slave in 1804 in Canajoharie, New York, but escaped to Canada after being sold to a third master. He joined the AME Zion Church in 1823, aided fugitive slaves during his time in New England, and helped to organize anti-slavery meetings when he served a Rochester congregation. Catherine Harris, born in Titusville, Pennsylvania in 1809, settled in Jamestown, New York. While working as a midwife, she housed both an AME Zion congregation and a station on the Underground Railroad in her home. Zionites also believed that educational elevation was integral to black freedom. Therefore, the 1848 General Conference ratified a Manual Labor School in Essex County, New York. Rush Academy would prepare candidates for the ministry and "elevate our whole people."[47]

Nonetheless, the two African Methodist bodies differed in three major areas. The AME Church celebrated its insurgent origins and its bold break with Wesleyan whites in Philadelphia. Though Zionites also fought against white ecclesiastical domination, their withdrawal was less rancorous and developed no narrative to match the dramatic hagiographies that AMEs told about Richard Allen and his fight for denominational independence. The geographical spread of the AME Church also exceeded the Zion organization. Superintendent Christopher Rush received a request to send a minister to Demerara in South America, and Zion's New York Annual Conference listed in 1848 a British North America Mission of seventy-two members in Halifax, Nova Scotia. But these church initiatives had a lesser impact than the AME's Canada Annual Conference and expansion elsewhere in the United States and in the Caribbean. Lastly, AME expansion benefited from the active evangelism and supervision of bishops and commissioned missionaries. In fact, Zion's 1848 Philadelphia Annual Conference "repudiate[d] the bishopric set up by any and every church" and affirmed the office of superintendent as preferable to a lifetime episcopacy; though both denominations established congregations in San Francisco in 1852, the AME General Conference sent follow-up personnel to start additional congregations in the region. Therefore, the two religious bodies, while deeply invested in the freedom pursuits of African Americans, had a disparate impact because of differences in geographical scope.[48]

---

[47] David H. Bradley Sr., *A History of the AME Zion Church, Part I*, 1796–1872 (Nashville, TN, Parthenon Press, 1956), 110–115; *Minutes of the General and the Several Annual Conferences of the African Methodist Episcopal Zion Church in America, 1848* (New York, G. W. Okie,1848), 7–9.

[48] *Minutes of the General and Several Annual Conferences, AME Zion Church* (1848), 11–12; *Minutes of the New York Annual Conference of the African Methodist Episcopal Zion Church*

ESCAPING SLAVERY AND EMIGRATION

The dispersed populations that Quinn, Ward, and other AME missionaries encountered, whether they were legally manumitted or were fugitives, migrated beyond the power of the proslavery South. Locating either in California or Canada seemingly protected them from slave catchers who indiscriminately kidnapped African Americans despite their legal status. The greater the distance from the slave states, the better were the opportunities to remain free. Those with lingering fears of vulnerability, however, were not reassured when the Fugitive Slave Act of 1850 was enacted. They knew that slave owners had received a guarantee in the US Constitution that their chattels would be retrieved and returned to their masters and mistresses. The 1793 proviso required federal officials to enforce this demand as the price that slave states demanded for their entry into the Union. The federal constitution affirmed that fugitive slaves had no right to be free, no matter where they resided.

This constitutional mandate received operational guidelines in federal legislation passed in Congress in 1850. Slave owners, who had complained that the constitutional statue was not effectively enforced, drew enormous satisfaction from the new law. Packaged as a part of the Compromise of 1850, a series of legislative acts to balance the interests of free and slave states, the Fugitive Slave Act compelled cooperation from law enforcement officials in all states and territories to capture and extradite runaways back to their owners. Widespread resistance stirred against the law, with some northern state legislatures enacting their own measures to circumvent the federal statute and individual citizens helping fugitives to escape. The Fugitive Slave Act also spurred AME growth and required the denomination to protect blacks who were fleeing "the slave power."[49]

Pittsburgh's Wylie Avenue congregation nervously anticipated the passage of the fugitive slave law. Though the legislation was enacted in September 1850, the congregation hosted a meeting of local blacks in July 1850, and they approved resolutions to thwart slave catchers coming into the city. The agenda of the 1851 New York Annual Conference was filled with references to the Fugitive Slave Act. One minister, Thomas Henson, reported on

In America, Church and Leonard Streets, city of New York, May 20th, 1848, 21; "Minutes of the Philadelphia Annual Conference (of the African Methodist Episcopal Zion Church), Philadelphia, Pennsylvania, May 6th, 1848," in the *Minutes of the General and Several Annual Conferences, African Methodist Episcopal Zion Church*, 19.

[49] Stanley W. Campbell, *The Slave Catchers: Enforcement of the Fugitive Slave Act*, 1850–1860 (Chapel Hill, University of North Carolina Press, 1970).

parishioners who "had fled to Canada on account of the Fugitive Slave Law." Bishop Quinn reminded delegates about "the difficulties we encounter from prejudice and persecution, the Devil and the Fugitive Slave Law." Moreover, the conference acknowledged "our dear brethren who have been exiled from their homes by the passage and enforcement of an exceeding[ly] cruel and oppressive enactment by Congress, known as the Fugitive Slave Bill." God, they believed, "will turn and overturn" this law so that "righteousness shall prevail throughout the earth." The 1853 Philadelphia Annual Conference was similarly outraged saying, "The passage of . . . that infamous bill of 1850 . . . makes devils blush . . . and] suffocates every principle of freedom." Daniel A. Payne observed that the new law generated a "bitter outburst of feeling against the United States." Its enactment "forced many of the best families of color to seek asylum in Western Canada, where they were safe" from slave catchers and their "bloodhounds." Therefore, Payne and others visited Dawn, a settlement of at least 500 expatriate African Americans at Dresden, Ontario, "to see if Canada would be a safe asylum for our people" seeking to escape the Fugitive Slave Act. With support from British and American abolitionists, Dawn, like other black settlements in Canada, resembled a "refugee" camp. Josiah Henson, himself a fugitive slave from Kentucky, was attracted to Canada and settled eventually among some fifty black families in Dawn. He influenced Harriet Beecher Stowe to pattern after himself her character Uncle Tom, in her 1852 best-selling novel *Uncle Tom's Cabin*. Henson, previously a Methodist minister, became the AME pastor at Dresden, where Payne believed blacks would be protected from the "slave power."[50]

AME declarations against slavery were expressed frequently and definitively in various venues throughout the antebellum period. An AME General Conference in 1820 denied fellowship to anyone who owned slaves. The 1850 Ohio Annual Conference, for example, called American slavery "a sin of the greatest magnitude" and a "crying evil of this nation." Moreover, "it is the duty of every Minister of the Gospel to cry against it." The 1852 New England Annual Conference would not "forget the forlorn and mournful condition of those of our brethren who are held in chains." Delegates prayed

---

[50] Blockson, *The Underground Railroad in Pennsylvania*, 153–154; *Minutes of the Annual Conference of the New York District of the African Methodist Episcopal Church* held in Bethel Church, Second Street (1851), 8–9, 19, 21; *Minutes of the Philadelphia District Annual Conference of the African Methodist Episcopal Church* (1853), 15; Payne, *History of the African Methodist Episcopal Church*, 252; Payne, *Recollections*, 66; Jared A. Brock, *The Road to Dawn: Josiah Henson and the Story That Sparked the Civil War* (New York, Public Affairs, 2018), 118; 124; 176.

that God would execute "righteousness for all them that are oppressed." The 1848 General Conference in expressing its disdain for slavery amended a resolution that called African Americans their "enslaved sisters and brothers." This terminology seemed to be an implicit acceptance of their degraded status. In asserting their full humanity and citizenship, revised wording defined them as "our people in free and slave States." The 1852 General Conference opposed "the enslavement of any portion of mankind as a sin of the first magnitude and we will seek, by all moral means, to maintain the constitutional position of our church, in regard [to opposition] to slavery."[51]

AMEs easily denounced slavery as "the highest violation of God's law" and "a shameful abuse of God's creatures." Delegates to the 1856 General Conference, however, addressed the harder issue of black slaveholders and their eligibility for AME Church membership. This issue crystallized because of denominational growth beyond the free states into slave territories within the expansive Missouri Annual Conference. "Abolitionist" clergy from such jurisdictions as the Philadelphia Annual Conference, for example, crafted a majority report that would deny fellowship to slaveholders and require the immediate expulsion of any persons who did not manumit their slaves. Because these delegates came from states where black bondage had been outlawed for decades, where abolitionism was strong, and where opposition to the 1850 Fugitive Slave Act was greatest, they wrote this resolution as though all slaveholders were white southerners. "The AME Church," they declared, "composed, as it is, of colored persons identified with slaves in chains, who never can be disseevered from them in their sufferings." The minority report, which the delegates adopted, balanced a forthright denunciation of slavery and a guarded condemnation of black slaveholders by allowing an ambiguous amount of time for these members to emancipate their chattel. They argued that some southern AMEs, themselves free persons of color, benignly purchased slaves in order to set them free. These transactions, at times, were formalized in front of "a civil magistrate" and executed on condition of repayment. A supporter of the minority report was

---

[51] Howard D. Gregg, *The AME Church and the Current Negro Revolt* (Nashville, TN, AME Sunday School Union, n.d.), 53; *Minutes of the Twentieth Ohio Annual Conference of the African Methodist E. Church (held at Bethel Church, Columbus, Ohio, August 1, 1850* (Pittsburgh, PA, *Christian Herald*, 1850), 14; *Minutes of the New England Annual Conference* (1852), 14; *Proceedings of the Eighth General Conference of the African M. E. Church* held in the City of Philadelphia, May 1, 1848, and continued in Session twenty-one days (1848) (Pittsburgh, PA, *Christian Herald*, 1848), 9; *Minutes of the Tenth General Conference of the African Methodist Episcopal Church* held in the City of New York, May 3–20, inclusive (1852) (Philadelphia, PA, Wm. S. Young, 1852), 5, 9.

loathed to "hinder such acts of mercy." Conversely, those who backed the majority report dismissed these seeming examples of magnanimity and cited AMEs who owned slaves, had sold them, and benefited from the profit. The denomination, they believed, was an anti-slavery church and should never equivocate on black freedom.[52]

Despite the passage of the minority report, the debate surrounding it revealed tensions between protecting the interests of territorial expansionists, who sometimes encountered black slaveholding members, and the greater need for unambiguous policies to realize black freedom. Though some equivocated on black slaveholders, abolitionist rhetoric and action played the broader role in defining the denomination's identity and praxis. The 1856 New England Annual Conference, adamant in its abolitionist principles, subtly defied the General Conference's minority report by shifting the debate about members who held slaves and to a emphasis to the conduct of clergy. "We will not admit," New England AMEs declared, "any slaveholder into our pulpits; either in principle or otherwise; we knowing him to be such, either white or black." Despite a debate that seemed to soften the emancipationist ethos of African Methodism, the denomination's expanding involvement in the Atlantic World, especially the creation of the British ME Church, showed that finding safe havens for free and fugitive blacks remained an AME priority. These initiatives demonstrated that black liberationist objectives stayed as a centerpiece to "the regular order" of the AME operations.[53]

Despite this important denominational debate, there was growing emigrationist energy generated from the worsening plight of African Americans during the 1850s. Beyond the enactment and enforcement of the Fugitive Slave Act of 1850, there were intense and violent conflicts about the extension of slavery into the territories showing that the "peculiar institution" was far from withering within American society. Rather the scepter of popular sovereignty, "bleeding Kansas," and the Dred Scott decision demonstrated that slavery was gaining a firmer grip where it existed and energized to spread into the Great Plains and Far West. At the same time, African Americans, who had been steadily fleeing to Canada, increasingly looked to Great Britain as a better protector of black rights than the United States.

---

[52] Payne, *History of the African Methodist Episcopal Church*, 336–338, 341.

[53] Ibid., 344; Also see Angell, "The Shadows of the Evening Stretched Out," 236–237; *Minutes of the Fourth Annual Conference of the New England District of the African Methodist Episcopal Church in America* held in Plymouth Hall, Boston, June 21–30, 1856 (Providence, RI, Knowles, Anthony, & Co., 1856), 13.

Its well-known history of abolitionism and suppressing the slave trade commended Canada to blacks as the nearest British possession where their rights would be affirmed.

This consciousness greatly influenced AMEs already living in Canada. African Methodism embodied the experiences and perspectives of these emigrant and fugitive peoples who had fled a republic that seemed increasingly acquiescent to slavery. Their denomination, though rooted in the United States, but serving a mobile membership, was expanding its base of operation to Canada. Since the British Empire afforded civic protections to AME ministers and members that American society denied to both free blacks and slaves, African Methodism could draw upon fresh sources of emancipationist energy and support from north of the border. That two of the three AME bishops, Quinn and Willis Nazrey, planned to reside in Canada suggested a serious contemplation of an alternative headquarters for AME governance.[54]

Hence, AME admiration for the British, especially after the passage of the Fugitive Slave Act, was frequently articulated. Quinn, for example, praised congregations at the 1853 Canada Annual Conference for celebrating the annual August 1 commemoration of the emancipation of slaves in the British West Indies. Similarly, at the 1854 Indiana Annual Conference he asked clergy to deliver a special sermon or lecture "in reference to the West India Emancipation." Moreover, the 1853 Canada Annual Conference resolved that "we have learned by long experience that the British government is the tried friend of the coloured race." Furthermore, Parliament was praised for the manumission of slaves in the West Indies and for suppressing slave trading in Africa. Equally important was British goodwill toward blacks who had settled in Canada. "By extending to us the hand of fellowship and throwing around us the arm of protection and providing a city of refuge for the bleeding slave [thus] escaping the man stealer," said the resolution, blacks should pledge loyalty to Queen Victoria and swear allegiance to "Her Majesty." Though the reception of blacks to various parts of Canada was occasionally unfriendly and at times British officials despaired of possible extradition and other international proceedings against fugitive slaves, African Americans still believed that greater security awaited them north of the border than in the United States.[55]

---

[54] Dennis C. Dickerson, *Religion, Race, and Region: Research Notes on AME Church History* (Nashville, TN, AME Sunday School Union, 1995), 58–59.

[55] Cited in Dickerson, *Religion, Race and Region*, 52–53; Robin W. Winks, *The Blacks in Canada: A History* (Montreal, McGill-Queen's University Press, 1971), 142–143.

Perhaps, the Philadelphia Annual Conference expressed what most AMEs believed about the magnanimity of the British. They commended them for their "benevolence exhibited in this time of peril and danger to the liberty of the coloured race in these United States." Unlike those in the American Colonization Society who tried to "force us from the homes of our youth and land of our birth to the shores of Africa" and unlike supporters of the federally enacted Fugitive Slave Act who exposed free blacks and slaves "to all the perils of interminable bondage," the British respected "the rights" of African Americans and judged racist American laws as examples "of barbarism" reminiscent "of the dark ages." Instead, the British showed themselves as protectors of blacks "by sheltering the panting fugitive when escaping from this land of blood" and "proved their Christian sympathy for us by opening their dominions and inviting us to the enjoyments of equal privileges with the natural born British subjects." These AMEs, pessimistic about their destiny in the United States, but determined to stand their ground, declared that "the entire treatment of the majority of the American people is, and has been such, that so long as slavery exists, and coloured people can be sold here, there never will be confidence enough reposed in them" to trust the benefits of repatriation across the Atlantic. Therefore, their best geographical option lay neither in the United States nor in Africa. Instead, the "renewal" of British "sympathy for us" and "inviting the long injured race" into Canada would offer them "the enjoyment of the blessings of liberty and equality."[56]

The deteriorating status of blacks in American society suggested that the stability of African Methodism was also at stake. Whatever the uncertainties for the denomination in the United States, its history of independence certainly could be sustained in Canada and national loyalties could be transferred to the British dominion. Because AMEs generally viewed Canada as a "genuine asylum of the oppressed," it seemed easy to accept from the Canada Annual Conference a petition "to set us apart as a separate body." Bishop Daniel A. Payne, presiding at the 1854 session, allowed an amendment to a new *The Book of Discipline* acknowledging "Queen Victoria as our rightful Sovereign" and noting that "British law throws the broad shield of equal protection over the life, liberty, and the personal happiness of all its loyal subjects without regard to the clime in which they were born, or the hue of their skin." Hence, the 1856 AME General Conference recognized the validity of the Canadian request "when we take into consideration the fact

---

[56] *Minutes of the Philadelphia District Annual Conference of the African Methodist Episcopal Church, 1851* (Philadelphia, William S. Young, 1851), 13–14.

that that country, unlike our own, gives full and equal privileges to all its subjects, and is an asylum from the shameful and unrighteous oppression of this government." With these declarations the Canada Annual Conference of the AME Church became the British Methodist Episcopal (BME) Church.[57]

Though Quinn was uneasy about the creation of the BME Church, he applauded the required intimacy between the two denominations. To sustain these close ties, "Bishop Quinn and a large number of old fathers ... begged" Nazrey to retain his episcopacy among the AMEs while presiding in the BME Church. Nazrey consented, and also helped to mollify a remnant of AMEs, especially in the maritime territories, who resisted a BME affiliation. Secondly, the credentials of clergy were interchangeable in each denomination and thus they could move back and forth between AME and BME annual conferences. These developments satisfied Quinn and established that the two sects would function virtually and interactively as a single religious body. Within eight years there were 3,000 BME members, sixty clergy, and forty-two congregations. Though the 1864 AME General Conference compelled Nazrey to relinquish his AME assignments, the two denominations continued symbiotically during the bishop's dual incumbency. The BME Church, another derivative denomination of African Methodism, defined its mission to evangelize blacks throughout the British Empire and spread to the Canadian maritime provinces, Bermuda, and Demerara (present-day Guyana). Despite the difference in name, the two religious bodies pushed complementary strategies to evangelize blacks in the Atlantic World and affirm their equal rights as citizens in the Americas.[58]

As AMEs searched for safe havens to secure black freedom, they carefully distinguished this objective from what the American Colonization Society tried to achieve. Founded in 1816, the ACS believed the solution to American slavery lay in the emancipation and expatriation of blacks to Africa, principally to Liberia. Eventually, slaveholders rearticulated ACS aims by stressing the removal of free blacks and leaving slavery intact. These conflicting motivations created an anomalous situation for AME leaders. Richard Allen, already an ally of Paul Cuffee in promoting African colonization, was initially receptive to the ACS. Non-elite blacks, however, suspected that they could be victimized by repatriation efforts and subjected to a coerced exit from the United States. Therefore, Allen, in recognition of these widespread suspicions, retreated from his supportive posture toward the ACS.

[57] Dickerson, *Religion, Race and Region*, 54; *Twelfth General Conference of the African Methodist Episcopal Church* held in Pittsburgh, PA, May 7, 1860, 29.
[58] Dickerson, *Religion, Race and Region*, 57–59; Winks, *The Blacks in Canada: A History*, 356.

Daniel Coker pragmatically drew funding from the Maryland Colonization Society to underwrite his emigration to Africa in 1820. Later, he supervised an ACS settlement in Liberia and cooperated with a British colonizationist and abolitionist in Sierra Leone. He also viewed black repatriation as the best way to circumvent the slavery and subjugation of blacks in the United States. Nonetheless, the cynical objectives of slave owners nullified the benign intentions of Allen and Coker, and discredited the ACS in the eyes of most AMEs.[59]

Some AMEs, however, still looked to Liberia as an escape from black oppression in the United States. The *African Repository*, an ACS periodical, reported in 1851, for example, that the *Liberia Packet* embarked from Baltimore on its tenth voyage with fifty-four emigrants on board. Though most were free blacks from Baltimore, the Maryland Colonization Society sponsored two from the state's Eastern Shore. William T. Catto, a supporter of African colonization, made a special appeal for J. M. Moore. This fellow minister, said Catto to the 1851 Baltimore Annual Conference, was "about to embark for Africa." Despite his emigration, Catto declared, "it is not his intention to relinquish his connection with our Church, but ever to continue with us." Therefore, Bishop Quinn certified that Moore would remain "a minister in good standing in the AME Church." Moore may have been responding to an appeal from James W. C. Pennington, a black Congregational minister who issued an appeal in the *Maryland Colonization Journal* for "Colored Preachers for Africa." He said that "well informed colored preachers of the gospel are what Africa now and ever has needed." These clergy, he continued, "will do the most effective work against Slavery in this country, and the Slave Trade in Africa."[60]

Moore, who sailed for Monrovia on July 20, 1851, came out of a complicated family situation, not unlike many other free blacks. Sailing with him were his wife, Comfort Moore, and their four children. Though Moore was born free in around 1812, Comfort, a literate woman, had been born in slavery in around 1816 and had been emancipated by a T. M. Moore. Their three older children were also born as slaves, but were later set free.

[59] Newman, *Freedom's Prophet*, 183, 202–204; Betty Thomas, "Daniel Coker," in Logan and Winston (eds.), *The Dictionary of American Negro Biography*, 119–120.
[60] *African Repository*, Vol. 27, No. 8, August 1851, 245; *Minutes of Thirty-Fourth Annual Conference of the African Methodist Episcopal Church for the Baltimore District* held in the city of Baltimore, MD, April 18, 1851 (Baltimore, MD, Sherwood & Co., 1851), 11; J. W. C. Pennington, "Colored Preachers for Africa," *Maryland Colonization Journal*, October 1847, 59–60. (Professor Richard J. M. Blackett of Vanderbilt University brought the Pennington article to my attention out of his own research.)

They were Matthias, aged eighteen, a bricklayer, Jacob, aged sixteen, and James, aged eleven. Their youngest son, Daniel, aged nine, was born after his mother was manumitted.[61]

The Moores were not the only Baltimore AMEs who espoused emigration to Africa. Moreover, they neither eschewed ties with the Maryland Colonization Society nor shunned its association with Liberia. At the 1852 Convention of the Free People of Color in the State of Maryland, James A. Handy, the presiding officer, praised "the infant republic of Liberia" whose "civil and Christian power [was] ordained by heaven for the redemption of Africa." He added that "emigration is the only medium by which the long closed doors of that continent are to be opened; by her own children returning." Through African American émigrés Africa would be "resuscitated, renovated, and redeemed." Handy, the son of a slave father and a free mother, was born in Baltimore in 1826. He prided himself on seeing the first four AME bishops, including the founder. He was baptized in 1833 and entered the ministry in 1860. Darius Stokes, formerly a minister at Bethel Church in Baltimore, declared at the convention that "as to going to Africa, he was in favor of any man going where he thought he could do better." Stokes had been expelled by Bethel's quarterly conference on some unspecified charge, but drew strong support for restoration in the Baltimore Annual Conference by fellow emigrationist J. M. Moore. Baltimore's AMEs conflated their espousal of emigration with colonizationist support for Liberia. Other AMEs, however, drew sharp distinctions between their own back to Africa initiatives and ACS sponsorship of black expatriation.[62]

Black opposition to colonization drew support from William Lloyd Garrison, the founder of *The Liberator* and the American Antislavery Society. In his *Thoughts on African Colonization*, Garrison said that the ACS, though it started as "a praiseworthy association," actually intended the deportation of free blacks as a means to strengthen slavery. He cited ACS overtures to slaveholders that said that "free people of color are a nuisance to us and [are] plotters of sedition among your slaves. If they be not speedily removed, your property will be lost and your lives destroyed." Because of these sympathetic communications with slave owners, numerous African Americans denounced the colonizationists. The 1851 Philadelphia Annual

[61] *African Repository*, Vol. 27, No. 9, September 1851, 283.
[62] *Maryland Colonization Journal*, August 1852, 227, 231–232 (courtesy of Richard J. M. Blackett of Vanderbilt University); Wright, *The Bishops of the African Methodist Episcopal Church*, 203–204; *Minutes of the Thirty-Fourth Annual Conference ... Baltimore District (1851)*, 5, 9–10.

Conference, for example, accused the ACS of pursuing a "detestable scheme" to remove "our people [from] this their native land." If free blacks were gone, slaveholders then would "hold our brethren the more quietly and safely in chains." Hence, AMEs should "spurn the advice of any and every man or minister, be he white or colored, who shall attempt to disturb and unsettle the institutions that exist among us by attacking the permanency of our people" in the land of their birth. Moreover, the AME Church, according to delegates, was threatened itself by colonization because "our religious and moral institutions must be disbanded" if the ACS was successful. Moreover, M. M. Clark, the *Christian Recorder* editor, visited the 1853 Philadelphia Annual Conference, and "in burning eloquence enchained the large audience in his rebukes and denunciations of the American Colonization Society." He also called the ACS an "insidious enemy of the colored American." Following Clark was the former Maryland slave, J. J. G. Bias, the physician-preacher-abolitionist. Bias excoriated "both Church and State" for their advocacy of "the doctrine of expatriation." Through an unholy alliance with "the African Colonization Society," religious and civic bodies joined "to expatriate the free colored population from this continent, where they are citizens by birth, to a land where they are utter strangers, and to [a place where there was] an unhealthy clime."[63]

These AMEs, while hostile to the ACS, were not opposed to black emigration, especially to territories within the western hemisphere. Some, however, eschewed expatriation to Liberia mainly because of its association with the ACS. AME emigrationists, whether they were integrationist or nationalist, generally espoused black self-determination and valued venues where black freedom would be secure. Hence, Bias told the Philadelphia Annual Conference to "look at Canada where the colored people have their rights and privileges as men." Moreover, "turn your attention," he said, "to the West Indies, that part, which is under [the] British Government, and there you will discover the rights and privileges of colored men." He also asked, "why cannot your attention be turned to those parts of the world which offer you liberty and happiness, where you are counted as men and not as dogs?" He expressed similar sentiments about Central and South America and Haiti. All of these destinations, Bias believed, were preferable to

[63] William Lloyd Garrison, *Thoughts on African Colonization, 1832* (New York, Arno Press, Reprint 1968), 3, 40–41; Payne, *History of the African Methodist Episcopal Church*, 250; *Minutes of the Philadelphia District Annual Conference* (1853), 14–15.

Liberia, "that hell of American prejudice," because they were free from colonizationist influences.[64]

Bias's worries about ACS ascendancy in Liberia and his support of black emigration within the western hemisphere showed that black self-determination was intrinsic to AME thought. This perspective derived from a history of AME autonomy and a record of its ambitious reach into the black Atlantic. Within this large geographical sphere AME clergy and laity tracked black mobility across the Americas and toward Africa to protect the physical, spiritual, and civic well-being of enslaved, fugitive, and emancipated peoples. Lewis Woodson, more than any other antebellum AME, articulated a capacious view of black self-determination that transcended both integrationist and nationalist ideologies. Blacks, in seeking and sustaining their freedom, Woodson declared, needed cohesive and morally grounded communities aimed at total self-sufficiency. Woodson, as an AME minister, valued the racial solidarity that African Methodism practiced and projected into the Atlantic World.[65]

Woodson, a mulatto born in Virginia in 1806, rose to prominence as an AME official and school founder beginning in the 1820s. In Chillicothe, Ohio, he helped to establish the African Educational and Benevolent Society. In Pittsburgh he served as pastor at Wylie Avenue AME Church, as secretary of the Ohio Annual Conference, and as a teacher at the school housed in his church. Martin R. Delany, the leading advocate of "a nationalist-emigrationist creed," an explorer in West Africa, and author of *The Condition, Elevation, Emigration, and Destiny of the Colored People of the United States*, was a Woodson student in Pittsburgh. Delany drew his racial ideology from Woodson and showed the breadth of his teacher's influence.[66]

Woodson, as a participant in the American Moral Reform Society, promoted thrift, upright conduct, and temperance as crucial to constituting blacks as a free people. He also supported "separate settlements" because racism prevented African Americans and whites from living together amicably and equally. Either Canada or the British West Indies or some rural location on the American frontier were desirable possibilities for black emigration. His parents, Thomas and Jemima Woodson, like the Baltimore couple in Brooklyn, Illinois, founded the all black Milton Township in

---

[64] *Minutes of the Philadelphia District Annual Conference* (1853), 15.

[65] See Floyd J. Miller, "'Father of Black Nationalism:' Another Contender," *Civil War History*, Vol. 17, No. 4, December 1971, 310–317; Gayle Tate, "Prophesy and Transformation: The Contours of Lewis Woodson's Nationalism," *Journal of Black Studies*, Vol. 29, No. 2, 209–233.

[66] Miller, "Father of Black Nationalism," 310–314.

Jackson County, Ohio, where "a church, day and Sabbath school" demonstrated the self-determination that he envisaged for the entire black population. He also believed that "without a national institution of some description our affairs can never attain any degree of consistence or permanence." These views explained why he remained in the AME Church until he died in 1878.[67]

Though Woodson clearly espoused nationalism, his stress on black self-determination realized in emigration to free territories was broad enough to embrace an integrationist such as Bias. Both AME clergy opposed colonizationists and the attempt of these whites to decide where blacks should emigrate and who among them should be free. Both Woodson and Bias supported the abolitionist movement and preferred that black emigrants should go either to Canada or the Caribbean or to the free states in the Old Northwest. The destiny discourse of Woodson and Bias reflected general denominational discussions about promoting autonomous black settlements in the Americas and black-led initiatives for African emigration. Other AME testimonies about these themes illustrated that Woodson and Bias were in the mainstream of their denomination's discussions about black self-determination.

ONWARD INTO THE SOUTH AND INTO THE CARIBBEAN

Because AMEs envisaged the black Atlantic as its sphere of operations and its mobile inhabitants as potential members, the 1860 General Conference established the Parent Home and Foreign Missionary Society. Delegates declared that AME clergy "do now see, in the keenest Christian anxiety the deplorable spiritual condition of our people-our brothers, 'bone of our bone and flesh of our flesh.'" The resolution observed that these persons "inhabit both hemispheres, North and South America, Africa, Asia, and the isles of the Sea." Therefore, AMEs extravagantly pledged to evangelize all of these areas and obey "the last command of our ascended Lord, 'Go ye into all the world and preach the gospel.'" Most AMEs, however, already had in mind the preferred areas within the Atlantic World that the church should target.[68]

---

[67] Ibid., 312, 315, 317; Tate, "Prophesy and Transformation," 224; cited in Sterling Stuckey, *The Ideological Origins of Black Nationalism* (Boston, MA, Beacon Press, 1972), 14.
[68] *Twelfth General Conference of the African Methodist Episcopal Church* held in Pittsburgh, PA, May 7, 1860 (Philadelphia, PA, Wm. S. Young, 1860), 26.

The geographical breadth of Africa diminished the AME preoccupation with ACS associations with Liberia. Furthermore, the proximity of the West Indies drew understandable interest from AMEs on the American mainland. The 1849 Baltimore Annual Conference, for example, recommended "a mission in the West Indies and Africa" and that this initiative should be "of highest importance to the Church and the world." Bishop Nazrey in 1853 said AMEs should "look after perishing Africa, the West India Islands, St. Domingo, and others." Nazrey had heard "the crying wants of many souls" and believed it "the duty of the AME Church to assist in sending the gospel to the heathens." At the 1860 General Conference Willis R. Revels urged interest in Liberia where the ME Church had been recently founded among "our downtrodden and abused race." Revels proposed "fraternal relations and intercourse ... between our brethren upon the two continents."[69]

Some AMEs who paid attention to the West Indies also included Central America as an area for possible expansion. At the 1852 General Conference a delegate from New Orleans commented on "his mission to Central America." He observed possibilities in Graytown in present-day Nicaragua where there are "great and opening advantages for usefulness in that country." He appealed "for the coloured people to go to that country." Hence, the 1857 minutes of the Missouri Annual Conference meeting in Louisville, Kentucky, listed a Central American Mission on its roster of appointments. Similarly, at the 1860 General Conference, Central America was mentioned again and delegates were told that "a strong effort should be made to establish ourselves there." Another report at the 1852 General Conference resolved "to form a mission in Central America" and to plant African Methodism in Jamaica. Again, at the 1860 General Conference delegates learned that Jamaica "presents a splendid field for missionary effort."[70]

AMEs, in discussing a mission to the West Indies, scarcely distinguished between islands under French or British influence. Rather, the region's reputation for protecting black freedom stirred their interest. A history of Haitian independence and British abolitionism commended particular locations in the Caribbean as desirable destinations for black emigration and

[69] *Minutes of the Baltimore Annual Conference of the African Methodist Episcopal Church* held in Baltimore, MD, April 21–30, 1849 (Pittsburgh, PA, Christian Herald, 1849), 8; *Minutes of the Annual Conference for the New York District, African Methodist Episcopal Church* held in Bethel Church, Second Street, New York, 1852 (New York, William S. Dorr, 1852), 6; *Twelfth General Conference* (1860), 13.
[70] *Minutes of the Tenth General Conference* (1852), 9–10; *Journal of Proceedings of the Third Annual Conference ... District of Missouri* (1857), 4; *Twelfth General Conference* (1860), 13.

AME evangelism. The 1851 New York Annual Conference impaneled a Committee on the West India Brethren, which proposed a communication to Haitian AMEs. They acknowledged that the Haitians "have long been neglected on our part" and that renewed "ties" would "cement the bond of union between us" Hence, Haitians were asked to send representatives to the 1852 General Conference. The 1852 New York Annual Conference "recognized and received" Daniel Shavers of Santo Domingo "as a minister and member." Shavers also requested an appointment "to the West Indies Islands" so he could evangelize Santo Domingo, St. Kitts, and Jamaica. At the 1860 General Conference the subject of Haiti was again addressed and described as part of an island "which looms up in the Atlantic Ocean and whose people have demonstrated the truth that colored men are capable of self-government." Haiti, the report said, "presents a very inviting field." British Columbia, a long distance from the Caribbean and another part of the British Empire, also appeared as an "interesting field" for AME expansion.[71]

These sentiments suggested that AMEs based in the United States seemed to adopt the stance of their BME counterparts in giving up on America. They could not, however, take this position lest they totally abandon the majority of blacks who were still in bondage. Quinn's slave state successes in the 1840s required AMEs to operate in the dangerous environs of slavery and evangelize far from the safe havens of British territories. This aggressive push into the South, though it avoided overt insurgencies against white power, remained focused at undermining the "peculiar institution." Therefore, delegates to the 1860 General Conference acknowledged the presence of African Methodism in the slave South and said it deserved as much attention as expansion into British territories. When they discovered that Nazrey was presiding among the BMEs in Canada, delegates worried if he would be prevented "from traveling and visiting our work in the Southern States."[72]

Still, the AME presence in the slave states was problematic for clergy whom bishops assigned to these border and southern regions. Some ministers encountered personal assaults to their status as free persons. For example, Turner W. Roberts, born into slavery in North Carolina, after manumission or escape, settled in Indiana and entered the AME itinerancy. He served as a pastor in Salem, Indiana, in 1847, and in 1848 was transferred

---

[71] *Minutes of the . . . New York District* (1851), 18–19; *Minutes of the Annual Conference for the New York District of the African Methodist Episcopal* held in Vine Street Church, Buffalo, NY (New York, William S. Dorr, 1852), 24–25; *Twelfth General Conference* (1860), 13.
[72] *Twelfth General Conference* (1860), 15.

to Kentucky. Roberts was misidentified in this slave state as a slave and placed on the auction block. A friend successfully bid on him and bought his freedom. Roberts left Kentucky and subsequently served in the Ohio and Illinois Annual Conferences, vowing to refuse any other appointments in a slave state.[73]

Notwithstanding Roberts's experience, AMEs remained committed to ministry in the slave South. For this reason, the New Orleans church attracted renewed interest from the denomination. The congregation of 1,500, though closed at one time by municipal authorities, showed the potential for AME growth despite its existence in a slave state. The parish, however, was connected to the Missouri Annual Conference, and representatives were "coming North every year" to attend the meetings. If a separate jurisdiction in the South was established, "more confidence of both colored and white persons" would result. A resident bishop would preside "without molestation and without being obnoxious to the laws of Louisiana and that region of [the] country." Hence, a resolution at the 1860 General Conference called for the creation of "The Louisiana Conference of the African M. E. Church." This action would help the denomination "to deflect the designs of their enemies, and enable them to defend themselves" against their detractors. Beyond the New Orleans work, said John Mifflin Brown, the former pastor of the city's St. James AME Church, "the States of Louisiana, Alabama, Tennessee, Mississippi, and other regions coming into the African M. E. Church" should constitute an expanded jurisdiction. Since AMEs already "live in the midst of trial and persecution," a formal organization would "place the church beyond the suspicion of those who would seek their destruction." Brown, who spoke from personal experience, had been jailed "because he was a free man from the North" who allowed slaves to attend his worship services. Nonetheless, in addition to his assignment at St. James Church, he started other churches in the New Orleans area. The insurgent "principles" that Brown stressed in his sermons appealed to "his suffering brethren" but disturbed whites in New Orleans. Though indigenous preachers might draw fewer suspicions than a northern outsider, such as Brown, the veteran preacher testified to AME possibilities in the Gulf and Mid-South regions.[74]

---

[73] Cory D. Robbins, *Reclaiming (The) African Heritage at Salem, Indiana* (Berwyn Heights, MD, Heritage Books, 1995), 77.

[74] Ibid., 25–26; John T. Jenifer, *Centennial Retrospect History of the African Methodist Episcopal Church* (Nashville, TN, AME Sunday School Union, 1916), 67; Wright, *The Bishops of the African Methodist Episcopal Church*, 112.

Hence, the cautious observations that AMEs espoused at the 1860 General Conference reflected the views of the free blacks who were the backbone of the New Orleans church. The city's sizable segment of free born and freed African Americans enjoyed a range of social and economic privileges that the majority white population could easily strip away. Maintaining African American organizations, especially churches, was among the responsibilities that they undertook. Historically, AME churches in slave cities depended on free black members to protect the temporal interests of these congregations. In Baltimore, for example, two leading congregations, Bethel and Ebenezer, throughout the antebellum period, specified that "none shall be eligible as trustees except freeman (who were) descendants of Africans." Free blacks, more than slave members, they thought, encountered fewer obstacles in transacting church business.[75] Since slaves probably belonged to the congregation and furtively attended services, AMEs either concealed or downplayed their presence and promised them no aid for either escape or rebellion. At least, that was their public position. Yet, in proposing to form a separate jurisdiction with an infrastructure of congregations, ambitious AMEs advocated an enhanced institutional presence in the southern states with a greater capacity to give slaves spiritual nurture, and perhaps surreptitious support to attain their freedom.

Maintaining an AME presence in the border states, especially as the Civil War approached, put the denomination under siege. As sectional tensions intensified in the two months preceding the firing on Fort Sumter in 1861, the Board of Police Commissioners in Baltimore, Maryland, placed restrictions on the meeting of the Baltimore Annual Conference. They pointed to a law that said "no free Negro belonging to, or residing in any other State, district or territory shall come into this State." While the penalty for the first offense was $20, the second violation was $500, with half of that amount allocated to the Maryland Colonization Society. The statute, the Baltimore police asserted, applied to the AME Church whose members lived in states that stretched across the Middle Atlantic to Ohio, and with the exception of Maryland were "prohibited, under the law, from visiting the city." The police would not "interfere with those who reside in the city if they feel disposed to

<hr/>

[75] See Ira Berlin, *Slaves Without Masters: The Free Negro in the Antebellum South* (New York, Pantheon Books, 1974); *The Constitution or Incorporation* is an extract from the records of the state of Maryland, printed by Order of the Bethel Church, Present Elder, the Rev. Edward Waters (Baltimore, MD, Woods and Crane, Printers, 1842), 7; *Constitution of the African Methodist Episcopal Ebenezer Church of the City of Baltimore* (Baltimore, MD, printed by Sherwood & Co., 1849), 4.

hold their Conference, but nonresidents will not be permitted" to come, and would be prosecuted if they did.[76]

In response, a committee from the Baltimore Annual Conference, which included John M. Brown, formerly of New Orleans, published in the *Christian Recorder* an address to bishops and clergy of African Methodism. Though they acknowledged "these precarious times" realized in the recent outbreak of the Civil War, the Baltimore Annual Conference met and published the proceedings of their meeting in the *Baltimore Sun*. Despite the forced absence of Bishop Payne, who lived in Ohio and was barred from attending, Maryland AMEs kept their jurisdiction intact. "We cherish ere another year shall pass away," they said, "that God will so arrange it that our bishops and brethren will be permitted to assemble together and do the business of [the] Conference without fear or molestation."[77]

Exploring expansion possibilities within the British Empire where slavery no longer existed, in the border and southern states where bondage continued to exist, and calls to consolidate gains in California and Haiti showed a denomination conscious of its diverse Atlantic World constituencies. The same 1860 General Conference that considered a separate Louisiana Annual Conference also "heard ... the voice of California saying, 'Come over and help us.'" A similar appeal was raised on behalf of Haiti. If episcopal visits to the Pacific Coast and Haiti were impossible, then a fourth bishop would be elected for these areas. In response the bishops promised to visit California twice before 1864 and to sail to Haiti "if the means are provided." There was no need therefore to elect another bishop to fulfill these directives. Delegates, in pressing the bishops on these issues, harnessed the denomination's emancipationist ethos to institutional expansion. The purpose of building the infrastructure of African Methodism lay in liberating blacks in the southern states or sustaining their freedom in the friendlier environs of the British dominions.[78]

Hence, AMEs, a people of shifting transnational loyalties, constructed themselves as a Creole church for the Atlantic World. The peoples of African descent who populated their pews and forged communities of slave escapees, emigrants, and expatriates attached themselves to African Methodism during their multifront exodus to safe havens in the Americas and Africa. Whether they migrated to Canada, sought refuge in Liberia, proposed settlements in the Caribbean, penetrated the slave South, or trekked to the

---

[76] *Baltimore Sun*, March 18, 1861 (courtesy of Professor Richard J. M. Blackett, Vanderbilt University); *Christian Recorder*, March 23, 1861.
[77] *Christian Recorder*, May 18, 1861.   [78] *Twelfth General Conference* (1860), 23.

American West, AMEs harnessed their expansion to its "mobile laity" and the pioneer preachers who followed them. The denomination's emancipationist ethos, though anchored in the abolition of slavery, also drew from multiple efforts to define and defend black freedom in settings of racial hostility and hegemony. Opposition to slavery, advocacy for the citizenship rights of free blacks, and support for emigration benefited from the backing of an independent black religious body. Therefore, AMEs adopted a freedom rhetoric and praxis even as the pressures of institutional governance and restrictions on female religious roles hindered the attainment of their liberationist goals.

3

"Welcome to the Ransomed," 1861–1880

"THE BATTLE CRY OF FREEDOM"

The antebellum period provided African Methodist Episcopalians (AMEs) with opportunities to tie their institutional development to the church's emancipationist ethos. Whenever these migrant Methodists settled in hostile areas in the Northeast and Midwest or identified with blacks in various slave settings, AME churches became known as outposts of black freedom and secret stations on the Underground Railroad. Institutional development was itself an assertion of black insurgency against established racial regimes that opposed African American equality. This pattern continued through the Civil War and Reconstruction era. Interpreting the war as an act of God's judgment against slave owners and black deliverance from bondage presented AMEs as constituting a freedom church. Its mission to evangelize, educate, and protect the political rights of the freed people also linked church expansion to the fulfillment of these emancipationist objectives. These goals were intrinsically aligned and showed African Methodism, despite displays of cultural and class elitism, as the people's church.

AME adherents envisaged their religious body as expanding its emancipationist energies for diverse African and Creole peoples in the Atlantic World. Despite powerful hegemonic structures sustaining the slave trade and slavery, ministers and members tried to circumvent them through escape and emigration to black enclaves on the American frontier or to Canada, the Caribbean, and Africa. AME churches, both directly and through derivative religious bodies, functioned as advocates and protectors for these fugitive and emigrant peoples. Moreover, they believed that their effort, though divinely assisted, also drew upon British state power, which favored freedom for blacks in North America. The outbreak of the American Civil War, like Armageddon, however, would determine whether anti-slavery or proslavery armies would triumph in the United States and free over 4 million African Americans. AMEs were sure that freedom forces, as instruments of divine deliverance, would manumit the slaves and entrust them to the denomination to evangelize and instruct them on how free people should live and develop. This task required a broader emphasis on expansion into the American South while maintaining ambitious plans for growth within the black Atlantic.

AMEs were certain that much of their future lay among southern blacks whose emancipation steadily unfolded during the course of the war. Though President Abraham Lincoln initially emphasized the preservation of the Union as his priority, African Americans, at the start of the hostilities, defined black emancipation as the nation's overriding objective. Hence, AMEs, in maintaining their emancipationist ethos, stood for immediate freedom whether blacks were escaping behind Union lines, settling in contraband camps, receiving manumission in the District of Columbia, benefiting from the Emancipation Proclamation, or taking their freedom through widespread wanderings away from the sites of their enslavement. As African Americans were freeing themselves, AME advocacy affirmed this reality that ex-slaves were creating for themselves and interpreted it as a prophetic fulfillment of a black jubilee. The *Christian Recorder*, the official AME newspaper, declared that "it is erroneous and short-sighted to say that this war is a useless expenditure of blood and treasure, and the victory of our forces a barren one, if slavery is not finally abolished." Elisha Weaver, the editor during the war, established the *Recorder* as the newspaper of record for African American issues. A few months before the firing on Fort Sumter, one reader told Weaver that "there has not been issued a paper under the auspices of our downtrodden people] to compare with it, either as regards its moral [instruction] or spirituality." Soon after the war, still under Weaver's editorship, the newspaper's record was validated as "devoted to the interests of the colored people."[1]

During the unfolding of black freedom from the outbreak of the war until its climax in various Juneteenth occurrences, AMEs implemented numerous

[1] Edward Ayers, *In the Presence of Mine Enemies: War in the Heart of America, 1859–1863* (New York, W. W. Norton and Company, 2003), 168–171; Armstead L. Robinson, *Bitter Fruits of Bondage; The Demise of Slavery and the Collapse of the Confederacy, 1861–1865* (Charlottesville, University of Virginia Press, 2005), 138–145; *Christian Recorder*, January 26, 1861, August 24, 1861, December 23, 1865.

geographical initiatives to offer what the historian Reginald F. Hildebrand described as its "gospel of freedom" to emancipated African Americans. Hildebrand observed that "emancipation made one a wholly new person" and "restore[d] the victims of slavery to full personhood and carr[ied] them to their rightful, equal place in the affairs of the nation." With the destruction of slavery, Hildebrand said, emancipation "destroyed an old world and brought a new experience," which the AME Church was peculiarly equipped to develop. It "was an independent black denomination established on the grand basis of Christian manhood and independence.'" African Methodism, during the Civil War and continuing through Reconstruction, would "undo the damage done by slavery and combat ongoing racial oppression."[2]

AMEs accelerated their advocacy of black emancipation after the Confederacy bombarded Fort Sumter in April 1861. President Lincoln's decision to raise troops to put down the southern rebellion and preserve the Union brought the issue of slavery front and center for African Americans and validated their support of the sixteenth president. A visiting AME minister told the congregation in New Bedford, Massachusetts, that "the hand of Providence was in the election of Mr. Lincoln to the Presidency" and that on Inauguration Day "the slaves were much engaged in prayer to God for him." Henry Dickerson, a local AME preacher in Woodbury, New Jersey, provided tangible support to the Union cause in 1862 when he leased his land for the training of the 12th Regiment of the New Jersey Volunteer Infantry. Later, during the war, David Smith, who served a church in the Washington DC area, recalled that "the Government took it for the use of the soldiers, but paid us well for its use." At the same time, blacks, not long after Lincoln authorized the defense of Fort Sumter, volunteered for the federal army in hopes of doing their part to destroy the "peculiar institution." Lincoln rejected them for military service, however, at least until later in the war. Slaves also took matters into their own hands and found refuge among advancing northern troops. Though Lincoln had promised a "hands off" policy on slavery, neither he nor others figured that the slaves themselves would aggressively undermine this directive. By July 1861, 850 slaves in the Hampton Roads region, for example, flocked to the nearest federal installation at Fortress Monroe, Virginia. Their actions compelled the commander, General Benjamin Butler, to classify them as "contraband of war" and beyond the reach of their slave owners. In these and other similar

[2] Reginald F. Hildebrand, "Richard Harvey Cain, African Methodism, & the Gospel of Freedom in South Carolina," *AME Church Review*, Vol. 117, No. 381, January–March 2001, 42–43.

acts of self-emancipation, blacks, at the start of hostilities, declared their liberation as the main objective of the Civil War.[3]

The *Christian Recorder*, which "deeply sympathizes with the oppressed of this land," reflected these perspectives and endorsed these on the ground realities. In May 1861 in an editorial entitled "The Hand of God," the *Recorder* saw "the Providence of God" in facilitating the start of the Civil War. "The course of events for the past eight months," declared the AME newspaper, "indicates most clearly the purpose of God to abettors of slavery." They "have resisted argument and appeal [and] by violence, bravado, [and] blasphemy have filled the measure of their iniquity." Hence, "the spirit of slavery culminated in the fact of treason and rebellion." The *Recorder* revealed the true character of the Confederacy in citing its declaration that "its cornerstone rests upon the great truth that the Negro is not equal to the white man; that slavery is his natural and normal condition." As far as the Confederacy was concerned, the war was being fought for "maintaining and perpetuating slavery." The Philadelphia Annual Conference concluded that "the present struggle, now raging in our beloved country [was] an evident manifestation that God will hear the cries and prayers of the oppressed, and 'will come down to deliver them.'" Moreover, the war signified a divine mandate for "the uprooting and destroying of slavery throughout the length and breadth of our land." Therefore, AMEs unequivocally concluded that the Civil War was all about slavery, and that it was God's will that blacks should be freed.[4]

Historian Eric Foner described Lincoln as "strongly antislavery, but he was not an abolitionist or a Radical Republican." Moreover, his evolution as an emancipator drew from perspectives that principled and persistent opponents of slavery articulated. Hence, the sixteenth president, Foner says, "came to occupy positions first staked out by" William Lloyd Garrison, Frederick Douglass, Sojourner Truth, Charles Sumner, and others who for decades called for the immediate end of slavery. AMEs understood Lincoln's emancipationist sensibilities even though he zigzagged on when to apply the full weight of office on behalf of black freedom. They surely tolerated the

---

[3] *Christian Recorder*, July 20, 1861; Benjamin Quarles, *Lincoln and the Negro* (New York, Oxford University Press, 1962), 66–69; City of Woodbury, *Community Bulletin* (June 6, 2016); David Smith, *Biography of Rev. David Smith of the AME Church* (Xenia, OH, Xenia Gazette Office, 1881), 92; Eric Foner, *The Fiery Trial: Abraham Lincoln and American Slavery* (New York, W. W. Norton and Company, 2010), 171.

[4] *Christian Recorder*, May 25, 1861; February 14, 1863; *Minutes of the Forty-Eighth Session of the Philadelphia District Annual Conference of the African Methodist Episcopal Church* (Philadelphia, PA. James S. Rodgers, 1864), 18.

President's view that the manumission of the slaves would proceed in incremental stages, but AMEs never stopped urging him to move faster on black freedom.[5]

Lincoln initially vacillated on slave manumission. In 1861 he reversed an emancipation order from General John C. Fremont, the Union commander in Missouri. Keeping the border states in the Union trumped black freedom and justified his firing of Fremont when the general refused to return slaves to their masters. The *Recorder* accused federal authorities of having "too much tenderness for rebels" in nullifying the Fremont proclamation. Lincoln's action, AMEs believed, was a "backward step." It was lamentable because the president would "dishearten the nation, [which was] freely offering its men and means to help the government in crushing [the] rebellion." Then, in the 1862 Second Confiscation Act, legislation that Lincoln opposed for technical reasons, while affirming the principle of freeing the slaves of Confederate loyalists, exempted fugitives in the border states.[6]

These considerations, however, did not thwart the President's efforts to end slavery in the District of Columbia. Years earlier, while a member of Congress, Lincoln said that slavery in the nation's capital should be abolished. Another congressman introduced such a bill in 1861, but Lincoln remained largely aloof from the debate, though he wanted to push the gradual emancipation of blacks with payment to slave owners and a "vote of the [white] people." Moreover, he thought it would be better if the District of Columbia or a border state had initiated black emancipation in these loyalist territories. Lincoln overcame these reservations and signed the bill. Hence, the District's 3,200 slaves were manumitted, their owners were compensated, and funds were appropriated to encourage black colonization either to Haiti or Liberia. Daniel A. Payne had been to the White House to urge Lincoln to sign the bill, saying that blacks looked to him to bring black freedom to fruition, at least in the nation's capital. Despite the compensation and colonization provisos included within the law, Payne and other AMEs embraced it as a significant step toward the total destruction of slavery.[7]

The Ohio Annual Conference praised "the abolishment of Slavery in the District of Columbia" and noted "with infinite delight this act by which the Manacles have been struck from the limbs of thousands of our Brothers and

---

[5] Foner, *The Fiery Trial*, xviii–xix.
[6] Foner, *The Fiery Trial*, 176–177; *Christian Recorder*, September 21, 1861; September 28, 1861.
[7] Foner, *The Fiery Trial*, 198–200; *Christian Recorder*, May 10, 1862; Quarles, *Lincoln and the Negro*, 104; John Hope Franklin, *The Emancipation Proclamation* (Garden City, NY, Anchor Books, 1963), 18.

Sisters, and we believe under God, this is but the entering wedge, which shall sunder this greatest of all iniquities." The *Recorder* added that "the slave master, slave-breeder, and slave-dealer are henceforth outlaws in the city of Washington." Because of the new law, "a great reproach has been finally wiped away." Moreover, "it is a great moral victory worth more than a dozen bloody triumphs on the field." The AME congregation in Terre Haute, Indiana, held a special service to thank God for this Civil War measure. In a resolution they commended Congress and praised President Lincoln as "a man acting with discretion, and aiming to do what is just and right to all men." The members also stated that "having been born on American soil ... we feel an attachment to this country, and will be loyal to its Government; though we have been deprived of many rights and privileges." Another AME thanked God "that liberty should be proclaimed through all lands, and while men oppressed us, with freedom He [God] blessed us, and severed vile Slavery's bands." Now he hoped that "the wronged millions throughout these dominions [shall] soon seek and find shelter 'neath Liberty's tree! And this land and nation, now with civil war raging, May, in truth and in deed, be the land of the free."[8]

Lincoln's subtle but steady push toward total black freedom reached another plateau in the Emancipation Proclamation. The recruitment of black soldiers increasingly became a military necessity especially because of the low enlistment of whites in the summer of 1862. This issue was linked to an expiring Confiscation Act, which was permitting Union generals to receive volunteers from among the contraband. Additionally, the victory of Union Army in Maryland at Antietam convinced Lincoln to issue a Preliminary Emancipation Proclamation in September 1862. Only slaves in those areas under Confederate control were affected and would be "forever free." Supporters believed that once slavery in the rebellious regions was undermined, it could not survive in the border states and sundry other locales. This blueprint became permanent when the historic Emancipation Proclamation was issued on January 1, 1863. This presidential directive that manumitted 3 million slaves also attended to military enforcement, allowing black recruitment into the Union Army.[9]

Despite Lincoln's ongoing interest in black colonization, attention to border state sensibilities about slavery, and abolitionist demands for an

[8] *Minutes of the Thirty-Second Session of the Ohio Annual Conference of the African M.E. Church* held in Zanesville, OH, April 15–23, 1862 (n.p., 1862), 19; Christian Recorder, April 26, 1862; May 17, 1862; August 16, 1862.
[9] Foner, *The Fiery Trial*, 216–218, 229–232, 240.

unequivocal black freedom, African Americans interpreted the Emancipation Proclamation as his latest effort to destroy the "peculiar institution."
The *Christian Recorder*, in recognizing the importance of the document,
reprinted it, and admitted that not all slaves had been set free. At the same
time, the AME organ declared that "those who are not immediately liberated
will be ultimately benefited by this act and that Congress will do something
for those poor souls who still remain in degradation. But we thank God and
President Lincoln for what has been done." A New Jersey subscriber rejoiced
because he "lived to see the day when a President of the United States, in the
exercise of a right, clearly guaranteed by the Constitution, dare wipe out with
one sweep, the foulest curse that ever stained the record of any people." He
added that "in breaking the bonds of the slaves, and letting the oppressed go
free, we believe Mr. Lincoln has fulfilled one of the great purposes an all-wise
Providence had in view, in permitting this civil war to afflict the people of
the United States." The AME congregation in Buffalo, New York, in echoing
these sentiments, hosted a community celebration "where all, irrespective of
sect, met and united in praise to God for the great work he had wrought."
Similarly, Henry M. Turner, the pastor of Israel Bethel in Washington DC,
hosted a celebration, and the Proclamation was read until exhaustion compelled a second attendee to finish the recitation. AMEs seemed unanimous
in crediting God, not Lincoln, for the Emancipation Proclamation. Despite
their acknowledgment of the president as a divine instrument who issued
this directive of limited applicability, AMEs broadly viewed the proclamation as a mandate for universal emancipation for which they had been
waiting. Additionally, AMEs at the 1864 General Conference, while acknowledging their seeming equivocation about the membership of slaveholders at
their 1856 meeting, thanked God for their present deliverance from slavery,
"an evil that had enwreathed the souls of our race and done its desperate
work there, upon the thoughts, the affections, the aspirations, the religion of
that image which God made like himself." Slavery, a "sin of which the very
booming cannon upon Sumter proclaimed" as dead, stood condemned
"before the bar of an insulted and outraged Christian world." Slavery was
a "sin, that before this General Conference shall meet again, shall be known
only as a dark page of history [and] as an evil of which the nation has at last
rid itself by the bloody arbitration of the sword."[10]

---

[10] *Christian Recorder*, January 3, 1863; January 31, 1863; February 14, 1863; Franklin, *The
Emancipation Proclamation*, 102–103; *Thirteenth General Conference of the African M.E.
Church* held in Philadelphia, PA, May 2, 1864 (Philadelphia, PA, William S. Young, 1864), 33.

AMEs were now assured that the Civil War was being fought for black emancipation and not exclusively for saving the Union. Hence, the 1864 Ohio Annual Conference acknowledged that "the dissolution of the Union is not the question now, but the dissolution of the wielded bands of Slavery." Delegates declared "that there is no redemption for our distressed land until we shall wipe from the escutcheon the foul and ruinous blot of human Slavery." This progression toward black freedom culminated on January 31, 1865 with congressional passage of the Thirteenth Amendment that abolished slavery altogether. Turner praised the amendment because it "wipes out the blot and heals the hideous canker which, for many years had preyed upon our beloved land." He added that "it guarantees freedom and equality to the human race, irrespective of color." Blacks, at a community meeting at Fleet Street AME Church in Brooklyn, New York, said "our thanks are due to Congress for the benefits bestowed in acts securing liberty to millions of our oppressed race." They also urged "the ratification of the same by [the] eighteen States of the Union."[11]

Lincoln, in authorizing Massachusetts Governor John Andrew to recruit black troops into the 54th Massachusetts Volunteer Infantry, signaled that ex-slave soldiers would have a role in bringing an end to slavery. Although blacks were already serving in units in Louisiana and South Carolina, the Andrew initiative was the president's first formal invitation to African Americans to fight in the Union Army. The number of black volunteers, who filled 175 regiments in the United States Colored Troops, swelled to 180,000. Their presence on the battlefield made them an indispensable force in defeating the Confederacy even while Lincoln, for a time, permitted racial disparities in pay between black and white soldiers.[12]

AMEs actively assisted in the recruitment of black troops for the Union Army, praised their performance in crucial battles, and endorsed clergy who volunteered as chaplains. In Maryland, for example, the Reverend Alexander W. Wayman confirmed that Maryland enlistees included many who were AMEs. "Late in the autumn of 1863," he recalled, "several companies went out of Bethel Church in Baltimore. It was a sad sight to see so many leaving the old citadel of African Methodism, but as they were going to obey their country's call, we gave them up." He added that "there were three class leaders who gave up their classes and took leave of them." Two of them

---

[11] *Christian Recorder*, March 18, 1865; April 15, 1865; *Minutes of the Thirty-Fourth Session of the Ohio Annual Conference of the African M. E. Church* held in Pittsburgh, PA, April 16–27, 1864 (Philadelphia, PA, Samuel Loag, Book and Fancy Job Printer, 1864), 19.

[12] Foner, *The Fiery Trial*, 187–188; Robinson, *Bitter Fruits of Bondage*, 188.

survived the war, but one "never returned." Nonetheless, more black troops were needed. Hence, Jabaz P. Campbell, another AME pastor, joined white speakers at the all black Sharp Street Methodist Episcopal (ME) Church in Baltimore trying "to raise colored troops for the army." Campbell hoped that by joining the army blacks would "have an opportunity to develop the truth of his equal manhood." Campbell acknowledged that there had been "tardiness" among Maryland blacks in responding to calls to enlist in the army. At various mass meetings exhortations from such advocates as AME minister Richard H. Cain had their effect, and "many of our young men came forward and gave to the Government agents their names." Campbell reported that in Baltimore "three thousand able-bodied colored young men have enlisted in the service of their country." "To arms to arms colored men," Campbell declared. He added "that God who has already done so much for us in this war . . . would do more," now that blacks had joined the Union forces. Black soldiers in April 1864 "marched in from their camp" into Baltimore to hear Wayman preach at Bethel Church from 1 Samuel 17:20, "and he shouted for battle." Bishop Nazrey, who presided in both the AME and British Methodist Episcopal (BME) denominations until 1864, was surely proud of his Canadian communicants who also joined the Union Army. One observer, in showing the bond between blacks on both sides of the border, noted that "your troubles are our troubles, your people are our people, your God is our God, and where you are buried, there we want to be buried."[13]

The bravery and sacrifices of black troops were extolled on the pages of the *Christian Recorder*. "Our colored soldiers," it said, "prove themselves to be men. There has been a good many examples in our civil war of the cowardice of white soldiers on both the Union and Rebel side, but here let it be remembered that in every engagement in which colored men have taken a part, they have done nobly." After Confederate sympathizers in the North blamed black soldiers for an unsuccessful Union attack on an installation in Petersburg, Virginia, the *Recorder* defended them. "Never did the famed Imperial Guard of Napoleon advance to certain death with a manliest intrepidity than did our heroic soldiers, both black and white." These troops encountered "an increasing tide of death," the *Recorder* declared, "until all hope was gone."[14]

[13] *Christian Recorder*, March 12, 1864; April 2, 1864; April 29, 1865; Alexander W. Wayman, *My Recollections of African M. E. Ministers or Forty Years' Experience in the African Methodist Episcopal Church* (Philadelphia, PA, AME Book Concern, 1881), 92–93, 95; Richard R. Wright, Jr., *The Bishops of the African Methodist Episcopal Church* (Nashville, TN, AME Sunday School Union, 1963), 124; 358–359.
[14] *Christian Recorder*, March 28, 1863; August 6, 1864.

One AME minister reported on the 54th Massachusetts Regiment and its involvement in a battle at Fort Wagner, South Carolina. He observed that "scores of these colored heroes were brought into [a hospital] and [were] bathed in blood." He "visited them" and then "spoke words of cheer, and asked God to sustain them." These men, he said, "had counted the cost and fought and bled from the deepest conviction of duty." When Confederate soldiers slaughtered black troops at the infamous Fort Pillow massacre near Memphis, Tennessee, in 1864, the attack of an overwhelming force of 6,000 compelled the surrender of the Union fort. According to the *Recorder*, "there ensued a scene which utterly baffles description." There was "indiscriminate butchery" toward the "wounded and already dying." Whites and blacks "were bayoneted, shot, or sabered, and even dead bodies were horribly mutilated," including some black women and children. Confederate journals wrongly accused black soldiers of "cruelty" and did not acknowledge that they, unlike southern soldiers, never disgraced the uniform they wear [or] the cause they maintain by such an atrocity as that of Fort Pillow." Turner encouraged black soldiers in their adherence to higher moral standards. Moreover, he opposed "the killing of all rebel prisoners taken by our soldiers" despite support from "an immense number of both white and colored people." He conceded that Confederate soldiers "have set the example, particularly in killing the colored soldiers; but it is a cruel one and two cruel acts never make one humane act." He added that "such a course of warfare is an outrage upon civilization and nominal Christianity and inasmuch as it is presumed that we would carry out a brutal warfare, let us disappoint our malicious [rivals] by showing the world that higher sentiments not only prevail, but actually predominate." The 1865 Ohio Annual Conference "viewed with pride and great pleasure, the gallant, heroic and daring deeds of the colored troops who have been engaged on the various fields of battle."[15]

AME pride in African American soldiers and their pivotal role in fighting against slavery extended to the few blacks who became army officers. Because whites preferred that blacks should not command Caucasian servicemen, the appointment of African American chaplains, an unprecedented development, did not violate their racial sensibilities. Out of 133 chaplains, however, only fourteen blacks received these coveted commissions. Although a majority of the Union's 180,000 black soldiers never saw any of the African American

---

[15] *Christian Recorder*, August 22, 1863; April 23, 1864; July 9, 1864; *Minutes of the Thirty-Fifth Session of the Ohio Annual Conference of the African M. E. Church* held in Delaware, OH, April 15–24, 1865 (Pittsburgh, PA, Publishing Committee: Samuel Watts, G. H. Graham and E. D. Davis, 1865), 28.

chaplains, the minority who interacted with them benefited from their spiritual, educational, and pastoral services. Among the fourteen chaplains, just
four were AMEs. Despite this small number, they provided the *Christian
Recorder* with eyewitness accounts about blacks fighting on the war front,
introduced countless ex-slave soldiers to African Methodism, and laid foundations for AME expansion in the postbellum South.[16]

David Stevens, Garland H. White, William H. Hunter, and Henry
M. Turner entered the military ministry and served in various regiments
in the United States Colored Troops. Stevens, the oldest of the four, was born
in 1803, was a boy drummer in the war of 1812, settled in Harrisburg,
Pennsylvania, and was appointed a chaplain in July 1863 to the 36th U. S.
Colored Troops. Both White, born in 1829 in Hanover County, Virginia, and
Hunter, born in 1831 in Raleigh, North Carolina, had been slaves. Hunter, for
example, entered the chaplaincy in affiliation with the First Maryland
Colored Troops, "the first chaplain of color" in the state. In sharp contrast
to both White and Hunter, Turner was born free in 1834 in Abbeville, South
Carolina. These chaplains, like other African Americans, believed that the
war was God's judgment against slavery and that it required them to recruit
black soldiers to fight in this righteous cause. Without hesitation Turner
urged free and contraband blacks to enlist in the 1st US Colored Troops,
which he organized at his Washington DC parish. Because he preached to
the recruits in their training camps and invited them to worship at Israel
Bethel, he asked Secretary of War Edwin M. Stanton on August 1,
1863 whether black regiments would be given "colored chaplains." In
response, Stanton, after receiving recommendations from a biracial group
of military, political, and clerical leaders, extended a chaplain's commission
to Turner. Though the *Christian Recorder* regretted that the DC pastor
would be gone from his extensive connectional and congregational activities,
he was going "to the battlefield . . . to administer to the necessities and wants
of the four millions of our race." Now, Turner and other blacks in the Union
Army, said the *Recorder*, have the "privilege to talk, [the] privilege to work
and [the] privilege to take up the musket and fight for [our] liberty."[17]

[16] Edwin S. Redkey, "Black Chaplains in the Union Army," *Civil War History*, Vol. 33, No. 4,
December 1987, 331–332; 350.

[17] Ibid., 350; James K. Bryant, "*The 36th Infantry United States Colored Troops in the Civil War:
A History*" (Jefferson, NC, McFarland, 2012), 66–67; Edwin S. Redkey, "Henry McNeal
Turner: Black Chaplain in the Union Army," in John David Smith (ed.), *Black Soldiers in
Blue: African American Troops in the Civil War Era* (Chapel Hill, University of North
Carolina Press, 2002), 338; Wayman, *My Recollections of African M.E. Ministers*, 89; Henry
M. Turner to Edwin M. Stanton, August 1, 1863; Salmon P. Chase to Edwin M. Stanton,

Turner's chaplaincy was another milestone in an already successful clerical career. Because he was never in bondage, he was free to function in the ME Church, South as an exhorter among slaves in the southeastern and Gulf states. When in New Orleans, he learned about the AME Church and in 1858 traveled to St. Louis to connect with the Missouri Annual Conference. After a transfer to the Baltimore/Washington DC area, he served well-established congregations including a church located near Capitol Hill. The former slave, Garland White, however, had a less auspicious start in ministry. He was sold from Virginia to Robert Toombs, a Georgia slaveholder who practiced law in Washington DC and served as a member of Congress representing a district in his home state. Probably because White was a house slave, he learned to read and write. These skills enabled him to qualify for the ministry just before his escape to Canada. He served AME congregations in London, Ontario, and later in Toledo, Ohio. Like Turner, White leveraged his ministerial status to recruit black soldiers in Ohio, Massachusetts, Rhode Island, New York, and especially in Indiana. Most of those who enlisted in the 28th US Colored Troops joined because of White. Despite requests to Indiana's governor and white officers assigned to the 28th, White's application for a chaplaincy was delayed. Appeals to Secretary of State William Seward, who knew White as both a slave and free man in Canada, helped to navigate his application through the War Department bureaucracy. In the interim he volunteered as a recruiter among Virginia and Maryland slaves and as a guide in Georgia for General William T. Sherman. Once the 28th filled its enlistment quota, White was appointed its chaplain in late 1864.[18]

AME chaplains, like their other black colleagues, praised the black troops and testified to their bravery and military proficiency. Turner, for example, reported from James River, Virginia, that the 1st US Colored Troops battled against the Confederate Army in what some thought was a losing encounter. Black soldiers, who generally "did all the fighting," Turner observed, comported themselves with superlative skill. He commended "the coolness and cheerfulness of the men, the precision with which they shot, and the vast numbers of rebels they unmercifully slaughtered, won for them the highest regard of both the General and his staff, and every white soldier that as on

September 4, 1863; Owen Lovejoy to Edwin M. Stanton, September 4, 1863, in Ira Berlin (ed.), *Freedom: A Documentary History of Emancipation, 1861–1867, Series III, The Black Military Experience* (New York, Cambridge University Press, 1982), 358–359; Edward A. Miller, Jr., "Garland H. White: Black Army Chaplain," *Civil War History*, Vol. 43, No. 3, September 1997, 203; *Christian Recorder*, November 28, 1863.

[18] Miller, "Garland H. White," 203–208, 210.

the field." Hunter, who Turner esteemed as "a model chaplain," served with
the 4th US Colored Troops and was "superintendent of all contrabands in
this department." In a dispatch from Petersburg, Virginia, Hunter defended
his regiment from a slanderous report that questioned their performance.
Black soldiers, he said, were "equal to the severest ordeal." He added "the
gallant 4th suffered dreadfully on that memorable day. We were the first to
leave the cover of the woods thereby suffering more than any regiment in
our division." Moreover, "our loss is estimated at about 150 in that charge,
and still we pressed forward until the outer works of Petersburg were ours,
and the order was given to halt." Hunter asked that the names of the black
soldiers who were killed and wounded should be listed in the *Christian
Recorder*. White, who was serving unofficially in the chaplaincy in the 28th,
endorsed Hunter's observations. "Those colored troops," he noted, came
from both northern and slave states and ensured that "the day is ours, and
Petersburg is sure."[19]

Black chaplains did more for African American soldiers than teaching
them to read and write, performing marriages, conducting religious services,
and visiting them in hospitals. AME chaplains, as blacks progressively
gained their freedom, became their advocates and defenders. Stevens, before
his retirement in June 1865, recalled numerous encounters with freedmen in
Virginia, Maryland, and Texas, and said they were "eager and anxious to
work and learn." Stevens, who had served for a time as pastor at Wesley
Union AME Zion Church in Harrisburg, Pennsylvania, where he housed
fugitive slaves, believed "we should send them ministers to take charge of
their churches and schools." Turner agreed. Hence, he wrote an open letter
to the bishops of the AME and AME Zion denominations because they were
negotiating organic union and "pledged themselves not to wrangle" but to
unite in preaching the gospel to the freedmen. Therefore, they needed to
know that the ME Church planned the absorption of black congregations in
the ME Church, South instead of yielding them to the African Methodists.
"This usurpation of power and church monopoly" by white Methodists,
Turner observed, "should be most vigilantly watched by us." Since "colored
soldiers" were "fighting the battles of this country and many of them are
members of the churches over which you preside," they had a right to attend
southern churches associated with black Wesleyan denominations.[20]

[19] *Christian Recorder*, June 25, 1864; July 16, 1864; August 20, 1864.
[20] Redkey, "Black Chaplains," 340, 342–343, 345–346; *Christian Recorder*, October 24, 1863;
October 1, 1864; October 21, 1865; Todd Mealy, *Aliened American: A Biography of William
Howard Day: 1825 to 1865* (Frederick, MD, America Star Books, 2010), 364.

White, like Stevens and Turner, hoped that his religious efforts would be foundational to further denominational development. "I have organized a thorough church system in my regiment," he observed, "and large numbers are coming in every day." The only problem, said White to the *Christian Recorder*, was "that none of our Bishops pay us that attention which might be extended toward us." He complained that "we get no books, tracts, periodicals, nor anything at all from our colored religious associations." Because he was the only black chaplain speaking about the "soul's salvation" of "some four or five thousand colored men," AMEs were missing a major evangelistic opportunity. Turner was similarly anxious about black soldiers and their salvation. Because of his regimental church he could attest to "the religious integrity of several in the regiment," but he needed more time" for catechesis. He, too, like White, lacked books to aid in the religious instruction of black troops.[21]

This seeming negligence, which White attributed to the AME bishops, was actually their single-minded focus on territorial expansion, a goal that the chaplains also embraced. Though the bishops urged prayer for "the special relations which the colored troops maintain both to the Army and the Government," Union military successes allowed for new initiatives to be realized on southern soil. Long before the end of hostilities, the bishops in their Quadrennial Address to the 1864 General Conference noted that "changes produced by the war in the South have again opened our churches in that region, so that we now have access to the city of New Orleans; and during the past year, our ministers have gone there and renewed their work." They added that "the cities of Memphis, Vicksburg, Little Rock, Columbia, and Natchez, have also been visited by our ministers with prospect of great success." These opportunities permitted them to revive a proposal offered at the 1860 General Conference to establish the Louisiana Annual Conference, which "would greatly enhance our interests in that section of the country."[22]

Even before his episcopal colleagues addressed evangelism among the freedmen, Willis Nazrey announced at the 1862 New England Annual Conference his intention to "send a Missionary to some part of the South." The Committee on Missions, in response to Nazrey, recommended a North Carolina and Virginia Mission and suggested an appropriation to support an evangelist in that appointment. Behind this entire effort was George A. Rue,

---

[21] *Christian Recorder*, August 20, 1864; Turner to the Adjutant General of the Army, June 29, 1865 in Berlin (ed.), *Freedom*, 626–627.

[22] *Quadrennial Address of the Bishops of the African Methodist Episcopal Church to the General Conference of 1864* (n.p., 1864), 1–2.

a native North Carolinian and a New England pastor. He planned to be that missionary, though he did not go to New Bern, North Carolina, until after the 1864 General Conference.

Nazrey, a bishop in both the AME and BME bodies, remained committed to an Atlantic World vision that embraced black Methodists in Canada and in new jurisdictions in the American South. The Baltimore Annual Conference, which also started missions in Virginia and South Carolina, helped the construction of an edifice in Alexandria, Virginia. Perhaps they were proudest of St. John's Chapel, a black congregation in Norfolk, Virginia, whose "Official Board" in 1863 voted unanimously to annul the discipline of the ME Church, South, and affiliate with the Baltimore Annual Conference. Reverend Alexander W. Wayman, who would be elected a bishop in 1864, led these 800 members into the AME fold. Other black congregations followed the lead of the Norfolk church. At an AME convention in eastern Virginia in December 1864, for example, were representatives from several churches and circuits, including Emanuel in Portsmouth whose membership numbered 500. All affirmed their allegiance to African Methodism and voted to "support the principles" of the denomination. The Baltimore Annual Conference supplied clergy from 1864 until Bishop Wayman organized the Virginia Annual Conference in 1867. The nine appointments stretched mainly from Port Royal in Caroline County and Fredericksburg southwards through Richmond into the Tidewater region.[23]

Although AMEs never doubted that the Union Army would defeat the Confederacy, they viewed General Robert E. Lee's southern surrender as evidence of divine deliverance achieved through the military ingenuity of General Ulysses S. Grant. "Steady and ever onward has been the march of the Union Army since its command was [en]trusted to Lieutenant-General Grant," noted the *Recorder*. "Not a mere game of chance was that strategic movement by which Lee, that most impenitent traitor, was so beautifully checkmated" and brought about his surrender at Appomattox on April 9, 1865. If Lee deserved dishonor, then President Lincoln was entitled to sainthood as God's instrument to end slavery. When he died as a result of assassination on April 15, 1865, DC's Israel Bethel Church resolved to mourn the slain president for six months. AMEs in Stockton, California, said,

---

[23] Cited in Dennis C. Dickerson, *A Liberated Past: Explorations in A.M.E. Church History* (Nashville, TN, AME Sunday School Union, 2003), 92–93; *Quadrennial Address of the Bishops*, 5; Israel L. Butt, *History of African Methodism in Virginia or Four Decades in the Old Dominion* (Hampton, VA, Hampton Institute Press, 1908), 32–33, 36–37; *Christian Recorder*, October 24, 1863; January 14, 1865.

"scarcely had we ceased rejoicing over the recent victories achieved by our noble chieftains, and at the moment when the heavens betokened freedom, was it that we received the news of the death of our beloved friend." Benjamin T. Tanner, the pastor at Frederick, Maryland, and later a bishop, said, "President Lincoln was truly a great man." Despite antiblack pressures "to prevent him from doing justice to the oppressed and enslaved," Lincoln resisted "and spake the word which has snapped asunder the fetters of millions of slaves and has armed 200,000 freedmen." Lewis Woodson coauthored a resolution at the 1865 Ohio Annual Conference that linked Lincoln's assassin to slavery's "dark and malignant spirit" that could "harden, deprave, and demoralize its votaries and render them capable of any act however desperate." Nonetheless, Jabaz P. Campbell, now a bishop, in this atmosphere of both triumph and tragedy, advised blacks to "rejoice in the advantages they had gained" and to "seek for more, until all the objections against their color were removed." He added that because "revolutions never go backwards," we "should elevate ourselves" and "act worthy of our new and growing privileges."[24]

The progression of black freedom through the DC Emancipation Act (1862), the Emancipation Proclamation (1863), decisive Union victories at Gettysburg and Vicksburg (1864), and the adoption of the Thirteenth Amendment (1865) required AMEs to discuss how the uplift of freed people would be accomplished. "From its beginning in 1863," argues one historian, "the AME Church's mission to the freedmen was deeply influenced by the ideology of the pre-Civil War moral reform movement." Because "human nature was perfectible," he said, and "if the social order ... were rearranged," ex-slaves could realize full freedom and citizenship. Therefore, while waiting for the war to end, AMEs, even as hostilities continued, commenced their mission to the freedmen. Hence, Bishop Payne addressed contraband blacks in Washington DC right after slavery's abolition in the District of Columbia on the matter of personal morality. In his sermon, "Welcome to the Ransomed," he admonished those who now "enjoy the boon of holy Freedom" that they should avoid "vice, licentiousness and crime." He challenged them "to be more than religious" and "to be godly." It was not enough to be "free in body," but one had to "seek to be free in soul and spirit." Establish

---

[24] *Christian Recorder*, April 29, 1865; May 20, 1865; June 3, 1865; *Proceedings of the Forty-Seventh Session ... Baltimore Annual Conference ... April 1864*, 29; *Proceedings of the Forty-Eighth Session of the Baltimore Conference of the African Methodist Episcopal Church*, April 13th, 1865 (Baltimore, MD, James Young, 1865), 9, 44; *Minutes of the Thirty-Fifth Session of the Ohio Annual Conference ... 1865*, 25.

strong households, he said, where children would be educated and habits of thrift and reliability to employers would be valued. These attributes and those of "godliness" and "honesty" were crucial characteristics that the AME Church would try to instill within the freed people.[25]

Additionally, education and the franchise became core to a meaningful freedom. Therefore, as that denomination started its early expansion into the South, schools were "connected" to new congregations. White support for this project came through funds from the American Missionary Association and the National Freedmen's Aid Society. The bishops, who solicited and welcomed this extramural assistance, reported in 1864 that "thousands of children and youth, of old men and old women, who exhibited an earnestness and aptness to learn" flocked to these facilities. Similarly, in the District of Columbia, schools "are crowded with children and youth who hunger and pant after knowledge." Surprisingly, this initiative convinced the bishops to consider cooperation with the ME Church "in our efforts to save the Freedmen of the South from ignorance and sin." The franchise, AMEs believed, would also help in achieving full black freedom. The Israel Lyceum at Israel Bethel Church, for example, described the Civil War as an effort "in which slavery attempt[ed] to assert her sway over liberty." For this reason AMEs in this DC church appealed to Congress early in 1864 to affirm that blacks should have "the unconditional right" to vote. They deserved the franchise because "our fathers, brothers, and sons now breathing the red flame of war on the battlefield" were fighting to end slavery and preserve American democracy.[26]

RECONSTRUCTION AND THE "GOSPEL OF FREEDOM"

The Reconstruction era provided AMEs with unprecedented opportunities to expand the denomination and broaden its "gospel of freedom." Because they anticipated an ample harvest from among the South's over 4 million ex-slaves, clergy flocked into the former Confederacy to build on earlier territorial initiatives and to energize existing efforts in evangelism, education, and citizenship training. Hence, in the 1860s through the 1870s, the southern wing of the AME Church grew into its largest branch, and its growing

[25] Clarence E. Walker, *A Rock in a Weary Land: The African Methodist Episcopal Church during the Civil War and Reconstruction* (Baton Rouge, Louisiana State University Press, 1982), 46; Daniel A. Payne, "Welcome to the Ransomed," in Milton C. Sernett (ed.), *African American Religious History: A Documentary Witness*, second edition (Durham, NC, Duke University Press, 1999), 233–236; 240.
[26] *Quadrennial Address of the Bishops*, 4–5; 7; *Christian Recorder*, January 23, 1864.

infrastructure of churches, schools, and civic associations established it as a major institutional presence in the southern states. Additionally, the "gospel of freedom," which AMEs promulgated, aimed to redeem blacks from slavery and its various social and psychological degradations. This ethos, which Reginald F. Hildebrand conceptualized, meant "that in the new era blacks had to become self-reliant, achieve upward mobility, and occupy positions of authority." AMEs and their Zion counterparts presented to prospective members an institutional heritage of "racial pride and independence" that freed people could embrace and emulate.[27]

Though such clergy as the chaplains Henry M. Turner, now stationed in Georgia, and William H. Hunter in North Carolina and George A. Rue, also in the old North State, had been busy with denominational expansion in these areas, the formal launch of the AME mission to the South formally started when Bishop Payne, in the company of a few other ministers, sailed from New York City and landed in Charleston in May 1865. Payne convened the first South Carolina Annual Conference at the city's "colored" Presbyterian Church. Out of this jurisdiction emerged districts for the Carolinas, Georgia, and Florida. Payne's successful meeting owed much to the recent evangelism of James Lynch from Baltimore and James D. S. Hall from New York at Port Royal, Beaufort, and Charleston. Though most of the 4,000 members who comprised the new AME jurisdiction came out of the ME Church, South, many of them had been drawn to African Methodism by Lynch and Hall. A New Jersey native, Theophilus G. Steward, also accompanied Payne to Charleston. After his arrival at Beaufort, he preached on June 18, 1865 a sermon titled "I Seek My Brethren." Drawn from Genesis 37:10, Steward explained why he, Payne, Lynch, Hall, and others were offering African Methodism to the freed people.[28]

Despite Steward's belief in the welfare of all humanity, he asserted that AMEs came to the South "to seek those who are our brethren by virtue of race." He said that these ties mattered "not because we care anything for races or nations," but because the freed people "have been and are yet in a great measure our brethren in affliction and that very affliction has served to

[27] Reginald F. Hildebrand, *The Times Were Strange and Stirring: Methodist Preachers and the Crisis of Emancipation* (Durham, NC, Duke University Press, 1995), 53, 55.
[28] Wesley J. Gaines, *African Methodism in the South or Twenty-Five Years of Freedom* (Atlanta, GA, Franklin Publishing House, 1890), 6; Benjamin W. Arnett (ed.), *Proceedings of the Quarto-Centennial Conference of the African ME Church of South Carolina, at Charleston, SC, May 15, 16 and 17, 1889* (privately printed by Bishop Benjamin W, Arnett, 1890), 40–41; Theophilus G. Steward, *Fifty Years in the Gospel Ministry* (Philadelphia, PA, AME Book Concern, 1921?), 43–50.

bind us together by the two-fold cord [of] sympathy for the oppressed and love of man." Steward also sought for those who were already Christians and Methodist members. To connect with these disparate brethren, AME evangelists were willing to search in "the cotton fields which they cultivated [and] the rice swamps [which] they watered and watched." They would also look into "the little huts wherein they dwelt," and other sites where "the bloodhounds that chased them, the swamps in which they, terrified and exhausted, took refuge." This search, said Steward, would also take them to the "great church edifices" that were "often built almost entirely by the African or colored children" who contributed their meager resources to sustain both black and biracial churches. Though he aimed "to organize them into churches and societies in accordance with the Methodist Discipline, and under the banner of the African Methodist Episcopal Church of the United States," Steward's mission was ultimately evangelistic. "Yet earnestly do I seek you to tell of Jesus," he said, "who was born in Bethlehem of Judea, lived a life of misery and discomfort, taken by wicked hands, crucified on Calvary's top to purchase for all men, redemption from the consequences of sin." The AME Church, he believed, by presenting Jesus as a fellow sufferer and victim of an evil hegemony, was the vehicle to save the freed people from sin and to unite them with a proud denomination capable of sustaining them in full spiritual and temporal freedom.[29]

Rapid expansion resulted from Payne's South Carolina initiative. Four contiguous states became flourishing venues of AME growth within a decade. Particular people established beachheads out of which AME expansion emerged. Rue was already at New Bern, but was joined by George W. Brodie at Raleigh and S. B. Williams at Wilmington, the state superintendents of the work in North Carolina. In South Carolina, where Richard H. Cain was superintendent and pastor of the populous Emanuel Church in Charleston, growth emanated from this port city to the Sea Islands, up the coast to Georgetown, and northwestward into the midlands at Columbia where Bethel Church started in 1866. Ex-slaves in Newberry, for example, brought African Methodism into the Upcountry. Formerly members of the ME Church, South, they notified the pastor at Columbia of their need for a preacher. Simon Miller was sent, organized them as an AME congregation in 1866, and assigned various local preachers to adjacent communities to start other churches. Similar patterns prevailed in Georgia and Florida with A. L. Stanford in Savannah, Henry M. Turner in Macon,

---

[29] Steward, *Fifty Years in the Gospel Ministry*, 43–46, 49–59.

and C. H. Pearce in Tallahassee as state superintendents at these emerging AME bastions.[30]

By the end of the decade Georgia became a separate annual conference, with churches spreading out from Savannah and Macon to Augusta, Columbus, Cuthbert, Albany, and Lumpkin. Two congregations in Atlanta affiliated in 1868 with the Georgia Annual Conference, including an antebellum parish in Marthasville, which incorporated in 1843 and grew into the influential Big Bethel Church. Similar growth occurred in Florida where Henry Call, while still in slavery and a member of the ME Church, South, learned about the AME Church in the aftermath of a Civil War battle. He had accompanied his Confederate slave master onto a Tennessee battlefield where a dead black soldier had an AME newspaper tucked in his uniform. After he returned to Florida, Call contacted William Steward, an AME minister in Jacksonville, to plant a congregation in Marianna in 1866. From there the church spread out from Tallahassee and from Quincy, and other neighboring cities.[31]

Subsequent expansion grew from beachheads in adjacent states between 1866 and 1868. These initiatives came from bishops, traveling missionaries, and local clergy and laity. African Methodism in Alabama, for example, had an abortive start in Mobile in around 1820 and succumbed to the opposition of slave owners. In 1867, Bishop Wayman, then serving in Georgia, sent nine preachers into the state to organize churches in six disparate locations. These congregations came together as the Alabama Annual Conference in Selma at Brown Chapel, the flagship church. When the Louisiana Annual Conference commenced in 1865, the jurisdiction included Louisiana, Mississippi, Arkansas, and Texas. Within these states, however, separate initiatives led to the founding of derivative divisions. The denomination entered Mississippi because of Henry "Pap(p)y" Adams, Sr. Born in Kentucky, Adams preached among slaves in Vicksburg and along with them affiliated with the ME Church, South. After he learned about the AME Church, he convinced his followers to join this black Wesleyan body. Hence, he contacted Page Tyler, a minister in the Missouri Annual Conference who had been appointed to the "Southern field," to start an AME congregation in Vicksburg. Bishop James A. Shorter in 1868 organized the Mississippi Annual Conference,

---

[30] Charles S. Smith, *History of the African Methodist Episcopal Church*, Vol. 2 (Nashville, TN, AME Sunday School Union, 1922), 517; 519; Arnett (ed.), *Proceedings of the Quarto-Centennial Conference*, 70–71.

[31] Gaines, *African Methodism in the South* , 15, 17; Charles S. Long, *History of the AME Church in Florida* (Philadelphia, PA, AME Book Concern, 1939), 55–57, 59.

beginning with ten appointments including two antebellum congregations in New Orleans. Similarly, the Tennessee Annual Conference, which started in 1867, drew from its organic beginnings in the Missouri Annual Conference. Page Tyler, reassigned to western Tennessee, organized St. Andrew Church in Memphis, and Jordan W. Early, the pastor at Asbury Chapel Church in Louisville, was reassigned to Nashville. This mission embraced ten counties in Middle Tennessee in 1868 and grew to several congregations in the Nashville area. One of the conference's founding congregations, Liberty Chapel, later renamed Bethel, started in 1866 with thirty members in the home of Ellen Calhoun. Moreover, a former slave, Liverpool Napoleon Merry, born in 1826 in Sumner County, Tennessee, had sued for his freedom in the 1840s. After meeting Bishop Daniel A. Payne in Nashville, he became a pastor successively at St. John in Nashville, in Clarksville, where he founded a school, and at Payne Chapel in Nashville. In 1867 Steven A. Patton, an Arkansas native, commenced preaching in Texas at Galveston, Austin, and in a small community near La Grange. Bishop Campbell, the prelate in the Louisiana Annual Conference, then appointed Houston Reedy to Galveston as a general missionary. Next, in 1868 Bishop James A. Shorter, with fifteen pastoral appointments, convened the first Texas Annual Conference. A local preacher, Nathan Warren, in cooperation with the Elrods, a black couple, organized an AME society in Little Rock, Arkansas, in 1866. Their effort laid foundations for the Arkansas Annual Conference, which Bishop Campbell launched in Little Rock in 1868.[32]

Who comprised the corps of AME clergy who spearheaded and sustained denominational growth? Some seventy-seven missionaries between 1863 and 1870 were involved in church expansion. Despite this probable undercount, most came from the Deep South and the Border states and a minority came from the North. There was a blend of persons who were free before 1861 and possessed of some formal or informal education. An uncertain number had been slaves and were familiar with the same bondage that many of their potential parishioners had experienced. Others had been soldiers in the

---

[32] W. H. Mixon, *History of the African Methodist Episcopal Church in Alabama with Biographical Sketches* (Nashville, TN, AME Sunday School Union, 1902), 29–30; Smith, *The History of the African Methodist Episcopal Church*, Vol. 2, 72; R. A. Adams (ed.), *Cyclopedia of African Methodism in Mississippi* (n.p., 1902), 13, 133; Sarah J. W. Early, *The Life and Labors of Jordan Winston Early* (Nashville, TN, AME Sunday School Union, 1894), 57–64; Virginia E. Cooper, "A Condensed History of Greater Bethel AME Church (Nashville)," unpublished MS; Paul Clements, "Liverpool Napoleon Merry," *The Nashville Prospect*, March 2018, 11; H. T. Kealing, *History of African Methodism in Texas* (Waco, TX, C. F. Blanks,1885), 26–27, 35, 37, 40; Richard R. Wright, Jr. (ed.), *Centennial Encyclopedia of the African Methodist Episcopal Church* (Philadelphia, PA, AME Book Concern, 1916), 10.

Union Army and a few were forced laborers for the Confederacy. A significant segment of Virginia's first-generation clergy either came from slave backgrounds or lived as free men among slave blacks. The "Father of African Methodism" in Virginia, Peter Sheppard, was born in 1816 in Norfolk and was converted in 1837. He joined the AME Church in 1864 and became a member of the Virginia Annual Conference in 1867. Whether he was a slave or a free man is unknown, but he was a founder of St. John Church in Norfolk and was pastor to several other congregations in Hampton, Farmville, Berkley, and other locations. George D. Jimmerson, born in 1849 in Salem, Virginia, to a slave mother, became a sharecropper after the Civil War on the farm of his former slave owner. He also attained an education from a white tutor and from the Richmond Colored Institute. He joined the Virginia Annual Conference in 1871 and was a pastor and presiding elder in both Virginia and North Carolina. Another former slave was Charles Henry Hunter, born in Montgomery County, Virginia, in 1843. He joined the AME Church in 1864 and the Virginia Annual Conference in 1872. A long roster of churches in the state claimed his pastoral energies, including a congregation at Roanoke that he organized.[33]

In the Mississippi Annual Conference was John H. Allen, born a slave in Virginia in 1819. He was sold in Norfolk in 1839 and then to New Orleans and on to Natchez ,where he was a dining room servant and coachman. Though he connected with the ME Church, South in 1843, he shifted to the AME Church in Natchez in 1864 and later organized a congregation at Woodville, Mississippi. John Knox Brooks, born in Washington, Mississippi, in 1844, served in the Union Army and was licensed as an AME preacher in 1869. He led in the construction of five churches. In South Carolina, D. J. Lites, born in Lexington County in 1848, had been sold three times as a slave. He became a blacksmith after the Civil War, joined the AME Church in 1869, and served several congregations. Similarly, Paul Harrel Johnson had been born a slave in 1840 in Charleston. He was raised as a companion to his slave owner's children and was therefore taught to read and learn carpentry. Though hired out, he remained in school, was certified as a master workman, and became a foreman in a shipyard where gunboats were built for the Confederate navy. A slave owner took Johnson with him to the Battle of Chickamauga in northwest Georgia, where he was attached to the Confederates until 1864 probably as a laborer. After the war, he joined Morris Brown AME Church in Charleston in 1867 and the South Carolina Annual

---

[33] Walker, *A Rock in a Weary Land*, 50; Butt, *African Methodism in Virginia*, 34, 63, 68–70, 71.

Conference in 1874. He served as a pastor at Edisto and as a presiding elder. These experiences in slavery and freedom and as military laborers and soldiers defined the profile of most AME missionaries and ministers in the postbellum period.[34]

New expansion opportunities in the South broadened the reach of the AME Church beyond the North and Midwest. The stretch of states from Virginia to Texas, with few exceptions, included no AMEs prior to the Civil War. Between 1866 and 1876, however, the denomination's membership grew from 50,000 to 206,331. These gains drew principally from the successful evangelization of ex-slaves, many of whom had belonged to the ME Church, South and who occupied a subordinate status in that Wesleyan body. The greatest growth occurred in South Carolina, which had 52,971 members in 325 churches in 1876. Georgia followed with 34,013 members in 289 churches. Florida and Tennessee trailed these states, but each exceeded the 9,472 members in the 121 churches in the Philadelphia and Pittsburgh annual conferences. Despite a spillover of communicants and congregations into neighboring Delaware and West Virginia, which were constituent parts of each jurisdiction, Pennsylvania had the largest aggregation of AMEs anywhere outside the South. Therefore, these demographic developments in the former Confederacy portended a significant shift in regional power within the denomination. The growing number of southerners increasingly demanded representation in the episcopacy and in other high denominational positions.[35]

The AME "gospel of freedom" was realized through the evangelism of ex-slaves and expressed in initiatives in both politics and education. Though affirmed as free through the Thirteenth Amendment, the freed people did not experience the reality of citizenship until 1867. Lincoln's Plan of Reconstruction, despite black emancipation, envisaged the colonization of African Americans outside the United States, proposed lenient requirements for the former Confederate states to reenter the Union, and offered no initiative for black political empowerment. "Lincoln," according to the biographer Eric Foner, "did not envision Reconstruction as embodying a social and political revolution beyond the abolition of slavery." His successor, Andrew Johnson, however, was far more deferential to former Confederates. He restored full

---

[34] Adams (ed.), *Cyclopedia of African Methodism in Mississippi*, 19–20, 33; Arnett (ed.), *Proceedings of the Quarto-Centennial Conference*, 341–343.
[35] Walker, *A Rock in a Weary Land*, 50; *The Sixteenth Session and the Fifteenth Quadrennial Session of the General Conference of the African Methodist Episcopal Church. Place of Session, Atlanta, Georgia. From May 1st to 18th, 1876*, 68.

political rights to all but a few of them and did not support black enfranchisement, in contrast to Lincoln who had envisaged suffrage for qualified
African Americans. In fact, Johnson allowed southern states to enact regres-
sive Black Codes to control black labor and to enforce vagrancy statues to
remand ex-slaves to work for former slave owners as punishment for so-
called violations. One correspondent to the *Christian Recorder* declared in
December 1865 "I earnestly hope that this session of Congress will consign to
the 'Tomb of the Capulets' all that has been done in the way of Black Codes.
We want nothing of the kind. Whatever is the law for the white man, must
be the law for the colored man, and when that is effected, then, and not till
then, will justice be rendered to all men."[36]

George A. Rue, the AME pastor at New Bern, North Carolina, agreed that
Johnson's Presidential Reconstruction, its leniency toward former Confederates, and its tolerance toward the Black Codes were antagonistic to black
freedom. He described southern rebels, for example, as "devils" who wanted
to "vent their spite upon . . . defen[se]less blacks . . . colored soldiers." Should
such "traitors to our country hold the balance of power again?" "No!" was
Rue's unequivocal answer. Therefore, he and other North Carolina blacks
called for a state convention both to protect their freedom and their prospects for the franchise. "We must be heard and we will be heard," Rue
declared. Hence, at a mass meeting at New Bern's AME Zion church, Rue
and three others were elected as delegates to represent their locality. To show
black Methodist unity, invitations to attend the September 1865 meeting
were suggested for Bishop Payne and Bishop J. J. Clinton, the respective
prelates of AME and AME Zion congregations in North Carolina.[37]

Raleigh's AME congregation, familiarly known as the Lincoln Church in
honor of the slain president, hosted the convention. James W. Hood, Zion's
state missionary and future bishop, was elected as the convention president.
Delegates "hailed" black emancipation, endorsed the Freedmen's Bureau,
called for schools to educate the state's 75,000 black children, and appealed
for "colored teachers" to guide black youth. Rue, Hood, and other attendees
envisaged their meeting as raising issues for a forthcoming state constitutional convention to consider. When congressional Republicans took
charge of Reconstruction in 1866, Rue, who died on December 22, 1866,
was affirmed in his fight for black civil rights.[38]

---

[36] See Phillip W. Magness and Sebastian N. Page, *Colonization after Emancipation: Lincoln
and the Movement for Black Resettlement* (Columbia, University of Missouri Press, 2011);
Foner, *The Fiery Trial*, 272; *Christian Recorder*, December 23, 1865.
[37] Dickerson, *A Liberated Past*, 95.   [38] Ibid., 95–96.

The assertion of legislative control over Reconstruction commenced in early 1866 right after Johnson vetoed an extension of the Freedmen's Bureau that Congress overrode. Moreover, in response, Radical Republicans enacted a civil rights bill to nullify the effects of the Black Codes. Additionally, they pushed a Fourteenth Amendment to establish black citizenship, and made it a criterion on which the former Confederate states would be readmitted to the Union. In 1867, Congress passed a law that divided the South into five military districts and stationed federal troops within these jurisdictions to protect African Americans from vigilante whites and such racist groups as the Ku Klux Klan. The Fifteenth Amendment was also enacted to insure the black franchise. These multiple measures established the environment for the entry of blacks into southern politics.[39]

Eric Foner conservatively estimated that 1,465 African Americans held federal, state, and local offices in the former Confederacy and in the District of Columbia and Missouri between 1867 and 1877. Disparities existed, however, among these several states because Reconstruction lasted for varying lengths of time, and the size of the black male voting population also differed in these respective locations. Approximately 237 of these officeholders were clergy, including fifty-three who were AME ministers. This political vanguard stood on the frontlines for a "gospel of freedom." Hildebrand observed that "for African Methodists politics was an indispensable weapon in the struggle to preserve emancipation and secure the rights, privileges, and protection of citizenship" for former slaves. Hence, politics became intrinsic to the bivocational profile of AME clergy during Reconstruction.[40]

Black officeholders at multiple levels of government played crucial roles in the body politic, enacting laws to establish public schools, financing internal improvements, and strengthening legal guarantees to undergird black citizenship. AME clergy and laypersons, some of whom made singular contributions to local, state, and national affairs, joined other black colleagues and white allies to reconstruct southern society. A select few among black politicians served in Congress. Among the sixteen was a small subset of officeholders with AME affiliations. One was Hiram Revels, an AME minister in the 1840s and 1850s and affiliated with the ME Church in the 1860s who represented Mississippi in the US Senate from 1870 to 1871. Jefferson

---

[39] See Eric Foner, *Reconstruction, America's Unfinished Revolution, 1863–1877* (New York, Harper & Row, 1988), 228–280.

[40] Eric Foner, *Freedom's Lawmakers: A Directory of Black Officeholders during Reconstruction* (New York, Oxford University Press, 1993), xiii, xxi; Hildebrand, *The Times Were Strange and Stirring,* 67.

Long, a layman and former slave born in Georgia in 1830, briefly represented his state as a congressman in 1870 and 1871 and was a delegate to the Republican National Committee (GOP) national conventions in 1872, 1876, and 1880. He was a member and trustee of an AME congregation in Macon whose pastor, Theophilus G. Steward, served from 1871 through 1873 on the state's Republican central committee. Steward recalled that Long, a merchant tailor, lost his largely white clientele because of his political activities. Like Long, Thomas Crayton, an AME minister born into slavery in Georgia in the 1830s, encountered stiff opposition to his civic involvements. He was a member of the Georgia constitutional convention in 1867 and 1868, and a member of the state legislature in 1870. In 1868, after he attended a GOP nominating convention, more than a dozen armed white men threatened to kill him. For a time he abandoned his home in Stewart County because of this encounter. This confrontation happened in the same year that Henry M. Turner and thirty-two other blacks were expelled from the Georgia legislature by former white allies in the Republican Party and hostile white Democrats. Richard H. Cain, one of the most prominent black politicians, however, was less embattled than his Georgia counterparts. He had been an AME pastor with previous service in Iowa and New York before going to Emanuel Church in Charleston. Cain, born free in Virginia in 1825, was elected to the South Carolina state senate for the 1868–1870 term. Though unsuccessful as a candidate for lieutenant governor in 1872, he served in Congress from 1873 to 1875 and again from 1877 to 1879.[41]

Other AMEs served at the local, county, and state levels as legislators and administrators of political and social welfare institutions. They were a blend of blacks born free before the Civil War both in the North and South and others who were born as slaves. George W. Brodie, born free in Kentucky in 1830, was an AME missionary to North Carolina. Appointed in 1867 to a state agency that oversaw voter registration, Brodie was named by the legislature in 1868 as the director of an insane asylum and in 1869 as an administrator of charitable institutions in Raleigh. Hugh Foley, a minister born free in Mississippi in 1847, taught in a Freedmen's Bureau school, was appointed in 1869 to the Wilkinson County Board of Supervisors, and was elected to the Mississippi legislature in 1870 and 1874. Ferdinand Havis, an AME layman, was born into slavery in Arkansas in 1846 as a son of his slave owner. He became a barber after attending a Freedmen's Bureau school. In 1871, he was elected to the Pine Bluff Board of Aldermen and reelected to

---

[41] Foner, *Freedom's Lawmakers*, 35–36, 53, 136, 180, 204, 215; Steward, *Fifty Years in the Gospel Ministry*, 129.

another four terms. He was a member of the Arkansas legislature, but resigned to serve as Jefferson County assessor from 1873 to 1877.[42]

Politics became intimately associated with African Methodism and was integrated into the ministerial profile of AME clergy. Not all AMEs, however, believed that politics and the ministry belonged together. One delegate to the 1872 General Conference offered a resolution that declared it "detrimental to the interests of our Church for our ministers to engage in politics." Therefore, "no one shall be allowed to be so engaged whilst holding a charge in [the] Church." Since the motion was tabled and allowed to die showed that these sentiments represented a minority view. Hence, Charles Pearce, familiarly known as "Bishop" Pearce within Florida AME circles, emerged as an influential figure in matters of church and state and typical of AME preacher-politicians. Born free in Maryland and an AME preacher from 1845, Pearce belonged to that corps of clergy who came south with Payne and whom the bishop dispatched to Florida. After Congress mandated voting for ex-slaves in 1867, the Florida Annual Conference, in the same year, became a separate jurisdiction apart from the South Carolina Annual Conference. Pearce and his colleagues, Robert Meacham, William Stewart, and William Bradwell, according to historians Larry E. Rivers and Canter Brown, Jr., recognized that their AME district "represented the sole organizational structure in the African American community that could touch a majority of black voters." This, of course, was a boon for the GOP. Moreover, Pearce led AMEs to choose sides within the Republican Party by favoring the radical faction. "Here Pearce," noted Rivers and Brown, "saw a chance for real victory for African Americans and the AME Church." About a third or eighteen out of forty-six of the delegates to the state constitutional convention, for example, were black. Approximately ten out of the eighteen were AME, including four clergy and six laymen. Pearce, not surprisingly, was named as temporary president of this 1868 convention, which wrote the new state constitution.[43]

Though AME clergy could not avoid disagreements with some white Republican allies and with each other, appointment or election to public office resulted from their extensive political activities. For example, Florida Governor Harrison Reed, to sustain himself in office, depended on an uneasy

[42] Foner, *Freedom's Lawmakers*, 26, 76, 98–99.
[43] *The Fifteenth Quadrennial Session of the General Conference of the African Methodist Episcopal Church. Place of Session, Nashville, Tennessee, May 6, 1872,* 134; Larry Eugene Rivers and Canter Brown, Jr., *Laborers in the Vineyard of the Lord: The Beginnings of the AME Church in Florida,* 1865–1895 (Gainesville, University Press of Florida, 2001), 32–34, 45, 50–52.

coalition between blacks and white conservatives. Hence, he appointed Pearce in 1868 as the school superintendent in Leon County and assigned Thomas W. Long, Pearce's AME associate, to the same post in Madison County. So, when an opposing GOP faction tried to depose Reed, Pearce mobilized black support in several counties for the governor. Furthermore, in return, legislation that they championed mandated racial integration in Florida public schools.[44]

Competition between politicians, even those in the AME Church itself, showed the extent of politicization within the denomination. In 1870 both Pearce, the presiding elder on the Tallahassee District, and Robert Meacham, a pastor from Monticello, vied for a congressional seat organized on the Panhandle for a black representative. Since Meacham received support from a white US Senator, Pearce backed a black state senator, Josiah Walls, who won the election. In 1870 there were seventeen blacks in the Florida House of Representatives, of whom four were AME. Later, the group included Josiah H. Armstrong, who served from 1871 to 1872 and then again from 1875 to 1876. Born in Pennsylvania in 1842, Armstrong served in the Union Army and subsequently settled in Florida. He was elected a bishop in later decades. Additionally, the state senate included both Pearce and Meacham and some AME laymen in this legislative body.[45]

"EDUCATION FOR FREEDOM"

Complicated political operations were largely avoided in education. In this sphere of AME activity, there was a singular objective and measurable results. Toward these ends, the freed people, to become strong Christians, full citizens, and economically emancipated, needed to be literate. Moreover, if African Methodism wanted intelligent leadership, its clergy and laity also required the highest possible training. Therefore, in 1863 Bishop Payne, in anticipation of a broad educational mission for African Methodism, purchased Ohio's Wilberforce University "to aid in the special work of enlightening and Christianizing the Freedmen." He added that "amid the smoke and fire of the war, the AME Church was the first to project and commence the founding of a collegiate institution for the superior education of those who are to be the educators of the Freedmen." Within a decade of its existence, said a report to the 1872 General Conference, Wilberforce "has developed itself from a mere common school into a young but vigorous

---

[44] Ibid., 56–58.   [45] Ibid., 74–75; Foner, *Freedom's Lawmakers*, 9.

University" growing to 125 after starting with fewer than a dozen students nine years earlier. Two classes had been graduated, including one in theology and the other from the Classical Department. Though Payne envisaged Wilberforce as the denomination's national university, educational demands in expanding southern territories motivated AMEs in these locales to establish regional institutions.[46]

Among the earliest of the southern schools was Payne Institute, founded in 1870 at Cokesbury, South Carolina. The Columbia District offered to purchase the land on which to build the facility. This South Carolina initiative, like those in other southern states, reflected regional pride as much as legitimate efforts to train teachers, preachers, and a literate black population. Therefore, delegates to the 1872 General Conference learned of other AME schools throughout the Confederacy and in some border states. Kentucky had high schools in both Louisville and Frankfort, and Alabama institutions were starting in Mobile, Cahaba, and Greenville. Twelve acres were purchased in Live Oak, Florida, for an institution specializing in classical and theological curricula. Several parochial schools in Georgia, maintained mostly by congregations, began in various leading cities including Atlanta, Macon, and Savannah.[47]

Wilberforce University, acknowledged as the denomination's flagship institution, received an annual appropriation of $5,000 during the 1872–1876 quadrennium. In 1876, the school had 10 faculty, 600 students, and assets of over $62,000. Payne Institute in South Carolina had similar promise with 80 acres of land, a building worth $2,500, 2 faculty, and 85 students. Delegates to the 1876 General Conference "hoped" that Payne "may be made a right arm of African Methodism in that portion of our country, if it is properly fostered." That, of course, would be hard to do because of the proliferation of other schools in the region. There were two educational initiatives in Texas, one in Washington County and the other in Galveston. Congregations such as Big Bethel in Atlanta and St. Paul in Raleigh continued their parochial schools, while the Kentucky Annual Conference sustained a high school in Louisville, though "its success is not encouraging." Other annual conferences including Baltimore, Louisiana, Tennessee, Mississippi, and Arkansas did the same in both mid-size cities and more

[46] Payne, "African M. E. Church in Its Relations to the Freedmen," 3, 5; *The Fifteenth Quadrennial Session of the General Conference, 1872,* 42–43.

[47] Joseph W. Morris, "Rise and Progress of Education in South Carolina" in Benjamin W. Arnett, Editor, *Proceedings of the Quarto-Centennial Conference of the African M. E. Church of South Carolina, at Charleston, S. C., May 15, 16, and 17, 1889, 1890,* 77–79; *The Fifteenth Quadrennial Session of the General Conference,* 1872, 43.

promising urban locations. Brown University in Tallahassee, Florida, replaced the earlier effort at Live Oak. The enterprising preacher-politician Charles Pearce solicited support from wealthy whites, including one who donated 640 acres in Volusia County for the school. The Brown Theological Institute received a state charter in 1873, but fiscal mismanagement ended the second of two initiatives undertaken for Florida AMEs. Bishop Payne probably did not regret the demise of the Brown venture and those in other states, because he and some others believed that Wilberforce deserved the entirety of AME support.[48]

These varied ventures and their uncertain prospects convinced the 1876 General Conference to elect a Commissioner of Education. He would work closely with the Financial Board "to increase the facilities within the reach of the masses of our people." Such serious observers as Bishop Payne, still persuaded that Wilberforce should have most of the denomination's educational energies, assessed its progress as unexpectedly modest. "During the last decade," he said, "more institutions of learning have sprung into existence than in any preceding it." He cited several that seemed on the way to success. "Several other schools," however, "have been named, some of which are only paper schools, while others have no existence even on paper." He observed that "the projects began before they were ready." Hence, "thousands of dollars have been spent in such fruitless effort." What these untutored pioneers did not realize was that "the founding of a college requires a great deal of forethought and preparation," as he had exhibited in launching and maintaining Wilberforce." Access to "a deep, long, and wide purse" was indispensable, especially in behalf "of a poverty-stricken and illiterate people."[49]

Reports to the 1880 General Conference seemed to sustain Payne's assessment. Wilberforce remained as the "first and chief educational center" of the denomination. Its strengthened faculty and facilities convinced the AME Educational Bureau to recommend reauthorization of the school's quadrennial appropriation of $20,000. Payne Institute maintained its standing as the southern counterpart to Wilberforce. Ten thousand dollars was recommended to purchase a new property in Spartanburg, South Carolina, and permission was given to sell the Cokesbury site to reestablish the school "in

---

[48] *The Sixteenth Session and the Fifteenth Quadrennial Session of the General Conference of the African Methodist Episcopal Church. Place of Session, Atlanta, Georgia, May 1–18, 1876,* 54–55, 91, 115–117; Long, *History of the AME Church in Florida* , 180–181.
[49] *The Sixteenth Session . . . of the General Conference, 1876,* 117; Payne, *Recollections* (1888), 231–232.

the new paradise." The Bureau declared, however, "that [as] soon as practicable, we will open schools in each episcopal district, especially in our Southern work, recognizing as we do the imperative necessity of training our people." For Payne, herein lay the problem of attempting the support of too many schools.[50]

This debate played out in the Arkansas Annual Conference where support for Wilberforce University was strong. A report at the 1879 session, for example, declared that "we today as a church have not a first-class school outside of Wilberforce University." When a motion was proposed to deposit an offering into "a nest-egg [for] an Educational Fund in the Arkansas Conference, and nowhere else," a substitute motion to send it to Wilberforce was advanced instead. Bishop John M. Brown, who favored the original proposal, said that "it is time to take steps looking to the founding of a State Annual Conference School in Arkansas." John T. Jenifer, the author of the alternate motion, strongly disagreed, saying "that the chief trouble with the colored race is that on the one hand they fail to do anything, and on the other they try to do too much." In reference to Wilberforce and a proposed Arkansas school, he said that the Ohio institution "is now a certainty, and is annually sending to Arkansas, as well as through the South, preachers and teachers; [but] she is now in need of means to assist her to do this work." To resolve this dilemma, Jenifer, who supported "State schools" and had worked "eight years ... to build up education in Arkansas," concluded that "the interest of Arkansas is as sacredly guarded at Wilberforce as in Arkansas itself." Despite this appeal, the resolution to withhold the donation from Wilberforce and to donate it instead to a state initiative was approved.[51]

Nonetheless, new and existing projects continued to attract the attention of denominational leaders on the connectional and conference levels. Though the school attached to Big Bethel in Atlanta continued in operation, another site was offered for sale "to our connection" in Newman, Georgia. In Texas, encouragement also was extended to a school in Waco in operation since 1877 and another one in Denison functioning since 1879. The Johnson School in Raleigh, which sat on property worth $1,800, thrived with 360 students, including fourteen who were studying theology. The 1880 General Conference requested annual conferences, rather than the denomination, to

[50] *Journal of the 17th Session and the 16th Quadrennial Session of the General Conference of the African Methodist Episcopal Church in the United States* held at St. Louis, Missouri, May 3–25, 1880 (1882) (Xenia, OH, Torchlight Printing Company, 1882), 162, 164, 166.
[51] *Minutes of the Eleventh Session of the Arkansas Annual Conference of the African Methodist Episcopal Church* held at Bethel Church, Little Rock, AK, March 10, 1879 (Atlanta, GA, Jas. P. Harrison & Co., Publishers, 1879), 4,12.

assume sole financial responsibilities for schools other than Wilberforce and Payne Institute.[52]

When the report of the educational bureau reached the 1880 General Conference delegates, they scaled back on the generous appropriations that the committee suggested. Wilberforce, the strongest institution, would receive $2,000 annually. Payne Institute and three other schools in Texas, North Carolina, and Florida were each granted $1,000 annually. There were not enough funds to support other less certain projects. Bishop Payne seemed right both in seeing education as an indispensable component of black freedom and admonishing AMEs to target their resources on fewer schools where results would be maximized. Benjamin F. Lee, the president of Wilberforce, declared where he thought national support belonged. "The AME Church," he said, "has several minor schools under the control of the Annual Conferences within whose territory they are located." Yet he added that "Wilberforce University is the intellectual arm of our Church, and the pride of our race."[53]

The mixed success of politics and education among ex-slaves led some of them to seek safer and more prosperous prospects in territories further north and west. The rise of the Redeemers abetted by the withdrawal of federal troops from the South after the 1876 presidential election, the increase of antiblack violence, and the emergence of the crop lien system showed that Reconstruction was coming to an end. Bishop Thomas M. D. Ward, while presiding in the 1876 Arkansas Annual Conference, acknowledged this sad reality. "We were told a few years ago," he said, "that the work was all done [and that] we might [as well] tear down our colored churches, close our schoolhouses, and abolish our distinct institutions because there should be perfect freedom and political and religious liberty" throughout the South. Ward concluded that the opposite was true. "The stern fact," he declared, "stares us in the face that the hatred to the black man is as deeply seated in the national heart today as in the dark ages of slavery." These "enemies," Ward warned, "are struggling to roll us back into the days of barbarism." Though the bishop believed "that the great American heart yet beats on the side of liberty" and that "hope" lay "in the strong arm of God," Reconstruction was over and blacks were less secure because of this development. These conditions, therefore, incentivized a migration of freed people out of Kentucky and Tennessee and the Gulf states to more hospitable locations west of the Mississippi River. Again, AME leaders trailed their

---

[52] *Journal of the 17th Session . . . General Conference*, 1880, 164–165, 167.
[53] Ibid., 74, 242–243.

Figure 3.1 Bishops of the AME Church, 1876 (Used with the permission of The Library Company of Philadelphia)

parishioners into virgin areas in Kansas, the Indian Territory, and wherever else opportunities seemed better than in the former Confederacy. All black towns, principally in the Great Plains, resulted from this emigration.[54]

Black town development drew from the initiatives of promoters of such settlements as Nicodemus, Kansas. They benefited from an 1844 law, which involved land speculators in the evolution of towns in the Trans-Appalachian West. Hence, the Nicodemus Town Company in 1877 laid foundations on 160 acres for this historic site. Six of the seven speculators were black and, according to one historian, "left their homes in the old South during the mid-1870s, searching for an open society where they could live and earn a living without fear of hostile whites." Moreover, "they were the precursors of the 'Exodusters'" who in 1879 and 1880 emigrated out of the South to Kansas and neighboring territories. Tired of racial repression,

---

[54] *Minutes of the Ninth Session of the Arkansas Annual Conference of the African Methodist Episcopal Church* held at Little Rock, Arkansas, November 9, 10, 11, 12, & 13, 1876 (Little Rock, AR, W. H. Windsor; 1876), 2.

persistent violations of their civil rights, and their inability to purchase land at reasonable rates, these immigrants lost faith in the promise of Reconstruction and settled in Nicodemus and other frontier locations. In Nicodemus they acquired homesteads, started a school, and established three churches including an AME parish. In 1879, the Kansas Annual Conference, itself only four years old, listed the Nicodemus Mission on its roster of appointments and attached it to a circuit with two other congregations.[55]

The Exoduster movement was another example of how AMEs tied themselves to initiatives aimed at enhancing black freedom. As a response to both the demise of Reconstruction and the white backlash against it, AMEs, in real time, discussed in the Kansas Annual Conference how the denomination should relate to this movement. At the 1879 session in Leavenworth, Bishop James A. Shorter convened a special forum to discuss "the great exodus movement." At first he reserved time for General Thomas Conway, an avid promoter of the "Kansas Fever," to address the AME meeting. Conway developed a charter-boat plan on the Ohio River to help marooned migrants. Although he failed to show up, the Reverend John Turner, a visitor from the Missouri Annual Conference, was ready to speak. Turner, who was "identified with the exodus movement in St. Louis" where many of the migrants were stranded, had gone to Washington DC to propose a plan to President Rutherford B. Hayes to help those in distress. He also worked with a local relief committee and made plans "for transporting the refugees in large numbers to Indiana, Iowa, and California." Turner declared that "this exodus is no impulse." Rather, the causes lay in "the dangers of the credit system [in] the South." He also commended the AME Church for its support of this grassroots initiative. The 1879 Pittsburgh Annual Conference also "took up the matter of the exodus." A resolution passed "favoring" the migration because of "the many ways which have been and are yet, in many instances, inflicted upon them by those who claim to have the controlling powers of the Southern States." Because "of the prejudice of a race which has and does yet refuse those political and material interests of our people as citizens," it seemed that "their course of emigrating is the best and what we believe to be the wisest" solution "to maintain their rights as American citizens." Additionally, the conference both "condemned" Frederick

---

[55] Kenneth M. Hamilton, *Black Towns and Profit: Promotion and Development in the Trans-Appalachian West, 1877–1915* (Urbana, University of Illinois Press,1991), 5–8, 17; Also see Nell I. Painter, *Exodusters: Black Migration to Kansas after Reconstruction* (New York, W. W. Norton, 1976), 3–68; *Proceedings of the Fourth Annual Session of the Kansas Conference of the African Methodist Episcopal Church* held at Leavenworth, KS, October 1–7, 1879 (Kansas City, MI, Press of Chas. Baker & Co., 1879), 27.

Douglass for his opposition to the exodus and concluded that they "do not look upon him as a safe and sound leader."[56]

Henry M. Turner, now an AME general officer, also told the Kansas Annual Conference that "he was in favor of the movement." He likened it to his long-standing advocacy of "emigration to Africa to build up a purely Negro nationality there." Not only was the exodus an "impulse of the people," but it drew "from the tenets of God." He lamented that blacks had been shackled with poor land, "robbed of what they earn[ed], and denied their rights." He reminded his listeners that the Illinois Annual Conference had passed resolutions "to maintain and aid" the exodus and "admonished the Kansas Annual Conference to [do the same and] look after the refugees." The AME missions officer, another visitor to the Leavenworth meeting, said that if the migrants "cannot enjoy their rights [in the South], they must leave." Since the United States was welcoming European immigrants, then "certainly the Negro" should "be permitted to move from one State to another." In response, the Kansas Conference noted that the exodus was "the best evidence of true manhood ever exhibited by the oppressed people of the South." Therefore, blacks should "never again rest contented in any locality where their rights are not respected." In relocating to Kansas and elsewhere, blacks should "become owners of land and producers as well as consumers as soon as possible." The achievement of these objectives obligated Kansas AMEs "to aid and assist our poor fleeing people whenever and wherever we can."[57]

Again, AMEs delivered their verdict on Reconstruction. "Regret it as we may," said two AME leaders, "we must confess that reconstruction of the Southern States upon a basis of freedom and equal rights is far from accomplished." They added that "the exodus of thousands of people from the land of their birth, and the restless desire of many more to leave, tells the story." That common experience was a narrative of "proscription-civil, social, [and] political – [this] is the story [that is] told, a story of privations and murders that ought to shock the National conscience from shore to shore." They concluded "that the exodus from the South of a portion of its oppressed people was only second in its beneficial influence upon the destiny of the race in America to emancipation itself." Moreover, in this trek out of

[56] *Proceedings of the . . . Kansas Conference, 1879*, 2, 5, 7; Painter, *Exodusters*, 225; 228–229; *Minutes (of the) Pittsburgh Conference of the AME Church* held at Erie, PA, September 11–17, 1879 (Pittsburgh, PA, Hagan & Co. Book and Job Printers, 1879), 14, 19.
[57] *Proceedings of the . . . Kansas Conference, 1879*, 7–8.

the South black migrants attracted material support and relief from AME churches through Illinois, Missouri, and Kansas.[58]

There were collateral benefits related to the exodus, especially for clergy. Some of them harnessed their vocational advancement to the migration. Oscar Hareins, for example, traveled to Kansas from Mississippi "with a company of immigrants." After his arrival in Kansas, Hareins, an ordained minister with a Baptist and a ME Church background, was accepted as an AME preacher. Perhaps his new denominational selection related to sectarian preferences among the Exodusters with whom he migrated and who might be potential parishioners.[59] Texas, however, seemed to occupy a peculiar position in the exodus movement. Though the state had been a part of the Confederacy and had been racially contested during Reconstruction, AMEs viewed it both as a destination for black migrants and as a place of escape. Clergy in both Texas and Kansas believed that the economic interests of migrants would be best served by settling in one or the other state. Moreover, congregations, some calculated, would be the unintended beneficiaries.

W. R. Carson, a delegate from the Northeast Texas Annual Conference to the General Conference of 1880, cosponsored a resolution that acknowledged a congressional investigation into "the cause and effect" of the "Kansas Fever." The motion, which was passed and tabled, proposed that a representative from each annual conference should "be appointed to report upon the exodus." In a later session, Carson, a Dallas resident and president of the Texas Farmers' Association, coauthored another resolution noting that "the colored people are moving from the South and desire to obtain homesteads." Instead of going to Kansas, migrants should go to northeast Texas, which "offers every inducement for emigrants to procure homesteads at easy rates." There was wide availability of "millions of acres of first class lands which can be obtained at prices ranging from 50 cents to $1.00 per acre, on ten years' time." Additionally, blacks would have a "guarantee of life and liberty" unavailable to them elsewhere in the South.[60]

An AME pastor in Parsons, Kansas, however, continued to stoke this interstate competition. "A great many come in Texas to settle in Kansas, he said, and of course [they were] spending almost [all] the means they had to come here." Though the expense of travel "leaves them very poor," the pastor observed, they acquired land, grew corn and cotton, and looked forward to a good crop. He believed "the prospect is as good" in Kansas as

[58] Ibid., 24.   [59] Ibid., 34.
[60] *Journal of the Seventeenth Session … General Conference, 1880,* 6, 23, 76.

any they could expect in Texas. "If this crop proves to be a good one," he observed, "Southern Kansas will be the place for emigrants from the South." Ultimately, the Parsons parish benefited because "our little church at this place," the pastor noted, "has begun to look up" because of new members from Texas.[61]

The "Kansas Fever," a consequence of a moribund Reconstruction, attracted AME endorsements and offers of relief. It showed how much the denomination attached its welfare and well-being to its mobile members emigrating out of the former Confederacy. Some believed, according to the *Christian Recorder*, that the election of James A. Garfield as the new Republican president "would put a stop to the exodus from the South, but it has not done so." Moreover, "as soon as the white rebels of the South learn a Negro's intention to emigrate they do everything in their power to annoy and harass them." AMEs were right to facilitate the exodus because many arrived in Kansas needing assistance, but eventually "they get off of the relief associations' hands." Moreover, "they never come back, and many of them own homes of their own within two years." The *Recorder* also noted that "the exodus of the Negro from the South is a movement of greater importance than is generally attached to it." Whites failed to understand that black labor had suffered "demoralization" because of the crop lien system and antiblack violence. "Southern whites," the *Recorder* said, "have got to give them protection or they will move North." Though "many now in Kansas would return to their old Southern homes if they were guaranteed protection to life, money, and their elective franchise," it seemed that blacks would greatly benefit by resettling in the "farming regions of the great North and the greater West."[62]

Some had already heeded this advice and took the denomination into virgin areas and advanced initiatives to expand black freedom. Ezekiel Gillespie, for example, was born in slavery in Tennessee in 1818, purchased his freedom, and migrated into the Old Northwest Territory prior to the Civil War. Though he lived briefly in Indiana, he relocated to Milwaukee, Wisconsin, in 1854. While working as a grocer, he involved himself with the Underground Railroad and defended an escaped slave who arrived in Racine, Wisconsin. In 1865, Gillespie and others signed and sent to the Wisconsin legislature a petition that requested black suffrage. Because Gillespie participated in 1849 in a failed attempt to win in a referendum, a local newspaper may have urged him to sue. This strategy worked, and in 1866 the

[61] *Christian Recorder*, August 19, 1880.   [62] *Christian Recorder*, December 16, 1880.

Figure 3.2 Ezekiel Gillespie won a lawsuit in the Wisconsin Supreme Court, 1865, for black enfranchisement and was a founder of St. Mark AME Church in Milwaukee (Used with the permission of the Wisconsin Historical Society)

state Supreme Court gave blacks the right to vote. This expansion of black political freedom extended to the social sphere as well. In 1866, Gillespie, a widower, married the widow Catherine L. Robinson, a staunch AME member from Lima, Ohio. Since no AME church existed in Wisconsin, Mrs. Gillespie persuaded her husband to spearhead the founding of a Milwaukee parish. In 1869, he wrote to Bishop Quinn, who quickly dispatched a minister to organize a congregation consisting of the Gillespies and six others.[63]

Like Gillespie, Biddy Mason was born in slavery in 1818, but in Mississippi. She was a chattel to three slave owners in three states. One of them fathered her three daughters and later converted to Mormonism. Therefore, they migrated westward to the Indian Territory and then to Utah. Brigham Young sent a group to southern California, which included Mason, to build a Mormon outpost. An effort to sell Mason into Texas drew intervention

[63] John Holzhueter, "Ezekiel Gillespie: Lost and Found," *Wisconsin Magazine of History*, Vol. 60, No. 3, Spring 1977, 179–184.

from a local sheriff, who stopped the transaction because California was a free state. Mason, a midwife and now a free woman, saved her earnings, and bought property in the fledgling Los Angeles. In 1872 she became a founder and benefactor of First AME Church, the city's earliest black congregation.[64] Gillespie and Mason typified AMEs, who while enlarging black freedom through their migration to the North and West, also established congregations as beachheads of black autonomy and racial solidarity. These ex-slaves embraced the same emancipationist ethos that influenced AME involvement in the Civil War and Reconstruction. Moreover, Gillespie's Wisconsin activities and Mason's experiences in the West reflected the same impulses that motivated the Exodusters who sought in Kansas a full and lasting freedom that they could not attain in the Reconstruction South.

"BRING US THE GOSPEL," TOO

The Atlantic World focus of African Methodism, though less emphasized during the Civil War and Reconstruction era, was not abandoned. While rapid growth throughout the South and the exodus westward claimed the lion's share of denominational attention, a vision for the full freedom of diverse African-descended peoples remained in AME consciousness. The same General Conferences that discussed and legislated on matters related to newly freed slaves also supported initiatives to push their religious body into territories outside the continental United States. At the 1872 General Conference meeting in Nashville, Tennessee, the first time ever in the former Confederacy, the missions secretary, James A. Handy, noted "in Africa, vast fields unoccupied already claim our attention. The cry of these millions is 'Bring us the Gospel!'" Moreover, "Cuba, Porto Rico, New Grenada, Central and South America all invite us to come." He added that "the age in which we live ... impels us to carry the glad tidings of salvation to every creature – even to Africans." Bishop Payne opposed such measures "on sending missionaries to Hayti and Africa." He said, "never would I consent to go or assist in sending anyone there until I could go all over the South to see my brethren." Evangelizing ex-slaves in the South and expanding outside the United States, according to Payne, was a zero-sum situation. The latter should not be pursued until the former had been accomplished. The thinking of the delegates, however, seemed in sync with Handy, because they

---

[64] Bobi Jackson, "(Bridget) Biddy Mason (1818–1891)," in Darlene Clark Hine, Elsa Barkley Brown, and Rosalyn Terborg-Penn (eds.), *Black Women in America: An Historical Encyclopedia*, Vol. 2 (Brooklyn, New York, Carlson Publishing,1993), 753–754.

agreed to another resolution in which the bishops would "have authority to organize mission Conferences in the West India Islands, and at any other point thought to be the most suitable by a majority of them." Going South and going to the Caribbean and Africa were integral to the Atlantic history of the denomination.[65]

Like missionaries from white American and European churches, some African Americans viewed overseas missions as an opportunity to Christianize and civilize people of African descent. Unlike their Caucasian counterparts, black missions advocates emphasized anticolonialism and supporting the full freedom of subject peoples. These concerns were foundational to their Atlantic World consciousness. Because Cuba became a venue for AME interest, the *Christian Recorder* focused on the War of Independence and the involvement of slaves seeking the overthrow of Spanish hegemony. Philadelphia blacks met at Bethel Church in 1873 "to sympathize with the patriots of Cuba in their struggle for independence, and longing to see the freedom of their five hundred thousand fellow men now held as slaves in that island." The *Recorder* recognized that the Cuban independence movement paralleled "our own disenthrallment and enfranchisement" during America's current Civil War/Reconstruction period. Hence, there was support for "the oppressed in every land and recognition of the suffering condition" of the Cuban slaves "of our race." Therefore the meeting "invoke[d] the spirit of our Christian Fathers" including Richard Allen and others who also gathered at Bethel decades earlier "to protest against 'American Slavery.'"[66]

Additionally, the wives of the bishops, in founding the Women's Parent Mite Missionary Society in 1874, declared their desire "for the evangelization of the world" and "for the universal spread of the gospel." Their "sympathies and prayers," however, were drawn towards Haiti because of the appeal coming from that feeble church, composed of our dear brethren on that historic island." Just as these women honored their founder, Richard Allen, they also acknowledged "the good and noble Toussaint L'Ouverture, and others whose blood flowed so freely for the emancipation of our race." They appreciated "the feeble band, residents of that island, lovers of Toussaint's ideas of liberty, and Allen's ideas of our holy religion, [which] ask us to aid them to[ward] a true understanding of the true Christ and his pure religion." Moreover, AMEs, in honoring Richard Allen and Toussaint L'Ouverture, in

[65] *The Fifteenth Quadrennial Session of the General Conference, 1872*, 81, 126; Payne, *Recollections*, 90.
[66] *Christian Recorder*, February 13, 1873.

the coming decades would add to the roster of heroes for black freedom in the Atlantic World the name of Antonio Maceo, a black leader in Cuba's ongoing struggle for independence.[67]

Handy observed that "we have but one foreign mission: the one in St. Domingo," the present-day Haiti. He added that "in that field faithful brothers are laboring, and although their success is apparently small ... when we consider properly the difficulties in the way, we feel that we have abundant cause to thank God that the little fire kindled forty-five years ago is still burning." Therefore, he "earnestly ask[ed] that something be done for St. Domingo." Problems in matching grandiose rhetoric with ample appropriations compelled delegates to entertain various methods to fund the mission. A motion was passed that attached the Santo Domingo Mission to the Philadelphia Conference, hoping that regular support could come from this source. Another resolution proposed to shift unclaimed funds for paying the expenses of absent delegates to the Haiti project.[68]

Delegates to the 1876 General Conference in Atlanta, the second consecutive meeting site in the South, heard less ambitious plans for overseas expansion than what was offered in 1872. Rather, attention was focused on support of the Haiti Mission and extending it to the rest of the island into the present-day Dominican Republic. First, delegates proposed that the Philadelphia Conference should be relieved of responsibility for Haiti, especially because the mission secretary had assumed the full obligation of funding the missionary society. Secretary George W. Brodie, despite bureaucratic resistance from some bishops and missionary society officers, tried to take charge of the Haiti Mission.[69]

Brodie endorsed the Reverend J. W. Randolph as the official AME missionary to Haiti. To meet his deadline for sailing to Port au Prince in November 1874, Brodie and Bishop John M. Brown mobilized monies from the missions office, the denominational treasury, and from the women's missionary society under the control of the bishops' wives. Brodie also traveled to various churches and conferences to solicit funds for Randolph's support. Some leaders, however, preferred someone other than Randolph. Moreover, the treasurer of the missionary society demurred on allocating monies until its president approved. A few bishops wanted the Reverend Charles W. Mossell to be appointed to the "Haytien Mission." Though Brodie drew contributions to support his mission from the American Bible

[67] *Christian Recorder*, May 14, 1874; April 8, 1897; July 15, 1897.
[68] *The Fifteenth Quadrennial Session of the General Conference, 1872*, 31, 92.
[69] *The Sixteenth Session ... of the General Conference, 1876*, 33.

Society and the American Missionary Association, he faced a stalemate between backers of Randolph and Mossell, the descendant of ex-slave and free blacks who had settled in Canada.[70]

Until this personnel issue was resolved, delegates at the 1876 General Conference recommended "that one of our bishops visit Haiti and Dominica within the next year." Though some had wanted Bishop Brown to go and establish a "Missionary Conference, "it was left to all of the bishops to decide which one of them would visit the island." Despite her role in the delay, Mary A. Campbell, a missionary society leader and wife of Bishop Jabaz P. Campbell, lamented that "some of the women of our church have become discouraged because no one has yet been sent to Haiti." That $600 had been raised showed that "we are ready to appropriate it as soon as a missionary is appointed." She added that "if a Missionary is sent to Haiti … much more will be raised by our society before the close of 1876." They were "anxious to do something in behalf of our brethren and sisters across the water." Despite these conflicts and delays, ministers and members were agreed that "the people of Hayti are calling for the AME Church to come and help them."[71]

Similarly, the 1876 delegates recommended "that an episcopal visit be also made to the Bahamas and Africa." To support the Bahama Islands initiative, these territories were added to the growing Florida Annual Conference. This momentum in AME expansion, especially, in the nearby Caribbean, sustained the church's robust Atlantic World vision and the view of itself as a diasporic denomination for black and Creole peoples. Still, the management of diverse peoples calling for "help" in Haiti, energizing embattled minister and members engaged in politics and education in the Reconstruction South, and supporting Exodusters heading for Kansas taxed the capacities of this ambitious religious body. These commitments, far from contracting the geographical reach of African Methodists, made them more determined to follow their constituents to wherever they went and to wherever they resided.[72]

Momentum for a capacious view of African Methodism continued through 1880. In that year, however, three bishops, Henry M. Turner, William F. Dickerson, and Richard H. Cain, were elected. Two of them, Turner of Georgia and Cain of South Carolina, emerged out of the recently organized southern wing of the denomination. Unlike Dickerson, a New York City pastor, Turner and Cain were veterans in southern secular politics who became spokesmen for newly enfranchised southern delegates who made

---

[70] Ibid., 97–102.   [71] Ibid., 37, 135, 155, 221.   [72] Ibid., 35, 120, 135.

their states power centers within the denomination. The short-lived Dickerson, a graduate of Lincoln University in Pennsylvania and the first bishop with an earned baccalaureate while presiding in southern jurisdictions and laying foundations for three colleges, faced opposition from constituents suspicious of his northern origins. William E. Johnson, a Cain ally in both church and secular politics, led a revolt of some South Carolina AMEs against Dickerson, accusing him of partiality in pastoral assignments for northern and Caribbean born preachers. Johnson, who dreamed of a separate AME Church in the South, established a splinter religious body named the Reformed Union Methodist Episcopal Church. Though the vast majority of South Carolina AMEs stayed loyal to Dickerson, Johnson embodied sectional sentiments, which remained a part of southern AME identity.[73]

These southern successes and the construction of a regional AME identity, while yielding an ample harvest of ex-slave members, broadened interracial and interethnic possibilities within AME evangelism. The experiences of James F. A. Sisson showed where a peculiarly southern black outreach facilitated a multiethnic ministry across a broad geographical terrain. Sisson, a white New Englander, joined the AME Church and played a frontline role in recruiting Virginia ex-slaves into the denomination. Subsequently, he served in Georgia and Arkansas and became a delegate to various General Conferences. At the 1876 General Conference, for example, he cosponsored a resolution to support the "Haytien Mission." He made his mark, however, in the Indian Territory, where he evangelized among diverse groups of Indians, some of whom were native Americans and others who had been black ex-slaves in the "Five Civilized Tribes." Many of those in both groups had migrated out of the South into the Indian Territory. At the 1879 Arkansas Annual Conference, Sisson declared that "the distances by horse are very great from among the Indian raised brethren to and from" the district meeting. Therefore, he offered a motion saying "that we can work more effectually through an organized effort in the Indian Territory" if an annual conference could be started near Atoka, an area of AME missionary activity. Hence, Sisson proposed at the 1880 General Conference the creation of the Indian Mission Annual Conference, and was surely pleased that an appropriation of $600 was recommended for education in that jurisdiction. One supporter declared that "an open door is before us in the Indian Territory, and we would be unwise if we do not enter soon." Hence, persons of Indian

---

[73] Dennis C. Dickerson, *Religion, Race, and Region: Research Notes on AME Church History* (Nashville, TN, AME Sunday School Union, 1995), 78–79, 85–87.

and African extraction, because of Sisson, became a part of an AME mission to ex-slaves of mixed heritage.[74]

Additionally, there was an unprecedented call to include the Chinese among the diverse peoples for whom the AME Church was established to reach. "We recommend," said one resolution at the 1880 General Conference, "that a movement be inaugurated in our California Conference" to initiate a "social contact of the educated men and women of our race with the Chinese of California" and "assist the Chinese in more rapidly assimilating our morals and our Christianity." That AMEs contemplated intimate interaction with the Chinese demonstrated an increased commitment to a Pacific Rim impact beyond the several black parishes already in existence in that region. This focus also expanded to British Columbia where other black, Indian, and Chinese residents could be claimed as potential parishioners.[75]

Sustained commitments to Haiti and Africa, however, carried over from the 1876 General Conference. Similarly, concrete steps were taken to inaugurate an AME mission in Africa. Charles and Ella Mossell displaced J. W. Randolph as the official missionaries to Haiti. Moreover, Bishop Brown and Reverend A. T. Carr in 1878 started a Liberian Mission Church in Charleston, South Carolina. These members, including the Reverend Samuel Flegler, the pastor, and some local preachers and class leaders within a group of thirty members, sailed for Monrovia, Liberia. In 1880 Flegler reported 283 members. The Mossells received denominational support for their ministry, and Flegler relied on funds from the South Carolina Annual Conference. Their efforts stirred one delegate at the 1880 General Conference to propose "a new missionary Bishop for Hayti and Africa." Since the initiative was reported "to be in a most flourishing condition," it seemed urgent for a bishop "to visit this missionary field" so that the venture would be "strengthened." Delegates also gestured to other territories in the Americas. The jurisdiction of the Louisiana Annual Conference, for example, was extended to Belize, Honduras, and the rest of Central America. Moreover, the bishops, in their quadrennial address, noted "the wail of perishing millions in the interior of the Continent of Africa, is the [same] Macedonian

---

[74] *The Sixteenth Session ... of the General Conference, 1876*, 155; *Journal of the Seventeenth Session ... General Conference, 1880*, 75, 84, 165–166; *Minutes of the Arkansas Annual Conference, 1879*, 13. See Christina M. Dickerson (Cousin), "The African Methodist Episcopal Church in the Indian and Oklahoma Territories, 1893–1907," *AME Church Review*, Vol. 123, No. 406, April–June 2007, 28–37 and her "Triangular Integration in a Black Denomination: James Sisson, African Methodism, and the Indian Mission Annual Conference," *Methodist History*, Vol. 53, No. 3, April 2015, 133–151.

[75] *Journal of the Seventeenth Session ... General Conference, 1880*, 167, 280.

cry" that had been applied to Haiti, in saying, 'come over and help us.'" One delegate believed "that the colored race in America is to do a large share of the work of redeeming the millions of souls in Africa."[76]

The evangelization of the Americas and Africa would bring to fulfillment what AMEs construed as their Atlantic destiny. Some of them saw the BME Church as their institutional vehicle to help achieve this objective. Hence, their goals could be harnessed to BME successes both in Canada and the Caribbean. Because both religious bodies acknowledged their intricate and interactive relationship, AMEs rationalized their view that what the BME Church claimed in British territories virtually accrued to African Methodism. In 1875, for example, Willis Nazrey, the former AME prelate who served the BMEs as their first bishop, died in Nova Scotia. Therefore, AME Bishop Alexander W. Wayman was invited to Ontario to preside at the BME General Conference. As presiding officer, he supervised the election of Richard S. Disney, a former AME minister, as Nazrey's successor and led in his consecration as the second bishop for the BMEs. In 1880 the BME Church was described as "the only legitimate daughter of African Methodism," a "planting of the venerated Richard Allen," and a partner in "the up building of the Church of Christ." Bishop Payne repeated these sentiments in saying that the BME Church was "our only legitimate daughter and all our affections are centered upon her." Delegates to the 1880 General Conference greeted his comments with "long continued applause." More clapping followed his reminiscence that he "was there when she was born," implying that BMEs were still tied to the parent AME body.[77]

Though some AMEs were sure about the mutual acceptance of their parent/offspring relationship with the BMEs, others saw ambiguity and uncertainty about the future of this derivative religious body. Founded as an institutional refuge for fleeing AMEs who settled in Canada to escape slavery and the oppression of free blacks, the BME Church extended its mission to other blacks in British colonies elsewhere in the Americas. Since AMEs also coveted these same territories, some conflicts arose between the two denominations. In 1868, the *Christian Recorder* queried about "what is to be the destiny of the British M. E. Church?" Now that the Civil War was over, would BME members return to the United States or "will they remain [and] become an integral part of the British American people." The

---

[76] Ibid., 50–51, 59, 84, 72–73, 91, 280, 287; Smith, *History of the African Methodist Episcopal Church*, Vol. 2, 127–128.

[77] *The Sixteenth Session . . . of the General Conference, 1876*, 220; *Journal of the Seventeenth Session . . . General Conference, 1880*, 62, 231.

Recorder, believing that BMEs would surely choose the latter, declared that blacks both in Canada and in the British West Indies seemed to be faring well and would see no need either to return or to emigrate to the United States. Hence, the BMEs, the *Recorder* advised, should "extend their organization among their fellow subjects of the British kingdom." The newspaper added that "there is an effectual door open to them, and the field is every [bit] as inviting as is our own Southern field." As related and parallel religious bodies, then "let the British M. E. Church, true to the genius of her nation, be the naval forces, while the AME Church will be the land; and let both land and naval forces meet and defeat their common enemy, sin."[78]

Some AMEs seemed content to evangelize exclusively in Haiti and Africa and to leave the British West Indies to the BME Church. Moreover, the BMEs, in fraternal addresses to AME General Conferences, stressed that the West Indies and Central America had become their "new field of labor" and included these territories in their Conference of the West Indies. AMEs, however, in an 1876 missions report, refused to honor the exclusive claims of the BME Church to the British West Indies. The BMEs, the report declared, should allow AMEs "to be relieved" from any agreement that kept them out of these areas of the Caribbean.[79]

Though the BMEs by 1876 had spread beyond Canada into Bermuda and British Guiana, talks commenced about the reunion of the two black Methodist bodies. The 1880 AME General Conference, after hearing Bishop Richard S. Disney discuss the condition of the BME mission in the West Indies, passed a resolution asking AME annual conferences to ratify a merger with its "only legitimate daughter." Many BMEs, whose ministerial credentials already had AME validation, saw no need to stay as a separate organization. The reasons that brought the denomination into existence had now disappeared. Hence, the AME General Conference dispatched messengers to the BME General Conference to show their willingness to move ahead with reunion and to "effect a modus operandi of cooperation in the missionary work in the West Indies and British Guiana." This "co-operation" was to "be known as the Reunion of the AME and BME Churches in America." At the next General Conference the two churches became one, and therefore the AME Church, which retained its denominational title, gained additional territories in Canada and new jurisdictions in Bermuda and British Guiana. Hence, those AMEs who viewed the BME Church as an

---

[78] *Christian Recorder*, September 26, 1868.
[79] *The Sixteenth Session ... of the General Conference, 1876*, 49–50; *Journal of the Seventeenth Session ... General Conference, 1880*, 135.

institutional means to fulfill Atlantic World expansion for their denomination were proven correct.[80]

As AMEs evangelized ex-slaves, they argued that among the competing Methodist bodies their denomination was the truest embodiment of the Wesleyan tradition. As the earliest exemplar of a "freedom church," AMEs contended that black emancipation could be affirmed and sustained through an affiliation with the heirs of Richard Allen. "The African Methodist Episcopal Church (A.M.E.), the African Methodist Episcopal Zion Church (A.M.E. Zion), the Colored Methodist Episcopal Church (C.M.E.), the Methodist Episcopal Church (M.E.), and the Methodist Episcopal Church, South (M.E. South)," said Reginald Hildebrand, "each offered southern blacks working models of what freedom could mean."[81] The two regional ME denominations were white controlled and the CME Church, a religious body that derived from a southern white Methodist organization, as far as AMEs were concerned, did not represent the racial independence and autonomy that their heritage embodied. AMEs, however, had a harder time in asserting superiority over the Zion Church. The longevity and freedom credentials of the AME Zion connection rivaled that of the Allenites. Hence, the AMEs resorted to an historical issue of polity by boasting they had proud black bishops, unlike the Zionites whose denominational leaders had been superintendents.

The amicable relationship between the ME Church, South and its offspring, the CME Church, established in 1870, was exploited by AME competitors. CMEs claimed that AME representatives took possession of church buildings and congregations that the ME Church, South intended for the CMEs. Hence, the CME bishops pleaded with the 1872 AME General Conference "to turn over to our church all the church property throughout the Southern States that belong to our church." They waited in vain for an answer. AMEs viewed them as an institutional vehicle for southern white paternalism, and their existence could circumscribe the new liberties now available to the ex-slaves. Although one CME historian correctly argued that the founders of the denomination expressed the same desire for racial independence and autonomy as the two African Methodist bodies, the

[80] *The Sixteenth Session ... of the General Conference, 1876,* 220; *Journal of the Seventeenth Session ... General Conference, 1880,* 76–77, 232–233.
[81] Hildebrand, *The Times Were Strange and Stirring,* xvii.

newest of the black Wesleyan denominations drew the derisive and unfair designation of "white folks' niggers" from aggressive AME rivals.[82]

The ME Church, with its anti-slavery heritage and in choosing black preachers to introduce the denomination to ex-slaves, had the advantage of greater economic resources in comparison to the AMEs. Although seemingly autonomous annual conferences gave blacks in the ME Church the guise of racial independence, AMEs were convinced that actual rather than virtual autonomy showed a complete break with southern slavery than what could be shown by the ME Church. African Methodists were present in the South, Hildebrand noted, "to regenerate a people" and to release them from any semblance of white control.[83]

The same arguments that AMEs developed against white affiliated rivals were less effective in criticizing the Zion Church. So, how could AMEs distinguish themselves from those whom Bishop Payne called the "twin sister" of the AME connection? Ex-slaves themselves were sometimes confused. Henry M. Turner, while stationed as a military chaplain in North Carolina, reported that in Charlotte "the colored people have a fine church, and are very intelligent. They have all united with the Zion church, and several said they thought they had joined the regular A.M.E. Church." He likely lamented that the AMEs did not establish their own congregation in Charlotte, an emerging New South city, until 1897. Nonetheless, there had been serious overtures for organic union between these black Wesleyan denominations. Each body believed in 1864 that the prospect of evangelizing four million ex-slaves required their united effort. Between 1864 and 1868 most AME quarterly and annual conferences voted against this. The same jurisdictions within the Zion Church, however, had voted favorably for merger. The Zionites had already yielded to AME demands that they abandon their four-year superintendency in favor of a lifetime episcopacy practiced from the beginning in the Allenite body. Nonetheless, organic union was killed. Although the *Christian Recorder* noted that "there are some who throw stumbling blocks in the way" from both sides, the failure to achieve union between two African Methodist bodies lay primarily with the AMEs. On the matter of the bishopric, despite Zion's acquiescence, AMEs proclaimed its superiority over its "twin sister."[84]

---

[82] *The Fifteenth Quadrennial Session of the General Conference, 1872*, 25–26; Hildebrand, *The Times Were Strange and Stirring*, 14, 22; Othal H. Lakey, *The History of the CME Church* (Memphis, TN, CME Publishing House, 1985, 15, 45.)

[83] Hildebrand, *The Times Were Strange and Stirring*, 50, 96–97.

[84] Daniel A. Payne, "The African M.E. Church in Its Relations to the Freedmen," 4; *Christian Recorder*, June 18, 1864; December 30, 1865; James A. Handy, *Scraps of African Methodist Episcopal History* (Philadelphia, PA, AME Book Concern, n.d., 246–247.)

AME attitudes toward the Zion Church and other Methodist bodies vying for the loyalty of ex-slaves seemed best expressed in the intemperate assertion of Jabaz Campbell who said that "we would like to have all the ground." AMEs thought of themselves as best suited to protect and promote an emancipationist ethos among the ex-slaves. Whether this involved politics, education, or the exodus movement, AMEs, through their proud heritage and contemporary praxis, thought they identified more broadly than the other Wesleyan bodies with the full freedom of former slaves. Such perspectives prevailed despite the presence of Zionites, black MEs, and CMEs in fighting for the franchise and starting black schools. This same grandiosity also extended to their involvements, both actual and aspirational, with peoples of African descent on both sides of the Atlantic. Whether it involved their benign relationship with the BME Church or its ruthless rivalry with the CME Church, AMEs, often selfishly and sometimes magnanimously, wanted "all the ground" to themselves.[85]

Despite a surfeit of pride among AMEs, the denomination's statistician showed them to be the largest of all the black Methodist bodies, but not by much. In 1881 there were 392,540 AME members, with the Zion denomination at a close second with 302,000 followers. Both African Methodist bodies, however, respectively outnumbered the 200,000 blacks in the ME Church and the 126,729 who belonged to the CMEs. Yet the AME mission was not over. The 1880 General Conference authorized the formation of nine new annual conferences. They largely came out of the continuing growth of members in the former slave states. These new annual conferences, almost exclusively in the South, included West Tennessee, South Arkansas, North Mississippi, East Florida, North Alabama, Northeast Texas, and Columbia (South Carolina). Hence, this increase, which put AMEs in striking distance of 400,000 members, became foundational to further growth in the South, the West, and elsewhere in the Atlantic World.[86]

---

[85] Cited in Walker, *A Rock in a Weary Land*, 82.
[86] Benjamin W. Arnett (compiler), *The Budget: Containing the Status of Methodism at the Second Ecumenical Conference of Methodism* held in October 7– 20, 1891 (Xenia, OH, Chew Printing, 1891), 64; Smith, *History of the African Methodist Episcopal Church*, 128.

4

∾

A Denomination in the Diaspora, 1880–1916

BUILDING A DENOMINATIONAL INFRASTRUCTURE

The ongoing growth of the African Methodist Episcopal (AME) Church within multiple constituencies in the black transatlantic required its advocacy and support for issues germane to black freedom. AMEs, for example, became frontline participants in struggles to protect black humanity in the American South, where the civil rights of the ex-slaves were receding, spoke as admirers of Antonio Maceo and other blacks fighting against Spanish colonialism in Cuba, and emerged as defenders of disenfranchised black and colored peoples against white settler hegemony in South Africa. As the denomination matured as an institution with a stable organizational framework and a solid infrastructure of program departments, schools, and transatlantic ministries, its leaders could confidently address black national and international interests and articulate positions, which commanded the attention of powerful whites on both sides of the Atlantic. These developments occurred as the franchise and other civic privileges became more racially restrictive for southern blacks and as various pan-African projects increasingly tied diverse black populations to the AME Church. Despite the breadth of the denomination's Atlantic consciousness, self-referential attitudes confined their success mainly to creolized peoples in the Caribbean and Africa and even among ex-slaves in the American South.[1] The identity of such populations exhibited cultural influences from several sources, of which the African background was only one. Nonetheless, as

---

[1] James T. Campbell, *Songs of Zion: The African Methodist Episcopal Church in the United States and South Africa* (New York, Oxford University Press, 1998), 97.

denominational governance and operations occupied church leaders, they neither neglected nor ignored pressing issues related to Afrocentrism and AME theological and racial identity, black emigration, and women's empowerment.

The episcopacy anchored AME ecclesiology from the first General Conference in 1816 through to its seventeenth session in 1880. Though these quadrennial meetings legislated policies and created departments for publishing and fiscal affairs, during the denomination's first six decades fourteen bishops governed a growing religious body and presided in far-flung states, a few Canadian provinces, and in some maritime locations. An increasing membership in an expanding geography, however, required additional agencies and personnel to manage the ambitious Atlantic reach of African Methodism. Hence, the AME Church, in the intervening decades between 1880 and 1916, established itself as a representative black institution whose discussions about racial identity and destiny and its assorted strategies deployed against segregation and colonialism reflected broader debates within the larger pan-African populations that the denomination served.

Twenty-five bishops, elected between 1884 and 1916, led the denomination during this period of bureaucratic consolidation, growth in the Caribbean and Africa, and engagement with several inexorable issues crucial to the well-being of blacks in the diaspora. In fact, their backgrounds reflected the diversity of African Methodism in the black Atlantic. Several had toiled as slaves and experienced a momentous transformation from bondage to freedom in the 1860s and 1870s, and articulated some of the paradoxical perspectives that derived from this transition. Though some, such as Evans Tyree, born in Tennessee in 1853, and James M. Conner, born in Mississippi in 1863, reached adolescence during the Civil War/Reconstruction period, others who became bishops were shaped as adults in the breathtaking shift from slavery to freedom. Wesley J. Gaines, for example, born a slave in 1840 in Georgia, had labored in three different locations including the plantation of the Toombs family in Wilkes County. Eager for an education, he learned the alphabet from a white child and studied from books that his father surreptitiously secured. He hid them from whites who would surely punish a slave for seeking an education. Despite this defiance, Gaines held in high esteem elite whites, including his slave owner, Robert Toombs, who served the Confederacy as Secretary of State. Though Gaines later became the proud pastor and builder of Big Bethel in Atlanta, reputed to be the largest black church in the South, his mixed feelings about Toombs showed the complicated relationships that slavery created between whites and blacks. Abram Grant seemed less forgiving and deferential to his slave master than was Bishop Gaines. Born in 1848 in Lake City, Florida, but sold at a slave auction in Columbus, Georgia, Grant became the property of Frank Ronluson, a man who owned five hundred slaves. The war, however, devastated all of his holdings and reduced him and his wife to near destitution. Years later, in 1896, Ronluson visited the South Florida Annual Conference where Bishop Grant was presiding, and announced his astonishment that someone who had been his chattel was now the "bishop of a great church." Though the irony of Grant in this exalted position reduced Ronluson to tears, the bishop magnanimously acknowledged him as a kind master. Yet he solicited no offering to aid this impecunious white man, but instead yielded the floor to his brother, Isaac Grant, who had been separated from the family forty years earlier and was anxious to share his recollections of another side of the slavery. Bishop Grant recalled that "the last I saw my brother" occurred when his slave-owner "sold him to the Slave Traders." Whatever pity Ronluson elicited from the bishop paled in comparison with the painful testimony about how slavery had torn apart the Grant family.[2]

Gaines and Grant stood in sharp contrast to William B. Derrick, Cornelius T. Shaffer, and Josiah H. Armstrong whose racial experiences did not include slavery, but drew from their military service in the Civil War. Derrick, born in Antigua in 1843, immigrated to the United States to fight in the US Navy, saw action on the flagship *Minnesota*, and participated in the legendary naval battle between the *Monitor* and the Merrimack. Shaffer, born in Ohio in 1847, joined the military in 1864 and was counted among the soldiers wounded in the war. Armstrong, born in Pennsylvania in 1842, enlisted in Regiment 3, Company A of the US Colored Troops in 1863 and was wounded at Morris Island, South Carolina. After a stay in a hospital, he was stationed at Beaufort, South Carolina, and then in Jacksonville, Florida. He fought in other battles in both Florida and Georgia, and worked as a cook and a teamster before attaining the rank of sergeant. He mustered out of the army in Florida in 1866.[3]

The denomination's Atlantic reach made possible the election of Charles S. Smith, J. Albert Johnson, and John Hurst to the bishopric. Smith, born in 1852 in Colborne, Canada, settled for a time in Alabama where he served in the 1870s in the state legislature. J. Albert Johnson, born in 1857 in Oakville,

[2] Richard R. Wright, Jr., *The Bishops of the African Methodist Episcopal Church* (Nashville, TN, AME Sunday School Union, 1963), 173–175, 191; Charles S. Long, *History of the AME Church in Florida* (Philadelphia, PA, AME Book Concern, 1939), 110–111.
[3] Wright, *The Bishops of the AME Church*, 77, 155, 301; Louisa R. Armstrong, Pension Claim; Luke Baker, Deposition B, May 16, 1913, Case of Louisa R. Armstrong; in Josiah H. Armstrong, *Military Pension Records* (Washington DC, National Archives, 1913).

Canada, was pastor to several British Methodist Episcopal (BME) congregations and transferred allegiance to the AME Church during the 1884 reunion. John Hurst, born in 1863 in Haiti, was sponsored as a student at Wilberforce University by AME missionaries. The election of other bishops showed the increased power of the southern branch of African Methodism. Morris M. Moore, despite his short-lived episcopacy, became a bishop in 1900 because of the consolidated influence of Florida in denominational affairs. The same was true in 1908 of Henry B. Parks, Joseph S. Flipper, and William H. Heard from Georgia. Similarly, the power of South Carolina catapulted into the bishopric Moses B. Salter in 1892, William D. Chappelle and Joshua H. Jones in 1912, and William W. Beckett in 1916. This diversity among the bishops reflected the same cross section of geographical origin and experiences present within the entirety of African Methodism. Hence, AME perspectives on racial identity and destiny, and debates about the best strategies to achieve black advancement, derived from these broad-based backgrounds present among AME ministers and members.[4]

To function as a bellwether of black debate and as a fulcrum for black development, a solid infrastructure for education, publishing, and domestic and global ministries needed to be in place. Therefore, in the 1880s and 1890s AME leaders focused on the consolidation of their multiple educational ventures, built impressive publishing plants in Philadelphia and Nashville, and organized various departments and subordinate bodies to support denominational personnel in their service to church members and the broader black population. Educational institutions, for example, rapidly proliferated in the growing southern branch of African Methodism. Driven by state pride and the urgent need to raise the ex-slave population to literacy convinced AME leaders to establish graded institutions from the elementary to the baccalaureate level. Decisions to shift schools to more favorable locations and to intensify funding commitments both from the national church and sponsoring episcopal districts coalesced into a denominational effort to regularize a church-wide educational ministry. Although several southern jurisdictions opened facilities to address educational deficiencies in their localities, succeeding General Conferences in the late nineteenth and early twentieth centuries selected schools that were worthy of consistent support and other institutions that deserved a lesser level of assistance.

---

[4] Wright, *The Bishops of the AME Church*, 92–93, 132, 234, 239–240, 242, 299, 318; Dennis C. Dickerson, *African Methodism and Its Wesleyan Heritage: Reflections on AME Church History* (Nashville, TN, AME Sunday School Union, 2009), 74–76.

Wilberforce University, which W. E. B. Du Bois described as the "prized child" of African Methodism, maintained its preferential position in denominational appropriations. During the 1880-1884 quadrennium, Wilberforce drew $5,342 for Wilberforce out of the AME treasury, more than for any other educational institution. Additional monies went to the school from the New Jersey and North Carolina Annual Conferences and from other supporters who funded the education of Haitian students. Just as southern districts exhibited regional pride in schools established in their areas, Wilberforce, despite its status as a connectional institution, received special attention from Ohio AMEs. President Benjamin F. Lee told the 1881 Ohio Annual Conference that Wilberforce "is your work" and "you should feel proud of this work." A respectable offering was collected in response. The Committee on Education at the 1882 session noted that the university had an indebtedness of $100,000 and that the Ohio Annual Conference had a "duty to support the institution and to do all in our power to make Wilberforce successful." This same committee reminded the 1883 session that "the twenty years of Wilberforce University, its sixty alumni and its ... active undergraduates make it an object worthy of the continued patronage given by this conference." Therefore, the Ohio Annual Conference committed to fund John Guillott of Haiti and immediately raise $500 because the school was "greatly embarrassed financially" and required emergency funds. Similarly, Payne Theological Seminary, which developed an institutional identity separate from Wilberforce in 1894, embraced a diasporic mission, despite its own fiscal challenges. An African, Moyazo Fanele Sakie, who adopted the name Daniel A. Payne, was presented as a ministerial candidate to the 1894 Pittsburgh Annual Conference. Bishop Benjamin W. Arnett said that Sakie's "intention is to attend" the seminary and then "return to his native land as a missionary."[5]

[5] W. E. B. Du Bois, *The Autobiography of W.E.B. Du Bois* (New York, International Publishers, 1968), 191; *Journal of the 18th Session and 17th Quadrennial Session of the General Conference of the African Methodist Episcopal Church in the World* held in Bethel Church, Baltimore, MD, May 5–26, 1884 (Philadelphia, Rev. James C. Embry, General Business Manager, 1884), 58, 80; *Minutes of the Fifty-First Session of the Ohio Annual Conference of the African Methodist Episcopal Church* held in Asbury AME Church, Middleport, Ohio, September 29–October 6, 1881 (Columbus, OH, J. F. Earhart Book and Job Printer, 1881), 17; *Minutes of the Fifty-Second Session of the Ohio Annual Conference of the African Methodist Episcopal Church* held in Quinn Chapel, Chillicothe, September 20–25, 1882 (Zanesville, OH, Visitor Power Press Print, 1882), 20; *Minutes of the Fifty-Third Session of the Ohio Annual Conference of the African Methodist Episcopal Church* held in Wayman Chapel, Hillsboro, September 19–24, 1883 (Zanesville, OH, Visitor Power Press Print, 1883), 19; *Minutes of the Twenty-Seventh Session of the Pittsburg(h) Conference of the African Methodist Episcopal Church*, held

Notwithstanding these sources of denominational support, Wilberforce, like other AME schools, remained impecunious and badly in need of an endowment of $500,000 to liquidate its debt and finance various improvements. The bishops, in their 1884 quadrennial report, believed that this level of funding was warranted because Wilberforce was "our most venerable institution of learning" and its seventy graduates and other alumni had "accomplished a vast amount of good." Bishop Payne concurred with his colleagues in wanting to establish the school as "a first-class college." Though reality belied the name "college," Payne preferred the designation so as to challenge AMEs to develop Wilberforce into "a first-class institution." "In order to perpetuate the AME Church," he said, "she must educate her own Children for the Christian ministry and for the School Room work of Christian education." The denomination, Payne noted, was "too poor to attempt to establish more than one college at a time." Hence, he voted for Wilberforce as the one college that deserved the church's full resources. He knew, of course, that southern competition for the denomination's educational dollars was intense and that an exclusive preference for Wilberforce was hard to attain.[6]

In some ways southern AMEs were heeding Payne's message that fiscal prudence required consolidation in their region's educational efforts. They received these same cues from the other bishops who in their 1884 quadrennial report named only three schools, besides Wilberforce, that deserved church-wide support. They lifted up Allen University in Columbia, South Carolina, Paul Quinn College in Waco, Texas, and Morris Brown College in Atlanta, Georgia. Although the education secretary acknowledged other institutions in North Carolina, Louisiana, Florida, Tennessee, Mississippi, Alabama, Kansas, and a second school in Texas, it appeared that the nine reverend fathers had picked only three schools with the same potential as Wilberforce University.[7]

The bishops believed that Allen University had special promise. After Wilberforce, it was "our next oldest institution of high grade." AMEs in South Carolina abandoned Payne Institute in Cokesbury, sold the property for $1,000, and transferred the funds to the new venture in Columbia, the state's capital city. The new location "reached a degree of success not

---

at Wayman's Chapel AME Church, Wheeling, West Virginia, October 3–7, 1894 (Altoona, PA, H & W. H. Slep, 1894), 5.

[6] *Journal of the 18th Session ... of the General Conference, 1884*, 116, 198, 201; Daniel A. Payne, "The Past, Present and Future of the AME Church," Second Paper, *AME Church Review*, April 1885, 314.

[7] *Journal of the 18th Session ... of the General Conference, 1884*, 117, 157–158, 160–162, 165.

attained by Payne Institute in ten years." Similarly, Paul Quinn College, unlike other AME initiatives in Texas, was "located in the very heart of a populous district." This factor convinced the bishops to recommend that the General Conference enact "wise legislation" for its benefit. Morris Brown College, though still in the planning stages, was situated in Atlanta on "a beautiful site" of 4 acres that was already paid for. "The work of instruction," the bishops were told, would start in September 1884. Optimism about these three institutions depended on closing schools in less desirable locations and reestablishing them in urban areas where students and financial support seemed more available.[8]

The AME education department followed the framework that the bishops recommended in 1884. This meant that denominational leaders, while they encouraged all educational initiatives, recognized that funds should only go to schools that had the singular focus of their respective districts and were situated in favorable locations. Hence, the Secretary of Education reported at the 1888 General Conference that seventeen schools operated within his oversight, but noted that "the smaller ones have not received any direct financial aid." The better schools, Wilberforce, Allen, Paul Quinn, Morris Brown, and the newly founded Kittrell College in North Carolina, had experienced "rapid development" and had found a "happy [physical] location." Moreover, "these institutions seemed to have reached a very fair degree of success in their work, and are now inspiring confidence both in their immediate localities and in the Church at large."[9]

Ohio AMEs, however, developed a steady source of funding for Wilberforce University beyond the church that no other denominational schools had cultivated. Like southern AMEs during Reconstruction, African Methodists in Ohio discovered that political involvement could yield important benefits to church constituents. When the 1883 Ohio Annual Conference convened in Hillsboro, for example, delegates learned that Civil War veteran and jurist Joseph B. Foraker, the Republican National Committee (GOP) candidate for governor, would be visiting the city. "It was unanimously agreed to visit him in a body" and to designate the pastor at Zanesville "to address the distinguished gentleman in behalf of the conference." Foraker received them and "delivered an address with which all were greatly pleased." Though Foraker lost, he won the next election in 1885, was

[8]   Ibid., 117, 155.
[9]   *Journal of the 19th Session and the 18th Quadrennial Session of the General Conference of the African Methodist Episcopal Church, in the World* held in Bethel Church, Indianapolis, Ind. May 7, 1888 (Philadelphia, Royal Printing Company, 1888), 145, 228.

reelected in 1887, and finished two terms in 1889. Hence, Ohio AMEs now had an influential political ally in the office of governor who could lend a powerful hand to help Wilberforce University.[10]

S. T. Mitchell, the president of Wilberforce and a former pastor in Cincinnati, and Benjamin W. Arnett, the financial secretary of the AME Church and an Ohio resident, generated support in the Ohio and North Ohio Annual Conferences for a bill in the state legislature to aid the oldest of AME institutions. The legislation called for a state subsidy for a "strengthened" normal department and for the creation of an industrial division at Wilberforce. The Combined Normal and Industrial Department (CN&I)would have a board of management comprising three members elected by Wilberforce trustees and three appointed by the Ohio governor and confirmed by the state senate. This arrangement for the seemingly autonomous CN&I circumvented possible charges of a church/state entanglement. The bill passed in 1887 with sponsorship from a state senate Democrat and a signature from Governor Foraker. CN&I, for example, received from the State of Ohio between 1887 and 1892 a total of $48,000.[11]

This infusion of state funds into Wilberforce allowed for a shift of attention to a needed expansion of the theological department. Hence, Payne Theological Seminary was created, and thereafter the 1892 General Conference authorized that "the regular appropriation hereafter made to Wilberforce University shall be applied to the maintenance" of the enhanced school of religion. The Education Department also maintained its hierarchy of support of $1,000 annually for Allen, Paul Quinn, Morris Brown, and the addition of Quindaro (later Western University) near Kansas City, Kansas, and Edward Waters in Jacksonville, Florida. Much lesser amounts, mostly around $250 annually, were disbursed to seven other schools in various southern states.[12]

Management of a far-flung aggregation of educational institutions sustained the AME commitment to freed people barely a generation removed from slavery. Stemming from both racial and denominational pride, glowing connectional and conference reports about these schools were often optimistic and at times exaggerated. The President of the West Tennessee College in Memphis, for example, boasted to the 1888 General Conference

[10] *Minutes of the Fifty-Third Session of the Ohio Annual Conference*, 1883, 3, 35.
[11] Benjamin W. Arnett (ed.), *The Centennial Budget*, 1887–1888fromn.p., 1888), 386.
[12] *Journal of the 20th Session and 19th Quadrennial Session of the General Conference of the African Methodist Episcopal Church in the World* held in Bethel Church, Philadelphia, Pennsylvania, May 2, 1892 (Philadelphia, Rev. James C. Embry, General Business Manager, 1892), 135.

that the school had "an outfit of volumes that would do credit to the [library] shelves of a DePauw or Princeton." The Committee on Colleges and Universities at the 1896 General Conference extended hearty commendations to the denomination's flagship schools. First, Wilberforce was congratulated for "securing" funding from the State of Ohio, and then Allen, Paul Quinn, and Kittrell in North Carolina were lauded for their strides "in the face of discouragement" and difficulty. For these top AME schools "we have nothing but words of praise for the earnest and effective labor of those institutions" and for their "magnificent reports." Moreover, these institutions, said Bishop Wesley J. Gaines in 1896, in service to a black Atlantic, boasted graduates "all over the land, in the isles of the sea, and in Africa."[13]

A Wilberforce professor, however, described the interior of the church's flagship institution. Just as a complimentary report on education was presented to the 1896 General Conference, W. E. B. Du Bois, soon to receive his Ph.D. from Harvard, arrived at Wilberforce to teach classics. "I knew something about Wilberforce," he said; "it was venerable and well known." Though he was disappointed that he would replace the distinguished Greek scholar, William S. Scarborough, who had fallen out favor in ecclesiastical politics, Du Bois remained committed because "the name of Wilberforce lured me." It was, however," a small colored denominational college married to a State normal school" and connected to a religious body that was "too poor to run the college." He added that "the State tolerated the normal school so as to keep Negroes out of other State schools." Moreover, Wilberforce, as the foremost school of the AMEs, became "the capital of the nationwide institution" and a venue for denominational politics. Bishops and clergy made a point of coming to commencements to do the business of the church. Trustees seemed more interested in this activity than in institutional oversight, and even some faculty "found it expedient to make powerful acquaintances" with the church hierarchy. Therefore, the Du Bois dream "to help build a great university" ran up against church politics, delayed payment of faculty salaries, and the dictatorial power of Wilberforce resident, Bishop Benjamin W. Arnett. Though Du Bois and other faculty prevented the appointment of the bishop's son and namesake as Professor of Literature, he knew that they had won a Pyrrhic victory against this blatant act of nepotism, and therefore his days at Wilberforce would be numbered.

---

[13] *Journal of the 19th Session and the 18th Quadrennial Session of the General Conference, 1888,* 236; *Journal of the Twentieth Quadrennial Session of the General Conference of the African Methodist Episcopal Church* held in St. Stephen's AME Church, Wilmington, NC, May 4–22, 1896 (1896), 22; 152.

Before his expected termination, Du Bois accepted in 1898 a lesser position at the University of Pennsylvania in order to escape certain vengeance from the bishop.[14]

Du Bois' assessment of Wilberforce was not at all far-fetched. His comments on the school's precarious financial condition, for example, were echoed in the report of the Committee on Education at the 1896 Ohio Annual Conference. Though students came to the school from twenty-five to thirty states in addition to past enrollees who had come from Canada, Mexico, the West Indies, and Africa, said the report, it was clear that the institution had enormous possibilities for service to the black Atlantic. The 1885 Ontario Annual Conference, for example, in response to a forceful address from President Mitchell, acknowledged "the amount of good work that has been accomplished by Wilberforce in behalf of the African Race on the American Continent." The delegates heartily endorsed the "great and important work" that Wilberforce could do for the Canadian church. Fiscal deficiencies, however, hampered what could be done for these broad constituencies. An Ohio Conference report said that "The extent of its usefulness is limited only by its meager amount of means. Had the university means commensurate with its capabilities and opportunities, it could do a wonderful work in educating and elevating our people."[15]

Du Bois most assuredly agreed. But, Harvard, Berlin, and Leipzig, where Du Bois had matriculated, were intrinsic to his academic pedigree, and he wanted to imprint their standards and aspirations onto Wilberforce. Mitchell, Arnett, and other AME leaders, however, had less grandiose objectives in mind. Equipping clergy, teachers, and other professionals with the requisite skills for these vocations were what Wilberforce supporters wanted to accomplish. The attainment of these goals required the mobilization of scarce resources from a religious body with ambitious Atlantic commitments. Yet these laudatory objectives were tied to undemocratic practices that offended academic purists such as Du Bois.

No one disputed that AME schools required endowments and other fiscal measures to fund their long-term viability. What denominational leaders achieved in the 1880s and 1890s, however, was an indispensable first step

<hr/>

[14] Du Bois, *The Autobiography of W.E.B. Du Bois*, 184–193.
[15] *Minutes of the Sixty-Sixth Session of the Ohio Annual Conference of the African Methodist Episcopal Church* held in Wayman Chapel AME Church, Hillsboro, Ohio, September 10–16, 1896 (Xenia, OH, Chew Printer, 1896), 26–27; *Minutes of the First and Second Session of the Ontario Annual Conference of the African Methodist Episcopal Church* convened at John St. AME Church, Hamilton, Ont., June 30, 1885 and at King St. AME Church, Amherstburg, July 1, 1886 (Hamilton, Ontario, H.A. Martin, 1886), 8, 11.

toward these objectives. Though it was hard to tame the intense regional pride and practical necessities that fueled the proliferation of southern schools, AME officials suggested a discipline of selective support only for institutions with promise and potential. This practice, while doing little to prevent episcopal districts from founding new schools, allowed some to wither for want of connectional contributions. Though that did not apply to some schools, such as Payne University, which started in 1889 in Selma, Alabama, and was adopted by the North Alabama Annual Conference, start-ups in other regions often faced bleak futures. Trustees of Turner College in Shelbyville, Tennessee, founded in 1886, sold the physical plant of the "starving little school" in the 1920s.[16]

Despite the ups and downs in educational consolidation, the denomination continued to strengthen its infrastructure and to establish other departments to serve the expanding needs of a growing Atlantic constituency. Therefore, agencies for publishing, church extension, and Atlantic expansion along with those in education contributed to the institutional maturation of African Methodism. AMEs, from their beginnings, required regular contact with printers who published for them hymnals, disciplines, general and annual conference minutes, and various periodicals including the *Christian Recorder*. A steady succession of book stewards, starting with Richard Allen, engaged individual vendors to print these AME books and newspapers, which were in turn sold to church constituents. Private contracting for these printing services prevailed until 1848, when the denomination established the Book Concern in Pittsburgh in 1848. moving it to Philadelphia in 1852 and locating it at 631 Pine Street. This historic address, where an impressive printing plant housed in a three story building was constructed in 1892, became a major venue for denominational publishing for several ensuing decades.[17]

AMEs undertook a second publishing enterprise in response to a resurgence of the Sunday School movement. Though prevalent among Southern Protestants in the post-Civil War period, it originated in eighteenth-century Great Britain and spread to the United States in the colonial and antebellum eras. In the South, as Sunday Schools shifted from religious instruction into

[16]   W. H. Mixon, *History of the African Methodist Episcopal Church in Alabama with Biographical Sketches* from Nashville, TN, AME Sunday School Union, 1902), 86–87; Reverdy C. Ransom, *The Pilgrimage of Harriet Ransom's Son* (Nashville, TN, AME Sunday School Union, n.d.), 265.

[17]   "Book Concern of the AME Church," in Richard R. Wright, Jr. (ed.), *Centennial Encyclopedia of the African Methodist Episcopal Church* (Philadelphia, PA, AME Book Concern, 1916), 293–294.

instruments for conversion in the mid-nineteenth century, the largest southern denominations, both black and white, fully embraced this evangelical
tool. Hence, the AME and AME Zion denominations, for example, testified
that most of their converts came out of their Sunday Schools. The AMEs
boasted 3,417 Sunday Schools in 1884.[18]

Charles S. Smith, born in Canada, spearheaded the Sunday School movement among African Methodists. The AME Council of Bishops appointed
him as corresponding secretary in 1882 and assigned him to establish a
Sunday School Union. He drew assistance mainly from southern annual
conferences that supported his publication of *Our Sunday School Review*, the
Jubilee Gem, and the "little catechism" drawn from (Bishop) *Turner's Catechism*. As Smith developed these instructional programs, he also focused
on the acquisition of a building to centralize and regularize AME Sunday
School Union initiatives. Initially, he started operations in his residence in
Bloomington, Illinois.

In January 1886 he moved to Nashville, Tennessee, to "have a more central
location" nearest to the majority of southern churches then supporting this
venture. Moreover, Smith cited the city's "commercial advantages, and also
its educational advantages, as it related to the intellectual development of the
colored people." Smith himself had matriculated in the medical department
of Central Tennessee College from which he earned in 1880 an MD degree.[19]

Because of the general popularity of the Sunday School movement, Nashville offered unusual business opportunities to AMEs beyond meeting their
own publishing needs. Smith hoped to "build up a trade that will be interdenominational in its influence." Specifically, the AME Sunday School
Union could "share the trade that is received by publishers from the
Sunday-schools of the several colored denominations." Because there were
generic materials that carry no "denominational title, imprint, or seal," then
it would be possible for AMEs to broaden their customer base "beyond the
bounds of our own Church."[20]

Smith knew these ambitions could only be realized if the AME Sunday
School Union was properly housed and equipped. Hence, he completed

---

[18] Sally G. McMillen, *To Raise up the South: Sunday Schools in Black and White Churches,
      1865–1915* (Baton Rouge, Louisiana State University Press, 2001), 11–14; *Journal of the 18th
      Session . . . of the General Conference, 1884*, 133.

[19] *Journal of the 18th Session . . . of The General Conference, 1884*, 117–118; Kenneth H. Hill,
      Charles Spencer Smith: A Portrait: Sable Son of God from Nashville, TN, AME Sunday
      School Union, 1993), 2, 9–10; *Journal of the 19th Session . . . of the General Conference,
      1888*, 177.

[20] *Journal of the 19th Session . . . of the General Conference, 1888*, 177.

negotiations on February 28, 1888 for a four-story building in downtown Nashville. The appraised price was $27,000, but Smith drew it down to $9,000, with $5,000 paid on the delivery of the deed and final payment in 1891. Smith asked the 1888 General Conference for funds "to properly fit up the building and put in printing material sufficient to do all our own work." Hence, he purchased over $5,319 in machinery and reported to the 1892 General Conference that charges for the equipment had been paid in full. These and other improvements, Smith declared, would provide AMEs with "a building adapted to our purposes." Moreover, this valuable real estate would be "the joy of the African Methodist Episcopal Church" and would help "in heightening the dignity of the Church."[21] Impressive dedicatory services were held in January 1889 and chronicled in a hardbound book that Smith printed in 1894. In providing a venue for the production of AME literature, said one bishop, Smith ranked in importance with AME church fathers whose labors were crucial "in promoting denominational success." Another bishop declared that the Sunday School Union would serve 400,000 AME members across the Atlantic World from the United States to Haiti, the West Indies, and Africa. A third bishop envisaged AME materials reaching the "mountains of the Cameroons and other portions of benighted Africa, that land where lives a race that has been under the dark cloud of barbarism," but also a place "where our fathers have lived."[22]

Although the newly constructed Book Concern of the AME Church in Philadelphia regularly published the *Christian Recorder*, the recently founded *A.M.E. Church Review*, and other volumes of hymns, liturgy, and polity, the bishops and Smith had a far greater vision for the Sunday School Union. They viewed African Methodism as exemplary of black independence and self-determination and its Sunday School Union as a vehicle to instill this pride in AME youth. To achieve this objective the publishing house would produce various genres in race literature to be included in Sunday School lessons, denominational history and theology, biography, and other publications that would demonstrate a black understanding of Biblical texts and promote AME identity. This literature aimed at educating the young and equipping the Church to lift black Atlantic populations to literacy and awakening them to their divinely directed destiny of freedom. The construction of the Sunday School Union also aligned AME institutional

---

[21] Ibid., 181–182; *Journal of the 20th Session ... of the General Conference, 1892,* 196; Charles S. Smith (compiler), *Dedicatory Services at the Publishing House of the AME Church Sunday School Union, Nashville, Tenn* from Nashville, TN, AME Sunday School Union, 1894), 7.

[22] Smith, *Dedicatory Services,* 9, 21, 25–26.

developments to its emancipationist mission within the black diaspora throughout the Americas and in Africa.

Hence, a Boston pastor, in addressing the 1897 Nova Scotia Annual Conference in Canada, noted "the possibilities of a people who, thirty-three years ago, on the very spot where their fore-fathers were sold as chattel, today own ... in the most central part of the city [of Nashville] valuable property." This Sunday School Union, he said, with slight exaggeration, was "the only department of its kind that any Church in the world possesses." Smith himself, in a missive to the Nova Scotia meeting, boasted that Union "periodicals have a circulation in almost every state and territory and in the West Indies and [in] West and South Africa." Its impact, he predicted, "shall be planted on every hilltop, and in every valley, and on the bosom of every plain, wherever a handful of colored children are to be found."[23]

Therefore, he developed a church-wide Children's Day as a fundraiser to support Sunday School publications. In the 1884–1888 quadrennium, for example, individual congregations raised nearly $16,000, and increased that amount to about $25,000 in the 1888–1892 period. To rouse denominational loyalty among the youth and raise consciousness about AME historicity, he promoted a tune that "more than a quarter of a million of African Methodist children [were] joyfully singing":

> Our Father's Church, our Mother's Church
> It is the Church for me;
> Our Father's Church, our Mother's Church,
> Mine ever more shall be.

This tune, Smith poetically declared, could be heard "from Dakota's icy mountain to Africa's golden strands, overlapping the isles of the sea, then stretching again from the eastern shores of our own land to the Golden Gate in the West." That the Sunday School Union served the black Atlantic was shown in Freetown, Sierra Leone, where "native African children have learned to shout "Hurrah for Allen's Sons" as they collected Children's Day offerings to send to Nashville.[24]

Smith was proud of the Atlantic reach of the Sunday School Union and its interdenominational impact. Moreover, Children's Day monies from across the AME connection enabled him to print more than 137,500 books in

---

[23] *Minutes of the Thirteenth Session of the Nova Scotia Annual Conference of the African Methodist Episcopal Church* held in Highlands AME Church, Amherst, NS, August, 25–29 1897 (Saint John, NB, Geo. A. Knodell, Printer, 1897), 16, 30.

[24] *Journal of the 20th Session ... of the General Conference, 1892*, 196–198.

1888 and another 218,000 in 1892. Additionally, he printed 48,000 Sabbath School volumes for the AME Zion Church. Moreover, he moved beyond producing the *Child's Recorder*, the *Teacher's Quarterly*, the *Scholar's Quarterly*, and *Lesson Papers* to publishing denominational and race literature to enlighten both AME youth and adults. Included among these volumes were Bishop Payne's long-awaited *History of the African Methodist Episcopal Church*, Vol. I, and *Poor Ben*, a biography of Bishop Arnett.[25]

The Sunday School Union was developing just as the bishops envisaged it. Bishop Arnett said that building the publishing house "has proved to be the Negro's opportunity, not only in developing his capacity, but in affording him the means of demonstrating his ability of self-government." Therefore, "come to the new Sunday School Union building," he said, "and see what we have accomplished." "See," he added, "what God has enabled us to do, and what we are doing for the moral, religious, and material development of the race." Furthermore, he noted that "God intends that this Church shall educate the Negro in self-respect, and that the hand that once held the hoe ... shall now use the pen with power, writing the deeds of black men and black women of the past in letters of living light." Bishop Grant concurred in saying that "we want to read race literature and have a little more race pride. If other races can be proud of themselves, we must learn to be proud of our development."[26]

Bishop Tanner believed that this race literature specifically involved AME history and biography. "As to biography," he noted, "what do we know of Allen, and the glorious fifteen who stood by [his] side and assisted in the work of our organization? What do we know of Morris Brown, and Waters, and that mighty Prince in Israel, William Paul Quinn?" He also asserted that "literature of the historic kind" was similarly needed. "Seventy years of work," he said, "in the North and South, in the East and the West, in the islands of the sea and Africa-fatherland! Seventy years of sowing in tares, and yet no history that the world can read!"[27]

Smith, all three bishops agreed, had made a major start in directions that they recommended. For example, in 1895 he published through the AME Sunday School Union *Glimpses of Africa: West and Southwest Coast*, and Tanner produced in the same year through the AME Book Concern *The Color of Solomon-What?* The denomination had two publishing plants housed in new facilities dedicated in 1889 and 1892 respectively. These departments showed a strengthened infrastructure for printing hymnals,

---

[25] Ibid., 198–199, 202–203.   [26] Smith, *Dedicatory Services*, 42, 52, 60.   [27] Ibid., 16–17.

disciplines, Sunday School books, periodicals, and race literature. These structures showed an institutional maturation that equipped AMEs to define blackness, to declare their autonomy, and to argue for black freedom in answer to the escalation in segregation and colonialism. Pursuing a black understanding of Biblical texts and presenting their own interpretation of black history were foundational steps in defending black humanity in an era of resurgent white supremacy on sides of the Atlantic. These publishing facilities, through the production of influential texts, enabled AMEs to show themselves as a reputable religious body whose traditional beliefs cloaked an insurgent pan-Africanism aimed at discrediting the surging racism then developing through American segregation and European colonialism.

A THEOLOGICAL AND AN AFRICANIST AWAKENING

A global mission to draw dark peoples into the same denomination animated African Methodism. Accompanying this pan-African consciousness was a vigorous theological discourse that defined the AME Church as an orthodox religious body steeped in a black Wesleyan identity. These theological components merged into an Ethiopian millennialism that gave urgency to an Atlantic outreach to populations of African descent on both sides of the ocean. Not until 1890, when James C. Embry, the manager of the AME Book Concern and elected a bishop in 1896, published *The Digest of Christian Theology*, did anyone write a systematic theology for the denomination. The book became a required text for AME ministerial candidates. Embry, a cleric of modest education, drew upon recognized scholars and the sermons of John Wesley to present basic Christian beliefs. His broad survey asserted that "our knowledge of God" was found "in the works of creation and the Bible." Notwithstanding the challenges from Darwinian science and the higher criticism," Embry viewed "the Bible as an authentic revelation from God because it gives us in a consistent, brief and perfectly credible way, the knowledge of God, the method of creation, and a scheme of moral duty that could never have been obtained in any other way."[28]

Embry described the attributes of God and provided an extensive explanation of the Trinity especially through a foundational scripture in 2 Corinthians 13:14 that cites the Godhead in "the grace of our Lord Jesus Christ, and the love of God, and the communion of the Holy Ghost." Embry subscribed

---

[28] Wright, *The Bishops of the African Methodist Episcopal Church*, 162–163; James C. Embry, *The Digest of Christian Theology* (Philadelphia, PA, AME Book Concern, 1890), iii–v; 5–6, 10.

to a high Christology that understood Jesus as standing above the mundane contexts of ordinary human affairs. Similarly, the Holy Ghost was a divine instrument through whom the Father and Son concretely dwelled among believers as Comforter and witness to the reality of the Godhead. Within the Trinity "the Father is such by paternity. The Son is God by filiation, and the Holy Ghost is God, and co-equal by procession." Through the rest of Embry's thorough volume, he presented orthodox discussions about divine providence, the promise of a Redeemer, human depravity, and God's provision and system for atonement. Though *The Digest of Christian Theology* functioned as an official theological text for African Methodism, the prolific Theophilus G. Steward published works that deepened the discourse that Embry's book inaugurated.[29]

Steward differed from Embry because he subjected traditional theology to challenges from modernity revealed in "industrialization, science, evolution, and biblical criticism." Hence, Steward developed what one scholar has described as a "rational orthodox theology." Steward, the pastor of several large congregations, embraced the evangelical theology that the AME Church espoused as a Wesleyan religious body. What ministers and members should preach in their salvific appeals, Steward believed, was traditional beliefs and doctrine leavened by modernist influences. In *Divine Attributes*, for example, Steward's description of God's characteristics resembled what Embry later published in *The Digest*. Unlike Embry, Steward engaged in some theological audacity in conceding, for example, an innate human capacity to recognize morality without the benefit of divine revelation. Moreover, in *Genesis Reread* Steward, while defending Biblical authority, reconciled scripture to Darwinian science on such matters as whether God took a literal twenty-four hours for each day of creation or accomplished the world's beginning within a metaphorical measure of time.[30]

Embry secured his theological training through intense tutorials from learned white clergy. Steward, after postponements during his early ministry, earned a seminary degree in 1880 at the age of thirty-seven from the Episcopal Divinity School in Philadelphia. The school promoted a liberal theology that grounded Steward's unorthodox perspectives on belief and doctrine. Though such serious thinkers as Bishop Tanner sometimes disagreed with some of his idiosyncratic views, Steward found common ground

---

[29] Embry, *The Digest of Christian Theology*, 15–55, 100–218.
[30] A. G. Miller, *Elevating the Race: Theophilus G. Steward, Black Theology, and the Making of an African American Civil Society* (Knoxville, University of Tennessee Press, 2003), xxiii, 56–58, 62–68; Embry, *The Digest of Christian Theology*, 15–27.

with Bishops Arnett, Tanner, and Turner as they coalesced fortuitously toward a theology that undergirded their church's transatlantic reach toward darker peoples.[31]

Embry's generic narrative on traditional Christian theology drew no direct connection to contemporary contexts of hegemony that darker peoples encountered. Steward, both experientially and intellectually, despite his modernist tendencies, appreciated the Afrocentric realities with which AMEs grappled. Steward had been a missionary among ex-slaves in the postbellum South and built a major church in Macon, Georgia, named in his honor Steward Chapel. He ministered in Haiti for six months and had prepared himself by learning French. This experience stirred a black nationalism that he expressed in a later publication, *The Haitian Revolution, 1791–1804*. The Haitian Revolution, like the American Revolution," he wrote, "was fought for citizenship rights, though the slaves in Haiti also sought "the right to own themselves." Additionally, the uprising, according to indigenous writers, was "the one ordeal through which the rehabilitation of the Negro Race has been accomplished." Charles W. Mossell, the veteran AME missionary in Haiti, shared Steward's views and expressed them in his own biography of Toussaint L'Ouverture. Mossell, Steward said, described "admirably the military genius of Toussaint and defend[ed] him against unjust attacks" from his detractors.[32]

Steward's theological temperament, unlike that of Embry, had enough breadth to accommodate Afrocentric impulses. These perspectives poured into an Ethiopian millennialism that Steward and other AME thinkers espoused. He and other black religious intellectuals, says one scholar, believed in a "pan African millennium" that would be "a future golden age continuous with a glorious African past accompanied by God's judgment of white society and Western Civilization." Steward, a theological modernist with pan-African sensibilities, criticized whites who racialized Christianity and construed it as a religion of a Caucasian "clan." His theological solution lay in his post-millennial perspective that the second coming of Jesus Christ would destroy "Anglo-Saxon culture" because of its failure "to effectively evangelize the world."[33]

[31] Embry, *The Digest of Christian Theology*, ii; Miller, *Elevating the Race*, 4, 42, 58.
[32] Miller, *Elevating the Race*, 3; Theophilus G. Steward, *The Haitian Revolution, 1791–1804* (New York, Thomas Y. Cowell Company, 1915), iv–v, vii–viii.
[33] Timothy Fulop, "The Future Golden Day of the Race": Millennialism and Black Americans in the Nadir, 1877–1901," *Harvard Theological Review*, Vol. 84, No. 1, 1991, 78; Miller, *Elevating the Race*, 76–78.

Despite the personal differences between Steward and Turner in the internal politics of the denomination, they and two other bishops, Benjamin W. Arnett and Benjamin T. Tanner, articulated Ethiopian millennialism. Though they emphasized disparate aspects of this perspective, these AME leaders put blackness at the center of their Biblical and theological views. In an address to the World's Parliaments of Religion in 1893 at the Chicago World's Fair, Arnett, in "Christianity and the Negro," asserted that "the Negro is older than Christianity." With every advance in human history, he said, "some reference to the Negro or his home, Africa" was presented. Therefore, "in the first days of Christianity" Africans were present among its principal "propagators." They included Luke the Cyrenian, the author of one of the synoptic gospels, another Cyrenian, Lucius, "one of the first teachers of Christianity," and Simon the Cyrenian who helped Jesus Christ carry the cross to Calvary. Tanner tackled white racialized interpretations of the Bible and criticized whites who hardly ever acknowledged Africans and other persons of color in the scriptures. Hence, he published in 1895 *The Color of Solomon-What?* in which he disputed his portrayal as a white man. Painstakingly, he deeply explored ethnological, linguistic, versional, and interpretive evidence that showed Solomon was not white. In the Biblical division of the races corresponding to Noah's three sons, Solomon belonged to the Shemitic or yellow race. Moreover, his heritage drew from the Hamitic or black race. Hence, Solomon was not white, but was a "colored" man who had "passion for women, manifestly of darker hue than were the women of Israel." The Queen of Sheba, an African, was his favorite.[34]

A derivative impact of AME intellectuals channeled through Tanner's son, Henry Ossawa Tanner, who attained international acclaim for his religious art especially after he permanently settled in Paris, France, in 1891. He participated in what historian David W. Wills characterized as the denomination's "black Christian culture." The religious themes in his artistic productions, according to most scholars, drew from the AME household of his father, Bishop Tanner, and his mother, Sarah E. Tanner, an ex-slave and leader in the Women's Parent Mite Missionary Society (WPMMS). Interspersed in the diverse genres of photography, sculpture, and painting that he mastered were several AME subjects, including individual portraits of his parents. After graduation from the Pennsylvania Academy of Fine Arts, he moved from Philadelphia to Atlanta to delve into photography, where he activated a methodology learned from his Academy professor,

---

[34] Dennis C. Dickerson, *A Liberated Past: Explorations in A.M.E. Church History* (Nashville, TN, AME Sunday School Union, 2003), 45–47.

Thomas Eakins. Eakins emphasized graphic depictions of people and lifelike
portrayals of bodily figures. Photography seemed a sensible vehicle to
capture realist representations of African Americans. Hence, Tanner traveled to Indianapolis to attend the 1888 General Conference. In a session
following his father's election to the bishopric, Tanner addressed the assembly "with respect to photographing the General Conference." In addition to
photography, he experimented with plaster molds of black people, including
a bust of Bishop Daniel A. Payne, who already had purchased some of his
nature paintings. Tanner's AME renderings blended with his other black art
done in the early 1890s. His paintings *The Banjo Lesson* and *The Thankful
Poor*, though they were familiar in form and content with other contemporary art, demonstrated Tanner's identification with the people in his father's
AME jurisdictions. At a time when minstrelsy and other degrading caricatures dominated depictions of African Americans, Tanner portrayed them in
their domestic and institutional settings as honorable and dignified human
beings. Whether it was the formal mien of AME officials, including both his
parents and Bishop Payne, or the proud proletarians who appeared in his
paintings, Tanner joined with other AME intellectuals in conceptualizing
and characterizing blacks as fully human and mirroring the image of God.[35]

Henry M. Turner, however, initiated a daring theological discourse
through a declaration in 1898 that "God is a Negro." Blacks, he said, had
"as much right biblically and otherwise to believe that God is a Negro" as
whites who pictured the Creator as "a fine looking, symmetrical and orna-
mented white man." White depictions of God showed "a white-skinned,
blue-eyed, straight-haired, projecting nose, compressed-lipped, and finely
robed white gentleman, sitting upon a throne somewhere in the heavens."
Turner recounted that all peoples portrayed God like themselves in their art,
carvings, and other aesthetic representations. Blacks, he noted, had a similar
right to sketch God to reflect who they were. Moreover, Turner observed, no
hope existed for any race "who do not believe that they look like God."[36]

The aggressive assertion of white hegemony in postbellum America and
during the "scramble" for Africa, while moving AMEs toward Ethiopian

[35] David W. Wills, "Aspects of Social Thought in the African Methodist Episcopal Church,"
Ph.D. dissertation, Harvard University, 1975, 43–44; Marcia M. Mathews, *Henry Ossawa
Tanner: American Artist* (Chicago, University of Chicago Press, 1969), 27, 32–33, 35, 40;
*Journal of the 19th Session and 18th Quadrennial Session of the General Conference of the
African Methodist Episcopal Church in the World* held in Bethel Church, Indianapolis, Ind.,
May 7, 1888, 63, 68; Dewey Mosby, Darrell Sewell, and Rae Alexander-Minter, *Henry Ossawa
Tanner* (New York, Rizzoli, [Philadelphia Museum of Art], 1992), 120.
[36] Ibid., 48.

Figure 4.1 Henry O. Tanner, portrait by Thomas Eakins (1844–1916), c. 1897, oil canvas, 24 5/8 × 20 1/8 in The Hyde Collection, Glens Falls, New York, The Hyde Collection Trust, 1971.16. Photograph by Joseph Levy

millennialism, also pressured them to revisit the meaning of their Methodism. They were proud of their inclusion in the First Oecumenical Conference on Methodism in 1881 in London, England. At this international gathering and at subsequent decennial meetings in 1891, 1901, and 1911, AME delegates in numerous public addresses expressed their fealty to Methodist belief and doctrine, and declared that their denomination was a thoroughly Wesleyan religious body. Bishop John M. Brown, for example, said AMEs had "the fire of enthusiasm that has fired up and stirred up other branches of the Methodist family for the salvation of the world." Additionally, they had bishops, class meetings, love feasts, and other aspects of polity and practice that had "given Methodism such grand success [through] the Spirit of our evangelistic efforts."[37]

Anyone visiting AME annual conferences could hardly miss the fervent renditions of "the old time Methodist hymns" whose lyrics inspired these spiritually uplifting services. Bishop Turner, who prided himself as a hymnologist, made certain that worship services always included Wesleyan selections when he was presiding in Georgia. The blend of Wesleyan hymnody and idiomatic black spirituality was witnessed, for example, at the 1898 North

[37] Ibid., 37–38.

Georgia Annual Conference where the church at Madison, Georgia, "was packed with people far and near." After a spiritually moving sermon was preached on "Wonderful Things," the sanctuary resounded with shouts of "amens" and "hallelujahs." The invitation to Christian discipleship was then extended to sinners, and "several fell at the altar begging for mercy." A preacher then "besought high heaven for mercy and grace for perishing sinners." The annual conference, said one observer, was a revival scene. An official from the Women's Home and Foreign Missionary Society sang "Some Mother's Child," which "bathed the congregation in tears and the old Methodistic fire evidently blazed in earnest upon the altar of our hearts. It was a Pentecostal scene" as "Bishop Turner, fired by his 'old time fire,' marched to the altar singing 'Come Sinners to the Gospel Feast,'" a familiar Wesleyan hymn. One person came and received salvation as Methodist lyrics climaxed in this outpouring of black Wesleyan spirituality.[38]

These marks of Methodism, though a part of normative black religious belief and practice, scarcely addressed the insuperable challenges confronting AME social holiness. It remained true that the denominational ethos that tied personal renewal to the transformation of their surrounding social environment was still operative in the late nineteenth and early twentieth centuries. Concern about an emerging Jim Crow regime in the American South and the European "scramble" in Africa energized these perspectives. At the same time, as Turner asserted, the tenets of Methodism required a connection to black religious identity as expressed in Ethiopian millennialism. Hence, Turner told the 1899 Georgia Annual Conference "I am a race man. Before I was a Methodist I was a Negro, and if the Methodist Church gets in the way of my loyalty to my race, then away with the Methodist Church."[39]

Turner's observations, though intemperate, tried to clarify how AMEs should envisage the insuperable issues associated with white hegemony. African Methodist worship with its creative blend of Wesleyan belief and hymnody and black religious idioms only partially represented AME mission and ministry. Actually, Turner and other AMEs affirmed the synergy that existed within their church's Wesleyan and black identity. Ethiopian millennialism and Methodist social holiness mobilized critiques of white supremacy and invigorated an AME determination to defend darker peoples on both sides of the Atlantic. AME theology, therefore, consisted of three

---

[38] Ibid., 57–58, 60.   [39] Ibid., 49.

interactive components including adherence to traditional theology, Ethiopian millennialism, and Methodist belief and practice.

Strands of anti-modernism drawn from Embry's traditional theology were reflected in the views of some AME clergy. Bishop Evans Tyree eschewed the new biblical criticism that Steward embraced. Tyree, a former slave, said "I represent a people of simple faith-people that believe in God. They believe the Bible and all it says. We do not doubt any part of it." Moreover, Tyree, a graduate of Meharry Medical College, noted "we believe that it is dangerous to tamper with the Holy Scriptures." Historian David Wills had in mind the perspectives of such scholars as Embry and Tyree when he observed "a steady shift toward conservatism" in AME theology. There was no successor to Steward, Tanner, and Turner, he said, to discuss theology and blackness with the same intellectual audacity as these theological stalwarts. Nonetheless, adherence to traditional theology, leavened by AME belief, blended with Ethiopian millennialism and Wesleyan social consciousness. A protective transatlantic reach to darker peoples and a search for strategies to transform oppressive societies also took AMEs beyond their traditional beliefs to test other ideologies aimed at black advancement.[40]

DIVERSE STRATEGIES TO FIGHT WHITE HEGEMONY

To oppose powerful nation-states active in creating and enforcing impregnable structures of segregation and subordination for darker peoples presented insuperable challenges to African Methodism. Both the United States and South Africa, the principal loci of racially oppressive systems, became major venues of denominational development. Therefore, clergy and laity devised a range of strategies to oppose, undermine, and circumvent oppressive policies aimed at black subjugation on both sides of the Atlantic. Between 1880 and 1916, legalized segregation, especially in the American South, and policies of separation and subordination in South Africa crystallized into hardened structures of discrimination designed for a racial caste system.

After the withdrawal of federal troops from the former Confederacy, white Redeemers moved to oust ex-slaves from politics and to "rig" the agricultural system to fix them in a condition as near to slavery as was legally feasible. Violence, especially from vigilante groups such as the Ku Klux Klan, intimidated and killed blacks. Lynching and other acts of barbarism showed

---

[40] Ibid., 39–40; Miller, *Elevating the Race*, 68–69.

the inhumanity that the South's racial regime regularly visited upon African Americans. Southern states, starting with Mississippi in 1890 and South Carolina in 1895, used understanding clauses, grandfather provisos, and poll taxes to restrict black suffrage. The Supreme Court in 1896 in *Plessy v. Ferguson* established the doctrine of "separate but equal" that permitted legalized segregation against blacks in every facet of their civic and social relations. The crop lien system reduced them to peonage and forced them into economic subservience to landowning whites.

This powerful tide of white supremacy affecting American society compelled blacks to explore diverse methods either to undermine or circumvent the emerging Jim Crow regime. Some AMEs, already proud of their institutional independence and their property holdings, believed their influence would improve the black condition. Benjamin F. Lee, soon to be a bishop, said in 1890 that the AME Church "has been to the Negro the rising of a new sun." He described the denomination as "infusing new hope into the heart of the Afro-American, developing influence into his heart, and patience and courage into his every movement." He added that "the erection of churches and parsonages, school houses and colleges all over the land has given assurance to those who doubt the ability of the Negro to organize and conduct business pertaining to materiality. Six million dollars worth of property settle this doubt, while the manly march of eleven bishops directly and settling nearly 3,000 churches must convince the most skeptical that governing ability is not wanting in the Negro American."[41]

Lee's commentary reflected what most AMEs said about the institutional significance of their denomination and its role as a protector of darker peoples. His perspective also mirrored the conclusion of one scholar, who argued that African Americans in the late nineteenth and early twentieth centuries deployed a strategy of institutional development, racial solidarity, and a deemphasis upon protest in favor of economic advancement as the best response to the rise of Jim Crow. Historian August Meier observed "by the last decade of the century it was clear that the main themes in Negro thinking on the race problem were that for the most part Negroes must work out their own salvation in a hostile environment and that, furthermore, they must be united in their efforts at racial elevation." Hence, their "emphasis" would be "self-help and solidarity" tied to an "economic approach." Booker T. Washington embodied these ideas and methodologies. Building Tuskegee

[41] B. F. Lee, "Introduction" in Benjamin W. Arnett (ed.), *Proceedings of the Quarto-Centennial Conference of the African M. E. Church of South Carolina at Charleston, S. C., May 15–17, 1889* (n.p., 1890), 6–8.

Institute from the ground up in rural Alabama starting in 1881, delivering his classic and accommodationist Atlanta Exposition Address in 1895, and founding the National Negro Business League in 1900 set the example and became platforms of influence for his brand of self-help and acceptance of the racial realities of a segregated South.[42]

Although blacks increasingly adhered to strategies of internal development, the tradition of protest and agitation, inherited from antebellum abolitionists, retained influential practitioners. The pervasive enactment of segregation statues, the epidemic of lynching, and widespread disenfranchisement reminded black leaders, both national and local, that these oppressive practices demanded loud and defiant responses. Some of them believed that Washington's racial conservatism signaled that blacks too easily acquiesced to racial subordination. To counter this impression the Afro-American Council in the 1890s branded itself as a civil rights organization. But W. E. B. Du Bois, William Monroe Trotter, and other "radicals" who formed the Niagara Movement in 1905 advocated unequivocal protest and agitation as their raison d'être. This initiative inspired in 1910 the founding of the National Association for the Advancement of Colored People (NAACP).

Washington became greatly familiar to AMEs. Bishop Tanner, like Washington, supported industrial education and believed blacks should aspire to land and business ownership. That Washington in 1891 hired his daughter, Halle Tanner Dillon, as Tuskegee's campus physician solidified their relationship. Washington persuaded a black Montgomery doctor to help her prepare for Alabama's state medical examination. Because "her sex and color will be against her," the bishop said he was deeply grateful for Washington's help. In 1894, Washington's article, "Taking Advantage of Our Disadvantages," was published in the *AME Church Review*. Though mindful of the racial prejudice that pervaded the South, Washington believed "every right of which we are now deprived can be secured through business development coupled with education and character." Blacks should "Get dollars. Get dollars!! And spend them wisely and effectively." Moreover, "there are one thousand places in the South where a colored man can take $600 and open a brickyard and in a few years grow independent, and when the colored man sells $10,000 worth of bricks to a white man and gets a mortgage on his house, this white man will not drive that Negro away from the polls." Without mentioning Washington's name, the 1900 General Conference

---

[42] August Meier, *Negro Thought in America, 1880–1915* (Ann Arbor, University of Michigan Press, 1963), 121.

responded to the ascendancy of Jim Crow, as did the Tuskegeean. A resolution declared that African Americans living in populous areas where they were subjected to discrimination in public places should "combine to furnish said accommodations for themselves." A commission was formed "to secure lands remote from any city, convenient for railroad transportation ... to erect an auditorium ... comfortable hotels to accommodate five thousand guests ... lay out a park, and plot a certain portion of ground to be sold for homes [and] to found and foster a community of prosperous colored people." Hence, AMEs were ready to hear Washington's address to the 1904 General Conference in Chicago. After his introduction, "the conference gave him a Chautauqua salute." The Tuskegeean praised the AME Church as "constructive and progressive." Moreover, his comments, wrote the conference secretary, pertained to "matters of vital interest to the race" and were "well-received." Bishop Abram Grant, a well-known Washington supporter, then called on all clergy and laity "who owned their homes to stand up" as a show of support for Washington's philosophy of self-help. "Almost the entire conference rose" and indicated to Washington that he had spoken to a friendly audience. Washington's strategy for racial uplift resonated with AMEs because Tuskegee reflected the same economic philosophy of self-help that Richard Allen pioneered in the Free African Society.[43]

AMEs also encountered the Washington program and persona through others whose views resembled those of the Alabama educator. William Hooper Councill, a founder of St. John AME Church in Huntsville, Alabama, in 1885, could have been mistaken for Washington himself. Born a slave in North Carolina and sold to a plantation in northern Alabama, he escaped to a Union army camp in Chattanooga. After the war, he attended an Alabama freedmen's school and attained additional training through

[43] William Seraille, *Fire in His Heart: Bishop Benjamin Tucker Tanner and the AME Church* (Knoxville, University of Tennessee Press, 1998), 83; Halle Tanner Dillon to Booker T. Washington, August 20, 1891; Benjamin Tucker Tanner to Booker T. Washington, August 20, 1891; Halle Tanner Dillon to Booker T. Washington, August 23, 1891, in Louis R. Harlan (ed.), *The Booker T. Washington Papers*, Vol. 3, 1889–1895 (Urbana, University of Illinois Press, 1974), 164–167; Booker T. Washington, "Taking Advantage of Our Disadvantages," *AME Church Review*, Vol. 10 (April 1894), 478–483, cited in Harlan (ed.), *The Booker T. Washington Papers*, Vol. 3, 409–411; *Journal of the Twenty-First Quadrennial Session of the General Conference of the African M. E. Church* held in the Auditorium, Columbus, OH, May 7–25, 1900 (Philadelphia, PA, AME Book Concern, 1900), 266–267; *Journal of the Twenty-Second Session of the General Conference of the African M. E. Church* held in Quinn Chapel AME Church, Chicago, Illinois, May 2–27, 1904 (Nashville, AME Sunday School Union, 1905), 106.

personal tutorials. Despite Ku Klux Klan threats, he operated schools in two Alabama counties. As a Republican operative and officeholder and as an intermittent ally of the Democrats, Councill leveraged his influence to become in 1875 the principal of the State Normal and Industrial School at Huntsville. His school, renamed Alabama State Agricultural and Mechanical College for Negroes, predated the rival Tuskegee Institute and gave him a platform for his own brand of racial accommodationism that exceeded Washington's deference to white authority.[44]

W. H. Mixon, the author of Alabama's AME history, admired Councill and included laudatory newspaper reports about him in his 1902 chronicle of the state's AME history. Councill said that God made no superior races and he refused to any general denunciation of all southern whites. Furthermore, he called for racial justice and pleaded, "give the black man a chance." Nonetheless, fellow blacks were astonished that Councill rationalized proposed educational restrictions on voters despite their discriminatory effect upon African Americans. Mixon seemed unaffected, however, by Councill's racially obsequious attitudes because of his role in leading and sustaining Alabama Agricultural & Mechanical.[45]

Mixon had similar sentiments about Washington, whom he met through Bishop Grant. Mixon visited Tuskegee as an AME representative at various events. Moreover, Mixon, who owned W. H. Mixon & Company: Dealers in Books and Stationery, embodied the entrepreneurial qualities that the Tuskegeean promoted among African Americans. Additionally, Bishop Grant, the prelate of Alabama from 1892 to 1896, had been a Washington supporter even before he catapulted to national prominence. He and Bishop Wesley J. Gaines testified alongside Washington before the US House of Representatives Appropriations Committee in favor of funding for the Cotton States and International Exposition in Atlanta in 1895.[46]

Grant's association with Washington continued despite his reassignment to the Midwest. Both men opposed African emigration, a position that put Grant at loggerheads with Turner. A Washington protégé told him in 1899 that an address Grant delivered "against emigration was superb." He added that Grant "will stop over in Atlanta" and "hit Bishop Turner's African emigration scheme [with] a whack." Grant, he said, "will kill it

[44] John David Smith, "William Hooper Councill," in Henry Louis Gates, Jr. and Evelyn Brooks Higginbotham (eds.), *African American National Biography*, Vol. 2 (New York, Oxford University Press, 2008), 448–449.

[45] Mixon, *History of the African Methodist Episcopal Church in Alabama*, 167.

[46] Dennis C. Dickerson, *Religion, Race, and Region: Research Notes on AME Church History* (Nashville, TN, AME Sunday School Union, 1995), 100–101.

wherever he speaks." Grant also lobbied Washington to persuade President Theodore Roosevelt to appoint William T. Vernon as Registrar of the Treasury. Vernon, later a bishop and president of the AME-supported Western University in Quindaro, Kansas, was a minister in Grant's episcopal district. Additionally, Grant cooperated with Washington's efforts to silence critics by controlling black newspapers. In 1905, for example, he told the Tuskegeean that the *Indianapolis Freeman* was for sale. Grant suggested that he, Washington, and two others, including H. T. Kealing, the editor of the *AME Church Review*, should each contribute to buying the newspaper.[47]

Other AMEs held Washington in high esteem, but would not eschew protest for black civil rights. Archibald J. Carey, Sr., the pastor at Quinn Chapel in Chicago and host to the 1904 General Conference, told two AME audiences that he supported the Tuskegeean and pledged to defend him against his Chicago critics. Hence, he opened his church to a meeting of Washington's National Business League. Nonetheless, Carey believed that protest was a needed strategy for black advancement. When the Illinois legislature in 1913 considered the passage of a Jim Crow bill, Carey, now pastor at the Institutional Church in Chicago, offered it as a venue to denounce the proposal. Other AMEs saw deficiencies in Washington's accommodationism and advocated direct confrontations against Jim Crow practices. Ida B. Wells-Barnett, who was a member of Bethel Church in Chicago in the 1890s, focused her energies on the scourge of lynching. Her investigations and several publications brought national and international attention to this racial crime. As a well-known journalist, women's club organizer, and protest advocate, her leadership stood in sharp contrast to the less confrontational stance of the Tuskegeean.[48]

Wells-Barnett, even after she forsook Bethel Church to join a black Presbyterian congregation, greatly admired Reverdy C. Ransom. She had cooperated with him in several protest activities in Cleveland and Chicago and shared his unfavorable views about Washington. More than any AME, Ransom, later a bishop, unequivocally rejected Washington's racial ideology.

[47] Robert Lloyd Smith to Booker T. Washington, October 12, 1899, in Louis R. Harlan (ed.), *The Booker T. Washington Papers*, Vol. 5, 1899–1900 (Urbana, University of Illinois Press, 1976), 229–230; Abram Grant to Booker T. Washington, November 1, 1905 in Louis R. Harlan (ed.), *The Booker T. Washington Papers*, Vol. 8, 1904–1906 (Urbana, University of Illinois Press, 1979), 244–245, 435.

[48] Dennis C. Dickerson, *African American Preachers and Politics: The Careys of Chicago* (Jackson, University Press of Mississippi, 2010), 36–37; Paula Giddings, *Ida: A Sword among Lions: Ida B. Wells and the Campaign against Lynching* (New York, Amistad, 2008), 172–174, 346–348, 407–408.

He noted there were leaders who said the African American "should accept in silence the denial of his political rights" and that he should "buy land and save money, but have no voice as to how the money he has accumulated is to be expended through taxation and the various forms of public improvement." In contrast, "there are others who believe that the Negro owes this nation no apology for his presence in the United States, that he should not yield one syllable of his title to American citizenship; that he should refuse to be assigned to an inferior plane by his fellow-countrymen."[49]

Ransom explicitly and directly criticized Washington when he declared:

> The Negro was told, if he would eschew politics, cease agitating for his rights, refrain from protesting and complaining against restrictions placed upon him, and devote himself to industry, through an industrial education in agriculture and the trades, he would be able to allay prejudice against him on account of color, because of his usefulness to the community in which he must reside. Dr. Booker T. Washington . . . is the chief apostle of this doctrine.[50]

These perspectives drew Ransom to like-minded critics of Washington who joined Du Bois and Trotter's Niagara Movement. At its 1906 meeting at Harper's Ferry, West Virginia, the site of John Brown's aborted raid on a federal arsenal to steal weapons to arm slaves, Ransom spoke on "The Spirit of John Brown." He denounced black leaders who have "no word of protest or condemnation for those who visit upon us all manner of fiendish and inhuman indignities" especially through the crime of lynching. While Washington's group pursued "money and property, the Niagara leadership does not believe in bartering its manhood for the sake of gain."[51]

Some AMEs broke conventional boundaries of racial discourse and introduced socialism as a solution to capitalist-based hegemony. Ransom expressed sympathy for socialism because it "places its chief value upon man." He noted that socialism motivated the "Carpenter of Nazareth" who esteemed humankind over "riches." Ransom added that socialism said "the rights of man are more sacred than the rights of property" and "the only sacred thing on earth is a human being." Blacks would benefit from socialism because this economic system safeguarded the interests of workers, and "the American Negro belongs almost wholly to the proletarian or industrial class." George W. Slater, an AME pastor in Iowa, promoted socialism by

---

[49] Giddings, *Ida*, 335, 378, 385–386; Reverdy C. Ransom, *The Spirit of Freedom and Justice: Orations and Speeches* (Nashville, TN, AME Sunday School Union, 1926), 12–13.

[50] Ransom, *The Spirit of Freedom and Justice*, 85.   [51] Ibid., 23.

publishing articles in socialist newspapers, delivering sermons, and selling his pamphlet "Blackmen Strike for Liberty." Booker T. Washington, he said, erred in his emphasis on industrial education, because whites would always "find an equal and sometimes superior competitor in the black man." Socialism was the better solution because "it stands for the collective owner-ship of the land and means of production by all the people for the good of all the people."[52]

Daring declarations about socialism had a marginal impact upon racial discourse among AMEs. The ideological binary between Washington accommodationism and Du Boisan agitation influenced what AMEs thought about the best method to achieve African American advancement. Washing-ton's perceived surrender to Jim Crow realities seemingly reaped an unusual virulence of racial violence perpetrated against blacks through the persist-ence of lynching and riots against persons and property in Atlanta, Georgia, in 1906 and Springfield, Illinois, in 1908. Moreover, Washington's well-known support of Theodore Roosevelt did nothing to prevent the president in 1906 from dishonorably discharging a unit of 167 black Buffalo soldiers for an alleged raid aimed at racist whites in Brownsville, Texas. In 1909, the launch of the NAACP, a derivative organization of the Niagara Movement, signaled a resurgence of black civil rights agitation. Du Bois, the editor of the group's influential journal, *The Crisis*, hastened Washington's declension as the unchallenged leader of African Americans.

In paying deference to this "great body," Washington expressed gratitude to the 1912 General Conference because AMEs had allowed him to speak to "several successive sessions" of their quadrennial conference. In noting the wide influence of "Negro bishops and Negro ministers," he pleaded with them to convince blacks to remain in rural areas where "the Negro ... is at his best in body, mind, and soul." Because the African American "follows the church building," then AMEs should "help to keep him in the land where he has a chance to grow a strong, healthy body and be away from the tempta-tions and complexities of large city life." He conceded that if a city church had "a strong, intelligent minister," then "the Negro [would] be tempted to leave the country and migrate to the city."[53]

[52] Reverdy C. Ransom, "The Negro and Socialism"; Philip S. Foner, "Articles of Reverend George W. Slater, Jr. Introduction"; George W. Slater, "Booker T. Washington's Error," in Philip S. Foner (ed.), *Black Socialist Preacher* (San Francisco, CA, Synthesis Publications, 1983), 286, 293–294, 303.

[53] *Journal of the Twenty-Fourth Quadrennial Session of the General Conference of the African Methodist Episcopal Church* held in Allen Chapel African M. E. Church, Kansas City, Missouri, May 5–23, 1912 (Nashville, TN, AME Sunday School Union, 1912), 371–372.

Despite the courtesies extended to Washington at the 1912 meeting, this same General Conference expressed views with greater congruence with the perspectives of Du Bois and Ransom than with those of the Tuskegeean. The bishops in their episcopal address acknowledged that if blacks were in a hurry to solve racial problems, then "let us hurry in the way of better schools, better religion, better homes, and more landowners." At the same time they said blacks had the right "to complain of their treatment in the lower courts," and they had a right to protest at discrimination in public transportation, especially from "ticket sellers and car conductors." Another committee said AMEs "cannot be indifferent . . . to the disenfranchisement of our race in the Southern States and the growing attacks upon our civil rights in every section of the country." The declaration continued by saying "we cannot ignore the injustice and discrimination done to our race in the Southern 'Jim Crow' laws, in mob violence, peonage, and numerous other discriminatory practices against the Negro citizens everywhere to exert themselves like men, against those who would rob us of our manhood rights and the priceless privilege of our citizenship." Notwithstanding this robust discourse about the racial destiny of African Americans, AMEs, like thousands of other blacks, lamented Washington's death in 1915. They heralded his multifaceted leadership in economic development and black institution-building. Most agreed with Mixon of Alabama who said that the Tuskegeean achieved "more for God and humanity than any" other of his contemporaries.[54]

Washington's 1912 General Conference speech also missed the mood of an AME leadership that possessed increased pride in its growing urban congregations in Chicago, Pittsburgh, and other industrial centers. Moreover, Ransom and such younger clergy as Richard R. Wright, Jr. already pioneered social gospel ministries that delivered a range of social and employment services to urban populations. These pastors were ascendant while such Washington allies as Bishop Grant and Bishop Gaines, both former slaves like the Tuskegeean, had died in 1911 and 1912 respectively. Ransom and Wright, drawing from the social gospel principles of Washington Gladden, Walter Rauschenbusch, and Graham Taylor, implemented pastoral strategies in practical Christianity for blacks who were newly arrived in Chicago. They believed that churches should focus as much on preaching as on worker advocacy for men, kindergartens and day care for children, and

[54] *Journal of the Twenty-Fourth . . . Session of the General Conference*, 1912, 84–85, 216; Kenneth M. Hamilton, *Booker T. Washington in American Memory* (Urbana, University of Illinois Press, 2017), 28. Also see Hamilton, *Booker T. Washington*, 21, 133–134, 153, 165, 184.

vocational training for women. With the permission of his bishop to relinquish his pastorate at Bethel, Chicago, Ransom founded the Institutional
Church and Social Settlement. With funds, disbursed by the 1900 General
Conference, he purchased the spacious Rail Road Chapel to house a congregation and numerous programs available "all day every day" to the city's
rapidly growing black population. Ransom told the 1904 General Conference
that Institutional's "day nursery cares for the children of mothers who are
compelled to go from home to work by the day" and "its gymnasium teaches
each child the value of a healthy and well developed body as well as a trained
mind." Moreover, "the employment bureau is securing work for the
unemployed." Wright, an AME student at the divinity school at the University of Chicago, was apprenticed at the Institutional Church. "My duties," he
recalled, "were to conduct the opening services of the religious worship on
Sunday nights, to sponsor a boys' club and to teach a girls' Sunday School
class." Later, his bishop assigned him to Trinity Mission, "a store-front
church." Trinity's location in a poor community populated with saloons
and houses of prostitution stirred Wright's social gospel consciousness. He
started a "community day nursery" for working mothers, a reading room,
and lectures on health education with a volunteer physician. "This pastorate
completely shifted my interest," he recollected, "from the theological to the
sociological point of view." He added that "the church must devote more
time to the social without of course neglecting the theological."[55]

The racial ideology of African Americans between 1880 and 1916, though
ranging from Washington's accommodationism and Du Bois' agitation,
aimed at restricting the impact of Jim Crow upon the black population. This
vigorous discourse involved AMEs whose theology included Ethiopian millennialism, which posited a glorious black past that presaged an equally
splendid destiny for darker peoples. Notwithstanding present adversities,
said a Wilberforce commentator in 1913, "the fundamental things are still
ours – the Home, the School, and the Church, and with these ... we are
surely justified in believing, on the ground of the achievements of these few
years of freedom, that we shall be able to remove every obstacle now athwart
the path of our progress." This same Ohio observer also declared that blacks,

[55] Wright, *The Bishops of the African Methodist Episcopal Church*, 178, 192; Reverdy
C. Ransom, *First Quadrennial Report of the Pastor and Warden of the Institutional Church
and Social Settlement to the Twenty-Second Session of the General Conference and to the
Connectional Trustees of the African Methodist Episcopal Church convened at Quinn Chapel,
Chicago, Illinois, May 1904* (n.p., n.d.), 3–4, 6; Ransom, *The Pilgrimage of Harriet Ransom's
Son*, 103–114; Richard R. Wright, Jr., *Eighty-Seven Years behind the Black Curtain* (Phila-
delphia, PA, Rare Book Company,1965), 94, 100, 104–105, 108–109, 114.

like "the descendants of Abraham ... have a mission to fulfill in this world [that is no] less sacred." He concluded "the past may belong to other races, but by the grace of God, the future is ours." AMEs would construct that future either through economic development or civil rights agitation. Whether through Washington's National Negro Business League or Du Bois' Niagara Movement, AMEs helped to energize both strategies, while developing their denomination as an influential institutional force active in realizing a future of freedom for darker peoples.[56]

In South Africa, where another version of Jim Crow or coerced segregation emerged at the same time as in the United States, an AME response was required. Though less developed, South African churches, within a dozen years after their merger with the AMEs, increased to three annual conferences. These jurisdictions grew alongside racially separate structures established through a unitary political system that coalesced in 1910. The British and the Afrikaners shared power within a racial hierarchy that subjugated the indigenous black population. These settler whites in 1913, for example, enacted the Native Land Act that segregated blacks into residential reserves, barred them from a range of public accommodations, and excluded them from the civic sphere. One historian, George M. Fredrickson, noted that these statutes curtailed "the power and privileges of the African majority to such an extent that the preservation of white minority rule would be absolutely assured."[57]

Fredrickson suggested that the term "segregation" may have been imported into South Africa from the American South. Nonetheless, the two systems differed in that blacks in South Africa resided exclusively in reserves and were barred from such economic arrangements as sharecropping in which their African American counterparts were overwhelmingly represented. Black laborers in South Africa could not reside on white-owned lands, but worked in cities as "migrant workers or provisional sojourners."

African Americans, however, both lived and worked in cities and could own or rent property if they had the resources. Despite these differences, blacks on both sides of the Atlantic were relegated to a racial caste system in which white economic and political privileges were aggressively preserved. The principal issue for AMEs in South Africa, as for blacks in the United States, lay in what strategies would allay or nullify the effects of impregnable

---

[56] *Journal of the Twenty-Fourth ... Session of the General Conference*, 1912, 84–85, 216.

[57] *Journal of Proceedings of the Eighty-Third Session of the Ohio Annual Conference of the African M. E. Church* held in St. Paul AME Church, Zanesville, Ohio, September 24–28, 1913 (Nashville, TN, AME Sunday School Union, 1913), 18–19.

structures of segregation designed to strip from them their citizenship and humanity.[58] Unfortunately, AMEs encountered hostile South African authorities that were suspicious of their institutional independence and possible insurgency. In these respects the ethos of Wesleyan social holiness embedded in the church's organizational DNA, though diffused in the United States through multiple racial advancement strategies, seemed a present threat in South Africa.

A report to the 1908 General Conference said that for six or seven years South Africans perceived "our Church with suspicion, as disseminators of disloyal and pernicious doctrines such as would cause disruption and stir insurrection against the Government, on the part of the natives." Because of the active opposition, the Council of Bishops sent Bishop William B. Derrick in 1906 to preside in the jurisdiction. That Derrick, unlike his two predecessors, was allowed to visit congregations in the Transvaal and the Orange Free State showed a preoccupation with practical education rather than political agitation. This strategy, which paralleled what Washington and some of his AME followers espoused in the United States, put at ease white South Africans who feared the presence of this proud and autonomous black religious body. Moreover, Derrick's focus on indigenous leaders who led in building schools demonstrated where AME energies would be directed.[59]

Derrick, despite deep involvements in politics, extolled black progress in both the economic and educational spheres. With a Washingtonian tone he told the 1905 Pittsburgh Annual Conference that African Americans, since slavery, had contributed $13 million for their education and accumulated "$995 million of property during the few short years of citizenship." He declared that "industry and activity are therefore essential to our progress as a people." Pittsburgh AMEs agreed that blacks were participants and beneficiaries from the nation's industrial advance. "Our race," they said, "has taken part in this, so that the great Wizard of Tuskegee has clasped hands with Wilberforce, Morris Brown, and Kittrell, and our various industrial schools, training our young men and women to higher usefulness along these lines." These perspectives framed Derrick's episcopal leadership in South Africa, where his educational emphasis assured whites that his activities were essentially benign.[60]

[58] George M. Fredrickson, *White Supremacy: A Comparative Study in American and South African History* (New York, Oxford University Press, 1981), 239–240.
[59] Ibid., 241–242.
[60] *Journal of the Twenty-Third Quadrennial Session of the General Conference of the African Methodist Episcopal Church* held in St. John AME Church, Norfolk, Virginia, May 4–21, 1908 (Nashville, AME Sunday School Union, 1908), 68; *The Biennial Convention and Thirty-*

Derrick, during two years, helped bring solvency to three schools and to position two of them for consolidation. Mainly through cooperation with indigenous leadership and the WPMMS, Derrick's Washingtonian posture defused some of the white opposition to AMEs in South Africa. An insolvent Bethel Institute in Cape Town, for example, was refinanced and drew an $800 annual allocation from the WPMMS. Marshall Maxeke and his wife, Charlotte Manye, who founded Wilberforce Institute in Transvaal, benefited from a tribal chief who donated a building worth $3,000. Another black South African, James Yapi Tantsi, was like Manye a graduate of Wilberforce University. He learned brick making and drew upon this skill to build another school named the Lillian Derrick School, in honor of the bishop's wife and onetime WPMMS president. Derrick's successor, J. Albert Johnson, later merged the Wilberforce and Derrick schools.[61]

The focus on education did not mean inattention to African rights. The best organized challenge to white political domination came from the African National Congress (ANC). Founded in 1912 with John L. Dube as its first president, the ANC, an expression of black consciousness, opposed the oppressive Native Land Act. There were several protest groups that predated the ANC, but most did not last. The group gave attention to the increasingly proletarianized black labor force and their raw exploitation by white political and economic interests. The ANC's mostly educated leadership class supported black labor strikes in 1913 and 1914 and spoke out against color restrictions in employment.[62]

South African AMEs, even those who endorsed Derrick's singular emphasis on education, had supported several organizations involved in native affairs and nationalist initiatives. In 1902, Charlotte Manye, for example, represented the Transvaal on the South African Native Commission and later joined the Transvaal Native Vigilance Association, a largely AME group. These political involvements led to her affiliation with the militant Native and Coloured Women's Association that in 1913 opposed laws that required blacks to carry passes in Bloemfontein. Later, she belonged to the ANC and became a founding member of the Bantu

Fifth Anniversary of the Women's Parent Mite Missionary Society, St. John AME Church, Cleveland, Ohio, November 11 to 14, 1909 (Philadelphia, PA, AME Book Concern, 1909), 39.
[61] *Journal of Proceedings of the Thirty-Eighth Session of the Pittsburgh Annual Conference of the African Methodist Episcopal Church* held in Bethel AME Church, Wilkes-Barre, PA, October 4–9, 1905 (n.p., Publishing Committee: C. J. Powell, D. S. Bentley, C. M. Tanner, Publishing Committee, 1905), 16, 45.
[62] *Journal of Proceedings of the Twenty-Third Quadrennial Session of the General Conference, 1908*, 68; *Biennial Convention and Thirty-Fifth Anniversary of the WPMMS, 1909*, 39.

Women's National League. Her husband, Marshall Maxeke, and James Tantsi, both educators on whom Derrick depended, attended the founding conference of the South African National Congress, an ANC forerunner. Selby Msimang and James Ngojo were AMEs whom one scholar described as ANC "radicals." Another ANC leader, Pixley Seme, received his education in the United States with AME assistance. While education was Derrick's strategy to minimize conflict with hostile white authorities, Manye and other advocates of education also aimed at political empowerment for their country's disenfranchised black proletariat.[63]

Whether in America or Africa, AMEs could not avoid the erection of segregated structures in the American South and in South Africa. Hence, their strategies of accommodation and protest each showed resistance to the stratified social order that triumphal whites determined to impose upon blacks. Whatever methodology that African Americans and Africans pursued to fight white supremacy invigorated their institutions and organizations and enabled them to undergird their activism. Therefore, AMEs, through their denominational infrastructure and through participation in various betterment and nationalist groups, mobilized educational, economic, and nationalist initiatives to attack segregation on both sides of the Atlantic.

MAINTAINING AN ATLANTIC PRESENCE

Developing structures within African Methodism aimed at servicing a growing pan-African constituency. There was an increased intensity in the church's consciousness of its transoceanic possibilities. Several bishops and delegates at the 1884 General Conference supported home missions efforts, but lamented their weak support for the African work. They also called for stepped-up assistance to Haiti and Santo Domingo.

The "foreign work," said Bishop William F. Dickerson, "has not accomplished all that we could desire." Insufficient funds did not provide "the means to carry forward the work as vigorously as necessary." Therefore, in Africa there was only a fragile foundation on which to build an AME presence. S. F. Flegler, who initiated the mission in Liberia, returned to the United States, and from 1881 "the work has been cared for by local brethren." Because European nations were colonizing Africa, Dickerson suggested "a vigorous, powerful forward movement" that would resemble a "Militant Church." He proposed "to plant firmly the banner of the African Methodist

---

[63] Peter Limb, *The ANC's Early Years: Nation, Class, and Place in South Africa before 1940* (Pretoria, Unisa Press, 2010), 76–77, 139, 143.

Episcopal Church upon the ramparts of the forts of the enemy [Europeans] on the shores and in the heart of Africa."[64]

The Congo, however, was a major worry. The Belgians and other European nations, beginning in 1884, colonized and ruthlessly exploited its peoples and natural resources. Bishop Thomas M. D. Ward, in the 1888 episcopal address, said that "the opening of the valley of the Congo brings to us increased responsibilities as well as enlarged opportunities." Ward regretted that Africa was being stolen through the barter of liquor:

> The rum fiend has already preceded us; Christian nations are its shippers. Shall we stand unmoved amid this moral desolation and fold our arms and moaningly say we are powerless, and thus permit the rum power to open wider the gates of hell? We must appeal to all races and classes of men to aid us in bruising this great red dragon. We must not halt, limp nor wince on this great theme; but write it in our book of laws, record it on our altars, send it out like a trumpet blast from our pulpits, *AFRICA must be Redeemed.*

This challenge required the same daring, noted Ward, as what "was shown by our men in the South" after the Civil War. The AMEs were a pan-African religious body needed as much in the Carolinas as in the Congo.[65]

Bishop Dickerson noted in 1884, however, that Haiti had received "more of our direct attention, and has shared more largely in our prayers and offerings than our work in Africa." Because Catholicism had biased Haitians with erroneous doctrines, the bishop said, AMEs needed to assist Charles and Mary Ella Mossell in this French-speaking black republic. His task was to preach to the adults while she taught the children in religious and secular subjects. It was recommended that her school at Port-au-Prince should be placed under "the immediate care" of the AME educational bureau. Santo Domingo, the former possession of Spain and the Spanish- speaking neighbor of Haiti, benefited from the United States Consul, the Reverend H. C. C. Astwood, who was an AME minister. The bishops commended him for "organizing and strengthening" African Methodism and for recruiting three preachers. These missionaries, especially "one of our Haytien students" worked "to bring the Gospel in all its fullness and power [to] the Dominican people." A church was planted in Barahona and in the capital, Santo Domingo City, where the congregation was outgrowing its "little chapel."[66]

[64] Ibid., 76, 78, 121; Campbell, *Songs of Zion*, 151.
[65] *Journal of the 18th Session ... of the General Conference, 1884*, 106.
[66] *Journal of the 19th Session ... of the General Conference, 1888*, 270.

Bishop Payne and a few others presented a dissenting view about AMEs acting on their pan-African consciousness. It was simply too expensive. He viewed the impending and unwise reunion with the BME Church as the right opportunity to illustrate his point. Existing AME commitments to its numerous schools, publishing plants and publications, and outreach to Africa and Haiti precluded additional obligations to "the vast British Empire" that the BMEs planned to evangelize. If the AMEs merged with their Canadian counterparts, African Methodism would have "for its field" global territories filled with "three hundred millions of men ... of every hue and color [and] of all ranks and conditions" throughout "Southern Africa, Southern Asia, and the great Islands of the Ocean." Payne opposed the AME Church turning "her back upon her own work at home and abroad to fritter away thousands of dollars upon the BME Church and the millions of inhabitants in its claimed territories.[67]

Payne's perspective, however, was a minority view. AMEs approved reunion and the BMEs, though split, also supported it. One BME from St. Thomas in the Virgin Islands, for example, was buoyed by the prospects "for men to go to foreign fields and give wings to the gospel and let it spread over the whole world." He also said that "this great purpose could be better effected after the consolidation of the two churches." When Bishop Disney for the first time presided in Indianapolis at the 1888 General Conference, he declared the AME Church as "the leading organization of colored men in this country" and "the greatest Church connection of the dark races." Moreover, Disney's tenure as a BME bishop and indispensable advocate of reunion enabled African Methodism to realize the territorial ambitions of both bodies. Not only did Disney bring with him the Ontario, Nova Scotia, and Bermuda Annual Conferences, but additional jurisdictions in the Caribbean and South America. He laid foundations for AMEs to claim the St. Thomas Annual Conference, whose reach stretched across Santa Cruz, Crab Island, St. John, Puerto Rico, "and all the Windward Islands north of Barbados." Disney also brought into African Methodism the Demerara Annual Conference, which included British, French, and Dutch Guiana, and Trinidad and Barbados.[68]

AMEs, coming out of the 1888 General Conference, recalled that "the South, with five millions, was open to us during the war." Now, the bishops declared, "the islands, South America, Mexico, Central America and Africa,

[67] *Journal of the 18th Session ... of the General Conference, 1884*, 106–107, 118; *Journal of the 19th Session ... of the General Conference, 1888*, 196.
[68] *Journal of the 18th Session ... of the General Conference, 1884*, 197–207.

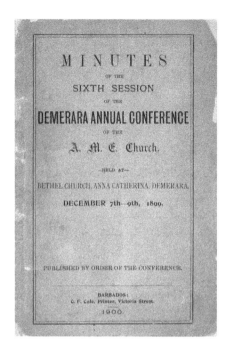

Figure 4.2 Front cover of the Demerara Annual Conference, 1890 (Author's private collection)

all and each is [an] inviting field." They added that "they are of the same blood and could soon be made to understand that their destiny was linked with ours." The AMEs "could do good work" in all of these territories, the bishops believed, "if we had the men and means." Toward that end the prelates recommended $3,000 annually to our African work," another $4,000 for the West Indies, $600 for the Indian Territory, and $800 for the Pacific work "so as to reach the thousands who are going there." These geographical ambitions aimed at fulfilling pan-African possibilities for full black freedom in multiple contexts of emancipation and post-emancipation and in colonial and postcolonial societies in which these diverse peoples struggled through their common heritage as slaves and victims of the slave trade.[69]

Moreover, Bishop Disney, coming from Canada, S. F. Flegler, a recent pioneer in Liberia, and the Mossells in Haiti, in crafting new geographical realities for their denomination, affected how AMEs envisaged themselves

[69] Ibid., 429–430; *Journal of the 19th Session . . . of the General Conference, 1888*, 40, 225–226.

and articulated their identity. Therefore, denominational rhetoric increasingly reflected a pan-African consciousness and acknowledged a growing AME Atlantic. For example, E. J. Gregg, the pastor of St. Stephen AME Church in Wilmington, North Carolina, in welcoming the 1896 General Conference, observed that "we can pray for the Queen ... welcome you, brethren from her Majesty's Dominion." Moreover, "we ask that the blessings of God may rest upon the Chief Magistrate of this nation," namely the President of the United States. He also declared that:

> We are exceedingly glad to welcome our brethren from the Fatherland, the land of hope-the home of the Negro; a land in which God has broken the shackles from the Negro. God will continue to raise that land [and] make it to prove the future land of the of the Negro, where he shall show his highest possibilities, where he will cease from being chased by murderers [and] where he will be recognized as a man. . .

Additionally, "we welcome you brethren from the Isles of the Sea, from our beloved Hayti, from our Bermuda, from all parts of the Caribbean [and] from Demarara. We welcome you as our brethren." Gregg showed that AMEs recognized their advance into the Atlantic and increasingly viewed African Methodism in this transoceanic context. Increasingly, Gregg's phraseology became a standard text in AME rhetoric.[70]

These patterns in AME expansion on both sides of the Atlantic were enabled by an infrastructure of annual conferences, church-wide agencies, and a heritage of pan-African interactions. In the late nineteenth century the buildup of new churches and conferences continued in the American South, extended through BME initiatives within the British Empire, and resuscitated out of earlier efforts in West Africa. W. H. Mixon in Alabama, J. Albert Johnson in Bermuda, and H. M. Steady in Sierra Leone showed in the 1880s and 1890s the breadth and diversity of the AME Atlantic and how the denomination's infrastructure helped in promoting simultaneous growth in disparate territories.

Though all three were born in the 1850s in different parts of the Atlantic World, and each was unfamiliar with each other's efforts, Mixon, Johnson, and Steady drew from the diversity of the African diaspora and helped to extend it into African Methodism. Winfield H. Mixon, for example, was born in Alabama in 1859 and became both the chronicler of AME history in his state and a participant in its steady growth during the final decades of the nineteenth century. The first Alabama Annual Conference convened in

---

[70] *Journal of the 19th Session ... of the General Conference, 1888,* 269, 281–282.

1868 with four presiding elder districts, but grew to three annual conferences and twenty-four presiding elder districts by 1900. Mixon himself, a veteran pastor and later a presiding elder, "organized so many churches that it was necessary to divide his district" and spin it off into separate jurisdictions. Because of Mixon's effective evangelism and that of others, the Alabama Annual Conference, which originated in the southern portions of the state, stretched northward into Birmingham and beyond. This required the founding of the North Alabama Annual Conference in 1878, and additional growth yielded the Central Alabama Annual Conference in 1891.[71]

Mixon viewed his state as having a distinctive experience worthy of an historical narrative that he hoped would "fertilize the roots of the stem" of the denomination. Hence, he published in 1902 through the southern-based Sunday School Union the *History of the African Methodist Episcopal Church in Alabama*. Such sentiments had already buoyed Mixon when the 1888 General Conference considered a southern venue for its next quadrennial session. Mixon, the presiding elder of the Selma District, and others in the North Alabama Annual Conference offered Selma as a desirable site for the church-wide meeting. Because Selma had "many trains running to and through it" and since blacks "own and control more real estate and comfortable homes than any city of its size in the South," it would be an ideal location for the General Conference. This same state pride also led Mixon to spearhead the start of Payne University in Selma in 1889. It would be "one of the greatest means for indoctrinating the faith and principles delivered to us by the fathers," he declared. Perhaps Mixon, as a widely traveled figure within the AME Church and seeing the breadth of African Methodism, wanted to testify to what his state uniquely contributed to that diversity.[72]

J. Albert Johnson, whose clerical career reflected the capacious reach of the AME Atlantic, experienced ministry in Canada, British Guiana, Bermuda, the United States, and South Africa. As a pastor, presiding elder, and bishop, Johnson understood better than most the extent of AME diversity through the five countries in which he served. Among his difficult assignments was the transition of Bermuda churches from their BME affiliation into an AME jurisdiction. Born in 1857 in Ontario, Johnson trained at the University of Toronto as a physician with hopes of becoming a medical missionary. He practiced medicine for a brief time in British Guiana before he accepted the call to preach in the BME Church. After he served several congregations in Ontario and Nova Scotia, the AMEs and the BMEs

[71] *Journal of the Twentieth ... Session ... of the General Conference, 1896*, 25–26.
[72] Mixon, *History of the African Methodist Episcopal Church in Alabama*, 17–18, 30, 43, 84, 95.

reunited. As pastor in St. Catharine, Ontario, he joined other BMEs in Canada, Bermuda, and British Guiana as they became African Methodists. To manage this denominational shift in Bermuda, Bishop Richard S. Disney, Nazrey's BME successor and now an AME prelate, transferred Johnson in 1886 from presiding elder of Ontario's Hamilton District to the island as the presiding elder and pastor to the flagship church, St. Paul in Hamilton.[73]

Though he sometimes complained about the lackluster performance of some pastors and their uncooperative congregations, in 1890 Bishop Tanner commended Johnson for "a very general growth" on the island. This included various physical improvements that Johnson completed at St. Paul. In 1891 Johnson endorsed an initiative from fellow clergy to start the Bermuda Collegiate Institute. As president of the trustee board, he traveled to England and Scotland to raise funds. As a result of these solicitations, Johnson wired £300 to the Bank of Bermuda for the school and attracted other contributions after his return. He finished six years in Bermuda in 1892 when Bishop Tanner appointed him to AME Union Church in Philadelphia.[74]

What Johnson found in Bermuda resembled what his AME counterparts experienced in the American South and South Africa. He encountered thick racial prejudices on the island especially within the religious community. He said that a white church where he was involved with an ecumenical service "treated me shabby because I am black." Moreover, in the educational sphere he attributed the reason for starting the Bermuda Collegiate Institute lay in "the unrighteous caste of the white population of the little island." Johnson labored among AME Anglophiles, but like Mixon in faraway Alabama, fought racism through the construction of AME churches and a parochial school to instill pride in a blackness tied to the autonomous legacy of their AME founder.[75]

Mixon and Johnson helped to develop African Methodism in regions where their predecessors and contemporaries established strong institutional foundations on which they could build. H. M. Steady, who rescued the AME mission in Sierra Leone from schism and demoralization, had no such advantages. John R. Frederick, a presiding elder in the New England Annual Conference, planted African Methodism in this Creole colony after his

[73] Ibid., 14–15, 18–19, 86.
[74] Dickerson, *African Methodism and Its Wesleyan Heritage*, 74–76; *Minutes of the First and Second Session of the Ontario Annual Conference of the African Methodist Episcopal Church Convened at John Street AME Church, Hamilton, Ont. June 30, 1885 and at King St. AME Church, Amherstburg, July 1, 1886,* 12.
[75] Dickerson, *African Methodism and Its Wesleyan Heritage*, 76–79.

arrival in 1887. The Wesleyan Countess of Huntingdon's Connexion met him with expectations to join the AME Church. Most were descended from blacks in Nova Scotia who immigrated to Sierra Leone in 1792. Several of them became AMEs. In 1895, Frederick reported nine congregations and 1,314 communicants. Sarah Gorham, a WPMMS member at Charles Street Church in Boston, became a missionary to Sierra Leone in 1888. Born in 1832, Gorham had already traveled in Liberia, where she also visited relatives who had settled there as emigrants. After going to Sierra Leone, she worked with the AME congregation at Magbele and focused on Temne women. Though the WPMMS observed that Frederick expected British assistance in securing land for AME schools, they believed that Gorham's arrival was a turning point for the mission. In awakening women to their role in aiding Sierra Leone, she persuaded female New Englanders "to purchase a boat by which the Missionaries could sail up into the interior." She died of malaria in 1894 and "became a martyr for the redemption of Africa." Frederick, how-ever, destroyed the thriving AME work by switching his allegiance in 1897 to the Wesleyan Methodists. In taking AME property and members with him, Frederick dealt a harsh blow to his former denomination. Steady, whom Frederick had licensed as a local preacher in 1891, was left "to pick up the pieces."[76]

Born in a Sierra Leone village in 1859, Steady's family was steeped in the Countess of Huntingdon's Connexion. He was educated in several Wesleyan and Anglican schools, and later supervised an Anglican institution until a Countess of Huntingdon's official invited him to teach at one of its facilities. When he disagreed with a Connexion doctrinal tenet, he became in 1890 a teacher at the Zion AME school and was ordained in 1893 as an AME minister. Steady became pastor at St. John Church and head of education at the Sierra Leone Annual Conference. When his congregation followed Frederick out of the AME Church, Steady turned to open-air preaching to attract new members to his splintered religious body. He succeeded in restoring Freetown's New Zion AME Church, and was appointed presiding elder in 1903.[77]

---

[76] Ibid., 78.

[77] L. L. Berry, *A Century of Missions of the African Methodist Episcopal Church* (New York, Gutenberg Printing Co., Inc., 1940), 136–137; *Report of the Board of Managers of the Woman's Mite Missionary Society of the African Methodist Episcopal Church, Philadelphia, from November, 1888, to November, 1892* (Philadelphia, PA, Pastoral Printing House, 1892), 7–9; Sylvia M. Jacobs, "Sarah E. Gorham," in Darlene Clark Hine (ed.), *Black Women in America: An Historical Encyclopedia*, Vol. I (Brooklyn, Carlson Publishing, 1993), 494–495; *Journal of the Twentieth ... Session ... of the General Conference, 1896*, 85.

Steady rehabilitated African Methodism in Sierra Leone with substantial WPMMS assistance. Between 1903 and 1907 he received quarterly allocations of $300 during each year. Sometimes additional monies were disbursed to particular parishes. After the Frederick schism, the number of congregations rose from zero to eight. Three were located in Freetown and the remaining five were in the interior up to 80 miles away from the capital city. He noted that the Ebenezer Canadian Church in Rotumba, for example, presented a special challenge. It was situated in "a Mo[h]ammed section" consisting of a small membership drawn from the ... slavetowns." Because of their irregular attendance, said Steady to WPMMS officials, he hoped to "remove the work to another centre." He was signaling that support for Sierra Leone still required their ongoing attention. The diversity of the AME Atlantic showed through the ministries of Mixon, Johnson, Steady, and others like them. With ministers and members located within the broad geography of the black Atlantic enabled African Methodists to address resurgent racism and its accompanying structures throughout the Americas and Africa.[78]

Henry M. Turner, whose episcopacy lasted from 1880 until his death in 1915, extended AME gains in the United States, Africa, and the Caribbean, and advanced pan-Africanism as a normative sensibility among African Methodists. After his chaplaincy in the Union Army and during his political career in Georgia, Turner facilitated the rapid growth of African Methodism in the state, reputedly recruiting thousands of ex-slaves and their preachers into the denomination. When he returned to Georgia as its bishop from 1896 to 1908, he presided over 140,000 members in nearly 1,000 congregations.[79]

Despite his Herculean labors in expanding the AME Church in the South and his fierce defense of black civil rights, Turner grew increasingly pessimistic about the attainment of African American equality in the United States. As a consequence, he advocated black emigration to Africa. His interest in the American Colonization Society, which predated the Civil War, was sustained during Reconstruction and its aftermath. Turner affirmatively viewed Africa both as a refuge for oppressed African Americans and as a symbol of black pride and the future possibilities of all African peoples. Because he perceived African Methodism as a divine instrument to achieve a

---

[78] "Rev. H. M. Steady," in Wright (ed.), *Centennial Encyclopedia of the African Methodist Episcopal Church*, 214.

[79] Mrs. I. M. B. Yeocum (compiler), *The Fourth Quadrennial Convention of the Women's Parent Mite Missionary Society of the African Methodist Episcopal Church, 1907* (Philadelphia, PA, AME Publishing House [Book Concern], 1907), 60–62, 101–107.

glorious black destiny, Turner thought that extending the denomination onto the "mother" continent would achieve these objectives. An official in the WPMMS, in reflecting the bishop's views, noted that "Africa claims our support as African Methodists, for are we not bone of her bone, and flesh of her flesh?"[80]

Turner knew about the AMEs who preceded him in Africa. When the Liberian Exodus Joint Stock Company transported several AMEs from Charleston to West Africa on the *Azor* in 1878, Turner was present to pray for the venture. Though he needed no encouragement to visit the region, he went there with the imprimatur of the Council of Bishops. His colleagues said that delegates at three earlier General Conferences directed one of them to travel to Africa "to look after our Church interests." Their episcopal address in 1896, in looking back on Turner's trip, never mentioned him as their designee, perhaps suggesting that the urgency to oversee the African mission was felt by all of the bishops rather than one. The bishops observed in 1892 that the unnamed Turner "was received by the ministry and people with great rejoicing and loud expressions of gratitude, because this the mother Church had remembered them, and sent one of her chief pastors to look after them." Subsequent reports to the 1896 General Conference credited Turner for undertaking the African assignment, and acknowledged that he had organized the Liberia and Sierra Leone annual conferences in 1891.[81]

The establishment of official jurisdictions in West Africa and the consolidation of AME expansion in that region was a major Turner contribution. In Liberia he found eleven appointments and in Sierra Leone he acknowledged the impressive beginnings of Frederick Mission between 1887 and 1891 with nine congregations. The jurisdictions numbered nearly 800 members and almost 1,000 communicants respectively. Inroads into the interior had already started. Now, the region was ready for a missionary bishop. For Turner, the painstaking construction of an AME presence in West Africa meant that an authentic pan-Africanism was being realized through African

---

[80] Stephen W. Angell, *Bishop Henry M. Turner and African American Religion in the South* (Knoxville, University of Tennessee Press, 1992), 68–80; Dickerson, *African Methodism and Its Wesleyan Heritage*, 113.

[81] Edwin S. Redkey, "Bishop Turner's African Dream," *Journal of American History*, Vol. 54, No. 2, September 1967, 273–274, 277; *Minutes of the Fifteenth Annual Meeting of the Women's Mite Missionary Society, Pittsburgh Conference Branch, African Methodist Episcopal Church* held at *St. James AME Church, E.E., Pittsburgh, PA, July 13, 14, 15 and 16, 1911* (n.p., Publishing Committee: Fern Hurrington, M. Levada Carter Norris, and Isetta M. Jefferson, 1911), 25.

Methodism. This was, however, only the first phase of his "African Dream."[82]

Just as Turner's West African initiatives benefited from other AMEs who went to the "mother" continent before him, he was similarly dependent on church developments that indigenous Africans inaugurated in South Africa. Mangena Maake Mokone and other blacks, formerly in the Wesleyan Methodist Church, established the Ethiopian Church and laid foundations for an eventual union with the AMEs. Their insistence on racial solidarity and institutional autonomy developed as a fortuitous reenactment of Richard Allen's St. George exodus in 1787. In a hagiographic account of the Ethiopian founder, a relative also noted that "Richard Allen sounded the call in 1816 in Philadelphia and Reverend Mokone in Africa sounded the call in 1892 in Pretoria for the Religious emancipation of the African Race." The common racial and religious origins of African Methodists on both continents resonated with ministers and members in the AME and Ethiopian churches and moved them, perhaps inevitably, toward merger.[83]

Mokone, as much as Turner, launched African Methodism in South Africa. He was born on June 14, 1851 in the Transvaal into one of the Bapedi tribes that had migrated from a coastal region in East Africa. Despite a venerable ancestry of chiefs and queens among the Bakone people, the ascendancy of Afrikaners in South Africa eroded the sovereignty of the region's indigenous populations. When the Swazis raided the farms belonging to his clan, Mokone joined others in a trek to Natal to purchase weapons to fight the rival tribe. Ironically, this search for arms introduced him to a broader and bleaker reality in southern Africa. However serious conflicts were between rival indigenous tribes, they paled in significance to the hegemony of settler whites of Dutch and English ancestry. Their stranglehold on economic and political power in South Africa, starting as early as the seventeenth century, increasingly marginalized African peoples in their own native lands. Mokone, as the South African economy diversified in its agricultural and urban sectors, worked in Natal on a sugar plantation, then in a bakery, and on into wage labor. In this context, he was introduced to the Wesleyan Methodists and answered the call to preach.[84]

---

[82] Redkey, "Bishop Turner's African Dream," 274; *Journal of the Twentieth Session and 19th Session . . . of the General Conference, 1892,* 23; *Journal of the Twentieth Quadrennial Session of the General Conference of the African Methodist Episcopal Church,* held in Stephen AME Church, Wilmington, NC, May 4–22, 1896, 1154–1155.

[83] *Journal of the Twentieth Session and 19th Session . . . of the General Conference, 1892,* 154–155.

[84] J. M. Mokone, *The Early Life of Our Founder (M. M. Mokone)* from South Africa, n.p., 1935), 18.

Mokone trained at a school in Pietermaritzburg, but while preaching between 1875 and 1879 worked as a carpenter. The Wesleyan Methodists raised him to full ordination in 1888 and assigned him to a congregation in Kilnerton, and then to Makanapanstad in 1889. Moreover, he started a church and a school in Pretoria, but he returned to Kilnerton in 1891 as the principal of another school. These varied experiences as a Wesleyan Methodist minister and educator, however, exposed him to a host of racial inequities that stirred him in ways reminiscent of the Richard Allen narrative. Hence, he and other dissidents bolted from their denomination in 1892, established the Ethiopian Church, and issued a Founder's Declaration of Independence whose fourteen points explained why an autonomous African religious body had become a necessity.[85]

Among the most egregious grievances that Mokone enumerated were the differentials in salary between whites and blacks, the practice of white pastors assigned to black congregations to live miles away from their parishioners, and the denial of monetary allowances for the families of "Native ministers" when the wives and children of white pastors experienced no such exclusion. Starting in 1886, Mokone noted, district meetings were racially segregated, and black jurisdictions "were compelled to have a white chairman and secretary." He added that "the Native ordained minister is of no use to his own people. He cannot exercise his rights as a minister or be placed in a position of trust." Often, "the candidates of whites will be placed over the black man as superintendent." White clergy also refused to interact with black members and "never go to visit the sick or pray for them, and when they die," they ask that "your Native minister must go to bury your own people." Because "no Native minister is honoured among the white brethren," Mokone spearheaded in Pretoria a separate Ethiopian Church.[86]

Word of Mokone's daring move spread throughout the Transvaal and other adjacent areas. In 1892, the minister at Marabstad observed "if Rev. Mokone is leaving the Wesleyan Church, I'm going along with him." The rest of his congregation followed him into the Ethiopian Church. Two local preachers elsewhere in the province in January 1893 also joined with Mokone. A black pastor in the Orange Free State, Jacobus G. Xaba, a Zulu, had been barred from his pulpit because of alleged disobedience to a white superior and then, with others, was arrested and incarcerated. Upon his release from custody, Xaba went to Pretoria to affiliate with the Mokone movement. Additionally, Joseph P. Kanyane, the leader of a dissident group

---

[85] Ibid., 5–6.   [86] Ibid., 7–9, 10–11.

of Anglican blacks, seemed no better off in their denomination than their counterparts in the Wesleyan Methodists Church. He, like Xaba and others, became the nucleus of the new Ethiopian Church.[87]

Mokone, like other indigenous Africans, envisaged Ethiopianism as their expression of religious and political nationalism. It was, according to one scholar, an urban phenomenon that reflected Mokone's own wanderings within South Africa, and therefore his church appealed to the "detribalized." In seeking affiliation with an older black denomination based among African Americans, the Ethiopian Church stretched beyond its assertion of independence to connect religiously to a black Atlantic body. They joined the AMEs to affirm themselves as a Creole people who stood above tribe and geography and to ratify their part in a denomination founded for the African diaspora.[88]

This connection was forged out of a series of fortuitous circumstances. As Mokone supervised the spread of the Ethiopian Church, Charlotte Manye, a part of his kin and kinship connections, left for the United States to study at Wilberforce University. There she learned about "the great AME Church." At the home of Manye's sister in Johannesburg, Mokone saw Bishop Turner's letterhead that Manye had obviously had sent. Mokone wrote to him about sending two of his ministers to Wilberforce for further training. Later Mokone must have been greatly pleased that the Pittsburgh Annual Conference Branch of the WPMMS joined with the Ohio and North Ohio divisions in funding Manye, whom they called "that noble hearted African," through her graduation from Wilberforce. Mokone also told Turner about the Ethiopian Church and that it "is entirely managed by us blacks of South Africa." Turner, already a force behind AME expansion in West Africa, viewed the communication from Mokone as an opportunity for additional growth on the "mother continent." Though the South African body had only seven ordained clergy and 2,500 members, Turner welcomed the prospect of bringing them into his denomination.[89]

If Mokone can be likened to Moses in pulling African Methodism into South Africa, then James Mata Dwane played the role of Joshua. Though he was older than Mokone, he functioned as his lieutenant and potential usurper in traveling to the United States in 1896 to effect amalgamation with the AME Church. He was a native of the Transkei out of the Gcaleka Xhosa tribe. His older sister who converted to Christianity paved the way for him to affiliate with the Wesleyan Methodists. Like Mokone, he was repulsed by the

[87] Ibid., 10–12.   [88] Ibid., 10, 12, 16–17.   [89] Campbell, *Songs of Zion*, 140.

racism that permeated church practices. Yet Dwane, who joined the Ethiopian Church not long before his departure for America, joined Charlotte Manye in experiencing what Mokone would never see, namely the sight of impressive church edifices and educational institutions autonomously operated by independent African Methodists. Manye remained in the United States and traveled within AME circles, and in 1900 participated in the annual convention of the WPMMS's Pittsburgh Conference Branch. Dwane, like Manye, saw what the AMEs had to offer. He met them at the imposing Mother Bethel Church in Philadelphia, other churches in New York, Washington DC, and on to Atlanta to meet Bishop Turner, Secretary of Missions Henry B. Parks, and Joseph S. Flipper, the pastor of Allen Temple, a leading congregation among Georgia AMEs. At a special session of the North Georgia Annual Conference, Turner ordained Dwane as an itinerant elder and authorized him to confer the same status upon other Ethiopian clergy. These actions would fully incorporate the Mokone movement into the AME Church.[90]

Turner also appointed Dwane as general superintendent of the AME Church in South Africa. After the Council of Bishops approved his visit to South Africa in 1897, he planned his trip for February 1898. His arrival sparked an electrifying response as blacks journeyed long distances to see a black bishop. He raised the number of ordained clergy to over fifty, authorized the founding of a school, and recognized the South African and Transvaal Annual Conferences. Most importantly, he named Dwane as a vicar bishop, a move that sidelined Mokone and angered fellow ministers.[91]

Nonetheless, Turner and Dwane in 1898 and 1899 experienced the exhilaration of the AME presence in South Africa. On the published minutes of Turner's Georgia annual conferences appeared his "Associate" the "Rt. Rev. James M. Dwane, Vicar Bishop," underneath his name. At the 1898 North Georgia Annual Conference Turner discussed his recent travels to South Africa and "the urgent necessity which forced him to ordain a vicar bishop"

---

[90] Mokone, *The Early Life of Our Founder*, 17; Angell, *Bishop Henry Mcneal Turner*, 225; *Minutes of the Twelfth Annual Meeting of the Women's Mite Missionary Society, Pittsburg Conference Branch, African Methodist Episcopal Church held at AME Church, New Castle, PA., July 2–6, 1908* (Pittsburgh, Nelson J. Miles, Printer, 1908), 22; *Minutes of the Fifteenth Annual Meeting of the Women's Mite Missionary Society, Pittsburgh Conference Branch, 1911* (n.p., Publishing Committee: Fern Hurrington, M. Levada Carter Norris, Isetta M. Jefferson, n.d.), 25.

[91] Campbell, *Songs Of Zion*, 123–125, 135; *Minutes of the Fourth Annual Convention of the Woman's Mite Missionary Society from held at Brown's Chapel A.M.E. Church, Allegheny City, Pennsylvania held July 5 to 9, Inclusive (1900)* (Pittsburg[h], Scott Dilbert, Printer, 1900), 30; Angell, *Bishop Henry Mcneal Turner*, 226, 229–230, 233.

and "the glorious future which awaited the African M.E. Church." Dwane, a late arrival to the meeting, addressed the assembly referring to AME Church influence "among the common people" and their tribal rulers in South Africa. He appealed for help to build a college and exposed the audience to his facility with the Kaffir, Zulu, and Dutch languages. In a later session, Dwane, "dressed in his episcopal robe," sang a hymn in "his native language," and then ascended the pulpit to preach. He refuted accusations that "Christianity has been more injurious to the natives of Africa than a blessing." Such charges surely applied to "the missionaries themselves," but not to the African Methodists who came to the "mother" continent as racial compatriots. Turner and Dwane showed that their partnership had yielded 10,800 members in two annual conferences.[92]

Dwane followed Turner to the 1898 Macon Georgia Annual Conference, where he preached again. "It is with difficulty," he said, that "I preach in English" because he was more accustomed to speaking in Kaffir. He drew praise, however, for his promise to translate into the "Kaffir tongue our book of discipline and liturgy." Secretary of Missions Henry B. Parks escorted Dwane to the 1898 Georgia Annual Conference "amid tremendous applause." The conference scribe wrote that "the majority of the brethren having never seen a native African [followed] every word of his captivating address." Dwane preached again, noting that "we in Africa are coming down from the trees of ignorance and superstition." He added "we want you, our brethren in America, to come down from the tree of dependence upon the white man" and recognize that blacks on both sides of the Atlantic should "trust each other more." Furthermore, he hoped that African Methodists would "come over and help us" as peers in the same denomination.[93]

The majority of the Council of Bishops approved Turner's appointment of Dwane as a vicar bishop despite a strong dissent from Bishop Wesley J. Gaines. The ensuing debate, however, proved futile. Dwane's elevation stirred discontent among his colleagues. Moreover, Dwane who was inept in his supervisory duties, resigned, left the AMEs, and joined the Anglicans. Despite the turmoil, Turner succeeded in winning the denomination's

[92] *Minutes of the Twenty-Sixth Session of the North Georgia Annual Conference of (the) AME Church* held in St. Paul AME Church, Madison, GA, November 9–15, 1898 (n.p., n.d.), 13–15, 24, 35.
[93] *Proceedings of the Macon (GA) Seventeenth Annual Session of the African Methodist Episcopal Church* held in Brown's AME Church, Dublin, GA, November 16–22, 1898, 29–30; Journal *of Proceedings of the Thirty-Third Session of the Georgia Annual Conference of the African Methodist Episcopal Church* held in St. Andrew's Chapel AME Church, Darien, GA, December 14–19, 1898, 26–30.

permanent commitment to South Africa. Mokone, for example, attended the 1900 General Conference as a delegate and along with J. Z. Tantzi was asked to address the assembly in their "native language." Their speeches followed a Kaffir selection, "Nkosi Yam Ubunditande," sung by the South African choir at Wilberforce University. Most importantly, one of the five bishops elected became South Africa's first resident prelate. That bishop, Levi J. Coppin, recalled that he "asked to be sent." Mokone joined others in consecrating him as the thirty-first bishop.[94]

The episcopal address at the 1904 General Conference commended Coppin on his "untiring zeal" supervising the AMEs in South Africa. Numerical growth was shown through the addition of three new annual conferences and expansion into Natal, Rhodesia, and other territories in British Central Africa. He launched Bethel Institute in Capetown in 1901, housed it in a ten-room brick building, and hired a faculty of eight to educate 350 students. This important development greatly pleased South Africans because their initial interest in the AME Church included support for their educational advancement. One of them said "give us ... a college or an educational institute that will enable us ... to stand on the same platform as the white race ... the same as the Negro is doing in America." Additionally, Coppin was proud of the *South African Christian Recorder*. The biweekly, which started in 1903, was printed in newly acquired facilities equipped with a modern press and other machinery. Besides the newspaper, the publishing house, a debt-free enterprise, also responded to the printing needs of South Africa's growing roster of congregations. Coppin, therefore, recommended that the newspaper should be granted official recognition, and its managing editor ranked as a general officer just as the editors of the denomination's other periodicals did. At the same time, Coppin tackled some intractable issues that drew colonial suspicions about the AME presence. Though AME clergy could not perform marriages, for example, Coppin believed "these hindrances will vanish" once the denomination became better established and won "the respect of the Government and of the religious world." Nonetheless, he successfully pressed authorities on licenses for at least a few AME preachers who tried fulfilling their matrimonial responsibilities.[95]

[94] Angell, *Bishop Henry McNeal Turner*, 234–235; *Journal of the Twenty-First Quadrennial Session of the General Conference of the African M. E. Church* held in the Auditorium, Columbus, OH, May 7–25, 1900, 32, 163, 294–295; Levi J. Coppin, *Unwritten History* (Philadelphia, AME Book Concern, 1919), 311.

[95] *Journal of the Twenty-Second Session of the General Conference of the African M. E. Church*, Chicago, Illinois, May 2–27, 1904, 80–83; Carol A. Page, "Colonial Reaction to AME

Coppin noted that diverse peoples affiliated with the AME Church. The Cape Colony, for example, consisted of members who spoke Dutch, English, and various indigenous languages. "Our English speaking preachers," he observed, "are confined to English speaking congregations, and these are but few." Therefore, the translation of the AME discipline and liturgy had become an urgent necessity. Coppin recalled an incident at an annual conference at Capetown that had interpreters for Dutch and Sikosa and other native languages. A participant from Bechuanaland (present day Botswana) protested, saying "there was no interpreting in his tongue." Fortunately, another attendee volunteered as an interpreter of the Bechuana language and other tongues represented at the meeting. Coppin's successors in South Africa also presided in annual conference sessions where multilingual renditions of hymns and scriptures were commonplace. In Kimberly, at the 1913 joint session of the Cape and Orange Free State conferences, with Bishop J. Albert Johnson in the chair, "Reverend B. L. Leshuta announced a hymn in se-Xosa and read a portion of Scripture in se-Suto." Next he "announced another hymn in se-Xosa and Brother P. N. Lesaba engaged in prayer in Dutch.[96]

Additionally, Coppin, having been a pastor to various urban congregations in the United States with diverse black constituencies, must have seen much that was familiar in South Africa. The Ethiopian Church and its successor AME congregations started in cities mainly around Pretoria and in the Witwaterstrand gold region surrounding Johannesburg and Cape Town. AME membership included recruits from European mission churches, nationalists who later founded native congresses throughout the country, and the chiefs and Christianized members of various tribes. For South Africans, the AME Church transcended their differences and according to one historian, the "blackness" represented by African Methodism was the glue that helped the denomination to thrive. Moreover, Cape Town's "emerging Coloured elite" joined the AME Church and "wore its affiliation with black America as a badge of distinction."[97]

Mindful of the growing diversity of African Methodism, the bishops urged an intra-racial integration of AMEs on both sides of the Atlantic that would

Missionaries in South Africa, 1898–1910," in Sylvia M. Jacobs (ed.), *Black Americans and the Missionary Movement in Africa* (Westport, CT, Greenwood Press, 1982), 180, 188.
[96] *Proceedings ... General Conference, 1904*, 82; Coppin, *Unwritten History*, 317–318; *Journal of Proceedings of the Joint Session of the Cape and O.F.S. Annual Conferences of the African Methodist Episcopal Church* held at Kimberly, October 21–26, 1913 (Cape Town, Citadel Press, 1913), 13.
[97] Campbell, *Songs of Zion*, 141, 163, 168.

be free of ethnic and cultural "antagonisms." They declared in 1900 that the denomination should "overcome these relics of disappearing and decaying barbarism that constitutes the chief apology for African Methodism's existence," which was "to break down the walls of tribal and even racial partitions." Whether African or African American, Cape Colored, Caribbean, or Xhosa, they belonged to one Creolized church founded to transcend these differences in region, language, color, and ethnicity.[98]

Perhaps the best barometer of AME activity lay with indigenous rank-and-file clergy. Though their bishop was African American, South Africans more decisively influenced denominational developments. The operations of Presiding Elder J. G. Xaba's Orangia District showed that the actions of indigenous leadership fixed the foundation from which AME growth would be shaped. At a 1902 conference Xaba urged acculturated Africans "to convert heathenism into Christ" and to "extend the Kingdom of Christ to the extremities of Africa." He added, "it is for us to evangelize and Christianize Africa."[99]

Xaba also acknowledged that AMEs remained vulnerable to white political and religious hegemony, and should mute the insurgent impulses intrinsic to their identity and ties to a proud and aggressive African American denomination. Hence, it seemed expedient to Xaba that AMEs should declare their "loyalty" because "we have been misrepresented to the [white] Government as rebels and enemies of white missionaries." His conciliatory tone drew from the difficulty of AME preachers to gain licenses to marry parishioners, to claim sites to build churches, and to aid refugees displaced because of the Boer War. Appeals for concessions and cooperation were Xaba's tactics for advancing AME interests. In reflecting this attitude the State of the Church report, for example, complained about the refusal of magistrates to allow AMEs to perform civil marriage ceremonies despite promises from "the Government" that the restriction would be removed. The report also noted "opposition in some of the Towns from the Municipal Authorities" to approve sites in the Orange Colony for AME edifices. Although African Methodism was both "recognized and tolerated," some city officials stopped the construction of AME churches. These circumstances generally drew from AME attempts to build on such enviable locations as crown lands

---

[98] *Journal of the Twenty-First Quadrennial Session of the General Conference of the African M. E. Church* held in the Auditorium, Columbus, OH, May 7–25, 1900, 332.
[99] *A Minute Book of the Orangia District Conference of the African Methodist Episcopal Church* held in Bloemfontein, September 3, 1902 (Bloemfontein, F. Wienand & Co., 1903), 5.

and in areas where nervous European missionaries feared competition from African Methodists.[100]

Lastly, the Boer War dislocated "our people" into refugee camps and dispersed them into other areas. AME clergy, "through the kind permission" of the head of the Native Refuge Camps in the Orange River Colony, were allowed "to travel among our congregations concentrated and scattered all over" the region. Hence, the Orangia District Conference expressed gratitude because clergy could be "at all times within the reach of their congregations, all over the native refuge camps." One pastor benefited from the relaxed travel restrictions as they resulted in sixty of his members departing a refugee camp for their "former homes." Similarly, another minister observed that "our refugee camp is being ... removed, people [were] being repatriated," and their lives were returning to normal both "spiritually and socially."[101]

Xaba recognized that the AME Church, while populous "among the cities and towns," must also have churches in the rural and refugee areas in South Africa. Moreover, he realized that this spatial distribution of AME members was accompanied by linguistic diversity. Like Coppin, Xaba responded by translating the AME liturgy into Sesuto and by printing baptismal certificates in Sesuto, Dutch, and English. Like his colleagues in other jurisdictions, Xaba realized that the AME Church in serving multiple black constituencies in South Africa reflected the same range of color and ethnic differences that appeared elsewhere within their transatlantic denomination.[102]

AME expansion into Africa highlighted the Creole character of African Methodism and credibly established it as a pan-African religious body. Bishop William W. Beckett articulated the meaning of this transatlantic connection when he addressed the 1916 joint session of the Transvaal, Natal, Cape, and Orange Free State Annual Conferences. Beckett, a native of Edisto Island, South Carolina, and born before the Civil War, declared "his gladness to come into the land of his ancestors" and that "his mother had often told him of the African tribe to which he belonged." Though he did not remember the name of the tribe, he "was very pleased to be among his own people in Africa." At the same time, denominational control, despite diverse but indigenous ministers and members in Africa, lay among African Americans. No African bishop or general officer would be elected within the foreseeable future, and denominational power centers in governance, finance, and publishing remained in the United States. Blacks, on both sides of the

[100] Ibid., 6, 14; Campbell, *Songs of Zion*, 181.
[101] *A Minute Book of the Orangia District Conference*, 1902, 14, 16, 20.   [102] Ibid., 5, 18, 19.

Atlantic, however, identified with each other for different but complementary reasons. Historian James T. Campbell, an insightful analyst of AME
development in South Africa, cited a knowledgeable AME who viewed the
history of the denomination as evolving through three stages. AMEs, he said,
believed God empowered Richard Allen to found their organization "to
demonstrate to the world the capacity of the Negro race variety for self-
government." Secondly, AMEs carried "the Gospel to the emancipated
Freedmen of the South," and thirdly, they turned "to redeem Africa, their
fatherland." In undertaking their African project, Campbell argued, AMEs
seemed less focused on Africa than on themselves. He added that "no matter
how sincere AME leaders were in their devotion to Africa, their interest
remained profoundly self-referential: Africa represented a field for African
American heroism, a vindication of centuries of suffering, a solution to the
riddle of black American experience." Furthermore, "Africans, if they
entered the picture at all, existed primarily as abstractions [and] imaginative
foils around which African Americans could define their own identity and
destiny."[103]

Africans, however, desired a connection to an African American religious
body. They shared the same view that the "mother" continent was a ripened
field for Christianity and that blacks on both sides of the Atlantic had been
"entrusted" with "the important work of spreading [Christ's] Kingdom in
Africa." Additionally, Africans realized that their outreach to the AME
Church irritated both the British and Afrikaners in South Africa and showed
an assertiveness that these settler whites eschewed. Their admiration of
African Americans and what they had achieved in less than fifty years after
slavery made it harder to justify the restriction of black rights in South
Africa. Moreover, as historian Carol A. Page has observed, "for AME
churchmen [in both America and Africa] the promotion of Christianity
was also the vehicle by which they could spread continental unity among
Africans."[104]

Turner's pan-African vision was not restricted to Africa, but shifted back
across the Atlantic to Cuba and Mexico. Though the Spanish-American War
provided opportunities to activate these initiatives in the Americas, other
contemporaries envisioned expansion within the western hemisphere before

[103] *Journal of Proceedings of the Joint Session of the Transvaal, Natal, Cape & Orange Free State
Annual Conferences of the African Methodist Episcopal Church* held at Bloemfontein
O.F.S.), November 29–December 3 1916 (Cape Town, Citadel Press, 1917), 12–13; Campbell,
Songs of Zion, 97.
[104] *A Minute Book of the Orangia District Conference*, 1902, 5; Page, "Colonial Reaction to AME
Missionaries," 181, 183.

and during Turner's episcopacy. In 1898, for example, the *Christian Recorder*, though acknowledging the AME presence in Africa and Haiti, published a special tribute from an official of the WPMMS to the Reverend H. C. C. Astwood. He and an assistant already were in Cuba "preaching and singing in Spanish in our missionary church." They, like their counterparts in the African and Haitian work deserved recognition and support.[105]

Astwood, like Frederick in Sierra Leone and Mokone in South Africa, expanded African Methodism and exhibited a consciousness of its pan-African possibilities as much as Henry M. Turner himself. Moreover, Astwood, Frederick, and Mokone, all born in colonial jurisdictions in the Caribbean and Africa, scarcely identified as missionaries like the Europeans, but functioned as acculturated blacks who viewed the AME Church as their vehicle to merge diverse black populations into an independent transatlantic religious body. Additionally, Turner, despite his commitment to African emigration, never lived in the overseas territories that he claimed as AME jurisdictions. Astwood, Frederick, and Mokone, however, settled among those whom they evangelized and developed African Methodism in interaction within their indigenous contexts. Because of these ministries the AME Church increasingly reflected the diverse languages and ethnicities that constituted the African diaspora.

Astwood leveraged his position in the United States consular service to advance African Methodism in the Caribbean. Perhaps his origins in the region spurred this commitment. He was born in 1844 at Salt Cay in the Turk Islands in the British West Indies. To recover from the death of his brother, Astwood settled first in Santo Domingo and then in 1874 in New Orleans. Before he joined the AME Church in Louisiana, Astwood, raised as an Anglican, left the Methodist Episcopal (ME) Church because of its discriminatory treatment of African Americans. Astwood blended his political and religious interests and rose rapidly through each. In the Turk Islands, as a youth, he served in the revenue service, and after his arrival in New Orleans he connected with P. B. S. Pinchback, Louisiana's first black governor. This political tie landed him as a US marshal and a reading clerk for the state senate. GOP President Chester A. Arthur assigned him as US Consul to Santo Domingo, and he remained in office through subsequent presidential administrations between 1882 and 1894. Parallel to his political ascent, Astwood also advanced in the AME Church. He was, according to the *Christian Recorder*, "a favorite" of Bishop Thomas M. D. Ward who

---

[105] *Christian Recorder*, November 17, 1898.

hired him as his private secretary and licensed him to preach. Just before going to Santo Domingo, Bishop John M. Brown ordained him as an itinerant elder in the New York Annual Conference and "commissioned" him to start AME churches in the Dominican Republic. Congregations at Santo Domingo, Marcoris, and Monti Christi resulted from this initiative.[106]

After Astwood completed his consular service in the Dominican Republic, he accepted successive pastorates in Harrisburg and Philadelphia, Pennsylvania. The outbreak of the Spanish-American War in 1898, however, awakened Astwood, Turner, and other AMEs to a resurgent pan-Africanism focused on the Caribbean and the rest of the Americas. Just as European colonialism in Africa stirred black opposition to white hegemony on the "mother" continent, imperialism within the western hemisphere and the Pacific became equally repugnant to advocates of black freedom.[107]

Initiatives in the Caribbean and South America had already been launched through the Demerara Annual Conference. In 1896, Bishop Turner deputized Reuben A. Sealy of Barbados to preside at the 1896 session. The jurisdiction embraced ten appointments, including four each in Barbados and British Guiana and two in Trinidad. At the 1899 meeting, Bishop Benjamin F. Lee proudly asserted that "the life and growth of our church are one of many evidences existing of the capacity of the peoples descended from Africans. It has proved a powerful excitant to those classes to self-support and self-advancement." The mission of the Demerara Annual Conference, he added, was "to bring to the saving knowledge of Jesus Christ ... the one race, united by common origin, common misfortune and common destiny." Because blacks had been "wronged" and because "the Ethiopian cannot change his skin, his misfortunes stand out in bold relief ... and are kept exposed by those who undervalue in him the image of God." Therefore, "it is for us [AMEs] an especial work in Christian responsibilities" to be present in the Caribbean and South America. Therefore, Sealy suggested initiatives for expansion to St. Kitts, Tobago, Antigua, Nevis, and St. Vincent, and that the mission at St. Thomas should be revived.[108]

Spain's suppression of rebels, including the famed black fighter Antonio Maceo, from the late 1860s to 1878, drew the attention from African

[106] *Christian Recorder*, July 26, 1883; March 16, 1896; April 16, 1896; *New York Age*, August 20, 1908.

[107] Lawrence S. Little, *Disciples of Liberty: The African Methodist Episcopal Church in the Age of Imperialism, 1884–1916* (Knoxville, University of Tennessee Press, 2000), 94, 107.

[108] *Minutes of the Sixth Session of the Demerara Annual Conference of the AME Church* held at Bethel Church, Anna Catherina, Demerara, December 7–9, 1899 (Barbados, C. F. Cole, 1900), 4–5, 13–14.

Methodists on the North American mainland. That slavery persisted in Cuba until its abolition in 1886 elicited no sympathy for Spain within the AME Church. Moreover, ongoing concern for black Cubans carried over into the 1890s. The 1896 General Conference, for example, resolved that the AME Church, "established upon the sacred principles of freedom and liberty," expresses the same "sympathy with the Cubans in their struggle for liberty and independence." The 1900 General Conference declared that the AME Church should offer itself as "a light worthy of being followed by the dark races and under God the means for elevating the Negro race." Though Cuba was Roman Catholic, the island "is of the dark race largely." When blacks were "left in the strong and greedy grasp of the Caucasian," whether American or Spanish, it was the duty of the AME Church to go "to their relief." One traveler in 1897 spoke at Bethel Church in Wilmington, Delaware, and in front of other AME audiences about the "the state of our people in Cuba." He said "the colored people are suffering the pangs of hunger and are being massacred."[109]

When the United States declared war on Spain because of the Spanish attack on the battleship *Maine* in Havana harbor, patriotism and the opportunity to prove their manhood and bravery stirred African American men. These same sentiments motivated AME military chaplains George Prioleau and Theophilus G. Steward in their recruitment of black soldiers to fight against the Spanish. At the end of the war, declared the *Christian Recorder*, these soldiers "will return to this country to resume the fight against American prejudice." The war also aroused feelings of solidarity with embattled black Cubans seeking self-determination. Similar sympathies were expressed for the Puerto Ricans and Filipinos whom Spanish overlords also exploited. Hence, AMEs viewed the war as a spur to evangelize Cuba and Puerto Rico, and secondarily their colored brethren in the Philippines.[110]

The bishops in their 1900 episcopal address noted the victory of the United States over Spain. As a result, the Americans now had jurisdiction over "many thousands of people, like ourselves, more or less Negro, and many thousands of others whose dark color renders them liable to similar contempt that [was] too often against the Negro." The bishops believed "all such peoples need to form that alliance which lifts them up to God, and thus

[109] *Journal of the Twentieth Quadrennial Session of the General Conference of the African Methodist Episcopal Church* held in St. Stephen AME Church, Wilmington, NC, May 4–22, 1896, 164–165; *Journal of the Twenty-First Quadrennial Session of the General Conference, 1900*, 329; *Christian Recorder*, November 18, 1897.
[110] *Christian Recorder*, June 9, 1898; Little, *Disciples of Liberty*, 95.

challenge and command the respect" from those who rule in American society. Hence, the AME Church would become guardians and protectors for the Cubans, Puerto Ricans, and Filipinos as American imperial interests encroached upon them. These conditions required AMEs to expand into these Atlantic and Pacific territories if these responsibilities were going to be fulfilled.[111]

Cuba and Puerto Rico had already drawn the attention of Secretary of Missions Parks, who proposed AME congregations for both areas even before the war began. Right after the US war declaration, the bishops selected Astwood to launch the AME mission to Cuba. His fluency in Spanish and his twelve years in the Dominican Republic were impeccable credentials. He accompanied the all black 8th Illinois Volunteers to the island, where he organized a congregation in Santiago and two in Havana. That Astwood remained only a short time in Cuba opened an opportunity that Turner was led to exploit.[112]

Turner presided in Georgia from 1896 to 1908, where African Methodism flourished among blacks many of whom were ex-slaves. His constituency of 139,284 in 919 congregations in 1906 enabled him to initiate an overseas outreach first to South Africa and later to former Spanish colonies in the Caribbean. Though the 1898 North Georgia Annual Conference commended Astwood's appointment, the bishop chose the Georgia Annual Conference as his locus for enhancing the AME mission to Cuba. Hence, Turner in 1900 selected D. S. Wells as presiding elder of Cuba and Puerto Rico and appointed nine missionaries to join him. Wells traveled 2,135 miles to numerous locations in Cuba and reported at the 1901 Georgia Annual Conference fifteen congregations, thirteen preachers, and 735 members. Like Astwood, Wells remained on the island for a limited time and returned to Georgia by 1903.[113]

Of course, it was not Turner's official responsibility to direct AME expansion to Cuba. Bishop Charles S. Smith, while Wells held an appointment to the island from Turner, visited Cuba twice between 1900 and 1904. Smith had been elected to the episcopacy in 1900 and was assigned to the Twelfth Episcopal District, a far-flung jurisdiction that included Canada, Bermuda, the West Indies, and South America. To these territories were added Hawaii, the Philippines, Puerto Rico, and Cuba. Smith's second visit to Cuba took

[111] *Journal of the Twenty-First Quadrennial Session of the General Conference, 1900*, 331.
[112] Little, *Disciples of Liberty*, 107; Dickerson, *Religion, Race, and Region*, 122.
[113] Benjamin W. Arnett (ed.), *The Budget of 1904* (Philadelphia, PA, E. W. Lampton and J. H. Collett, 1904), 161, 163; Dickerson, *Religion, Race, and Region*, 123–124.

him through the heart of the island from Havana to Santiago." The Santiago province," he observed, was "decidedly favorable for our success" and was "the black belt of Cuba" where most slaves had been held in bondage. Blacks were also "largely in the majority" in this area. Despite Smith's intermittent presence and the short stay of Astwood and Wells, the Cuba mission was without any sustained indigenous leadership and, therefore, had few prospects for success. Nonetheless, the recent 1900 General Conference, more than others previously held, revealed an enlarged global consciousness among AMEs and how much they viewed themselves as protectors of non-white peoples. There had been invitations from "our brethren in the West Indies and South America," said one report to the quadrennial meeting, and there were predictions that "the dusky sons of India and the yellow men of China, Japan and [K]orea-in a word, the dark races of all the world – will welcome our organization amongst them." The mission to black Latinos was a concrete expression of this transnational awareness and determination to evangelize partners "to learn with us to worship the true God," and to honor the man that God "raised up to be the instrument in establishing the AME Church, even our own sainted [Richard] Allen."[114]

Turner, however, focused on black Latinos within the western hemisphere. For example, out of the same Georgia Annual Conference from which Wells was sent to Cuba, Turner appointed J. R. Cox as the presiding elder of Mexico. In 1906 Cox expressed optimism about AME prospects because the ME Church, South, its competitor, was "trying to discriminate against color the same [as] they do in the States." If the AMEs would establish a chair in Spanish at one of its colleges, then trained missionaries could "soon overcome this republic." Turner's definition of pan-Africanism as inclusive of black Latinos throughout the region proved contagious in the Georgia Annual Conference. At the 1906 session, a pastor called on AMEs to expand further into South America and especially focus on Brazil.[115]

These activities in Cuba and Mexico reflected the efforts of others in the Americas. David Patterson Talbot served in British Guiana and spread the denomination to Dutch Guiana. Born in British Guiana in 1877, Talbot was educated at Morris Brown College and Turner Theological Seminary, where he earned degrees in pedagogy and theology. He received both ordinations from Bishop Turner in 1903 and 1905 respectively. After his return to British

---

[114] Dickerson, *Religion, Race, and Region*, 122; *Journal of the Twenty-First Quadrennial Session of the General Conference, 1900*, 174, 192; *Proceedings (of the) Twenty-Second Session (of the) General Conference, 1904*, 84.

[115] Dickerson, *Religion, Race, and Region*, 126–127.

Guiana in 1906, he established Turner Monumental Church in Wakenaam, Essequibo. While sailing back from the 1912 General Conference, the boat docked at Paramaribo, Dutch Guiana, where an English-speaking clergyman invited him to evangelize in the Dutch colony. Talbot accepted, and started AME congregations and schools in Paramaribo and Nieuw Nickerie.[116]

Pushing AME development outside the United States became a preoccupation beyond the episcopacy and moved into other strata within the church's leadership. Jennie Bumry, the president of the WPMMS's Pittsburgh Branch, for example, declared in 1902 that the Macedonian call came through bishops in Africa, the Caribbean, and the Pacific that AMEs should be "special instruments in the evangelization of the darker races." Another WPMMS official from West Virginia said AMEs should make "good use of the opportunities in Cuba, Porto Rico, the Philippines and the numerous isles of the sea." This consciousness for a global solidarity of dark peoples permeated African Methodism and stretched across the church's ministry and membership.[117]

AME evangelism also extended to American Indians, including their communities of mixed black and indigenous populations. Former slaves to Indians, black migrants from the American South, and the indigenous peoples living in the Indian Territory responded to AME emissaries coming mainly from Arkansas. The Indian Mission Annual Conference grew to about twenty congregations between its start in 1879 and 1900. These churches were located on Creek lands and others were among the Choctaw and Cherokee. In the Creek nation there were AME congregations in all black settlements in Red Bird, Boley, and Clear View. They consisted of "Freedmen" who had been the slaves of Indian masters. One of these black Indians, J. A. Broadnax, became a presiding elder in this jurisdiction. Congregations also spread to the neighboring territory, where in 1895 the Oklahoma Annual Conference was established. The congregation at Guthrie, for example, founded in 1888, consisted of black migrants seeking to settle on

---

[116] Information provided to the author by Bishop Frederick H. Talbot, nephew of Reverend David P. Talbot.

[117] *Minutes of the Sixth Annual Convention of the Woman's Mite Missionary Society, Pittsburg [h] Conference Branch of the African Methodist Episcopal Church* held at AME Church, Brownsville, PA, July 3–6 Inclusive, 1902 (n.p., Publishing Committee: Lillian S. Dorkins, M. Levada Carter, & Libbie Skinner, 1902), 10; *Minutes of the Fourth Annual Convention of the Woman's Mite Missionary Society, Pittsburg[h] Conference Branch of the African Methodist Episcopal Church, Allegheny City, PA,* held July 5 –9, inclusive, 1904 (n.p., Publishing Committee: Lillian S. Dorkins, Libby Skinner, & M. Levada Carter, 1904), 44.

"new Indian lands." They faced, like others in the Indian Territory, the same racism from which they fled in the postbellum South.[118]

Like Broadnax, John Hall, an Ojibwe in Michigan, embraced African Methodism because its capacious Creole identity easily accommodated Indians with either tribal or mixed characteristics. In 1890 Hall, who joined the Michigan Annual Conference in 1887, became its "Indian Missionary." He was formerly an interpreter in Canada for the Indian mission of the Wesleyan Methodist Church. He was dismayed because these Wesleyan whites disrespected Ojibwe religious practices. AMEs, on the other hand, worshipped through rituals that appeared familiar to Hall. "We are not ashamed to shout when the Great Spirit comes into our hearts," Hall observed. His statement, most contemporary commentators would have argued, could have described an AME service. Moreover, Hall called AMEs his cousins, a term of crucial familial significance according to his biographer. Hall, she said, "unambiguously identified with an African American denomination and deployed the language of kinship to articulate his connection with members" of the AME Church.[119]

The "Indian Missionary" for AMEs in Michigan Hall reported in 1892 that he evangelized the Indian population at several sites including the Isabella settlement, Osceola, Aug-gans-te-gang, and De-wah-ne-gang. His effort yielded only fourteen Indian converts, but in 1894 he started a congregation at Athens, Michigan. Though less successful than missions in the Indian Territory and Oklahoma, Hall's ministry showed that AMEs included Indians in their vision of themselves as a church for those colonized by Euro-American hegemony.[120]

WOMEN AND AFRICAN METHODISM

The martyrdom of Sarah Gorham and the presence of Charlotte Manye as bridges between African Methodism in America and Africa illustrated the increased visibility and importance of women in church affairs. Levi J. Coppin, then editor of the *AME Church Review*, in his 1888 memoir of Catherine S. Campbell Beckett, said "from the very beginning women have

[118] Christina M. Dickerson, "The African Methodist Episcopal Church in the Indian and Oklahoma Territories, 1893–1907," *AME Church Review*, Vol. 123, No. 406, April–June 2007, 29–31, 32–34.
[119] Christina Dickerson-Cousin, "'I Call You Cousins': Kinship, Religion, and Black-Indian Relations in Nineteenth-Century Michigan," *Ethnohistory*, Vol. 61, No. 1, Winter 2014, 80–81, 87.
[120] Ibid. 88, 90–91.

been conspicuous in the history of the AME Church." The broad impact of the two missionary societies as incubators of denominational leadership and influences in church expansion on both sides of the Atlantic showed that women focused as much on issues of empowerment within the AME Church as on the dehumanizing effects of a resurgent racism upon disparate black populations throughout the Atlantic World. AME women, operating autonomous missionary organizations and in seeking ordination, created contested venues in which they asserted power in identifying initiatives and objectives for the mission and ministry of their church.[121]

In writing about the Women's Auxiliary of the National Baptist Convention (NBC), Evelyn Brooks Higginbotham said it exhibited a separatist consciousness at its founding in 1900, four years after the NBC was established. Though some of the founders were married to prominent preachers, Nannie H. Burroughs and her leadership cadre were either unmarried or unconnected to any clergymen. Hence, they were free to develop an autonomous body that maintained their treasury and priorities independent of male control. The launch of the two AME missionary groups occurred during this same era. Though viewed as subordinate bodies, these women governed themselves through their own slate of officers. While they gestured to male authority and selected leaders who had familial links to the denominational hierarchy, AME missionary societies, like their Baptist counterpart, raised and disbursed their own funds to their chosen projects.[122]

Both AME missionary societies owed their existence to general officers who believed that women should fund AME expansion outside the United States. Benjamin T. Tanner, the editor of the *Christian Recorder*, appealed to bishops' wives to organize and lead the WPMMS. Similarly, William B. Derrick, himself a West Indian and the Secretary of Missions, drew a hearty endorsement from Bishop Turner to start in 1893 the Women's Home and Foreign Missionary Society. While the older group, prevalent in the northern states, focused on Haiti, the Dominican Republic, and Sierra Leone, the second organization, predominant in the southern states, supported Turner's initiatives in West and South Africa.[123]

Leadership in the WPMMS lay with the wives and relatives of bishops and other clergy. The presidency of the national organization, for example,

---

[121] Levi J. Coppin, *In Memoriam of Catherine S. Campbell Beckett* (n.p., 1888), 106.
[122] Evelyn Brooks Higginbotham, *Righteous Discontent: The Women's Movement in the Black Baptist Church, 1880–1920* (Cambridge, MA, Harvard University Press, 1993), 155–159.
[123] Wright, *Centennial Encyclopedia of the African Methodist Episcopal Church*, 325–326; Sara J. Duncan, *Progressive Missions in the South and Addresses* (Atlanta, GA, Franklin Printing and Publishing Company, 1906), 90–91.

alternated among them. Sarah E. Tanner, wife of Bishop Tanner, presided as president at the first connectional convention in 1895, and at the second quadrennial meeting Florida Grant, the wife of Bishop Grant, succeeded her. Lillian Derrick, wife of Bishop Derrick, replaced Grant and served until 1907. An acting president, Carrie Cuff, functioned until Mary F. Handy, widow of Bishop Handy, presided from 1911 for the following two decades. Integral to the WPMMS infrastructure was Catherine S. Campbell Beckett, the wife of a pastor. Most importantly, she was the daughter of Bishop Jabaz P. Campbell and WPMMS founder, president, and treasurer, Mary A. Campbell. Fanny Jackson Coppin, the wife of Bishop Coppin, who was principal of Philadelphia's Institute of Colored Youth, remembered Beckett as a graduate of the school in 1872. Coppin recalled that Beckett was present when the WPMMS was started and noted her role in various offices. Similarly, Isabelle Tanner Temple, another pastor's wife and daughter to Bishop Tanner and perennial WPMMS president, Sarah Tanner, maintained a long and active participation in the organization, including the presidency of the Pittsburgh Annual Conference Branch. At the 1907 quadrennial meeting, for example, she served as first vice president at the same time that her mother was treasurer.[124]

These familial leadership patterns spilled over into endogamous practices connected to the episcopacy. To be a bishop's wife required the performance of duties beyond conventional marital responsibilities, including WPMMS involvements. Perhaps that led Bishop Grant to marry the sister of his recently deceased wife, Florida. The new Mrs. Grant, Louisa Rebecca Armstrong, was herself the widow of Bishop Josiah H. Armstrong. Bishop Turner married Mrs. Harriet Wayman, the widow of Bishop Alexander W. Wayman. She had been the WPMMS president from 1878 to 1883, and was expected to aid Turner's efforts to strengthen the Women's Home and Foreign Missionary Society. Mary A. Campbell, nearly ninety years old and Bishop Campbell's widow, reminded the 1907 WPMMS convention about the close ties between the wives of the bishops and their missionary organization. She credited her husband and Bishop John M. Brown with calling the women together to support the AME presence in the Atlantic

[124] Richard R. Wright, Jr. (compiler), *Encyclopedia of African Methodism* (Philadelphia, AME Book Concern, 1947), 424, 569; Octavia W. Dandridge, *A History of the Women's Missionary Society of the African Methodist Episcopal Church, 1874–1987* (n.p., 1987), 6; Coppin, *In Memoriam of Catherine S. Campbell Beckett*, 41, 43, 45, 47; *Journal of Proceedings of the Fourth Quadrennial Convention of the Women's Parent Mite Missionary Society of the African Methodist Episcopal Church (1907)*, 1; Alma A. Polk, *Twelve Pioneer Women in the African Methodist Episcopal Church* (n.p., 1947), 31.

World, especially the quarterly contributions that were going to Sierra Leone. Now, "only two of the original founders [were] living, Mrs. Bishop Brown and myself."[125]

Bishops' wives appeared at WPMMS conventions as denominational leaders who hardly hid their tie to the episcopacy. At the 1903 meeting, for example, Mary F. Handy, the wife of Bishop James A. Handy, had to her credit the organization of the Baltimore Annual Conference Branch during her husband's incumbency as presiding prelate. She counted heavily on the support of the wives of Bishops Brown, Wayman, and Campbell. Serving as 1903 convention vice presidents were Lillian Derrick, Sarah E. Tanner, and Mary Lee, another cadre of bishops' wives. Mayme S. Beckett, the granddaughter of Bishop Campbell, was the assistant secretary. Moreover, there was a special protocol where the bishops' wives were addressed as "Mrs. Bishop." Hence, as Bishop Arnett presided, he called the names of Mrs. Bishop Derrick, Mrs. Bishop Tanner, Mrs. Bishop Lee, and Mrs. Bishop Handy along with various pastors' wives and the well known Wilberforce professor, Hallie Quinn Brown. This title, "Mrs. Bishop," used in this missionary society context, allowed them to function with the concrete prerogatives of their husbands' office. South African AMEs memorialized Fanny Jackson Coppin in 1913 by naming a newly constructed dormitory at their Evaton school in the Transvaal in her honor. Coppin "was the only one, thus far, of the Bishops' wives," they said, "who came to Africa."[126]

In their vigorous support for AME expansion in the Caribbean and Africa, WPMMS leaders, including the bishops' wives, reflected the same Atlantic consciousness that shaped the ethos of their denomination. Mrs. Bishop Derrick, in her 1903 presidential report, for example, restated the WPMMS commitment to Sierra Leone. A letter from Charlotte Manye in South Africa was read in which she commended various groups including "Missionary Mite" branches for funding her educational projects. Starting in January 1903, with the permission of a tribal chief, Manye opened a school with twenty-five students. Because physical punishment from African males was

---

[125] Wright, *The Bishops of the African Methodist Episcopal Church*, 360; *Journal of Proceedings of the Fourth Quadrennial Convention of the WPMMS, 1907*, 66.

[126] *Journal of Proceedings of the Third Quadrennial Convention of the Women's Parent Mite Missionary Society of the African Methodist Episcopal Church* held in Wylie Avenue AME Church, Pittsburgh, PA, November 5–9, 1903 (n.p., Publishing Committee: M. Levada Carter, Libbie Skinner & Emma Chambers, 1903), 2, 12–13; Polk, *Twelve Pioneer Women*, 21; Wright, *The Bishops of the African Methodist Episcopal Church*, 207; *Journal of Proceedings of the Joint Session of the Cape and O.F.S. Conferences of the African Methodist Episcopal Church*, 1913, 24.

meted out to them for pursuing an education, some girls would no longer attend. "It would have made your heart ache," Manye said, "to see their backs and to know that they were lashed because their fathers want to sell them for so many head of cattle." The children "sit on the floor and the floor is of mud and clay." In her plea to the WPMMS, Manye said "I need the aid of my mothers. Let each member of the society, if possible, adopt a boy or girl." In response, Jennie Bumry, the president of the Pittsburgh Branch, "stated one box and one barrel had been made ready for Africa by the women of her branch." A Tennessee delegate added that

> Africa especially claims our support as African Methodists, for are we not bone of her bone, and flesh of her flesh? And our church being African from Bishop to sexton should Be profoundly interested in the redemption of her peoples.[127]

This sentiment suggested that the terminology "missionary society," a nomenclature adopted from Euro-American religious bodies, was a misnomer and a misleading description of how AME women actually viewed their transatlantic ministries. Charlotte Manye and her girls' education project in South Africa, for example, was far from being a missionary initiative through which culturally superior African Americans deigned to assist their African clients. Rather, Manye was a colleague in the Atlantic world of African Methodism partnering with the WPMMS to lift other females to higher levels of education that white hegemony and black male sexism denied to them.

Their male colaborers expressed the same egalitarian view when notified that M. M. Mokone and J. Z. Tantsi of South Africa, in route to the 1900 General Conference in Columbus, Ohio, "suffered shipwreck, narrowly escaping with their lives." A committee that included W. H. Mixon of Alabama proposed that Mokone and Tantsi should receive an appropriation from the denominational treasury to replace their belongings. They were "our brethren from South Africa" who were coming "to legislate with us for the best interest of this great church." Because Mixon also held this same unbiased perspective about AME women, he agreed with an observer of the 1907 WPMMS convention, who praised the organization as "a body of women who compose so largely the wives of the ministers of the AME Church" in addition to those who were spouses to bishops. She added "by coming in contact with such women we get breadth and we get strength."

---

[127] *Journal of Proceedings of the Third Quadrennial Convention of the WPMMS*, 1903, 14, 18–19, 76.

Despite these spousal connections and their subordinate relationship to the male-dominated General Conference and to the Secretary of Missions, the WPMMS functioned autonomously by raising and disbursing their own funds and channeling them to particular persons and projects. In 1900, for example, monies were allocated to two Caribbean clergy, Reuben Sealy in Barbados and T. L. M. Spencer in Trinidad, and also to H. M. Steady in Sierra Leone. The following year, Sealy received $100 to build a school in Upper Collymore. Additional gifts in 1902 went to Sealy and Spencer, while $500 was sent to Bishop Coppin in South Africa and $200 to his new presiding elder, Carlton Tanner, the son of a bishop and WPMMS treasurer.[128]

Those who received WPMMS monies singularly acknowledged the missionary women as the source of their supply. Steady, who wrote on Sierra Leone in 1907, noted his "pleasure to forward you a precise report of the work, whose main support has been assigned you by the authorities of our Church." He was wise to mention the Florida Grant Mission at Turnbo, named for the late WPMMS president. He needed funds to reopen "this operation" owing to its "destruction by fire." Mrs. Bishop Tanner, the bursar, in response, validated that quarterly payments had gone to Steady and that he showed "what business exactness the Rev. Steady accounted to the treasurer for the moneys sent to him" for the several congregations he supervised. Besides Steady in West Africa, the "never ceasing energy the Auxiliaries and Branches" of the WPMMS supported personnel in the "Barbados Isles, the Bahamas, and Bermuda" in addition to Charlotte Manye and M. Tantsi in South Africa.[129]

The WPMMS operated as an influential component within the AME Church. Because its top leadership exercised power that drew from the authority that their husbands held, those who were addressed as "Mrs. Bishop" performed in the organization the same prerogatives that were vested in their spouses. Emilie Townes, a scholar of womanist ethics, suggests that "sexism," however, was "more powerful and it showed up" in what the bishops' wives were called. These women, Townes adds, while reminded that their husbands were in charge, claimed power for themselves

[128] *Journal of the Twenty-First ... General Conference, 1900,* 117, 202–203; *Journal of Proceedings of the Third Quadrennial Convention of the WPMMS, 1903,* 16–17; Dennis C. Dickerson, *Religion, Race, and Region: Research Notes on AME Church History* (Nashville, TN, AME Sunday School Union, 1995), 101–102; *Journal of Proceedings of the Fourth Quadrennial Convention of the WPMMS, 1907,* 29, 40.

[129] *Journal of Proceedings of the Fourth Quadrennial Convention of the WPMMS, 1907,* 60–62, 75.

Figure 4.3 Wives of the AME bishops at the 1900 General Conference in Columbus, Ohio. Standing, left to right: Clara Moore, Ellen Lucretia Tyree, Christine S. Smith, Louisa Rebecca Armstrong, Lillian Derrick, Harriet Wayman, Anna Marie Shaffer, Fanny J. Coppin; seated, left to right: Mary Handy, Florida Grant, Sarah E. Tanner, Julia Gaines, Mary Louise Arnett, Mary L. Lee, Priscilla Salter (Author's private collection)

in the midst of their autonomous missionary organization. The growing presence of female evangelists, however, challenged this leadership model embodied in the bishops' wives, and it enhanced the meaning of women's autonomy. A subtle subversion bubbled beneath the surface of the amicable relationships between the wives of the bishops and pastors and compelled interactions with deferential, but determined women preachers. Most prominent among them were Amanda Berry Smith and Nora F. Taylor, well-known evangelists who were dually involved in WPMMS affairs and preaching in venues across the United States and abroad.

Smith, born to Maryland slaves in 1837, married an AME preacher. After her sanctification, she was involved, mainly in the 1880s, with the holiness movement traveling in Europe, India, and Africa as an evangelist. She settled in Chicago in 1892. Though her ministerial credentials derived from her AME affiliation, she knew that male opposition to female preachers was strong. At the 1872 General Conference, for example, a male minister accused her of promoting female ordination. "The thought of ordination," she said, "had never once entered my mind for I had received my ordin-ation" from a divine source. Nevertheless, she was well known to several bishops and their wives and received endorsements for her preaching and participation in the WPMMS. At the 1893 Third Episcopal District meeting in Columbus, Ohio, she led the devotions and was described as "a true evangelist called by God." In sharing reminiscences of her "stay in Africa," Smith expressed the same Atlantic consciousness as the bishops' wives. At the 1895 meeting Mrs. Bishop Wayman praised Smith because of what "she had done for Home mission work by raising eight orphan children." The *Christian Recorder*, in noting her presence at the meeting, proudly presented:

> Mrs. Amanda Smith, the great evangelist, [as] a woman who without education or means [and being] impressed by the Spirit to go to work for God, has traveled over two continents and surprised the world by her wonderful power in Biblical explanations, clear forceful preaching and wonderful evangelistic power. Any audience is glad to listen to her. Her name draws hundreds, and judgment day alone can tell the souls which have been brought to Christ through her efforts. She is known as a woman mighty in word and deed [and] one who has received an unction from the Holy One.[130]

Clergy at the 1896 Pittsburgh Annual Conference acknowledged Smith as an evangelist of international standing and validated her role in AME ministry and missionary activity. Bishop Benjamin F. Lee declared "we have a great occasion, a great opportunity, [and] a great personage [in] Mrs. Amanda Smith, one of the greatest women of the age, having traveled over three continents." Smith, whose remarks resembled a sermon more than a saluta-tion, read the seventeenth chapter of John and described it as an "interces-sory prayer in which Jesus prays for his people [and] his followers." She then shifted to "a very practical, definite and impressive exhortation combined with a pointed personal testimony" about "her entire sanctification." Women preachers, from Jarena Lee to Smith herself, more consistently than male clergy reminded AME audiences about this core Wesleyan tenet embedded in their belief.[131]

[130] Amanda Berry Smith, *Amanda Berry Smith: An Autobiography: The Story of the Lord's Dealings with Mrs. Amanda Smith: The Colored Evangelist* (New York, Oxford University Press, 1893, 1988), 17, 57, 77, 84, 113, 199–200, 255–506; *Christian Recorder*, July 20, 1893; November 14, 1895.

[131] *Minutes of the Twenty-Ninth Session of the Pittsburg[h] Annual Conference of the African Methodist Episcopal Church* held in St. Paul's AME Church, Washington, PA, October 8–14, 1896 (n.p., Publishing Committee: David F. Caliman, William H. Palmer, & Price A. Scott, 1896), 17.

Before she left the conference, Smith addressed the assembly again, sang her "favorite hymn," and "as she passed out of the Church, the Conference sang, 'Meet Me There.'" This moving act of respect was concretized in a resolution and in a donation to aid Smith's missionary project for orphans. The Pittsburgh Conference, said the resolution, was "honored as well as blessed by the presence of the greatest woman Evangelist of the Christian world in the person of Sister Amanda Smith." Because she was establishing a Colored Orphan's Home in Chicago, the conference endorsed the initiative and appropriated a small sum to help the launch of her venture. Though she lacked ordination, Smith, who was not a bishop's wife, created ministries in evangelism and in the social gospel that established compelling clerical credentials for herself and other female preachers that male colleagues both respected and affirmed.[132]

Smith and Nora F. Taylor at the 1907 WPMMS meeting paired together as delegates respectively representing the Ohio and the Chicago jurisdictions. Taylor, herself a female preacher, was a close friend to Smith. Taylor was made conspicuous at the convention when asked to sing and pray. Born in 1870 in Missouri, she migrated to Kansas City and later to Chicago where she joined Quinn Chapel. Bishop Grant "authorized" her as a "singing evangelist" in her annual conference and then she was permitted to preach, lecture, and to do missionary work. One observer who saw her at a Chicago area WPMMS meeting testified that Taylor "stirred the women with her fervent oratory into paroxysms of emotion." Like Smith, she traveled extensively, including to numerous Midwest locations. She was president of the WPMMS at Quinn Chapel and head of the Chicago division in the Iowa Annual Conference.[133]

Ransom, who knew Taylor, understood the implications of her presence in the WPMMS and as an AME female leader. "The women of the race," he said, "should take confidence from what her life achievements have demonstrated." He added that Taylor was an obscure church member possessed "with limited education, without influence or influential friends. She was not the wife of a bishop, prominent church official or of a man of any business or public importance. Her husband was just a plain working man." Nonetheless, Taylor, through "the sheer forcefulness of her personality and by the

---

[132] Ibid., 18–19, 68.
[133] *Journal of Proceedings of the Fourth Quadrennial Convention of the WPMMS, 1907*, Delegate roll page, 59; Jualynne Dodson, "Introduction" in Smith, *An Autobiography*, xxxviii; Dickerson, *A Liberated Past*, 138–139; *Christian Recorder*, July 18, 1901; Wright, *Eighty-Seven Years behind the Black Curtain*, 114.

complete consecration to God of her physical strength and her natural gifts of mind and spirit," became "the most popular, the most influential and the most universally beloved woman of her day."[134]

Ransom also linked Taylor to Smith because both derived their influence from their own preaching abilities, and not from their spousal connections. "As an evangelist," he declared, "the late Amanda Smith is the woman Sister Taylor can be most nearly compared." He said that "Amanda Smith was one of the greatest Evangelists of her day regardless of color or of race. In moments of great elation her face would often become transfigured with the overshadowing presence of the spirit of God. She was a saint." He added "Nora F. Taylor was her legitimate successor in her day and generation. We have seen Sister Taylor go up on the wings of the spirit until she would be transformed [with] her face shining with divine light until the whole audience would be caught up under the spell of manifestation of the divine presence." Similarly, the WPMMS's Pittsburgh Branch described Taylor as a "local church member and officer, and as a preacher, evangelist, traveler, lecturer, missionary and loyal church worker," all roles that she constructed for herself and not from spousal status. Therefore, "hers was a life of incomparable worth" and "her labor in America, in Bermuda, and in Africa made her the foremost woman in the AME Church."[135]

The subtle construction of alternate models of female autonomy was reinforced through the Women's Home and Foreign Missionary Society (WHFMS). Though Smith and Taylor drew support for their preaching from the WPMMS, the WHFMS, as it expanded within the South, benefited from the advocacy of female evangelists. A different leadership pattern developed in the WHFMS, the second, but equally influential, female organization. Though its members espoused the same pan-African perspective that permeated the WPMMS, this group, despite its closeness to Bishop Turner, became a venue for women whose leadership depended less on clergy connections and for those who were seeking ministerial recognition.

After its founding in 1893, Turner harnessed the organizational energies of the WHFMS to his initiatives in West and South Africa. Because the WPMMS mainly spread in northern and in some border states and neglected most of the South, the WHFMS viewed the southern states as available

---

[134] Reverdy C. Ransom, "Nora F. Taylor," in *AME Church Review*, Vol. 40, No. 158, October 1923, 91–92.

[135] Ibid.; *Minutes of the Twenty-Eighth Annual Convention of the Women's Mite Missionary Society, Pittsburgh Conference Branch [of the] African Methodist Episcopal Church* held in Park Place AME Church, Homestead, PA, July 10, 11, 12, 13, 1924 from Franklin, PA, *The New-Herald Press*, 1924), 10.

for its own expansion. In 1896 the Reverend Lillian Thurman, "a wonderful gospel preacher" and an experienced Michigan evangelist, became the "first general superintendent" of the WHFMS. Her successor, Sara Duncan, recalled that Thurman "for about six months traveled and organized in the South and West" until she resigned to take a pastorate. Duncan, who assumed her duties in 1897, reported to the 1900 General Conference that Thurman deserved commendation for coming to Georgia and Alabama to join Bishop Turner in launching the WHFMS. Because Thurman was a native Canadian and lived in Michigan, southern women wanted someone from their region to replace her.[136]

Between 1897 and 1900, Duncan traveled "15,698 miles, lectured to 416 audiences, organized 318 societies, re-established twenty-two auxiliaries, and juvenile [units], appointed organizers and presidents in each [of the] Presiding Elder Districts" in Georgia and Alabama. Similar progress happened elsewhere in the South, especially Florida, Kentucky, Mississippi, Arkansas, and the Carolinas. Duncan observed that Africa, "being our most important field," would have assistance for "the thirty ministers and 400 members with teachers and schools in West Africa, whose flag is waving and hands uplifted, shall not cry in vain." She also noted "South Africa, with the help of the women and children in America, shall show to the world what is meant in holy writ, 'Ethiopia shall stretch forth her hand.'"[137]

Unlike the WPMMS, the first two presidents of the WHFMS personified a different leadership model. Thurman, though her brother, Charles S. Smith, served as a general officer and later a bishop, developed her own persona as an AME leader. Her exposure to a national AME audience occurred in 1889 when she spoke at the dedication of the Sunday School Union. In her address on "Women" Thurman paid tribute to black women, some of whom were AME, who contributed to African American advancement. She mentioned Sojourner Truth, the abolitionist, Sarah J. Earley and Frances Ellen Watkins, fellow temperance advocates, and Hallie Quinn Brown and Fanny Jackson Coppin, both educators. Though she celebrated her brother and others who built the publishing house, "we must not forget the many efforts that have been made on the part of women of the Church for the purchase of this building as well as what they have done for humanity." Widely known as an evangelist in the Michigan Annual Conference, Thurman conducted

[136] Duncan, *Progressive Missions in the South and Addresses*, 101, 135; Bettye Collier-Thomas, *Jesus, Jobs, and Justice: African American Women and Religion* (New York, Alfred Knopf, 2010), 159–160.
[137] Duncan, *Progressive Missions in the South and Addresses*, 85, 87, 91.

revivals at several churches during the 1890s. In these contexts Turner became familiar with her ministry and chose her to head the WHFMS.[138]

Duncan, Thurman's successor, born in Cahaba, Alabama, in 1869, claimed in her family background "three colored men who were members of the [state's] First Constitutional Convention." Duncan was taught by tutors and educated at Knox Academy in Selma, where she was also a teacher. In 1889 she married Robert Duncan of Rome, Georgia, where she was a principal. They resettled in Selma where her husband operated a printing business. Her conspicuous participation in Selma at the WHFMS's first state convention led Turner to appoint her to follow Thurman as general president.[139]

Turner brought to the WHFMS issues that showed it as different from the WPMMS. He reinforced the pan-African vision already embedded in the AME ethos and espoused in the WPMMS. The WHFMS, however, targeted Turner's West and South Africa missions and supported them with the same vigor that the WPMMS pursued in Haiti and the Caribbean. Most importantly, he responded to southern AME women who had been excluded from leadership in the WPMMS and appointed Sara Duncan as president and empowered her and other female southerners. Moreover, Turner, in a maverick move at the 1885 North Carolina Annual Conference, ordained Sarah Ann Hughes as an itinerant deacon, impressed that as an evangelist Hughes had productively served as a pastor to various congregations. At Wilson Mills, North Carolina, for example, Hughes led the congregation in constructing a new edifice. His successor, Bishop Campbell, however, rescinded the Hughes ordination. Though the 1888 General Conference upheld Campbell's action, female evangelists were affirmed in their status. Hence, Turner and other bishops, though still appointing them to churches mainly in less desirable locations, discovered, as in the case of female evangelists in Georgia, that they could be helpful in spreading and promoting the WHFMS. Hence, the rise of women's missionary societies intersected with the increase of female preachers.[140]

Turner's advocacy for Hughes coincided with a broader discourse about women's ordination in other white and black Wesleyan bodies.

[138] Smith, *Dedicatory Services*, 74–78; Dickerson, *African Methodism and Its Wesleyan Heritage*, 85.
[139] Duncan, *Progressive Missions in the South and Addresses*, 12–13, 201.
[140] Stephen W. Angell, "The Controversy over Women's Ministry in the African Methodist Episcopal Church during the 1880s: The Case of Sarah Ann Hughes," in Judith Weisenfeld and Richard Newman (eds.), *This Far by Faith: Readings in African American Women's Religious Biography* (New York, Routledge, 1996), 95–96, 103, 105.

Conventional perspectives, reflected in Daniel A. Payne's 1889 book *A Treatise on Domestic Education*, illustrated male AME thinking on the subject. Christian motherhood was Payne's ideal and the best duty that women perfomed for the church. With regard to John and Charles Wesley, "their feet were set in the right path by the consummate prudence and skill of their pious mother," Susannah Wesley. Though both parents were "co-laborers," Payne believed, "the mother is the special teacher and educator of her own child." He added that "if she be wise, how she can affect earth and heaven, both time and eternity, by her diligent, daily prayerful teachings, and her Christian examples of holiness and self-abnegation." Women need not become ministers because motherhood was their singular and highest calling. Payne, argued historian Julius H. Bailey, "viewed the licensing of female preachers as a threat not only to the family, but to his sense of male authority." Bailey correctly contended that Payne and other male AME leaders defined Victorian womanhood as meaning "maternal responsibilities and the care of the home as] paramount to any other pursuit." Benjamin T. Tanner opposed Hughes's ordination because Jesus shunned women as his preachers and disciples. He said in 1898 that Turner's action "is one that Christ did not order, if we are to take his course in His selection of the Twelve and of the Seventy as expressive of His mind." These same perspectives motivated the Methodist Episcopal Church in barring the ordination of two women in 1880. The Methodist Protestant Church, however, ordained one of them, Anna Howard Shaw, but withdrew it in 1884.[141]

Turner's rationale for Hughes's ordination was in part pragmatic. Because her pastoral successes happened in North Carolina where AMEs trailed the AME Zion Church in membership, Turner was convinced that female ministers such as Hughes could challenge the Zion ascendancy in the Old North State. Ironically, some Zionites, such as Turner, promoted women's ordination to address a similar problem of "too much useless male timber lying around in all our conferences." The 1898 ordination of Mary J. Blair Small, the wife of a bishop, in the Philadelphia–Baltimore Annual Conference, occurred in this discursive context. The ordination of Julia Foote followed in 1900 in the New Jersey Annual Conference. In becoming elders

---

[141] Daniel A. Payne, *A Treatise on Domestic Education*fromCincinnati, OH, Cranston & Stowe, 1889), 3, 121–122, 135–136, 139; Julius H. Bailey, *Around the Family Altar: Domesticity in the African Methodist Episcopal Church, 1865–1900* (Gainesville, University Press of Florida, 2005), 4, 45; Benjamin T. Tanner, *Dispensations in the History of the Church and the Interregnums*, Vol. I (n.p., 1898), 133–134; "Timeline of Women in Methodism," www.umc.org/who-we-are/timeline-of-women-in-methodism.

in the AME Zion Church, Small and Foote laid to rest whether women were entitled to full clerical standing in an historic Wesleyan body.[142]

Though the AMEs revoked the Hughes ordination and restricted women to the lower office of evangelist, Turner maintained his advocacy for women preachers by deploying them to building the WHFMS. While presiding in Georgia from 1896 to 1908, some female evangelists doubled as WHFMS organizers. A. E. Duncan, in the Southwest Georgia Annual Conference, filled these roles. In 1898 she organized twenty-three local branches with 487 members. Her preaching also drew new AME members, and outside Georgia Duncan, "by the inspiration of the Holy Spirit," delivered sermons elsewhere in the South and in the Midwest. Other female evangelists, Angeline E. Brown and Virginia Drinkard, like Duncan, reported at the 1904, 1905, and 1906 sessions of the Southwest Georgia Conference on WHFMS funds they raised. Additionally, Brown in 1904 preached fifty-two sermons and conducted fifteen praise services.[143]

Just as Amanda Berry Smith and Sarah Ann Hughes encountered opposition to their presence in ministry, A.E. Duncan was similarly criticized in Georgia. A minister in the Macon Georgia Annual Conference accused her of saying "hard things about our Church" and about Morris Brown College. A committee investigated the charges, found them true, and recommended against her preaching in their jurisdiction. Moreover, the Southwest Georgia Conference to which she belonged was informed about these findings. Presiding D. S. Wells, a Turner confidante, however, defended Duncan and no action was taken against her.[144]

Despite the attacks on Duncan and similar accusations against another evangelist, Mrs. Ryals in the Southwest Georgia Conference, Turner stayed committed to female preachers because of their involvement in the WHFMS. Millie Wolfe, the most prominent among Georgia's female evangelists and WHFMS supporters, drew from Turner the same advocacy in authenticating her ministry as he had done with Sarah Ann Hughes. He provided her with several opportunities to preach at various sessions of the Georgia Annual Conference. At the 1904 session of the district's WHFMS, for example, Wolfe

---

[142] Angell, "The Controversy over Women's Ministry," 102–103; Martha S. Jones, "'Too Much Useless Male Timber': The 'Man Question' in the Woman Ordination Debate in the African Methodist Episcopal Zion Church," *AME Church Review*, Vol. 118, No. 385, January–March 2002, 61; Sandy Dwayne Martin, "The African Methodist Episcopal Zion Church and the Women's Ordination Controversy, 1898–1900: A Case Study on the Value of Racial Inclusivity in Religious Studies," *Journal of the Interdenominational Theological Center*, Vol. 21, Nos. 1 and 2, Fall 1993/Spring 1994, 108, 111.
[143] Dickerson, *A Liberated Past*, 127–128, 131.   [144] Ibid. 132–133.

commented on "the many sacrifices which she had made for the cause of sacred missions" and reported on her travels as an evangelist. In 1905 she preached in three of Georgia's annual conferences and one in Kentucky, in which she logged 334 sermons and attracted 115 new AME members.[145]

Though barred from ordaining any other women, Turner still authorized Wolfe to go through the regular process to become an itinerant elder. She was admitted on trial to the 1899 Georgia Annual Conference and was approved all the way to Fourth Year Studies at the 1903 session. Though she pursued the same course of study as her male peers, they were ordained and she was not. When Wolfe asked to relocate to the Iowa Annual Conference in 1904, Turner granted her request and she was transferred as a virtual ordinand to another jurisdiction.[146]

Sara Duncan agreed that the denomination's two missionary societies should be linked to female preachers. Their homiletical and organizational skills benefited both groups. Moreover, each would seem vulnerable to a different and subversive model of women's leadership. Duncan explained the unexpected convergence between the WPMMS and the WHFMS on the matter of female preachers. In her *Progressive Missions in the South* she commended the WPMMS's Nora F. Taylor, "the great evangelist, sweet singer and one who works untiringly for the cause of missions." Additionally, "many souls have been brought to Christ by her preaching." Concerning Millie Wolfe in the WHFMS, Duncan noted she "has done more in the State of Georgia for the cause of Christ, starting mission points, building churches, and saving souls, than any other woman of her day and generation." Duncan added, in deference to male clergy, that Wolfe "does her work in a womanly way. She dresses the same, takes the women as her associates, and never tries to get away from her sex." Nonetheless, "some of her sermons have [been] published," especially "Scriptural Authority for Women's Work in the Christian Church."[147]

Turner and Duncan were obviously aware that regional differences existed between the two missionary societies and that there was no "Mrs. Bishop" as an officer in the southern-based group WHFMS. Turner's four marriages, three of which left him widowed, testified to the absence and the low profile of his spouses in either missionary group. Eliza Ann Peacher Turner, his first wife, a South Carolinian and mother of their several children, seldom traveled with him to his far-flung episcopal assignments. Her obituary in 1889 made no mention of any WPMMS affiliation and she died before the WHFMS was founded. Martha Elizabeth DeWitt Turner, his second wife, to whom he was married for nearly a decade, was a Georgia native who was

---

[145]   Ibid. 129–130, 133.   [146]   Ibid., 130–131.
[147]   Duncan, *Progressive Missions in the South and Addresses*, 179, 213–214.

reared near Philadelphia. She was the first bishop's wife ever to affiliate with the WHFMS. Instead of contending for the presidency, she restricted her activities to the subordinate chapters of the organization. She was president of the local WHFMS at Big Bethel in Atlanta, and a year before her death in 1898 Mrs. Turner headed the Georgia state affiliate. Turner, in marrying Harriet Ann Elizabeth Wayman, tapped the widow of Bishop Alexander Wayman to share his interest in the WHFMS. Born in 1828 in Baltimore and married in1864 to a recently elected and widowed bishop, Harriet Wayman was among the cohesive cadre of bishops' wives who founded the WPMMS. She apparently had little, if any, involvement with the WHFMS because she died within a few years of marrying Turner.[148]

Sara Duncan never mentioned Harriet Wayman Turner as a contributor to the WHFMS. There seemed to be no need because Laura Lemon, a confidante to Henry and Martha Turner, became her dependable channel to the bishop. Lemon was born in Atlanta in 1880 and educated locally at Clark College and Morris Brown College. In 1897, Martha Turner asked her to work as an assistant secretary to the bishop and to serve as her companion. After the death of Martha Turner, Lemon became the bishop's chief secretary for the Sixth Episcopal District. In 1902, clergy in the Atlanta Annual Conference urged her selection as president of the WHFMS for that jurisdiction. They supported her by increasing their annual allocation to the branch. After the death of Harriet Wayman Turner, Lemon married Bishop Turner and was elected in 1908 to succeed Duncan as WHFMS president. Ironically, Bishop Turner's death on May 18, 1915 was followed by Laura Turner's demise on October 11, 1915.[149]

Sallie G. Simmons, the WHFMS vice president and the wife of a South Carolina pastor, replaced Turner. Though Simmons inherited 43 annual conference branches, 1,322 congregational societies, and 13,591 members, the WHFMS remained the smaller of the two AME missionary societies. The WPMMS had 22,000 members and raised $65,553 between 1911 and 1916, while the WHFMS, during a similar period, raised $34,695. These disparities paled in importance to the broader reality that these missionary women as much as the male leaders of the AME Church commonly viewed their denomination as a transatlantic religious body.[150]

---

[148] *Christian Recorder*, November 19, 1885; July 25, 1889; January 20, 1898; February 10, 1898; Wright, *The Bishops of the African Methodist Episcopal Church*, 337.

[149] Duncan, *Progressive Missions in the South and Addresses*, 137-139; Wright, *Centennial Encyclopedia*, 320.

[150] Polk, *Twelve Pioneer Women*, 23; Wright, *Centennial Encyclopedia*, 320; *Journal of the Twenty-Fifth Quadrennial Session (Being the Centennial Session) of the General Conference of the African Methodist Episcopal Church, Philadelphia, Penn., May 3rd to May 23rd, 1916* (Philadelphia, AME Sunday School Union, 1916), 358-360.

The establishment of women's missionary societies in the historic black Methodist and National Baptist religious bodies accompanied the rise of a nationally organized black women's club organization and increased black involvement in the Young Women's Christian Association (YWCA). Then in 1896, out of preexisting state and local organizations, emerged the National Federation of Afro-American Women, later renamed the National Association of Colored Women (NACW), into the forefront of African American leadership. The women's clubs joined the fight against lynching and female suffrage, causes that member Ida B. Wells-Barnett of Chicago, an intermittent AME, nationally championed. The organization also engaged in a range of self-help projects and social services especially for poor and working women. AME women, either in the WPMMS or in the WHFMS, extended their activities to NACW programs and governance. An early endorsement came from the WPMMS's North Ohio Annual Conference branch. Sadie J. Anderson, the corresponding secretary, noted that in recent years there had been an "epiphany of [the] woman" and that "now the dear brothers hail with joy the dawn of the day of the systematically organized efforts of their sisters."[151]

An AME of formative NACW influence was Lucy Thurman, the National Superintendent of the Women's Christian Temperance Union work among Afro-Americans. A Washington DC affiliate, the Lucy Thurman Union, like numerous other groups, paid to the NACW an initial affiliation fee. The unit addressed the disproportionate black population "in our jail and workhouses" and its program to "help our women to understand the significance of physical training as a temperance measure and a most important factor in hygiene and health reform." Thurman spearheaded and became president in 1898 of the Michigan State Federation, a NACW group that addressed lynching and the convict lease system. Thurman, who was elected in 1906 as the NACW's third president, at an earlier national meeting, motioned for financial assistance for "Mother Harriet Tubman," the aged abolitionist, to attend the proceedings. Thurman's successor, Elizabeth Carter, a large presence in Bethel Church in New Bedford, Massachusetts, was the first recording secretary in 1896 and then presided as fourth president over the NACW's 45,000 members from 1908 to 1912. Later, she married the widowed Bishop William S. Brooks. Mamie Robinson Fletcher Ross, who was married to Bishop Isaac N. Ross, formerly the pastor of Metropolitan AME Church in Washington DC, like Thurman, the sister to Bishop Charles S. Smith, was "an enthusiastic member" of the NACW. Thurman's sister-in-law, Christine Shoecraft Smith, while her husband supervised the AME Sunday School Union, started a women's club in Nashville in 1896 and immediately connected it to the NACW. Later, she became a WPMMS president. Joining these leading AME women was Alice Dugged Carey, an educator at Morris Brown College and pastoral spouse, who directed the NACW's rescue work.[152]

Similarly, less visible AME women blended their missionary society with NACW activities. Hattie Lucile Buren simultaneously served as president of the WPMMS' Missouri Annual Conference Branch and as treasurer of the Missouri State Federation of Women's Clubs. In the same way, Mamie J. Brockman Butler was president of the WHFMS's Mississippi Annual Conference Branch and secretary of Mississippi's State Federated Clubs and organizer of its charitable and literary divisions. Unlike Buren and Butler, Leanna C. Snowden was not married to a minister but was spouse to a mail carrier. Nonetheless, she became president in 1912 of the WPMMS's Kentucky Annual Conference Branch and elected a delegate to the organization's 1916 convention in Detroit. Concurrently, she served as the first president of the City Federation of Women's Clubs in Lexington, Kentucky, and first vice president in NACW's state affiliate.[153]

Involved AME women also energized the YWCA and its network of local divisions. In New York City, for example, Sadie Battles, while prominent in the WPMMS's New York Annual Conference Branch, also chaired a special YWCA committee charged with fundraising for the move of the black Manhattan affiliate uptown into Harlem. Emma Ransom, visible and influential in the WPMMS and formerly the kindergarten supervisor at Chicago's Institutional Church, accompanied her husband to New York City where he became the pastor of Bethel Church. Immediately, she delivered speeches for both suffrage and YWCA meetings. In 1909 she began a fifteen-year tenure as president of the volunteer management committee for the black Manhattan branch. Christine S. Smith, already active in the WPMMS and the NACW,

---

[152] *A History of the Club Movement among the Colored Women*, 35, 57, 78; Bettye Collier Thomas, *Jesus, Jobs, and Justice: African American Women and Religion* from New York, Alfred Knopf, 2010), 282–283; Giddings, *Ida*, 493; Wright, *The Bishops of the African Methodist Episcopal Church*, 110; Ransom, *The Pilgrimage of Harriett Ransom's Son*, 144; Wright, *Centennial Encyclopedia of the African Methodist Episcopal Church*, 191–193; Wright, *Encyclopedia of African Methodism*, 255–256; Duncan, *Progressive Missions in the South and Addresses*, 130.

[153] Wright, *Centennial Encyclopedia of the African Methodist Episcopal Church*, 52, 54, 211.

chaired the Detroit YWCA's committee of management of the Lucy Thurman Branch. Beyond these missionary ministries, AME women, through the NACW and the YWCA, became "political" actors in their support for female suffrage and reform initiatives to address the condition of African Americans. Moreover, AME, NACW, and YWCA leadership constituted an interlocking network of elite women that included their counterparts in the AME Zion and National Baptist bodies. These church-based women deployed sundry quasi-religious and service bodies to operationalize their vision for a social and political order to empower women and all their segregated and colonized kinfolk in the black Atlantic.[154]

Though the denomination boasted 548,355 members in 1916, that same year the Secretary of Missions lamented that in the "foreign fields" of the Caribbean, South America, and Africa, the AMEs numbered only 22,900. South Africa claimed nearly all of the membership with 18,573, with West Africa and Jamaica a distant second and third, with 1,548 and 1,055 respectively. Though perception scarcely matched facts on the ground, denominational rhetoric still connected the Americas to Africa, thus advancing the claim that AMEs hoped to realize religious dominance within the Atlantic World.[155]

At the centennial General Conference in 1916 Bishop Parks, in the quadrennial sermon, credited clergy with the spread of AME "operations to every state in the Union, West and South Africa, Haiti, Santo Domingo, Bermuda and South America." Parks and his colleagues echoed his observations in their episcopal address and recalled John Allen, the son of the founder, who extended the AME presence to Haiti and used his facility in French and Spanish to advance African Methodism. "The study of Spanish and French, and some of the African tribal languages," they said, "should now be taken up in order to better prepare the church to carry on its foreign work." They also noted that AMEs in the United States should be attentive to "our kindred beyond the sea," should do more and more for the redemption of Africa," and "grasp the outstretched hand of Ethiopia" to sustain AMEs on both sides of the Atlantic.[156]

---

[154] Judith Weisenfeld, *African American Women and Christian Activism: New York's Black YWCA, 1905–1945* from Cambridge, MA, Harvard University Press, 1997), 56–57, 91–92; Ransom, *First Quadrennial Report*, 11; Wright, *Encyclopedia of African Methodism*, 256; Glenda Elizabeth Gilmore, *Gender and Jim Crow: Women and the Politics of White Supremacy in North Carolina, 1896–1920* (Chapel Hill, University of North Carolina Press, 1996), 15, 200.
[155] *Journal of the Twenty-Fifth Quadrennial Session . . . of the General Conference*, 1916, 351.
[156] Ibid., 53, 290, 307.

5

෴

Into the Second Century: Migration, Depression, and War, 1916–1945

The Centennial General Conference of African Methodism opened on May 3, 1916 in Philadelphia at Mother Bethel Church. This towering edifice was situated on the same property on which the congregation built its first structure in 1794. After the traditional singing of Charles Wesley's "And Are We Yet Alive," Bishop Joseph S. Flipper delivered an opening prayer to commemorate this historic meeting and to thank God for this "spot where our founder and first Bishop organized this branch of Thy Zion." He was grateful "for that spirit which Richard Allen manifested to the world, when he with a few others, in 1787, rose from their knees in St. George Church, and marched out to stand up for manhood Christianity, believing that 'God made out of one blood all men to dwell upon all the face of the earth.'" Flipper also asked the Lord to "bless our brethren from West Africa, South Africa and South America and the isles of the sea, and may they realize as they meet with us here and elsewhere and labor with us, that we are brothers and sisters [from the same] home land."[1]

Among the many delegates, all of them men, were leading clergy and a lesser number of lay delegates, who were equally distinguished. They included John M. Avery, an officer and director of the North Carolina Mutual Life Insurance Company in Durham, North Carolina, Charles V. Roman, a physician and professor at Meharry Medical College in Nashville, Tennessee, and Reuben J. Gardner from the all black Mound Bayou,

---

[1] *Journal (of the) Twenty-Fifth Quadrennial Session [Being the Centennial Session] of the African Methodist Episcopal Church, 1916*, 43–45.

Mississippi, and an official with the Yazoo & Mississippi Valley Railway. This august body transacted the business of the denomination in the stately "mother" church of African Methodism located in Philadelphia's downtown historic district. They also celebrated the independence and self-sufficiency of their transatlantic religious body, believing that it was a bulwark for protecting blacks in the diaspora and promoting their well-being.[2]

Lurking on the horizon, however, were several inexorable events related to two world wars, migration, Garveyism, and depression that would transform the global landscape in which the African Methodist Episcopal (AME) Church would operate between 1916 and 1945. As World War I was unfolding, the bishops seemed prescient in realizing the complicated and confounding challenges that lay ahead of their denomination. "One sure interpretation of these things," they declared in 1917, is that "these things are hard to understand" and therefore "God is calling aloud for a closer walk with him." As a faith declaration, the bishops were correct, but they seemed bewildered as to how to retrofit African Methodism, both structurally and intellectually, to navigate the new realities flowing from these unprecedented developments.[3]

In the late nineteenth and early twentieth centuries racism morphed into advanced systems of segregation and colonialism on both sides of the Atlantic, and proactive AMEs adopted strategies to resist and overcome these hegemonic structures. Beginning in the early twentieth century, however, AMEs experienced the unparalleled challenges that world wars, unprecedented demographic movements, resurgent black nationalism, and economic crisis would produce. These overwhelming forces required solutions beyond what they had previously devised. Though institutionally mature and stable with half a million members, more than 6,000 churches in almost every state, and an impressive infrastructure of denominational departments, AME leaders adhered to an erroneous belief that these organizational achievements immunized them from these imminent societal and global changes. Their institutional responses were at times belated, inadequate, and too reliant on routine rhetoric about the diagnosis and cure for black oppression. Whatever was lacking in organizational initiatives and strategies, this large denomination included well-qualified personnel, both

[2] Ibid., 11, 16, 18; Richard R. Wright, Jr. (ed.), *Centennial Encyclopedia of the African Methodist Episcopal Church* (Philadelphia, PA, AME Book Concern, 1916), 30, 94, 190–191.
[3] "Address of the Council of Bishops, AME Church," *Christian Recorder*, August 16, 1917, cited in Milton C. Sernett (ed.), *African American Religious History: A Documentary Witness* (Durham, NC, Duke University Press, 1985), 42.

in the clergy and laity, who maintained a tradition of AME social holiness and who pressed their leaders to develop innovative proposals to modernize African Methodism.

Though war was a normative feature in the human experience, none had the broad moral impact and the incomparable carnage associated with World War I. Competing nation-states pursuing power and territory, settling old scores, and asserting claims of self-determination pushed the Triple Entente and the Triple Alliance into an irreversible conflict that culminated in the violence of war. A villainized Germany along with its ally, Austria-Hungary, were pitted initially against Russia, but mainly in opposition to England, France, and the United States that were fighting "to make the world safe for democracy." The resulting casualties of 37 million people, including 10 million military fatalities and 7 million civilian deaths, stirred revulsion from a range of religious bodies. Beginning with the Quakers through their American Friends Service Committee to the Fellowship of Reconciliation and to the Mennonites and some Pentecostal bodies, including the all black Church of God in Christ, pacifism, embodied in resistance to all war, became a permanent part of twentieth-century religious discourse. A derivative idea and moral methodology, nonviolence, also emerged out of this discursive development.[4]

Notwithstanding the unimaginable slaughter that happened in World War I, AMEs maintained an ambivalent posture toward war. On multiple levels, war, though it was a repulsive display of human depravity, provided freedom opportunities for African Americans and vocational possibilities in military chaplaincy for black clergy. Broader concerns about the morality of war itself seldom displaced these pragmatic considerations. AMEs embraced the Civil War in the 1860s and the Spanish-American War in 1898, and boasted a prestigious roster of AME chaplains from Henry M. Turner in 1863 to George A. Singleton in 1918. Singleton, for example, was assigned to the 317th Engineers of the 92nd Division during World War I and was stationed in France. Similarly, J. Acton Hill, a well-known Kentucky pastor, was a World War I chaplain and a first lieutenant. Moreover, two AME agencies appropriated special funds "to the chaplains of our Connection to work in the United States Army." Additionally, during World War I various

---

[4] Joseph Kip Kosek, *Acts of Conscience: Christian Nonviolence and Modern Democracy* (New York, Columbia University Press, 2009), 4, 21, 23–26, 34–42; Theodore Kornweibel, Jr., "'I Thank My God for the Persecution': Conscientious Objection in the Church of God in Christ," in Paul N. Alexander (ed.), *Pentecostalism and Nonviolence: Reclaiming A Heritage* (Eugene, OR, Pickwick Publications, 2012), 39–63.

AME ministers entered the military. Frederick D. Coleman, a licensed Kentucky preacher, for example, became in 1918 a soldier in both England and France in the 814th Pioneer Infantry, Company E. Furthermore, some current bishops were themselves veterans or related to army officers. Bishop Cornelius T. Shaffer, for example, was a Civil War veteran and Henry O. Flipper, the brother to Bishop Flipper, was the first black graduate of West Point. At Wilberforce University, the denomination's flagship institution, President Grover Cleveland assigned Lieutenant John Alexander to establish a military science department. After Alexander's sudden death, Colonel Charles Young, the third black graduate of West Point, succeeded him. While stationed at the school, Young organized the 9th Ohio Battalion of Colored Soldiers that later fought during the Spanish-American War. Through the World War I period AMEs boasted that "there is only one colored institution that has a United States Military Department," namely Wilberforce University. Benjamin O. Davis, a captain of the US Calvary, was Professor of Military Science and Tactics during World War I.[5]

Whatever reservations AMEs officially expressed about World War I, scarcely anyone offered any pacifist perspective. Denominational leadership was simply too invested in the military to develop any anti-war views. Though racism marred the career of Henry O. Flipper and Charles Young, who faced racist attempts to force him into a premature retirement, AMEs, while critical of army segregation and other racist practices, leveled no charge against war itself. Hence, prominent clergy offered moral circumlocutions that pondered the human failings that caused war, but avoided any outright condemnation of militarism itself. Just a few weeks after the war began, the 1914 Pittsburgh Annual Conference observed that in the European conflict "the allied powers are in a death struggle for supremacy." The reason, these AMEs believed, drew from "the rebel spirit [that] is uppermost in man." They added "it is the adoption of methods distinctly un-Christian in the attempt to adjust the difficulties between man and man, and between

[5] Richard R. Wright, Jr., *The Bishops of the African Methodist Episcopal Church* (Nashville, TN, AME Sunday School Union, 1963), 30–31, 301, 331; *The Autobiography of George A. Singleton* (Boston, Forum Publishing Company,1964), 89, 96; Richard R. Wright, Jr. (compiler), *Who's Who in the General Conference, 1924* (Philadelphia, AME Book Concern, 1924), 212; *Journal of the Twenty-Sixth Quadrennial Session of the General Conference of the African Methodist Episcopal Church* held in St. Louis, MO, May–18, 1920 (Nashville, TN, AME Sunday School Union, 1922), 330; Richard R. Wright, Jr. (compiler), *Encyclopedia of African Methodism* (Philadelphia, PA, AME Book Concern, 1947) 70; A. S. Jackson, *Department of Education, African Methodist Episcopal Church, Ninth Quadrennial Report, General Conference*, St. Louis, MO, May, 1920, 11; *Wilberforce Bulletin*, Summer Session Number, June 19–July, 1916, April 1916, 6.

nation and nation." The solution lay in taming "the rebel heart," rather than developing a countervailing force through pacifism. In showing uncertainty about the war AMEs, with apocalyptic undertones, queried "who can tell? . . . what seer can penetrate the gathering gloom and tell what the coming day will be?"[6]

The bishops also lacked a moral methodology through which war could be critiqued. In their 1916 episcopal address they realized that World War I "became so large and far reaching that the average mind could not so grasp its import as to properly diagnose its cause, forecast its extent, or properly define its ultimate result." So what was their recommendation? "Let's get back to the Bible," they declared." "He who proclaimed the doctrine of peace on earth and good will toward men," continued the prelates," is Himself the Prince of Peace, and has all the ages at His command to carry out His righteous purposes in the government of this world." Again, in 1920, the bishops acknowledged "the distress, bloodshed, confusion, and carnage brought on by the Worldwide War." At the same time AMEs were proud that "during the recent world war, 400,000 Negro men, undaunted, went forth to battle, and 'Over There,' and, here in camps, and other places, they fought." Again, denominational leaders issued no verdict on the morality of war itself, unlike the small but growing number of Christians, outside African Methodism, who opposed violence of any kind.[7]

Though opposition to armed conflict in favor of pacifism scarcely characterized AME perspectives about the carnage resulting from combat, a single voice proposed a way other than the violence of war to settle international disputes. Reverdy C. Ransom, the editor of the *AME Church Review*, was among the first black intellectuals to recognize Gandhi's nonviolence in India as a moral principle and praxis grounded in spirituality. He understood it as a strategy to advance the interests of aggrieved peoples and as an effective force that would avoid the violence of war. In "Gandhi: Indian Messiah and Saint," Ransom identified him as "the new 'Light of Asia,' [who] would deliver his countrymen from the rule of British imperialism, not by violent resistance, but through the peaceful method of non-cooperation." Ransom also noted "the Western nations, claiming to be Christian through the centuries, have rejected the doctrine of non-resistance by Christ.

---

[6] *Minutes (of the) Forty-Seventh Session of the Pittsburgh Annual Conference (of the) African Methodist Episcopal Church* held in Bethel AME Church, Williamsport, PA, October 7–11, 1914 (Philadelphia, PA, AME Book Concern, 1914), 49.
[7] *Journal (of the) Twenty-Fifth Quadrennial Session, 1916*, 307, 310; *Journal of the Twenty-Sixth Quadrennial Session of the General Conference of the African Methodist Episcopal Church, 1920*, 120, 212.

Even to this day they are unable to think of concerted resistance save in terms of war." In 1931 Josephus R. Coan, an AME seminarian at Yale Divinity School, joined with his five black classmates in sponsoring a conference on "Whither The Negro Church." The black students, including Coan and their white faculty adviser, concluded that Gandhi resembled Jesus in espousing the superiority of nonviolence over the weaponry of violence.[8]

AFRICAN METHODISM AND THE BLACK MIGRATION

The practical effects of war on African Americans rather than pacifism preoccupied AME leaders. The bishops, for example, were pleased that their colleague, William W. Beckett, elected in 1916, sailed to South Africa "although World War I was raging and the Atlantic Ocean was infested with German submarines." Charles S. Smith, another bishop, abbreviated his visit to Bermuda "owing to uncertainty re[lated to] steamboat accommodations" between the island and New York City caused "by strenuous war conditions." At the same time, the black migration from the rural South to the urban and industrial North and the violent response of white workers drew an increased share of the church's attention. AME clergy had long known that their "mobile laity" and their peripatetic movements directly affected the vibrancy of their congregations. Whether in the antebellum escape of free and slave blacks to the safer environs of the North, Canada, and Liberia or in the postbellum Exoduster movement out of the South into Kansas and the Great Plains, African Americans, many of them AMEs, seemed always to be an "unsettled people." As they moved slowly but steadily into areas that promised work in mills, mines, and other industrial sites, preachers tied their ecclesiastical successes to the economic opportunities available to their parishioners and hoped to realize the demographic benefits resulting from black migration.[9]

In the 1890s, in the two decades before the World War I era migration, work sites in West Virginia and in western and northeastern Pennsylvania

---

[8] Reverdy C. Ransom, "Gandhi: Indian Messiah and Saint," *AME Church Review*, Vol. 38, No. 150, 87; "Whither the Negro Church?" Seminar held at Yale Divinity School, New Haven, CN, April 13–15, 1931, 3, 5, 37–38, 42, 47–48.

[9] Wright, *The Bishops of the African Methodist Episcopal Church*, 93; *Minutes of the Thirty-Fourth Session of the Bermuda Annual Conference of the African Methodist Episcopal Church held at St. John's AME Church, Bailey's Bay, July 19th to 23rd, 1917* (Hamilton, Bermuda, S. S. Toddings-Mid-Ocean Press, 1917), notes page. "Unsettled people" is a term borrowed from Rowland Berthoff, *An Unsettled People: Social Order and Disorder in American History* (New York, Harper & Row, 1971).

beckoned to black workers. The presiding elder on the Allegheny District in the Pittsburgh Annual Conference observed in 1894, for example, that "our people are laboring people and as labor has been scarce and money hard to get, our financial reports will not come up to our former standard." Therefore various presiding elders during this period observed that job prospects for their members would determine whether their congregations would flourish or decline. When strikes, recessions, and racial exclusion from organized labor occurred, they lamented these developments and their negative impact on AME churches. At Brownsville, Pennsylvania, "the people have not done what they would like to do, in way of support, owing to the long coal strike among the miners." This condition, which persisted into 1895, caused one commentator to observe that the "times have been hard in Brownsville this year, [with] but few of the men having steady work." The presiding elder of the Wheeling District in 1894 recalled that blacks had been barred from digging coal before "the great miners' strike," but "there are now employed two thousand men in different localities" probably because they had been strikebreakers. He noted that at Coketon, West Virginia, "we met quite a number of this class from the south, several of whom had been members of our church." The miners wanted assurances that "as soon as [they were] well settled they will try and support a church of their choice."[10] Similarly, the presiding elder on the Allegheny District noted that on the West Newton Circuit in western Pennsylvania "there [are] but a very few people" primarily "because the mills, having moved away, left little work for them." As a result the people "removed also, which leaves our church at this point very weak."[11] In northeastern Pennsylvania "many of the people are leaving Williamsport on account of scarcity of work." The presiding elder observed that "the lumber business has almost become a thing of the past; consequently we are looking for a thinning out" of the black population.[12]

AME clergy also realized that work place discrimination and exclusion from organized labor created additional sources of economic vulnerability

[10] *Minutes of the Twenty-Seventh Session of the Pittsburg(h) Conference of the African Methodist Episcopal Church* held at Wayman's Chapel AME Church, Wheeling, West Virginia, October 3–7, 1894 (Altoona, Pennsylvania, H. & W. H. Slep, 1894), 44, 50; *Minutes of the Twenty-Eighth Session of the Pittsburg(h) Conference of the African Methodist Episcopal Church* held at Bethel AME Church, Wilkes-Barre, Penna., October 10–14, 1895 (Altoona, Pennsylvania, H. & W. H. Slep, 1895), 38.

[11] *Minutes of the Twenty-Seventh Session of the Pittsburg[h] Conference*, 1894, 45.

[12] *[Minutes of the] Thirty-Second Session [of the] Pittsburg[h] Annual Conference [of the] African Methodist Episcopal Church, Brownsville, PA, October 12th–17th, 1899* (n.p., Publishing Committee: P. A. Scott, S. P. West, & T. J. Askew, 1899), 12.

for their "mobile laity." Presiding Elder William H. Brown of the Pittsburgh District told the 1897 session of his annual conference that "our people have a hard way to make their living. The workshops are still closed against the men of color and open to the foreign white man, citizen or no citizen of this country. Just as soon as he strikes the shores of America, if he is white, the shop doors are open to him. He can get the best jobs ... all of which is denied to the colored man." Brown criticized Pittsburgh clergy because they were "fearless in attacking every sin of every kind, except prejudice proscription in labor." Brown's colleague, Cornelius Asbury, the presiding elder of the Allegheny District, at this same annual conference, observed how labor strikes affected members within his jurisdiction. "A large portion of the district," he said, "lies in the mining section where bituminous coal is taken from the depths of the earth, and this section has been seriously affected by the strike which lasted about three months." Rather than castigate the exclusionary policies of many labor unions and the strikes that often left unemployed AME members in the Ohio Valley, the annual conference proposed a conciliatory posture toward organized labor. "We extend to our laboring organizations throughout this country," declared the resolution, "our sympathy in their efforts to get better wages, urging at the same time an opening of the doors of organized labor to the Negroes of America, and pray that strikes and all such disturbances may soon be things of the past."[13]

That AME churches in the Northeast and Midwest were captives of business cycles, and labor unrest in mass production industries were reflected in the observations of western Pennsylvania clergy. Presiding Elder Richard H. Bumry of the Washington District observed in 1914, for example, that a mission had been organized at Bentleyville. The congregation, he believed, had "a promising outlook, if industrial conditions do not become such as to compel people to seek new fields of labor." Bumry, who had worked in the 1880s in Pittsburgh at the Black Diamond Steel Works and at the Oliver Wire Mills, also said in his Pittsburgh Annual Conference report that the financial condition in several churches was "somewhat impaired, owing to the industrial conditions prevailing throughout the district." The churches that he supervised in the Monongahela Valley and in Fayette County "derive their support directly from the mill and mine industries." Bumry, as he informed his bishop who resided in Chicago and not in Pittsburgh, said "the mines, mills and coke ovens in this region have had a

[13] *Minutes of the Thirtieth Session [of the] Pittsburg[h] Annual Conference* held in Euclid Ave. AME Church, Pittsburg(h), PA, October 7–13, 1897 (n.p., Publishing Committee: D. F. Caliman, Price A. Scott, & R. H. Bumry, 1897), 8, 16, 36.

dull and unprofitable season. The coke ovens have been closed for months. Many of the mines have been shut down during the entire year and the mills working one and two shifts and for weeks idle." He added that a number of congregations "received the full effect of this depression."[14]

World War I, in unleashing an unprecedented black migration out of southern agriculture into northern industry, nullified Bumry's apprehensions about his vulnerable AME congregations. His prescient colleague on the Allegheny District in 1909, for example, had noted that St. Paul Church in McKeesport, Pennsylvania, "is situated in the center of an iron and steel manufacturing district, and is now beginning to look out from under the clouds of adverse conditions" caused by a recession. The coming of World War I helped to change the financial fortunes of churches in McKeesport and other industrial communities along the Three Rivers. Despite initial neutrality in 1914 and a delayed declaration of war in 1917, United States defense industries mobilized production and personnel based on the possibility of American military involvement. While industries geared up for the manufacture of munitions and other military ordnance, the steady supply of European immigrants, who mainly came from the affected war areas, shrank. Hence, this reliable pool of labor that had populated the ranks of unskilled and semiskilled occupations of foundries, factories, and mines sharply declined. At the same time floods, boll weevil infestation, and falling cotton prices pushed blacks from southern farmlands and readied them for recruitment for industrial labor in countless destinations in the Northeast and Midwest. Moreover, the scourge of lynching exasperated African Americans and tired them of the egregious racial oppression that became commonplace in the South. While blacks showed their patriotism during the war, said delegates to the 1918 North Georgia Annual Conference, "helpless members of the race have been burned to death, hanged to limbs and riddled with bullets by infuriated mobs without the semblance of a trial, and in not a single instance have the lynchers been apprehended and made to pay the penalty of their crime." W. E. B. Du Bois reported that the AME Ministers' Alliance in Birmingham, Alabama cited seven causes of the migration, including "[racial] prejudice, disfranchisement, Jim Crow cars, lynching, bad treatment on the farms, the boll weevil, [and] the floods of 1916" that destroyed their crops. Therefore, 400,000 African Americans between 1914 and 1917 resettled in the North's innumerable industrial communities

---

[14] *Minutes [of the] Forty-Seventh Session of the Pittsburgh Annual Conference [of the] African Methodist Episcopal Church*, 1914, 87–88; Wright, *Centennial Encyclopedia of the African Methodist Episcopal Church*, 51.

and thousands more migrated through the 1920s and swelled the black population in major northern cities and in their neighboring satellite towns.[15]

AMEs recognized that World War I thrust African Americans toward a new threshold of economic opportunity. Delegates to the 1917 Ohio Annual Conference, for example, acknowledged that "prejudice still lives, but the monster must struggle against the flame and gas and smoke of world war which are weakening the monster's hold upon the industrial structure of society." They added that "approximately 75,000 skilled workmen of color have migrated northward within the last two years. They have found higher wages [and] they have supplied technical ability" in the nation's war effort. A pastor in the Pittsburgh Annual Conference recalled, "the boys of the South were prepared industrially" for the opportunities that the migration offered. Therefore, "when the World War was on, the boys of the South walked in[to] the various positions in the North." At the same time AME leaders at the 1920 General Conference realized that they could not sit on the sidelines and do nothing to bring aid to the thousands who were migrating. Hence, some funds for ministries outside the United States were shifted to the Home Mission Field to help "take care of our people who have left their Southern homes and [have] come North among strangers." As the migration resumed in the early 1920s, the 1924 General Conference said the "exodus" was a movement "the like of which has not been witnessed within the bounds of any nation since history began." They were abandoning "untoward conditions" in the South and "moved like the tramp of an invading army toward the promised land of better education, good wages, unrestricted use of the ballot and a larger measure of freedom." African Americans "registered their eternal protest against proscription, peonage, disfranchisement, Judge lynch and Ku Kluxism." Hence, AMEs acknowledged "this great migratory movement" and pledged to aid blacks in their resettlement in the North. The ministry was therefore advised "not to fail in its effort to employ all the arms of effective, social service" to the migrants.[16]

---

[15] *Journal of Proceedings of the Forty-Second Session of the Pittsburgh Annual Conference of the African Methodist Episcopal Church* held in Brown [Chapel] AME Church, North Side, Pittsburg[h], October 6–11 inclusive, 1909 (n.p., Publishing Committee: C. J. Powell, T. J. Askew, P. A. Scott, W. B. Anderson, D. S. Bentley, & W. S. Lowry, 1909), 18; *Journal of Proceedings of the North Georgia Annual Conference of the African Methodist Episcopal Church* held in Bethel AME Church, Dalton, GA (beginning November 7, 1918), 30–31; Reverdy C. Ransom, "The Voice of the Press on the Negro Exodus from the South," *AME Church Review*, Vol. 34, No. 133, July 1917, 23.

[16] *Journal of Proceedings of the Eighty-Seventh Annual Session of the Ohio Conference of the African Methodist Episcopal Church* held in St. Paul AME Church, Columbus, OH,

The observations of contemporary African American scholars brought clarity about the causes and impact of the black migration. Among them were three AME scholars visible to both church and public audiences. All of them earned Ph.D.s from the Ivy League, realized that black workers were writing a new chapter in their economic history, and admonished their denomination to be cognizant of this transformation. Richard R. Wright, Jr., a 1911 Ph.D. in sociology from the University of Pennsylvania and editor of the *Christian Recorder*, had published several peer-reviewed studies about black labor, including "One Hundred Negro Steelworkers" (1914). Wright, as an advocate of black migration, disagreed with numerous black newspapers and leaders who opposed the exodus. Wright declared in 1917 that "if a million Negroes moved north and west in the next twelve months, it will be one of the greatest things for the Negro since the Emancipation Proclamation." The *Recorder* also argued that the migration "was best for the Negro-Americans, the nation, and the South" mainly because "migration through all time has been a great solver of problems." Blacks, Wright believed, "would get [a] better education in the North," become voters, earn higher wages, and join labor organizations. To the doubters he "begged them to welcome their brother from the South." Wright also recognized that "the mobile laity" belonging to the AME Church, beyond the influence of any prelate or preacher, was a part of "the movement North" and was "unorganized." He reminded AMEs that "100,000 Negroes have moved without any leader, without any organization, and with nothing but an individual motive." He believed that such a large number of African Americans, if organized into a proletarian group, "could get back our franchise; we could do away with segregation, and we could protect ourselves against injustices." Additionally, Wright, a practitioner of the social gospel since his seminary days at the University of Chicago, advised black churches in the North to address the multiple needs of the migrants. Hence, as an officer in the Interdenominational Ministerial Alliance in Philadelphia, he supported initiatives to aid black newcomers with jobs and housing.[17]

September 12–16, 1917 (Philadelphia, PA, AME Book Concern, 1917), 33; *Official Minutes of the Pittsburgh Annual Conference, Third Episcopal District, AME Church,* held in Bethel AME Church, Meadville, PA, November 10th–November 14th, 1926 (New Castle, PA, Expert Printing Company, 1926), 14; *Journal of the Twenty-Sixth ... General Conference, 1920,* 270; *Journal of the Twenty-Seventh Quadrennial Session of the General Conference of the African Methodist Episcopal Church* held in Louisville, KY, May 5 including the 21st, 1924, 397.

[17] Richard R. Wright, Jr., *Eighty-Seven Years behind the Black Curtain* (Philadelphia, PA, Rare Book Company,1965), 94–96, 310–312, 314; Francine Rusan Wilson, *The Segregated Scholars: Black Social Scientists and the Creation of Black Labor Studies, 1890–1950* (Charlottesville,

Sadie Tanner Mossell, the granddaughter of Bishop Benjamin T. Tanner, was another expert observer of the black migration. In earning a Ph.D. in 1921 in economics from the University of Pennsylvania, Mossell wrote a dissertation entitled "The Standard of Living Among One Hundred Negro Migrant Families in Philadelphia," which was published that same year in *Annals of the American Academy of Political and Social Science*. She examined whether the wages that migrants earned were sufficient to sustain them in their new northern environment. Mossell calculated that 40,000 blacks, "chiefly from the agricultural districts of Mississippi, Alabama, Florida, Georgia, and South Carolina," settled in Philadelphia between 1916 and 1918. They found employment in various industrial sites ranging from women working in knitting mills to men laboring for the railroads, steel plants, and munitions factories. She investigated 100 families, their household budgets, and expenditures. Though she described the newcomers as culturally different from the indigenous black population and noted that "the migrants retarded the steady march of progress of the colored people in Philadelphia," Mossell was mindful of what "obstacles" hindered their advancement. Migrants had families that were too large to maintain a fair standard of living, engaged in "unwise spending" in their choice of rental properties, and made poor decisions in the purchase of insurance. She also acknowledged that racial discrimination in a host of social and economic areas negatively affected the newcomers.[18]

Mossell, who called herself "a true daughter" of African Methodism, believed that churches should help southern migrants in their adjustment to the North. Housing was a special concern. "Conditions in the city were deplorable," she wrote. She cited newspapers that reported on "Negroes [who were] herded together like cattle" with some residing in remarkably tiny quarters where "twenty men slept on the floor [because] no beds were provided." She said the church "could help by building houses instead of expensive church edifices at a cost of hundreds of thousands of dollars." Mossell also believed churches should "instruct its members as to how to buy

University of Virginia Press, 2006), 151; Richard R. Wright, Jr., "One Hundred Negro Steelworkers," in *Wage Earning Pittsburgh*, The Pittsburgh Survey (New York, Charities Publication Committee, 1914), 97–110; Genna Rae McNeil, Houston B. Roberson, Quinton H. Dixie, and Kevin McGruder, *Witness: Two Hundred Years of African-American Faith and Practice at the Abyssinian Baptist Church of Harlem, New York* (Grand Rapids, MI, William B. Eerdmanns Publishing Company, 2014), 108; Ransom, "Voice of the Press on the Negro Exodus from the South," 22.
[18] Sadie Tanner Mossell, "The Standard of Living among One Hundred Negro Migrant Families in Philadelphia," *Annals of the American Academy of Political and Social Science*, Vol. 98, Child Welfare (November 1921), 173–175, 178–179, 216–217.

food, insurance, [and] housing" and prevent their "unwise spending." This intervention by the churches could be enhanced by a vigorous "government economic involvement in the housing market."[19]

A third AME scholar, Charles H. Wesley, viewed the migration as a watershed in African American labor history. Wesley, according to one biographer, believed that blacks should "control their own destiny." He was successively the pastor to two congregations in Washington DC between 1918 and 1928, taught at Howard University and earned the Ph.D. in history from Harvard. His book, *Negro Labor in the United States, 1850–1925: A Study in Economic History*, published in 1927, had been his doctoral dissertation. Wesley delved into the mechanics of the migration and the chronological stages of the exodus. He noted two periods of migration in 1916–1919 when the defense needs of World War I required an enhanced pool of workers and in 1921–1923 when there was continued decline in European labor now mandated in federal immigration restriction legislation. In each case "Negro laborers were not chosen because of preference for them but because of necessity." Though he conducted thorough research in government data and reports from numerous social agencies, Wesley, like Mossell, interviewed the migrants themselves. "I personally questioned a large number of immigrants," he said, as they came into Union Station [in Washington DC] in order to secure at first-hand the causes for their movement." They noted the "push" factors of economic exploitation, racial violence, and Jim Crow laws in the South and the "pull" factors embedded in the new social and economic opportunities available to them in the North.[20]

Like other AME scholars and clergy, Wesley recognized that there "was a state of unrest among the Negro population of the South" accompanied by high expectations of what the "Promised Land" in the North offered to them. "The wage difference between the North and the South," Wesley observed, "played no little part in causing the migration." He disagreed with Mossell by noting that migrants "had not been unthrifty workers," but had "brought their life savings with them." He discovered that many of them had sold

[19] Francine Rusan Wilson, "Sadie T. M. Alexander: A 'True Daughter' of the AME Church," *AME Church Review*, Vol. 119, No. 391, July–September 2003, 40, 42; Mossell, "The Standard of Living among One Hundred Negro Migrant Families," 175, 217–218; Julianne Malveaux, "Missed Opportunity: Sadie Tanner Mossell Alexander and the Economics Profession," *Papers and Proceedings of the Hundred and Third Meeting of the American Economic Association*, Vol. 81, No. 2 (May, 1991), 310.

[20] Wilson, *Segregated Scholars*, 170; Charles H. Wesley, *Negro Labor in the United States, 1850–1925: A Study in American Economic History* (New York, Vanguard Press, 1927), 283–284, 291–292.

property and "with this money, homes were purchased and the foundation was laid for new economic futures in a freer environment." He commended black workers because the "closed door" to northern mills and factories was "slowly being pushed open by Negro labor-the door to larger industrial opportunity." Hence, he admonished racially exclusive labor unions that "the use of the Negro as a strikebreaker" as in the strikes in numerous industries in 1919 "and his increasing employment shows the great danger to Labor [unions] from a lack of organization" of the African American worker.[21]

Wesley could claim partial credit for the heightened consciousness in the Baltimore Annual Conference about black migration. At the 1923 session delegates adopted Wesley's analysis of the exodus and noted that the "new migration is on since the last Conference met." Klan terrorism and poor economic conditions continued to push blacks out of the South to northern destinations. The report acknowledged the "new wave of Negro migration, some of which are passing through the confines of the Baltimore Conference." In response Wesley and three other members of the resolutions committee proposed that the Baltimore Conference "shall seek out and bring into the church the migrants who are coming north in great numbers and that we shall give them otherwise every reasonable aid." Not only did Wesley influence AMEs in his area toward greater awareness of the migration, but the importance of his book was highlighted in the *Christian Recorder*. In 1927, the newspaper said, "every minister of our church ought to have a full understanding of the history of Negro labor, and the problems with which we as a race of working people are now confronted." Wesley, who would become in 1928 a presiding elder in the Baltimore Annual Conference, "has done a valuable service not only to historical research but a very practical service for his people."[22]

That AME members were a "mobile laity" was a fact well known to presiding elders in northern industrial regions. Though this demographic reality had shaped the AME experience throughout its history, church leaders were reawakened to this historical phenomenon during

[21] Wesley, *Negro Labor in the United States*, 292–294, 305–306.
[22] *Minutes of the One Hundred and Sixth Session of the Baltimore Conference of the African Methodist Episcopal Church* held in Trinity AME Church, Baltimore, MD, April 25–29, 1923, 60–61; cited in Charles H. Wesley, *A Stranger in One's Own Land: Autobiography of Charles H. Wesley*, unpublished MS, compiled and edited by Constance Porter Uzelac, Fort Lauderdale, Dorothy Porter Wesley Research Center, 2011, Chapter 10, n.p; Janette Hoston Harris, "Charles Harris Wesley, Educator and Historian, 1891–1947," Ph.D. dissertation, 1975, Howard University, 112–113.

World War I. Whether the migration was desirable and to be encouraged or a dubious movement that deserved no endorsement influenced the ambivalent response of some within the episcopacy. Inexplicably, the bishops in 1917 said they were unaware of "the cause or causes of the exodus," though they recognized "the unsettled condition of our people." Whatever the reasons, the impact seemed a zero sum outcome for the denomination because "our [southern] church work is situated in the very heart and center of the portions deserted, and those [northern cities] to which many thousands [have] come." A report to the 1917 North Ohio Annual Conference affirmed this observation. "Our Church," it said, "must prepare to adjust itself to the decrease in its membership in one section and its increase in another." Moreover, "there is a duty laid upon us that we have never had before." That meant taking "an active interest" in (new) moral and racial issues in addition to "industrial adjustments" of those migrating AMEs. The bishops declared that researchers should "discover the causes of [the current] unrest and find a remedy." If an explanation for the migration was identified, the bishops believed, then the "restlessness would cease, and the conditions [would] become settled." At the same time they conceded that the exodus would continue as long as there was for blacks "an opportunity to make a living, to enjoy [the] privileges of [being] citizens of a democracy, a chance to educate their children, and [to] feel that measure of security as to life, which alone can bring contentment." These unsettled conditions would also allow African Americans to "move freely from place to place as business or inclination may suggest." At least the bishops knew it would be hard to ignore this new sense of freedom that black southerners were experiencing.[23]

The black migration was a transformational challenge that appeared to bewilder some bishops and clergy. Clearly, the laity ignored those clergy who discouraged the exodus. Instead, they maintained networks that had long facilitated chain migration and responded to railroad and industry agents who offered "transportation" and employment in burgeoning foundries and factories outside of the South. This process, in which black southerners eagerly participated, unexpectedly shifted the landscape on which their denomination would operate. As these rapid changes were occurring, Bishop Flipper and his Georgia constituents tried to make sense of their impact

---

[23] Address of the Council of Bishops, AME Church, 1917, 40–41; *Minutes (of the) Thirty-Sixth Session of the North Ohio Conference of the African Methodist Episcopal Church* held in North St. AME Church, Springfield, OH, September 19–23, 1917 (Philadelphia, PA, AME Book Concern, 1917), 79.

upon their episcopal district. At the 1916 North Georgia Annual Conference, Flipper, whom the "Georgia Regulars" familiarly called "Big Brother" and "Honest Joe," showed that he understood immigration and the war and their relationship to the black migration. "There are two great disturbing elements before the public at present," he said," one is the European war, the other the exodus of Negroes from the South." He added that "the European war has called many foreigners to their native countries to defend their colors; and northern industry has been hampered by the exodus of foreigners, and being hampered makes a demand on the Southern Negroes, thereby opening a door hitherto closed against us." In a jeremiad, Flipper declared that "the death of men on European battlefields is the resurrection of the southern Negro. We have been shut out from laboring in the North, by discriminating industrial unions. This exodus makes the white man in the South begin to appreciate our industrial value." A few weeks later at the Macon Georgia Annual Conference he offered additional comments on "the restless condition of our people and the emigration of many to the North." He was "glad some of our people were going. We had as well freeze in the North as to be murdered in the South." Nonetheless, Flipper said, "he [himself] was not going because he didn't like northern customs," perhaps a reference to his brother's experience with racial discrimination at West Point. He believed that "this is the 'Hand of God' [in] opening the door of industry to the Negro and not the love of the North for the Negro."[24]

These observations, made at the start of the Great Migration, stirred a different response from Flipper as the exodus from Georgia started to take a toll on AME membership. He told the 1921 Georgia Annual Conference "I am happy that I am not afraid of the KKK [Ku Klux Klan]. Jesus is marching. I am going to stay here. I am not going East, West, North or South. I am going to put my trust in God and I am going to win." He added, however, that "this white man is not so bad ... we have plenty of good white friends." He remembered "I was a slave. The master did not whip us. Our fathers and mothers troubled God on the throne until the gates of slavery set free four million." Moreover, Flipper believed "all white

---

[24] Wright, *The Bishops of the African Methodist Episcopal Church*, 164; *Journal of Proceedings of the Forty-Fourth Annual Session of the North Georgia Conference of the African Methodist Episcopal Church* held in Turner Chapel AME Church, Marietta, GA, October 25–29, 1916 (Nashville, TN, AME Sunday School Union, 1917), 14; *Journal of Proceedings of the Thirty-Fifth Session of the Macon Georgia Conference of the African Methodist Episcopal Church* held in Wesley Chapel AME Church, Milledgeville, GA, November 15–19, 1916 Nashville, TN, AME Sunday School Union, 1917, 22.

folks in the South do not hate the Negro and all white folks in the North do not love the Negro."[25]

Whatever the economic and social explanations that caused the migration, Flipper thought that the South was better overall for African Americans. Because of such views, Ransom, writing in the *AME Church Review*, said that the denomination was weakened when episcopal leaders were "regarded as a 'Northern' or a 'Southern Bishop.'" He said that "one of the best things that could happen to the First and Third Episcopal Districts would be to assign to them men like Bishops Flipper and [William D.] Chappelle, practically all of whose ministry has been confined to the South." These districts, which drew thousands of black migrants, were centered respectively in the Northeast and in the Ohio River Valley. Flipper, a "Southern Bishop," would be better balanced if he understood the "mobile laity" that abandoned Georgia for Philadelphia and Pittsburgh. Moreover, he seemed oblivious to what Alain Locke observed in the *New Negro* that "it is the rank and file who are leading, and the leaders who are following."[26]

The clergy in Flipper's district, while in sync with his commentary about the migration, did not accept his nostalgic appraisal of the South. Carlton M. Tanner, an Atlanta pastor and the son of a bishop, observed at the 1916 Macon Georgia Annual Conference that "many of our people are going North on account of the unrest in this part of the country, and ought to go." His observation seemed apropos because at the 1917 session of the same annual conference other ministers also acknowledged "the unsettled condition of our people on account of which many are leaving this section of our country and are seeking homes where the climate and customs are very different." The migration, they hoped, would "prove the indispensability of the Negro in the South as nothing else could." At the same time the "exodus" would lead to "problems varied and serious." Pastors such as Tanner believed that the denomination's missionary department should "look after them" after they arrived in the North. Similarly, Richard H. Singleton, the pastor of the populous St. Phillip Church in Savannah, responded in 1917 to three of his members who asked him to write letters of transmittal for them to Mother Bethel in Philadelphia alerting the congregation about their

---

[25] *Journal of Proceedings of the Fifty-Fourth Annual Session of the Georgia Annual Conference [of the] African Methodist Episcopal Church held at Bethel AME Church, Statesboro, Georgia, November 23rd to 27th, 1921* (Nashville, TN, AME Sunday School Union, 1922), 50.

[26] Reverdy C. Ransom, "Bishop C. T. Shaffer," *AME Church Review*, Vol. 36, No. 141, July 1919, 307; Alain Locke, *The New Negro* (1925), 7.

migration to the city. These were developments that no bishop or pastor could prevent.[27]

Pastors at the 1916 Georgia Annual Conference noted their "churches have lost a great many of their best members by the removal of a great number to the North seeking employment." Moreover, the closing of "saw mill plants and turpentine stills where we once had large memberships" compelled "our people to move away seeking employment." As a result "we have at some places empty church houses," and at other locations there were "only a few families left." By 1917 in the Southwest Georgia Annual Conference, dollar money, the funds paid into the denominational treasury, declined more than $600. This happened because "more than a thousand of our best paying members" joined the migration. The 1922 Georgia Annual Conference similarly said "we have lost hundreds of our best members by immigration." Clergy noted "the boll weevil has caused a shortage in many of the points in the conference." They lamented that "the Negro who is naturally adapted to farms because of his environments and training finds it difficult and danger-ous to live in certain sections of the south only as a serf, because of Klanism and Mob Violence, of which he is the main prey." Hence a way must be found so that needed labor will not be intimidated or driven from the community where they can best serve." No matter how little or how much Flipper and Georgia ministers understood the "exodus," the laity, without heeding their commentary, still headed North and pressured African Meth-odism to adjust to new social and demographic realities.[28]

Ransom was right in identifying Flipper as an AME fixture in the South. Had he served elsewhere, his perspectives on the migration might have been modified. William H. Heard, another Georgian, a fellow student with Flipper at Atlanta University, and elected to the bishopric with him in 1908, had been committed to preside in Mississippi, but the 1920 General Conference

---

[27] *Journal of Proceedings of the Thirty-Fifth Annual Session of the Macon Georgia Conference, 1916*, 31–32; *Journal of Proceedings of the Thirty-Sixth Annual Session of the Macon Georgia Annual Conference of the African Methodist Episcopal Church* held in St. Peter's AME Church, Fort Valley, GA, November 15–18, 1917 (Nashville, AME Sunday School Union, 1918), 57; Robert Gregg, *Sparks from the Anvil of Oppression: Philadelphia's African Method-ists and Southern Migrants, 1890–1940* (Philadelphia, PA, Temple University Press, 1993), 162.

[28] *Journal of Proceedings and Year Book of the Fifty-First Session of the Georgia Annual Conference [of the] African Methodist Episcopal Church* held in St. Paul AME Church, Brunswick, GA, November 22–26, 1916 (Nashville, TN, AME Sunday School Union, 1917), 50; Reverdy C. Ransom, "Travel Talks," *AME Church Review*, Vol. 33, No. 131, January 1917, 171–172; *Journal of Proceedings of the Fifty-Fifth Session of the Georgia Annual Conference of the African Methodist Episcopal Church* held in St. Paul AME Church, Brunswick, GA, November 22–26, 1922 (Nashville, TN, AME Sunday School Union, m.d.), 54, 64.

assigned him to the Northeast. "I did not ask to come to you," said Heard to the 1920 Philadelphia Annual Conference, but "I agreed to come." Once he moved to Philadelphia, Heard developed a pragmatic response to the "exodus." "The migration of our people from the South," he observed," compels us to build large churches in the large cities."[29]

Heard fulfilled his promise to Decatur Ward Nichols, a son of a veteran South Carolina minister and a recent graduate of the seminary at Drew University in New Jersey. He appointed Nichols in 1926 to serve the eighteen members at the Emanuel Mission in New York City. Like Nichols, the membership was "made up principally of people who went to New York City from South Carolina and most of them were members of [the] great Emanuel Church in Charleston." Since Heard remarked that Bethel was the only large AME Church in Manhattan and that he wanted "to establish a second great church" in the heart of the metropolis, the best opportunity seemed to lie in developing Emanuel. If Nichols could locate an appropriate edifice to purchase, Heard committed the First Episcopal District to match the $10,000 that Nichols resolved to raise. Because each fulfilled the terms of their agreement, Nichols acquired a Jewish synagogue "in the heart of the black-belt of New York City," retrofitted the sanctuary, and developed in the ensuing decade a congregation of 2,400 members. Such developments as the Emanuel project moved the 1926 Philadelphia Annual Conference to commend Heard's leadership in the District and to note that "many new churches have been erected and bought, housing thousands of African Methodists coming from the South."[30]

Another Flipper protégé, Archibald J. Carey, Sr., like Heard was a native Georgian, a fellow alumnus of Atlanta University, and a pastor in the North during the migration. When he led a congregation in Athens, Georgia, Flipper was his presiding elder. After a successful pastorate in Jacksonville, Florida, he was transferred to Chicago and successively led Quinn Chapel, Bethel, and Institutional. The growth of these congregations drew from the steady influx of blacks that swelled to a flood of people during the war. In

---

[29] *Journal of Proceedings of the One Hundred and Fourth Session of the Philadelphia Annual Conference of the African Methodist Episcopal Church* held in Bethel AME Church, Steelton, PA, June 9–15, 1920 (n.p., 1920), 36.

[30] Jeanette T. Johns, *The Upward Journey: A Centenarian's Chronicle: Personal Stories of Bishop Decatur Ward Nichols, Revered Clergyman of the African Methodist Episcopal Church* (Nashville, TN, AME Sunday School Union, 2002), 28–30; "Spurious Evangelists," *AME Church Review*, Vol. 43, No. 171, 166; *Journal of Proceedings of the One Hundred and Tenth Annual Session of the Philadelphia Conference of the African Methodist Episcopal Church* held in Mt. Pisgah AME Church, Philadelphia, PA, May 12–16, 1926 (n.p., 1926), 51.

1918 Carey became a presiding elder and oversaw the expansion of several Chicago churches. The Hyde Park congregation, for example, was relocated into a new building and it was "crowded to overflowing" when Carey came for an official visit. Bishop Levi J. Coppin and Carey dedicated a new edifice for Wayman Chapel on the city's North Side. During Carey's two years as presiding elder, pastors on his district bought over $100,000 in church property.[31]

St. James Church in the East End of Pittsburgh in 1915 inaugurated the St. John Mission and housed it in "a beautiful little building." The presiding elder told the 1917 conference that "the work is growing numerically and [holds] promises for a great church in the future." At the 1919 meeting it was reported that "the people are loud in their praise for the work accomplished this year." The pastor "is building up a substantial membership and we can hope for a great church in this part of the city." St. John, however, still relied on financial support from St. James, which paid its indebtedness of $700. Nonetheless, the presiding elder presented a resolution that same year saying that St. John "has shown phenomenal growth and gives promise to becoming able soon to operate successfully as a separate and distinct organic unit." With reduced assistance, St. John "may reasonably be expected to develop into a flourishing society." Therefore, St. James was requested to transfer the title of the St. John edifice to the Mission itself. A continuous black migration sustained expectations for St. John's future as it did for congregations elsewhere in the North. Joseph Gomez, assigned to Bethel AME Church in Detroit in 1919, attracted a large share of black migrants. Within a month of his arrival, morning services spilled over into a second service held in the Bethel basement. A newer and bigger edifice was needed. In 1921 Gomez inaugurated the "New Bethel" project. "It was initiated in one of the greatest real estate deals," a congregation history said, "made by colored people in Detroit and the largest of any congregation." Bethel bought a lot in a white neighborhood for $40,000 and an existing structure on the property for $12,000. "A magnificent brick building, with its large stained glass window and towering steeple," was dedicated at a cost of $300,000 in 1925 for a membership of 3,520. Ransom concluded in 1923 that in Detroit and Chicago AMEs had been especially vigorous in their response to the migration. "In Detroit, within the past four years," he observed, "five or six new churches have been formed, with memberships from one to eight hundred."

[31] Dennis C. Dickerson, *African American Preachers and Politics: The Careys of Chicago* (Jackson, University Press of Mississippi, 2010), 19–20, 29.

In Chicago, he said, "a score of African Methodist churches, with pastors and workers, are on duty every day among the new comers in their midst."[32]

Ransom endorsed these initiatives. "The Corporations and Industrial Concerns," he observed, "will take care of the purely material or economic side" of black migrant issues, "but the moral and social aspects in the movement of so many thousands into a new and strange environment, remains the work of the church and kindred organizations." He added that "the AME Church has the intelligence, the capacity and the ability to cope with the present situation." Ransom recommended that AME districts outside the South should shift a part of their denominational assessments to the Secretary of Missions to fund church expansion and "stipends" for ministers who would serve the newcomers. "This is the day of great opportunity," he said, to help African Americans "in the crowded communities and around the industrial plants where our men, women and children live and work."[33] At the same time, Carlton M. Tanner, disappointed that some bishops had not given sufficient attention to the "emigration of our people from the South," reported "certain sections of the southern states have been almost depopulated of our people." As a consequence, "thousands of them are being lost to our Church." He suggested the establishment of a national Service Bureau to monitor the migration and to deploy ministers in the North "to meet incoming trains and give assistance to these persons."[34]

These developments convinced other AMEs that the exodus, if clergy were vigilant, would spearhead unprecedented membership growth in their respective areas. Since blacks were settling into mill and factory labor, this signaled their permanent presence in steel, auto, mining, rubber, and electrical manufacturing. "In northern industries to which [the Negro] has come," noted one AME report, "industrial institutions are doing many things to induce him to stay." The African American worker, the report

---

[32] *Official Minutes of the Fiftieth Session [of the] Pittsburgh Annual Conference*, 1917, 53; *Journal of Proceedings of the Fifty-Second Annual Conference of the Pittsburg[h] Conference of the African Methodist Episcopal Church* held in Washington, PA, October 22, 1919 (Philadelphia, PA, AME Book Concern, 1919), 47, 79; Annetta L. Gomez-Jefferson, *In Darkness with God: The Life of Joseph Gomez, A Bishop in the African Methodist Episcopal Church* (Kent, OH, Kent State University Press, 1998), 73, 81–82, 94; *An Historical Sketch Published on the Occasion of the Eightieth Anniversary of Bethel AME Church, Detroit, Mich., 1841–1921*, 11; Reverdy C. Ransom, "Moral and Social Responsibility Increased by Larger Industrial Opportunities," *AME Church Review*, Vol. 40, No. 158, October 1923, 97.

[33] Reverdy C. Ransom, "The Church and the Exodus," *AME Church Review*, Vol. 34, No. 133, July 1917, 33–35.

[34] Carlton M. Tanner, "A Service Bureau," *AME Church Review*, Vol. 34, No. 136, April 1918, 248–249.

continued, "is a necessity" especially if "he [is] granted all the rights and privileges of any other people." Women, as much as male clergy, urged the AMEs toward a heightened awareness of the migration. The president of the Pittsburgh Conference Branch of the Women's Parent Mite Missionary Society (WPMMS) observed in 1917 "in many places the field for [the] Social Missionary has broadened" because "our people are coming north by the thousands." She said that "local societies can greatly assist the Pastor in looking after these people." Hence, she beckoned members to "ask your pastor how you can help him? Let us be awake to the opportunities around us for doing real service for God and His Church." In noting the ongoing urgency of the exodus and its impact on AME congregations, a delegate from the steel town of Braddock at the 1918 Pittsburgh Branch Mite Missionary meeting discussed "The Opportunity and Migration Among Colored People."[35]

Presiding elders, who were on the ground observers in 1917, noted the derivative impact of the migration upon church growth. The presiding elder of the Cleveland District told the 1917 North Ohio Annual Conference that increased accessions were attributable "to the influx from the South." Proudly, he added that "a great deal of missionary work has been done to get them to become members." Another presiding elder in the Pittsburgh Annual Conference reported that at St. James in the city's East End "the membership is almost doubled" to 689, and that there were "more members than seating capacity" within the sanctuary. As a result, "the pastor and congregation are looking forward for another site in order to accommodate the people." At Westinghouse, an electrical manufacturing plant, a retired pastor had been "looking after this [new] work," which included thirty-eight men and a Bible class. These migrants, either single or married with wives and children still residing in the South, buoyed the expectation of the area presiding elder, who said that "we will be able to organize here." Elsewhere in western Pennsylvania another presiding elder declared "we have organized new work in the district in every place we could." He reported at the 1917 Pittsburgh Annual Conference that "we have quite a nice organization

---

[35] *Journal of Proceedings of the Third Session of the Pennsylvania Annual Conference, Third Episcopal District, AME Church* held in St. Paul AME Church, McKeesport, PA, October 29–November 2, 1924 (n.p., 1924), 31; *Minutes of the 20th Annual Convention [of the] Women's Mite Missionary Society, Pittsburgh Conference Branch, African Methodist Episcopal Church* held in the Bethel AME Church, Franklin, PA, July 5, 6, 7, 8, 1917 (n.p., 1917), 9; *Minutes of the 22nd Annual Convention [of the] Women's Mite Missionary Society, Pittsburgh Conference Branch, African Methodist Episcopal Church* held in the Bethel AME Church, Williamsport, PA, July 4, 5, 6, 7, 1918 (n.p., 1918), 7.

at Ellwood City" in addition to new congregations at Ford City and Farrell, all of which started with at least twenty-five members. At the 1918 meeting, the presiding elder of the Allegheny District noted the start of "four mission points" in the twin towns of Tarentum and New Kensington and at Creighton and Wilmerding. In a region populated by a large number of small industrial communities, the district's increased membership of 760 during the previous two years reflected broader growth within the Pittsburgh jurisdiction. Though most migrants settled in the Northeast and Midwest, some ventured to the West Coast. The Reverend W. G. Fields in 1925, for example, transferred from the West Alabama Annual Conference to the California Annual Conference and was appointed to a church in Santa Barbara. Moreover, "many of our people are moving to Sacramento, and the future for African Methodism is bright" for the St. Andrew congregation.[36]

Another consequence of the migration was a division of the Pittsburgh Annual Conference to accommodate growth within the jurisdiction. The conference, since 1907, when it spun off its West Virginia congregations into a separate judicatory, stretched from Pittsburgh and its environs northward to Meadville and Erie and northeastward to Scranton and Wilkes-Barre and numerous other towns throughout these regions. With new congregations emerging along the Three Rivers in western Pennsylvania, the three presiding elders had expanded oversight of these industrial communities and concomitant obligations for churches outside these areas. Therefore, the Pennsylvania Annual Conference was organized in 1921 in Scranton and held its first session in 1922 in Wilkes-Barre. Because of membership increases in the Pittsburgh area, some of these congregations were detached from the Pittsburgh Conference and added to the Pennsylvania Conference to lend numerical strength to the new jurisdiction. The 1924 General Conference ratified these actions.[37]

---

[36] *Minutes [of the] North Ohio Conference, 1917*, 67; *Journal of Proceedings [of the] Fiftieth Session [of the] Pittsburgh Conference, African Methodist Episcopal Church* held in Brown Chapel AME Church, Pittsburgh, PA, October 3–7, 1917 (Philadelphia, PA, AME Book Concern, 1917), 41–42, 51, 53, 123; *Journal of Proceedings of the Emergency Executive Committee of the Fifty-First Annual Session of the Pittsburg[h] Conference of the African Methodist Episcopal Church* held in St. Paul AME Church, Washington, PA, Wed., Thurs., October 30–31, 1918 (Philadelphia, PA, AME Book Concern, 1918), 31–32; *Journal of the Twenty-Seventh Quadrennial Session of the General Conference of the African Methodist Episcopal Church* held in Louisville, Kentucky, May 5 including the 21st, 1924, 163; Minutes of the Sixtieth Session of the California Annual Conference of the African Methodist Episcopal Church held in San Francisco, CA, September 23–27, 1925 (Nashville, TN, AME Sunday School Union, 1925), 8, 22.

[37] *Journal of Proceedings of the First Session of the Pennsylvania Annual Conference, Third Episcopal District-AME Church* held in Bethel AME Church, Wilkes-Barre, PA, October

Presiding elders, standing on the frontlines of the migration, observed the adjustment of their congregations to demographic developments growing out of the exodus. While some churches grew and various clergy inaugurated programs to accommodate black newcomers, others were ineffectual in meeting the challenge to increase their memberships. In his 1917 report to the Pittsburgh Annual Conference, R. H. Morris observed that "many thousands of our people have found work and homes in the bounds of the Allegheny District. We have looked after their welfare and have taken quite a few of them into our churches. Ministers from the South have come to our district; some with transfers and we have tried to make them feel at home in our churches." He added "the financial condition of our people was never better in many years. Work is plentiful and wages are good and all who want work can get it." He maintained this optimism in 1918 when he reiterated that "the financial condition of the people [because of the migration] has greatly improved. Work has been plentiful and wages [are] good" and thriving churches were the result.[38]

Morris's colleague, W. H. H. Butler on the Washington District, lamented, however, that the glass factory town of Charleroi "like many other appointments on this district," had experienced a "great spiritual dearth." He said that "few converts have been added to the church nor has any considerable increase been made to the membership although many people from the South have settled down in that vicinity." Similarly, Presiding Elder W. H. Truss admonished those on his Pittsburgh District that "our people from the South seem to be standing alone waiting for some one to extend them their hand and bid them welcome." If AMEs would embrace the migrants, he believed, "our churches will not have so many empty pews for they will come to us from every quarter." Truss seemed sensitive to this issue perhaps because of his proletarian pursuits. A decade earlier, when he served a pastor at Bellevue, Pennsylvania, Truss supported himself as an employee of the Pennsylvania Railroad. Hence, both presiding elders were queasy about the reception migrants would receive at such socially prestigious congregations as Bethel Church in Pittsburgh. Despite a sizeable membership of 728, elite light-skinned members were proud of their class and color, and endorsed

---

25–29, 1922 (n.p., 1922), 56–57; *Journal of Proceedings of the Third Session of the Pennsylvania Annual Conference*, 1924, 5.

[38] *Journal of Proceedings of the Fiftieth Annual Session [of the] Pittsburgh Conference*, 1917, 41–42; *Journal of Proceedings of the Emergency Executive Committee of the Fifty-First Annual Session of the Pittsburg[h] Conference*, 1918, 28.

Bethel's practice of seating light-skinned and dark-skinned members apart from each other.[39]

Similarly, at Mother Bethel in Philadelphia Robert J. Williams, appointed pastor in 1916, battled an entrenched "old settler" faction that was unsympathetic to any vigorous outreach to newcomers. Evans Tyree, the bishop who assigned him to the denomination's flagship congregation, wanted a more socially conscious church that would be receptive to the migrants. At the 1918 Philadelphia Annual Conference a committee of clergy noted "the increase in membership in this section has been very large" in part "because of the unprecedented unrest in the Southland among our people and the consequent migration" to the North. They said that "this has at once presented a sociological question which gives the Church much to do." Therefore, "the corralling and holding of these brethren has caused our wide-awake Bishop, Evans Tyree, to appoint a committee to devise ways and means to at once provide for city missions and [other efforts] to secure these to the Church." The 1921 annual conference, in response to General Conference legislation, proposed the start of a Social Service Committee that the bishop would appoint. It would cooperate with public and private agencies and would hire a social worker to serve recent migrants in the Philadelphia region.[40]

Sundry examples of inhospitality at the two Bethels in Pittsburgh and Philadelphia showed that members in some AME churches were late in realizing that they could not ignore the irreversible forces that the migration unleashed. Absorbing new members who were southern and rural, addressing their condition as industrial employees, and helping them to reconstitute their social and religious communities required an urgent magnanimity that caught some congregations off-guard. Some churches, however, were alert to the task that lay ahead of them. Delegates at the North Ohio Annual Conference resolved that "we [should] avoid as much as possible the

[39] *Journal of Proceedings of the Fiftieth Annual Session [of the] Pittsburgh Conference, 1917*, 36, 49; *Official Minutes [of the] Forty-First Session, 1908, Pittsburg[h] Conference [of the] African Methodist Episcopal Church*, 88; Dennis C. Dickerson, *Out of the Crucible: Black Steelworkers in Western Pennsylvania, 1875–1980* (Albany, State University of New York Press, 1986), 65.
[40] Robert Gregg, *Sparks from the Anvil of Oppression: Philadelphia's African Methodists and Southern Migrants, 1890–1940* (Philadelphia, PA, Temple University Press, 1993), 175–189; *Journal of Proceedings of the One Hundred and Second Session of the Philadelphia Annual Conference of the African Methodist Episcopal Church* held in Bethel AME Church, Wilmington, DE, May 16–19, 1918 (n.p., 1918), 33; *Journal of Proceedings of the One Hundred and Fifth Session of the Philadelphia Annual Conference of the African Methodist [Episcopal] Church* held in Mt. Olive AME Church, Philadelphia, PA, May 18–22 (1921, Philadelphia, PA, AME Book Concern., 1921), 37.

reference to such expressions as 'Southern Negroes and Northern Negroes,' and seek to remove any thought of section or difference." Moreover, AMEs should "care for a people to whom we are obligated." Henry Pinckney Jones, pastor at St. James, Pittsburgh, addressed these issues in the opening sermon at the 1917 Pittsburgh Annual Conference. In preaching on "The Poor Neglected," Jones, who previously served in the Chicago Annual Conference as the assistant pastor to Reverdy C. Ransom at the Institutional Church and Social Settlement, brought a social gospel consciousness to this Pittsburgh audience. He criticized the "Formalism" of AME services and the irrelevant emphasis upon "Fashion" saying that "too many stay away because they have not clothes to wear" and "because the service is 'too high' [or] too stiff." That the poor refused to "hear the gospel," he said, was "one of the greatest of our religious problems." Jones added "we must study their needs" and "interest ourselves in their every-day life problems." At this same conference other clergy said in a report that the exodus provided blacks with the opportunity to show that they were "dependable, industrious and capable, giving free exercise of citizenship rights, the education of their children under conditions impossible in sections from which they have come, and the creation of an atmosphere of confidence and self-respect which cannot be other than salutary." They also noted that "our task is to convince them that [their] new liberty and freedom must not be taken for license; that industry, education and morality must stand guard over the door of their new habitat if they would continue to enjoy the confidence of their new friends and neighbors." It was declared that the churches and ministers of this section are alive to this vital matter and will prove equal to this tremendous responsibility." Presiding Elder Truss, who was similarly optimistic, rejoiced because "we are having a great revival in industry at this time, and many of our people are employed." He noted that "east of Altoona [Pennsylvania] the brickyards are open to our men and very comfortable homes are being erected for their families." He was happy that "among the many that are coming here we [are] find[ing] some very good Methodists."[41]

Recessions interrupted the migration and affected the supply of new members available to strengthen existing congregations and to populate new ones. At the 1922 Pittsburgh Annual Conference the presiding elder of

---

[41] *Minutes of the Thirty-Eighth Annual Session of the North Ohio Conference of the African Methodist Episcopal Church* held in Payne's Chapel AME Church, Hamilton, OH, October 8–12, 1919 (Philadelphia, PA, AME Book Concern, 1919), 76; *Journal of Proceedings of the Fiftieth Annual Session [of the] Pittsburgh Conference, 1917,* 8–-9, 49, 58; Wright, *Who's Who in the General Conference,* 1924, 69–70.

the Allegheny District reported that "the industrial conditions have been such as to cause a spirit of unrest" within this jurisdiction. Church members left "seeking work" elsewhere, and this had been "materially felt in the milling and mining regions." In these areas "the closing of the mines and mills, and the railroad shopmen's strike was indeed distressing to many of our people." He named eight industrial communities where "this continuous non-employment seriously [a]ffected our churches." The 1924 session of the Pennsylvania Annual Conference received a similar report saying "this has been a year of slow business. The principal industries such as [the] Steel Mills and Coal Mines have not been in full operation and most of our people were out of work."[42]

Conditions seemed the same at the 1924 Pittsburgh Annual Conference, where the presiding elder of the Washington District was "happy to report an increased tendency" of migrants to connect with area AME churches. Because of the recession these new members, however, "have returned, either to their former homes, or have gone to some other fields where the industrial conditions are more healthful." He added, "our mills and mines are still working on one-third time" and "in many instances entire departments have been closed." Moreover, "at least sixty percent of the mines have been closed down for the past 14 months." He noted that this "distressing economic condition has played havoc with the pay envelope and in turn [a]ffected seriously the finances of the churches." The presiding elder, however, hoped for "a full resumption of both mills and mines in the early part of 1925."[43]

Nonetheless, these periodic downturns did not break the continuity of the migration through its second stage in the 1920s and did not undermine the broad impact of the exodus upon African Methodism. Even as mills and mines in western Pennsylvania experienced slowdowns, other industrial plants within the region and elsewhere in the Northeast and Midwest stayed at full employment and beckoned migrants to these new locations. Black southerners frequently moved from Pittsburgh to Cleveland and perhaps

[42] *Journal of the Fifty-Fifth Annual Session of the Pittsburgh Conference of the African Methodist Episcopal Church* held in Park Place AME Church, Homestead, PA, November 1–5, 1922 (Philadelphia, PA, AME Book Concern, 1922), 33; *Journal of Proceedings of the Third Session of the Pennsylvania Annual Conference, Third Episcopal District, AME Church* held in St. Paul AME Church, McKeesport, PA, 40.

[43] *Journal of Proceedings of the Fifty-Seventh Session of the Pittsburgh Annual Conference, Third Episcopal District, African Methodist Episcopal Church* held in Wayman Chapel AME Church, New Brighton, PA, November 5–9, 1924 (New Castle, PA, Expert Printing Company, 1924), 24–25.

onto Chicago, Detroit, or Philadelphia. The exodus, while bringing in new AME members, also replenished ministerial ranks with transplanted southern preachers and intensified efforts to align the interests of black workers with those of their new employers. Despite recessions that periodically slowed the migration, the exodus continued through the rest of the decade and created in the urban and industrial North new arenas of denominational activity.

Looking back on more than a decade of migration and especially on the 1920s, the bishops in their episcopal address at the 1928 General Conference said the denomination "has grown," that "many new churches have been built," and "many souls have been received into the connection." They also believed the migration had resulted "in good to our race variety." They also said "the migrants were invited to join existing churches of our denomination in localities where they settled, and wherever this was not practicable they organized and built new churches of our denomination, which everywhere are thriving." They declared "they are our kith and kin and we are happy to receive them and cause them to be one with us."[44]

Though annual conferences in the four episcopal districts covering the Northeast and Midwest had an ample corps of clergy, some southern AME ministers became migrants themselves. At the beginning of the migration Bishop Flipper, for example, gave transfers to northern annual conferences to seventeen clergy in the Southwest Georgia Annual Conference. Several wanted to follow their members and, with support from colleagues in the South and the North, settled in northern cities and various mill and factory towns. Others were proletarian preachers who were bivocational and in search for jobs in mass-production industries. Clergy in western Pennsylvania noted that "ministers from the South have come to our district [and] some with transfers." Moreover, "we have tried to make them feel at home in our churches." That surely applied to William Thomas, a South Carolina migrant who arrived in Duquesne, Pennsylvania, in 1923 to work in the local steel mills and who became the assistant pastor at Payne Chapel Church. Various ministers transferred into northern annual conferences as fully ordained clergy, but were subjected to a probationary period. That was the situation for W. W. Johnson, an elder in the South Florida Annual Conference, who joined Bethel, Pittsburgh, and was received on trial into the Pittsburgh Annual Conference. T. A. Carthan, an AME evangelist from Georgia, "knowing that so many of my people migrated North, I came that

---

[44] *Journal of the Twenty-Eighth Quadrennial Session (of the) General Conference of the AME Church, Chicago, Illinois, May 7–23, 1928*, 92.

I might help to gather them back to the fold." After he settled in Michigan, local AME clergy did not welcome him. No pastor, he said, "would have me to run [a] single [revival] meeting for them." He added that "had I been given a chance" by these ministers, "I could have succeeded."[45]

Others started their ministerial training in annual conference courses of study in the South and proposed to finish after a transfer into the North. El(l)is King was a traveling deacon in the Mississippi Annual Conference and sought admission into the North Ohio Annual Conference in 1919 pending "evidence" of his ordination status. Similarly, W. M. McClendon, an elder in the Northeast Mississippi Annual Conference, was admitted on trial to the 1919 Pittsburgh Annual Conference. Washington Bennett, who studied at the AME-sponsored Central Park Normal and Industrial School in Savannah, was admitted to the Pennsylvania Annual Conference in 1924. Appearing with Bennett were William Bullock, educated at Allen University in South Carolina, and Edward Wilson, schooled in Virginia and supplying St. John's Mission in Pittsburgh. Wilson's death in 1925, however, cut short his ministry. Bishop Flipper, despite his ambivalence about the migration, transferred W. H. Hunter, a native of Eatonton, Georgia, to the Pittsburgh Annual Conference where he was fully ordained in 1919. Others, such as Henry Y. Tookes, transferred from Daytona Beach, Florida, to become pastor at the Bethel Church in Chicago in 1927. Bishop A. L. Gaines purchased a synagogue, the Sinai Temple, for $450,000 to rehouse the congregation. Tookes "responded to the S.O.S." from Gaines to serve Bethel's 2,500 members and lead them from a temporary worship site to their renovated edifice. Moreover, Tookes was a popular preacher, whose exuberance when singing his favorite "I'm on my way up there to my Father's House" stirred his parishioners with "so much shouting that the Doxology could not be sung," and "many chairs [were] broken." Tookes was catapulted to a visible leadership role in the Chicago Annual Conference, where he became a delegate and host to the 1928 General Conference, and he was elected to the episcopacy in 1932.[46]

---

[45] Ransom, "Travel Talks," 171; *Journal of Proceedings of the Fiftieth Annual Session [of the] Pittsburgh Conference, 1917*, 41, 62; Dickerson, *Out of the Crucible*, 70; *Minutes of the Thirty-Eighth Session of the Michigan Annual Conference of the African Methodist Episcopal Church* held in First Community AME Church, Grand Rapids, MI, September 10–14, 1924 (Nashville, TN, AME Sunday School Union, 1924), 37.

[46] *Minutes of the Thirty-Eighth Annual Session of the North Ohio Conference of the African Methodist Episcopal Church* held in Payne's Chapel AME Church, Hamilton, OH, October 8–12, 1919 (Philadelphia, PA, AME Book Concern, 1919), 22; *Journal of Proceedings of the Fifty-Second Annual Conference of the Pittsburg[h] Conference of the African Methodist Episcopal Church* held in Washington, PA, October 22, 1919, 125; *Journal of Proceedings of*

J. H. Flagg and Isaac S. Freeman were also migrant ministers who pursued bivocational opportunities that the exodus offered them in western Pennsylvania. Each found jobs in the steel industry and admission to ministerial orders in the Pittsburgh Annual Conference. Moreover, they contributed much to the expansion of the denomination in founding new congregations. Flagg migrated in 1916 from Enterprise, Alabama, where he was a blacksmith, to Johnstown, Pennsylvania. Apparently he was already fully ordained as his name appeared on the roster of traveling elders in the minutes of the 1917 Pittsburgh Annual Conference. At that meeting Flagg, credited as founder of the Johnstown mission, was appointed officially to serve the thirty-two charter members. By 1919, Johnstown had lost "many of our people," probably because of a postwar recession. Nonetheless, the congregation, now with someone else as pastor, expressed "a willingness to press forward." Flagg, in the meantime, became a conference evangelist without a church assignment. By 1923, Flagg became a pastor at Huntington, Pennsylvania, but relinquished the appointment because of ill health. Unlike Flagg, Isaac S. Freeman, an AME minister from Blakely, Georgia, experienced chain migration first by going to Philadelphia and then moving in 1924 to Woodlawn, later known as Aliquippa, in the Beaver Valley in western Pennsylvania. He became an employee at the nail mill at the local Jones & Laughlin steel facility. Also in 1924, Ebenezer AME Church started with thirty-four members, and Freeman, the founder, was formally assigned as pastor. The presiding elder reported "we will soon have a church erected on the lot we are buying." Moreover, Freeman was reassigned to Woodlawn, where he was stationed through the late 1920s. Flagg and Freeman had a counterpart in William T. Coleman, who migrated in 1919 from Alabama to Beloit, Wisconsin. His degrees from Tuskegee Institute prepared him for employment at the Fairbank Morse plant where engines were manufactured. After pastorates in Wisconsin and neighboring cities in Illinois and Indiana,

the Third Session of the Pennsylvania Annual Conference held in St. Paul AME Church, McKeesport, PA, October 29–November 2, 1924, 42; Official Minutes of the Pennsylvania Annual Conference, Third Episcopal District, AME Church [held in] St. Paul AME Church, Uniontown, PA, November 3–7, 1926, "Our Honored Dead" (New Castle, PA, Expert Printing Company, 1926), n.p.; Who's Who in the General Conference 1924 (1924), 78; Wright, The Bishops of the African Methodist Episcopal Church, 327; Journal of Proceedings of the Forty-Fifth Annual Session of the Chicago Conference of the African Methodist Episcopal Church held in Ebenezer AME Church, Evanston, IL, September 21–25, 1927 (Nashville, TN, AME Sunday School Union, 1927), 15, 48–49, Statistics/West Chicago District; Singleton, The Autobiography of George A. Singleton, 143; Journal of the Twenty-Eighth Quadrennial Session [of the] General Conference of the AME Church, Chicago, Illinois, May 7–23, 1928, 9.

Coleman organized an AME congregation in Kenosha, Wisconsin, that was later named in his honor.[47]

Hence, it was not unusual for proletarian preachers to double as ministers and industrial employees in mill and factory communities in the North. They joined with elite, full-time clergy in flagship congregations to constitute a two-tiered ministry much like their counterparts in the South, where educated clergy were stationed at significant urban congregations and other ministers, usually farmers, served in smaller, rural parishes. What was different in the North was the common fealty by both classes of clergy to industrial employers, whose policies determined whether parishioners would be gainfully employed contributors to their economically vulnerable congregations. When the 1922 Pittsburgh Annual Conference convened at Park Place Church in Homestead, Pastor Harrison G. Payne, with the consent of "officials of the Carnegie Steel Works," arranged a tour for the delegates to see the "mammoth plant" where innumerable AMEs labored. This gesture showed that clergy recognized the link between a thriving workplace and well-supported churches, and that their interests in a sober, reliable and thrifty labor force were closely aligned with the concerns of mill managers. Moreover, AMEs took note of employer support of the religious activities of newly arrived migrants. A presiding elder in the North Ohio Annual Conference, for example, observed that at Airline Junction near Toledo there were well-attended services and a Sunday School. Because of this development "the railroad officers agreed to build a union church" that would also include the AMEs.[48]

Both employers and clergy, out of mutual self-interest, developed social service initiatives aimed at providing needed amenities to black newcomers. These programs, they hoped, would encourage the permanent settlement of migrants in their new social and economic environment. Since the nineteenth century companies had funded a range of initiatives called welfare capitalism that offered recreation, housing, health services, and other programs to win the loyalty of laborers and discourage membership of

---

[47] Dickerson, *Out of the Crucible*, 69; *Journal of Proceedings of the Fiftieth Annual Session [of the] Pittsburgh Conference, 1917*, 53; *Journal of Proceedings of the Fifty-Second Annual Conference of the Pittsburg[h] Conference, 1919*, 4, 34, 47; *Journal of Proceedings of the Third Session of the Pennsylvania Annual Conference, 1924*, 11, 41; *Journal of Proceedings of the Fifty-Seventh Session of the Pittsburgh Annual Conference, 1924*, 23; *Official Minutes of the Pittsburgh Annual Conference, 1926*, 3, 19; Wright, *Encyclopedia of African Methodism*, 71.

[48] *Journal of Proceedings of the Fifty-Fifth Annual Session of the Pittsburgh Conference of the African Methodist Episcopal Church* held in Park Place AME Church, Homestead, PA, November 1–5, 1922 (Philadelphia, PA, AME Book Concern, 1924), 49; *Minutes [of the] Thirty-Sixth Annual Session of the North Ohio Conference, 1917*, 71.

independent unions. Employers, in implementing these measures, hired black welfare officers. These social workers recruited southern black workers, administered housing, managed athletic teams, and functioned as liaisons with black churches. George Foster Jones, the black welfare officer at the Carnegie steel plant in Clairton, Pennsylvania, until his death in 1925, was the chorister in the town's First AME Church. He also led a "colored community chorus" that drew support from his church and other black congregations. As supervisor of the steel plant's community center, he often invited black clergy to preach to black workers. Charles Broadfield, born in 1897 in Hampton, Virginia, and educated as a blacksmith at Hampton Institute, was the fourth black welfare officer at the Carnegie steel works in Duquesne, Pennsylvania. After he served in World War I and migrated in 1921 to Duquesne to become a steelworker, he ascended to his social work position in the late 1920s. He had charge of the mill's black baseball team and recommended blacks for jobs at the Duquesne plant. Because he supervised the mill's community center and belonged to the local Payne Chapel AME Church, Broadfield invited the congregation to worship in the facility after members, most of whom were recent migrants, outgrew their church building.[49]

Elsewhere, employers directly deployed congregations and their pastors to fulfill functions that black welfare officers performed for steel managers in western Pennsylvania. In 1911 the Reverend J. P. Q. Wallace started a social service department at Bethel AME Church in Detroit. "With the coming of our people in large numbers," beginning in 1916, a labor and housing bureau was established. In March 1917, for example, 197 men and 189 women found jobs through Bethel. In 1920 the department was rehoused in a building next to the edifice, with additional activities that the city's Recreation Commission funded. Another Bethel pastor, William H. Peck, starting in 1928, joined black clerical colleagues at Second Baptist Church and St. Matthew Episcopal Church in worker recruitment for the Ford Motor Company.[50]

Housing, however, proved especially troublesome for black migrants. One presiding elder in the Pittsburgh Annual Conference noted in 1917 that "we are sorry that homes cannot be secured for them as they are compelled to live in unsatisfactory places." Though some ministers had done much to

[49] Dickerson, *Out of the Crucible*, 106, 110–111.
[50] Milton C. Sernett, *Bound for the Promised Land: African American Religion and the Great Migration* (Durham, NC, Duke University Press, 1997), 145; *An Historical Sketch . . . of the Eightieth Anniversary of Bethel AME Church, Detroit, Mich., 1841–1921* (n.p., 1921), 10; August Meier and Elliott M. Rudwick, *Black Detroit and the Rise of the UAW* (New York, Oxford University Press, 1979), 17–18.

"alleviate this congestion," much still needed to done. Those at the 1923 meeting were reminded that "our people from the south-land" continued their migration and poured into the mill communities in Homestead, Duquesne, Clairton, Donora, and Monessen. Although migrants were "doing well" in their jobs, poor housing threatened their "permanency" in the area. "The housing conditions," it was said, "are miserably inadequate." This was a crucial matter bearing on the churches because it affected the "permanency" of their members, who were apt to migrate elsewhere or return to the South. Hence, Pastor Payne at Park Place, Homestead and "a committee of our church" took up "the question of housing" with steel employers. Out of this initiative Payne organized a real estate agency to find residences for sale or rental to blacks "on low monthly installments." Delegates to the 1924 Indiana Annual Conference were similarly grieved about poor housing conditions for the migrants. These "problems," they said, "are taxing the most consecrated minds." In 1925, they developed a solution that mirrored what some AMEs in western Pennsylvania were doing. The delegates thought "these newcomers should be encouraged to buy homes for themselves on the small payment down and monthly installment plans, and in this way become property owners."[51]

These actions echoed the social gospel initiatives that Reverdy and Emma Ransom inaugurated at the Institutional Church in Chicago in 1900.[52] When the couple relocated to New York City, where he was editor of the *AME Church Review*, they founded and operated between 1913 and 1924 the Church of Simon of Cyrene. In the "Black Tenderloin" in lower Manhattan, he observed, "it is hell," and thus he and Emma Ransom offered a "lifeline to the poor human derelicts who have suffered moral shipwreck and have been dragged by the treacherous undertow of degeneracy and vice." As in Chicago, the clergy and their congregations "rarely, if ever venture" to help

---

[51] *Journal of Proceedings of the Fiftieth Annual Session [of the] Pittsburgh Conference, 1917*, 50; *Journal of Proceedings of the Fifty-Sixth Annual Session of the Pittsburgh Conference of the African Methodist Episcopal Church* held in Bethel AME Church, Pittsburgh, PA, November 7–11, 1923 (Philadelphia, PA, AME Book Concern, 1923), 51–52; Dickerson, *Out of the Crucible*, 57; *Journal of Proceedings of the Eighty-Sixth Annual Session of the Indiana Conference, African Methodist Episcopal Church* held in Bethel AME Church, Indianapolis, Indiana, September 24–28, 1924 (n.p., 1924), 42; *Proceedings of the Eighty-Seventh Annual Session of the Indiana Conference, African Methodist Episcopal Church* held in Allen Chapel AME Church, Terre Haute, IN, September 23– 27, 1925 (Nashville, TN, AME Sunday School Union, 1925), 45–46.

[52] *First Quadrennial Report of the Pastor and Warden of the Institutional Church and Social Settlement to the Twenty-Second Session of the General Conference and to the Connectional Trustees of the African Methodist Episcopal Church* convened at Quinn Chapel, Chicago, Illinois, May, 1904, 2, 4, 6–7.

such persons. With thirty members in a rented storefront, the Ransoms held nightly worship services and outreach to prostitutes, gamblers, drunkards, and petty criminals.[53]

Ransom established a paradigm of social gospel practice that influenced other AMEs. His model unwittingly reinforced the welfare capitalism that employers sponsored in the mill and factory communities in which black migrants were settling in the 1910s and 1920s. The 1924 General Conference, perhaps with Ransom's work in mind, declared "the church, with its various auxiliaries, [and] social settlements ... are accepting the challenge of the new social conditions with a seriousness, which shows the full comprehension of the situation." The Pennsylvania Annual Conference resolved that "the social message of the gospel should be heralded as never before." Moreover, it said that "social service work should not be considered a work which the church is assisting other agencies." Rather, "there is a demand for a social programme, built up, and fostered by the church [itself]." Similarly, delegates at the Pittsburgh Annual Conference, even as the migration was lessening in the late 1920s, believed that newcomers should be welcomed and "these strangers could be sought and looked after by the pastors and a small committee," who would show that "the church is concerned about their material as well as their spiritual well-being." Alexander J. Allen, later a bishop, was among several pastors who already pursued what Ransom pioneered in Chicago and New York City. At his modest sized church in the coal-mining community of Connellsville, Pennsylvania, Allen led the congregation in making "needed improvements" to the physical plant. Included in these renovations were "modern conveniences for social and community uses." Too few AME clergy emulated the Ransom and Allen initiatives. A committee at the 1924 South Ohio Annual Conference observed that "the migration of colored people" put "great demands" on AME congregations. Unfortunately, "in every large center our facilities for religious work are inadequate for our needs."[54]

---

[53] Reverdy C. Ransom, *The Pilgrimage of Harriet Ransom's Son* (Nashville, TN, AME Sunday School Union, n.d.), 228, 231–234.

[54] *Journal of the Twenty-Seventh Quadrennial Session of the General Conference, 1924*, 401; *Official Minutes [of] the Seventh Annual Session of the Pennsylvania Annual Conference of the African Methodist Episcopal Church* [held in] Calvary AME Church, Braddock, PA, October 10–14, 1928 (Philadelphia, PA, AME Book Concern, 1928), 22; *Official Minutes of the Pittsburgh Annual Conference, Third Episcopal District, African Methodist Episcopal Church* [held in] Bethel AME Church, Wilkes-Barre, PA, October 2–6, 1929 (n.p., 1929), 43–44; *Journal of Proceedings of the Fifty-Second Annual Conference of the Pittsburg(h) Conference, 1919*, 37; *Proceedings of the Third Annual Session of the South Ohio Conference of the African Methodist Episcopal Church* held in Quinn Chapel AME Church, Wilmington, OH, October

Additionally, the migration compelled a convergence of two issues to which AME ministers and migrants needed to respond. White and immigrant industrial workers, accustomed to a small minority of black laborers in the mass production industries, jealously guarded their ascendancy in northern mills, mines, and factories. With the sudden surge of black newcomers in the 1910s and 1920s, the African American population expanded in workplaces and neighborhoods that Caucasians claimed as their own. A growing black presence in both venues angered whites who responded violently and who defiantly defended exclusionary policies in labor unions. The reality that blacks were becoming a permanent population in northern urban and industrial communities, however, required AME leaders to condemn white on black violence while hoping for an end to racial discrimination within organized labor.

AME clergy, mindful that the migration directly affected the demographic vitality of the denomination, vigorously addressed the violence perpetrated again African American migrants and challenged unions to open up to the increasing numbers of black industrial workers. They surely knew about how white workers responded to the black migration. On May 28 and July 2 1917, white workers in East St. Louis, Illinois, objected to the arrival of black laborers at the Aluminum Ore Company as strikebreakers. Black newcomers regardless of gender or generation were assaulted, their homes burned, and some were lynched. In 1919 in Chicago, one of several cities where riots occurred, whites and blacks clashed because migrants encroached onto a beach that was supposedly segregated. Nearly forty people were killed, most of them black, and hundreds were injured. Archibald J. Carey, Sr., then a presiding elder in the Chicago Annual Conference, joined other African American leaders who cooperated with the mayor and governor to restore order. Though Carey walked the streets in the "Black Belt" to urge calm, he blamed white antipathy toward blacks as the cause of the riot.[55]

In 1917 in the *AME Church Review*, Ransom, while supportive of the migration, affirmed that blacks "will find race prejudice and discrimination" in the North, and as more African Americans settled in various communities that discrimination would intensify. Emma Ransom deplored the riots and declared at the 1919 convention of the WPMMS "if all ministers would take a stand, the conscience of the country would be awakened." Bishop Charles

22–26, 1924 (n.p., Publication Committee: O. W. Childers, J. B. Harewood, M. M. Lewis, n.d.), 37.

[55] See Elliott M. Rudwick, *Race Riot at East St. Louis*, July 2, 1917 (Carbondale, Southern Illinois University Press, 1964); Dickerson, *African American Preachers and Politics*, 38.

S. Smith, in a reflection about the "Red Summer," addressed Bethel AME Church in Detroit in November 1919 on "The First Race Riot Recorded in History." "The four main causes of bloodshed and strife among men, he declared, "are tribalism, intra-racialism, religious fanaticism, and race antagonism." Often violence against blacks came through an "armed mob" attacking "a defenseless individual." Nonetheless, "the new Negro," the bishop said, "does not hate any element of the white people." Instead, "he hates injustice, oppression, discriminatory laws and practices, [and] unequal opportunity in the field of industrial and economic endeavor." There could be no democracy or righteousness in American society, he asserted, as long as mobs "delight in making bonfires of human bodies." The 1919 North Ohio Annual Conference believed "the Race Riots have grown out of the influence of Southern propaganda upon the irresponsible white men of these northern communities and the presence of Southerners of decided Southern spirit in our midst, and it is their aim to terrorize the colored people and leave the impression that the Negro is no more safe in the North than in the South." They urged Congress to enact a bill that a Kansas senator introduced, calling for an "investigation of the Race Riots." Similarly, AMEs at the 1927 Ohio Annual Conference deplored the persistence of antiblack sentiments in the North. In Indiana, for example, "a great migration" of "poor white Southerners" affected a state that was historically associated with the Underground Railroad and "Quaker ideals." Moreover, "this influx of Southern sentiments and ideals," they said, "has changed the North almost into another South." In Indiana, the KKK was trying to transform the state's abolitionist heritage into an antiblack bastion. These factors, AMEs believed, contributed to hostile responses to the black migration.[56]

Blacks also encountered violence during widespread labor strikes in 1919. Cooperation with the war effort, requested by federal authorities, convinced union leaders to postpone their wage demands and continue, uninterrupted, the production of military ordnance. Within months of the armistice in November 1918, there were over 3,000 strikes and lockouts involving more

---

[56] Reverdy C. Ransom, "The Negro in the North," *AME Church Review*, Vol, 33, No. 131, January 1917, 152; Dovie King Clarke, Sadie J. Anderson, and Mattie J. Ford (compilers), *The Seventh Quadrennial Convention of the Women's Parent Mite Missionary Society of the African Methodist Episcopal Church, 1919* (Jacksonville, FL, Edward Waters Press, 1919), 54; Charles Spencer Smith, *The First Race Riot Recorded in History* (n.p., Commission on After-War Problems of the African Methodist Episcopal Church, January 1920), 5, 7, 9, 11; *Minutes of the Thirty-Eighth Annual Session of the North Ohio Conference, 1919*, 75; *Minutes [of the] 97th Annual Session [of the] Ohio Annual Conference [of the] African Methodist Episcopal Church* held in North Street AME Church, Springfield, OH, October 12–16, 1927 (n.p., 1932), 33–34.

than four million workers. In several industries, especially in iron and steel, black workers became strikebreakers against racially exclusionary unions. In some plants violence between unionized whites and nonunion blacks occurred. Delegates to the 1919 Pittsburgh Annual Conference were surely aware of the steel strike that happened at the same time as the AME meeting. Because the Amalgamated Association of Iron, Steel, and Tin Workers did not recruit actively among newly hired black steelworkers, migrants either were opposed or ambivalent toward the strike. Nonetheless, Pittsburgh Conference delegates seemed buoyed by a recent development at the national meeting of the American Federation of Labor (AFL). A black AFL delegate advanced a resolution, which the organization accepted, that said black members would be welcomed "without prejudice." AMEs urged "our brothers to take immediate advantage of this splendid opening." The 1922 Pittsburgh Conference recognized that "ninety per cent of our people belong to the wage-earning class." Delegates advised that "our people should not be made the pawn in labor disputes between capital and labor whether they be unionized or unorganized." A consensus, it seemed, was developing in African Methodism against black workers filling the role of strikebreaker and preferring that they should, where possible, belong to unions.[57]

Already, the bishops had realized that the unsettled condition of Labor "[a]ffects the Negro more seriously than any other race variety" mainly because they, like "the majority of the members of the African Methodist Episcopal Church belong to the laboring class." The prelates recognized that "the better the working condition of the Negro, the higher [the] wages [and the wider] the open door of opportunity to labor." Hence, "all [will] tend to better prepare him to contribute more liberally to the financial enterprises of the Church." This institutional self-interest led episcopal leaders "to appoint a Labor Commission, consisting of three bishops, three Elders and three prominent labor leaders, whose duty shall be to collect data and facts as to labor conditions in general, and that of Negro labor in particular." Moreover, the commission would compile "a list of industrial plants, employing Negro labor and those who do not and seek through every and all honorable means, a wider door of opportunity for Negro laborers, and such an adjustment and relation as will give them equal wages for equal work."

---

[57] Dickerson, *Out of the Crucible*, 85–92; *Journal of Proceedings of the Fifty-Second Annual Conference of the Pittsburg[h] Conference of the African Methodist Episcopal Church* held in Washington, PA, October 22, 1919, 59; *Journal of Proceedings of the Fifty-Fifth Annual Session of the Pittsburgh Conference*, 1922, 43.

The bishops, at least implicitly, conceded the necessity of blacks seeking an alliance with labor unions.[58]

Denominational leaders, despite disruptions in membership in the South, believed that the migration was a net plus for African Methodism, though some, such as clergy at the 1924 Michigan Annual Conference, believed "the transient church is proving quite a problem." They acknowledged that in the South "entire churches are being depleted over night" owing to the migration. What was needed was for the denomination to disburse "a special appropriation" for jurisdictions "into which our people are fastly coming" and put into "responsible hands to enable a congregation" to serve the migrants. They noted that "in the city of Detroit, the progress has been phenomenal" but not enough had been done. "We need," they declared, "fourteen large first class churches that we may be able to give religious homes to the many souls pouring into our city." The same cautious optimism marked the episcopal address at the 1928 General Conference, which noted that "the AME Church has grown substantially during the quadrennium. Many new churches have been built [and] many souls have been received into the connection." The bishops concluded "this migration was greatly and permanently resulting in good to our race variety." They observed that "the suppression, oppression and repressing of our people in the South by the dominant race has caused them to migrate." Though they left homes, property, and family, most migrants "came away feeling that they were achieving a better country and a better condition of life." The bishops admitted, however, that "for want of money we were hardly able to provide churches adequate to their needs, but everywhere they were sought after by our preachers and members and made welcome." Therefore, there was a "great expansion of our church in the North and Northwest." The prelates confessed, however, that the migration "apparently decreased our membership in the South, but others seem to have taken their places so rapidly that the migrants have scarcely been missed so that our general increase has been constant but not so large as we would wish." On that the bishops were unwittingly on target, in noting that the AME Church had reached a point of numerical stalemate.[59]

[58] *Journal of the Twenty-Sixth Quadrennial Session of the General Conference, 1920,* 204–205.
[59] *Minutes of the Thirty-Eighth Session of the Michigan Annual Conference of the African Methodist Episcopal Church* held in First Community AME Church, Grand Rapids, MI, September 10–14, 1924 (Nashville, TN, AME Sunday School Union, 1924), 48; *Journal of the Twenty-Eighth Quadrennial Session [of the] General Conference, 1928,* 92.

AME membership, according to the US religious census, totaled 494,777 in 6,608 congregations in 1906. Parishioners grew substantially to 548,355 in 6,633 congregations by 1916. During the Great Migration, however, there was a modest rise in the number of congregations to 6,708 by 1926, but AME membership dipped slightly to 545,814. Essentially, the size of the denomination, despite the migration, remained essentially the same. The exodus had essentially been zero sum for African Methodism. Charles H. Wesley, now a presiding elder and a professor of proven proficiency with statistical data, minimized the decennial decrease of 2,541 AME members. These numbers, he said, were "accounted for on the basis of the migration and the methods in which the statistics were handled by the individual ministers." Nonetheless, Wesley relied on the federal census report as an authoritative source. In a speech in 1931 to the Ecumenical Council on Methodism, he cited as reliable the AME statistics in the census of religious bodies.[60]

Similarly, the bishops realized that the census reported a membership decline, but they, unlike Wesley, rejected the findings as inaccurate. "The publication," they said, "is unfortunate and misleading." They observed that "while members have been lost in some places, in other places there have been gains, so that our church is much stronger today than it has ever been." Both the bishops and the historiographer W. H. H. Butler, previously a presiding elder in the Pittsburgh Annual Conference at the start of the World War I migration, believed that "secretaries of annual conferences" were responsible for providing the "correct number of ministers and members" to AME leaders, and perhaps some conveyed mistaken information. Moreover, Butler declared that he had not received from responsible officials, including the bishops, either "with certainty or regularity," statistical data from the church's respective jurisdictions. That probably explained why the religious census was mistaken. From his own tabulations, however, in 1931 Butler tallied AME membership in the Americas and Africa as 783,358 in 7,398 congregations. These calculations sustained the AME Church as the largest of the African American Methodist bodies and showed the "Herculean task confronting us if we would remain dominant as sons of Richard Allen in the field of religious teaching for persons of Negro lineage." He said that "if we are to gain and hold the masses of our Race variety, we

[60] Bureau of the Census, US Department of Commerce, *Religious Bodies, 1936*, Vol. II, Part 2, Denominations K to Z (Washington DC, Government Printing, Office, 1941), 1179; Charles H. Wesley, "The Negro Church as A Factor in American Religious Life," *AME Church Review*, Vol. 45, No. 180, April 1929, 224; Charles H. Wesley, "A Decade of Methodism in the Western Section as It Relates to the Negro Population," *AME Church Review*, Vol. 48, No. 193, July 1932, 11.

must be alert to keep them fully informed of our activities and plans for strengthening the walls and enlarging the borders of our Zion." Butler's census rather than the numbers from the US Bureau of Census became what AMEs repeated to internal and external audiences. While visiting an annual conference a month after the 1932 General Conference adjourned, John R. Hawkins, the denomination's financial secretary, in extolling AME strength, called attention to its numerical standing of "more than 700,000 members." Clearly, Hawkins was taking his cue from Butler.[61]

Notwithstanding Butler's boosterism, the AME Church lost ground in the shifting religious landscape among African Americans. The migration occurred within a compressed period of more than a decade. Within this limited time, rapid and palpable transformations took place in black religion. In all of the major northern cities to which southern migrants came, they encountered AME congregations of proud longevity and varying degrees of class and color pretensions. Some members, though a part of the working class, possessed northern genealogies, at times less than a generation or two, but still more than the new arrivals from presumably less cultured southern rural backgrounds. AMEs arriving in Chicago, for example, learned about Quinn Chapel AME Church, founded in 1847. The formidable three story Gothic edifice occupied a full city block. With both derision and awe, it was called a "swank" church that was not for the "common herd." Though it grew during the migration, Quinn Chapel, whose AME services were typically "sedate and formal," did not attract as many new members as the more popular Olivet Baptist Church. Together, Chicago's several AME churches increased by 5,000, but Olivet, a single congregation, equaled that number on its own.[62]

St. Mark AME Church in Milwaukee, established in 1869, had a reputation for catering to those of "high skin-color" and a "middle class orientation." Although its services were "emotionally and physically subdued," the congregation provided the migrants with an industrial employment bureau and a social service center. Perhaps St. Mark members viewed newcomers in the same way as their condescending counterparts at St. John AME Church, Cleveland as a "new burden." There were, of course, AME congregations, often in satellite industrial communities, whose small membership and

[61] *Journal of the Twenty-Ninth Quadrennial Session [of the] General Conference of the AME Church, May 2–16, 1932, Cleveland, OH*, 102, 536–538; *Journal of the Eighty-First Session of the New England Annual Conference of the African Methodist Episcopal Church* held in the Loring Street AME Church, Springfield, MA, June 23–26, 1932 (n.p., 1932), 22.
[62] Allan Spear, *Black Chicago: The Making of a Negro Ghetto, 1890–1920* (Chicago, University of Chicago Press, 1967), 178.

familial atmosphere appealed to some migrants. At the same time, Presiding Elder James G. Robinson of the Detroit District observed in his 1922 report to the 1922 Michigan Annual Conference that congregations in Ypsilanti and Ann Arbor consisted of "quiet, reserved people" who likely eschewed the exuberant expressions of religiosity prevalent among recent black migrants. At Park Place in Homestead, Pennsylvania, Dr. Harry M. Hargrave, a physician and church officer, played the violin during worship. At Avery Chapel in Oklahoma City, Dr. William Haywood, a dentist, who conducted the choir, insisted on singing anthems. Moreover, he had Handel performed, and in cooperation with the organist drew upon the psalms to provide lyrics for various selections. Haywood also eschewed Negro spirituals and did not tolerate any hint of influence from any popular music. Ralph Ellison, who became the famed black author of *Invisible Man* and a connoisseur of jazz, attended Avery Chapel as a child. He remembered that if Haywood encountered any popular "music or notated scores," he would have surely "destroyed them and scattered the pieces." Baptist churches and newer holiness, Pentecostal, and Spiritualist congregations, some of them storefronts, benefited from AME aloofness from the musical tastes of rank-and-file newcomers who chafed under such worship restrictions that music directors such as Haywood zealously enforced. But, Langston Hughes, like Ralph Ellison baptized at St. Luke AME Church in Lawrence, Kansas, where his family were members from the 1880s, encountered African Methodism as a normative marker for black religious and cultural respectability. Ellison pushed against this standard through an embrace of jazz. For Hughes, however, the doctrine of salvation through Jesus Christ, as explained from the St. Luke pulpit, informed his later literary productions. The "religious themes" in Hughes' writings, said one scholar, "shows that he was 'working out his salvation.'" These characteristics of respectability integral to African Methodism, influenced the accomplished novelist and founder of the Black Arts movement John O. Killens. Though he became an unbeliever, despite his matriculation both at Morris Brown College and Edward Waters College, his later literary career owed much to his upbringing at Steward Chapel AME Church in Macon, Georgia. There his mother was president of the Paul Laurence Dunbar Literary Club in which discussions of black writers always occurred.[63]

---

[63] Joe William Trotter, *Black Milwaukee: The Making of an Industrial Proletariat, 1915–1945* (Urbana, University of Illinois Press, 1985), 129; Kimberly L. Phillips, *Alabama North: African American Migrants, Community, and Working-Class Activism in Cleveland,*

AMEs had a prescribed order of service. Though idiomatic music often punctuated the worship experience, it appeared within the liturgical boundaries of traditional hymnody, the doxology, Decalogue, scriptural selections and litanies, and sermons that were homiletically sound but sometimes enthusiastic. The majority of Baptist churches, and all of the holiness, Pentecostal, and Spiritualist churches engaged in spiritual spontaneity through music, personal testimonies, glossolalia, shouting, and exuberant responses to loud and emotional preaching. These worship practices better suited the preferences of southern black migrants including some of whom were AME. Although exuberant worship services also happened in various AME congregations, seldom did they match the freedom and uninhibited zeal of the newer religious bodies. Moreover, AME annual conferences had the final say on whether congregations could be organized and admitted into the denomination. These procedures caused AMEs to respond less effectively to the migration than those churches with looser or independent ecclesiastical structures. Wallace D. Best concluded that "as a religious diaspora, southern migrants established their churches as islands of southern religious practice and community. More than an economically and socially derived phenomenon rooted in the exigencies of urban life, storefront churches (and other upstart congregations) were evocative of an uprooted and re-gathered religious community."[64]

African Methodism possessed other vulnerabilities in the area of mass black religion. AMEs who became well-known revivalists included H. Franklin Bray, who emulated such popular white contemporaries as Billy Sunday. Bray and the few AMEs like him did not preach to large crowds using the latest in organizational and communications apparatus that came to characterize modern evangelism. Instead, they pursued a traditional revival format of a singular focus on the particular congregations that sponsored them. Bray, a veteran pastor and presiding elder in Kentucky and in the West, when he preached in 1919 at Park Place Church in the Homestead, billed himself as the "Rocky Mountain Evangelist." His

1915–1945 (Urbana, University of Illinois Press, 1999), 166; *Minutes of the Thirty-Sixth Session of the Michigan Annual Conference* held in Quinn Chapel AME Church, Flint, MI, September 13–17, 1922 (Philadelphia, PA, AME Book Concern), 1922, 45; Lawrence Jackson, *Ralph Ellison: Emergence of Genius* (New York, John Wiley & Sons, 2002), 27; Wallace D. Best, *Langston's Salvation: American Religion and the Bard of Harlem* (New York, New York University Press, 2017), 1–3, 5; Keith Gilyard, *John Oliver Killens: A Life of Black Literary Activism* (Athens, University of Georgia Press, 2010), 14, 30–33.
[64] Wallace D. Best, *Passionately Human, No Less Divine: Religion and Culture in Black Chicago, 1915–1952* (Princeton, NJ, Princeton University Press, 2005), 65.

photograph and biography in the widely distributed *Who's Who in the General Conference [of] 1912* and in the 1916 volume, the *Centennial Encyclopedia of the African Methodist Episcopal Church*, provided publicity for Bray, but limited his appeal to AME-sponsored revivals. Martha Jayne Keys, a Kentucky evangelist and pastor, was similarly familiar to AMEs. *Who's Who in the General Conference [of] 1924* noted Keys "has traveled extensively and has held revival campaigns in most of our largest churches as well as small ones, and thousands of persons have been converted." However large were the crowds that Bray and Keys, both graduates of Payne Theological Seminary, attracted, they scarcely broke denominational boundaries to conduct a broader evangelism beyond familiar AME terrain.[65]

The Church of God in Christ (COGIC), which was steadily growing beyond its founding environs in the Mid-South and in the Mississippi Delta, moved with the migration into the fertile soil of the urban and industrial Northeast and Midwest. Ready with free-wheeling worship, physical demonstrations of deep spirituality, and an emphasis on glossolalia, COGIC, unlike AME evangelists, cast a wider net through tent revivals to southern migrants beckoning them to join the denomination. These tent revivals, reminiscent of John Wesley's open air preaching, took worship out of the sanctuary and into the streets, and showed COGIC's lack of pretension and an easy accessibility for black newcomers. For example, Otha M. Kelly, a COGIC member, migrated from Mississippi to Chicago in 1917. After working at several jobs, including employment in the stockyards, and finding a COGIC congregation to join, Kelly became an evangelist in the 1920s. He started preaching in a borrowed tent and "within 13 days," he said, "there were already enough people 'saved' to begin a church which I promptly set up in a storefront." Moreover, he traveled to Milwaukee, Detroit, Buffalo, New York City, and various locations in the South. In 1930 Kelly logged 20,000 miles. He drew crowds in "city after city" where "many people responded to my straightforward old-fashioned holiness way of preaching." He said, "I believed as they did in a Bible-centered, solid ministry, preached by a clean-living Christian."[66]

No doubt, Kelly stressed in his revivals baptism by the Holy Ghost with the manifestation of speaking in tongues. He presented this spiritual gift in

---

[65] Richard R. Wright, Jr (compiler), *Who's Who in the General Conference [of] 1912* (1912), 39–40; Richard R. Wright, Jr. (ed.), *Centennial Encyclopedia of the African Methodist Episcopal Church (1916)*, 268; Dickerson, *Out of the Crucible*, 70; Richard R. Wright, Jr (compiler), *Who's Who in the General Conference [of] 1924*, 151–152.

[66] Otha M. Kelly, *Profile of a Churchman: The Life of Otha M. Kelly in the Church of God in Christ* (Jamaica, NY, K & C Publishers, 1976), 28–63.

such unpretentious settings as tents and storefronts. Music in services he conducted probably included lyrics such as "Yes Lord," which grew out of the folk religious culture of African Americans and were presented in a simpler, a cappella style that was easier to apprehend than AME hymnody. These aspects of COGIC religious practice could be found within African Methodism, especially in the South, but generally AMEs, perhaps unwittingly, ceded this ground to Kelly and other COGIC competitors.

The slowness of AMEs in adapting to the new media that the migrants increasingly embraced to service their religious needs stifled denominational growth. Records and radio broadcasts saturated and steadily homogenized the black religious culture with gospel music and exuberant folk preaching that scarcely included any AME input. Thomas Edison's invention of the phonograph in 1877 later made records a major medium for religious music. Initially, various black and white record labels promoted blues and jazz music, but in 1925 Evangelist Calvin Dixon became the earliest black minister to put his sermons on "wax." Dixon's action, said one scholar, signified "the emergence of black sermons as a modern commodity." This medium overwhelmingly appealed to black holiness and Pentecostal preachers, who recorded sermons and worship services, and this helped them to outdistance the AMEs and other mainline churches in reaching the mass of black religious consumers. For example, one COGIC preacher, F. W. McGee in both Des Moines and Chicago used his recorded sermons and services to facilitate his evangelism and church planting among migrants in these Midwest locations.[67]

Radio, of course, was the best medium to reach a black religious population. Again, AMEs failed either to dominate or participate in this aspect of mass black religion. In Chicago, for example, Pastors Clarence Cobbs of the First Deliverance Spiritualist Church and Elder Lucy Smith of All Nations Pentecostal Church in the early 1930s started weekly radio broadcasts of the former's prosperity sermons and the latter's "southern vernacular preaching" and her congregation's "emotionally demonstrative worship." This medium, one scholar observed, "heralded this new religious culture" that AMEs had no role in developing.[68]

There were other tectonic shifts in the black religious culture that left AMEs behind. Popular black religious music was developing mainly from

---

[67] Lerone A. Martin, *Preaching on Wax: The Phonograph and the Shaping of Modern African American Religion* (New York, New York University Press, 2014), 11, 32, 62–63, 71, 84, 90, 110–114, 116–119.
[68] Best, *Passionately Human, No Less Divine*, 115.

the pen of Charles Albert Tindley, the pastor of the all black East Calvary Methodist Episcopal Church, renamed Tindley Temple, in Philadelphia. In 1906 and 1907 Bishop Turner endorsed Tindley's "Stand By Me" and "By and By, When the Morning Comes." Bishop Coppin was especially enamored with singing "By and By." These compositions caught on among other AME worshippers and blended with the traditional Wesleyan hymns that they sang. Less familiar than Tindley was James S. Hatcher, an AME pastor in Virginia and dean at the denomination's Kittrell College in North Carolina. He wrote "I Cannot Drift," featured in successive editions of the *AME Hymnal*, in addition to "Come to Me" and "Yet Will I Rejoice." However popular Tindley was, his lyrics, though thematically reminiscent of slave sorrow songs and similar in beat to the secular blues, his "Take Your Burden to the Lord" and "Beams of Heaven" never blended with black urban music. Moreover, Hatcher, like Tindley, believed that religious music is "the vehicle and conservator of doctrine. The best way to teach people theology and doctrine is in song." These two African American Methodists, in their compositions, while sustaining the musical genres that Charles Wesley, Isaac Watts, and John Newton contributed to evangelical Protestantism, adopted none of the cultural influences that stood outside the religious heritage.[69]

Neither Tindley nor Hatcher embraced the urban blues. This popular musical form that Georgia migrant Thomas Andrew Dorsey played in Chicago during the 1910s and 1920s morphed into the gospel blues that he popularized in Baptist circles through his classic "Precious Lord, Take My Hand." Gospel choirs grew out of this development and transformed the black religious culture. Though AME congregations later embraced the gospel blues and instituted gospel choirs, African Methodism did not drive or influence these movements, nor were they popularly associated with them.[70]

Kelly and other clergy in the newer black churches pursued ministries mainly focused on preaching holiness and intensifying the religious experience of their followers. This emphasis had a wider appeal than what was

---

[69] Dennis C. Dickerson, *A Liberated Past: Explorations in AME Church History* (Nashville, TN, AME Sunday School Union, 2003), 64; Wright, *Who's Who in the General Conference [of] 1924*, 194; James S. Hatcher, "I Cannot Drift," in *The Richard Allen AME Hymnal* (Philadelphia, PA, AME Book Concern, 1946), 311; James S. Hatcher, "The Contribution of Church Music to Church Worship," *AME Church Review*, Vol, 34, No. 135, January 1918, 163; *The Episcopal Address Presented by Bishop M. H. Davis to the Thirty-Second Quadrennial Session of the General Conference of the African Methodist Episcopal Church at Philadelphia, Pennsylvania, May 1944* (Nashville, TN, AME Sunday School Union, 1944), 22.

[70] Best, *Passionately Human, No Less Divine*, 102–117.

offered by most AME ministers, though there were exceptions to this pattern. Some AME services, though expressed within the denomination's liturgical boundaries, resembled what Kelly presented to his jubilant listeners. At the 1924 Indiana Annual Conference, for example, a minister led the congregation in singing Tindley's "Take Your Burden to the Lord" and then "a Pentecostal wave of spiritual enthusiasm engulfed the assembly." Nonetheless, Kelly's AME generational peers in the Chicago area included highly educated clergy such as William A. Fountain, Jr., the son and namesake of a bishop, and Frederick D. Jordan, later a bishop and the son of a professor. Both were born in Georgia and were alumni in 1919 and 1925 respectively from Garrett Biblical Institute, a Methodist seminary at Northwestern University in nearby Evanston, Illinois. Garrett's curriculum reflected liberal Protestantism, whose core lay in Biblical criticism and the social Gospel. Deep experiential religion and practical Christianity, however, defined the range of ministry in migrant era churches. One emphasized emotionalism in worship and the other, though it valued evangelistic preaching, attempted effective and holistic ministry. COGIC leaned toward the former and most AME congregations tended toward the latter. Holiness, glossolalia, and intense spirituality were delivered to religious consumers in tent revivals, such as those that Kelly sponsored, on records, such as those of F. W. Mc Gee, and the radio broadcasts of the "vernacular southern preaching" of Lucy Smith. These conveyed to migrants a version of African American Christianity that was both familiar and intimate. The spirited but erudite sermons of Fountain at Ebenezer AME Church in Evanston and Jordan at St. Paul AME Church in Chicago accompanied social gospel sensibilities that migrants accepted and appreciated. The 1924 General Conference endorsed this perspective, saying "the migrant has conditions that are new and bewildering to him, so that the ministers of the AME Church will find a new class to deal with, and they will have to establish social centers, build more churches, and create a condition to satisfy this new element, for those people will need teaching economically, socially, politically, and morally." The migrants received these messages, however, from AME preachers and parishioners whom they generally perceived as either detached or unreachable. Hence, Kelly, the son of a Mississippi farmer, and his holiness and Pentecostal colleagues became dominant on Chicago's shifting religious landscape more than such Garrett-trained AMEs as Fountain and Jordan.[71]

---

[71] *Journal of Proceedings of the Eighty-Sixth Annual Session of the Indiana Conference, African Methodist Episcopal Church, 1924*, 11; Dennis C. Dickerson, "William A. Fountain, Jr., Rufus E. Clement, and the Making of the Atlanta University Center," *AME Church Review*,

Far from being a boon to African Methodism, the migration, while maintaining the denomination as a major organization, left it in a less commanding position on the black religious landscape. Its impressive infrastructure and the visibility of its educated clergy in politics and social holiness initiatives sustained the AME Church as an important factor in African American religious life. With respect to religious loyalties within the black population, however, the denomination had a decreased membership share because of new religious groups and the emergence of a mass religious culture in which African Methodism played either a marginal or nonexistent role. Perhaps, the perspectives of R. R. Downs, a veteran pastor, explained why AMEs were at times oblivious to the new religious realities that the migration created. Though concerned about AME growth in Harlem, Downs decried the very practices that had the biggest appeal to migrants. He advised against unwise variations from the recommended AME order of service. For example, "the singing of 'jazz hymns' destroy[s] the dignity and solemnity of the service [especially] during the communion." He believed "the whole object is to, seemingly, get the people noisy and in a high state of ecstatics, to screaming and hollering." These "jazz hymns," a recent blend of popular secular styles with religious music, apparently had a widening appeal to some AMEs. Downs concluded that "this religious habitude or noisy form of worship, beyond doubt, pleases a large number of people," but AMEs should resist these encroachments upon "the value of order and quietness."[72]

AFRICAN METHODISM AND GARVEYISM

While the migration was stirring upheaval in the AME Church, Garveyism intervened and complicated the loyalties and identities of African Methodists. This movement, aimed at the redemption of Africa and mobilizing black opposition to colonial and racial subjugation, also mimicked AME activity in the Atlantic World and reminded ministers and members about these facets of their emancipationist heritage. Hence, the same pan-Africanist energies and social holiness objectives that defined African Methodism were harnessed to Marcus Garvey's Universal Negro Improvement Association

---

Vol. 117, Nos. 379/380, Fall 2000, 21–22; Wright, *The Bishops of the African Methodist Episcopal Church*, 168, 170, 244–245; *Journal of the Twenty-Seventh Quadrennial Session of the General Conference, 1924*, 181.

[72] R. R. Downs, "The Best Means of Redeeming African Methodism in Harlem," *AME Church Review*, Vol. 43, No. 171, January 1927, 155, 157.

(UNIA). Moreover, Garveyism attracted as members mobile black populations migrating out of the South into the Northeast and Midwest as well as
emigrants involved in broader movements within the African diaspora
leaving the Caribbean, Central and South America, and Africa for destinations elsewhere in the Americas and Europe.

Marcus Garvey, born in Jamaica in 1887 and baptized in the Wesleyan
Methodist Church, founded UNIA in 1914. This pan-African organization
derived from Garvey's travels through Central and South America, parts of
the West Indies, and Europe. "I asked," he said, "where is the black man's
Government? Where is his King and his kingdom? Where is his President,
his country, and his ambassador, his army, his navy, his big men of affairs?"
Because Garvey saw during his travels blacks in colonized and subordinate
conditions, he resolved, "I will help to make them" a respected people. That
would be the task of UNIA, whose mission was to redeem Africa from
European colonial rule and unite people of African descent throughout the
diaspora. With a base in New York City, in the 1920s Garvey claimed
6 million UNIA members in 900 branches.[73]

Garvey could scarcely develop UNIA without an encounter with the AME
Church. A few months after the organization started, Alfonso Dumar spoke
at a UNIA meeting. Dumar, who founded the AME Church in Jamaica in
1912, urged Garvey to shift his operations to the United States, where the
chances of success were greater. This influential endorsement came from a
General Conference delegate elected successively for the 1916, 1920, 1924, and
1928 meetings. In 1917 Bethel Church in Harlem hosted 2,000 people at a
UNIA mass meeting. At another rally at New York City's Palace Casino a
roster of speakers, including Reverdy C. Ransom, endorsed UNIA objectives.
Not unlike Garvey, Samuel E. Churchstone Lord, a St. Vincent native and
superintendent of the AME Church in Haiti, said in 1918 "that as a race the
Negro or African people are entering upon a new era." Echoing Garvey, Lord
observed that in the United States and the West Indies young blacks were
"unversed" about "the grandeur and prestige" of black heroes and heroines.
This history, Lord declared, would be "guide-posts for our present achievements and an earnest [predictor] of our future accomplishments." Philip
Van Putten, a long-time leader of AMEs in the Dominican Republic and
Haiti, belonged to UNIA. Born in 1889 in the French West Indies and reared
in the Virgin Islands on St. Thomas Island, Van Putten was licensed to
preach in the AME Church in 1914 in the Dominican Republic and was fully

[73] Marcus Garvey, "The Negro's Greatest Enemy," in Robert A. Hill (ed.), *Marcus Garvey and UNIA Papers*, Vol. I, 1826–August 1919 (Berkeley, University of California Press, 1983), 5, 10.

ordained later in 1923 at the New York Annual Conference. In 1920 he represented the Dominican Republic at the UNIA convention. Joseph Gomez, the pastor of the teeming Bethel Church in Detroit, opposed Garvey's "Back to Africa" program because in the United States "too much blood had been spilled in the struggle for freedom, [and] too much sweat [had been] poured into [the] making of this country for the Negro to give up his rightful place." Nonetheless, Gomez, born in Antigua in 1890, reared in Trinidad, and an immigrant to the United States in 1908, credited Garvey with interpreting theology to "answer the longing hearts of the Negro race." Garvey deployed a rhetoric that resonated with AMEs and tapped into their rich heritage of black autonomy. Hence, about fifty AME clergy comprised one-fifth of the organization's 250 ministerial supporters. This group, perhaps, more than the AME laity, was aware of the denomination's presence not only across the United States, but also in numerous nations and colonized areas in the Americas and Africa.[74]

AMEs may have interpreted Garvey's UNIA slogan, "One Aim, One God, One Destiny," as a politicized version of the Atlantic ambitions of their racially proud and independent religious body. Perhaps Garveyism appealed to AME clergy because UNIA spread into many of the same places where African Methodism already existed. One scholar has written that "Garveyites, stretching across the African diaspora, were connected by a vast and sustained project of network building." Moreover, "they pursued a common set of aims, structured around broad appeals to pan-Negro unity, political education, and racial pride; and that they shared a common understanding about the opportunities presented by global events, and a faith in the liberatory implications of racial organization." Though he argues "Garveyism was an organic mass politics," there was something within it

[74] "Newspaper Reports," "America's Bitter Race War," "Among the Negroes of Harlem," in Hill, *Garvey Papers*, Vol. I, 73–74, No. 1, 222, 239; Richard R. Wright, Jr. (compiler), *Sixteenth Episcopal District of the African Methodist Episcopal Church* (n.p., 1964), 85; *Journal [of the] Twenty-Fifth Quadrennial Session of the General Conference, 1916* (Nashville, TN, AME Sunday School Union, 1916), 26; *Journal of the Twenty-Sixth Quadrennial Session of the General Conference, 1920* (Nashville, TN, AME Sunday School Union, 1922), 28; *Journal of the Twenty-Seventh Quadrennial Session of the General Conference, 1924* (Philadelphia, PA, AME Book Concern, 1924), 23; *Journal of the Twenty-Eighth Quadrennial Session [of the] General Conference of the AME Church, Chicago, Illinois, May 7–23, 1928* (Nashville, TN, AME Sunday School Union, 1928), 24; S. E. Churchstone Lord, "Essential Requirements in the Uplift of the Negro Race," *AME Church Review*, Vol. 34, No. 135, January 1918, 154–155; Wright, *Encyclopedia of African Methodism*, 592; Wright, *Sixteenth Episcopal District of the African Methodist Episcopal Church*, 19–20; Gomez-Jefferson, *In Darkness with God*, 1, 14, 17, 103; Randall K. Burkett, *Black Redemption: Churchmen Speak for the Garvey Movement* (Philadelphia, PA, Temple University Press, 1978), 9.

that resonated with AMEs. Perhaps Garveyism strikingly mirrored the racial ethos of African Methodism itself. Garvey's ambitious Black Star Line, his influential newspaper, the *Negro World*, the parallel African Orthodox Church (AOC), and a focus on the rehabilitation of Africa reflected historic perspectives and practices of the oldest of black religious institutions.[75]

That Garveyism excited some AME preachers and some of their proletarian parishioners seemed related to what they understood as similarities between UNIA and their denominational heritage. The bishops at the 1920 General Conference, for example, reminded themselves and the delegates that they "in almost every instance, [had] taken the initiative in the cause of the Negro Race" thus maintaining their traditional role as the defenders of blacks in the Americas and Africa. J. G. Robinson, Ransom's successor as editor of the *AME Church Review*, echoed these sentiments, saying the bishops "are the greatest factors in the elevation of the Negro Race." Additionally, in 1922 the *Christian Recorder*, while lamenting some of Garvey's financial ineptitude, declared that if he succeeded "in one-half of his undertaking[s], within the next ten years, he will have accomplished the greatest thing in Negro history since Richard Allen established the AME Church." Hence, some AMEs viewed as complementary their affiliation with both Garveyism and African Methodism. A congregation in Michigan, however, went further than most in blending Garveyism with African Methodism. The presiding elder in 1922 reported that the parish in River Rouge, a small mission of nineteen parishioners, was thoroughly Garveyite. "The members of Marcus Garvey's organization," he said, "seem to control the church and the charter hangs back of the pulpit." He added that "the pastor can do nothing at any time, if the Garveyites object." Without a pastoral change, the prospect for the mission "is not too enticing." By 1924, with a different pastor, the congregation, now numbering fifty, "is in a good spiritual and financial condition." The Garveyite influence had been reduced or eliminated.[76]

---

[75] Adam Ewing, *The Age of Garvey: How a Jamaican Activist Created a Mass Movement and Changed Global Black Politics* (Princeton, NJ, Princeton University Press, 2014), 5–6.

[76] *Journal of the Twenty-Sixth Quadrennial Session of the General Conference, 1920*, 205; *Journal of Proceedings of the Eighty-Sixth Annual Session of the Indiana Conference, African Methodist Episcopal Church, 1924*, 11; "Editorial," Christian Recorder, March 11, 1922, cited Hill, *Garvey Papers*, Vol. IV, September 1, 1921–September 2, 1922 (1985), 566; *Minutes of the Thirty-Sixth Session of the Michigan Annual Conference, 1922*, 49, Statistical Table, unnumbered; *Minutes of the Thirty-Eighth Session of the Michigan Annual Conference, 1924*, 56, Statistical Table, unnumbered.

More than any other UNIA member, Richard H. Tobitt embodied a blended Atlantic AME and Garveyite identity. He was born in 1873 in Antigua where he became a teacher. Later, he emigrated to Canada and to the United States, and graduated from Mico College in Jamaica. Tobitt's career as an educator and AME minister developed in Bermuda. The British long had been negligent in providing public schools for the mostly black inhabitants of their Atlantic colony. As early as 1891, when J. Albert Johnson, now a bishop, raised funds in Great Britain for the Bermuda Collegiate Institute, AMEs had been trying to fill the void in the island's educational system. After arriving in 1911, C. A. Stewart, a transfer from the Nova Scotia Annual Conference, started a high school at St. George AME Church. He hired Tobitt in 1912 as principal for the St. George School.[77]

When Tobitt was introduced to the 1912 Bermuda Annual Conference, he heard fellow Antigua native, William B. Derrick, the island's presiding bishop, say that "His Majesty has no more loyal subjects [than] the ministers and members of the AME Church." Derrick, who lived in Flushing, New York, also "declared his attachment to England and emphasized the fact that her government is the best and greatest in the [world]." Tobitt, like others who attended the conference, knew that the bishop's hyperbole may have assuaged the sensitivities of watchful colonial officials, but hardly addressed the reasons why Stewart brought him to the St. George School. Instead, Tobitt realized that he was now a part of a palpable AME insurgency against British neglect of black education in Bermuda. In fact, the report on education at this same meeting said "Bermuda as a British colony is the only one which undertakes compulsory education, without a school building owned by the colony for the training of her young." Because education in Bermuda was "meager," a public school system "in its entirety" was needed. To achieve this objective teachers should go on strike, and Tobitt hoped "the offsprings of the coloured race [would] be there" and African Methodism would be clearly seen playing its potent part in bringing about a public school system." At the 1914 Bermuda meeting Stewart, chair of the education committee on which Tobitt served, proposed a resolution that was "signed by nearly every member of the Conference," which called for "a free Public School System for the colony with equal advantages for both races, white, as well as coloured." After the adoption of the resolution another minister moved that

---

[77] "Report of a Meeting at Liberty Hall," Hill, *Garvey Papers*, Vol. 2, No. 1 August 27, 1919–August 31, 1920 (1983), 496; *Minutes of the 29th Session of the Bermuda Annual Conference of the African Methodist Episcopal Church held at Hamilton, Bermuda, from July 29th to August 5th, 1912* (Hamilton, Bermuda, S. S. Todding-Mid-Ocean Press, 1912), 3, 11.

the resolution should "be given publicity through the press." Hence, AME defiance toward British educational failures in Bermuda framed Tobitt's entry into African Methodism. Already in 1912, he was one of Stewart's fifty members and probationers at St. George and the principal, in charge of sixty students. He commented at this same meeting about "the serious duty of teachers to mould the minds [of students] and thus control the destiny of [the] people."[78]

In the ensuing eight years Tobitt rose in the Bermuda Annual Conference as a pastor, educator, and advocate of the Atlantic World identity of African Methodism. These blended pursuits facilitated his acceptance of Garveyite ideology. Before the 1913 Bermuda Annual Conference convened, Tobitt supplied the pulpit at St. David's Mission. The presiding elder later reported that Prof. R. H. Tobitt "has had a degree of success along all lines," including five conversions and three accessions, and a total of fifteen members and probationers in this small congregation. "Prof. Tobitt," he said, "is an excellent scholar and a diplomat and I believe success awaits him in the Church, if he will join the Conference and put himself in position where God and the Church could use him." Not surprisingly, Tobitt asked Haitian-born Bishop John Hurst, and the delegates at the 1913 conference to admit him as a ministerial candidate.[79]

Tobitt's threefold activities included qualifying for full ordination, serving as a pastor, and participating on the conference education committee. At the 1914 Bermuda meeting he received the good news that the Committee on Admission "found him to be proficient" and recommended him to be admitted on trial to the annual conference, the first official step to ordination. His continuing candidacy compelled the committee to report in 1916 that Tobitt, in showing "an efficient knowledge of the subjects" in the conference's ministerial training course, qualified him for his first ordination as an itinerant deacon. At this same meeting Tobitt asked to take the exam for Third Year Studies and speed up his eligibility for his second ordination. Although his request was denied, the 1917 Bermuda Annual Conference approved him for Fourth Year Studies and advanced him for candidacy as an itinerant elder "having [already] passed a satisfactory examination."

---

[78] *Minutes of the 29th Session of the Bermuda Annual Conference, 1912*, 3–5, 8, 11, 14–15, 22; *Minutes of the Thirty-First Session of the Bermuda Annual Conference of the African Methodist Episcopal Church held at Somerset in Allen Temple, July 23rd to 27th, 1914* (Hamilton, Bermuda, S.S. Todding-Mid-Ocean Press, 1914), 10–11).

[79] *Minutes of the Thirtieth Session of the Bermuda Annual Conference of the African Methodist Episcopal Church held at Richard Allen AME Church, St. George, July 24th to 28th, 1913* (n.p., 1913), 5, 9–10, 18.

In 1918 he was "quite proficient and capable in the courses prescribed." Hence, the "decision as to ordination of Bro. R. H. Tobitt [will] be wholly at the pleasure of the Bishop."[80]

Tobitt, while he matriculated in the AME ministerial curriculum, maintained high visibility in the proceedings of several sessions of the Bermuda Annual Conference. At the 1916 meeting, for example, Tobitt collected subscriptions for AME periodicals and he belonged to two fundraising committees. He also delivered a "a practical paper on Education," and he discussed his familiarity with an island reformatory and how it was different from an "Industrial Institution." Moreover, he believed "the latter institution" was "preferable" for the rehabilitation of inmates. Similarly, at other annual sessions of the Bermuda Conference Tobitt played significant roles. In 1918 he served on several committees including the Committee on Sunday Schools. In the State of the Church report he showed his understanding of the Atlantic reach of African Methodism. He praised the denomination for "rising up like a pyramid of strength to combat the mammon of unrighteousness." He noted "her voice is heard" whether in the United States, West and South Africa," and "to come nearer home-in Canada, Bermuda, Jamaica, Hayti, Barbados, British and Dutch Guiana, and Trinidad."[81]

Tobitt's entry into the AME Church exposed him to its layered operations and ecclesiastical infrastructure. Though pedagogy rather than preaching brought him to Bermuda, Tobitt exhibited a deep spirituality that suited him for a pastorate. At the start of his ministry, for example, Tobitt expressed "his trust in God" and "his desire to become an instrument in His hands." He brought these attitudes to his appointment at St. David's, a mission congregation where he maintained its viability and potential for growth. Commentary from Tobitt's presiding elder and reports in the Bermuda Conference minutes commended Tobitt's efforts

---

[80] *Minutes of the Thirty-First Session of the Bermuda Annual Conference, 1914*, 19; *Minutes of the Thirty-Third Session of the Bermuda Annual Conference of the African Methodist Episcopal Church held at St. Paul's AME Church, Hamilton, July 20th to 24th, 1916* (Hamilton, Bermuda, S. S. Todding-Mid-Ocean Press, 1916), 14, 27; *Minutes of the Thirty-Fourth Session of the Bermuda Annual Conference, 1917* (Hamilton, Bermuda, S. S. Toddings-Mid-Ocean Press, 1917), 33; *Minutes of the Thirty-Fifth Session of the Bermuda Annual Conference of the African Methodist Episcopal Church held at Allen Temple, Somerset, August 8th to 11th, 1918* (Hamilton, Bermuda, S. S. Toddings-Mid-Ocean Press, 1918), 31; *Minutes of the Thirty-Sixth Session of the Bermuda Annual Conference of the African Methodist Episcopal Church held at St. Paul's, Hamilton, Bermuda, Beginning Thursday, July 17th, 1919* (Hamilton, Bermuda, S. S. Toddings-Mid-Ocean Press, 1919), 7.

[81] *Minutes of the Thirty-Third Session of the Bermuda Annual Conference, 1916*, 4, 8, 10,14; *Minutes of the Thirty-Fifth Session of the Bermuda Annual Conference, 1918*, 2,11, 27, 39.

at the fledgling parish.[82] Nonetheless, in 1919 Tobitt, because of a setback, recommended that St. David's, where he had a small membership, and another Bermuda congregation should borrow funds from the denomination's Church Extension Department to improve their physical plants.[83]

What Tobitt learned during his initial years of active involvement in the Bermuda Annual Conference was a deep understanding of African Methodism as a transnational body and as a potentially insurgent force against colonialism. His ministerial colleagues, impressed with his educational attainments, assigned the writing of important conference reports to Tobitt. In them he discussed the Atlantic reach of the AME Church and its opposition to the inadequate educational policies of Bermuda's colonial rulers. Tobitt commended African Methodism because it upheld "the motto of her founder and pioneer the illustrious Bishop Richard Allen-'God Our Father, Christ Our Redeemer, and Man Our Brother.'" Moreover, the denomination "wherever oppression of mankind and the progress of sin are to be crushed, and liberty, religious, educational or civil is to be gained, the AME Church takes her stand."[84]

AME activism, Tobitt discovered, was normative behavior for his Bermuda colleagues. He commended them for their campaign "to reclaim the vagrant youths of this colony and to provide for the public welfare." They were consistent critics of colonial authorities because of the island's educational deficiencies. "In the fight for educational reform," he said, African Methodism "sets a pace by producing in the field men of mark who are capable of holding their own with credit." At the 1918 and 1919 meetings of the Bermuda Conference, Tobitt (who wrote the reports on education) both reflected black discontent with the colonial educational system and commended AME efforts in supplementing what little the British provided. "Education locally," Tobitt observed, "leaves much to be desired." Though he acknowledged improvements in schools that received colonial aid, Bermuda, it seemed, was the only British colony that lacked "a public school building of its own." He added that "nothing but a Free Public School

[82] *Minutes of the Thirty-First Session of the Bermuda Annual Conference, 1914*, 3, 25; *Minutes of the Thirty-Fifth Session of the Bermuda Annual Conference, 1918*, 20.
[83] *Minutes of the Thirty-Sixth Session of the Bermuda Annual Conference, 1919*, 11, 16, Table: A-Numerical Statistics of Churches and Sunday Schools; *Minutes of the Thirty-Third Session of the Bermuda Annual Conference, 1916* (Hamilton, Bermuda, S. S. Toddings-Mid-Ocean Press, 1916), 13; *Minutes of the Thirty-First Annual AME S[unday] S[chool] Convention and Teachers' Institute of the Bermuda Annual Conference held at Warwick AME Church Mission, Warwick (East) on September 7th, 1916* (Hamilton, Bermuda, S. S. Toddings-Mid-Ocean Press, 1916), 43, 49.
[84] *Minutes of the Thirty-Fourth Session of the Bermuda Annual Conference, 1917*, 18–19.

System" can address "this defect." Only "the people themselves, by proper agitation, legislation, and sacrifice" could achieve this objective.[85]

Tobitt concluded in 1919 that educational progress in Bermuda over the years was "lacking." The British provided no facility to house an elementary school and there were "no High Schools and Grammar Schools beyond private and aided institutions, no Colleges and Universities, in short, no real educational facilities for betterment of the people." As a result, black Bermudans immigrated to the United States in a similar way to contemporary black southerners who settled in northern American cities. To address the education issue, Tobitt suggested an upgrade in Bermuda's status within the British Empire to that of a crown colony. This change would create "central schools" where there could be no race discrimination [and] no payment of school fees by parents and guardians for the elementary education of their children." Conditions were better in Barbados, Tobitt believed, where there was a "Free Public School System because blacks belonged to a "local parliament" and there was "no race discrimination so rampant" as in Bermuda. He also proposed that blacks in Bermuda should cooperate "and agitate wisely for things we need."[86]

Because of this persistent problem, Tobitt noted, "the AME Church, despite her shortcomings, has been the pioneer of higher education in Bermuda, so far as her coloured population is concerned." AMEs brought educators, such as Tobitt himself, from "sister colonies of the West Indies" who taught in such schools as "'St. George's High School' in the East, a 'Sandys Grammar School' in the West, [and] radiating from the Centre-a 'Berkeley Institute.'" Without African Methodism, black education on the island, no thanks to the British, would have been seriously restricted.[87]

Tobitt did more than hurl polemics at the British, but he engaged in insurgency on his own. Because of colonial neglect, "the work of educating the natives in Bermuda has fallen in the hands of the [scho]ol teachers." In order to officially empower them, Tobitt "formed what is called a Teachers Union which is working for a better condition." He also defied colonial authorities because "they heap upon us books that have been written by white men and books that give inspiration to the white boy." He observed that "the colored boy reads about what white men have done and then he thinks that honor is only for the white boys." To address this problem, Tobitt told "our children that there are black heroes as well as white heroes." Hence,

[85] Ibid., 19; *Minutes of the Thirty-Fifth Session of the Bermuda Annual Conference, 1918*, 24.
[86] *Minutes of the Thirty-Sixth Session of the Bermuda Annual Conference, 1919*, 20–23.
[87] Ibid., 22.

at the St. George School, he taught students about "such great men like Toussa[int] L'Ouverture, Frederick Douglass, Crispus Attucks and such great men belonging to our race, so that the colored child can aspire [like] some of their own race."[88]

Tobitt seemed second to none in his admiration of African Methodism. The denomination's transnational presence and the insurgent impulses of its ministers and members impressed him. That Bermuda AMEs showed no reluctance in criticizing the deficient educational policies of the British revealed their distaste for the continued colonialism imposed on their island. These racial realities reinforced Tobitt's attachment to African Methodism and attracted him to Garveyism. UNIA mirrored African Methodism in its pan-Africanism and in its antiracist and anticolonial ideology. Perhaps, as a politicized version of the AME Church, UNIA easily secured Tobitt's commitment. Belonging to both organizations, however, became for him increasingly problematic. Though Tobitt's blended AME and Garveyite identities complemented each other, it was difficult for him to participate fully in the two demanding groups.

At the 1920 Bermuda Annual Conference, Tobitt was probably present when Bishop James M. Conner declared "that all the coloured people of the world belong or should belong to the African Methodist Episcopal Church, and that it was the duty of our pastors everywhere to gather all our people ... and teach them the Fatherhood of God and the universal brotherhood of man." The ex-slave bishop spoke words that Tobitt himself could have uttered. But how to realize the pan-African objective of black empowerment required the political praxis that Garveyism offered through its mass mobilization of African peoples throughout the diaspora. Facilitating that task, however, pulled Tobitt away from his parish and undermined his relationship with his new presiding elder, E. D. Robinson.[89]

Robinson raised reservations at the 1920 Bermuda Conference about Tobitt's ministerial efficiency. The case was referred to the judiciary committee, but Tobitt insisted that "his cause" should be considered publicly "in open Conference." Robinson accused Tobitt of going to the United States on July 27, 1920 "representing a secular organization," and thus abandoning the St. David's Mission. Though Tobitt "acknowledged his guilt and begged to be forgiven," he accused Robinson of personal animosity toward him.

[88] "Reports of the Convention," Hill, *Garvey Papers*, Vol. II, 520–521.
[89] *Minutes of the Thirty-Seventh Annual Session of the Bermuda Annual Conference of the African Methodist Episcopal Church held at Richard Allen Church, St. Georges, Beginning Thursday, October 7th to 9th* (n.p., 1920), 4.

Nonetheless, Bishop Conner, "in his fatherly and unbiased manner, remonstrated with Bro. Tobitt, advising him that he should know the law of the church more thoroughly and thus avoid such a serious breach." Despite the reprimand, the bishop showed conciliation and permitted Tobitt to deliver the benediction to end the session.[90]

Perhaps Conner noted some subtle differences between the oral presentation of Tobitt's case and the more serious accusations permeating the presiding elder's written report. It said, "Rev. R. H. Tobitt, a teacher in St. Georges [High School], began the year and remained in charge until the 27th of July 1920, at which time he left his work without permission or even discussing the matter with his Presiding Elder and left for New York to attend a secular convention." What had not been discussed "in open Conference," according to Robinson, was that he "received a card on the same day he [Tobitt] sailed saying that he would be absent in the United States during his vacation and that he had made provision for his charge." Robinson said that "on examination we found the work had not been properly provided for." So, while Tobitt was away, the presiding elder assigned a replacement pastor because of whom "this work is now progressing splendidly" and was under the "watch care" of a larger congregation. In a final swipe at Tobitt, Robinson spoke more broadly about the quality of Tobitt's overall ministry, concluding "we are convinced after watching the work for nearly four years that it will never prosper in the hands of supplies [like Tobitt] who are unable to give it their attention."[91]

Though Robinson refused to name the "secular organization" that claimed Tobitt's larger loyalty, everyone at the annual conference probably knew that he was referring to UNIA. In this the presiding elder spoke for a segment of AMEs who were opposed to Garvey and eager to take aim at Tobitt. Bishop Smith, Conner's predecessor, unapologetically denounced the Jamaican leader. While presiding in Bermuda, Smith, a Detroit resident, wrote in 1919 to the notorious US Attorney General, A. Mitchell Palmer, saying that the *Negro World*, the UNIA newspaper, was "calculated to breed racial and international strife." He added that he had met the editor, probably Garvey himself, and concluded "he is an adventurer and a grafter bent on exploiting his people to the utmost." Smith also suggested that Garvey should be "deported as an undesirable." The bishop, a native Canadian whose earlier jurisdictions included Cuba and South Africa, possessed the same pan-

[90] *Minutes of the Thirty-Seventh Annual Session of the Bermuda Annual Conference of the African Methodist Episcopal Church, 1920*, 4, 7–8.
[91] Ibid., 15–16.

African vision for African Methodism as did Conner and Tobitt, but he envisaged no possible alignment between his denomination and UNIA. This attitude greatly influenced his dealings with Tobitt. When Smith visited Bermuda in March 1920, he denied him full ordination by refusing "to elevate Rev. R. H. Tobitt to elder's orders" on the flimsy premise of "non-necessity." Within a few months, however, Conner succeeded Smith in Bermuda, and despite Tobitt's eviction from his pastorate at St. David's Mission, allowed him to function in the annual conference and serve on the resolutions committee.[92]

After presenting the resolutions, Tobitt remained on the floor and addressed Bishop Conner. He admitted to being a member of an organization that seemed to draw criticism and unwanted attention to the AME Church. Therefore, Tobitt, "being an AME preacher and considering that the said organization was a worthy one which would afford him a larger scope for usefulness among his people, he desired to remove all responsibility from the church for his actions and restore her to public confidence." Then Tobitt surprisingly "begged that he be allowed to withdraw from the Conference." When put to a vote, the delegates granted his request to sever his ties with the Bermuda Annual Conference. A sympathizer, however, "expressed regret that Bro. Tobitt should take such a step, and suggested that he reconsider his decision before it was too late." Tobitt disagreed. He "had thoroughly weighed the matter and was prepared to carry out his present decision."[93]

What lay behind the dramatic events at the 1920 Bermuda Annual Conference was Tobitt's public embrace of Garveyism. In the period leading up to the meeting, he delivered a lecture at St. Paul AME Church in Hamilton on a familiar Tobitt topic, "Is Education Necessary to the Negro?" After he finished, someone gave him Garvey's widely circulated newspaper. From it, Tobitt said, "I caught his vision and became a ready disciple of Garveyism." UNIA held "the Master Key," he believed, "to the correct solution of the vexed race problem of the world." When he organized a Bermuda branch of the UNIA at St. David's Mission, his troubles began. Later, Presiding Elder Robinson called out UNIA in a letter to the British colonial secretary. He "assailed the Marcus Garvey [movem]ent" and said that "[it] is a very

---

[92] Bishop C. S. Smith to A. Mitchell Palmer, Attorney General, June 25, 1919, Hill, *Garvey Papers*, Vol. I, 446; *Minutes of the Thirty-Seventh Annual Session of the Bermuda Annual Conference, 1920*, 9,14, 16–17.

[93] *Minutes of the Thirty-Seventh Annual Session of the Bermuda Annual Conference, 1920*, 9–11,16.

dangerous movement, in that it arouses antagonism [amo]ng races wherever it goes." Robinson, and maybe Bishop Conner, blamed Tobitt for the retaliation of British authorities against an AME school. The British denounced Tobitt's signature on a UNIA declaration of rights for peoples of African descent and described the document as "antagonistic to the existing order." This resulted in a cut off of funds to the AME sponsored St. George School because "Tobitt was no longer a fit person to be entrusted with the education of children."[94]

Despite Robinson's actions, other AMEs in Bermuda agreed with Tobitt's persistent criticism of British neglect of black education, notwithstanding colonial aid to church-sponsored schools. Though this insurgent impulse stirred little support for Garvey himself, it showed that Garveyism as an ideological critique of colonialism had some resonance within African Methodism. Unafraid to state his opposition to the British in Bermuda itself, Tobitt also denounced them in the United States. During his AME contretemps in Bermuda, he addressed UNIA's 1920 convention and listed British racial practices. Though Bermuda had a parliament, the population, which was 75 percent black, had "only two colored representatives and one of them is dubbed by the natives as 'the white man's tool.'" Moreover, "in the 'Courts of Justice' the people who are condemned by the law are subject not only to fine[s], but after being imprisoned for a certain number of years, [these persons were] flogged, as they do in some parts of Africa." These punishments, Tobitt observed, sometimes applied to such misdemeanors as stealing a bicycle. Additionally, Bermuda blacks were mostly farmers. White farmers, often with access to their own ships, easily transported their produce to New York while black farmers usually waited at the Customs House or at the wharf for available vessels. Frequent delays led to a decreasing value for their crops. Hence, UNIA's Black Star Line was needed to break "the shipping trade [that] is monopolized by the white man." The dockyards, though owned by the British employed an impressive number of blacks whom the British encouraged to train in vital trades. "You can find," Tobitt said, "engineers, fitters, [and] plumbers of all descriptions," all of whom could help in the Black Star Line.[95]

---

[94] Randall K. Burkett, *Garveyism as a Religious Movement: The Institutionalization of a Black Civil Religion* (Metuchen, NJ, Scarecrow Press and The American Theological Library, 1978), 26–27; Edward Robinson to Colonial Secretary, Bermuda, October 18, 1920; General James Willcocks, Governor to Viscount Milner, Secretary of State, Colonial Office, November 2, 1920, Robert A. Hill (ed.), *Marcus Garvey and Universal Improvement Association Papers*, Vol. XII, The Caribbean Diaspora, 1920–1921 (Durham, NC, Duke University Press, 2014), https://books .google.books.

[95] "Reports of the Convention," Hill, *Garvey Papers*, Vol. II, 519–521.

Tobitt, who entered fully into his UNIA activities, was Garvey's appointee as leader of the Eastern Province of the West Indies. In his report to the 1921 UNIA convention, Tobitt discussed his travels in Philadelphia and Brooklyn and in the Bermuda and the Caribbean. He encountered, as in Bermuda, hostile colonial officials. In Trinidad, for example, he was refused permission to enter the colony. In 1924 Tobitt sailed for Great Britain as the UNIA ambassador whose duties related to that country's black population. He requested an interview with the Prime Minister and Secretary of State so he could present his credentials.[96]

Despite Tobitt's efforts to pursue pan-Africanism in both the AME Church and UNIA, he seemed unable to avoid interpersonal friction with a few AMEs, such as Robinson and Garvey himself. Already sensitive to dissent, Garvey, who battled James W. H. Eason, an AME Zion minister and critic, also identified Tobitt, a furloughed AME, as an untrustworthy associate. He was friendly with Garvey's erstwhile mentor, Duse Mohamed Ali, himself a prominent pan-Africanist, and promoted him for a larger role in UNIA affairs. Like many others, Tobitt seemed disappointed in Garvey's poor business acumen. Whatever the breaking point in the relationship, Garvey accused Tobitt for alleged mishandling of UNIA funds. Garvey may also have been irked about Tobitt's ordination as a priest in the AOC, whose assertive archbishop, George A. McGuire, another Antiguan and former AME minister, raised him to this new clerical status. Tobitt traveled in the West Indies as a Garvey emissary and as McGuire's general missionary "for religious awakening among our people." Garvey, who stopped McGuire from establishing the AOC as the official church of UNIA, may have suspected Tobitt of competing loyalties.[97]

Whether out of necessity or nostalgia, in 1926 Tobitt returned to the Bermuda Annual Conference to seek reinstatement. Though he was introduced initially as a visitor, the Committee on Admission later reported that Tobitt should be "readmitted [as] a member of the Conference. After the motion passed, Bishop William T. Vernon "imparted" to Tobitt "some wise

---

[96] "Convention Reports," August 8–13, 1921, Hill, *Garvey Papers*, Vol. III, September 1920–August 1921 (1984), 646; *Morning Herald*, January 25, 1924; Marcus Garvey to J. H. Thomas, British Colonial Secretary, January 25, 1924; "British Colonial Office Report on the UNIA," February 1924, Vol. V, September 1922–August 1924 (Berkeley, University of California Press, 1986), 548–549; 560–561.

[97] "Address by Marcus Garvey," August 11, 1924, Hill, *Garvey Papers*, Vol. V, 698; Judith Stein, *The World of Marcus Garvey: Race and Class in Modern Society* (Baton Rouge, Louisiana State University Press, 1986), 144–149; Richard Newman, "Introductory Essay: The Origins of the African Orthodox Church," in *The Negro Churchman*, Vols. 1–4, 1923–1926 (Millwood, NY, Kraus Reprint, 1977), iii–iv, ix.

and fatherly counsel [and then] warmly welcomed him back" into the jurisdiction. His readmission seemed unremarkable because he was already supplying the Warwick Mission. He was reassigned to Vernon Temple at Southampton East and in 1927 Mt. Zion Church was added to his pastoral responsibilities. Next, he went to St. John's at Bailey's Bay.[98]

After he was readmitted to the Bermuda Conference as an itinerant deacon, Tobitt was ordained as an itinerant elder at the 1927 session. Now that he was fully ordained, he was thoroughly integrated as a leader in the conference as though he never had left. At the 1927 meeting, for example, the bishop appointed him to the finance committee, and he resumed his interest in the AME position on education in 1928. At the 1929 session Bishop Joshua H. Jones asked Tobitt to preside briefly while he attended to another conference matter.[99]

While Tobitt transferred to the New York Annual Conference in 1930, he maintained his connection to Bermuda AMEs, saying in a letter to the 1933 meeting "that you are not forgotten." He also commended their bishop, William H. Heard, whose jurisdiction included both New York and Bermuda, noting that islanders should "give him your maximum support." Tobitt, who was secretary of the New York Conference and a pastor on Staten Island, shared Atlantic and UNIA affiliations with his Georgia-born bishop. In 1895 Heard was appointed as the United States Minister to Liberia, and after his election to the episcopacy was assigned to West Africa. In 1922 he received an award from UNIA "because of the great work done by him in Africa among the native people there." Perhaps, this common Garveyite connection explained the mutual esteem between Tobitt and Heard.[100]

---

[98] *Minutes of the Bermuda Annual Conference, Forty-Third Session, African Methodist Episcopal Church, Allen Temple AME Church, Somerset, Bermuda, Friday, May 21st, 1926* (n.p., 1926), 6–7, 15; *Minutes of the Bermuda Annual Conference, Forty-Fourth Session, African Methodist Episcopal Church, St. Paul's AME Church, Hamilton, Bermuda, Friday, April 22nd, 1927* (n.p., 1927), 11; *Minutes of the Bermuda Annual Conference, Forty-Sixth Session, African Methodist Episcopal Church, Bethel AME Church, Shelly Bay, Bermuda, Thursday, December 18th, 1929* (n.p., 1929), 6.

[99] *Minutes of the Bermuda Annual Conference, Forty-Fourth Session, 1927*, 3, 12; *Minutes of the Bermuda Annual Conference, Forty-Fifth Session, African Methodist Episcopal Church, Richard Allen AME Church, St. Georges, Bermuda, Thursday, August 16th, 1928* (n.p., 1928), 6; *Minutes of the Bermuda Annual Conference, Forty-Sixth Session, 1929*, 9.

[100] *Minutes of the One Hundred and Eighth Session of the New York Annual Conference, African Methodist Episcopal Church held at St. John's AME Church, New York City, May 28 to June 1, 1930*, 12; *Minutes of [the] Bermuda Annual Conference, Fiftieth Session, African Methodist Episcopal Church, Bethel AME Church, Shelley Bay, Bermuda, April 1933* (n.p., 1933), 13; *Official Journal of the New York Annual Conference of the African Methodist*

Because AME identity was sometimes reflected in black nationalism, African Methodists other than Tobitt and Heard acknowledged these attributes within Garveyism. Richard R. Wright, Sr., a Philadelphia banker and the father and namesake of the editor of the *Christian Recorder,* said in 1921, amid cheers at a local UNIA assembly, that "there have been only two great Negro movements in the history of America." One of them "was started in Philadelphia in the year 1787 and is known as the African Methodist Episcopal Church, and the other movement is the Universal Negro Improvement Association, both organizations being owned and controlled by Negroes."[101]

Emma C. Kinch, a New Jersey native and a veteran AME missionary to West Africa, supported UNIA's objective of African redemption and ridding the continent of European colonialism. From 1908 to 1910, with sponsorship of the WPMMS, Kinch served in Liberia where in 1909 she established in Monrovia the Eliza Turner Memorial School, which initially had twenty students. Kinch attended a meeting of the East Pittsburgh District at the Pittsburgh Annual Conference in 1913, where she spoke about "Africa: Its Customs and Needs." As a delegate to the 1919 WPMMS convention, Kinch urged conference branches "to become better acquainted with Missions" especially through "Mission Study classes." She pushed this initiative because white missionary women believed it "utterly impossible . . . to teach Negro women missions." Moreover, she thought "the AME Church is by ties of blood and racial affiliation especially fitted by Providence to participate largely in the salvation of our brothers and sisters in the fatherland." In front of a Garveyite audience at the UNIA-owned Liberty Hall in New York City in 1920, Kinch showed how her AME membership aligned with the Black Nationalist organization. She said, "you have never enjoyed your manhood until you have walked in Liberia and have come in contact with the black President of that country." Kinch advised blacks to "join hands and back up the man [Marcus Garvey] who is leading us out of this wilderness into the Promised Land." Kinch maintained her AME visibility as the denomination's supervisor of missionary work among young people. In a visit to the 1924 Indiana Annual Conference she discussed funding for a project in South America. Bishop Heard introduced her to the 1932 New

---

Episcopal Church, Minutes of the One Hundred and Twelfth Session held at Macedonia AME Church, Flushing, Long Island, NY, May 24–27, 1934 (Philadelphia, AME Book Concern, 1934), 34, 53; William H. Heard, *From Slavery to the Bishopric* (Philadelphia, PA, AME Book Concern, 1924), 45, 78; Burkett, *Garveyism as a Religious Movement,* 139.
[101] Burkett, *Garveyism as a Religious Movement,* 137.

England Annual Conference as a woman "known from coast to coast, in Africa, and the isles of the sea as a leader and organizer and a preacher of note."[102]

A cross section of clergy in both the Caribbean and the United States conflated the black nationalist sensibilities of African Methodism with UNIA. West Indians, an example being Tobitt, migrated in and out of the AME Church during their involvements either with UNIA or with the parallel AOC. John Gibbs St. Clair Drake, born in Barbados, was fully ordained in 1912 on his native island. For a time in the 1920s he was a pastor to a Baptist congregation in Pittsburgh while serving as an international organizer in UNIA. Again, like Tobitt, he returned in the 1930s to the AME Church as a pastor and presiding elder throughout the Northeast. Reginald G. Barrow was also born in Barbados and was ordained as an Anglican priest. After he was assigned to a parish in St. Croix in the Virgin Islands in 1918, Barrow took note of the "poor conditions under which the majority of people" lived. Hence, he supported the Labor Union of St. Croix and challenged planters and plantation owners to raise the wages of their under-paid workers. His criticism of economic overlords was enhanced when he joined with labor activists in publishing a newspaper. When employers complained to Barrow's bishop, he was ordered to end his insurgent activities. When Barrow refused, he was forbidden in 1920 to preach to his parishioners. As a result, 800 members left with Barrow and followed him into the AME Church. The Labor Union, Barrow's allies, assisted with a donation of 3 acres of land on which to build St. Luke AME Church. Barrow became pastor at St. Luke and at Bethel AME Church in Christiansted, and the presiding elder on the island until 1922. Additionally, he served the AME Church in the 1920s as a dean and professor at the denomination's Lampton College in Louisiana and at Edward Waters College in Florida. In 1925 Barrow, who had become a priest in the AOC, was consecrated in New York City as an AOC bishop. Other ministers of greater visibility included Milton H. Mickens, who had been a leading pastor in Seattle, Washington

---

[102] Burkett, *Black Redemption*, 43–45, 49; Wright, *Centennial Encyclopedia of the African Methodist Episcopal Church*, 144; *Journal of Proceedings of the Forty-Sixth Session of the Pittsburgh Annual Conference of the African Methodist Episcopal Church* held in St. Paul AME Church, Uniontown, PA, October 8–12, 1913 (Nashville, TN, AME Sunday School Union, 1913), 51; *The Seventh Quadrennial Convention of the Women's Parent Mite Missionary Society of the African Methodist Episcopal Church, 1919* (Jacksonville, FL, Edward Waters College Press, 1919), 44, Appendix; *Journal of Proceedings of the Eighty-Sixth Annual Session of the Indiana Conference, 1924*, 11; *Journal of the Eighty-First Session of the New England Annual Conference of the African Methodist Episcopal Church* held at Loring Street AME Church, Springfield, MA, June 23–26, 1932 (n.p., 1932), 11.

and later Huntington, West Virginia, and C. A. Wingfield, a prominent pastor in Georgia and secretary of a UNIA unit.[103]

The Garvey movement, notwithstanding the involvement of some important clergy, was an authentic grassroots movement. Though no formal denominational endorsement came from any General Conference, no annual conferences, or from the Council of Bishops, an undetermined number of rank-and-file AMEs were excited by Garvey. The cities and industrial communities where southern black migrants settled were especially locations of UNIA growth. Gary, Indiana, a center of steel production, had a large UNIA membership. Henrietta Redd, a member of the AME Church, belonged to the UNIA division and reported at the 1924 National Convention in New York City that "the two organizations [were] working satisfactorily together." In Ohio industrial communities in Cleveland, Akron, Canton, Lorain, Toledo, and Youngstown, UNIA divisions were organized in the same setting where well-established AME congregations already existed. Similarly, in western Pennsylvania UNIA divisions started in Pittsburgh and in a long roster of coal and steel towns. Each had a large population of black migrants, many of whom attended the AME congregation located in each of these locations. As in Gary, Indiana, there was a likely overlap in AME and UNIA membership.[104]

Pan-Africanism became a rhetorical trope for some AMEs. Ransom recalled at the General Conference of 1920 that William T. Vernon, a candidate for the bishopric, won supporters because of his speech that featured "his tricks of oratory and the blackness of his skin." Before an audience of delegates Vernon tried "to conjure" the memory of Henry M. Turner, the pan-African prelate who had died a few years earlier. Vernon, in a vulgar display, "spread his legs wide apart as though to stand astride the world [and] then rocking himself from side to side, he cried, 'Turner, shake two Continents!'" Then, again, he shouted, "Turner, shake two Continents!" Vernon was referring to Turner's transatlantic ministry in "Africa and America." Ransom believed that Vernon, a Republican National Committee (GOP) operative and former Registrar of the US Treasury, was making a

---

[103] Wright, *Encyclopedia of African Methodism* (1947), 98–99; Dickerson, *Out of the Crucible*, 80; *Negro Churchman*, August 1925, October 1925; Burkett, *Garveyism as a Religious Movement*, 144, 149; Wright, *Sixteenth Episcopal District of the African Methodist Episcopal Church* (n.p., n.d.), 103–104; Wright, *Centennial Encyclopedia of the African Methodist Episcopal Church*, 159, 253.

[104] "Convention Report," August 4, 1924, Robert A. Hill (ed.), *Marcus Garvey and Universal Negro Improvement Association Papers*, Vol. V, September 1922–August 1924 (Berkeley, University of California Press, 1986), 654; Tony Martin, *Race First: The Ideological and Organizational Struggles of Marcus Garvey and the Universal Improvement Association* (Dover, MA, The Majority Press, 1986), 366–367.

Figure 5.1 Bishop William T. Vernon, Mrs Emily Embry Vernon, and AMEs in southern Africa, 1920–1924 (Used with permission from the Bishop William T. Vernon Collection, University of Kansas Libraries, Kenneth Spencer Research Library)

"grotesque appeal" that "swept the house with tumultuous applause." Vernon's histrionics resembled exactly what critics said about Garvey. Vernon, like Garvey, boasted of his black skin, "rubbing his cheeks to call attention to his obvious color" while seeking the votes of General Conference delegates. Garvey also believed he was "turning the tables" on mulattoes whose favored status in his native Jamaica and seeming entitlement to leadership among African Americans in the United States stirred his criticism and derision. Vernon was probably taking a posthumous swipe at the Caucasian features of the recently deceased Bishop Shaffer and the light skin of his episcopal rival, Archibald J. Carey, Sr. and his wife, who was accused sometimes as passing for white. These tensions, according to Charles H. Wesley, existed in the AME Church. "Paint the Bench Black," a reference to the bishops and the issue of skin color, was a perspective often whispered within denominational circles, Wesley noted. Nonetheless, both Garvey and Vernon were serious pan-Africanists. Vernon, for example, succeeded in his election to the episcopacy and assumed a pan-Africanist mien through his assignment to the Transvaal, Cape Colony, Orangia, Natal, and Zambezi Annual Conferences in southern Africa.[105]

---

[105] Ransom, *The Pilgrimage of Harriet Ransom's Son*, 262; Wesley, "The Negro Church as a Factor in American Religious Life," *AME Church Review*, April 1929, 225–226; Dickerson, *African American Preachers and Politics*, 43; *Journal of the Twenty-Sixth Quadrennial Session of the General Conference*, 1920, 5, 157.

The AME Church fully functioned as a pan-African body in ways that the contemporary Garvey movement envisaged for itself. Diasporic and multilingual demonstrations, for example, were a part of the regular order at AME General Conferences. At the 1924 meeting in Louisville, Kentucky, six South African representatives, for example, were introduced and "sang two selections in their native tongues." Emily Embry Vernon, the daughter of Bishop James C. Embry, served with her husband Bishop Vernon in southern Africa. She read a paper to the assembly on "Women's Work in South Africa." The president of the WPMMS presented M. V. F. Smith, a student in Dutch Guiana, to sing "in her native language." Additionally, the Secretary of Missions, E. H. Coit, in his quadrennial report, showed expenditures of $115,418 that funded programs and personnel, mostly indigenous, in West Africa, South Africa, the Caribbean, South America, and Bermuda. In Trinidad, for example, where Garvey's UNIA grew to thirty chapters by the early 1920s, the AME Church operated the Gaines Normal and Industrial School. The Reverend W. H. Mayhew and other indigenous West Indians managed the institution and invited in 1931 the Director of Education of this British colony to review the school's progress. At a meeting at Metropolitan AME Church in the island's Newtown area, Mayhew reported on the 118 students and their matriculation in Gaines's "large and airy" building.[106]

A PAN-AFRICAN RELIGIOUS BODY

John A. Gregg embodied the transatlantic identity of African Methodism. Gregg, born in Kansas in 1877 and a graduate of the University of Kansas, was a veteran of the Spanish-American War and was quartermaster-sergeant of his regiment in Santiago, Cuba. He was best known among AMEs as president of Edward Waters College and then Wilberforce University. He was recently elected as a bishop and president-designate of Howard University in 1924 and 1926 respectively. Because his episcopal assignment to South Africa took precedence, he refused the honor of becoming Howard's first African American president. His predictable decision derived from his two years in South Africa in 1904 to 1906, when he founded an AME school in Chatsworth in the Cape Province. As a youth, he testified, "AFRICA! AFRICA! How that word has always thrilled me since as a boy of six in

---

[106] *Journal of the Twenty-Seventh Quadrennial Session of the General Conference, 1924*, 73, 137, 223; *Trinidad Guardian*, July 16, 1931 (courtesy of Professor Richard J. M. Blackett, Vanderbilt University); Kim Johnson, "How Marcus Garvey Influenced Trinidad," August 23, 1998, www.trinicenter.com/moreHowMarcus GarveyinfluencedTrinidad.htm.

my father's home." Though the AME Church, he said in 1920, eschewed entry "in the political life of South Africa other than as religious activity does and should," Gregg echoed the objectives of the same anticolonial insurgency that informed Garveyism. He noted that in South Africa, for example, "one hears much of the 'Ethiopian Movement.'" He added that the European imperialist that acquires "these colonies ... against the will of the people thus governed, has continually to watch every movement ... that it may not develop into a storm which might sweep everything before it." Now, he was returning in 1924 to the "mother" continent as South Africa's AME prelate.[107]

Gregg showed his immersion in African Methodist issues on the "mother" continent in a lengthy letter to his episcopal colleagues in 1926. He thanked them for special allocations to satisfy the financial obligations for building a new edifice for Bethel Memorial, the flagship congregation in Cape Town, South Africa. Within two years Gregg would dedicate the cathedral structure to house the large, though mostly colored membership. He noted that Francis H. Gow, who had previously received regular stipends from the Department of Missions, now got less lucrative quarterly payments. Nonetheless, "I am pleased," Gregg declared, "that African Methodism is holding its own in this sub-continent." He added, "I raised some funds during my stay in America" to supplement denominational funding.[108]

Gregg reported on a convention of the Women's Home and Foreign Missionary Society (WHFMS) in Bloemfontein, "and it was the best in the history of the church here. More than 400 women gathered from all parts of our work, two women walking nine days to attend from Basutoland." In the Transvaal, "we then visited Wilberforce Institute, Johannesburg, Boksburg, Krugersdorp and several points in the colony." Additionally, he observed "new laws and especially the segregation policy have very much disturbed our people. Many have been compelled to move from the farm and vast sections of the diamond mining areas have simply been denuded of Native population. Naturally, our churches in these localities have suffered greatly." South Africa's "mobile laity," unlike contemporary black migration in the United States, moved under duress, and Gregg had no strategy to oppose state policies that uprooted AMEs and depopulated areas where the

---

[107] Wright, *Centennial Encyclopedia of the African Methodist Episcopal Church*, 99–100; Wright, *The Bishops of the African Methodist Episcopal Church*, 199–200; John A. Gregg, *Africa and a Way Out*, delivered at the Bishop's Council, Baltimore, MD, February 13, 1920, Bethel AME Church (n.p., Edward Waters Print, 1920), 6, 13–14.

[108] @John A. Gregg to [The] Bishops [of the] AME Church in Council Assembled, Jacksonville, Fla., USA, December 21, 1926," Private collection of the author.

church had been established. "Nevertheless," Gregg reported, "we are pushing forward and even in the face of those hardships something is being
accomplished." The following week, he noted, "I shall dedicate a new church
at Dordrecht, another at Potchefstroom, another at Upington, and . . . four
other churches ready for dedication in the [Orange] Free State."[109]

Gregg participated in a subtle insurgency against white-controlled evangelization on the "mother" continent. The Council of Bishops chose him as
the AME representative in Belgium at the International Conference on the
Christian Mission in Africa. There were 250 delegates, "about 20 of whom
were of our Race Group." Gregg reported that the AME presence "gave our
Church special standing, particularly with the South African delegation,
which was quite large." Gregg served on the Committee on the American
Negro and Africa, which forced the Conference to adopt an audacious
resolution. The first section demanded that African Americans "should be
permitted by governments and encouraged by missionary societies to play
an increasingly important part in the evangelization of Africa." In the second
section committee members sought assurances that African Americans
should be affiliated with "responsible societies of well-established and recognized standing." Hence, Gregg was proud that "every turn our Church was
accepted" as a religious body that met these criteria.[110]

Black nationalist sensibilities that permeated African Methodism were
negotiated and pursued within the denomination's far-flung presence
throughout the diaspora. The importance of Garvey's politicized version of
pan-Africanism lay in its influence upon several freedom movements in
ensuing decades against racism and colonialism in the Americas and Africa.
Though UNIA included the Black Star Line, the *Negro World*, and divisions
and branches spread across the black Atlantic, its infrastructure hardly
matched the organizational breadth and stability of the AME Church. The
denomination's heritage of racial pride, autonomy, and on the ground
institution building was influential in seeding and laying foundations for
insurgent initiatives against white supremacy on both sides of the Atlantic.
In 1936, for example, the bishops denounced the Italian invasion of Ethiopia
and pledged to assist American Aid for Ethiopia. The prelates praised
"Christian Emperor Haile Selassie" because he was the "leader of one of
the oldest Christian nations in the world." Bishop Ransom, preaching at the
1936 General Conference, denounced "the Christian nations of Europe,"
saying they "have ravaged and torn Africa apart." Italy's invasion of "the

---

[109] Ibid.   [110] Ibid.

ancient Kingdom of Ethiopia" illustrated this sad situation. "Africa knows," he said, that "white nations who send her missionaries are really there to subjugate her people and to exploit the land." The challenge to confront colonialism lay with the AME Church. Therefore, Ransom queried, "is our present missionary machinery equal to the task?" Just as AMEs populated the staff and membership of the National Association for the Advancement of Colored People (NAACP) and the National Urban League, the church's clergy and communicants also affiliated with UNIA. In movements to fight Jim Crow and racial inequality, whether embodied in racial oppression in the United States or in the Caribbean or in Africa, AMEs and Garveyites, who were sometimes allies and at other times dually aligned with membership in both organizations, reinforced the black nationalist influence of both African Methodism and Garveyism.[111]

Charles H. Wesley, in this post-Garvey era, also reflected normative AME thinking about black consciousness and how it had been realized in the denominational heritage. Writing in his 1935 biography *Richard Allen: Apostle of Freedom*, the first scholarly study of the AME founder, Wesley described him as "the first organizer of Negro unity and race solidarity in the United States." For this "oppressed, exploited group" Allen developed a "philosophy" that stressed "that Negroes had to be made group-conscious, and, that not until then would they begin their march towards freedom by their own efforts." Moreover, Wesley believed that AMEs advanced from the establishment of a lasting ecclesiastical organization to seeking broader protections for blacks in the diaspora. Daniel Coker, Allen's denominational cofounder, drew "inspiration" from starting a connectional body in 1816 to expansion to the "mother" continent. Coker settled in Sierra Leone in 1821 and launched derivative congregations in the region. Wesley, in his foreword to Clara E. Harris's history of the WPMMS, referred to Psalm 68:31. He said that "the Old Testament prophecy that 'Ethiopia'-the spiritual motherland of the darker races of Africa-should soon stretch forth her hands unto God seemed to be a challenge to the more favored darker peoples of America to help to bring on the day of Africa's awakening." He also declared in an introduction to L. L. Berry's *A Century of Missions of the African Methodist Episcopal Church, 1840–1940* that from "the days of Daniel Coker

[111] *The Episcopal Address Presented by Bishop William Alfred Fountain, Sr., A.M., D.D., LL.D. to the Thirtieth General Conference of the African Methodist Episcopal Church, New York City, May 6, 1936* (Philadelphia, PA, AME Book Concern, 1936), 68-69; *Journal of the Thirtieth Quadrennial Session of the General Conference of the African Methodist Episcopal Church* held in The Rockland Palace, New York City, May 6–18, 1936, 32.

to the present day, the redemption of Africa and Africa's people scattered in other parts of the world has seemed to be a supreme and ultimate purpose of our leadership." These perspectives from this presiding elder and professor, who in 1932 lost an election to the episcopacy, explained the readiness of AMEs to continue its reach into the black Atlantic and revive its mission to Cuba.[112]

The ongoing pan-Africanism of AMEs lay behind their presence in Cuba starting in 1898. Sustaining the mission in the ensuing decades, however, proved problematic. White missionary groups, with corporate support from such businesses as the influential United Fruit Company, disadvantaged AME initiatives. They harmed the denomination when they withheld contributions in favor of white religious organizations and refused them assistance in establishing places of worship. Moreover, the defeat of an armed black rebellion in 1912 aimed at political empowerment showed that AMEs lacked an island infrastructure either to encourage this movement or to benefit from this surge of black consciousness. The denomination's future, said W. H. Mayhew, the Spanish-speaking superintendent of the AME Caribbean work, lay in "arousing racial consciousness" among Afro-Cubans. Too few personnel, however, made it difficult to realize what Mayhew envisaged for the Cuban mission. A second opportunity seemed available when a special AME Commission to Cuba arrived on the island in January 1939. For two Commission members, Bishop Gregg and Bishop Noah W. Williams, both veterans of the Spanish-American War who had been detailed to Cuba, the trip was a homecoming of sorts.[113]

John H. DeVeaux, an adventurer and a Caribbean native, probably born in the Bahamas, appealed to the 1938 summer session of the Council of Bishops to visit Cuba. In addition to a letter, DeVeaux, who was the Deputy Supreme Chancellor of the Knights of Pythias in Havana, enclosed photographs of the activities of his fraternal organization. He urged AME representatives to survey "the field" and realize "a splendid opportunity" for "our Methodism there." He seemed to have an endorsement from Colonel Batista,

[112] Charles H. Wesley, *Richard Allen: Apostle of Freedom* (Washington DC, Associated Publishers, Inc., 1935), ix–x; Charles H. Wesley, "Foreword," in Clara E. Harris, *The Woman's Parent Mite Missionary Society of the African Methodist Episcopal Church, 1824–1827–1874–1935* (n.p., 1935), 5; Charles H. Wesley, "Introduction," in L. L. Berry, *A Century of Missions of the African Methodist Episcopal Church, 1840–1940* (New York, Gutenberg Printing Co., Inc., 1942), vi.
[113] Jualynne E. Dodson, "Encounters in the African Atlantic World: The African Methodist Episcopal Church in Cuba," in Lisa Brock and Digna Castaneda Fuertes (eds.), *Between Race and Empire: African Americans and Cubans before the Cuban Revolution* (Philadelphia, PA, Temple University Press, 1998), 91–96.

who aspired to political power through his active participation in a 1933 coup that put him as head of the military and in 1940 as president. Generating goodwill toward the AME Church could have helped in currying favor with the presidential administration of Franklin D. Roosevelt (FDR). Perhaps DeVeaux's inroad to the AME officialdom may have involved his son, John A. DeVeaux, from whom he was estranged. The junior DeVeaux was fully ordained into the AME ministry in 1932 by Reverdy C. Ransom, now a bishop and a member of the Commission to Cuba. When the bishops and other AME leaders arrived in Havana, they "received a welcome from [the] military forces by the personal adjutant of Colonel Batista." DeVeaux also presented a letter asking for certain financial aid for some economic venture." Bishop William A. Fountain had already sensed "that the group that sponsored our coming was more political and business than spiritual." Nonetheless, Fountain felt "it would be advisable to establish some work, even a small mission." Church treasurer Hawkins said the visit entailed only a "survey." The Commission, he believed, "should study what the people of Cuba have to offer and that we should make no commitments as far as our Church is concerned."[114]

DeVeaux unfolded plans for the Commission that he hoped would overcome the skepticism of some of its members about himself and the venture that he proposed. He stressed the relevance of Cuba's black heritage and the role of blacks in fighting for the country's independence from Spain. Hence, DeVeaux guided the Commission to various shrines of Cuban independence throughout the island and to meetings with a wide range of provincial and municipal officials. Among the several receptions, the Commission attended one in Pinar del Rio province where they visited the Halls of the Western Athenas and the Maceo Societies, named for the Afro-Cuban leader in the independence movement. Wreaths were laid at monuments for Jose Mari, Antonio Maceo, Mariana Gomez, Maceo's mother, and at the Battleship Maine Memorial. At Matanzas, the Commission reported "a great throng awaited us at the Hall of the 'Union Matancera' society where the mayor greeted them for the city and the provincial governor." Another large group greeted them in Colon City. In Santa Clara "we were pleasingly surprised to

[114] John [H.] DeVeaux in the Florida Passenger Lists, 1898–1964, Selected Passenger Lists and Manifests, National Archives, Washington DC; John [H.] DeVeaux in the 1910 United States Federal Census; Census Place: Miami, Dade, Florida; Roll: T624_158; Page 12A; Enumeration District 0055; FHL microfilm: 1374171; *Proceedings of the Mid-Summer Session of the Council of Bishops, African Methodist Episcopal Church in Kittrell, College, Kittrell, North Carolina, August 18–19, 1938,* 3; *Minutes of the Council Of Bishops, AME Church, Dallas, Texas, February 16, 1939,* 3–4; Wright, *Encyclopedia of African Methodism,* 96.

find a large picture, about five by eight feet, directly over the mayor's seat, of a colored Cuban woman, who had done much toward financing the Cuban revolution, and also a colored woman [was] one of the Council members."[115]

Evidence of Batista's support of the AME mission occurred during the visit to Santa Clara, when the Commission was told that Americans were "their best friends" and where they "were escorted to the Army Headquarters, where the Chief of Staff and his officers gave us a fine welcome." Moreover, the Great Maceo group and the La Belle Union hosted a banquet for the AMEs. Similarly, at Camaguey City "large numbers of Cubans" greeted them, including the Victoria Society and the Maceo Sons. After a long journey to Santiago, on the eastern part of the island, the Commission went to another army headquarters. Bishops Gregg and Williams, however, "visited their old camp ground where they saw service during the War of Cuban Freedom." With Bishop Tookes accompanying them, the threesome, repeatedly reminded about Antonio Maceo, could hardly miss the contrived linkage between themselves and their black Cuban compatriot.[116]

The robust itinerary through Cuba produced the desired effect upon the Commission and among Cubans genuinely interested in joining a proudly black religious body. After the Commission's return to Havana, they met and discussed "our intended visit with Co. Batista" and plans for an AME worship service. At the Methodist Episcopal Church, after Bishop Williams's sermon, Bishop Ransom referred to the AME "goodwill tour" in Cuba and said that the Commission had no intention "of proselytising members from other churches." Then Ransom "presented the invitation, and led by Mr. John H. DeVeaux a large number united with the AME Church." Bishop Fountain next "read them into the full membership [of] the Church."[117]

Before leaving Cuba, the Commission placed the Reverend L. T. Holly, one of those who joined the AME Church at the Havana service, "in temporary charge of the work." Holly, "a regularly ordained minister of the Anglican Church," was fifty-five years old. He and DeVeaux appeared before the Commission and they "promised to work together." Initially, they were told "to organize the groups into working units, with Mr. DeVeaux serving in the capacity of temporal adviser or trustee," but it was later resolved "that all instructions to Rev. Holly and Mr. DeVeaux be held in abeyance until after the Bishops' Council." Nonetheless, Treasurer Hawkins, though skeptical at first, "felt that this step taken in Cuba was one of the most vital in the history of the Church."[118]

---

[115] *Minutes of the Council of Bishops, February 16, 1939*, 4.   [116] Ibid., 5.   [117] Ibid.
[118] Ibid., 6–7.

Instead of Holly and DeVeaux, Jose W. Jarvis, a presiding elder in the Pittsburgh Annual Conference, became the superintendent in Cuba. Jarvis, a Caribbean native, spoke Spanish and received from Treasurer Hawkins a monthly salary of $100 from July 11, 1939 to May 1940. Secretary of Missions Berry also paid him $50 monthly during the same period. Hawkins allocated $800 "to assist in opening at once churches in Cuba," and five bishops in large districts promised to repay that amount to the denominational treasury. Within a month of his arrival Jarvis, accompanied initially by Bishop Ransom, leased an edifice in Havana with a seating capacity of 600. Furthermore, he opened a church in Santiago with four Sunday Schools and a parochial school affiliated with it. He also planted congregations in Camaguey and Santa Clara. Bishop Gregg, in the Episcopal Address to the 1940 General Conference observed that "more than a million people in Cuba are without a Church" and "they have invited us to come." He added "Our Church is the only Negro denomination operating in Cuba and Dr. J. W. Jarvis is the only duly accredited Negro minister of any denomination" on the island. Gregg and his colleagues believed "Cuba has enough to engage the full-time services of a Bishop and all the workers he can possibly command." Hence, the four members of the Cuban delegation, including Jarvis and DeVeaux, witnessed the assignment of newly elected Bishop Alexander J. Allen to a Caribbean and South American district that included Cuba. At the Bishops' Council on February 14, 1941, Bishop Allen presented for full ordination a physician, Arturo Tellezla Torre, who became the superintendent of the Cuba initiative.[119]

THE GREAT DEPRESSION

The overlap of World War I, the Great Migration, and the Garvey era, all with transformative effects on African Methodism, scarcely ended before the economic crisis of the 1930s. Whatever the improvements in the lives of blacks moving to northern cities and industrial communities, either from the American South or the West Indies, their ambitious vision for diasporic empowerment in the black Atlantic suffered a major setback. Garvey's

---

[119] Berry, *A Century of Missions*, 203–204; Wright, *Sixteenth Episcopal District*, 109; *The Episcopal Address Presented by Bishop John Andrew Gregg, A.M., D.D., LL.D. to the Thirty-First Quadrennial Session of the General Conference of the African Methodist Episcopal Church at Detroit, Michigan, May, 1940*, 41–42; *Journal of Proceedings of the Thirty-First Quadrennial Session of the General Conference of the African Methodist Episcopal Church* held in Ebenezer AME Church, Detroit, MI, May 1–15, 1940 (Philadelphia, PA, AME Book Concern, 1940), 16.

deportation in 1927, the result of the muscle-flexing of federal power in Washington DC through pervasive surveillance, and the stock market crash of 1929 plunged blacks into the same economic vulnerability that they suffered as southern sharecroppers and low paid, landless workers in the Caribbean and Africa.

The Great Depression hit the American population hard, but its devastating effects were greater among African Americans. In both the agricultural and industrial sectors of the economy blacks were affected far more negatively than were whites. Of all African Americans 56 percent were rural residents and 40 percent were employed as farm workers. As a result of the depression in 1934, the income of blacks was 73 percent of that of whites in the agricultural sector. The industrial sector had 12 million workers who were unemployed in an economy that in 1933 experienced a 30 percent decline in the gross national product, from $104 billion to $75 billion. Black unemployment, according to estimates from the National Urban League, ranged between 30 to 60 percent more than the figure for whites. African Americans on relief in 1933 were 17.8 percent of the black population in comparison to 9.5 percent among non-blacks. In Detroit, a recent destination for thousands of black migrants, the black population of 4 percent of the total of city residents, filled 25 percent of the relief rolls.[120]

AMEs acknowledged the stock market crash and the ensuing depression that it precipitated. They knew first hand about its severity because Treasurer Hawkins was compelled "to reduce the salaries of the Bishops and General Officers." Despite their awareness of the unprecedented downturn, AMEs showed, like most politicians including President Herbert Hoover, too little in innovative thinking about how to halt the deepening economic crisis. Delegates to the 1930 Pittsburgh Annual Conference noted that "wages have been at their lowest ebb [in] many years [and] unemployment is the issue of the day. Industry has lagged and agriculture has been greatly [a]ffected by the drought." Moreover, "the stock market has had the greatest slump in years [and] banks have failed in many sections." Delegates observed that the Hoover administration had "ceased optimistic predictions of an early return of prosperity." Pittsburgh AMEs could only hope that the nation "will maintain faith in God, confidence in themselves and in the Government" and as a result "a reasonable prosperity will ensue." Similarly, the 1932 New England Annual Conference said the nation was "facing one of the most complex and confusing conditions in the annals of the human race ... a condition

---

[120] Raymond Wolters, *Negroes and the Great Depression: The Problem of Economic Recovery* (Westport, CT, Greenwood Publishing Corporation, 1970), 7–8, 83, 91.

that seems to baffle the most skillful financier and the lords of industry." Delegates noted "that all human skill and endeavor has failed; millions of dollars by the state, municipalities and federal government have been appropriated to save the people from famine, ruin and poverty almost without avail." The solution, they naively believed, lay in the AME motto, "God Our Father, Christ Our Redeemer, and Man Our Brother." Invoking this denominational credo "would sweep this depression from the face of the earth" and restore prosperity and "social and domestic fellowship."[121]

Other AMEs gave greater attention to the depression's direct impact upon their parishioners and their economic environs. At the Macon, Georgia, Annual Conference delegates observed that the economic situation stirred "a restlessness among the people and migration continues among our group." Moreover, "employment is very dull at this time in the cities and on the farms, due to retrenchment on railroads and other large corporations." Further, they noted that "rural churches more and more are being depleted and this phase of church activity should not be overlooked, but a special committee should be appointed to report on church degeneration." Delegates to the North Ohio Annual Conference meeting in the steel and coal community of Steubenville, Ohio said that "Unemployment [a]ffects the Negro first and worst hence is a burning question and is seriously telling upon the work of the Church of Jesus Christ everywhere, for without money our work will fail and if our people do not have it, then the Church cannot get it."[122]

The bishops also lamented that "thousands of industrious laborers have been unable to get work. Self-respecting men and women have been forced to take a place in the bread line and wait to have food doled out to them from soup kitchens. "A general officer, concerned about clergy hard hit by the depression, called on the denomination "to remove AME ministers from the bread line." A special committee at the 1932 General Conference blamed the "continuation" of the depression on "the hoarding of wealth by

[121] *Episcopal Address, Thirty-First Quadrennial Session of the General Conference, 1940* (n.p., 1940), 42–43; *Official Minutes of the Pittsburgh Annual Conference, Third Episcopal District, African Methodist Episcopal Church, Trinity AME Church, Pittsburgh, PA, September 24 to September 28, 1930* (n.p., 1930), 33–35; *Journal of the Eighty-First Session of the New England Annual Conference, 1932,* 37.

[122] *Journal of Proceedings of the Forty-Eighth Annual Session of the Macon Georgia Conference of the African Methodist Episcopal Church* held in Allen Temple AME Church, Cordele, GA, November 19–24, 1930, Nashville, AME Sunday School Union, 1930, 49; *Minutes of the Forty-Ninth Annual Session of the North Ohio Conference of the African Methodist Episcopal Church of the Third Episcopal District* held in Quinn Chapel AME Church, Steubenville, OH, October 1–5, 1930, 34.

individuals, which has crippled the industry of the country and caused the closing of numerous banks." AMEs took note of President Hoover's Reconstruction Finance Corporation (RFC). With $2 billion, the RFC was designed "to relieve the frozen assets of the banks, and the sale of bonds to bring hoarded wealth into circulation." This initiative, however, had "very little effect in relieving the situation."[123]

Far from standing on the sidelines, AMEs readily responded to the privations around them. At Allen Chapel in Kansas City, Missouri, where Joseph Gomez had been appointed as pastor in 1928, operated a food kitchen in the church basement in the early 1930s, and also provided cots and showers for the homeless. In addition, Gomez established a Social Service Bureau to locate jobs and housing for the needy. He was transferred to St. Paul in St. Louis, Missouri, where his predecessor, Noah W. Williams, now a bishop, had built a community center. This made much-needed services available to those who were hard hit by the depression. A. Chester Clark, who served as pastor at Bethel in Baltimore between 1930 and 1933, led the congregation in sponsoring a soup kitchen that reportedly fed "thousands of the unemployed." The New York Annual Conference in 1934 cooperated with a Welfare Relief organization affiliated with the state of New York in operating "the set-up work" program. The headquarters was located in Harlem at St. John's AME Church. A conference committee declared that "with full cooperation of all we hope to make this a great success."[124]

Hoover, a Republican, was hardly lax in responding to the Great Depression. The stimulative impact of the RFC, various public works projects, and federal contributions to state relief programs, however, inadequately addressed the depth of the economic crisis. Nonetheless, some AMEs such as J. G. Robinson, the editor of the *AME Church Review*, remained loyal to the Republicans during the 1932 presidential election. He also feared embarrassment for the "Jim Crow Democratic Negro," who would be snubbed and denied a "share of Federal appointments." Hoover, according to his AME loyalists, lost to FDR, the Democrat, owing to "unemployment and [the] other hardships of the Depression," which "led people to just want a change." Now it was time "to rebuild the Grand Old Party and make it once more the party of Lincoln." Any African American who voted for the

[123] *Journal of the Twenty-Ninth Quadrennial Session [of the] General Conference of the AME Church*, **1932** (Philadelphia, PA, AME Book Concern, 1932), 115, 261, 213.
[124] Gomez-Jefferson, *In Darkness With God*, 113, 131–132; Mankekolo Mahlanggu-Ngcobo, *The Preaching of Bishop John Bryant* (Baltimore, MD, Victory Press, 1992), 94; *Minutes of the One Hundred and Twelve Session of the New York Annual Conference, 1934*, 75.

Democrats, according to some, did not understand "what Self-Respect means." The election of FDR, however, brought to the presidency a pragmatic politician and a practitioner of eclectic strategies to lift institutions and individuals from economic collapse and privation. Through the 1930s the First New Deal and the Second New Deal spearheaded massive programs to rehabilitate agriculture and industry, to put the jobless back to work, and to institutionalize a range of initiatives to address unemployment, unionization, and old age security.[125]

Roosevelt, in the first 100 days after his inauguration in March 1933 and with unusual cooperation from Congress, signed into law the Agricultural Adjustment Act (AAA), the National Industrial Recovery Act (NRA), and the Federal Emergency Relief Administration (FERA), all of which directly affected African Americans. The AAA posited that farm income and crop prices would improve through reductions in cultivable acreage. Farmers, therefore, received federal payments for land that lay fallow. The NRA imposed corporate regulations upon production to stabilize prices through respective industry codes on wages and hours, the output of goods and services, and fair competition. FERA expanded on Hoover initiatives by paying the unemployed to build schools, roads, bridges, and public works. Most blacks in agriculture occupied the lowest stratum in farm labor. About 70 percent worked as general laborers, sharecroppers, and share tenants, and another 10 percent were cash tenants. Despite the AAA, the income of blacks remained below that of whites. The program's stress upon acreage reduction discriminated rampantly in favor of landowners who received payments neither to plant nor harvest crops. As vulnerable black farm laborers they were often displaced and seldom received their share of federal funds.[126]

The NRA, especially among southern blacks in low wage work in tobacco, lumber, fertilizer, laundry, and iron and steel, were paid a racial differential that compensated them at lesser pay than that of whites. This disparity, employers argued, had been a time-honored policy because black workers, though less efficient, would be saved from losing their jobs. These lower wages were also justified because the cost of living for blacks was lower than for whites. Moreover, Section 7a of the NRA, which authorized the bargaining rights of unions, empowered the AFL, a craft-dominated group that traditionally excluded blacks. Additionally, the AFL largely ignored workers in the mass production industries with their heavy representation of African

---

[125] J. G. Robinson, "Editorial-That Democratic Landslide," *AME Church Review*, Vol. 48, No. 194, October 1932, 3–4.

[126] Wolters, *Negroes and the Great Depression*, 7–9, 13, 27, 31.

Americans. FERA, despite the black civil rights sympathies of Harry Hopkins, the director, feared the same southern white congressmen who restricted the positive impact of the AAA and NRA. Hence, Hopkins had mixed results in bringing relief benefits to blacks. Although executive orders barred racial discrimination, officials at the local level often disobeyed these directives and either excluded or reduced black participation in FERA initiatives.[127]

These important components of the First New Deal suppressed black participation, and AMEs recognized that Southern Democrats were the stumbling blocks. African Methodists in the Georgia Annual Conference observed that "our President seems to be willing to give equal justice to all, but he is helpless." Discriminatory practices from officials "entrusted to make the just distribution of government affairs in this country" prevented the full inclusion of African Americans. The Second New Deal agenda, however, especially after 1935, produced better results for African Americans. Harold Ickes, the Secretary of the Interior had already stopped segregation in his division's cafeterias and bathrooms, and barred employment to any whites refusing to work with blacks. The Public Works Administration (PWA) that he supervised drew skilled and unskilled blacks to construction projects, and some of them gained entry to affiliated craft unions that were usually off limits to African Americans. Additionally, PWA housing included blacks above their percentage in the general population, while some other units had integrated occupancy. Moreover, the United States Housing Authority built 122,000 units between 1937 and 1942, and 41,000 of these went to African Americans.[128]

The enactment of the National Labor Relations Act in 1935, however, generated another transformative shift among African Americans equal to the impact of the Great Migration. When in 1935 the Supreme Court in the Schechter case invalidated the NRA and its Section 7a clause, which energized union activity, Senator Robert F. Wagner of New York resurrected the proviso in new legislation, familiarly known as the Wagner Act. The labor law motivated John L. Lewis of the United Mineworkers and others to found the Committee on Industrial Organizations (CIO). Starting in 1936, Lewis led broad-based organizing drives, heavy with experienced Socialist and

---

[127] Ibid., 98–99, 101, 103, 172–175; Harvard Sitkoff, *A New Deal for Blacks: The Emergence of Civil Rights as a National Issue: The Depression Decade* (New York, Oxford University Press, 1978), 44, 49.

[128] *Proceedings of the Sixty-Seventh Session of the Georgia Annual Conference of the African Methodist Episcopal Church* held in Gaines Chapel AME Church, Waycross, GA, November 28–December 2, 1934 (n.p., 1934), 45; Sitkoff, *A New Deal for Blacks*, 67.

Communist operatives, in such mass production industries as auto, steel, rubber, and electrical manufacturing. These mills and factories, located in major industrial areas of the Northeast and Midwest, were populated with black migrants who settled into these occupations during the World War I and 1920s era. The CIO unions could not realize their organizing objectives unless the mass of black workers in these industries became members. As a result, blacks formed a large and visible presence in important CIO groups, whose ties to FDR's Democratic political coalition became indispensable.

Despite the benefit that African Americans derived from the New Deal, AMEs were neither oblivious to broader societal injustices against blacks nor to federal programs that reflected these patterns of racial inequities. In 1932 the bishops deplored the continued scourge of lynching as a "social disease" and urged "the enactment of State and national anti-lynching statutes to punish mobs and indemnify the families of mob victims." Perry B. Jackson, a former Ohio state legislator, an assistant police prosecutor in Cleveland, and a delegate to the 1936 General Conference, authored the resolution condemning Congress for failing to bring to a vote the Costigan–Wagner bill, a strike "against the atrocious lynching evil." Jackson, a Republican, urged AMEs to telegram the majority leaders in both Houses and President Roosevelt to act on the legislation in the current congressional session. He also joined two others in commending "the wonderful work that the NAACP is doing to eliminate lynching, mob violence, and to bring about a better understanding between the races." The Episcopal Address to the 1936 General Conference, in expressing regret about the Scottsboro case, noted that "there are a few people who have not bowed their knees to the Baal of Injustice." In 1931 nine black males, nearly all of them minors, faced false accusations in Scottsboro, Alabama, of raping two white women of questionable character. All were convicted and eight were sentenced to death. The Supreme Court twice set aside the convictions and the bishops noted that a new trial was scheduled in 1936. They affirmed "the innocence of the defendants and called on citizens of the South and North alike to help to remove an injustice, which can bring only injury to the entire nation."[129]

Few AMEs believed that the same racial discrimination that permeated American society left New Deal programs unaffected. Hence, they joined

---

[129] *Episcopal Address by Bishop W. Sampson Brooks to the Bishops, General Officers and Members of the Twenty-Ninth Quadrennial Session of the General Conference of the African Methodist Episcopal Church, 1932, Cleveland, OH, May 2–16, 1932* (Philadelphia, PA, AME Book Concern, 1932), 45–46; *Journal of the Thirtieth Quadrennial Session of the General Conference, 1936*, 121, 123; *The Episcopal Address, Thirtieth General Conference, 1936*, 71–72.

with other African Americans in criticizing the New Deal initiatives that excluded, segregated, or limited the involvement of blacks. In 1933 John P. Davis, a black attorney, and Robert C. Weaver, a black economist, organized the Joint Committee on National Recovery. They proposed to monitor NRA codes to insure the full integration of blacks. In 1934 Presiding Elder Charles H. Wesley was appointed to the Joint Committee as a representative both for the AME Church and the Alpha Phi Alpha Fraternity. He was placed on the Executive Committee and agreed with the impaneling of subcommittees on the Public Works Administration, the Homestead Subsistence Codes, the Federal Relief Administration, and other facets of the NRA. He also endorsed a Protest and Actions Committee. Similarly, concerning NRA the bishops said that "we cannot say that under it the Negro is getting a square deal." The Economic Security Act, enacted in 1935, established Social Security to provide old age pensions, support for the unemployed, and funds for survivors of deceased spouses or parents. Excluded from this largely working-class legislation were service and agricultural laborers who were disproportionately black. This stirred ire from Sadie Tanner Mossell Alexander, now a lawyer and married to a fellow

Figure 5.2 Sadie Tanner Mossell Alexander, an expert observer of the black migration and a member of President's Committee on Civil Rights, Truman Presidential Administration, 1947. (Used with Permission from the University Archives and Records Center, University of Pennsylvania)

attorney. At the 1935 black Elks convention, Alexander "severely criticized the Economic Security Act as detrimental to our group."[130]

The New Deal, a special moment in American history that in many respects was without precedent, revealed partisan divisions within AME ranks. They included those who were loyal to the Lincoln legacy in the GOP, others who were open to the innovative ideas of a new Democratic president, and a few with socialist sympathies who advised more social welfare, but were supportive of the leftward tilt of various New Deal policies. Notwithstanding this vigorous discourse, grassroots AMEs, especially those in the industrial proletariat, voted with their feet, responded to CIO organizers in the mass production industries, and created new pro-union realities that the church hierarchy was compelled to acknowledge.

Robinson, an Arkansas native and the *Review* editor, tilted the AME periodical toward the GOP. Moreover, his wife was an activist Republican who had been an assistant sergeant at arms at the 1924 Republican National Convention. Nonetheless, Editor Robinson, though still expressing Republican sympathies, acknowledged FDR as "a man of action, and his policies psychologically," he thought, "have had a beneficial effect." Nonetheless, Robinson criticized the NRA saying "I doubt whether [there was] anything more destitute of reason [and] more devoid of any sound philosophic basis than the NRA [that] was ever foisted upon people." Despite "the NRA and other regulations," Robinson believed, "prosperity will return." It would happen "by Divine decree" rather than government action. Moreover, Robinson did not forget that FDR was a Democrat and that his party had been no friend to African Americans. He was especially disturbed about Roosevelt's plan in 1937 to reorganize the Supreme Court with additional justices. The Court had invalidated signature elements of the New Deal including NRA, and FDR wanted more justices who would vote to uphold his policies. Robinson reminded *Review* readers that the Court, in recent decades, had safeguarded the rights of African Americans in border and southern states where Democrats were dominant. In 1917 the Court ruled as unconstitutional a residential segregation ordinance in Louisville, Kentucky, and in 1919 the justices commuted the death sentences of twenty-two blacks for alleged guilt in the Elaine, Arkansas, riot. In the 1930s the justices at

[130] Wolters, *Negroes and the Great Depression*, 110–113; Wesley: *A Stranger in One's Own Land*, Chapter 13 (n.p.); *The Episcopal Address, Thirtieth General Conference, 1936,* 70; *Minutes of the Thirty-Sixth Annual Meeting, Grand Lodge, Improved Benevolent and Protective Order of Elks of the World, Convened in Masonic Temple, Washington, DC, August 26–31, 1935* (n.p., 1935), 9.

whom FDR directed his hostility "twice saved the lives of the 'Scottsboro Boys'" and set aside "the outrageous sentence passed on Angelo Herndon," a black Communist who had been organizing the poor and unemployed in Georgia. Hence, Robinson advised against any blanket endorsement of Roosevelt as action favorable to blacks. He remained tied to a political party whose southern wing was implacably opposed to African American advancement.[131]

Delegates at the 1935 Chicago Annual Conference reflected Republican perspectives, and showed disappointment about racial inequities that were pervasive in various New Deal programs. They denounced FDR and Congress because they had "not hesitated to enact any legislation, however, hurtful, however subversive to [the] principles of government, as laid down in the Constitution." They also said that "experiments have been made of the most hurtful kind" and some of them affected African Americans. They noted "in southern states an inequality of wages is in force." Moreover, there were "Negroes being forced to accept less than whites on similar projects and in many instances [they were] given no work as long as whites can be found to take the jobs." AMEs also lamented the negative impact of FDR's farm program, saying in the North Ohio Annual Conference that it "has not done very much for the Negro farmer." They noted that in the South "where he is to get pay from the government the landowner takes it and he has no redress." A Maryland minister was similarly unimpressed with FDR, saying that his reelection victory in 1936 showed that the electorate was "under a spell of Hysteria caused by a Federal dole. The people reelected its socialist President on a Democratic ticket." He greatly lamented that "nine million Negroes in the South who suffer shamefully the prejudice of the white Democratic South." An Alabama pastor, J. S. Brookens, during the 1936 election, declared FDR "the direct object of my denunciations." He discovered that blacks were excluded from Roosevelt's Warm Springs, Georgia Foundation for infantile paralysis. Brookens, whose son suffered from the same affliction that had put Roosevelt in a wheelchair, thought that the president "was most responsible" for the discrimination at the polio treatment facility. Brookens "could not understand how he could assent to the exclusion of little Negro boys and girls who suffered" from his same

[131] "Mrs. J. G. Robinson," *AME Church Review*, Vol. 54, No. 124, January–February–March 1938, 38; Wright, *Encyclopedia of African Methodism*, 243; J. G. Robinson, "God's Answer to the Madness of Economic Theorists," *AME Church Review*, Vol. 50, No. 201, July–August–September 1934, 14–15, 17; J. G. Robinson, "The President, the Supreme Court and the Negro," *AME Church Review*, Vol. 52, No. 211, January–February–March 1937, 167–168.

affliction. While FDR ignored the charges, "certain Negro publications" that supported the New Deal strongly denounced Brookens. Though Roosevelt, in subsequent years, set up a separate "Negro Warms Springs at Tuskegee Institute," this did not excuse the original discrimination of which the president was guilty. For these reasons the Democrats, according to AMEs such as Brookens, remained suspect.[132]

That many AMEs preferred the Republicans also drew from institutional interests. Two denominational schools, Wilberforce University near Xenia, Ohio, and Western University in Quindaro, Kansas, each housed normal and industrial departments funded by their respective state governments. The GOP in these states, while at times losing to the Democrats, usually had dominance in both the governorships and legislatures in Ohio and Kansas. To maintain uninterrupted appropriations for Wilberforce and Western and patronage for trustee and administrative positions, AME leaders carefully navigated the intricacies of politics in these states. The Combined Normal and Industrial Department (CN&I) at Wilberforce started in 1887 at the initiative of AME Reverend Benjamin W. Arnett, a Republican state legislator, in cooperation with GOP Governor Joseph Foraker. The CN&I operated under a state-appointed trustee board that yielded general oversight to the university president, who was always chosen by the church. One historian noted that the church trustees "always viewed the state division "as an integral part of the overall school," while "the state board viewed it as a separate entity." Nonetheless, some church trustees ingratiated themselves to Ohio political leaders for fear of losing the large state allotments that benefited the entire university. Moreover, state trustees were similarly solicitous to politicians because they coveted their positions on the CN&I board. President Gilbert H. Jones informed the 1932 General Conference that the church had twenty-eight faculty and forty-three staff while CN&I had thirty-six faculty and seventy-six staff. He also commented favorably about "the support and cooperation between the church and the State." The election in 1936 of D. O. Walker, a Cleveland pastor and a Democrat as the Wilberforce

[132] *Journal and Year Book of the Fifty-Third Annual Session of the Chicago Conference of the African Methodist Episcopal Church* held in Quinn Chapel AME Church, Chicago, IL, September 18–22, 1935 (n.p., 1935), 39; *Minutes of the Fifty-Sixth Annual Session of the North Ohio Conference of the African Methodist Episcopal Church* held in Bethel AME Church, Akron, OH, September 29–October 3, 1937 (Nashville, TN, AME Sunday School Union, 1937), 55; Lincoln Criglar, "Nineteen Thirty-Six Review," *AME Church Review*, Vol. 53, No. 212, April–May–June 1937, 198; Wright, *Encyclopedia of African Methodism*, 49; J. S. Brookens, "The American Negroes' Warm Springs," *AME Church Review*, Vol. 56, No. 148, July 1945, 12–13.

president, maintained comity between the church and state departments probably because the governor, Martin L. Davey, a Wilberforce supporter, was also a Democrat. When John W. Bricker, a Republican, was elected governor in 1939, conflict stirred between him and Walker. Bishop Ransom, the chair of the church trustees and himself a Democrat, recalled that he and President Walker "represented" to the GOP "an invasion of vested, political power" because "no spot in Ohio was so completely owned and controlled by the Republican Party influence as was Wilberforce." Ultimately, Walker's resignation was demanded lest "the state would withhold the money (amounting to more than fifty thousand dollars) it paid to the university for professional services." Walker resigned, Ransom noted, because Wilberforce was not "financially prepared to have a complete break with the state." Democrats lost this round at the state level, but better days had arrived for them nationally.[133]

Western University, established in 1874, received a state appropriation in 1899 for an industrial department. In 1932 AMEs were reminded that "for a number of years efforts had been made by Dr. W. T. Vernon and Rev. J. R. Ransom to secure help from the legislature, but these were in vain until the attention of Governor W. E. Stanley [a Republican] was attracted." Western's initial allotment of $10,000 started a continuous connection between the AME Church and the State of Kansas. In a report to the 1932 General Conference, it was noted that since 1899 "the university and the State Industrial Department have worked in cooperation, to the advantage of both." Like Wilberforce, Western had both church and state trustees each with sensibilities about the political currents in their state. GOP ascendancy in Ohio, Kansas, and other states laid claim to some AME loyalties that Roosevelt's New Deal seriously challenged.[134]

Notwithstanding historic Lincoln loyalties to the GOP and complicated institutional interactions with state Republicans, the Democrats, thanks to the New Deal, made inroads to black voters. Lax advocacy for the rights of African Americans had already eroded that attachment to the GOP. Prescient delegates at the 1930 Pittsburgh Annual Conference, for example, criticized President Hoover for advancing an antiblack nominee to the United States Supreme Court and for too few black appointments to federal positions. "The general political situation," the AMEs said, "constrains us to

[133] Gomez-Jefferson, *In Darkness with God*, 188–189; *Journal of the Twenty-Ninth Quadrennial Session, General Conference, 1932*, 384; Ransom, *The Pilgrimage of Harriet Ransom's Son*, 282–283; Wright, *Eighty-Seven Years behind the Black Curtain*, 208.
[134] *Journal of the Twenty-Ninth Quadrennial Session, General Conference, 1932*, 410–411.

remind this GOP that the New Negro is thinking new and that he is no longer bound to the party that WAS the party of Lincoln." In the words of Harvard Sitkoff,[135] the Roosevelt Administration presented to African Americans a New Deal for blacks. Despite the presence of racism in several New Deal programs, blacks generally believed the benefits of Roosevelt recovery and relief outweighed the disabilities that their discriminatory policies imposed upon them. Delegates at the 1936 General Conference reflected the growing consensus of African Americans about the New Deal:

> Government agencies have supplied millions of jobless people with employment. The huge relief program, as provided by the Administration has taken sufficient care of the needy. Thousands of homes have been redeemed and modernized under the Federal Housing Administration; also thousands of farms have been refinanced and improved through the Farm Loan Corporation. Our banking system has been strengthened and made more secure. The New Deal has unmistakably served a splendid purpose.

They also anticipated the passage of Social Security and Unemployment Insurance legislation and how they would likely spearhead "an early return of prosperity." The severity of the depression, says Lizabeth Cohen who examined its impact in Chicago, undermined the efficacy and reliability of social institutions upon which workers had depended. The New Deal, because of "the loss of faith" in churches and other traditional institutions, filled the void that religious leaders discovered they could not address. Black workers in Chicago in other industrial and agricultural sites ultimately concluded "our survival depends on a strong federal government and [on] the Democrats." The church, while important, could not match what the federal welfare state could now provide often through various state and municipal agencies. A. Philip Randolph, a socialist who was proud of his AME heritage, acknowledged that in New York City the black church fed depression sufferers. "In many instances," he observed, "the church has relied upon the general fund supplied by the city" that deployed congregations as "a convenient agency" to deliver these services.[136]

---

[135] Sitkoff, *A New Deal for Blacks*, 9.
[136] *Official Minutes of the Pittsburgh Annual Conference, Third Episcopal District, African Methodist Episcopal Church [held at] Trinity AME Church, Pittsburgh, PA, September 24 to September 28, 1930* (n.p., n.d.), 37–38. See Harvard Sitkoff, *A New Deal For Blacks: The Emergence of Civil Rights as a National Issue*, New York, Oxford University Press, 1978. *Journal of the Thirtieth Quadrennial Session, General Conference, 1936*, 112; Lizabeth Cohen, *Making a New Deal: Industrial Workers in Chicago, 1919–1939* (New York, Cambridge University Press, 1990), 249, 261; A. Philip Randolph, "The Negro Church and Economic

George W. Slater, a veteran Iowa minister and a socialist like Randolph, understood the new reality of the welfare state better than most. He and a colleague in the Northwestern Annual Conference called the New Deal a "rebirth of liberty." "This freedom," they said, "demands the stress of human values; business for the use and convenience of the people than for profit; the equitable distribution of all and every kind of production." Moreover, this rebirth of liberty:

> calls for such economic security in which every man shall be guaranteed a good living when forced out of work, real security in old age, during sickness, guaranteed a good home, plenty of clothing, and good and satisfying food. This new freedom stresses the fact that the individual shall not be left to his own initiative, his own skill and power nor that of any particular group, but that he shall have the protection and fostering care of both his local and federal government.[137]

Obviously, Slater and others in the Northwestern Annual Conference had been won over by FDR. He and two other colleagues wrote that Roosevelt was "both a revolutionist and reformer." They could have added that the president was a pragmatist because he, according to their assessment, shifted "to the right or to the left wing, politically, socially and economically, only so far as a practical intelligent electorate will support him." These farm-belt AMEs revealed their leftist sensibilities in acknowledging Francis Townsend's "Old Age Pension proposition." They also acknowledged Father Charles E. Coughlin's "doctrine of his social security associations," Huey Long's "far-reaching 'Share the Wealth' proposition," and others who were pushing Roosevelt further toward more social welfare and wealth distribution. But, FDR, a master of the art of the possible, according to these clergy, had pushed proposals to reconstruct American society as far as they would go. Slater and others, in the end, were satisfied because blacks, despite imperfections in the New Deal, were the beneficiaries.[138]

By no means were AME leaders caught off guard as African Americans shifted their allegiance from the party of Lincoln to the Democrats. They began to court Bishop Ransom during the presidential campaign of 1928.

Relations-I," in *Whither the Negro Church?* seminar held at Yale Divinity School, New Haven, CT, April 13–15, 1931, 7.
[137] *Minutes of the Eighteenth Annual Session of the Northwestern Conference of the African Methodist Episcopal Church* held in Bethel AME Church, Davenport, IA, September 7–11, 1938 (n.p., 1938), 60–61.
[138] *Minutes of the Fifteenth Annual Session of the Northwestern Conference of the African Methodist Episcopal Church* held in St. Paul AME Church, Des Moines, IA, September 10–15, 1935 (n.p., 1938), 67–68, 70.

James A. Farley, the campaign manager for Democratic nominee, Alfred E. Smith, asked Ransom "to do missionary work among our people to break old political ties." The long-term benefit, Ransom recalled, "was to awaken Negroes politically to be conscious of the fact that they could break their slavish adherence to the Republican Party." Additionally, Bishop John Hurst, an NAACP board member, connected to Smith's campaign through the organization's assistant secretary, Walter White. White started the National Negro Independent "Al Smith" Association and placed Hurst's name on the letterhead. Voting Republican was a hard habit for most AMEs to break. The 1928 Nebraska Annual Conference warned against supporting Al Smith because he was aligned with southern segregationists. Moreover, Smith, if elected president, would appoint Supreme Court justices who resembled the infamous Roger Taney who ruled against Dred Scott. Therefore, the conference "Report on the State of the Country" endorsed a "vote for Hoover." Such sentiments, however, waned after FDR's vigorous response to the Great Depression. Richard R. Wright, Jr., still the editor of the *Christian Recorder* and a "nominal independent Republican," decided to give Roosevelt a chance and voted for him in 1932. In 1936, Wright noted, "I gave my services to the Democratic party because I felt that it would be a calamity not to reelect Mr. Roosevelt." Though Wright, now a bishop, like many blacks, believed "the Democrats were the chief political enemies of my people," with wins in Congress "they would be in a position to block legislation which [would aid] Negro-Americans in getting a fair deal." The New Deal, however, included legislation that "benefited my people as well as the nation." All the Republicans could say was that Lincoln "freed the Negro from slavery." That was not enough any more. Hence, Wright became head of the "colored committee" of the Good Neighbor League, an organization that Eleanor Roosevelt led. Wright wrote "Why the Colored Man Should Vote for Roosevelt," and reported that the one million copies of the pamphlet could not meet the demand. A rally at Madison Square Garden in New York City, two months before the election, drew thousands, and they heard a special message sent from President Roosevelt. Additionally, such pastors as P. A. Pitts in New England actively supported FDR in 1936 by serving as Director of the Speakers Bureau of the Democratic National Campaign Committee in charge of the Massachusetts Division of Colored Voters.[139]

---

[139] Ransom, *The Pilgrimage of Harriet Ransom's Son*, 280; Kenneth R. Janken, "Walter F. White, Bishop John Hurst, and the Election of 1928," *AME Church Review*, Vol. 117, No. 383, July–September 2001, 33; *Minutes of the Sixth Annual Session of the Nebraska Conference of the Fifth Episcopal District of the African Methodist Episcopal Church* held in

These AME spokesmen, while influential within some segments of their denomination, were hardly needed to encourage blacks to vote in 1936 for FDR. One polling organization found that 76 percent of all northern blacks cast their ballots for Roosevelt. In most northern cities the black vote for the president was at least 60 percent, and in Chicago his share of black votes increased from 23 percent in 1932 to 49 percent in 1936. Similarly, in Philadelphia black vote totals rose in the same period from 30 percent to 64 percent. AMEs in the Georgia Annual Conference, buoyed by Roosevelt's reelection, cheered his statement at the dedication of a building at Howard University: FDR said that "there should be no forgotten men and no forgotten races." These African Methodists thought "with such a man at the helm of the United States ship, we cannot but look for a safe voyage and sure landing of every American, be he white or black." Some AMEs, however, such as J. G. Robinson, regretted the 1936 election returns, saying that in the North "I am alarmed to think of Negroes up here voting the Democratic ticket." Robinson feared that "the Democratic party in the South will hang a rope around the Negro's neck and with the other hand hug him in the North." He defiantly declared that "any Negro who supports the Democratic Party becomes void of Race love." Robinson's view, however, increasingly became a minority perspective. The political landscape among African Americans was being transformed, and they were becoming a part of Roosevelt's Democratic coalition that would influence black politics for years to come. This support did not spare Roosevelt and his congressional allies from continued agitation from AMEs to protect black civil rights. The 1937 New York Annual Conference, for example, praised the House of Representatives for passing the Gavagan anti-lynching bill and urged the Senate to do the same. The bill never reached FDR for his signature and scarcely tested his resolve to champion protections for the physical safety of African Americans.[140]

Roosevelt's reelection, with a strong black vote, also reverberated at state level. In 1934 AMEs in Georgia, learning that Arthur Mitchell, a black

Bethel AME Church, Leavenworth, KS, September 12–16, 1928 (Nashville, TN, AME Sunday School Union, 1928), 39; Wright, *Eighty-Seven Years behind the Black Curtain*, 208–210; Wright, *Encyclopedia of African Methodism*, 224.

[140] Sitkoff, *A New Deal for Blacks*, 95–96; *Proceedings of the Sixty-Eighth and Sixty-Ninth Sessions of the Georgia Annual Conferences of the African Methodist Episcopal Church, 1935 and 1936* (Philadelphia, PA, AME Book Concern, 1936), 83–84; J. G. Robinson, "Just a Few Dots – That's All," *AME Church Review*, Vol. 53, No. 213, October–November–December 1937, 267; *Official Journal of the New York Annual Conference of the African Methodist Episcopal Church Bring Minutes of the One Hundred and Fifteenth Session, May 19th to May 23rd, 1937* held in The Israel AME Church, Albany, NY (n.p., 1937), 18.

Democrat in Chicago, was elected in a "landslide" to succeed in Congress a black Republican, said it "marks a new and startling epoch in the world as relates to our race group." Mitchell, they noted, "will be the first Negro Democrat that has ever sat in this great body of lawmakers in this country." In Ohio Governor Davey, a Democrat, appointed Bishop Ransom to the Board of Paroles and Pardons. As a result, leading clergy at the 1937 North Ohio Annual Conference, in a letter to Davey, declared their "appreciation for the recognition of the race in the appointment" of their bishop. Moreover, they said, "a grateful constituency will keep in mind this act of recognition to a people never wanting in loyalty." Moreover, politicians who belonged to the AME Church began filling the ranks of Democratic Party officeholders. The Committee on the Condition of the Negro in the United States at the 1940 General Conference saluted "two Negro State Senators" who were "members of our great denomination." The report referred to Charles A. Diggs in Michigan and William Wallace in Illinois, Democrats who represented districts in Detroit and Chicago respectively. This acknowledgment came from the lead author of the report, William T. Andrews, a General Conference delegate and a Democratic member of the New York State Assembly. Although Andrews and his committee chronicled the persistence of racial discrimination in several spheres of American society, the Roosevelt administration, they said, had done much to ameliorate the black condition. For example, "federal aid and other public funds are being provided to erect low-cost housing for our people, as well as for others and that we, because of our greater need, have shared and benefited in greater proportion than our population ratio would have indicated." While the GOP still contended for AME support, Democrats fought just as hard to maintain their gains within the denomination and among blacks generally. At the 1940 General Conference, for example, Bishop David Henry Sims, a Republican, presented a GOP delegation that included a member of the Republican National Committee. This was after Edgar G. Brown, an Advisor on Negro Affairs in the Civilian Conservation Corps, had spoken as a representative of the Roosevelt Administration.[141]

Integral to the Roosevelt political coalition was organized labor, especially the new CIO unions whose launch depended greatly on black industrial

---

[141] *Proceedings of the Sixty-Seventh Session of the Georgia Annual Conference of the African Methodist Episcopal Church, 1934* (n.p., n.d.), 45; *Minutes of the Fifty-Sixth Annual Session of the North Ohio Conference of the African Methodist Episcopal Church, 1937* (Nashville, TN, AME Sunday School Union, 1937), n.p.; *Journal of Proceedings of the Thirty-First Quadrennial Session of the General Conference of the African Methodist Episcopal Church, 1940*, 18–19, 84, 114, 116.

workers, many of them AMEs. Supporters of the Wagner Act within the denomination, including some who were socialists, encouraged its advancement and facilitated efforts to develop unionized African Americans into an influential constituency both within the Democratic Party and organized labor. Ransom, who during the CIO organizing drives endorsed this major move toward industrial democracy, reminded representatives of leading black religious bodies that "95% of our members are laborers." Because his district included the mill and mining areas of Ohio, West Virginia, and western Pennsylvania, he asserted that "we should aggressively fight to secure for them, along with others, industrial justice and economic opportunity." AMEs in Ransom's North Ohio Annual Conference were bothered by Communist influences in the CIO and the aggressive tactics of sit-down strikes, a methodology that the church could not "indorse." At the same time, they agreed with the emerging consensus about "the right to strike and the right of collective bargaining." There was no such ambiguity among delegates at the 1937 Michigan Annual Conference, the center of the auto industry. They backed "collective bargaining which heretofore has been regarded as the exclusive right of white workers but today our group has been benefited to a great extent." Further, they observed that "this tendency towards white recognition of mutual interest with Negro workers" was a desirable development.[142]

Randolph, the labor organizer and the socialist son of a Florida pastor, more than any other AME pushed his denomination into a broad recognition of the proletarian character of African Methodism. "The actual economic power in the Negro church," he told black seminarians at Yale, "is the hands of the working class masses." Hence, "the economic control of the Negro church is working class in nature." The clergy, he also noted, "has a working class background" because none of them "come from homes that rest upon an income derived from rent, interest, and profits." Even the few like Richard R. Wright, Jr., whose father and namesake operated a Philadelphia bank, had no "control over any productive or distributive enterprises employing large numbers of workers." Such ministers and members at best were a petit bourgeoisie. Because of this view the passage of the Wagner Act

---

[142] Reverdy C. Ransom, "Annual Address to the Fraternal Council," *AME Church Review*, Vol. 53, No. 213, October–November–December 1937, 266; *Minutes of the Fifty-Sixth Session of the North Ohio Conference, 1937*, 55; *Journal of the Fifty-First Annual Session of the Michigan Conference of the African Methodist Episcopal Church* held in Turner Chapel AME Church, Fort Wayne, IN, September 1–5, 1937 (Nashville, TN, AME Sunday School Union, 1937), 59.

seemed to Randolph an opportune moment to help develop an energized black proletariat to enact economic justice for African Americans.[143]

Hardly a regular churchgoer and, at times and incorrectly, called an agnostic or atheist, Randolph respected African Methodism because it produced the militant Henry M. Turner and his defiant parents, who seldom bowed to egregious racial practices in their native South. Equally important was Randolph's admiration of Richard Allen. The rise of the AME founder from slavery to a courageous religious organizer among African Americans was a paradigm that Randolph himself emulated. Additionally, the emancipationist influences of both the American and French Revolutions that were so crucial to Allen's understanding of his religious and civic selves were similarly influential in Randolph's ethical development. His conversion to socialism made him inpatient with churches, both black and white, in their deference to capitalist power. After Randolph, now a New York resident, and Chandler Owen founded *The Messenger*, a self-described radical magazine, he put his ideas into practice in 1925 in organizing the Brotherhood of Sleeping Car Porters (BSCP) and winning recognition for the all-black union in 1937. He was disappointed that too many within the black clergy, including AME Bishop Archibald J. Carey, Sr., opposed unions either because they were paid saboteurs or were beneficiaries of corporate philanthropy. He was heartened, however, that some AME clergy, who were his generational peers supported him. In around 1920 Joseph Gomez twice opened Bethel Church in Detroit to Randolph to espouse his socialist views. H. Allen Garcia, Caribbean born like Gomez and pastor at Bethel in Buffalo, New York, invited Randolph in 1921 to speak on "Proposed Solutions to the Negro Problem." In the address Randolph advised black workers to "band themselves together and become an important factor in the industrial and economical world." Charles H. Wesley, a presiding elder in the Baltimore–Washington DC area agreed to chair a BSCP meeting in the nation's capital in 1933. Randolph thanked Wesley for his "interest and cooperation."[144]

In 1936 Randolph founded the National Negro Congress (NNC), a federation of several black civil rights, religious, and fraternal groups. Wesley

---

[143] Randolph, "The Negro Church and Economic Relations," in *Whither the Negro Church?*, 5.

[144] Cynthia Taylor, *A. Philip Randolph: The Religious Journey of an African American Labor Leader* (New York, New York University Press, 2006), 39, 50–42, 84, 224; Randolph, "The Negro Church Economic Relations," in *Whither the Negro Church?*, 8; Gomez-Jefferson, *In Darkness with God*, 73; Chandler Owen to Joseph Gomez, February 21, 1920 (letter in possession of the author); Monroe Fordham, *A History of Bethel AME Church, Buffalo, New York, 1831–1991* (Buffalo, NY, Bethel History Society, 1978, 1991), 26–27, 42; Wesley, *Stranger in One's Own Land*, unpublished MS, Chapter 15 (n.p.).

reported that the inaugural meeting in Chicago drew 817 delegates representing 585 organizations. Though he affiliated the BSCP with the craft-oriented AFL, Randolph, with backing from the NNC, joined John L. Lewis, who donated $1000 to the NNC, in the unionization of workers in the mass production industries. Hence the NNC cooperated with the Steelworkers Organizing Committee (SWOC) in Cleveland, Pittsburgh, and other industrial communities to plan recruitment strategies aimed at black laborers. The NNC served as a liaison between SWOC and black steelworkers and disseminated information to black newspapers and churches. Whether in launching the BSCP or in his advocacy of the CIO, Randolph believed that the black church generally, and his own AME Church in particular, should identify as proletarian bodies. "The minister," said Randolph at Yale Divinity School, "should play a big part in the labor movement because 99% of his members are laborers."[145]

Though Gomez, Garcia, and Wesley constituted a minority of AME clergy who had visibility as advocates of organized labor, thousands of rank-and-file AME members throughout the industrial Northeast and Midwest affiliated with the CIO. The vast majority was like Carl O. Dickerson, an active member of Payne Chapel AME Church in Duquesne, Pennsylvania, who in 1936 became an employee at the local Carnegie steel plant. Born in 1914 in Alabama, he migrated with his parents to western Pennsylvania in 1922. When SWOC, with assistance from nearby locals of John L. Lewis's United Mineworkers, came through the Monongahela River Valley to sign up CIO members, Dickerson and others readily joined. He became active in Local #1256 and Dickerson, like other black steelworkers in Philadelphia, Gary, Youngstown, and Chicago, was elected to an office. This new reality in the religious and economic lives of AME members made them a part of a newly constituted coalition of FDR supporters who helped in empowering the labor movement, a major objective of Roosevelt's welfare state. Randolph energized this proletarian project because of the massive black migration, the influential BSCP, and an invigorated New Deal. As a result of these developments, Randolph, together with Ransom, Gomez, Wesley, and other AME leaders, pushed workers' rights into the consciousness of African Methodism.[146]

---

[145] Dickerson, *Out of the Crucible*, 136–137; Charles H. Wesley, "The Negro Has Always Wanted the Four Freedoms," in Rayford W. Logan (ed.), *What the Negro Wants* (Chapel Hill, University of North Carolina Press, 1944), 103; Randolph, "The Negro Church and Economic Relations," in *Whither the Negro Church?*, 7

[146] Carl O. Dickerson, interviewed by Dennis C. Dickerson, Philadelphia, PA, October 5, 1975.

WORLD WAR II

The outbreak of World War II furthered the transformation of the environment in which African Methodism operated. The denomination, Wesleyan
in origin and proudly black and autonomous, developed these complementary characteristics across its long history. A dual focus on societal reconstruction throughout the Atlantic World and independent institutional
governance continued to shape the AME historical narrative. The migration,
the depression, and two world wars, however, compelled responses to these
enigmatic events that challenged the savvy of both ministers and members
who had to navigate these historic changes. At the same time that these
societal pressures pressed upon the AMEs, they had to manage their
sprawling religious body through several internal crises. The simultaneous
demands to broaden social holiness initiatives while administering complicated institutional conflicts bifurcated different cadres of clergy and communicants, who mobilized their energies either toward black advancement
or organizational business. AMEs such as A. Philip Randolph and Archibald
J. Carey, Jr., while respectful of the institutional achievements of African
Methodism, emphasized the denomination's insurgent tradition against
racial and economic exploitation. Conversely, leaders such as Reverdy
C. Ransom and Charles H. Wesley, despite their energetic commitment to
the social holiness ethos of the AME Church, devoted increased attention to
the institutional affairs of the denomination. Though these involvements
involved traditional mission objectives, the clash between divergent policy
preferences and large but prickly personalities created damaging strains
within the AME organization.

Despite the shifting societal and global surroundings in which African
Methodism operated, Charles S. Spivey, Sr., the Yale-trained Dean of Payne
Theological Seminary, praised the church's institutional resilience. "The
Church of Jesus, as it was conceived and set in operation by Allen," he wrote
in 1942, "is still a living power for God and righteousness in a crooked and
perverse generation." The denominational treasury disbursed "dollar
money" that did "more work for racial development than any dollar which
Negroes spend." Within the black Atlantic, he said, "that dollar works
mightily for God and the race" whether in higher education or in building
churches, clinics, and secondary schools. Notwithstanding its identity as a
denomination for the black diaspora, African Methodism, an orthodox
Christian body, was incubated within "American democracy." In spite of
"past and present injustices and inequalities," the United States offered "the
largest measure of freedom for our church to work" in order "to bring [the]

influence of the teachings of Jesus to bear upon the government." This perspective, which forbade any sympathy or support for Communism, Nazism, and Fascism, predictably allied the denomination with the western democracies.[147]

Though the AME Church, since World War I, had declared that peace was preferable to war, neither its leaders nor its rank-and-file members, with some exceptions, were pacifist. The moral clarity of World War II and the "menace of isms" showed the evil of newly established totalitarian regimes and how they threatened the survival of the western democracies and the lives of darker peoples. Although lynching, legalized segregation, and colonialism compromised the moral standing of the United States and its European Allies, these pernicious practices, while similarly serious when compared to Nazism and Fascism, did not require the same military action to dismantle them. Nonetheless, AMEs, like other African Americans, believed that global racism, whether prevalent within Allied nations or within the Axis Powers, demanded their dual attention and robust opposition. In the 1930s murderous dictators Adolf Hitler in Germany, Benito Mussolini in Italy, and Joseph Stalin in the Soviet Union ruthlessly maintained themselves in power, massively killed domestic opponents and vulnerable minorities, especially Jews, and violated or attacked the sovereignty of other nations. Hitler successively annexed Austria and invaded Czechoslovakia, Poland, and France, Mussolini seized Ethiopia, and Stalin signed with Hitler a Nazi–Soviet Non-Aggression Pact.

In the same month the Nazis marched into Paris, May 1940, Bishop Gregg, speaking for his colleagues in their Episcopal Address, explained why the specter of the "isms" imperiled world peace and compelled AME support for the Allies. An AME pastor preaching at the 1940 Pittsburgh Annual Conference commented on "the ravages of war in Europe being launched by Adolf Hitler." He likened the German dictator to King Belshazzar of Babylon and inferred that the same divine judgment that the prophet Daniel pronounced upon the ancient monarch would be applied to the Nazi leader. He and other AME clergy were confronted with the same question that black educator Horace Mann Bond posed to Africans Americans in "Should the Negro Care Who Wins the War?" Writing in 1942 in the *Annals of the American Academy of Political and Social Science*, Bond said "the nearly thirteen million Negroes who are Americans have every reason to view with deep alarm the imperfections threatening the American ideal."

---

[147] Charles S. Spivey, *A Tribute to the Negro Preacher and Other Sermons and Addresses* (Xenia, OH, Eckerle Printing Co., 1942), 195, 197; *The Episcopal Address, 1940*, 22.

Blacks, despite their victimization in American society, "may be depended upon to fight to preserve and extend that credo" of freedom that defined the national principles. Though no blacks wanted to be scapegoats in case of an American defeat, they still believed in the promises of liberty contained in the Declaration of Independence and the Bill Rights that the Axis Powers defiantly denied. Nonetheless, delegates to the 1943 Macon Georgia Annual Conference wondered "what shall be the Negro's lot in [the] social and political set-up in the postwar society."[148]

Communism, though opposed to any "distinctions among men on the grounds of race or color," asserted the Episcopal Address of 1940, was antireligious. "Communism has rejected Christ," the bishops said, "suppressed the Church, banned religion, and has refused to recognize God as Creator." While most AMEs belonged to the working class and constituted an inviting pool of recruits, it was important to note that Communism offered "a Godless State, where the lives of the people are regimented and controlled by the designs of men." Nazism was similarly undesirable because the German Third Reich attempted "to build a State upon the Nordic myth" that "would exclude all races except people of pure Germanic blood." That State "would exclude people of Negro blood or make them subjects to the same ruthless persecution that it visited upon our Jewish brethren." Milton S. J. Wright, an AME member and Wilberforce professor who had earned a Ph.D. in economics in 1932 at the University of Heidelberg in Germany, echoed these episcopal admonitions about Nazi racism. Prior to Hitler's election in 1933 as Chancellor of Germany, Wright, in a jocular but innocent statement, speculated on a possible assassination of the Nazi leader. This off-the-cuff remark from Wright while still in the country attracted the attention of Hitler's storm troopers, who whisked him off to an audience with Hitler. During this peculiar encounter, Hitler told Wright that blacks seemed surprisingly acquiescent to their oppression in the United States and would remain a subservient people. This exchange, which surfaced right after the

[148] *The Episcopal Address presented by Bishop John Andrew Gregg, A.M., D.D., LL.D. to the Thirty-First Quadrennial Session of the General Conference of the African Methodist Episcopal Church at Detroit, Michigan, May, 1940* (n.p., 1940), 21–22; *Official Minutes of the Seventy-Third Annual Session of the Pittsburgh Annual Conference of the African Methodist Episcopal Church of the Third Episcopal District* held in Bethel AME Church, Wilkes Barre, PA, September 24–29, 1940 (n.p., n.d.), 13; Horace Mann Bond, "Should the Negro Care Who Wins the War?" *Annals of the American Academy of Political and Social Science*, Vol. 223, September 1942, 82–84; *Official Journal of the Sixty-Second Annual Session of the Macon Georgia Conference of the African Methodist Episcopal* held in Stewart Chapel AME Church, Macon, GA, November 24–28, 1943 (n.p., 1943), 10.

start of World War II in an *Ebony* magazine article, reinforced for blacks that racism lay at the core of Nazi ideology.[149]

Fascism, not unlike the other two totalitarian regimes, the Episcopal Address recounted, "exercises a control over the economic and religious life, and the social activities of its people so complete as to hinder the free development of human personality" and nullify "the teachings of Jesus laid down for his servants to follow in building the Kingdom of God among men." Despite the "menace of isms," the western democracies were also imperfect. Europeans, for example, had ravaged Africa and "divided it among themselves," and in the United States Jim Crow fixed African Americans in a second-class status. But embedded in their democratic principles lay opportunities to challenge and change noxious racial policies that were harder to achieve in totalitarian societies. Because of "the triumph of totalitarian leadership on the Eastern hemisphere," resolved the 1940 Michigan Annual Conference, "the system of democracy within our own borders will be imperiled." Hence, AMEs opposed, said the bishops in their 1944 Episcopal Address, the "Communism of Russia, Fascism in Italy, Nazism in Germany, [and the] Discrimination and Prejudice of America."[150]

As the possibility of an American entry into World War II became evident, Roosevelt, in a special message to Congress in January 1941, outlined the liberties that the nation would defend against authoritarian powers. These Four Freedoms included the freedom of speech, the freedom of religion, the freedom from want, and the freedom from fear, all tenets that were inimical to totalitarian states. In the same month that Roosevelt declared the Four Freedoms, Bishop Sherman L. Greene appointed the Reverend Howard Thomas Primm to the populous Union Bethel Church in New Orleans. Immediately, Primm, a rising star among AME pastors, initiated plans to build a social service center named the Four Freedoms Building. During the war, as Primm raised funds for the structure and repeatedly referred to the Four Freedoms project, he and Union Bethel members sacralized the themes that justified the war against Nazism and Fascism. In appropriating these alliterative principles, these AMEs showed that Roosevelt's rhetoric was attracting support for Allied war aims. Hence,

[149] *The Episcopal Address Presented by Bishop John Andrew Gregg, May 1940,* 22–23; Robert Fikes, "African American Scholars of the German Language and Culture," *Journal of Blacks in Higher Education,* No. 30, Winter 2000–2001, 109.

[150] *The Episcopal Address,* 1940, 22–23; *Journal of the Fifty-Fourth Annual Session of the Michigan Conference [of the] African Methodist Episcopal Church* held in Quinn Chapel AME Church, Flint, MI, August 1940 (n.p., 1940), 63; *Episcopal Address,* 1944, 22.

African Methodism, with scarce dissent, was "all in" with fighting totalitarianism on the basis of the Four Freedoms.[151]

The bishops further validated this view in a February 1941 letter to Roosevelt. They told him that during the denomination's existence across 125 years it "has always cooperated and will always cooperate with the president and [the] administrative government of the United States." Because the church's ministers and members "are interested in the cause of humanity and democracy," the bishops wanted information about the national defense and how they could "offer our services in whatever way you may desire." The bishops also wanted to recommend someone in the clergy or laity to a federal commission for national defense because "the AME Church was interested" in a wartime role. A response came in July 1941 when FDR, through the Office for Emergency Management of the Executive Office of the President, appointed Bishop Ransom to the Volunteer Participation Committee in the Office of Civilian Defense. Ransom, one of a committee of forty-five, had specific duties in the Fifth Corps area in the Midwest.[152]

The bishops were also careful not to endorse war, but to recognize that it was at times necessary to pursue if freedom was at stake. They declared, "we do not bless war, but we uphold our National Defense self-preservation." They said, "the members of the AME Church are part of a loyal group of Americans whose fathers obtained their freedom at the point of a sword." Moreover, the specter of Nazism and Fascism threatened "the ideals of our American Democracy" and our "religious freedom." Therefore, the bishops had "no other choice but to call upon the members of our church and race to contribute in every way possible to support the program of our government for National Defense." The bishops, because they aspired to the "goal of national unity" wrongly stated that while racial discrimination still occurred in the military, "instances of bias are decreasing." As the fight against American racism continued, whites, they said, should be reminded that "our race has never produced a traitor to our country's flag."[153]

After the Japanese bombed Pearl Harbor on December 7, 1941, Roosevelt requested and received from the US Congress a declaration of war. Days later, because the Germans declared war against the United States, Congress

[151] *Footprints of Service: Paths Made by Howard Thomas Primm as Seen and Witnessed by Others* (Nashville, TN, AME Sunday School Union, n.d.), 29, 31.
[152] *Proceedings of the Winter Session of the Council of Bishops, African Methodist Episcopal Church in New Orleans, Louisiana, February 13–14, 1941* (typescript), 14; Ransom, *The Pilgrimage of Harriet Ransom's Son*, 293–294.
[153] *Proceedings of the Winter Session of the Council of Bishops, African Methodist Episcopal Church in New Orleans, Louisiana, February 13–14, 1941*, 13–14.

also granted authorization to the President to battle the Nazis. AMEs, just like the rest of the nation, without a whiff of pacifism, mobilized their constituency to fight the Axis Powers and provide tangible support to black soldiers. William P. Stevenson, a prominent Philadelphia pastor, joined Local Draft Board #32 of the Selective Service System. Ernest L. Hickman, a Chattanooga pastor, a member of the Civilian Defense Council, delivered a radio address on "The Negro's Part in the War Effort." The laity sustained a similar level of support for the war. Roscoe Draper, a lifelong AME from Bryn Mawr, Pennsylvania, became a flight instructor at Moton Field at Tuskegee Institute in 1942. He taught civilian pilots and military cadets who constituted the all-black Tuskegee Airmen. Moreover, the episcopacy vigorously backed national defense through Bishop John A. Gregg, who traveled to several war fronts to boost the morale of blacks in the military, and Bishops George E. Curry and David H. Sims, who reminded AMEs to buy War Stamps and War Bonds. The 1944 Episcopal Address restated this support in saying AMEs should "continue buying United States War Bonds." At the 1942 New Jersey Annual Conference Bishop Sims also received an official from Fort Dix in New Jersey who "pleaded" for black military participation. In 1943 the bishops resolved that black soldiers should receive 100,000 free copies of Bishop Wright's pamphlet about Richard Allen and that the American Bible Society should donate 100,000 scripture portions. Additionally, the Council directed Bishops Wright and Decatur Ward Nichols to visit as many army camps as possible. Furthermore, AME officials, as in previous wars, endorsed the military chaplaincy for eligible clergy and urged members, some of them students in AME schools, to enlist in the armed forces.[154]

Further evidence of AME investment in World War II and a nonexistent pacifism lay in the innumerable families that supported the involvement of close relatives in the armed forces. Madison Carey, Jr., the grandson and nephew of the two Archibald Careys, one a deceased bishop and the other a

[154] Wright, *Encyclopedia of African Methodism*, 140–141; 263; Communication from Roscoe Draper to the author, November 12, 2015; see John A. Gregg, *Of Men and Arms* (Nashville, TN, AME Sunday School Union, 1945); *Minutes [of the] Bishops Council, AME Church* [held in] St. John AME Church, Birmingham, AL, February 17 & 18, 1944, 5; *Episcopal Address, 1944*, 52; *Journal of Proceedings of the Thirty-Second Quadrennial Session of the General Conference of the African Methodist Episcopal Church held with The Arena, Philadelphia, PA, May 3–14, 1944*, 41; *Proceedings of the Mid-Summer Session of the Council of Bishops, African Methodist Episcopal Church in St. James AME Church, St. Louis, Missouri, June 24–25, 1943*, 11; *Journal of Proceedings of the Seventieth Session of the New Jersey Annual Conference of the African Methodist Episcopal Church* held in Mt. Zion AME Church, Plainfield, NJ, May 1942 (n.p., 1942), 14.

leading Chicago pastor, fought the Japanese in Burma. Two of Bishop Alexander J. Allen's four sons wore the army uniform. Samuel W. Allen was drafted in 1942 and was attached to the Adjutant General's Corps, and G. Wesley Allen served in the Philippines as a first lieutenant in the Artillery Division. Eugene A. Adams, Jr., the namesake of the denomination's Secretary of Education, attained the rank of technical sergeant and was stationed overseas with an engineering corps. For more than two years he was stationed in the China–Burma–India operations.[155]

The welfare of 125,000 blacks in the military drew the attention of the major African American denominations, including those in the AME Church. These religious bodies were organized into the Fraternal Council of Negro Churches, which Bishop Ransom had founded in 1934 and was now headed by Bishop James A. Bray of the Christian Methodist Episcopal (CME) Church. The council secretary, Bishop Wright, approached the White House proposing that a representative from the Fraternal Council should be sent to both the Pacific and the European/North Africa/Near East war fronts to visit and encourage the morale of African American troops. Hence, Bishop Gregg, mainly because of Wright's lobbying, was selected for these extensive shuttles across both the Pacific and the Atlantic oceans. After consultation with an aide to Roosevelt and with the military's chief of chaplains, Gregg left to "carry personal greetings of the President" and from the Fraternal Council to black men and women in uniform.[156]

Between July 1943 and February 1944, accompanied by Chaplain John Allen DeVeaux, the disaffected son of the bishop's Cuba guide in 1939, Gregg visited on two separate tours war fronts widely dispersed across the globe. They interacted with black troops, all of whom were restricted to segregated units, inspected their projects in engineering, construction, chemical decontamination, and various ordnance responsibilities. They also interviewed white and black officers, including chaplains and the legendary General Douglas MacArthur. A bonus involved meeting AMEs in the military and denominational sites in South Africa and Liberia.

These tours, proposed originally by Gregg in April 1943, were made easier for him by his attaché, Chaplain DeVeaux. After AME pastorates in the Ohio River Valley, DeVeaux became a regimental chaplain for the 24th, 25th,

---

[155] Dickerson, *African American Preachers and Politics*, 70; *Boston Globe*, October 4, 2015; *Vineyard Gazette*, December 2, 2010; Wright, *Encyclopedia of African Methodism*, 23; Charity Adams Earley, *One Woman's Army: A Black Officer Remembers the WAC* (College Station, TX, Texas A & M University Press, 1989), 105.
[156] Gregg, *Of Men and Arms*, vii.

and the 368th Infantry. Moreover, he was post chaplain at Fort Huachuca in Arizona and chaplain for the 93rd Division. He was raised in 1942 to the temporary rank of major in the US Army. The start of the Gregg/DeVeaux journey initially took them to inspect a Negro unit at Hamilton Field near San Francisco and then on board a B-34 bomber headed to Honolulu, Hawaii. Before their departure for the island of Canton in the Pacific theater, they toured Pearl Harbor where the Japanese recently had attacked. Once they landed at Canton, they were 600 miles from a Japanese base on Gilbert Island. Then, on their next stop in Australia, they met General MacArthur, the Commander-in-Chief of the Southwest Pacific.[157]

In New Guinea the bishop was especially impressed with vital engineering tasks that black soldiers undertook. He observed them operating "pile drivers, bulldozers, steam shovels, tractors" and other power machinery "all under the direction of Negro Corporals, Sergeants, and Lieutenants." He added that "the whole water purification plant, upon which the lives of all the soldiers of that area depended, was in the hands of Negroes." Furthermore, he saw, "a Chemical Warfare Service of Negroes repairing gas masks and conditioning various forms of equipment." He also reported on "a hillside where Negro men with surveyor's instruments, glasses, and drafting boards, were laying out terrain for roadways, runways and revetments [or barricades]." Additionally, he laid a wreath on the grave of the first soldier killed in New Guinea, an African American private, William M. Clemons of Texas.[158]

After they completed their Pacific tour, Gregg and DeVeaux returned to the War Department in Washington DC for authorization to visit war fronts in Europe and North Africa. After stops in Newfoundland and Scotland, they landed in England for trips to London and Liverpool. They visited an ordnance depot and a chemical facility where 1,000 troops, consisting of separate units of whites and blacks, were stationed. After flying to North Africa and landing in Morocco, they went through Marrakesh and then Casablanca, where they attended a worship service conducted by an AME chaplain, Wesley B. Nash of South Carolina. At their next stop in Oran, they met nine black chaplains and their units at Biggers Chapel, a worship site named for a black soldier killed in that area. While talking with a general, Gregg noted the lack of recreational facilities for black soldiers. "When we left," the bishop observed, "we had every assurance of better recreational advantages for the seven hundred Negro soldiers under his command."

[157] Ibid., 1, 5–9, 11, 13, 22–23; Wright, *Encyclopedia of African Methodism*, 96.
[158] Gregg, *Of Men and Arms*, 45–46, 48, 52.

Gregg also recommended "the presence of some colored Red Cross Workers" who "would make them feel at ease."[159]

At Bizerte, Tunisia, Gregg had a meeting with "Negro Captains" and preached to over 2,000 soldiers. The bishop had additional meetings, and said that at a hospital visit he saw "many patients from the battle fronts, wounded, maimed, and blinded"; this encounter "brought the horrors of this awful war very close. He added that "late into the night" he and DeVeaux conversed with two colonels about bringing "interracial goodwill and comity" between blacks and whites in the military and in the homeland. The following day bishop and chaplain consulted with "eighteen Negro Commissioned Officers." After his arrival in Italy, Gregg was informed that Captain C. B. Hall had received from General Dwight D. Eisenhower a decoration "for being the first Negro to shoot down a Nazi plane in a dog fight and to miraculously escape from two others who were chasing him." In Egypt, Gregg and DeVeaux told a general that "Negro M.P.s could greatly aid him in settling the difficulties with Negro troops, who felt that they were not [being] properly protected by white M.P.s." This negligence usually occurred when "pugnacious New Zealanders" "assault[ed] American troops when they meet in 'pubs' and elsewhere."[160]

After stops in India and Sudan, Gregg went to South Africa, where he added denominational business to his agenda. Josephus R. Coan, the AME superintendent, and Francis H. Gow, the pastor at Bethel AME Church in Cape Town, prepared for his arrival. Because Bishop Frank Madison Reid, Sr. was prevented from reaching his jurisdiction, Gregg, with a military escort, substituted for his colleague in dedicating two buildings at Wilberforce Institute in the Transvaal and ordaining forty-one new ministers. Right after the bishop ended these war front inspections, President Roosevelt wrote to Gregg on March 17, 1944, thanking him for visiting "the Negro men and their commanders in our armed forces" and commending him for "this definite contribution to the morale" of blacks in the military.[161]

Few AME leaders could interact with African Americans in the military and advocate on their behalf with the same proximity that Gregg and DeVeaux had available to them. That did not mean, however, that bishops, educators, and pastors lacked other institutional mechanisms to acknowledge and facilitate the mobilization of AMEs to fight against Nazism and Fascism. The bishops gave special attention, for example, to the recruitment and endorsement of military chaplains. AME schools hosted military

[159] Ibid., 82–83, 102–104, 107, 109, 111, 114, 116–117, 119.   [160] Ibid., 121–122, 127–128, 133.

[161] Ibid., 167, 176–177, 221; Wright, *The Bishops of the African Methodist Episcopal Church*, 294.

training programs especially for potential black officers and became entry points for black females to join the Women's Army Corps (WAC). Some pastors, such as the minister at Scranton, Pennsylvania, in his report to the 1943 Pittsburgh Annual Conference, submitted rosters of members who paid their denominational assessments. This particular pastor subdivided the roll and saluted an impressive forty-five parishioners, "our soldier boys" whose contributions of Dollar Money were celebrated. One of them, a woman, was probably enlisted in the WAC. Chaplains also checked in with their annual conferences to report on their activities. One of them, First Lieutenant J. Julian Jenkins, stationed at Fort Francis E. Warren in Wyoming, noted it as "a new assignment and a larger job." He paid to the 1944 Pittsburgh Annual Conference denominational assessments for himself and his wife, and said that five conversions and four reclamations had occurred soon after his arrival at the base. Previously, in 1943 he had served at Fort Riley, Kansas, "as the only Negro chaplain to thousands of soldiers." Similarly, Chaplain Andrew Johnson, formerly the pastor to three Ohio congregations, discharged financial obligations to the 1944 North Ohio Annual Conference to maintain his standing in the AME clergy. Starting in 1940, he had been a chaplain for the Civilian Conservation Corps in upstate New York and later, in 1941 and 1942, he was regimental chaplain for the 366th Infantry at Fort Devens in Massachusetts and then Assistant Division Chaplain for the 92nd Division at Fort McClellan in Arkansas.[162]

The bishops agreed that military chaplaincy provided their clergy with a direct involvement in national defense through their caring for a countless corps of blacks in the armed forces. Moreover, these chaplains personified, as did their counterparts from other white and black denominations, the consensus present within these religious bodies that war was the preferred instrument to defeat the Axis Powers. As a result there were in excess of 8,000 Christian and Jewish clergy who served as World War II chaplains. Some, such as Lewis McGee, an AME pastor in the Midwest, started as World War I chaplains. McGee joined the 92nd Infantry Division in 1918,

---

[162] *Official Minutes of the Seventy-Sixth Annual Session of the Pittsburgh Annual Conference of the African Methodist Episcopal Church of the Third Episcopal District* held in St. James AME Church, Pittsburgh, PA, September 21–26, 1943 (n.p., 1943), 74–75; *Minutes of the Seventy-Seventh Annual Session of the Pittsburgh Annual Conference [of the] African Methodist Episcopal Church of the Third Episcopal District* held in Brown Chapel AME Church, Pittsburgh, PA, September 19–24, 1944 (n.p., 1944), 33; *Minutes of the Sixty-Third Annual Session of the North Ohio Conference [of the] African Methodist Episcopal Church* held in Community AME Church, Cleveland, OH, September 26–October 1, 1944 (Cleveland, OH, Babby's Printing Co., 1944), 19; Wright, *Encyclopedia of African Methodism*, 160–161.

and after World War II began volunteered as a chaplain in the 95th Infantry Division; he was stationed in Belgium. Months before the Japanese attack on Pearl Harbor, the bishops learned from an Episcopal Church prelate in Phoenix about the need for chaplains for black soldiers at Fort Huachuca, Arizona. In the following year, 1942, another communication came to the AME episcopal leaders from a chaplain in the 25th Infantry at this same installation asking them to "give religious support to the men in arms." The bishops assured the chaplain that "we are ready to give whatever aid" that was necessary. Perhaps he did not know that the Council of Bishops already had impaneled a Committee on Chaplains with Bishop Wright as chair.[163]

Through this committee the bishops were deeply engaged in finding chaplains for the armed forces. In June 1941 they advanced the applications of five AME clergy, including George Dewey Robinson, a graduate of the School of Religion at Howard University, and Californian Alvia A. Shaw. In 1942 Shaw attained the rank of first lieutenant, then was promoted to captain, and served with the famed 369th Division in the Pacific. Bishop Wright also traveled to Washington DC to report that eight slots had been filled and that the bishops needed to find four more applicants. "We want the best available men," pleaded the Committee.[164]

An energized episcopacy in 1943 facilitated the expansion of AME military chaplains to fifty-four. Notwithstanding this impressive effort, the bishops' Committee on Chaplains reported the need for another forty-two. Each bishop, therefore, was called to nominate "three eligible persons" to fill the denominational allotment. Bishop Gregg and Chaplain DeVeaux had already echoed this concern about the black chaplain shortage during their wartime visit to Hawaii. After they addressed a worship service that all the chaplains attended, they discovered that the two hundred blacks at the army base had "no Negro Chaplain." Once chosen and commissioned, the bishops committed to supplement their supplies and to designate a responsible AME official to report on the activities of the chaplains and their whereabouts. They would receive portable communion sets and receive communications

[163] Edwin S. Gustad and Leigh E. Schmidt, *The Religious History of America* (San Francisco, Harper San Francisco, 2002), 329; Mark D. Morrison-Reed, *Black Pioneers in a White Denomination* (Boston, MA, Beacon Press, 1980, 1984), 115, 117; *Proceedings of the Winter Session of the Council Of Bishops, February 13–14, 1941*, 9; *Proceedings of the Mid-Summer Session of the Council of Bishops, African Methodist Episcopal Church in Allen Temple AME Church, Cincinnati, OH, June 25–26, 1942*, 9.
[164] *Proceedings of the Mid-Summer Session of the Council of Bishops, African Methodist Episcopal Church in Avery Chapel AME Church, Oklahoma City, Oklahoma, June 26–27, 1941* (typescript), 10–11; *Christian Recorder*, July 2, 1968; Wright, *Encyclopedia of African Methodism*, 250.

from an appointed head of the Commission on Army and Navy Chaplains whose expenses the denominational treasurer would fund.[165]

The Bishops Council delegated to the Committee on Chaplains, consisting of Bishops Wright and Nichols, authority "to approve" AME chaplains. These chaplains were mainly in the army, except for James Russell Brown who served in the navy and Fred E. Stephens, "the 1st Negro Chaplain of the only Negro service unit in the Air Corps," the forerunner to the Air Force. Similarly, Julius C. Carter, another army chaplain, was dispatched to the 2nd Air Force in Colorado Springs, Colorado. Additionally, several chaplains in these various military branches received special training at the Chaplains School at Harvard University. Andrew L. Johnson, who was promoted in 1942 to captain, became a section leader for forty chaplains in the Harvard program. Some chaplains were dispatched overseas, including Warren J. Jenkins who was attached to the 870th Engineers and went with his unit to Australia. P. C. Watkins, assigned to the 93rd Division, went with them to the southwest Pacific. Paris V. Sterrett, while a part of the 366th Infantry, "was wounded in North Africa" and was "honorably discharged on account of his injuries."[166]

Military chaplaincy, in the view of the bishops, attained such ecclesiastical importance that in 1944 the Council instructed Bishop Gregg to request from the War Department a roster of AME chaplains in the Regular Army. Those who appeared on the list would be designated as official members of the upcoming General Conference. When the legislative body convened in Philadelphia, on a motion by Bishop Monroe H. Davis and an Arkansas delegate, "all Chaplains of the Armed Forces were granted seats in this General Conference." As a result, ten military chaplains were received as official delegates.[167]

Officials at AME colleges joined the bishops in the recruitment of defense workers and black officers for the armed forces. Wilberforce University had a contract with Patterson Field to train airplane and auto mechanics at a renovated campus facility. At a cost of $75,000, modern engines were made available for this vocational training initiative. Moreover, Charles H. Wesley, now the president of the denomination's flagship institution, approved the

[165] *Proceedings of the Mid-Summer Session of the Council of Bishops, June 24–25, 1943*, 10–11; Gregg, *Of Men and Arms*, 90.
[166] *Proceedings of the Mid-Summer Session of the Council of Bishops, June 24–25, 1943* (typescript), 11; Wright, *Encyclopedia of African Methodism*, 63, 160-161, 263, 288-290, 347.
[167] *Minutes [of the] Bishops' Council, AME Church [in] St. John AME Church, Birmingham, Ala [bama], February 17–18, 1944*, 3; *Journal of Proceedings of the Thirty-Second Quadrennial Session of the General Conference, 1944*, 12–13.

organization of a Reserved Officer Training Program along with relevant course offerings. Furthermore, an Army Specialized Training Program was inaugurated, which made Wilberforce only one of seven black colleges with this course of study. Additionally, Georgia Myrtle Teal, Dean of Women at Wilberforce, endorsed two recent alumnae for the WAC. They were Jamye Coleman, the daughter of a leading Nashville pastor, and Charity E. Adams, the daughter of a general officer. Coleman declined the recommendation, but Adams became one of nearly forty women who completed special training in 1942 at Fort Des Moines, Iowa.[168]

At Adams's graduation, she received a commission in the 1st Company, 3rd Platoon as the first African American officer in the Women's Auxiliary Army Corps. As the commanding officer of Company 8, disparagingly identified as a unit of "colored girls," Adams assumed additional duties as a convoy officer for women dispatched to Fort Huachuca, Arizona, and to Staten Island. Although few army bases accepted black women and a limited number of jobs were available for these professionally trained WACs, Adams eked out opportunities as a training supervisor at a Pentagon site in developing course materials for women officers serving overseas. At the same time she tried to get more black women placed in motor transport training, a vocation that was "lily-white." Moreover, she inspected forts in the Northeast and in North Carolina, visited various units of black WACs, and worked as a summary court officer.[169]

Because black newspapers criticized the army about the absence of black WACs serving overseas, despite the assignment of whites to these locations, Adams in 1944 was dispatched to Europe and stationed on January 25, 1945 to London. After assignments to Paris, Adams met two convoys of black WACs who disembarked in Glasgow, Scotland. Adams, the ranking officer over five companies in the 6888th Central Postal Directory in Birmingham, England, was charged with getting mail to American troops on the European front. Already a major, Adams and her unit, after the German surrender to the Allies, moved to Rouen, France. In 1946 Adams mustered out of the military at the rank of lieutenant colonel. Her ongoing activities and achievements were communicated to AMEs through her presence at a congregation in Des Moines and through a visit to Fort Des Moines by Bishop Gregg and a delegation of leading pastors in his Midwest jurisdiction. Olivia J. Hooker, a survivor of the Tulsa race riot of 1921 and rooted in the

---

[168] Wesley, *A Stranger in One's Own Land*, Chapter 17, 246; Wright, *Encyclopedia of African Methodism*, 23, 70, 301.
[169] Earley, *One Woman's Army*, 43–44, 54, 64, 79, 90, 92–93, 97, 101.

city's Vernon AME Church, like Adams, pioneered as an African American woman in the United States military. Though legislation was enacted in 1942 to establish the United States Coast Guard Women's Reserve, it barred black women. When the racial restriction ended in 1944, Hooker and four other African Americans in February 1945 enlisted in the reserve unit.[170]

Deep institutional engagement in support of ministers and members in the armed forces and unambiguous endorsements of the war aims of the federal government masked marginal voices in favor of pacifism. Bayard Rustin, an alumnus of Wilberforce University and a tenor and soloist in the Wilberforce Quartet, was raised in the AME and Quaker home of his grandparents in West Chester, Pennsylvania. That his grandmother knew Richard R. Wright, Jr., a Wilberforce trustee, enabled Rustin to receive a music scholarship to the school. His matriculation in 1932–1933 ended for one of a few possible reasons. They included his homosexuality, leading a strike over the low quality of the food, and losing his scholarship because he refused to join the campus Reserve Officers' Training Corps. Later, he registered in 1940 as a conscientious objector and joined the pacifist Fellowship of Reconciliation and the War Resisters League. Continued refusal to heed the draft landed him in a federal penitentiary in 1944. These experiences deepened his activism in numerous nonviolence and peace movements. Archibald J. Carey, Jr., though he supported American involvement in World War II, welcomed to Woodlawn AME Church in Chicago a small group of pacifists involved in nonviolent protests against racial discrimination. Bernice Fisher, one of the founders of this newly established organization, the Congress of Racial Equality, joined Woodlawn as the congregation's first white member. She encouraged another pacifist to attend and develop, like Fisher, much admiration for Carey's timely and provocative sermons. She frequently debated with her pastor about the morality of war and whether she should register for the draft.[171]

Despite the presence of a pacifist consciousness in disparate AME venues, these perspectives scarcely affected church support for the war against the Axis Powers. Most importantly, the Roosevelt administration was mindful that numerous denominational leaders endorsed its ongoing New Deal initiatives and that transferred church support to FDR's wartime

[170] Ibid., 87, 118, 121, 127, 135, 138–140, 144, 147, 149–151, 161; *New York Times*, January 22, 2002; *Christian Recorder Breaking News*, November 23, 2018; Olivia J. Hooker, https://storycorp sorg-staging.s3.amazonaws.com/uploads/HookerMBBfinal-1mp3.
[171] Jervis Anderson, *Bayard Rustin: Troubles I've Seen* (New York, HarperCollins, 1997), 22–23, 31, 35, 66–67, 98–101, 108–109; Dickerson, *A Liberated Past*, 164.

mobilization. Hence, federal officials regularly appeared at denominational meetings to cement their alliance with AMEs and win over or neutralize Republicans, such as Bishop Sims, within this major ecclesiastical constituency. Mary McLeod Bethune, the unofficial head of Roosevelt's "Black Cabinet" and director of the Division of Negro Affairs in the National Youth Administration (NYA), disbursed funds to construct buildings on the Wilberforce University campus for various vocational programs. In 1942 she transferred ownership of these facilities to the university, a move that enabled President Wesley to convert them into dormitories. Bethune's NYA colleagues maintained the agency's connection to AMEs through the war period. While she negotiated the Wilberforce deal, these NYA officials appeared in 1942 before the Bishops Council to solicit their approval of the bureau's national defense initiatives. Bishop Tookes motioned that the bishops should "support the government in this defense program." At this same meeting, Bethune's boss, Aubrey Williams, the NYA's executive director, also won the endorsement of the bishops for NYA's wartime activities. Bethune herself appeared before the Council in 1943, representing the NYA. The AME interaction with this federal agency buoyed one Arkansas minister, Vince M. Townsend, who praised the NYA for "the fine help given us in the education of the Negro youth." He added that "every school among us has students whose education is being paid by the government."[172]

Other federal agencies sent either communications or officials to solidify ties with the AME Church. The head of the Civilian Conservation Corps Camps for Negroes assured the bishops that local pastors conducted worship services for black soldiers with assigned duties at these facilities. Bishop Gregg received a notice from the AAA about funds that were available for rural community development and rural home beautification in various episcopal districts. An AAA official also requested the bishops to endorse its program "to have farmers increase their production for war purposes." The bishops were told emphatically that aid would be given to farmers "irrespective of race or creed." The visit of Eleanor Roosevelt to the 1944 General Conference in Philadelphia climaxed for AMEs the desire of the Roosevelt administration to retain black support for its New Deal and national defense policies. After Sadie Tanner Mossell Alexander, now the

<hr />

[172] Wesley, *Stranger in One's Own Land*, Chapter 17, 246; *Proceedings of the Mid-Winter Session of the Council of Bishops, African Methodist Episcopal Church in Bethel AME Church, Baltimore, Maryland, February 19–20, 1942* (typescript), 2, 7; *Proceedings of the Mid-Winter Session of the Council of Bishops, African Methodist Episcopal Church in St. John AME Church, February 18–19, 1943*, 2; V. M. Townsend, *Fifty-Four Years of African Methodism* (New York, Exposition Press, 1953), 153–154.

attorney for the Council of Bishops, responded to the First Lady's speech, "Mrs. Roosevelt withdrew amid applause" from the AME crowd.[173]

FDR's administration, in both depression and war, seemed above partisan politics, and its AME support blurred the lines between church and state. At least, that was the view of Townsend of Arkansas. The Roosevelt presidency tried "to alleviate human suffering," "advance agriculture," and did "the fine and needed work in defense preparation." AMEs, he declared, "cannot afford to be unconcerned and indifferent in government matters-especially in this defense movement." African Americans should "turn a deaf ear to Communist and foreign propaganda" and "stand as one in this mighty struggle against all of the enemies of democracy."[174]

Beyond the cozy relationships forged between the Roosevelt administration and the AME Church, World War II had derivative effects upon African Methodism far more important than vocational gains for chaplains and funds distributed from domestic and war mobilization programs. Despite the war, AME congregations, especially in urban areas, continued a steady growth. Anchored principally in social gospel ministries and civic engagement, such churches as Woodlawn in Chicago and Union Bethel in New Orleans grew and housed extensive social service organizations. At Woodlawn, through the 1930s and early 1940s, the membership grew from 40 to 1,500 mainly because of its socially conscious ministries. Pastor Archibald J. Carey, Jr., a member of the Midwest Conference on the Negro and the War, developed the West Woodlawn Club for Service Men, a group of draftees and other military personnel. Additionally, he founded the American Veterans Committee in which Carey, also a practicing attorney, provided legal advice to those embroiled in court martial proceedings. Howard Thomas Primm at Union Bethel in New Orleans located in its Four Freedoms Building the Sarah Allen Child Development Center, day care to aid working mothers, and a Harvest Ministry that facilitated his participation in municipal affairs. Primm's seemingly prescient programs in later years led his eulogist, Bishop John Hurst Adams, to characterize his multiple ministries as "The Primm Paradigm." This template, reminiscent of

[173] *Proceedings of the Mid-Winter Session of the Council of Bishops, African Methodist Episcopal Church in Avery Chapel AME Church, Oklahoma City, Oklahoma, June 26–27, 1941* (typescript), 8; *Proceedings of the Mid-Winter Session of the Council of Bishops, Baltimore, Maryland, February 19–20, 1942*; *Minutes [of the] Bishops Council, Birmingham, Alabama, February 17–18, 1944* (typescript), 5; *Proceedings of the Mid-Winter Session of the Council of Bishops, Nashville, Tennessee, February 18–19, 1943* (typescript), 2; *Journal of Proceedings of the Thirty-Second Quadrennial Session of the General Conference, 1944* (n.p., 1944), 17.
[174] Townsend, *Fifty-Four Years of African Methodism*, 153.

Ransom's Institutional Church and Social Settlement and parallel to Carey's Woodlawn Church, was reflected in other congregations that expanded because of World War II.[175]

In 1943 Bishop Sims reported to the Bishops Council that the First Episcopal District was "growing both in numbers and finances." The reason lay with the "large groups of our people [who] were migrating into the District influenced by defense work needs." What was occurring at St. Matthew Church in Philadelphia must have been foremost in his mind. In 1939 he appointed Mahlon M. Lewis to the 1,600 member congregation, where he led in building a massive physical plant that was "paid in full." Lewis, the contractor and a laborer on the project, then grew the membership to 3,000 and hosted the 1944 General Conference. The M. M. Lewis Community Center housed a boys' club that helped hundreds of youth in the West Philadelphia area and Lewis's other ministries moved the Slowe Post of the Veterans of Foreign Wars to honor him in 1945. Elsewhere in the District, Sims similarly declared "war conditions brought about the migration of many of our people from the South to the [North] East." Since "many of them settled on the East side of New York City," this factor required "the purchase of a church building" for the Zion Mission to accommodate "a large number of our people from the South."[176]

Notwithstanding Roosevelt's favorability among African Americans, AMEs, like other blacks, adopted the Double V for Victory slogan during World War II. To fight Nazism and Fascism overseas also required concomitant efforts to eradicate racism and segregation in the United States. Arthur S. Jackson, Hawkins's successor as AME treasurer, declared in 1942 that blacks in the military "fight for a liberty in which they so meagerly share, and yet they fight that this cruel thing of enslaving tyranny shall hide its hideous face in eternal defeat." He hoped through an Allied victory "that race hate and race antagonism shall be driven back into their serpentine forms [and] that all good democratic governments may spurn and despise them." The Baltimore Annual Conference advised no "let-up on our insistence for full equality of opportunity," while also remembering "our duties as citizens of this, the World's greatest Democracy." The Pittsburgh Annual Conference lamented that blacks "are sacrificing their lives upon the nation's altars [and] upon the many far-flung battlefields of the world for the cause of freedom

[175] Dickerson, *African American Preachers and Politics*, 67–68; Wright, *Encyclopedia of African Methodism*, 62; *Footprints of Service*, 31–32.
[176] *Proceedings of the Mid-Winter Session of the Council of Bishops, Nashville, Tennessee, February 18–19, 1943* (typescript), 2, 10–11; Wright, *Encyclopedia of African Methodism*, 184.

and democracy." Nonetheless, "the Negro both at home and abroad is still the victim of prejudice, hate, and discrimination" and "is denied the very thing he is fighting and dying for." The Northwestern Annual Conference said, "we cannot fight to crush Nazi brutality abroad, and condone race riots and race discrimination at home." The North Ohio Annual Conference hoped "that God will hasten the day when our boys will come marching home with the coveted goal of victory." At the same time, "we shall fight on the home front until the hydra headed cobra of race is completely destroyed."[177]

Because of the persistence of Jim Crow practices in both civilian and military agencies, the Roosevelt administration and Congress drew sharp criticism from the AMEs. Sensing the coming of war, the 1940 Michigan Annual Conference said that "congressional dilatoriness in dealing with the important items of the equalization of Negroes in the armed forces of the government and the anti-lynch bill [are] an occasion for serious disappointment." The delegates resolved to send "a forceful and unequivocal letter to the president and Congress urging a speedy passage of the bills now pending in relation to these two important subjects." They also suggested the appointment of a biracial commission "to advise all [federal] administrative departments" on issues pertaining to African Americans and a black Special Assistant to the Secretary of War. The Northwestern Annual Conference expressed similar concern about the treatment of blacks in the armed forces where they encountered the "indignities of Segregation and Discrimination" and endured "a constant recurrence of brutalities and murders by Civilian and Military police." Roosevelt, as "Commander-in Chief," they observed, "has the full power to end" these practices" Therefore, AMEs "call on him to use that power now."[178]

---

[177] L. Brackett Kinchion, *The Life and Works of Arthur Smith Jackson* (Nashville, TN, AME Sunday School Union, 1944), 92–93; *Official Journal and Minutes of the Twenty-Sixth Session of the Baltimore Annual Conference of the African Methodist Episcopal Church* held in Trinity AME Church, Baltimore, MA, May 5–9, 1943 (Nashville, TN, AME Sunday School Union, 1943), 43; *Minutes of the Seventy-Seventh Annual Session of the Pittsburgh Annual Conference [of the] African Methodist Episcopal Church of the Third Episcopal District held in Brown Chapel AME Church, Pittsburgh, PA, September 19–24, 1944* (n.p., 1944), 42; *Minutes of the Twenty-Third Annual Session of the Northwestern Conference of the African Methodist Episcopal Church* held in Payne Chapel AME Church, Waterloo, IO, September 8–13, 1943 (n.p., 1943), 41; *Minutes of the Sixty-Third Annual Session of the North Ohio Conference [of the] African Methodist Episcopal Church* held in Community AME Church, Cleveland, OH, September 26–October 1, 1944 (Cleveland, OH, Bagby's Printing Co., 1944), 40.

[178] *Journal of the Fifty-Fourth Annual Session of the Michigan Conference (of the) African Methodist Episcopal Church* held in Quinn Chapel AME Church, Flint, MI, August 1940

Charity Adams discussed her own first-hand experiences with Jim Crow in the WACS. She objected to segregation even when her complaint threatened her promotion. WAC headquarters and the White House, "attributable in part to the recommendation made to the president by his Negro advisor," set up "a Negro training regiment, parallel to the regular training regiment, in order to provide promotional opportunities for Negro officers." Adams disagreed because top officers of the black unit would be reserved for whites. Though offered the position of commanding officer of the Negro regiment, Adams "wanted no part of it." She added, "I want to make it as a WAC and not as a Negro WAC officer." Because of racial realities, she also knew that "regimental commander" would be off limits to her because of Jim Crow.[179]

The Roosevelt administration was similarly deficient in barring employment discrimination in burgeoning defense industries. In 1941 Michigan Annual Conference delegates saw that "thousands of foreigners and [white] natives have found employment and given precedence over Negro laborers" thus making "the problem of work and wages among us is at its critical stage." Specifically, the conference recalled examples "of the exclusion of Negro skilled workers from certain defense industries and of the frequent refusal to admit qualified Negro students into training and apprenticeship programs." They noted "some corporations of national importance receiving large government contracts" and then showing "themselves unwilling to employ skilled Negro workers." Unfortunately, "companies manufacturing aircraft, automobiles, and gasoline motors are among those where such discriminatory conditions prevail." Especially egregious was the shipbuilding industry, in which there was "an excellent record of colored men" performing at a high level in the previous world war. "This is no time," delegates declared, "to compromise with race prejudice and its attendant discriminations in industrial defense programs."[180]

The discontent that pervaded the Michigan Annual Conference, a diocese where innumerable defense industries were located, reflected the militancy of A. Philip Randolph, the influential labor leader. Randolph, who viewed himself as an Richard Allen heir, announced in January 1941 that 10,000 blacks would march on Washington DC to demand "the Right to Work and

---

(n.p., 1940), 64, 66; *Minutes of the Twenty-Third Annual Session of the Northwestern Conference, 1943*, 44.

[179] Earley, *One Woman's Army*, 100.

[180] *Journal of the Fifty-Fifth Annual Session of the Michigan Conference of the African Methodist Episcopal Church* held in Community AME Church, Jackson, MI, August 27–31, 1941 (n.p., 1941), 72, 74–75.

Fight for Our Country." Because Randolph's idea drew increased support during the next six months, he organized in July 1941 the Negroes' Committee to March on Washington for Equal Participation in National Defense. Moreover, 100,000 became the number of marchers who would be mobilized to demonstrate in the nation's capital for employment equity in war industries. To head off Randolph's plans, however, FDR issued Executive Order 8802, which established a Fair Employment Practice Commission (FEPC) to penalize defense plants for discriminatory treatment against blacks and others. To monitor the agency Randolph kept in operation his March on Washington Movement (MOWM).[181]

While Randolph was gathering support in early 1941, the Bishops Council resolved "not [to] endorse the movement of the 'March on Washington' because of the temperament of the times." On this matter, however, Randolph had greater sway among rank-and-file AMEs and showed the bishops to be out of step with most members in the denomination. Archibald J. Carey, Jr., for example, invited Randolph to Woodlawn in Chicago to explain the objectives of MOWM. The FEPC, which Randolph's initiative drew from the Roosevelt administration, attracted conspicuous support from Dwight V. Kyle, the pastor at Avery Chapel in Memphis and son-in-law to Bishop Wright. Similarly, a FEPC investigator monitored the efforts of the Reverend B. M. McLinn, the pastor of St. Paul in Washington, Pennsylvania, and another minister who worked to end discrimination against black workers at various plants in their locale.[182]

The militancy of Randolph and various AME clergy reflected this common impulse to hold FDR to a higher bar of black advocacy than the denominational hierarchy seemed inclined to do. While they acknowledged the benefits of the president's New Deal and his wife's conspicuous support of African American civil rights, much unfinished business remained in black advancement. When historian Rayford W. Logan assembled a cross section of black leaders to opine in *What the Negro Wants* (1944) about the civic standing of African Americans, AMEs were well represented among the fourteen contributors. Each expressed views that were insurgent and beyond the usual partisan jockeying between the competing promises of the political

[181] Cynthia Taylor, *A. Philip Randolph: The Religious Journey of an African American Labor Leader* (New York, New York University Press, 2006), 130, 132–134, 137.
[182] *Proceedings of the Mid-Summer Session of the Council Of Bishops, Oklahoma City, Oklahoma, June 26–27, 1941* (typescript), 7; Taylor, *A. Philip Randolph*, 169; Wright, *Encyclopedia of African Methodism*, 191–192, 590; Dennis C. Dickerson, "The Black Church in Industrializing Western Pennsylvania, 1870–1950," *Western Pennsylvania Historical Magazine*, Vol. 64, No. 4, 343, October 1981.

parties. Not surprisingly, Randolph stressed MOWM as an all Negro movement committed to nonviolent mass mobilization, a tactic that the bishops
initially eschewed. MOWM, beyond its demands for equal treatment of
blacks in the military and in the workplace, suggested that race riots in
Detroit in 1943 and other cities required attention to labor, economic, and
law enforcement issues. MOWM, Randolph asserted, "is determined to fight
to abolish Jim Crow through nonviolent, good will, direct action, or constitutional [dis]obedience."[183]

Willard S. Townsend, president of the United Transport Service
Employees of America, held an honorary degree from Wilberforce
University and joined Woodlawn Church in Chicago because of Archibald
Carey, Jr.'s racial militancy and support for organized labor. He strongly
criticized the AFL because it facilitated discrimination against blacks in craft
and semicraft occupations. He also noted "union-management 'conspiracies'
to eliminate Negroes from certain skilled well-paying jobs." He held up
the CIO as providing hope for black workers. As secretary of the CIO
Committee to Abolish Race Discrimination, Townsend credited the
federation "as a national bulwark in the struggle to extend the democratic
process into every phase of American life." He called on FDR to appoint "a
Negro as a Vice Chairman of the War Manpower Commission with equal
supervisory powers . . . as [the] Assistant Secretary of Labor" for oversight of
black participation in defense industries.[184]

Charles H. Wesley reminded readers of the Logan volume that blacks, in
responding to the Detroit race riots, concluded 'I would rather die for
democracy here than in Germany.' African Americans, Wesley said, "want
to secure freedom and democracy for the rest of the world but they also want
these here at home." He agreed with Randolph and Townsend that "the
Negro wants [the] freedom to work and to maintain with others, the
accepted American standard of living." Moreover, Wesley queried, for
"whose freedom" was the United States fighting? He asked whether it was
"the freedom of a peace to exploit, suppress, exclude, debase, and restrict
colored peoples in India, China, Africa, [and] Malaya?" He hoped World
War II would emancipate the world from "racial arrogance, economic
lordships, and social differentiation." The war, he believed, should liberate

---

[183] A. Philip Randolph, "March on Washington Presents Program for the Negro," in Rayford
W. Logan (ed.), *What the Negro Wants* (1944), 154, 156, 162.
[184] Dickerson, *African American Preachers and Politics*, 97; Willard S. Townsend, "One
American Problem and a Possible Solution" in Logan, *What the Negro Wants*, 110, 177,
187, 350–351.

from colonialism peoples of color in empires that Europeans and Asian powers, whether in the Allied or Axis alliances, built on the backs of vulnerable populations. Similarly, Randolph said "the colored people of Asia, Africa, and Latin America will measure the genuineness of our declarations about a free world to the extent that we create a free world within our own borders."[185]

Such clergy and laity as Wesley and Randolph, drawing from the AME ethos of social holiness, believed that reform of racially unjust structures and practices would result in lives of equity and flourishing for fellow church members and the communities of which they were a part. Though they thought that an autonomous African Methodism with its impressive institutional operations testified to a tradition of black pride and independence, they also were heirs to Richard Allen, the "apostle of freedom," who viewed the church as having an equally crucial role as a defender of segregated and colonized peoples. The bishops gestured to this tradition in 1943 when they, in response "from a student movement in Ohio," agreed "to write senators of their respective states to abolish the Poll Tax in the Southern States" and kill statues designed to disenfranchise black voters. E. A. Adams and John H. Lewis, both deeply involved in AME institutional affairs, became equally conspicuous in advancing black civil rights. The same was true of L. C. and Daisy Bates, lay persons well known for their protests against racial violence.[186]

Adams, a general officer, was well known in Columbia, South Carolina, as the former pastor of the city's Bethel Church and through his affiliations with Victory Savings Bank, Waverly Hospital, and Allen University. He was part of a vanguard of African American leaders in South Carolina who were energized in the 1930s through the 1940s in militantly pressing for black civil rights. In 1934, for example, Bishop Noah W. Williams supported a NAACP drive in Darlington and refused to hold an annual conference in Clinton because of a lynching. R. W. Mance, a ministerial leader in the South Carolina Annual Conference, headed the State Negro Citizens Committee that urged FDR to support the Costigan–Wagner anti-lynching bill. These examples of black militancy led to the organization of the eight NAACP chapters into the South Carolina Conference of the NAACP. Adams's

---

[185] Wesley, "The Negro Has Always Wanted the Four Freedoms"; Randolph, "March on Washington Presents," in Logan, *What the Negro Wants*, 110–111, 161–162.

[186] *Proceedings of the Mid-Winter Session of the Council of Bishops [of the] African Methodist Episcopal Church in St. John AME Church, Nashville, Tennessee, February 18–19, 1943,* (typescript), 9.

activities emerged out of the state's invigorated black leadership. He and other black clergy in Columbia identified police brutality as a major issue. Hence, they organized patrols to follow municipal and military police from Fort Jackson to monitor their behavior and eliminate the abuse of African Americans. This pressured the military to put black military police on the streets and later to arm them to assist in equitable policing within the African American population. In 1942 Adams, who was president of the Columbia NAACP, encountered the Ku Klux Klan. The hooded hate group surrounded the Adams home and that of James M. Hinton, the NAACP state president. Adams, despite this show of force by the Klan, entered his home and took out "his double-barreled shotgun and shells" and waited them out. Early the next morning the Klan left, but not because of any invention from Columbia police.[187]

Similarly, John H. Lewis, a Georgia-born pastor and former president of Morris Brown College, was thrust into major civil rights activity in Arkansas. The Yale-trained Lewis, as principal of Paul Laurence Dunbar High School in Little Rock, became involved in the NAACP campaign for teachers' salary equalization. The movement stretched across Texas, Maryland, South Carolina, and other southern states where black teachers earned less than whites of similar qualifications. Susie Morris, a teacher at Lewis's school, and other members in the all black Little Rock Classroom Teachers' Association, backed a lawsuit in 1942. At the hearing in 1943 for *Morris* v. *Williams*, Lewis asserted that Morris was entitled to a top rating for salary purposes.[188]

Dissatisfaction with the white resistance to the suit deeply disappointed Lewis and compelled his resignation from Dunbar. His son, the historian David Levering Lewis, recalled the toll this activity took on the Lewises. "Our family," he said, "went from the top of the social heap to pariah status in the dominant community and to an awkward presence as unemployed among its our racial group." Lewis's denomination, however, came to the rescue with the presidency of the AME-sponsored Shorter College in North Little Rock. He brought along John Gipson, the head of the black teachers' group.

[187] Wright, *Who's Who in the General Conference*, 1924, 115; Edwin D. Hoffman, "The Genesis of the Modern Movement for Equal Rights in South Carolina, 1930–1939," *Journal of Negro History*, Vol. 44, No. 4, October 1959, 356, 363, 367–368; interview with John Hurst Adams, Seattle Civil Rights & Labor History Project, University of Washington, June 24, 2005, Earley, *One Woman's Army*, 62–63.

[188] Wright, *Who's Who in the General Conference*, 1924, 31; John A. Kirk, "The NAACP Campaign for Teachers' Salary Equalization: African American Women Educators and the Early Civil Rights Struggle," *Journal of African American History*, Vol. 94, No. 4, Fall 2009, 534–538, 541.

Morris was vindicated, however, in 1945, when an appeals court validated Lewis's testimony that the salary disparity that she suffered was unlawful.[189]

Lucious and Daisy Bates, members of Bethel Church in Little Rock, joined Lewis as local AME militants during the World War II period. As publishers of the *Arkansas State Press*, which they established in 1941, they informed their statewide readers about the urgency of civil rights issues. In 1942 they led in publicizing the shooting death of Sergeant Thomas P. Foster by a white policeman. The Foster murder was another example of violence being visited upon black soldiers stationed on army bases in the South. The persistent efforts of the Bates couple, in cooperation with the Negro Citizens' Committee and the NAACP, attracted the attention of the federal government. Though the policeman was not indicted, the Bates newspaper continued coverage of police abuse of black soldiers and civilians. Black law enforcement officers were recommended for policing in predominantly black precincts. Just like Randolph, Adams, Lewis, and the Bates couple, whether their involvement was connectional or congregational, constructed themselves as AMEs through an adherence to an Allenite model of Wesleyan-based activism. For all of them, renewal from sin, experienced through the salvific process, overflowed into impulses to reconstruct creation away from unjust structures and practices of social sin. Archibald Carey, Jr. best summarized AME religiosity in saying that Richard Allen was "a fighter against segregation" who was involved in "making a kingdom of man [into] a kingdom of heaven."[190]

INTERNAL STRAINS

Archibald Carey identified a serious "fault line" in African Methodism. Numerous ministers and members, like Carey himself, participated broadly within denominational affairs, but put greater emphasis upon an AME witness beyond their sectarian activities. Some balanced both while others stressed one over the other. The bishops, for example, tasked with overseeing a large and expansive religious body, gave only periodic attention to issues pertaining to black advancement. Instead, they grew increasingly preoccupied with the powers and prerogatives of their episcopal office. Moreover,

[189] Ibid., 542; David Levering Lewis, "At the Top of the Bottom in the Segregated South," in *Class Matters* (New York, Macmillan, 2005), 142; John A. Kirk, *Redefining the Color Line: Black Activism in Little Rock, Arkansas, 1940-1970* (Gainesville, University Press of Florida, 2002), 43.
[190] Kirk, *Redefining the Color Line*, 44, 47-51; Dickerson, *African American Preachers and Politics*, 83.

scores of candidates aspiring to the bishopric and other ecclesiastical positions, though at times conspicuous in black activism, allocated less and less time to these pursuits and more to the business of institutional operations and contending for high office. Those within the organized lay were similarly focused on internal AME activities. Launched in 1912 as the Layman's Missionary Movement and reorganized in 1916 as the Connectional Lay College, the group agitated for a greater role in denominational governance. At the 1928 General Conference they gained equal representation as General Conference delegates, an improvement over the token ceiling of three representatives from each annual conference. In 1936 they won the right to serve on the Episcopal Committee, which evaluated the ongoing fitness of bishops including fixing the time of their retirement and assigning and reassigning them to respective episcopal districts. The presence of John R. Hawkins as education secretary and later as treasurer signified the rise of lay power in the connectional church. The treasurer's position had been a stepping stone for clergy to win the bishopric, but after Hawkins served from 1912 to 1939, all of his successors came from the laity.[191]

Though the two missionary societies, the WPMMS and the WHFMS, merged in 1944, the former which was northern-based and dominated by bishops' wives, and the latter that was southern-based with a broader diversity of officers, were arenas for intense electoral competition. Lucy M. Hughes of Texas, head of the WHFMS since 1923, was elected president of the new Women's Missionary Society, and Christine S. Smith of Michigan, head of the WPMMS since 1931 and widow of Bishop Charles S. Smith, became the disgruntled general secretary of the WMS. Like contenders at General Conferences for the bishopric and the general officership, competitors for high positions in the lay organization and in the Women's Missionary Society viewed these activities as the essence of their AME identity. Moreover, institutional strains growing out of the Sunday School Union, how bishops exercised their authority, and the impending split at Wilberforce University, however, interacted with the denomination's routine internal politics. Electoral victories over some factional foe remained normative in AME operations. Bishop Ransom fretted that abuses in episcopal authority and perhaps the other developments at the Sunday School Union

[191] Howard D. Gregg, *History of the African Methodist Episcopal Church* (Nashville, TN, AME Sunday School Union, 1980), 301–304; George A. Singleton, *The Romance of African Methodism* (Boston, MA, Exposition Press, 1952), 168. They included A. S. Jackson, an educator, Robert W. Mance, a physician, A. G. Gaston, a businessman, Joseph C. McKinney, an engineer, and Richard Allen Lewis, a mortician.

and Wilberforce University created situations in which "our integrity and capacity for self-government were seriously challenged."[192]

Ira T. Bryant joined John R. Hawkins as an influential lay leader in the connectional church. He was the son of an Alabama pastor, M. E. Bryant, who became in 1888 the first editor of the *Southern Christian Recorder.* Bryant, a monotype printer at the United States Government Printing Office, served as his father's successor as business manager of the newspaper and was himself elected in 1908 as secretary-treasurer of the Sunday School Union. He transformed the modest Nashville facility that Charles S. Smith acquired into an impressive physical plant. Bryant's preoccupation, however, lay in vilifying various bishops for financial mismanagement and alleged "abuse of power." He championed voiceless poor preachers and their destitute families left behind by their demise. Though offended bishops persistently opposed him through the 1920s and 1930s, they faced in Bryant a formidable opponent. Because of his control and purchase of additional AME properties, he could not be easily dismissed. Furthermore, he published *The Young Allenite,* which held up the bishops "to special ridicule." One observer noted that because Bryant's publication "did not reach enough people," he added to "the Sunday School quarterlies with as much as thirty-six pages of [disparaging] cartoons of bishops and other leaders." Bishop Monroe H. Davis specifically accused Bryant of defaming the bishops as "thieves, rogues, hogs, money hogs and grafters." Bryant also placed the Sunday School Union beyond episcopal control through a change in the charter that permitted him to select members of its board of managers, some of whom were bishops who were allied with him.[193]

Bryant's derogatory descriptions about rank-and-file clergy boomeranged among delegates at the 1936 General Conference and strengthened the candidacy of E. A. Selby, who defeated him for reelection. Bryant wrongly contended, however, that the General Conference had no power to oust him since that authority had passed to the Union's separate board. Hence, he refused to relinquish the Nashville publishing house and forced Selby to

---

[192] Singleton, *The Romance of African Methodism,* 77–78; Octavia W. Dandridge, *A History of the Women's Missionary Society of the African Methodist Episcopal Church, 1874–1987* (n.p., 1987), 9–11; Alma A. Polk, *Twelve Pioneer Women in the African Methodist Episcopal Church* (n.p., 1947), 8–10, 14–16; Ransom, *The Pilgrimage of Harriet Ransom's Son,* 306.

[193] Wright, *Centennial Encyclopedia of the African Methodist Episcopal Church,* 50–51, 360; Ransom, *The Pilgrimage of Harriet Ransom's Son,* 264–265; *Proceedings of the Called Session, Council of Bishops in St. Paul AME Church, Tampa, Florida, February 25–27, 1932* (n.p., n.d.); Andrew White, *Lest We Forget: A Brief Review of the Bitter Struggles and Heartaches Suffered by the AME Sunday School Union* (Nashville, TN, AME Sunday School Union, n.d.), 3–4; Monroe H. Davis, *The Sunday School Union Spotlight* (n.p., n.d.), 4, 6.

operate in Philadelphia at the AME Book Concern. Therefore, Sunday School literature and other publications emanated from two denominational locations without any clear indication of who was the general officer in charge. Though marathon court proceedings ultimately substantiated Selby's right to occupy the Nashville facility, Bryant continued the publication of articles denouncing some bishops and other church leaders. He seemingly trespassed onto the site of the 1944 General Conference and was arrested. He failed to appear in court after posting a bond of $4,000 and was described by Bishop Wright as "a fugitive from justice." Moreover, E. A. Selby secured a new charter to operate the legitimate AME Sunday School Union and barred Bryant from using AME logo. Nonetheless, Bryant persisted in publishing "his *Bootleg* Sunday School Literature" under the discredited Allen Methodists Sunday School Union.[194]

Bryant's raw rhetoric challenged what he viewed as the unchecked authority of the episcopacy. That William T. Vernon and the innocent Joshua H. Jones had been suspended from the bishopric at the 1932 General Conference for alleged power abuses and financial irregularities seemed to validate Bryant's position. Charles Leander Hill, an accomplished scholar, accepted as legitimate the premise of Bryant's crude criticisms of the bishops. While Bryant disparaged some bishops as lacking integrity, Hill believed that whatever their misconduct it drew from a fundamental misunderstanding of the episcopacy within the Protestant tradition.

Hill, the Dean of Turner Theological Seminary in Atlanta between 1933 and 1944, was a Reformation scholar, philosopher, and an ordained AME minister. A graduate of the college and seminary at Wittenberg University and the recipient of a Ph.D. from Ohio State University, Hill, while on a fellowship at the University of Berlin in 1931–1932, deepened his queries about Martin Luther's Reformation protégé Philip Melanchthon. Hill's fluency in Latin and German enabled him to translate into English Melanchthon's 1521 doctrinal treatise, *The Loci Communes of Philip Melanchthon*, also the subject of his 1938 doctoral dissertation.[195]

Hill, well known as a gifted preacher, addressed the Connectional Council in 1944 in Birmingham. This organization of rank-and-file clergy and laity convened concurrently and at the same site as the Council of Bishops.

[194] Davis, *The Sunday School Union Spotlight*, 3, 20; *Journal of the Thirtieth Quadrennial Session of the General Conference of the African Methodist Episcopal Church, New York City, May 6–18, 1936*, 89; Kinchion, *The Life and Works of Arthur Smith Jackson*, 78; Wright, *Encyclopedia of African Methodism*, 567; White, *Lest We Forget*, 10–11.
[195] Arthur P. Stokes, "Charles Leander Hill: Profile of a Scholar," an address delivered before a symposium of the Charles Leander Hill Day Memorial Convocation, May 9, 1984, 2–4.

Hence, with bishops present in the audience, Hill spoke on "The Episcopacy-Its Functions, Its Authority, Its Limitations." In the primitive church, he said, the bishopric, described interchangeably by the Greek terms *episcopos* and *presbyteros*, denoted a functional office for those who administered the Eucharist and other religious duties. Starting in the second century, however, the bishopric became identified exclusively as an episcopacy whose descent derived directly from the apostles and prophets. They embodied the unity of the church and through them God imparted divine grace to the ecclesia. In the sixteenth century Martin Luther rejected this formulation and proposed "the universal priesthood of Christian believers" in place of a sacerdotal order of bishops and their exclusive claim to apostolic succession. American Methodists followed Luther's lead in viewing the bishopric as itinerant and presbyterial, whose roles lay in teaching and defending doctrine and performing administrative functions.[196]

Hill suggested that Henry M. Turner's ill-fated musings about a House of Bishops headed by an archbishop and possessed of legislative powers similar to the General Conference increasingly skewed how AME bishops envisaged the episcopacy. Turner's influence, according to Hill, precipitated "an unbridled usurpation of authority not vested in the office of the Episcopacy coupled with an attitude and an interpretation of the Episcopacy which logically leads back into Roman Catholicism." Some bishops believed that the laying on of hands upon ordinands conferred special graces that only they were equipped to convey. To the contrary, Hill asserted, that "whatever grace a Bishop has, it is not due to the fact that he is a Bishop, but because he is a Christian." Moreover, he lamented that some in the episcopacy "flaunt themselves as earthly princes vested with special powers and authority." He likened them to the dictatorial governments against which blacks were fighting in World War II. Such bishops, he said, "have fast turned their superintendency into a [balled] fist, totalitarian, fascist regime," and their "staff has become transformed into a club to bludgeon the heads of the clergy." He explained that the AME episcopacy was not an order, but an office best understood as an itinerant superintendency. Additionally, the Council of Bishops, contrary to Turner's vision, had no legislative or judicial

---

[196] Charles Leander Hill. "The Episcopacy-Its Functions, Its Authority, Its Limitations," in E. A. Adams, Sr. (Compiler and Ed.), *Year Book and Historical Guide to the African Methodist Episcopal Church* (Columbia, South Carolina, Bureau of Research and History, 1955), 33–35.

functions because the General Conference alone possessed those powers. The Council, he declared, could only "make recommendations to the general church."[197]

Bryant's *The Young Allenite* and Hill's "The Episcopacy" in their polemical critiques about how bishops exercised power showed them as the first cause of the denomination's internal turmoil. There were, however, more benign testimonies about the bishops and their understanding of the episcopacy as an office held by itinerant elders whose posture among other ordained clergy was that of "first among equals." Following Bishop Vernon's suspension from the episcopacy in 1932, for example, Bishop Gregg appointed him to a pastorate in Topeka, Kansas. Gregg's action resembled how Richard Allen and Morris Brown served simultaneously as the pastor of "Mother" Bethel in Philadelphia and as bishops, and how Edward Waters resigned the episcopacy to return to a pastorate in Maryland. Gregg and Vernon, notwithstanding the controversial circumstances surrounding the latter's suspension, affirmed that the bishopric was an office in line with Hill's definition. Additionally, Hill's protégé, Charles S. Spivey, Sr., the Dean of Payne Theological Seminary, declared that the autocratic actions generally ascribed to the bishops did not apply to all of them. With respect to "Bishops Gregg, Ransom, Wright, and [Noah W.] Williams," he said, "nothing of the driving, clubbing, harsh attitude" usually associated with their colleagues described their behavior. "In all of their dealings, particularly with that large group of our ministry," these bishops "were indeed "fathers [in] God." Notwithstanding the ameliorative perspectives such as those that Spivey expressed, the bishops still were stunned by Hill's critique. Hence, in Birmingham at one session of the Council of Bishops, the prelates recommended the deletion of a clause in AME law "which make other denominations believe that our Bishops are tyrants, traitors, or crooks." It seemed that the cumulative effect of the Bryant attacks and the freshness of the Hill address compelled this response.[198]

Despite Hill's critique and Spivey's selective defense of the episcopacy, ingrained habits of institutional behavior pitted bishops against those who circumvented their intrusive oversight especially of AME educational

---

[197] Ibid., 36–37, 39.
[198] John A. Gregg to William T. Vernon, 1933 (in the author's possession); Spivey, *A Tribute to the Negro Preacher*, 249; *Minutes [of the] Bishop's Council [at] St. John AME Church, Birmingham, Alabama, February 17–18, 1944* (typescript), 3.

DR. CHARLES H. WESLEY
College president and Historian

Figure 5.3 Charles H. Wesley, scholar, pastor, presiding elder, president of Wilberforce University (used with permission from prints and photographs, Moorland-Spingarn Research Center, Howard University)

operations. Charles H. Wesley, though refusing the Wilberforce presidency in 1932, accepted the offer in 1942 to head the Ohio institution. Though Wilberforce still consisted of a church-supported College of Liberal Arts and a state-funded CN&I department, Wesley still functioned within a milieu that bishops and their handpicked trustees controlled. Howard D. Gregg, an education professor and AME minister whom Wesley persuaded to leave Howard University with him in 1932 to head the CN&I, described the denomination's tight supervision of the university's two divisions. "The Bishop of the Third Episcopal District," Gregg noted, "had complete control of all affairs at Wilberforce University. He could not only designate who was to be elected president of Wilberforce but he could also designate who was expected to be elected superintendent of the C. N. & I Department." This was accomplished through the bishop's selection of nominees to the university board of trustees. Moreover, the bishop named six of the nine trustees of the CN&I department while the Governor of Ohio selected three. The bishop and the Wilberforce president were also ex-officio members of the state board. During Wesley's presidential tenure that bishop was the venerable octogenarian Reverdy C. Ransom.[199]

[199] Howard D. Gregg, *History of the African Methodist Episcopal Church* (Nashville, TN, AME Sunday School Union, 1980), 326, 347.

Wesley was hardly naïve about AME politics and how it could politicize Wilberforce affairs. He also knew that bishops sometimes sustained their influence over AME colleges through the appointment of their sons as presidents of schools in the districts over which they presided. One of Wesley's immediate predecessors at Wilberforce was Gilbert H. Jones, the son of Bishop Joshua H. Jones in the Third Episcopal District. Moreover, Wesley's contemporaries in AME college presidencies were William A. Fountain, Jr. of Morris Brown College, the son and namesake of Georgia's presiding prelate, and Sherman L. Greene, Jr., the president of Campbell College in Mississippi, where his father and namesake was the bishop. Hence, Wesley crafted, in writing, specific conditions that would govern his acceptance of the Wilberforce presidency. Though several items pertained to compensation, housing, and other amenities, Wesley was equally concerned with matters of governance. He wanted formal election to the presidency by both the church and state boards. As a result, a Joint Executive Committee from the two boards consisting of six trustees, five of them AMEs, made the actual offer to him. Then, the full board, again with AME majorities in each body, including nine bishops, Wesley recalled, "elected me." It appeared to him that "the President was to be the major executive official of the university, provided the bishops would withhold their power of actions in times of decision." This, he believed, was a breakthrough in Wilberforce history.[200]

Wesley, who made himself a familiar figure at AME meetings, leveraged these appearances to generate denominational funds to support Wilberforce. Wesley, while acknowledging regular appropriations from three AME jurisdictions, proposed, like Bishop Payne in the nineteenth century, that Wilberforce should be "a connectional institution." After making this declaration to the 1943 Michigan Annual Conference, delegates commended Wesley for his "soul absorbing educational passion [and] his forceful presentation, bordering on the evangelical." He advanced a motion at the 1944 General Conference that each bishop and episcopal district should raise monies to retire the indebtedness at Wilberforce. After the motion passed, Bishop Nichols recommended the establishment of a connectional board of trustees. Later, at the 1944 Chicago Annual Conference, Wesley praised AMEs for help in reducing the Wilberforce debt by $37,000 with $89,000 remaining to be paid. Ultimately, this burdensome obligation was liquidated

[200] Wesley, *A Stranger in One's Own Land*, Chapter 17, 242–243.

in 1946, with Bishop Ransom and Wesley doing the ceremonial burning of the mortgage.[201]

Notwithstanding Wesley's amicable interactions with the AME hierarchy, trouble brewed beneath the surface of a seeming coalescence of Wilberforce's church and state divisions. Complaints about several of Wesley's administrative and personnel decisions stirred opposition among some faculty in the College of Liberal Arts. The summer session functioned poorly, there was neglect of the *Negro College Quarterly*, and he fired the Dean of Women, Georgia Myrtle Teal, who in 1944 married Bishop Ransom, the incumbent trustee board chair.[202]

Most seriously, Wesley acquiesced to proposals to reduce the AME presence on the state board. Wesley, some contended, endorsed a bill in the Ohio legislature that would give the governor eight rather than six members with the church appointing a lone ninth member. The accrediting agency, the North Central Association of Colleges and Schools, allegedly wanted this action but that seemed untrue. In actuality, argued some Wilberforce faculty, the CN&I, now known as the College of Education and Industrial Arts, would become "an exclusive Negro school" aimed at shifting black enrollments away from Ohio State University.[203]

Wesley pushed back on these charges, saying "I am opposed to and will have no part in the operation of a so-called Jim-Crow institution." He added, "I had no part either in the presentation or advocacy of the present bill." Nonetheless, he concurred with the idea that the Ohio governor should increase the number of his appointments to Wilberforce's state board. It was undesirable that AME bishops should "control not only the College of Liberal Arts," but the College of Education and Industrial Arts as well. Wesley also recoiled at accusations of disloyalty to African Methodism. "I was born in the AME Church," he declared. Moreover, he grew up next

---

[201] *Journal of the Fifty-Seventh Annual Session of the Michigan Conference of the African Methodist Episcopal Church* held in St. Stephen AME Church, Detroit, Michigan, August 24, 1943 (n.p., 1943), 76, 92; *Journal of Proceedings of the Thirty-Second Quadrennial Session of the General Conference, 1944*, 41–42; *Journal and Year Book of the Sixty-Second Annual Session of the Chicago Annual Conference of the African Methodist Episcopal Church* held at Arnett AME Church, Chicago, Illinois, September 12–17, 1944 (Nashville, TN, AME Sunday School Union, 1944), 22; Wesley, *A Stranger in One's Own Land*, Chapter 17, 251.
[202] Milton S. J. Wright, "The Wilberforce Dilemma: A Critical and Objective Evaluation of Dr. Wesley's Administration," *Wilberforce University Bulletin*, Vol. 32, No. 4, January 1948, 18, 20.
[203] Ibid., 28.

door to his home congregation, Quinn Chapel in Louisville, Kentucky, and he boasted of a grandfather who was an AME minister. "The only biography they have [*Richard Allen: Apostle of Freedom*], Wesley asserted, was written by the president of this university." and it was listed in the 1936 *AME Doctrine and Discipline* as required reading for ministerial candidates.[204]

Nonetheless, Milton S. J. Wright, speaking for Wesley's faculty opponents in the College of Liberal Arts, conceded the president's several accomplishments between 1942 and 1944. These achievements mainly pertained to the accreditation of the "University and the College of Education and Industrial Arts by the American Association of Teachers Colleges." There were innumerable liabilities, however, that made the Wesley presidency "a sad story indeed." The most egregious failing was the loss of accreditation from the North Central Association. The agency "put almost the entire blame [for] the conflict between the two boards for [the] withdrawal" of accreditation. Moreover, D. Ormonde Walker, a previous Wilberforce president, attributed the loss of accreditation both to Wesley's actions and some practices that carried over from earlier administrations. Though twenty-four relatives worked on the faculty and staff, including family members of the three bishops, Wesley hired twelve of this number inclusive of his daughter as an instructor in music. Additionally, the prevalence of departmental libraries, beyond the control of the university librarian, and low rates of faculty and student use of library books were noted as institutional deficiencies. Wright blamed Wesley's poor presidential decisions as the real problem, and he was greatly bothered that "Dr. Wesley was continually playing politics and gradually building himself strong with the state board." Hence, the loss of accreditation and increased state control of the College of Education and Industrial Arts precipitated in 1947 an abrupt dismissal of Wesley as the Wilberforce president and orders to vacate the premises within twenty-four hours.[205]

"Members of the AME Church," Wesley said, "you have made a mistake." He showed his loyalty to the denomination when he located a new building that the state funded on "church ground." He added, "do you suppose I would have labored ... if I did not have the best interests of the school at heart?" In a clear admonition to the bishops, Wesley said that "the

[204] Wesley, *A Stranger in One's Own Land*, Chapter 17, 252, 252, fn7; Gregg, *A History of the African Methodist Episcopal Church*, 353; *The Doctrine and Discipline of the AME Church* (Philadelphia, PA, AME Book Concern, 1936), 483.
[205] Wright, "The Wilberforce Dilemma," January 1948, 15–17, 26, 28; D. Ormonde Walker, *The Struggle for Control of Wilberforce University, An Address before the St. James Literary Forum, Cleveland, OH, April 27, 1947* (n.p., 1947), 8–10.

presidency of Wilberforce is not like a pastor's position. That position can be sent on Sunday to the woods and be kept there. We cannot permit Wilberforce to become like that." For those who believed that Wesley himself still aspired to the episcopacy, he said, "I do not want to be a bishop." Instead, he established a rival state-supported institution next door to Wilberforce that was eventually named Central State College.[206]

The church board, in two perfunctory explanations, accused Wesley of being "out of harmony" with the ideals and spirit on which Wilberforce was founded" and that he had showed himself "incapable of maintaining the ideas of student morality and religion in education." Bishop Ransom, in his autobiography, refused comment because he was "too close to the event and was too active in the issues that led to the split." Notwithstanding his direct involvement in the ousting of Wesley, he hoped that "the State of Ohio shall not be allowed to establish a Negro 'Jim-Crow school'" on land formerly attached to the Wilberforce campus. Only Bishop Gregg knew that Wesley was not Ransom's preference for the Wilberforce presidency. In 1942, after Wesley issued his demands for an incumbency free from ecclesiastical politics, Ransom confided in Gregg that he wanted Charles Leander Hill to head his alma mater. After Wesley's ousting, Hill, the pastor of Bethel Church in Columbia, South Carolina, was tasked to rebuild "the church side" of the Wilberforce schism. Though D. Ormonde Walker, later a bishop, agreed that Ohio should not establish "a separate institution of learning for Negroes," he recommended the ouster of ill-willed black politicians from the state board and a corresponding reduction in the number of bishops and clergy on the church board and the addition of a "wider range of trained and intelligent citizens from various parts of the country" to represent the AMEs. The firing of Wesley, however, prevented a Walker compromise from reaching fruition. Wesley crossed the "ravine" that divided the church campus from the state side and founded a larger and better-funded Central State College.[207]

Though a convergence of conflicting church and state interests lay behind the 1947 split, the fissure had at its core Wesley's perception of overreach by AME episcopal power. What happened at Wilberforce contrasted sharply with the negotiated separation that occurred a few years earlier between Western University and the State of Kansas. Bishop Williams led in ending the church/state relationship that resulted in AMEs gaining all properties

[206] Gregg, *History of the African Methodist Episcopal Church*, 353–354.
[207] Ibid., 351; Ransom, *The Pilgrimage of Harriet Ransom's Son*, 320; Handwritten note from Reverdy C. Ransom to John A. Gregg (1942) in the author's private collection; Walker, *The Struggle for Control of Wilberforce University*, 16.

that had been jointly occupied. Nonetheless, the Wilberforce split became the latest example of serious stresses within AME episcopal governance. As the Wesley controversy was unfolding the seeming corruption of Bishop David H. Sims in the Northeast hurled the denomination into an unprecedented extra session of the General Conference.[208]

Sims presided in the First Episcopal District that included large congregations in such major cities as Boston, New York City, and Philadelphia. Other bishops viewed the jurisdiction as a "delectable plum" that Sims exploited for his own aggrandizement. He levied illegal assessments upon the churches to support such "pet" projects as his Paradise Lakes development in New Jersey. Those levies amounted to annual contributions of $10 from each member. These payments drew frowns from Ransom, who said Sims could raise within a quadrennium an impressive $1 million. "The protests," Ransom reported, "became so vocal that certain ministers in the New York area appealed to the Council of Bishops in the spring of 1945," demanding that Sims should be removed. The situation was made urgent with congregations refusing to recognize Sims's authority, including a large church that withdrew to affiliate with another denomination. Moreover, Bethel Church in Harlem lost 1,000 members because of the Sims assessments.[209]

A committee of twelve bishops came to New York City on a fact-finding mission and concluded that the Empire State needed a new bishop. When Wright was appointed, Sims secured a court injunction to block the assignment. At this point the Council of Bishops ordered Sims to stand trial in an AME proceeding. Sims and his faction of colleagues, known as the "Axis" bishops, along with 100 followers, stormed into the assembly and forced the trial to move to another New York church. A disruption also occurred at this second site. Ransom recalled that "they burst in upon the legal proceedings, and by noisy and boisterous conduct, and menacing attitudes that threatened physical violence, broke up the orderly proceedings of the trial."[210]

As a result, a call was issued for a special session of the General Conference to meet in Little Rock, Arkansas, on November 20, 1946. Further efforts by Sims to secure injunctions to prevent the meeting of the General Conference and judicial actions by the Council of Bishops to resist Sims's actions led a federal judge to instruct the competing parties to settle the conflicts by using their own ecclesiastical machinery. At the Little Rock meeting Sims

---

[208] *The Episcopal Address Presented By Bishop M. H. Davis to the Thirty-second Quadrennial Session of the General Conference of the African Methodist Episcopal Church at Philadelphia, Pennsylvania, May 1944*, 20–21.

[209] Ransom, *The Pilgrimage of Harriet Ransom's Son*, 307–308.   [210] Ibid., 308–309.

and his "Axis" colleague, Bishop George E. Curry, were expelled from the episcopacy, and Bishop Davis was temporarily suspended.[211]

Bishop Wright lamented that the Council of Bishops in 1945 and 1946 "sank to its lowest level and temporarily lost its hold on its own ministry and people." On one hand, he included in his assessment Sims's malfeasance and the faction of bishops who supported him. At the same time, Wright chided Sims for spearheading the election in 1940 of Decatur Ward Nichols to the bishopric. But Nichols, according to Wright, wanted to dislodge Sims from the First Episcopal District and to displace him as the AME's preeminent spokesman in the GOP. The presence of Bishop Wright and Bishop Sherman L. Greene's in a divided First District was only temporary, and they became placeholders for Nichols who received this assignment at the 1948 General Conference.[212]

The resort to external judiciaries to settle internal disputes convinced delegates at the 1946 special session of the General Conference to propose a "Judicial Court or Council" to adjudicate governance issues. Originally, it was recommended that the council would judge appeals on the constitutionality of any acts of the General Conference while being "answerable" to that same body, which could reverse "by majority" any of its rulings. The 1948 General Conference considered "a bill establishing a court of adjudication" as a "final tribunal of appeals on all questions of law." Any alleged abuses committed by any officer or body within the denomination related to "Mis-Feasance, Mal-Feasance, Mal-administration, or Treason" would be subject to the jurisdiction of the Judicial Council, which would "in NO way conflict with laws adopted by the General Conference." At the 1952 General Conference Attorney Herbert L. Dudley, the president of the Connectional Lay Organization, called for the third reading of the Judicial Council bill. Despite some parliamentary disputes and some amendments, including those that unambiguously made the body subject to the General Conference and limited it to appeals, the law was enacted. The legislation brought a modicum of order to settling institutional disagreements and averting the most serious threats to AME self-government, such as that experienced in the Sims case.[213]

[211] Ibid., 309.
[212] Wright, *Eighty-Seven Years behind the Black Curtain*, 271; Charles Leander Hill, *He Followed His Star: A Pen Portrait of the Life, Personality, and Chief Exploits of William Alfred Fountain, Sr.* (Nashville, TN, AME Sunday School Union, 1987), 121–123.
[213] Townsend, *54 Years of African Methodism*, 44–45; *Proposed Judicial Administration as Presented to the African M. E. Church at the 33rd Quadrennial Session of the General Conference, Kansas City, Kansas, May, 1948*, 2–3, 13; *Official Minutes of the Thirty-Fourth Session of the General Conference of the African Methodist Episcopal Church held at Chicago, Illinois, May, 1952*, 200–204, 211, 215.

AMEs, however, paid a price for these large institutional distractions. Episcopal power, whether described by Ira T. Bryant in his polemical caricatures or through Charles Leander Hill's scholarly analysis, stood in the way of an energized insurgency against racially oppressive structures and practices. Seeming patriotism masked in quid pro quos with the Roosevelt administration dulled AME criticism of the president's weak opposition to Jim Crow. Moreover, an attenuated public theology resulted from an increased immersion in internal institutional conflicts where the overreach of episcopal power lay at the core. The Bryant and Hill critiques, far from being specific only to the 1930s and 1940s, showed that frontline black leadership that had once emanated from the episcopacy shifted almost exclusively to rank-and-file pastors and parishioners. Such ministers and members and sundry intellectuals helped to invigorate the civil rights movement in the United States and independence movements in Africa and elsewhere in the black Atlantic.

6

ɢᴡ

Freedom Now! Civil Rights, Black Power, and Anticolonial Insurgencies, 1945–1976

STRAINS IN THE AFRICAN METHODIST SOCIAL CREED

Internal tensions within the ecclesiastical operations of African Methodism coexisted with the broad activism of African Methodist Episcopal members (AMEs) in civil rights, Black Power, and anticolonial insurgencies. The bishops and other clerical and lay leaders whose vocations focused on denominational affairs contrasted with militant ministers and members who defined African Methodism through a praxis that aimed at societal reconstruction in the United States and ending colonialism in Africa. The objectives of denominational governance, however, diverted attention away from energized opposition to hegemonic structures and practices that harmed AME constituencies. Though the maintenance of African Methodism as a proud and independent religious body remained as a worthwhile demonstration of black self-determination and institutional autonomy, this preoccupation caused some leaders to extend only perfunctory support to significant initiatives against white supremacy. Some clergy, however, balanced their immersion in denominational affairs with social activism. Such ministers similarly advocated significant reform within the AME Church to effect fiscal accountability and greater democracy in ecclesiastical governance.

Notwithstanding the factional fights in the late 1940s that led to the special session of the General Conference and to the split at Wilberforce University, AMEs, in a range of venues, challenged segregation and systemic discrimination on the streets, in the courts, and at other levels of government. Others, including Afrocentric intellectuals and activists on both sides of the Atlantic who opposed colonialism, joined in sustaining the ethos of social holiness that

366

Richard Allen, Jarena Lee, Morris Brown, and Denmark Vesey exemplified in the first decade of the denomination's existence.

Within denominational circles after World War II there was a wide awareness that the ethos of AME activism was being embodied far more in the insurgency of A. Philip Randolph, Sadie T. M. Alexander, Archibald J. Carey, Jr. and other AMEs of both national and local significance than in the ecclesiastical hierarchy. Moreover, the growing intensity of an emerging civil rights movement in which AMEs played an integral role required a manifesto that provided denominational leaders with an opportunity to endorse this burgeoning black militancy. The enactment of an African Methodist Social Creed at the 1952 General Conference aimed to highlight the insurgent character that lay within the denominational DNA. The social creed hardly eliminated tensions that pulled some AMEs to focus on internal activities and others who believed that their "parish" lay beyond the sectarian boundaries of their religious body. Instead, this General Conference mandate served as a reminder to AMEs that multiple issues pertaining to civil and human rights and peace and global security in an age of atomic power and ascendant Communism demanded their attention and involvement.

The creed drew from the aging but still supple mind of Bishop Reverdy C. Ransom. Now a nonagenarian, Ransom, perhaps sobered by the sad spectacle of the special session of the General Conference in 1946 and his embarrassing involvement in the Wilberforce split in 1947, viewed the social creed as an opportunity to resuscitate what he surmised as an increasingly insular denomination. The manifesto, though it addressed doctrinal and family life issues, also provided guidance both to the clergy and the laity, whose energies sometimes split between immersion in denominational politics and a broader beckoning to societal reconstruction. Though these two tendencies, at times, resulted in an uneven blending of both, a well-articulated social creed could clarify exactly where AME activity should be directed.

God's universal laws that formed the basis for "peaceful relations among men and nations" were foundational to the African Methodist creed. Flowing from that was "the sacredness of human personality," a personalist theology reflected in the writings of Howard Thurman, George Kelsey, and other black religious intellectuals. This "oneness of the human race" provided no support to "racial prejudice and discrimination" and declared that such attitudes and actions were "injurious to the unity of mankind." Hence, "all members of the human family should be accorded equal opportunities for educational, social, and cultural development in accordance with their capacities and inclinations." To achieve a just and lasting peace, AMEs, in echoing Randolph and Bayard Rustin, endorsed the use of "nonviolent methods." The creed also gestured toward the recent campaign for a permanent Fair Employment Practice Committee (FEPC) and ongoing efforts to establish such agencies on the state and municipal levels. No one should be denied, the manifesto asserted, "the right to earn a living because of race, creed, or color." After the General Conference enacted these statements of principle, the bishops requested "an annual reading of this Social Creed in all our churches and Sunday Schools."[1]

To facilitate the dissemination of the African Methodist Social Creed, it was expanded and published as a pamphlet. Moreover, a paragraph of explanation accompanied the several bullet points elaborating on the denomination's staunch stand against racial segregation and discrimination. The creed denounced housing bias that barred blacks from "more desirable residential sections" and "segregation in our tax supported public schools, colleges, and universities." Though opposed to a "godless Communism that seeks to dominate The Free World," AMEs showed their proletarian consciousness in recognizing that "over ninety per cent" of its membership was "laborers" who possessed the right "to collective bargaining." Additionally, the FEPC, the brainchild of A. Philip Randolph, deserved congressional approval because employment discrimination "places an economic handicap" upon African Americans and bars their admission "into the great [main]stream of our Social, Industrial, Economic, and Cultural Life."[2]

Similarly, unjust incarceration harmed African American advancement. "Chain gangs, prison camps, and jails," the creed declared, "annually hold thousands of Negro prisoners who have committed no crime, but only misdemeanors or trivial offences such as 'Imprudence to an officer of the Law.'" Though the denomination had long supported temperance, the creed acknowledged dope as a new scourge that, along with alcohol, should be treated as enemies of the "home" and other venues of African American life. While AMEs were hardly ever pacifist, the creed asserted "we cannot follow the Prince of Peace while advocating or supporting war." With the specter of advancing Communism emanating from the USSR, China, and Korea, "the world is organized today, under the high tension and strain concerning the

---

[1] *Official Minutes of the Thirty-Fourth Session of the General Conference of the African Methodist Episcopal Church held at Chicago, Illinois, May 1952*, in *Combined Minutes of the General Conferences, African Methodist Episcopal Church, 1948–1952–1956* (Nashville, TN, AME Sunday School Union, 1956), 172–173.

[2] *The African Methodist Social Creed* (Nashville, TN, AME Sunday School Union, n.d.), 5, 9–10.

imminence of war." It was important for AMEs to "stand for peace" and fight "for the preservation of freedom and justice for all."[3]

AMEs realized that an awareness and engagement with pressing domestic and international issues in the post-World War II era made preoccupations with internal ecclesiastical intrigues increasingly untenable. There were, however, members and ministers whose activities already reflected principles that were articulated in the creed. Proletarian parishioners, for example, fought racial discrimination at industrial and military sites in such disparate locations as western Pennsylvania and Bermuda. Carl O. Dickerson, an involved member of Payne Chapel in Duquesne, Pennsylvania, protested bias against blacks at his own Carnegie steel plant even when his local union, in which he was an officer, eschewed the issue. His activism led to an appointment in 1948 to the District 15 wage policy committee of the United Steelworkers of America (USWA). In the same year, he joined picketers at a USWA convention in Atlantic City, New Jersey where union officers were lodged at the exclusive Traymore Hotel. They protested the hotel sign that read "NO NEGROES, NO JEWS, AND NO DOGS." Dickerson and the other black USWA members forced union officials to move to a nondiscriminatory hotel. Similarly, militant John Hughey, whose three brothers were AME pastors, started work in 1947 at the Carrie Furnaces in Rankin, Pennsylvania. Hughey objected to the displacement of black laborers by white employees and technological innovations in the departments where African Americans had been dominant. Bermuda's Kingsley Tweed was described as "a charismatic, articulate young carpenter with a pronounced call to the AME Church ministry." Tweed, in 1952, as an employee at the United States Kindley Air Force base, joined the Bermuda Industrial Union. He was fired and blacklisted because he led twenty-two others in protesting the racially biased conduct of their employer.[4]

Like the laity, the clergy, even as ecclesiastical responsibilities required their attention, engaged in broader spheres of activity. J. Solomon Benn, a presiding elder in the Philadelphia Annual Conference, was a Republican (GOP) candidate in 1950 for the Pennsylvania legislature. Moreover, an AME protégé of Charles Leander Hill, the president of Wilberforce University, lobbied in 1953 for his appointment as Governor of the US Virgin Islands.

[3] Ibid., 11.
[4] Dennis C. Dickerson, *Out of the Crucible: Black Steelworkers in Western Pennsylvania, 1875–1980* (1986), 179–180, 225; Ira P. Philip, *The History of the Bermuda Industrial Union: A Definitive History of the Organized Labour Movement in Bermuda* (Hamilton, Bermuda, Bermuda Industrial Union, 2003), 110.

These parishioners and preachers envisaged themselves as distinctively AME in their varied public involvements. The creed, in trying to speak the realities that rank-and-file AMEs experienced apart from the church's organizational operations, played some part in preparing African Methodism for the challenges of the civil rights movement.[5]

Nonetheless, the task of governing African Methodism, itself an achievement in black sovereignty, stood in tension with more energetic efforts to fight the same hegemonic forces that required the founding of the AME Church in a previous century. As black freedom movements gained momentum both during and after World War II, the dual obligations of institutional maintenance and insurgent activity split the clergy and the laity between those who emphasized one commitment over the other. Though some exerted themselves in both pursuits, church insiders, who demanded total allegiance to institutional affairs, compelled choices that marginalized social holiness objectives. The ministerial trajectories of Isaiah H. Bonner of Alabama and Joseph A. De Laine of South Carolina illustrated these tendencies within the denomination.

Bonner was born in Camden, Alabama, in 1890. Through the northern-based Presbyterian Church, USA, he received B.A. and B.D. degrees at Knoxville College and ordination in the Presbytery of Tennessee. Despite these Calvinist connections, especially in supplying the pulpit at the historically black Shiloh Presbyterian Church near his campus, Bonner also received a license to preach at Bethel AME Church in Knoxville and served an AME congregation in nearby South Pittsburg, Tennessee. After teaching at a Presbyterian preparatory school in Alabama and securing a full AME ordination, Bonner launched a successful ministerial career in the state, most notably in Mobile, from where he was elected to the episcopacy in 1948. He was assigned to South Africa just as the Afrikaner-dominated Nationalist Party ascended to power and imposed an unusually rigid and oppressive apartheid system of racial separation upon the nation's black majority.[6]

Historically, South Africa's British and Boer officials had always been suspicious of the AMEs because of their American-based bishops, their heritage of black autonomy, and their opposition to antiblack policies in

---

[5] J. S. Brookens, "Negro Candidates of the Republican Party," *AME Church Review*, Vol. 59, No. 165, April–June 1950, 11–14; Dennis C. Dickerson, *African American Preachers and Politics: The Careys of Chicago* (Jackson, University Press of Mississippi, 2010), 147.

[6] *AME Christian Recorder*, May 8, 1978; *The Aurora*, November 1908; January 1909; June 1912; November 1913; February 1914; June 1914 (Knoxville, TN, Knoxville College Archives); Richard R. Wright, Jr., *The Bishops of the African Methodist Episcopal Church* (Nashville, TN, AME Sunday School Union, 1963), 94–95.

both the Americas and the colonized areas of Africa. Though the British-dominated Cape Colony legitimized the denomination in 1899, complaints from diverse European clergy and hostile local officeholders, especially in Natal, the Transvaal, and the Orange Free State, were uncomfortable with the "Ethiopianism" that AMEs embodied. Because resident Bishop Levi J. Coppin made futile attempts in the early 1900s to quiet indigenous African Methodist ministers who were opposed to white rule, distrust of the denomination remained operative during subsequent decades, particularly when Bonner sought entry to South Africa in 1948 and tried to stay for an extended time.[7]

As a result, presiding elders in Cape Province in 1949 asked South Africa's Minister of the Interior to allow Bonner to remain in the country until 1952 to handle an enormous backlog of church business. Bonner's predecessors, owing in part to World War II, had been unable to travel to South Africa for over a decade. These indigenous clergy emphasized to the apartheid government that Bonner's "work deals purely with the spiritual upliftment of the church members and as head of the AME Church he is bound to preach nothing but peace and goodwill to all men." Bonner echoed these same sentiments, saying in a letter to nation's AME clergy that "as your Bishop and leader, I am asking you not to make your church a political organization. As ministers and disciples of our Lord, we must follow his way to conquer. We can only win by love and not by force. Be ye, therefore, preachers of LOVE. HATE NO MAN. God is still ruling the world. Let us serve God in sincerity and in truth and he will fight our battles for us." Therefore, Bonner informed one presiding elder that his principal focus would be a church building program to erect "many new churches in needy places." As a result Bonner built seventeen new edifices in South Africa and in northern and southern Rhodesia, territories that were also a part of his assignment. Additionally, Bonner Hall, built as a classroom facility and dormitory, was constructed in the Transvaal at the AME-sponsored Wilberforce Institute.[8]

[7] Carol A. Page, "Colonial Reaction to AME Missionaries in South Africa, 1898–1910," in Sylvia M. Jacobs (ed.), *Black Americans and the Missionary Movement in Africa* (Westport, CT, Greenwood Press, 1982), 181, 190–192.
[8] I. H. Bonner to Fellow Worker in Christ, n.d., *Easter M. Gordon Collection*, Korresp: 1948–1977, Leer NR 55; I. H. Bonner to Easter M. Gordon, August 22, 1949; Korresp: Bishoppee Bonner, 1949–1954, Leer NR 29; I. H. Bonner to Presiding Elders, Pastors, Missionary Presidents and Members, September 5, 1950, Korresp: 1948–1977, Leer NR 55, Institute for Historical Research, University of the Western Cape, Bellville, Cape Province, Republic of South Africa; Wright, *The Bishops of the African Methodist Episcopal Church*, 95.

Bonner, while mindful of apartheid's pernicious development in South Africa, believed that building and maintaining AME infrastructure ranked higher than "political" activities that directly challenged the nation's racially unjust regime. He adopted the same posture during his tenure as the bishop in segregated South Carolina between 1952 and 1960. Pressure from an aggressive pro-segregationist governor, George B. Timmerman, was exerted upon Allen University, where Bonner was board chairman. Timmerman demanded the dismissal of three faculty members whom he accused of leftist and integrationist advocacy. The governor correctly surmised Allen's vulnerability because it depended on the state for certification of its teacher training program. President Frank Veal, fearing this revocation, fired the professors and deleted from the university catalogue any mention of the campus National Association for the Advancement of Colored People (NAACP) Youth Council. Despite these conciliatory moves, the state still revoked the teacher accreditation program because the American Association of University Professors criticized the breaches of academic freedom at Allen that Timmerman had caused. Nonetheless, both Bonner and Veal had buckled to the governor by acquiescing to the firing of the three professors, thinking that these terminations would preserve this vital academic center.[9]

Bonner, whether in South Africa or South Carolina, seemed averse to confrontations with state power and restricted his activity to protecting AME denominational interests. Though motivated by his reverence for the AME past and pride in its Atlantic reach, Bonner believed that he should emphasize the expansion and maintenance of the ecclesia. He had not yet realized that the black struggle for freedom had shifted gears and was now in an emergent, transatlantic phase of insurgent opposition against segregation, colonialism, and its newest manifestation apartheid. While Bonner seemed disengaged from these developments, Joseph A. De Laine, his generational peer, understood these new challenges that flowed from the emancipationist ethos of African Methodism.

Like Bonner, De Laine was a black Southerner. He was born in 1898 in South Carolina just as legalized Jim Crow was reinforcing the subjugation of African Americans through political disenfranchisement and peonage. De Laine, the son of an AME minister, was educated at Allen University and served several congregations in the state. Trained as a teacher, he was a bivocational clergyman who, while leading a church in his native Clarendon

---

[9] Sandra Archer Young, "The Rhetoric of Segregation, Subversion, and Resistance: Allen University vs. the State of South Carolina," *AME Church Review*, Vol. 121, No. 399, July–September 2005, 21, 23–24, 26, 29–34.

County, was principal at the Scott's Branch School in Summerton. He belonged to an increasingly combative corps of black South Carolinians who grew the number of NAACP chapters in the state from the three in Charleston, Columbia, and Greenville in 1930 to eighty-six by 1954. Within a similar period of time the membership expanded from 800 to 14,237. Fear that whites would succeed in labeling the NAACP as Communist, such leaders as E. A. Adams, who taught De Laine at Allen University, used the pseudonym Negro Citizens Committee to mask their insurgent activities. Through this guise Adams and others convinced De Laine to start a NAACP chapter in Clarendon County in 1942. With assistance in 1943 from two other AME pastors, they recruited six supporters as endorsers for a NAACP charter. Because some reluctant black ministers withdrew their churches as possible meeting sites, the pastor at St. Mark AME Church in Summerton, Edward Frazier, opened the doors of his small parish to the NAACP.[10]

De Laine's illness, however, demoralized the chapter until he revived it in 1947 and gained a new charter in 1948. Additionally, he attended a seminar at Benedict College where a NAACP official, James Hinton, an Adams protégé who had urged De Laine to found a NAACP branch, spoke about racial inequality in the state's public schools. No South Carolinians, he lamented, had been willing to spearhead a test case about discrimination against black students in school bus transportation. As a pastor and principal in Clarendon County, De Laine volunteered to find plaintiffs for a suit. After meetings were held at some local AME churches, the ill-fated Pearson case emerged. Abandoned because of a technicality, De Laine, in cooperation with the national NAACP, developed *Harry Briggs Et Al* v. *Clarendon County Board Of Education.*[11]

The Briggs case landed in a federal district court in Charleston where a three judge panel heard arguments. In a two to one decision the court sustained the denial of bus transportation to Clarendon's black students. The lone dissenter, Judge J. Waites Waring, already on record for the desegregation of the College of Charleston and the University of South Carolina, declared in the Briggs case that "segregation in education can never produce equality." Such a system, he said, "is an evil that must be eradicated," and therefore "segregation is per se inequality." De Laine's push elicited this compelling legal language from Waring, and helped the NAACP

[10] Dennis C. Dickerson, *A Liberated Past: Explorations in AME Church History* (Nashville, TN, AME Sunday School Union, 2003), 185–186, Ophelia De Laine Gona, *Dawn of Desegregation: J. A. De Laine and Briggs V. Elliott* (Columbia, University of South Carolina Press, 2011), 18.
[11] Dickerson, *A Liberated Past*, 188.

in bundling the Briggs case with similar suits that the organization brought to the United States Supreme Court.[12]

The origin of the lead case coming out of Topeka, Kansas, resembled the Briggs suit in South Carolina. In both places AME clergy, situated far from the locus of ecclesiastical rank, responded to prodding from the NAACP to challenge school desegregation. The initial attack against Topeka's segregated public educational system started in 1948 when the president of the local NAACP challenged the adherence of school officials to the separate but equal doctrine of *Plessy* v. *Ferguson* (1896). In 1950 the branch secretary asked Walter White, the national executive director, to support a suit to end the segregated schools in the Kansas state capital, and as a result Robert L. Carter became the liaison between the national NAACP and its Topeka chapter.[13]

The branch secretary herself volunteered as a plaintiff on behalf of her daughter, whom she attempted to enroll at a white school close to their home. Additionally, Oliver L. Brown, who was not a NAACP member, was selected as a complainant. Though an assistant to the pastor at Topeka's St. John AME Church, Brown also worked as a unionized welder at the repair shops of the Atchison, Topeka and Santa Fe Railway. Hence, he was not subject to the same economic reprisals that could affect potential plaintiffs in more vulnerable occupations. Though described by some as lacking "militancy," another observer said that Brown "was no longer willing to accept second class citizenship" and now "wanted to be a whole man."[14]

Because Brown's daughter, Linda, walked to a segregated school that was nearly a mile from their residence, her father took her to a white school that was closer and better equipped. When Brown left the principal's office after a predictable rejection, he became "quite upset." He testified in 1951 at the US District Court for Kansas in *Brown* v. *Board of Education of Topeka* that he was a taxpayer and that his daughter had a right to attend a school nearest their home on a non-racial basis. Another seven plaintiffs gave similar testimonies. Nonetheless, a unanimous decision was delivered finding no discrimination in the Topeka public schools. Hence, the Briggs and Brown cases, filed within two months of each other, together with suits from Prince Edward County, Virginia, Washington DC, and Delaware landed as a

[12] Tinsley E. Yarborough, *A Passion for Justice: J. Waties Waring* (New York, Oxford University Press, 1987), 172–173, 196.
[13] Richard Kluger, *Simple Justice: The History of Brown* v. *Board of Education and Black America's Struggle for Equality* (New York, Alfred Knopf, 1975), 392–394.
[14] Ibid., 395.

unified suit at the US Supreme Court. The ultimate ruling on May 17, 1954 in the combined cases, whose shortened title was *Brown* v. *Board of Education* et al., declared as unconstitutional public school segregation.[15]

De Laine paid a heavy price for steering the Briggs case into the hands of the NAACP. In 1950, for example, Bishop Frank Madison Reid, Sr. transferred him to Lake City, South Carolina, where he would be lesser known and theoretically safer than in Clarendon County. Nonetheless, De Laine questioned the bishop on wisdom of this move because the area was known as a "KKK hole." Bishop Reid, however, refused to budge because the Lake City parish required a pastor of De Laine's experience and ability. Moreover, Reid reasoned that the NAACP, which now had the Briggs case, had sidelined De Laine. When E. A. Adams learned about the transfer, he recognized the irony, and told De Laine "Lake City is Hell. Just go on to Hell and God will bring you out all right."[16]

In October 1951 the De Laines' Summerton home was torched while local firemen looked on without offering any assistance. The De Laine property, they said, lay outside their jurisdiction. In Lake City, in the year following the Brown decision, a White Citizens Council was organized. The inaugural meeting drew "several hundred white men" who heard a lawyer declare that "the nigger preacher y'all are feeding is the real backbone of the desegregation movement. Y'all got to get rid of him before y'all can stop the others." That same night, De Laine's daughter recalled, "night riders took to their cars" and commenced their first act of vandalism by hurling a ketchup bottle onto the family residence. A few nights later a window was broken. Days later, rocks were thrown at the house. While he was away attending the 1955 Palmetto Annual Conference in Charleston, De Laine's church was set afire and "reduced almost to rubble." At this point Bishop Reid informed De Laine that Bishop Decatur Ward Nichols was offering him a church in the Northeast as an escape from South Carolina. De Laine refused, saying "I'd rather stay where I am and fight it out."[17]

Perhaps De Laine too hastily rebuffed these offers of rescue from the two bishops. Upon his return to Lake City, he heard rumors that he was unsafe. Despite entreaties from his wife, Mattie, and again from Bishop Reid to leave Lake City, De Laine, with a gun in hand, refused to be chased away. The harassment continued, however, with shooting around the minister's home. These ominous happenings in 1955 finally convinced him to flee and drive out of town "like a madman." In Florence, South Carolina, both NAACP and church officials facilitated his exit out of the state, enabling him to avoid a warrant for his arrest on a trumped up charge.[18]

De Laine arrived in Trenton, New Jersey, and from there Bishop Nichols drove him to New York City. Nichols' successor, Bishop George W. Baber, assigned him in 1956 to Buffalo, New York to organize the city's second AME congregation to accommodate transplanted South Carolinians. The congregation took the name De Laine-Waring AME Church to commemorate the crucial players in the *Briggs* v. *Elliot* case. Baber transferred De Laine to New Rochelle in 1957, and to Brooklyn in 1960, these being two congregations of modest size. Disappointed that more favorable pastoral appointments were unavailable to him, De Laine asserted bitterly that "it appears like what the church did for us was an extension of the work of the white citizens council." His failure to be elected as editor of the *AME Church Review* reinforced his hurt that AMEs would not reward him for his frontline involvement in the civil rights movement. Notwithstanding De Laine's long series of articles published in the *Christian Recorder* titled "Our Part in a Revolution," AMEs did not formally acknowledge his courageous adherence to their church's liberationist legacy.[19]

Brown, initially an unlikely warrior for black advancement, fared no better in becoming an AME hero deserving of denominational reward and recognition. He moved on from the ministerial staff at Topeka's St. John Church to the pastorate of the smaller St. Mark AME Church in another section of the city. While De Laine lived on until 1974, dying in his mid-seventies, Brown died prematurely in 1961 in his early forties. The ministry of Brown and De Laine, though disconnected in terms of ecclesiastical governance, conformed to what several commentators described as the rebirth of Allen's social insurgency. De Laine, for example, "hurled the first serious blow in modern times against [the] entrenched evil of school segregation" that embodied the Allen legacy.[20]

E. A. Adams, now the denomination's historiographer, "tipped his hand" in a volume he published in 1955. Though never mentioning De Laine, whom he counseled and helped to protect his real estate holdings, Adams expressed his unambiguous preference for an energized AME social holiness over an exclusive focus on insular institutional affairs. Hence, in the *Year Book and Historical Guide to the African Methodist Episcopal Church*, published during the era of burgeoning black civil rights militancy, Adams characterized the denomination as having a "long and colorful history of service to

[18] Ibid., 181–187, 189.   [19] Dickerson, *A Liberated Past*, 194–197.
[20] Howard D. Gregg, *The AME Church and the Current Negro Revolt*, (n.p., n.d.), 7, 17.

and redemption of a people." Perhaps his extensive interactions with De Laine moved him to say that within African Methodism "there is an even greater potential for service, redemption and Christian leadership within our church yet to be fulfilled." Sadie T. M. Alexander, the activist AME attorney, agreed. In 1952 she acknowledged De Laine's fight for "the elimination of segregated schools" and expressed her concern "for the safety of his life and that of his family" as terrorists "burned to the ground" his farm "and every building on it." Her Charleston informants told Alexander that "he is marked for death." Archibald J. Carey, Jr., the pastor at Quinn Chapel in Chicago and an alderman, validated the views of Adams and Alexander, saying that AME clergy should pattern their ministries after Richard Allen and become "dedicated not only to the calling of God but to the service of

Figure 6.1 AME bishops praying at the Supreme Court in commemoration of the *Brown* v. *Board of Education of Topeka* case outlawing school segregation. Standing, left to right: Bishops F. D. Jordan, H. T. Primm, W. R. Wilkes, I. H. Bonner, A. J. Allen, Frank M. Reid, Sr., Decatur Ward Nichols, S. L. Greene, R. R. Wright, Jr., G. W. Baber, Carey A. Gibbs, E. C. Hatcher, Joseph Gomez (Reprinted from Jeanette T. Johns, *The Upward Journey: A Centenarian's Chronicle: Personal Stories of Bishop Decatur Ward Nichols, Revered Clergyman of the African Methodist Episcopal Church* (Nashville, TN, AME Sunday School Union, 2002)

man." All AME ministers, Carey recommended, and also the laity, should be officers in their local NAACP and Urban League affiliates "and all other movements for civic improvement or human freedom."[21]

CARRIERS OF THE ALLEN ACTIVIST LEGACY

The civil rights movement drew from a minority of ministers and members largely exclusive of the episcopacy. Their visible leadership and participation in this new phase of the black freedom struggle established a sharp contrast between themselves and other AMEs who preferred involvement with the machinations of denominational politics, including efforts to reform church governance. The presence of critical clergy and laity in "the coming of age of civil rights" as a national issue showed these leaders to be both pivotal and indispensable. Though A. Philip Randolph, Sadie T. M. Alexander, and Archibald J. Carey, Jr. distinguished themselves in the separate spheres of grassroots mobilization and government advocacy, they played essential roles in advancing black civil rights. Their activism was informed by what E. A. Adams described as "translating [AME] History into Action" and fulfilling "the vision and greatness of [Richard] Allen and [Daniel A.] Payne."[22]

Randolph, through the March on Washington Movement (MOWM), introduced the methodology of grassroots mass mobilization into the black freedom struggle. This foundational technique, which mirrored Gandhian nonviolence, decisively influenced the civil rights movement. Having achieved a wartime Fair Employment Practices Committee, Randolph maintained this nonviolent strategy through the 1940s and 1950s to press for other civil rights objectives. In sustaining MOWM, Randolph also strengthened his clerical and church relationships and educated them about mass grassroots action.

MOWM, while monitoring FEPC's anti-discrimination activities in wartime defense industries, also opposed other acts of bias against African Americans. Several examples of racial violence in the South, for example,

[21] Gona, *Dawn of Desegregation*, 117; E. A. Adams, Sr. (Compiler and Ed.), *Year Book and Historical Guide to the African Methodist Episcopal Church* (Columbia, South Carolina, Bureau of Research and History, 1955), n.p.; Sadie T. M. Alexander, "Untitled Address, circa 1952," 12–13, *Sadie Tanner Mossell Alexander Papers*, Box 63, Folder 33, University Archives & Records Center, University of Pennsylvania, Philadelphia; Dickerson, *African American Preachers and Politics*, 83.
[22] See Harvard Sitkoff, "Harry Truman and the Election of 1948: The Coming of Age of Civil Rights in American Politics," *Journal of Southern History*, Vol. 37, 1971, 597–616; Adams, *Year Book and Historical Guide*, n.p.

convinced Randolph to mobilize prayer protests, especially among black preachers and parishes in New York City, to call attention to these deadly civil rights violations. Additionally, MOWM's initial emphasis on the FEPC had a derivative impact upon statewide initiatives to enact anti-employment discrimination statues. Despite a promise to Randolph from President Harry Truman that the agency would be "an integral part" of his postwar "reconversion program," the federal FEPC expired in 1946. This important MOWM initiative came to an end because a bill to establish it as a permanent agency received weak support from Truman, who allowed it to die without a fight in the US Senate.[23]

For this reason, John Adams, an AME presiding elder in the Nebraska Annual Conference and a senator in the state's unicameral legislature, revived the Randolph initiative. Adams replaced his son and namesake as a legislative representative of an Omaha district, and was elected and reelected six times starting in 1949. During his incumbency the presiding elder introduced a bill for a Nebraska FEPC, but was rebuffed because fellow legislators argued that municipal agencies would be more effective in ending employment discrimination. Whitney M. Young, Jr., the executive director of the Omaha Urban League between 1950 and 1953 and a member of St. John AME Church, understanding this subterfuge, proposed that the Omaha city council should pass a FEPC ordinance. The efforts of both Adams and Young, though unsuccessful, showed the reach of Randolph's influence.[24]

Randolph's push for grassroots pressure for government action to safeguard black rights continued in the 1950s and 1960s. With support from organized labor in 1957, he joined with Roy Wilkins of the NAACP and Martin Luther King, Jr., head of the newly founded Southern Christian Leadership Conference, in staging a grassroots Prayer Pilgrimage for Freedom in Washington DC. Randolph, who formally rejoined African Methodism in 1957 at Bethel Church in Harlem, drew ministerial support for the march and for its emphasis on securing the suffrage for disenfranchised African Americans. This pattern was replicated in 1963 in the massive March on Washington for Jobs and Freedom. Randolph, the titular head of the march, pitched the idea to the "Big Six" civil rights leaders in the NAACP, Congress of Racial Equality (CORE), Southern Christian Leadership

---

[23] Cynthia Taylor, *A. Philip Randolph: The Religious Journey of an African American Labor Leader* (New York, New York University Press, 2006), 151–153; William C. Berman, *The Politics of Civil Rights in the Truman Administration* (Columbus, Ohio State University Press, 1970), 33–34.

[24] Dennis C. Dickerson, *Religion, Race, and Region: Research Notes on AME Church History* (Nashville, TN, AME Sunday School Union, 1995) 109–110.

Conference (SCLC), National Urban League (NUL), Student Nonviolent Coordinating Committee (SNCC), and the National Council of Negro Women, and they attracted broad-base support from labor, religious, and other activist organizations. The 250,000 marchers exerted public pressure upon Congress to enact President John F. Kennedy's omnibus civil rights proposals. Lyndon B. Johnson, the successor to his martyred predecessor, signed this landmark legislation into law on July 2, 1964 in part thanks to the Randolph-inspired march.[25]

Just as Randolph stirred grassroots blacks in pressing for their civil rights, Sadie T. M. Alexander helped in mobilizing federal support for these same objectives. During the 1940s Alexander, beyond her role as a major attorney for the AMEs, became increasingly influential through involvements in the NAACP, NUL, the National Council of Negro Women, and the National Bar Association. Visibility in these major black organizations together with her experience as assistant city solicitor in Philadelphia made her a compelling choice in 1947 for the President's Committee on Civil Rights. President Truman received from the panel a hard-hitting report, *To Secure These Rights*, which laid bare with blunt descriptions the indignities and discriminatory practices imposed on African Americans. Alexander and Channing Tobias, a Christian Methodist Episcopal (CME) minister and a high-level Young Men's Christian Association official, the only two blacks out of the fifteen on the commission, communicated with black organizations to solicit their input into their investigations.[26]

Alexander, a board member of the NUL, pressed the committee administrator to invite testimony from this major organization. She insisted "that the League [should] have an opportunity to present the result of its 35 years in the field of industrial relations." Alexander was alarmed that "not a single organization working in the field of Negro concern has submitted a memorand[um]." Moreover, Alexander used her leverage to urge federal intervention into a case of anti-black violence. She told the committee chair about a lynching in Greenville, South Carolina, and said that "if the Justice Department had a division equipped with men skilled in the law involving civil rights," then inept FBI agents could surrender these investigations to legal professionals. Specifically, Alexander wanted officials in the Department of Justice to recommend the elevation of civil rights out of the Criminal Division into a special Division of Civil Rights headed by an

[25] Taylor, *A. Philip Randolph*, 176–179, 203–218.
[26] Francille Rusan Wilson, "Sadie T. M. Alexander: A 'True Daughter' of the AME Church," *AME Church Review*, Vol. 119, No. 391, July–September 2003, 44–45.

assistant attorney general. The opening of regional offices in various parts of the South would bolster the effectiveness of the division and would signal increased federal scrutiny of civil rights violations. She proposed that African Americans should flood the president with communications to "let him know it is their will" that these actions should be taken. Alexander also wanted Truman "to appoint a permanent committee on civil rights" to continue the work of their special task force.[27]

Alexander described her participation on the Truman panel as "one of the greatest privileges of my life." G. James Fleming of the Race Relations department of the American Friends Service Committee (AFSC) acknowledged her "very vigorous role on the committee" and praised the "straightforward, thorough-going, and challenging" report that drew from the panel's investigations. Alexander, while functioning in a federal bureaucratic setting, helped to amplify black civil rights as an urgent issue in the US body politic.[28]

While Alexander served on the Truman panel, the welfare of African Methodism was never far from her consciousness. Fall out from the 1946 special session of the General Conference again plunged the denomination into the Court of Appeals to fight an injunction to stop a meeting of the Council of Bishops. Though a court decree allowed the bishops to convene, Alexander, who was their attorney, recalled that the suit was "consuming all of my time and energy" and was preoccupying her five stenographers in typing "various briefs and pleadings." Hence, Alexander, because of the AME litigation, declined to attend an honorific dinner feting her for accomplishments on the Truman committee and in other spheres of civil rights activity. "When the very existence of my church is threatened," she told Channing Tobias, no "personal tribute" would preempt her effort "to adequately protect my church." The heritage of sovereignty and social holiness, the two complementary characteristics of African Methodism, mattered much to Alexander, and both required and received from her energized involvements. Similar commitments also drove Archibald J. Carey, Jr., who, like Randolph and Alexander, contributed much to civil rights advancements.[29]

[27] Sadie T. M. Alexander to Lester B. Granger, February 26, 1947; Sadie T. M. Alexander to Robert K. Carr, March 15, 1947; Alexander to Carr, April 28, 1947; Box 39, Folder 39; Alexander to William H. Gray, Jr., November 10, 1947, Box 39, Folder 40, *Alexander Papers, UARC*, University of Pennsylvania, Philadelphia, PA.

[28] Alexander to Gray, November 10, 1947, Box 39, Folder 40; G. James Fleming to Sadie T. M. Alexander, November 7, 1947, UPT 50 A3745/Truman Commission Scrapbook, Oversize Box 4, *Alexander Papers, UARC*, University of Pennsylvania, Philadelphia.

[29] Alexander to Channing H. Tobias, February 18, 1947, Box 39, Folder 39, *Alexander Papers, UARC*, University of Pennsylvania, Philadelphia.

Carey, immersed in AME affairs, like Alexander, held two successive pastorates in Chicago, served as a delegate to AME General Conferences, and was elected president of the Connectional Council. His activism, which ranged from advocacy of grassroots mass mobilization to eliciting civil rights measures from government, reflected tactics that Randolph and Alexander respectively pursued. Beyond his support of Randolph's MOWM, Carey's political activities mandated the same grassroots mobilization that protest marches generated. Hence, his candidacy for the Board of Alderman in Chicago in 1947 required him to organize potential constituents and community groups to push for his election. With his parishioners at Woodlawn AME Church as his political base, Carey extended his reach in the Third Ward to an interdenominational clientele and to a variety of African American civic and labor groups. After beating a fellow AME, Carey focused in 1948 on banning racial discrimination in publicly aided housing. Though the Carey Ordinance was not enacted, he gained a national reputation for forthright civil rights advocacy.[30]

National Republicans, mainly because of energetic black officeholders and candidates, hammered Democrats on their vulnerable civil rights record. They especially focused on the failure of President Truman to press Congress on a permanent FEPC and the persistent practice of levying poll taxes to prevent blacks from voting in the Democratic-dominated South. In a bold move in 1950 the GOP sponsored four black candidates for Congress running on platforms of invigorated civil rights advocacy. Besides the two contenders in Philadelphia and New York City, the other two were AME clergy, William Hodge in Cleveland and Carey in Chicago. All of them lost, with Carey defeated by a well-entrenched black Democratic congressman, William L. Dawson. Because he retained his position as alderman, Carey remained as one of the few GOP officeholders in Cook County, Illinois. He was well positioned, therefore, to speak at the 1952 Republican National Convention that met in Chicago.[31]

Carey's speech, a fortuitous classic and template for Martin Luther King, Jr.'s more famous "I Have a Dream" oration, reviewed why Republicans were better on civil rights than the Democrats and why the GOP should reclaim its historic role as protectors of black freedom and guardians of the rights of other populations of color. African Americans, like other Americans, sang with patriotic fervor:

[30] Dickerson, *African American Preachers and Politics*, 95–103.
[31] Ibid., 105–111, 117.

My country 'tis of thee
Sweet land of liberty
Of Thee I sing.
Land where my fathers died
Land of the pilgrim's pride
From every mountain side
Let freedom ring.

He then added:

That's exactly what we mean-from every mountain side, let freedom ring.
    Not only from the Green Mountains and the White Mountains of
Vermont and New Hampshire; not only from the Catskills of New York;
but from the Ozarks in Arkansas, from the Stone Mountain in Georgia,
from the Great Smokies of Tennessee and from the Blue Ridge Mountains
of Virginia – Not only for the minorities of the United States, but for the
persecuted of Europe, for the rejected of Asia, for the disfranchised of South
Africa and for the dis-inherited of all the earth-may the Republican Party
under God, from every mountain side, LET FREEDOM RING![32]

For Carey, pursuing black civil rights through partisan involvements, with
validation from energized black voters in Chicago's Third Ward, led him to
vest high hopes in the GOP presidential candidate Dwight D. Eisenhower.
Because Carey backed a winner, he was appointed to a brief term as
Alternate Delegate to the United Nations between September 12 and December 9, 1953. In 1955, Eisenhower asked Carey to serve as vice chair of the
newly impaneled President's Committee on Government Employment
Policy. The group was charged to investigate and settle cases of racial and
religious discrimination in federal employment. When the chair died in 1957,
Carey succeeded him and thus became one of the highest-ranking African
Americans in Ike's presidential administration. Carey held hearings across
the country and he personally intervened to settle sundry cases of racial
injustice. He believed that his historic meeting with the president and his
cabinet in 1960 to outline plans for increased cooperation with departments
and agencies in rooting out discriminatory practices within the federal
bureaucracy counted as a notable achievement. Despite the effectiveness of
Randolph's methodology of grassroots mass mobilization, Carey, like Alexander's role in the Truman administration, leveraged his position in the
Eisenhower presidency to promote government employment equity for
African Americans.[33]

[32] Ibid., 119.   [33] Ibid., 132, 134–137.

Randolph was right in observing that the grassroots mass mobilization could draw upon the untapped energies of black churches to invigorate opposition to legalized segregation. His prayer protests and ministerial alliances in the 1940s presaged in the 1950s an unexpected convergence between growing black impatience with the daily indignities of Jim Crow and the rise of southern black congregations determined to protect militant ministers and members in their challenge to segregated structures. Black churches constituted a base of support for newly organized community-based groups that replaced NAACP chapters recently outlawed by southern state legislatures. Hence, these organizations, with black churches behind them, helped to fund a succession of bus boycotts in southern cities that applied effective economic pressure upon once smug defenders of white supremacy.

Aldon Morris correctly credits black churches as the funding source for the mass mobilization that lay behind clergy-led boycotts starting in Baton Rouge in 1953, Montgomery in 1955, and Tallahassee in 1956. AMEs, along with ministers and members in other religious bodies, played crucial roles within this grassroots phase of the civil rights movement. Rosa McCauley Parks in Montgomery and King Solomon Du Pont in Tallahassee were among the indispensable contributors to the growing black militancy against Jim Crow.[34]

Rosa Parks has been immortalized as the "mother of the modern civil rights movement" because of her brave refusal to relinquish her seat to a white man on a Montgomery bus on December 1, 1955. This single act of defiance galvanized the city's black population, who saw her arrest as the "final straw" in a long series of discourtesies and discriminatory treatment by the Montgomery City Lines. A bus boycott was called and was coordinated by the newly formed Montgomery Improvement Association and its charis-matic president, Martin Luther King, Jr. Notwithstanding King's leadership role and the NAACP's Supreme Court suit, *Gayle v. Browder*, which invali-dated Alabama's Jim Crow statues on November 13, 1956, Parks was import-ant beyond her symbolic standing in her local community.

The Parks encounter on the Montgomery bus, though unplanned, was grounded in two decades of activism in Alabama that owed, in part, to her AME heritage. Parks, from her hometown congregation, Mount Zion in Pine Level, to St. Paul Church in Montgomery, regularly attended services and imbibed the message that Jesus Christ died for the sins of humanity, and for

[34] Aldon Morris, *The Origins of the Civil Rights Movement* (New York, Free Press, 1984), 1–76.

that reason Richard Allen stood for the dignity of African Americans. Therefore, AMEs were obliged to correct the blot of slavery and racial injustice in God's creation. Just as Christ redeemed humankind from personal sin, believers were charged with removing sin from their surroundings. Hence, Parks, who as a stewardess at her Montgomery church prepared the Eucharist for consecration and distribution by her pastor, experienced personal renewal through her participation in the sacrament. In seeking the same renewal in her surroundings, she reenacted this ritual through her NAACP activities and pursued societal renewal by challenging segregation.

Parks embodied in the Montgomery movement years of previous civil rights involvements that contributed to the successful bus boycott. When she met Raymond Parks, whom she married in 1932, he was participating in the National Committee to Defend the Scottsboro Boys, the persecuted black men who had been unjustly convicted for the rape of two perjured white women. Her husband, said one biographer, "helped to radicalize Rosa Parks during the Great Depression" with talk about "NAACP strategies for helping blacks win the right to vote and gain entry to local hospitals" in Alabama. Rosa Parks was similarly aware that President Franklin D. Roosevelt had integrated military bases such as Maxwell Field in Montgomery, where she in 1941 was employed as a secretary. The irony of riding on a segregated bus to a federal job at an integrated facility was not lost on Parks.[35]

Parks's experience with integration led to her defiance of bus driver James F. Blake in 1943. Blake was known as a tobacco spitting "vicious bigot" who regularly "cursed at 'nigras' just for the fun of it." He insulted black women by calling them "bitch" and "coon." Parks, already familiar with his antiblack vulgarity, refused to obey his order to disembark from the bus, after paying her fare and reboarding through a rear door. Coincidentally, Blake's bus was the same one she boarded in 1955, though in the intervening years Parks made a point to avoid him.[36]

The denial of voting rights to African Americans motivated Parks in the 1940s to join the NAACP. At the Montgomery Branch she became involved immediately in a voter registration drive. Twice in 1943 she tried to register and again in 1944. Astonishingly, Parks was told that despite having a 1933 high school diploma, she flunked a literacy test. Wise to the subterfuges that had been used to prevent her registration, Parks circumvented them and

[35] Douglas Brinkley, *Rosa Parks* (New York, A Lipper/Viking Book, 2000), 40–42, 44.
[36] Ibid., 57–60.

passed the test in 1945. She paid the poll tax and voted in the state's 1946 gubernatorial election.[37]

Parks's militancy in the 1940s, while evident in her determination to vote and to defy bus driver Blake, escalated in a more daring encounter with racial violence in the case of Recy Taylor in Abbeville, Alabama, in 1944. After leaving a church service, Taylor, married and the mother of an infant, accompanied two other blacks, a mother and son, on the journey to their respective homes. Surprisingly, seven armed white men drove toward them to accost Taylor, and accused her of assaulting a white boy in a nearby town. Despite her denial and efforts by her male companion to protect her, Taylor was pushed into the car and driven to a remote location. She was ordered to disrobe while a rifle was pointed at her. Six men took turns to rape her. When the news of the crime reached the office of the Montgomery NAACP, local president E. D. Nixon sent Branch Secretary Parks to Henry County to investigate. Parks, after speaking with Taylor, established the Alabama Committee for Equal Justice for Mrs. Recy Taylor.[38]

Though racially flawed judicial proceedings scuttled the Taylor case, Parks tried to mobilize alliances with several groups such as the Southern Negro Youth Congress, whose members included a professor and president of Tuskegee Institute. These affiliations helped to spread information about the egregious treatment that Taylor received in the local court. Coverage of the case was also transmitted through the *Pittsburgh Courier* and the *Chicago Defender*. Parks's committee, despite charges against it as a Communist front organization, persisted in its national campaign to publicize how sexualized violence victimized black women. Though Alabama state officials never intervened in the Taylor case and allowed her attackers to escape conviction, these experiences matured Parks into a seasoned organizer and activist.[39]

Even before the Montgomery bus boycott ended, AMEs at the 1956 General Conference hailed Parks as a denominational heroine. According to Bishop George W. Baber, a former pastor at Ebenezer in Detroit and a 1940s veteran of the city's civil rights committee, Parks reenacted what Richard Allen had done in 1787. "Richard Allen's spirit walked out at Philadelphia," the bishop declared, "and more recently he walked out in Montgomery." Additionally,

[37] Ibid., 40–42, 47, 50, 56, 60.
[38] Danielle L. McGuire, *At the Dark End of the Street: Black Women, Rape, and Resistance – A New History of the Civil Rights Movement From Rosa Parks to the Rise of Black Power* (New York, Alfred Knopf, 2010), xv–xvii, 13.
[39] Ibid., 13–16, 26, 36.

Bishop Isaiah H. Bonner introduced the Reverend Ralph W. Hilson, the pastor at Montgomery's St. John Church AME Church, "who spoke on 'The Battle of Montgomery'" and recounted the contributions of Rosa Parks, "a Stewardess of the AME Church." He asserted "that 50,000 people of Montgomery walked off the bus with her." Hilson, a member of the Montgomery Improvement Association executive board, also solicited monies for the boycott in the North and mobilized support from Alabama AMEs for those who would "walk in dignity rather than ride in shame."[40]

Despite the pride in Parks from Baber and Hilson, these denominational cheerleaders defined her narrowly in symbolic terms, thus sidestepping, perhaps unwittingly, her long and daring experience as a fighter against Jim Crow. Sitting in the General Conference audience as these tributes were paid to an absent Rosa Parks was King Solomon DuPont, a delegate from the Florida Annual Conference. He was present at the Miami meeting three weeks before two female students from the all black Florida A & M University defied segregation statutes and sat in the white section of a Tallahassee bus. To support the student boycott, the Reverend C. K. Steele, a Baptist pastor, organized the Inter Civic Council (ICC). DuPont, a fellow ICC organizer, was elected vice president. Likely, he understood better than the other AMEs on the General Conference podium the deeper importance of Parks's activism and that of his own.[41]

Just as the example of Parks's Klan-hating grandfather helped to ignite her militancy, DuPont's restive slave grandfather influenced his grandson's defiance of his city's Jim Crow transit system. Their activist lineage, stretching three generations back to slavery, indelibly affected Parks and DuPont. Reared in the household of his grandfather Edwards, a mulatto and former slave, Parks observed his challenge to racial mores, such as firmly shaking hands with whites and insisting that they call him by his surname. His contempt for white supremacy also showed through his loaded rifle whenever Ku Klux Klan (KKK) violence threatened him. Perhaps his support of Marcus Garvey and black nationalism presaged Parks's later sympathies for the militancy of Malcolm X.[42]

---

[40] "Official Minutes of the Thirty-Fifth Session of the General Conference of the African Methodist Episcopal Church which convened in Miami, Florida, May 1956 at Dinner Key Auditorium," in *Combined Minutes of the General Conferences*, 338, 384; Gregg, *The AME Church and the Current Negro Revolt*, 31.

[41] "Official Minutes . . . General Conference, 1956," 321; Glenda Alice Rabby, *The Pain and the Promise: The Struggle for Civil Rights in Tallahassee, Florida* (Athens, University of Georgia Press, 1999), 16, 22.

[42] Brinkley, *Rosa Parks*, 22–25, 191–193.

Figure 6.2 King Solomon Dupont, Tallahassee bus boycott leader, 1956; pastor of Fountain Chapel AME Church, Tallahassee (from the Florida Memory State Library & Archives and offered under the Creative Commons Public Domain, Mark 1.0)

Similarly, DuPont's civil rights involvements drew from his recalcitrant grandfather, whom he said "resented the whole idea of slavery." Despite having his owner's name, Archie Skulls, he escaped, along with his brother, to a swamp that became for them like a maroon. After being there for several months, the brother returned, and Skulls, who remained at large for a little while longer, also came back. He did not plan, however, to stay a slave. A deal with his owner allowed him, after finishing his daily chores, to hire out to split fence rails. These wages enabled him to buy his freedom, and at his master's request to change his name, after a divine revelation, to King Solomon DuPont. The site where DuPont prayed became family property and the name passed on to a third generation. This apocryphal account energized the Reverend King Solomon DuPont and convinced him "to dislike discrimination in any form."[43]

As a Tallahassee bus boycott leader, DuPont, who served as pastor of Fountain Chapel AME Church from 1950 to 1958, endured police interrogations about ICC operations. When municipal officials offered a compromise of "first come, first served" within the same segregated seating system,

[43] *Washington Afro-American*, October 2, 1956.

DuPont described it as merely "a step toward an agreement." Steele and ICC's 1,000 assembled followers, however, rejected any segregated arrangement and DuPont agreed. In fact, when the buses stopped running, DuPont assured boycotters that the ICC had enough station wagons, drivers, and dispatchers to accommodate Tallahassee's 10,000 boycott supporters. Moreover, he asserted that if the carpools ceased to operate, "I wouldn't ride the bus" even if whites sat on the top of the bus and let blacks take the seats. On another occasion, as boycott solidarity waned, DuPont declared his preference to "die and go to Hell before he would ride the bus again."[44]

In December 1956, after seven months, the boycott ended. Nonetheless, fines had been levied upon some ICC officers for their involvement with carpools that were used to transport boycotters. The integrated seating that the Supreme Court mandated a few months earlier in the Montgomery case also affected Tallahassee. DuPont was emboldened to seek election to the city commission in 1957. Because racial threats were hurled at him, Fountain Chapel members volunteered to guard the DuPont residence. Though he lost the election, his tally of 2,405 votes included an astonishing eighty-seven votes from whites.[45]

In different spheres of activity through their involvements in a range of organizations, AMEs in particular locales, like Parks in Montgomery and DuPont in Tallahassee, played pivotal roles in the civil rights movement. Though hardly singular in their significance in these respective communities, such activists as Daisy Bates in Little Rock, John H. Wheeler in Durham, and Andrew White in Nashville became indispensable leaders in advancing black civil rights. After the Supreme Court's Brown decision, Daisy Bates, the State President of the Arkansas NAACP since 1952, expressed cautious optimism for compliance because the Little Rock school board offered a gradual plan for desegregation. The Arkansas NAACP Legal Defense Committee, however, sued the school district in a federal appeals court demanding in 1957 the immediate integration of Little Rock schools. When Governor Orval Faubus ordered state troops to prevent nine black students from entering Little Rock's Central High School, Bates became the adviser to the students. She opened her home as their headquarters, requested police protection for them, and asked clergy to be their escorts.[46]

---

[44] Ibid.; Rabby, *The Pain and the Promise*, 22, 29, 42.
[45] Rabby, *The Pain and the Promise*, 60–61.
[46] Daisy Bates, *The Long Shadow of Little Rock* (New York, David McKay Company, 1962), 47, 49, 52, 62, 65–66, 89).

The students came to the Bates home each day after school to debrief about their encounters. In this context she hosted James M. Lawson, Jr., the southern regional secretary for the FOR and a minister in the all black Central Jurisdiction of the Methodist Episcopal Church. Lawson, like Bates, listened to the nine students about their daily experiences and then advised them about how to handle the harassment of white students, many of them egged on by outside adult racists. When Minnijean Brown was expelled for retaliating against the physical abuse and verbal taunts of these white students, Bates enlisted Drs. Kenneth and Mamie Phipps Clark to arrange her transfer to the private New Lincoln School in New York City. Bates and three of the Little Rock Nine, including Ernest Green, Melba Patillo, and Gloria Ray, drew encouragement from Rufus K. Young, their pastor at Little Rock's Bethel AME Church. Young, said one observer, took "a vigorous out-in-the-open pro-school integration stance." Z. Z. Driver, another AME pastor, was similarly militant in accompanying his parishioner, Minnijean Brown, and the other eight students to Central High.[47]

After President Dwight D. Eisenhower dispatched federal troops to compel the entry of the Little Nine into Central High, the local city council ordered Bates's arrest for refusing to reveal the names of NAACP members in accordance with a recently enacted ordinance. She was released on bond after police took her into custody. In addition to her arrest, Bates recalled that she was "singled out for 'special treatment'" or harassment. The KKK burned crosses on the Bates property, rocks were hurled into the house that she shared with her husband L. C. Bates, and gunshots were fired. Moreover, in Ouachita County, Arkansas she was twice hanged in effigy. Because of her frontline involvement in the Little Rock desegregation case, Daisy and L.C. Bates lost advertisers and other business for their outspoken newspaper, the *State Press*. Their business was forced to close in 1959. Pennie Esther Gibbs, the wife of Bishop Carey A. Gibbs, the AME prelate of Alabama, believed that the activism of Daisy Bates deserved recognition from AMEs. When the State of the Country report at the 1957 North Alabama Annual Conference failed to mention her name and her title as State President of the Arkansas NAACP, Gibbs objected and demanded an acknowledgement of Bates's civil rights leadership.[48]

[47] Ibid., 116–121; Dunbar H. Ogden, *My Father Said Yes: A White Pastor in Little Rock Integration* (Nashville, TN, Vanderbilt University Press, 2008), 37, 149; Gregg, *The AME Church and the Current Negro Revolt*, 24.
[48] Bates, *The Long Shadow of Little Rock*, 107–108, 110–111, 151–152, 176, 178; "Minutes of the Seventy-Ninth Annual Session of the North Alabama Conference of the African Methodist Episcopal Church held at Grant Chapel AME Church, Birmingham, Alabama, November

Like Bates, John Hervey Wheeler, while embedded in several business and black betterment pursuits in Durham, North Carolina, became a critical influence in its local civil rights struggles. Wheeler, the president since 1952 of the black Mechanics and Farmers Bank, while preferring ordered social change, recognized grassroots protest as a legitimate tactic to advance African Americans. Wheeler, who possessed an impressive AME pedigree, was born in North Carolina at the campus of Kittrell College. Both parents, John L. Wheeler, the president of the AME school, and Margaret Hervey Wheeler, had been educated at Wilberforce University. The elder Wheeler, whom W. E. B. Du Bois taught at Wilberforce, left Kittrell to become an agent in the Raleigh office of the Durham-based North Carolina Mutual Life Insurance Company. After a transfer to Atlanta, the Wheelers attended the populous Big Bethel AME Church and their son graduated from the local Morehouse College. The younger Wheeler then settled in Durham where he worked for North Carolina Mutual and ascended the hierarchy of Mechanics and Farmers Bank. Moreover, he became active as treasurer and trustee in Durham's St. Joseph AME Church where his wife, a physician's daughter, was nurtured.[49]

Like others in Durham's black elite, Wheeler participated in the 1940s in the Durham Committee on Negro Affairs, which focused on racial inequities in the local public schools and expanding black employment opportunities. When the Supreme Court decreed school desegregation in the Brown decision, Wheeler, as a member of the North Carolina Council on Human Relations, pressed the governor to empanel a committee to advise him on compliance. He also belonged to the North Carolina Commission on Interracial Cooperation, an affiliate of the Southern Regional Council (SRC). Such organizations, according to sociologist Aldon Morris, functioned as "movement halfway houses" that provided financial support and personnel to activist civil rights organizations. The SRC offered information through studies and surveys about the condition of the black population. Between 1954 and 1961 Wheeler served as the SRC treasurer. Promoting school desegregation and pushing state officials toward a speedy acquiescence to the Brown decision energized his SRC participation. His large presence in the North Carolina Democratic Party and in the SRC brought him to the

6–10, 1957," in *Combined Minutes of the 1957 Conferences of the Ninth Episcopal District (African Methodist Episcopal Church), Bishop Carey A. Gibbs* (Nashville, TN, AME Sunday School Union, n.d., 129.

[49] Brandon Kyron Lenzie Winford, "'The Battle for Freedom Begins Every Morning': John Hervey Wheeler, Civil Rights, and New South Prosperity," Ph.D. dissertation, University of North Carolina, Chapel Hill, 2014, 10, 21, 31, 37, 53–54, 65, 90–91, 115–117, 124–125, 410.

attention of newly elected President John F. Kennedy. Because of a SRC report that recommended various civil rights initiatives that the Kennedy administration should undertake, JFK appointed Wheeler in 1961 to the President's Committee on Equal Employment Opportunity.[50]

Notwithstanding, Wheeler's commitment to broadening black economic prospects, school desegregation remained core to his civil rights pursuits. This objective required support for ongoing court action and vigorous lobbying at the state and federal levels. This focus on public schools often influenced Wheeler's views on other tactics used to push black advancement. He backed, for example, the Royal Ice Cream sit-in in Durham in 1957 that a white Methodist minister, Doug Moore, also endorsed. A fellow St. Joseph Church member, William A. Marsh, Jr., acted as the attorney for the demonstrators who were arrested for trespassing. Moreover, Wheeler, as a member of the Durham Committee on Negro Affairs, vacillated about supporting the boycott because of possible white outrage that could damage school desegregation efforts. Nonetheless, he endorsed Durham's student sit-ins in 1960 by going to the site of the demonstrations and publicly declaring them as a valuable tool to fight for black equality, saying that student led movements deserved adult backing.[51]

Two clergy, W. H. Hall and Andrew White, explicitly identified with the moral methodology of nonviolence. Hall, the pastor of Zion Chapel AME Church in Hattiesburg, Mississippi, energized a local movement for civil rights, but enlisted outside experts to educate himself and other activists about nonviolent direct action. James M. Lawson, Jr. of the Fellowship of Reconciliation (FOR), as he had done in Little Rock, became a resource for Hall, the leader of the Mississippi Christian Movement Conference. In 1959 Hall attended in Atlanta the SCLC-sponsored Institute on Nonviolence and met Lawson, who commended him for his activism. "It was particularly good to see another Methodist minister," Lawson said, who was "active in the field of genuine racial change." Hall, a resident in a state notorious for its racial brutality, was special to Lawson because "as I travel about the South, I have discovered that far too few Methodist ministers are concerned for this area which does so much harm to the South." He thought that Hall might be interested in

[50] Ibid., 3, 156, 167–170, 229–230, 341–342; Morris, *The Origins of the Civil Rights Movement*, 139–173.

[51] Winford, "The Battle for Freedom Begins Every Morning," 285–286, 290–292, 295–298, 318; *A Celebration of Life for William A. Marsh, Jr.*, Funeral Program, November 24, 2018, St. Joseph AME Church, Durham, North Carolina.

hearing Lawson on "the biblical-theological basis to nonviolence," a topic that was "neglected in our Institute."[52]

Lawson asked Hall to settle on a date to travel to Hattiesburg and indicate "what kind of leadership you expect me to give." Lawson planned to discuss "What is the Gospel Amid Racial Hatred?" to preface a discussion about nonviolence. When he came for the workshop, however, "the attendance was small." Because he remained impressed with Hall, Lawson promised a follow-up visit in the hope that the pastor would use "basic Christian methods of evangelism" to elicit a better response from residents, especially from the clergy. He told Hall that he would conduct "another workshop on nonviolence for local people in your city or simply for the members of your church?" Lawson also tantalized Hall with a possible lecture on "some good Wesleyan history" maybe "on John Wesley and his handling of conflict." Lawson's eagerness to work with Hall seemed urgent. The pastor's recent reassignment to Hattiesburg in 1959 by Bishop Frederick D. Jordan, a civil rights advocate, "means that for at least another year, you are in the city where you have some roots from which to work."[53]

As a general officer in charge of Christian education, Andrew White occupied an office in Nashville, Tennessee, at the denomination's international publishing house. Additionally, he had been licensed to preach in Washington DC by Charles H. Wesley, the well-known presiding elder and educator. Moreover, White and Kelly Miller Smith, pastor of Nashville's First Baptist Church, Capitol Hill, matriculated at the School of Religion at Howard University at different times during the incumbency of Benjamin E. Mays, Howard Thurman, and William Stuart Nelson. These scholars emphasized the training of an "insurgent Negro professional clergy" committed to the destruction of Jim Crow energized by the moral methodology of Gandhian nonviolence. Grassroots mobilization, which White undoubtedly learned at Howard, depended on "Christian nonviolent direct mass action," a praxis that blended with his understanding of Allenite activism. Richard Allen, he said, identified with his "dehumanized" followers who "needed to be organized and needed to have a Christian guiding principle of action." White claimed that "the AME Church has never strayed from the course charted by Richard

[52] James M. Lawson, Jr. to W. H. Hall, August 4, 1959, FOR I, FOR Out 1959 Folder, Box 36, *James M. Lawson, Jr. Papers*, Vanderbilt University Special Collections and University Archives, Nashville, TN.
[53] Lawson to Hall, August 4, 1959; James M. Lawson, Jr. to W. H. Hall, August 31, 1959; James M. Lawson, Jr. to W. H. Hall, October 21, 1959, FOR I, FOR Out 1959, Box 36, VUSCUA.

Allen" in "fearless battles against the enemies of human dignity and civil liberties."[54]

White and Smith in 1957 traveled to Atlanta for the inaugural meeting of the SCLC. Impressed with the Montgomery Improvement Association that sustained the 381-day bus boycott and other local organizations that jointly launched the SCLC, the two clergymen returned to their city to establish in 1958 the Nashville Christian Leadership Conference (NCLC). With Smith as president and White as secretary, the NCLC became the organizational umbrella for the student sit-ins at Nashville's downtown department store lunch counters from February 13 to May 10, 1960. With sponsorship from NCLC and FOR, James M. Lawson, Jr. conducted nonviolent workshops that trained students for their successful encounters with business and civic officials and with the violent defenders of Jim Crow.[55]

In 1963 White, after he served as financial secretary and second vice president, succeeded Smith as NCLC president. He observed that the persistence of segregation required a fresh emphasis on black economic development. He also believed that NCLC should redouble its efforts to attract "a mass of people" to the organization. To address this issue, he urged in 1964 that black churches in Nashville should play a larger role in "rallying the masses." Additionally, White doubled down on NCLC's commitment to nonviolence, saying that the group "was waging a nonviolent conscience pricking battle against racial injustice and segregation."[56]

White, who pushed for broader black employment in local and state government and cooperation with SCLC's operation economic division, Operation Breadbasket, said little to AMEs beyond his locale about his frontline civil rights leadership. In his widely read 1965 publication, *Know Your Church*, White included a section on "The Desegregation Fight." He heralded Bishops Frank Madison Reid, Sr. in South Carolina and Frederick D. Jordan in Mississippi and Louisiana for never yielding "one inch of ground" to white segregationists. Yet White, unlike Bates who in 1962 published *The Long Shadow of Little Rock*, said nothing about his sustained participation in the consequential Nashville Movement. It seemed more important to White to celebrate the denomination's episcopal leadership

---

[54] Randall M. Jelks, "Benjamin Elijah Mays and the Creation of an Insurgent Negro Professional Clergy," *AME Church Review*, Vol. 108, No. 387, July–September 2002, 32–38; Dennis C. Dickerson, *African Methodism and Its Wesleyan Heritage: Reflections on AME Church History* (Nashville, TN, AME Sunday School Union, 2009), 192; Andrew White, *Know Your Church Manual* (Nashville, TN, AME Sunday School Union, 1965), 8–9.

[55] Dickerson, *African Methodism and its Wesleyan Heritage*, 187–188.   [56] Ibid., 188–189, 192.

rather than the diverse strands of Allenite activism that he, Bates, and Wheeler embodied.[57]

CRAFTING AN INSTITUTIONAL RESPONSE TO
THE CIVIL RIGHTS MOVEMENT

Notwithstanding the tensions between denominational politicians and social activists and the efforts of some who overlapped both categories, AME leadership could scarcely ignore the burgeoning civil rights movement. Pressing issues and interactions with movement leaders, some of whom were AME ministers and members, compelled the denomination's cooperation and financial support in ending Jim Crow. For example, Walter White, executive director of the NAACP, addressed the 1952 General Conference about the "Race Question" and how the two world wars "destroyed forever [the concept of] racial superiority. Now the struggle included opposition to Communism, colonialism, and race prejudice. He proudly announced that southern blacks were surmounting the hurdle of poll taxes, with 125,000 of them obtaining "poll tax receipts for voting." In response Bishop Joseph Gomez "pledged the support of the great AME Church to the NAACP."[58]

In a later session Bishop Reid presented Judge J. Waites Waring. Already, in 1950, J. S. Brookens, editor of the *AME Church Review*, praised Waring for a decision that "broke the back of the white Democratic primary." Brookens declared that "it is the work Divinity for a South Carolina white judge" who "opened the doors of the Democratic Party to all citizens regardless of color, not only in the South Carolina, but throughout the South." In his lone dissent in 1952 in the Clarendon County suit in *Briggs* v. *Elliott*, however, Waring laid a foundation for the Supreme Court's Brown decision two years later, Waring repeated to delegates that segregated schools "can never be equal." In his address "The Church and Social Justice," Waring told AMEs that both political parties should assert in their platforms their unequivocal opposition to racial discrimination. Moreover, he said, "we've got to find out where candidates stand on Civil Rights before we endorse anyone." Because "two-thirds of the world is made up of dark-skinned people," the United States should recognize that "true democracy" was undermined "when this

---

[57] Ibid., 189–190; White, *Know Your Church*, 84–85.
[58] "Official Minutes of the Thirty-Fourth Session of the General Conference of the African Methodist Episcopal Church held at Chicago, IL, May 1952," in *Combined Minutes of the General Conferences*, 169.

evil [racial discrimination] exists in our nation." Both parties should also "deplore and condemn all attempts to discriminate for or against any of our citizens by reason of religion, race, or ancestry." This meant a guarantee of the right to vote, equal employment opportunity, and "the right to security of person and property." Building on President Harry Truman's 1948 executive order to desegregate the military, Waring called for "the immediate integration of all personnel in all of the armed services." He also advocated provisions in all federal contracts against racial bias. Delegate Archibald J. Carey, Jr., after praising the judge, "moved that the General Conference" should adopt Waring's proposals.[59]

Waring's address synthesized what was already a consensus among AMEs. In the 1952 presidential election year, the Indiana Annual Conference, for example, declared that "the party or candidate who thinks enough of human rights to speak in definite terms regarding Civil Rights and the FEPC" would get "the Negro vote." They also recognized that Supreme and Truman administration actions in attacking poll taxes, ensuring access to previously all white public colleges and universities, and ending race restrictive covenants in housing and military desegregation showed recent gains in black civil rights. The Indiana conferees also noted that the "USA is a long way from attaining the brotherhood of man."[60]

When Bishop Bonner acknowledged Alabama's AME activists at the 1956 General Conference, he reflected the denomination's broader awareness that the civil rights movement was "up and running." Though the Reverend Fred Shuttlesworth, the state's most militant opponent of Jim Crow, while abandoning his early AME affiliation to become a Baptist, found allies in Birmingham in his former denomination with Samuel M. Davis, a pastor, W. E. Shortridge, a mortician, and A. G. Gaston, the millionaire businessman and AME general officer. Besides Rosa Parks, Bonner also recognized Autherine Lucy, who had just desegregated the University of Alabama and Nathaniel Howard of Tuscaloosa, who rescued Lucy from a mob opposed to her court ordered enrollment. Bishop Carey A. Gibbs, Alabama's AME prelate, gestured toward this militant mood. He impaneled a committee at the 1957 North Alabama Annual Conference to write a resolution "protesting inhuman practices and other evils directed against colored people in

[59] J. S. Brookens, "Judge Waring," *AME Church Review*, Vol. 59, No. 164, January–March 1950, 5; *Official Minutes of the Thirty-Fourth Session of the General Conference, 1952*, 192–193.
[60] *Official Minutes of the 114th Annual Session of the Indiana Conference of the African Methodist Episcopal Church* held in Allen Temple AME Church, Marion, IN, September 24–28, 1952 (n.p., n.d.), 52–53.

Alabama." Gibbs instructed the group, after a conference vote, to send the resolution to Governor James "Big Jim" Folsom.[61]

Bonner's nod to Parks and Lucy mirrored other stands taken at the 1956 General Conference that showed AMEs as supportive and conversant with pressing civil rights issues. The episcopal address advocated a permanent FEPC, and delegates approved resolutions calling for a Civil Rights Committee of the AME Church. In enacting a resolution in favor of "desegregation," AMEs readied themselves for a speech from Thurgood Marshall of the NAACP Legal Defense Fund. Marshall, the head counsel who argued the Brown case, addressed the AME assembly on "Desegregation and Discrimination" in which he "gave a factual discourse" about achieving integration. After the speech, the AME treasurer and delegates then serving as NAACP branch presidents lifted an offering for the organization. Bishop Sherman L. Greene, Sr. announced that another offering for the NAACP would be collected on the following day. Moreover, Bishop Reid "urged all to join [the] organization."[62]

Marshall's presentation affirmed the view of some AMEs that the Brown decision would encounter stiff resistance and unanticipated consequences. AMEs in the Colorado Annual Conference believed that hostility to Brown was "the dying economy of white supremacy." Martha Jayne Keys, a Louisville pastor and delegate to the 1956 General Conference, commented at the 1954 West Kentucky Annual Conference that the Brown decision was stirring opposition. Her concern was focused, however, on "what will become of our race teachers? Will they be integrated into white schools?"[63]

Additionally, massive resistance in Prince Edward County, Virginia, displaced discussions about the pace of desegregation and where the teachers would be assigned. When the Virginia legislature allowed local communities to close public schools to thwart compliance to the Brown decision, Prince Edward County in 1959 shut down its entire school system. In response the

---

[61] *Official Minutes of the General Conference 1956*, 394; Andrew M. Manis, *A Fire You Can't Put Out: The Civil Rights Life of Birmingham's Fred Shuttlesworth* (Tuscaloosa, University of Alabama Press, 1999), 39–40; "Minutes ... North Alabama Conference, 1957," in *Combined Minutes of the 1957 Conferences of the Ninth Episcopal District*, 132–133.

[62] *Official Minutes of the General Conference 1956*, 375–376, 383.

[63] "Journal of Proceedings of the Seventieth Annual Session of the Colorado Conference of the African Methodist Episcopal Church held in Tanner Chapel AME Church, Phoenix, AZ, September 12–16, 1956," in *The Combined Minutes of the Conferences of the Fifth Episcopal District, African Methodist Episcopal Church* (Nashville, TN, AME Sunday School Union, 1956), 181; "Minutes of the Seventy-Fourth Session of the West Kentucky Annual Conference held in St. James AME Church, Mayfield, KY, October 20–24, 1954," in *Minutes of the Conferences of the Thirteenth Episcopal District (African Methodist Episcopal Church), 1954* (Nashville, TN, AME Sunday School Union, n.d.), 34, 40, 48.

pastor at Beulah AME Church in Farmville, Alexander I. Dunlap, and his
Baptist colleague, L. Francis Griffin, Jr., with permission from Bishop Reid,
now presiding in the Second Episcopal District, enrolled sixty-three students
from Moton High School in Prince Edward County in the high school
division of Kittrell College in North Carolina. They were charged half-
tuition, but those unable to pay still could matriculate. In some cases, Griffin
paid their expenses. Hence, several received their high school diplomas from
the AME school.[64]

Just as the 1956 General Conference affirmed its alignment with the legal
and legislative methodologies of the NAACP, the 1960 General Conference
extended similar support to the NUL and its institutional and interracial
alliances. Though Executive Director Lester Granger, an Eisenhower Republican, seemed uncomfortable with street demonstrations, a new generation
of leaders in local affiliates emerged who wanted the League to reflect, in
tone and tactics, the insurgent energies of civil rights activists. Additionally,
delegates, while endorsing the League, an organization in leadership transition, created a structure to function as a liaison between the denomination
and the civil rights movement.

Alexander J. Allen, a delegate from the Pittsburgh Annual Conference and
son of Bishop A. J. Allen, proposed a resolution to celebrate the League's
"record of inter-racial achievement." Allen, the executive director of the
Pittsburgh Urban League from 1950 to 1959 and newly transferred to the
League's national office, wrote that "the achievements of the Urban League
have been especially successful in combating racial discrimination in
employment, in vocational guidance for youth, and in the general improvement of living conditions affecting the American Negro population."[65]

Allen's temperate language masked his history of activism that matched
the militancy of the current civil rights struggle. While Allen, a graduate of
Wilberforce and Yale Divinity School, was an official in the Baltimore Urban
League in the 1940s, he endorsed a march to Annapolis, the Maryland state
capital, to demand the enforcement of equal employment and housing
opportunities for blacks. Moreover, he belonged to a Disturbed Committee
of young local League executives who pushed for a more activist posture in
the national organization and greater cooperation with the NAACP. These

---

[64] www.motonmuseum.org/kittrell-junior-college-reunion-the ame-connection; Kristen Green,
*Something Must Be Done About Prince Edward County: A Family, A Virginia Town, A Civil
Rights Battle* (New York, HarperCollins, 2005), 104.
[65] *Official Minutes of the Thirty-Sixth Session of the General Conference, AME Church,
May-1960, Shrine Auditorium, Los Angeles, California* (Nashville, TN, AME Sunday School
Union, 1960), 23.

Figure 6.3 Exterior view of Bethel AME Church, Wylie Avenue at Elm Street, Hill District, August 1955. Gelatin silver print (gift of the Estate of Charles) "Teenie" Harris, 1996

objectives resonated with Allen because his father, during his pastorate in Columbus, Ohio, was twice elected president of the local NAACP branch. Allen was pleased that Granger's successor, Whitney M. Young, Jr., a colleague in the Disturbed group and an erstwhile AME member when he served League affiliates a decade earlier in St. Paul, Minnesota, and Omaha, Nebraska, began to move the national organization to more activist involvements. Allen wanted to affirm that "the program of the Urban League enjoys the cooperation and support of the African Methodist Episcopal Church [and] its ministers and its laymen." On hand to support the resolution was Allen's uncle, Nimrod Allen, a delegate from the Ohio Annual Conference and the founder and executive director of the Columbus Urban League.[66]

---

[66] Dennis C. Dickerson, *Militant Mediator: Whitney M. Young, Jr.* (Lexington, University Press of Kentucky, 1998), 85–86, 116–118, 130–131; *Official Minutes of the General Conference 1960*, 23, 50, 83–84, 92, 240–241; Wright, *The Bishops of the African Methodist Episcopal Church*, 42.

Frederick C. James, a delegate from the Northeast South Carolina Annual Conference and pastor of Mt. Pisgah AME Church in Sumter, complemented Allen's focus in generating AME support for civil rights organizations. James believed, however, that the denomination needed its own activist agency to intersect with the initiatives from frontline organizations. James, a native South Carolinian, after studying for the ministry at Dickerson Theological Seminary at Allen University, transferred in 1944 to the School of Religion at Howard University. William Stuart Nelson, the dean, already a proponent of nonviolent direct action, sustained the school's reputation for training what he described as "moral engineers." Nelson, as all students at the seminary knew, had been awarded an AFSC fellowship to administer in India its Calcutta Service Unit. There, Nelson studied Quaker pacifism and met Mahatma Gandhi. Beyond Nelson's influence, James also enrolled in a new course on social ethics that strongly informed his ministry. Though he received his divinity degree before Nelson's return, awareness of Gandhian nonviolence filled the atmosphere of the School of Religion despite the dean's sabbatical leave.[67]

James returned to South Carolina to teach at Allen University, to serve as dean at Dickerson seminary, and to accept successive pastorates. Because the activism of AME clergy from Columbia to Clarendon County received endorsements from Bishop Reid, James heard him declare at the Northeast South Carolina Annual Conference a few months after the Brown decision that "we have got to play a part in making integration work." Taking this cue, James in 1958 launched a bold but ill-fated campaign to be elected to the Sumter city council. Then, at the seat of the 1960 General Conference in Los Angeles, he offered a resolution to establish a Department of Social Action as an integral part of the AME infrastructure.[68]

James's bill proposed that the commission, in conducting studies and issuing directives and positions, "shall assist in the direction of the African Methodist Christian social witness in all matters relating to human relations and Christian citizenship." A consultant, whom James originally thought

---

[67] *Official Minutes ... of the General Conference*, 1960, 32; Frederick H. Talbot (compiler), *Forward in Faith: Bishop Frederick Calhoun James: The Story: A Faithful Bishop's Witness & Work* (n.p., 2011), 185; Dennis C. Dickerson, "William Stuart Nelson and the Interfaith Origins of the Civil Rights Movement," in R. Drew Smith, William Ackah, and Anthony G. Reddie (New York, Palgrave Macmillan, 2014), 57–72; William Stuart Nelson, "Theological Education for Ministers," 1–3, *William Stuart Nelson Papers*, Box 392/1933, Theological Education for Ministers Folder, Moorland Spingarn Research Center, Howard University, Washington, DC.

[68] Talbot, *Forward in Faith*, 185, *Norfolk Journal and Guide*, November 6, 1964.

should be a general officer, would head the department and report to the General Board, a newly established administrative unit. Moreover, the consultant would operate with an annual budget of $5,000 and "shall be ever conversant with issues" in the realm of social action. Beyond the connectional office, each annual conference and each congregation would empanel their own Committee on Social Action. The annual conference committee would share its yearly report with the denominational officer.[69]

Some denominational politicians feared that James, with the stature of a general officer, would attain a visibility comparable to that of leading civil rights activists. They preferred that he should have the less lofty title of social action consultant. James, however, brought energy to the position but restricted his activity to supporting the programs of existing civil rights organizations and not to any distinctive AME actions. His denominational detractors seemed satisfied that any of his movement aspirations were kept in check. Nonetheless, James officially showed that the denomination stayed abreast of shifts in the black struggle for freedom. With the launch of sit-ins and other student led demonstrations starting in Greensboro in February 1960 and spreading to Nashville and Memphis, Tennessee, and to Rock Hill and Columbia, South Carolina, and other southern cities, AME college students joined their peers in exerting fresh pressure upon segregationist practices. Sit-ins in Nashville between February and May 1960, for example, drew participants from Tennessee Agricultural & Industrial, Fisk, Meharry Medical College, and the American Baptist College. James M. Lawson, Jr., through a series of nonviolent workshops, equipped them to occupy and desegregate downtown lunch counters. Among several AMEs was Novella McCline, a Tennessee A&I undergraduate who sat in at the Woolworth's lunch counter. James understood that black activism had moved to a higher gear of militancy and was likely aware of the lunch counter sit-in at Eckerd's drugstore in Columbia on March 14, 1960. Simon P. Bouie, a student at Allen University and later an AME pastor, and Talmadge J. Neal, a student at Benedict College, demanded service while occupying a booth. After they refused to leave, the police arrived and charged them with trespassing. Because of their arrest and conviction, Bouie and Neal fought the case all the way to the United States Supreme Court, which exonerated them in 1964. Because of this new phase of civil rights activism, James urged the 1960 General Conference to "take commendable cognizance of the hundreds of students from our churches and other churches of this our land, who by their 'sit-in' and 'stand-up'

[69] *Official Minutes ... of the General Conference, 1960*, 180–181.

protests against segregation" exhibit "their dignity in the process of their protests." Archibald J. Carey, Jr. commended Nashville clergy at a Chicago NAACP dinner for supporting the student sit-ins and marching "in front of a downtown department store," and he noted that "sit-ins have emerged in Savannah, Georgia." He said that "people everywhere have caught the spirit of freedom."[70]

James and Carey reflected the same consciousness that other AMEs expressed for increased pressure against Jim Crow practices. This view mirrored what a contemporary Methodist ethicist said about the sit-ins as "a stirring in this land" and "as a form of Christian action." Just before the 1960 General Conference students at the AME supported Daniel Payne College in Birmingham participated in the local sit-in movement. Fred Shuttlesworth of the SCLC-affiliated Alabama Christian Movement for Human Rights, impressed by the Greensboro student sit-ins, encouraged similar activism among students in Birmingham at the CME-sponsored Miles College and at Daniel Payne College. Because they were drawn to a voting rights campaign, a Miles student leader, starting on March 1, 1960, spearheaded a Prayer Vigil for Freedom that protested a filibuster by southern congressmen opposed to the proposed Civil Rights Act of 1960. Student demonstrators from both black Methodist schools carried signs saying "The Law of God Will Be Fulfilled." Birmingham police arrested twelve of them, and though they were not charged, one of the protesters together with his mother and sister were beaten by deputies.[71]

Another series of student protests began on March 30, 1960. Demonstrators, including ten Daniel Payne students, targeted five Birmingham department stores where they sat in and demanded service at the lunch counters. After their arrest and a night in jail, Howard D. Gregg, Daniel Payne's president, and Samuel M. Davis, a local pastor whose son was a student protest leader, signed bonds for their release. Moreover, Gregg imposed no disciplinary penalty on the students. These events and others like them helped to frame James's General Conference resolution backing the sit-in movement.[72]

[70] Ibid., 230; *Connect*, June 14, 2018; *Columbia Business Report*, October 23, 2017; https://supreme.justia.com/cases/federal/us/378/347/case.html; "Archibald J. Carey, Jr. File, 100-8261-3479," in *Archibald J. Carey Domestic Security Investigation (FBI) File*—100-CG-20875.PDF (courtesy of Professor Lerone A. Martin, Washington University)

[71] Paul Ramsey, *Christian Ethics and the Sit-In* (New York, Association Press, 1960), x; Glenn T. Eskew, *But for Birmingham: The Local and National Movements in the Civil Rights Struggle* (Chapel Hill, University of North Carolina Press, 1997), 148–149.

[72] Gregg, *The AME Church and the Current Negro Revolt*, 33; Eskew, *But for Birmingham*, 149–150.

Similarly, the 1960 West Tennessee Annual Conference meeting in Memphis observed that "sit-ins, wade-ins, and knee[l]-ins are rampant all over the South." Delegates were aware that "young people, tired of waiting, weary of insults and filled with the world wide urge for freedom, are on the march." Moreover, "many have been arrested, others will be, but such is the price of freedom." Therefore, "the church must lend its full support to these" protesters. Perhaps conferees referred to Ernestine Lee, a student at Owen Junior College and a member of Memphis's Providence AME Church. She was among forty student activists who in March 1960 were arrested for their sit-ins that aimed to integrate two public libraries. Lee's six sisters emulated her and became involved in other sit-ins and kneel-ins to desegregate local lunch counters and churches.[73]

AMEs in Jackson, Mississippi, played a significant role as backbone for the Jackson Movement. The initiative drew from the Tougaloo College NAACP, the West Jackson Youth Council, the Jackson NAACP, and the NAACP at the AME-supported Campbell College. A boycott that focused on Jackson's Capitol Street businesses was planned. The demands included equality in hiring and promotion in local businesses, addressing black customers with titles of respect, service on a first come/first served basis, and the elimination of segregated drinking fountains, bathrooms, and lunch counter seating. By January 1963 Medgar Evers, Mississippi's NAACP field secretary, reported that a selective buying campaign and picketing had started. A sit-in at Woolworth's occurred on May 28, 1963 after months of economic pressure on downtown stores. An interracial group of protesters endured physical attacks and suffered injuries.[74]

Conspicuous in his support of the sit-ins was G. R. Haughton, the pastor of Jackson's Pearl Street AME Church, whose doors were opened for a mass meeting on the day that the protesters were attacked. Haughton and various NAACP leaders addressed the overflow crowd. Haughton and five other leaders had met the Jackson mayor and reported on his acceptance of the sit-in demands except for school integration, which was deemed a judicial matter. The other grievances pertained to desegregation of public facilities, hiring of black police, and the removal of segregation signs. Like President

---

[73] "Minutes of the West Tennessee Annual Conference of the African Methodist Episcopal Church, Eighty-Sixth Session held in Ward Chapel AME Church, Memphis, TN, November 15–19, 1960," in *West Tennessee Annual Conference, African Methodist Episcopal Church, Official Journal, Rt. Rev. E. L. Hickman, 1959, 1960, 1961* (n.p.), 42; *Memphis Commercial Appeal*, March 26, 2017; *Memphis Daily News*, April 21, 2017.

[74] M. J. O'Brien, *We Shall Not Be Moved: The Jackson Woolworth's Sit-In and the Movement It Inspired* (Jackson, University Press of Mississippi, 2013) 90–91, 96, 100, 115, 125–126.

Gregg at Daniel Payne College in Birmingham, Charles A. Jones, the dean and chaplain at Campbell College, strongly supported the demonstrators and warned the mayor to keep his promises.[75]

Between the 1960 and 1964 General Conferences Frederick C. James helped to found the Sumter Movement and to serve as its chairman. The Sumter Movement, starting in 1963, was the successor group to the short-lived Sumter Citizens Committee, whose inability to overcome white obstruction of interracial negotiations, required that local blacks adopt a different strategy. As a result, the Sumter Movement, "stimulated by the youth and the spirit of CORE," a group that James had supported, pursued a militant methodology. Hence, James led a movement that embraced non-violent direct action and other related tactics to attain the desegregation of lunch counters, hotels, motels, and various public and private facilities.[76]

This CORE influence drew from James's acquaintance with James Farmer, CORE's executive director and the son and namesake of his New Testament professor at the School of Religion at Howard University. When CORE sponsored Freedom Rides in 1961 to test whether integrated facilities were available between Washington DC through the southeastern seaboard and Gulf states, the interracial bus riders were hosted along the way at James's Mt. Pisgah Church in Sumter. When CORE developed "an exciting documentary motion picture, 'Freedom Ride,'" to chronicle this historic but dangerous journey, James, as head of the AME Social Action Commission, sponsored it. The flyer invited viewers to "witness to its fullest the beatings, violence, and Bus burning in Anniston, Houston, and Shreveport that shocked the nation and led to a change in policy of the Interstate Commerce Commission ruling in restaurants and terminals in more than 85 cities and communities." Monies from the film "will be used to fight the last desperate struggles of the dying evil of segregation." The flyer carried the conspicuous imprimatur of James's social action office.[77]

Notwithstanding the importance of the Sumter movement and James's alliance with CORE, the Birmingham campaign of 1963, which drew national notice and prodded President Kennedy to introduce landmark civil rights legislation to Congress, became a cornerstone event in the leadership of Martin Luther King, Jr. and the organizing acumen of Fred Shuttlesworth. A. G. Gaston, the secretary-treasurer of the AME

[75] Ibid., 114, 148–149.
[76] "The Sumter Movement, Sumter, South Carolina," February 15, 1964, *F. C. James Papers*, private collection, Columbia, South Carolina.
[77] *Core Presents-"Freedom Ride,"* F. C. James Papers, Columbia, SC.

Department of Church Extension, while disinclined to demonstrate himself, became a benefactor to the Birmingham campaign. King's held strategy meetings in the A. G. Gaston Motel, a site that was subsequently bombed. When arrested, protesters required $237,000 in bail money, Gaston provided $160,000 in bond guarantees. When King was jailed, Gaston advanced $2,500 for bail to effect his release. Though he counseled that demonstrations should yield to "the conference table," Gaston leveraged his wealth to underwrite the Birmingham campaign, thus enabling protesters to return to the streets to demonstrate. By the time the 1964 General Conference convened in Cincinnati, the civil rights struggle already bore the imprint of James, Gaston, and other AMEs who strengthened the infrastructure of the black freedom struggle.[78]

James submitted his first social action report and resolutions to the Cincinnati assembly. They included proposals to support the major civil rights organizations, voter registration initiatives, and passage of Kennedy's comprehensive civil rights bill. He pressed the General Conference to ask Congress for a "speedy and unhampered passage of Civil Rights Bill 7152." He urged "the speedy exercise of the Senate's right of cloture" against recalcitrant southern senators and their allies trying to stop through [the] filibuster and "crippling amendments" to what would become the Civil Rights Act of 1964. He also said that AMEs should cooperate with the NAACP's lobbying activities in federal, state, and local legislatures for civil rights laws and anti-discriminatory statutes on employment, support for direct action campaigns, and paying for life memberships in the NAACP.[79]

In offering unequivocal support for the pending civil rights bill in Congress, James echoed the bishops and leading AMEs who were prominent in the black struggle for freedom. The Council of Bishops, speaking through Bishop George W. Baber, declared "that the AME Church [should] employ all of the resources at its command to impress upon Congress" a demand for the prompt passage of the benchmark civil rights bill. The bishops also said that James's Social Action Commission should be "empowered" to recommend plans to support President Lyndon B. Johnson's legislative package of civil rights and other economic and social welfare bills. Moreover, Archibald J. Carey, Jr. relayed a message to the General Conference from A. Philip

---

[78] A.G. Gaston, *Green Power: The Successful Way of A. G. Gaston* (Troy, AL, Troy State University Press, 1968), 118, 121, 123, 125.

[79] Frederick C. James, *Social Action in the AME Church*, 1960–1964, F. C. James Papers, Columbia, SC.

Randolph that each US senator should receive a telegram from the AME assembly urging "immediate enactment of the civil rights bill."[80]

Additionally, James wanted AMEs to incorporate social action into regular denominational operations. Therefore, congregations and annual conferences were expected to integrate into their ministries Christian citizenship activities, intergroup participation, and self-help and self-improvement initiatives. Christian citizenship included local church involvement in voter registration and interactions with elected officials about support of civil rights, housing, and equal employment opportunity legislation. Intergroup cooperation meant alliances with institutions and agencies that would facilitate desegregation. This also included assistance from AME congregations in showing and promoting CORE's film on the "Freedom Ride."[81]

Because the Free African Society, out of which the AME Church emerged, emphasized self-help and self-improvement, James proposed diverse means to include these objectives as a part of denominational social action. His recommendations about church credit unions and "projects to combat juvenile delinquency" pertained to what he believed blacks could do for themselves. Additionally, he indicated that NAACP membership and "selective buying and purposive patronage" where blacks spend their monies where they were respected "comprised a core principle in self-help and self-improvement."[82]

Because James viewed Richard Allen as the "father" of the modern civil rights movement, he proposed the development of a film on "The Richard Allen Story." Other AMEs echoed his perspective about their denomination as an incubator of black protest. To show that the denomination was inextricably linked to "the current Negro revolt," AMEs defined Richard Allen and his walkout from St. George Church in 1787 as antecedent to the civil rights movement. When the bishops in 1963 visited the White House, Bishop Eugene C. Hatcher declared to President Kennedy that Allen was "an architect of minority [advancement] techniques" and pioneered "organized protest." During the 1964 General Conference four delegates, including Rufus K. Young, the Arkansas pastor who backed the Little Rock Nine, commended the "well planned nonviolent demonstrations" shown in the 1963 March on Washington and pointed to the AME Church as an example of "effective protest against racial segregation." When Martin Luther King, Jr.

[80] *Official Minutes of the Thirty-Seventh Session of the General Conference [of the] AME Church held at The Cincinnati Gardens, Cincinnati, Ohio, Beginning May 6, 1964* (n.p., n.d.), 13, 89.
[81] *Core Presents-"Freedom Ride."*   [82] James, *Social Action in the AME Church.*

was assassinated in 1968, a joint session of the Philadelphia and Delaware Annual Conferences described the slain civil rights leader as an heir to the AME founder.[83]

Additionally, AMEs at the 1964 General Conference signaled their identification with the frontline leadership of the civil rights struggle. James delivered an enthusiastic introduction of Martin Luther King, Jr. just before his evening address to the AME assembly. Though he had delivered this speech, "Remaining Awake Through a Great Revolution," it conveyed, perhaps unwittingly, an insinuation that AME leaders were standing on the sidelines of the civil rights movement. While no bishop had a high profile in the black freedom struggle, King surely knew that James, Carey, Daisy Bates, Randolph, and maybe his nemesis, Roy Wilkins, envisaged themselves as energetic heirs to Allen's social holiness. More than the bishops, these AMEs were the contemporary carriers of Allenite activism. Throughout the 1964 General Conference, either their presence or the mention of their names signified deep denominational involvement in a "revolution" in which they were fully awake. The General Conference scribe reported that "the large crowd," however, "was inspired" by King despite having to pay an admission fee.[84]

After the King speech, Daisy Bates asked delegates to approve a "Civil Rights Day." Bates presented Roy Wilkins, a fellow AME, with a merit award. Other civil rights honorees were selected from the respective eighteen episcopal districts. Bishop Gibbs, for example, presented A. Philip Randolph, a fellow Florida native and a member of Bethel in Harlem, for an award for spearheading the 1963 March on Washington. James introduced Mississippi native H. Hartford Brookins, the pastor of First Church in Los Angeles and founder of the United Civil Rights Committee, a group that pressed the Los Angeles mayor to address housing, education, and law enforcement issues. Brookins also pushed for black representation on the Los Angeles city council, a move that resulted in the election in 1963 of his parishioner, Thomas Bradley. Notwithstanding Brookins's prominence, a fellow pastor, L. Sylvester Odom at Ward AME Church in Los Angeles, could also have been the honoree. Odom was president of the Western Christian Leadership

[83] Ibid.; Gregg, *The AME Church and the Current Negro Revolt*, 52–53; *Official Minutes ... General Conference 1964*, 168–169; "[Minutes of the] 152nd Session of the Philadelphia Annual Conference and the 45th Session of the Delaware Annual Conference held jointly at St. Matthew AME Church, Philadelphia, PA, April 17–21, 1968," in *Combined Minutes of the 1968 Annual Conference, First Episcopal District, African Methodist Episcopal Church, Bishop John D. Bright, Sr.* (n.p., 1968), 254.
[84] *Official Minutes ... General Conference 1964*, 80.

Figure 6.4 Rev. Martin Luther, King, Jr., Rev. (later Bishop) Frederick C. James, and Attorney (later Judge) William Mcclain at the 1964 General Conference in Cincinnati, Ohio) (used with permission from Bishop Frederick C. James, Columbia, SC)

Conference, the regional affiliate of King's SCLC. Odom was probably disqualified because of his candidacy at this same General Conference for editor of the *Christian Recorder*. Another King protégé, W. E. Shortridge, a member of Bethel AME Church in Ensley, Alabama, and the first president of the Lay Organization of the Ninth Episcopal District, however, was honored posthumously. He had combined visibility as a member of the AME Judicial Council and as treasurer of Shuttlesworth's Alabama Christian Movement for Human Rights and an executive board member of SCLC.[85]

When President Johnson signed the all important Civil Rights Act two months after the 1964 General Conference, this celebrated event became another in a series of seminal benchmarks in the ongoing struggle for black civil rights. Before AMEs reconvened in Philadelphia for their 1968 General

[85] Ibid., 89–90; *Manual and Directory of the Ninth Episcopal District Laymen's Organization of the African Methodist Episcopal Church* (1960), 3 (courtesy of Wayman B. Shriver, Birmingham, AL); *Doctrine and Discipline of the African Methodist Episcopal Church, 1956* (Nashville, TN, AME Sunday School Union, 1956), 611; *Doctrine and Discipline of the African Methodist Episcopal Church* (Nashville, TN, AME Sunday School Union, 1960), 665; http://www.blackpast.org/aah/brookins-hamel-hartford-1926; George Meany to L. Sylvester Odom, June 16, 1961, Clayborne Carson (ed.), *The Papers of Martin Luther King, Jr.*, Vol. 8, January 1961–August 1962 (Berkeley, University of California Press, 2014), 250, fn.3; *The Sphinx*, May 1960, 20.

Conference, African Americans, including some African Methodists, either shaped or responded both to federal initiatives and grassroots pressures to enfranchise blacks and to end poverty within the black population.

After the passage of the 1964 law, insuring the right to vote became the next objective in African American advancement. Vernon Jordan and Johnny and Clara Barbour played crucial roles in laying foundations for this energized campaign in the civil rights movement. Jordan, an attorney and lifelong AME, had been the NAACP's Georgia field director and a staff member in the SRC. This had been involved in the Voter Education Project (VEP), a nonpartisan, foundation funded agency aimed at black voter registration. In 1964 Jordan became acting VEP director and later head of the organization. His duties lay in distributing funds to southern groups working to expand the black electorate.[86]

Barbour, an up and coming Mississippi minister, arrived in Jackson from Greenwood in 1957 to attend Campbell College. On the AME campus he became president of the NAACP intercollegiate chapter and joined with three others to spearhead a bus sit-in. While he was pastor at Allen Chapel in Meridian, Barbour served as coordinator for voter registration and education for the Mississippi NAACP. Barbour admitted that "we were frightened" because "bombs" already had been hurled in his direction. "I went to my little church one Sunday," he said, "and they had thrown a bomb in the window because we were housing things for the civil rights movement." Moreover, "a guy called and said that he was going to burn a cross on my lawn. I never shall forget that," Barbour declared. Nonetheless, he persisted in his activism. "We had to meet and we had to do a training process of getting people to register and to vote," he recalled. Barbour "even carried them" to the application site "because people were afraid." He secured "transportation and [would] physically stand behind them while they would register to vote." The training included "telling people how to mark ballots, how to fill out applications ... particularly old people who were willing" to register. He also taught them how to answer possible questions that were posed to them.[87]

Additionally, Clara Barbour, his wife, did street canvassing among potential voters, although she "mainly stayed in the office" and did coordination for the local voting registration campaign. At headquarters, in a building

[86] Vernon E. Jordan, Jr., with Annette Gordon-Reed, *Vernon Can Read: A Memoir* (New York, Public Affairs, 2001), 145, 173–177.
[87] An Oral History with Reverend Johnny Barbour, Jr. and Clara M. Barbour, interviewed by Donald Williams, Tougaloo College Archives, Civil Rights Documentation Project, 1999.

owned by a black pharmacist, she "answered phones and helped to get out material" mostly in the form of flyers. Clara Barbour remembered singing "at some rallies when Dr. King came," but like her husband she confessed that "a lot of times I was scared."[88]

The efforts of veterans in black voter registration, examples being Jordan and the Barbours, flowed into what President Johnson proposed in a federal voting rights bill and the mobilization to support this initiative from SCLC and SNCC. Both organizations, in their focus on voter registration in Selma and surrounding Dallas County, Alabama, stirred violent responses from racist whites in law enforcement. Broad national attention on Bloody Sunday on March 7, 1965 preceded additional television coverage of the Selma to Montgomery march that started a few weeks later. An influential speech from King, after the five-day march on a 54-mile trek to the Alabama state capital, spurred President Johnson and Congress to act on the historic Voting Rights Act that was signed on August 6, 1965.

P. H. Lewis, pastor of Brown Chapel in Selma, facilitated these voting rights demonstrations. The stately edifice served as a meeting place for mass rallies, lodging for protesters, and as a makeshift outpatient facility for those injured by the aggressive violence of horse mounted police at the Edmund Pettus Bridge. Among the thousands of participants in the Selma to Montgomery march were R. W. Hilson, a presiding elder in Birmingham and a King protégé during the Montgomery bus boycott, Howard D. Gregg, the Daniel Payne College president and supporter of student protesters, and the president of the school's NAACP chapter.[89]

RESPONSES TO BLACK URBAN ISSUES

Days after the voting rights law was signed, the focus of the black freedom struggle shifted to the urban pathologies that pervasively afflicted African Americans. The outbreak of the Watts riots in Los Angeles on August 11, 1965, though hardly the first black urban rebellion in the 1960s, dramatized issues surrounding substandard schooling, inadequate housing, and police abuse among black city residents. H. Hartford Brookins, still the pastor at Watts's First AME Church, told the Commonwealth Club that "Watts is dilapidated and old, 46.9% of its dwelling units were built in 1939 or before." He added that "Watts is poor" and "the unemployment is twice that of the Caucasian community." Brookins also said that "strained relations exist

[88] Ibid.   [89] Gregg, *The AME Church and the Current Negro Revolt*, 42–43.

between the Negro community and the Los Angeles Police Department." His colleague, Henry W. Murph, the pastor since 1950 at Watts's Grant AME Church, also lamented these underlying causes of the rioting. Murph, a native South Carolinian, positioned Grant as a food distribution site and himself as a negotiator between justifiably angry young blacks and heavily armed National Guard troops who patrolled the riot-torn area.[90]

Though Brookins, Murph, and other AME leaders, as tactical centrists, eschewed the violence flowing out from the riots, they acknowledged that white racism created and sustained black ghettoes. President Johnson's Kerner Commission articulated this view, which Roy Wilkins, a critic of the riots, also expressed. Wilkins, a member of Bethel Church in Harlem, spoke at the 1968 General Conference and discussed his roots in the AME Church. He "reviewed the incidents of the Chicago riots in past years and the present social unrest," saying that he agreed with the Kerner Commission "that the prejudiced white group is responsible for the city riots today." After the enthusiastic response to Wilkins's speech, Bishop Hubert N. Robinson, who extended his commendations to the NAACP leader, asked delegates to give "a most liberal contribution" to the centrist organization.[91]

AME leaders adopted the same posture toward black urban unrest expressed by Wilkins and Murph, who was elected a bishop at the 1968 General Conference. While understanding the causes of black rioting, they still preferred the judicial and legislative tactics of the NAACP to which they pledged continued support. This affinity for the NAACP was normative for African Methodists. As the largest of civil rights organizations, the NAACP's 1,500 branches across the United States extensively involved both AME clergy and laity. The network of AMEs in the Chicago NAACP is illustrative. Carl Fuqua, the assistant minister at Archibald J. Carey's Quinn Chapel, became the executive director of the city's NAACP branch in 1959. Already, he had been a NAACP official in North Carolina while he was a dean at the AME-supported Kittrell College. He inherited a fractured affiliate that included disenchanted critics who eschewed the partisan connections of some officers and who viewed Fuqua as an establishment choice because of his ties to Carey. Nonetheless, Fuqua inaugurated a drive to expand chapter membership to 35,000. Chicagoans should join the NAACP, he said, because the organization was equipped to address racial inequalities

---

[90] H. H. Brookins, "Watts Close-up-A Lesson for Other Cities," *AME Church Review,* Vol. 87, No. 227, January–March 1966, 41–42, 44; *Los Angeles Times,* November 2, 2006.
[91] *Official Minutes of the Thirty-Eighth Session of the General Conference [of the] AME Church, May 1–14, 1968, Philadelphia, PA* (n.p., n.d.) 127.

"through legal redress, protest, and political action." In recruiting 20,000 new members Fuqua could claim some success in generating grassroots support for his initiatives. His branch objectives also included special programs to activate NAACP youth councils, agitation for an Illinois FEPC, and addressing ongoing segregation in the Chicago public schools. Though he endorsed youth activism, he disagreed with their tactic of doing wade-ins to desegregate local beaches. He advised regular and sustained protests instead of "weekends only" demonstrations.[92]

During Fuqua's tenure, which ended in 1964, Samuel S. Morris, the pastor of Chicago's Coppin Memorial AME Church, served as branch president, and Robert Thomas, Jr., pastor of the city's Bethel AME Church, played a similarly large role in branch affairs. This network of AMEs in the Chicago NAACP reflected the denomination's support of the organization throughout the United States. The New York Annual Conference, like the rest of the First Episcopal District, for example, paid in 1967 its portion for a life membership in the NAACP for their prelate, Bishop John D. Bright. These involvements showed the strength of ties between the AME Church and the NAACP.[93]

Though NAACP methodologies appealed to AMEs, they also recognized, in part because of the riots, that poverty aggravated the social and economic ills that powered racial inequality. In addition to the NUL, the SCLC acknowledged these linkages and addressed the lack of economic opportunities for blacks. Hence, SCLC in 1962 launched in Atlanta Operation Breadbasket and spread it to Chicago in 1966 with Jesse Jackson as its director. Ralph D. Abernathy recalled that John A. Middleton, the pastor of Atlanta's Allen Temple AME Church, became the first president of Operation Breadbasket and hosted the organizational meeting at his church.[94]

President Johnson energized these anti-poverty efforts when he, in 1964, declared a War on Poverty. He charged R. Sargent Shriver in the Office of Economic Opportunity (OEO) and other federal agencies with frontline responsibilities to relieve privation among whites, especially in Appalachia, and blacks in urban ghettoes. In Seattle, for example, John Hurst Adams, the

[92] Dickerson, *African Methodism and its Wesleyan Heritage*, 200–207.

[93] Ibid., 204, 206; "Official Minutes of the One Hundred Forty-Fifth Session of the New York Annual Conference, African Methodist Episcopal Church, 1967," in *Combined Minutes of the First Episcopal District, African Methodist Episcopal Church, 1967, Bishop John D. Bright, Sr.* (n.p., 1967), 190.

[94] Merlisse Ross Middleton, *Reflections on the Man: John Middleton* (Nashville, TN, AME Sunday School Union, n.d.), 35.

pastor of First AME Church from 1962 to 1968 and son of activist general officer E. A. Adams, became chair of the Central Area Civil Rights Committee. Adams and another local leader, Walter Hundley, started the Central Area Motivation Program and they respectively served as first chairman and the first executive director. They flew to Washington DC to meet their senator, Warren Magnuson of Washington, to get funding from Shriver's OEO. Magnuson called, and Shriver immediately funded Seattle's anti-poverty agency. Other AME clergy, observed Bishop Joseph Gomez, served "with distinction" in various divisions within OEO, especially on such "poverty boards" as the Community Action Program." During the late 1960s Gomez said that "this outreach effort is expanding as the church strives to carry the Ministry to the doorsteps of the poor."[95]

The involvement of Middleton, Adams, and other AMEs in anti-poverty initiatives, though happening in disparate locales, converged into broad backing for black economic empowerment. These commitments were anchored, at least in part, in the denomination's consistent advocacy in the 1940s and 1950s for federal and state FEPCs and other anti-discrimination measures to protect their white collar and blue collar parishioners. Archibald J. Carey, Jr. became a well-known guardian of black federal workers in his position as a head of Ike's committee against racial bias in government employment. Moreover, there was pervasive AME support for the massive March on Washington for Jobs and Freedom. Similarly, the Memphis Movement in 1968 blended black civil rights and African American labor advancement.[96]

Nonetheless, the Memphis Movement was different because it involved low wage, nonunion blacks. They lagged far behind their counterparts in the unionized black precincts of Chicago, Detroit, Pittsburgh, and other industrial centers in the North and West. Though employed, these black Memphians, populated the ranks of the poor. The condition of black sanitation workers and their pursuit of better pay and union recognition from a racially recalcitrant municipal government galvanized into a major "I Am a Man" movement. Martin Luther King, Jr., at the invitation of James M. Lawson, Jr., the principal tactician in the Nashville Movement and now pastor of Memphis's Centenary Methodist Episcopal Church, focused national attention on the black sanitation workers' strike.

---

[95] Seattle Civil Rights & Labor History Project-University of Washington, Video Oral History-Bishop John Hurst Adams, depts.washington.edu/civilr/Adams/.htm; Joseph Gomez, *Polity of the AME Church*, 1971, 85.

[96] Dickerson, *African American Preachers and Politics*, 134–145.

King, who was devoting increased attention to poverty and economic inequality in American society, viewed his involvement in the Memphis strike as a precursor to a Poor Peoples' March on Washington DC. AME clergy in Memphis, H. Ralph Jackson and Henry L. Starks, joined Lawson and other clergy, including Malcolm Blackburn, the white pastor of Clayborn Temple AME Church, in vigorous support of black sanitation workers and King's objective to focus national attention on the desperate condition of the working poor.

The strike started in a tragic occurrence that put on public display the exploitative and humiliating circumstances that black workers endured. Memphis sanitation employees received no overtime pay. When residents refused to put out garbage for pick-up, sanitation laborers had to retrieve the refuse from wherever the containers were located. Sometimes they had to gather up the rubbish themselves and then had no facility to clean their hands before eating their lunches. When it rained, the garbage men were often dismissed from work without compensation.[97]

What precipitated the strike of over 1,300 garbage workers occurred on January 31, 1968. Heavy rains caused two black laborers to take cover from the bad weather near the garbage machinery. They became entangled in a faulty truck, which caught and killed them. These normative conditions and the tragedy that was visited upon the two sanitation employees triggered the involvement of Local 1733 of the American Federation of State, County, and Municipal Employees (AFSCME). Mayor Henry Loeb, when presented with grievances from the garbage collectors and from their unrecognized union, refused to negotiate. The walkout, said Loeb, was unlawful. After an unsatisfactory meeting between Loeb and officials of the AFSCME union officials joined the sanitation workers in a downtown march.[98]

AFSCME support, while crucial in pressing for the right to represent the garbage collectors, relied on the cooperation of black clergy who had organized Community on the Move for Equality (COME) to function as an auxiliary strike committee. Lawson's ties to King and his strategic advice, though critical, drew from the strong backing of Jackson and Starks. Both AME ministers became frontline leaders and denounced Loeb's race-based resistance to a mostly black labor movement. Jackson, a COME cofounder, along with other clergy participated in daily marches to Memphis city hall. Jackson also chaired the Platform Committee for the mass rallies at various

[97] Hattie E. Jackson, 65 Dark Days in '68: Reflections: Memphis Sanitation Strike (Southaven, MI, The King's Press, 2004), 2.
[98] Ibid., 2–5.

churches. As an AME general officer who supervised the Minimum Salary Department, Jackson opened its building as a headquarters and when necessary a makeshift clinic for demonstrators injured by the police.[99]

Though Jackson embodied Allenite activism, he channeled it through the nonviolent methodology that lay at the core of the civil rights movement. He had participated, for example, in the 1966 James Meredith March Against Fear. While never abandoning nonviolence, the sanitation strike and the violent response of Loeb's police force radicalized the sharply dressed middle-class minister. Jackson recalled his birth in Birmingham and his "30 years of discipline" as a black Alabaman. When a Memphis policeman "gassed and maced" him during a march, Jackson became as "mad as hell." Because police action "baptized him into the world of the working poor," he became an unwavering advocate of the garbage employees. He was appalled, for example, about the "type of wages and salaries they received [and] the type of homes they live[d] in." These occurrences constituted a rude awakening for this denominational executive. He also criticized white preachers for their aloofness toward the struggles of the black working poor, saying that they were "unfit for the honor of minister." Additionally, he condemned the refusal of Loeb and other officials to negotiate with their sanitation employees. The strike would not end, he said, until concessions were yielded to the strikers. At one point, Jackson challenged Loeb face to face to "agree to a dues check-off and union recognition." The mayor wouldn't budge.[100]

Starks, a native Memphian and the pastor of the city's St. James AME Church, joined Jackson and other black clergy in visible support of the strike. Starks, however, was radicalized in a different way from Jackson. A deceased parishioner had been a garbage collector who had no fringe benefits. Despite his poor health, he received no sympathy from his employer, who scarcely provided him with any time off to convalesce after two surgeries. Similarly, another deceased member, also a sanitation worker, could not earn a transfer to less strenuous duties despite a bad back. In the end Starks mourned the premature death of this member, who had been forced to find other low-paying jobs to support his nine children. The treatment of these parishioners educated Starks about the plight of the black working poor and the 'slave mannerisms' that characterized their interactions with their municipal

---

[99] Ibid., 78, 88, 106, 115, 352.
[100] Michael Honey, *Going Down Jericho Road: The Memphis Strike, Martin Luther King's Last Campaign* (New York, W.W. Norton & Company, 2007), 191, 207–208, 211, 215, 260, 326, 457, 488.

employers. The "I Am a Man" mantra that mobilized the strikers, Starks believed, broke a psychological shackle that these laborers had carried. Additionally, Starks, like Jackson, though a veteran of past civil rights marches, was astonished when Memphis police sprayed mace on the demonstrators.[101]

Starks and other black ministers, because of an unintentional invitation, interacted with the all white Memphis Ministers Association, and witnessed first hand their surprising indecision about the strike. Not until the King assassination did some of these clergy exhibit any repentance or understanding of what was happening in their city. A Greek Orthodox priest prostrated himself before Starks, begging pardon for the indifference of white clergy to the condition of black Memphians. Starks, however, already thought that his time seemed better spent with the all black Interdenominational Ministerial Alliance, in which he served as president and whose membership overlapped with COME.[102]

The grassroots Memphis movement exerted an irresistible pull upon the AME colleagues of Jackson and Starks. Though less visible, Miller A. Peace, the Mississippi-born pastor of Avery Chapel, and Malcolm Blackburn, the Canadian-born pastor of Clayborn Temple, also expressed predictable outrage over the plight of black garbage collectors. Their protests, however, drew from a normative AME impulse to advance black civil rights and to mobilize these energies in support of the working poor. Hence, Peace, a strike backer and an avid student of black history, drew no distinction "between the role of [the] church or the Civil Rights Movement" in fulfilling his "higher calling." Blackburn, who was white, declared that the sanitation workers "were our people." In identifying with them he recited their prayer, which said in part, "give us this day our Dues Check-Off" and "we forgive those who [use] MACE against us." This rhetorical commitment to the strikers was concretized in opening Clayborn Temple to several rallies and providing refuge and medical assistance to injured marchers fleeing from the police.[103]

After King's assassination, Jackson, at a mass meeting on April 7, 1968, urged participation in a memorial march to honor the slain SCLC leader. Days later, on April 16, an agreement between the City of Memphis and AFSCME was announced at Clayborn Temple. Local 1733 of the sanitation

[101] Ibid., 54–55, 206–207, 212.   [102] Ibid., 151, 153, 169, 449, 455.
[103] Jackson, 65 Dark Days in '68, 6, 99; Richard R. Wright, Jr. (compiler), Encyclopedia of African Methodism (Philadelphia, PA, AME Book Concern, 1947), 220; Honey, Going Down Jericho Road, 215, 243, 260, 353.

workers was recognized as the bargaining agent for the garbage collectors, a pay raise was granted, and safer working conditions were achieved. The Memphis movement, which King envisaged as a prelude to a national Poor Peoples campaign, reverberated among African Methodists. The involvement of Jackson, Starks, and other Memphis AMEs in the sanitation workers strike signaled to their denominational colleagues that the economic empowerment of the working poor and others in poverty had become an urgent priority within the civil rights movement.[104]

Frederick C. James, through the Social Action Commission, understood and endorsed this shift in the black freedom struggle. Despite King's death, declared his SCLC successor, Ralph D. Abernathy, the planned Poor Peoples March in Washington DC would still occur. In response, James urged the 1968 General Conference to support the SCLC campaign. He submitted a resolution that said the AME Church "has maintained a steadfast commitment to the ideals of social justice for all people of all races, of all classes, and of all creeds." Moreover, "the cry of the poor, the cry of the hungry, the cry of the disadvantaged, the cry of the dispossessed, the cry of the disenfranchised as well as the cry of the lost have always been the cry of the African Methodist Episcopal Church." Hence, the General Conference offered "its sincere and prayerful endorsement and also its active support to 'The Poor Peoples March on Washington.'" After James presented the motion, General Officer H. Ralph Jackson, who seconded the resolution, reminded delegates about the Memphis sanitation workers strike and "the need to assist the poor and the disadvantaged [who] should get the attention of the Church and the Nation." Starks, a delegate from the West Tennessee Annual Conference, provided another second to the motion. In addition a delegate from the Delaware Annual Conference supervised an offering "to assist the March of the Poor."[105]

Both Whitney M. Young, Jr. of the NUL and A. Philip Randolph had, prior to the Memphis sanitation workers strike, presented detailed proposals for black economic development. In 1964 Young offered a Domestic Marshall Plan that would disburse $145 billion over ten years to eliminate ghettoes and establish economic parity for African Americans. Though this was rumored to be the template for President Johnson's War on Poverty, Young was challenging the federal government to provide for blacks the same as had been done through the Marshall Plan for rebuilding Europe after World War II. Similarly, in 1966 Randolph recommended a Freedom

[104] Jackson, 65 *Dark Days in '68*, 41, 47–48, 53.
[105] *Official Minutes . . . General Conference 1968*, 42, 98, 183.

Budget costing $185 billion over a decade that would economically empower the black population.[106]

Taking cues from the National Council of Churches and President Johnson's National Advisory Commission on Civil Disorders, James and the AME social action department engaged the discourse on the economic empowerment of the poor, especially in riot-torn cities across the United States. Therefore, James proposed that the 1968 General Conference should approve Randolph's Freedom Budget idea. The plan, James said, called for full employment, "decent and adequate wages," eliminating "slum ghettoes," and improvements in housing, medical care, and public school education. James asserted that the AME Church "recognized that the crisis problem of the cities cannot be met without massive action on economic issues." The Freedom Budget, he believed, advanced correct solutions to address the needs of the disadvantaged.[107]

James, having energized the Social Action Commission as a visible component of the connectional church, sought its permanent integration into the denominational infrastructure. He offered a resolution that recognized "the need for immediate concentrated efforts by the AME Church in the area of Human Rights and Social Justice" through an "allocation of $32,000 for Social Action." The proposal also called for a Department of Social Action with a full-time director rather than a part-time consultant. James, a 1968 candidate for the episcopacy, continued as a South Carolina pastor and in this part-time social action position. Bishop Frederick D. Jordan, however, accepted a special assignment in both ecumenical affairs and "Urban Ghetto Ministry."[108]

The social action energy of African Methodism morphed into housing partnerships between the denomination and the federal government. In the New York Annual Conference, Bishop John D. Bright formed a nonprofit housing corporation that explored "the continued need for Middle-Income housing and the federal government's willingness to finance these developments under the auspices of a nonprofit organization." The Philadelphia and Delaware Annual Conferences in joint session praised Bright for the "low cost housing [that] has been built under his leadership." Most significantly, he led in "opening the Sarah Allen Home to minister to the sick, the aged, and to the infirm," though at the 1968 General Conference its operations were shifted to the Women's Missionary Society. Additionally, General Officer H. Ralph Jackson, through the Department of Minimum Salary,

[106] Dickerson, *Militant Mediator*, 255; Taylor, *A. Philip Randolph*, 223.
[107] *Official Minutes . . . General Conference 1968*, 257–258.   [108] Ibid., 170, 251, 256.

believed the denomination should be involved in providing low-rent housing to the poor. Hence, in cooperation with the federal Department Housing and Urban Development, Jackson initiated projects in Memphis, New Orleans, Louisville, Seattle, and Bowling Green, Kentucky.[109]

Moreover, the Second Episcopal District comprising Maryland, the District of Columbia, Virginia, and North Carolina had ten low-income housing projects. The Fifth Episcopal District, stretching westward from Missouri to the Pacific Coast, had eight projects, including low-income housing units in St. Louis and Denver. Bishop Gomez identified specific congregations in Detroit, East Chicago, Indiana, Tuskegee, Alabama, Columbus, Ohio, and Fort Worth, Texas, as sponsors of low-income housing. These broad initiatives convinced Gomez to recommend that the denomination should name a full-time housing secretary.[110]

Most AME clergy scarcely resembled Frederick C. James and H. Ralph Jackson in their frontline activism and their conscious emulation of their denominational founder. While ministers frequently gestured to the AME ethos of Allenite insurgency and often identified with national and local civil rights organizations, their roles were mostly marginal and secondary to involvements with internal denominational affairs. Few contemporaries understood these phenomena better than Vernon Jordan, who as an attorney and NAACP official accompanied one of the two black students admitted in 1961 to the University of Georgia past a hostile white crowd. After his tenure with the Voter Educational Project, he became executive director in 1970 at the United Negro College Fund and in 1972 was appointed Whitney Young's successor at the NUL.

During his adolescence in Atlanta, Jordan, who had participated in an oratorical contest sponsored by Georgia's State Negro Voters League, was told that he would be a preacher. His mother, Mary Belle Jordan, an active member in the city's St. Paul AME Church, wanted her son to eschew ministry in their denomination. He should not, she believed, "spend his life" as a sycophant to a bishop. She also deplored "the political maneuvering within the AME Church," and she feared that if her son entered this system of hierarchy "it would take a lot energy to negotiate that structure."[111]

[109] *Official Minutes ... New York Annual Conference 1967*, 175; *Philadelphia/Delaware Annual Conference Minutes 1967*, 257; *Memphis Commercial Appeal*, August 88, 1980, Joseph Gomez, *Polity of the AME Church*, (Nashville, TN, Division of Christian Education of the African Methodist Episcopal Church, 1971), 87.
[110] Gomez, *Polity of the AME Church*, 87–89.   [111] Jordan, *Vernon Can Read*, 51–52.

Jordan, however, "liked the idea of becoming a preacher" because the black church figured largely "in the spiritual and political life of the black community." While an undergraduate at the Methodist affiliated DePauw University, Jordan, with a group of fellow students, visited Union Theological Seminary in New York City where their intellectual appetites were whetted through encounters with Reinhold Niebuhr and Paul Tillich, both internationally known theologians. Trip sponsors hoped that Jordan and the others "might get a call from the Lord" to preach. Though this divinely inspired call to preach failed to materialize, Jordan regretted that "no preacher in the AME Church ever took a real interest in me or in the other youngsters in the church." He agreed with his mother that AME clergy "were so busy running for bishop that there was no time for mentoring young people." He added "no one came up to me and said, 'this is what it is like to be a preacher.' Had they done so, the law as a profession might have had some serious competition." Nonetheless, Jordan believed that if he had entered the ministry "I know I would have had a church that combined a spiritual message with a lot of community outreach."[112]

The absence of AME mentors probably pertained to pastors at Jordan's home congregation. Some potential AME advisors who lived in Atlanta and were known as local civil rights activists were inaccessible to Jordan. Harold I. Bearden, pastor of Big Bethel starting in 1951, used the city's black radio station, WERD, to preach sermons that put his congregation at "the vanguard of the civil rights movement." Big Bethel member, Jesse Hill, an executive in the Atlanta Life Insurance Company, was involved with Atlanta University Center professors Whitney Young, M. Carl Holman, and Samuel Z. Westerfield in publishing a report through their Atlanta Committee for Cooperative Action titled *A Second Look: The Negro Citizen in Atlanta*, which showed the realities of segregation in "the city too busy to hate." Hill also chaired the Atlanta All-Citizens Registration Committee aimed at increasing black voting.[113]

After the Supreme Court in 1956 invalidated segregation on Montgomery, Alabama, buses, several black ministers in Atlanta, led by William Holmes Borders of Wheat Street Baptist Church, notified municipal officials of their intention to desegregate city buses. This group of pastors included Benjamin

[112] Ibid., 52–53.
[113] Gregory D. Coleman, *We're Heaven Bound!: Portrait of a Black Sacred Drama* (Athens, University of Georgia Press, 1992), 177; Dickerson, *Militant Mediator*, 109–111; Martin Luther King, Jr. to Jesse Hill, Jr., January 28, 1959, Clayborne Carson (ed.), *The Papers of Martin Luther King, Jr.*, Volume V, *Threshold of a New Decade*, January 1959–December 1960 (Berkeley, University of California Press, 2005), 114–115.

Gay of Antioch AME Church in Decatur, who joined his colleagues in forming the Triple L movement. Gay recalled that they "boarded the bus" and "rode downtown" while "all of the passengers except one got off as they saw us taking front seats."[114]

Jordan seemed unaware of the civil rights involvements of these AMEs in hometown Atlanta. Nonetheless, he "remained active in the AME Church" even though his spiritual advisors, Gardner Taylor and Howard Thurman, were ordained as Baptist ministers. Jordan, who poured the ethos of Allenite activism into his lay vocations, met the like-minded John H. Wheeler, also an AME layman, through their affiliation with the SRC. Wheeler, Jordan said, "mentored me and often sent me to represent him on the national commissions on which he sat. He would be an adviser and confidant to me for many years."[115]

Whether they were clergy, such as Bearden and Gay, or laity, such as Hill and Wheeler, these carriers of an AME activist legacy informed the institutional culture of the denomination. Too often, as Mary Jordan observed, these impulses became secondary to the political business of denominational governance and contests for office and power. At other times, though ministers like Bearden and Gay vied for the episcopacy, they still provided energetic support to movements for black civil rights. Although no AME clergy mentored Jordan, Wheeler, a layman of enviable AME pedigree, facilitated his rise to leadership in the civil rights cause. Though not determinative of particular ideological preferences, their AME identity, a cultural marker of background and heritage, helped to frame their public commitment to black advancement.

RECKONING WITH CIVIL RIGHTS OPPONENTS

Nothwithstanding their pivotal contributions to the civil rights movement, some in the clergy and laity succumbed to disguised but destructive associations with federal contacts who disparaged the black freedom struggle. FBI Director J. Edgar Hoover, while he disdained Martin Luther King, Jr. and engaged in a sustained campaign to discredit him, still maintained a cordial relationship with the outspoken Martin Luther King, Jr. supporter, Archibald J. Carey, Jr., the pastor of Quinn Chapel in Chicago. Hoover was

---

[114] James W. English, *Handyman of the Lord: The Life and Ministry of Reverend William Holmes Borders* (New York, Meredith Press, 1967), 89–90; Benjamin Gay, A *Retrospective Review of my Ministry* (n.p., n.d.), 4–5.
[115] Jordan, *Vernon Can Read*, 53, 177.

convinced that the Communist Party was manipulating the civil rights movement and duping some of its leaders and participants into espousing an anticapitalist ideology. Carey, like innumerable other African American spokespersons, had been subjected, at times unknowingly, to steady FBI surveillance of their militant black advocacy from the 1940s through the 1960s. Because Carey, who was also an attorney, seldom eschewed associations with leftist allies, including the National Lawyers Guild and some labor groups, sundry FBI informants wrongly concluded that he was among the "outstanding members of the Communist Party representing trade unions and both races." Other informants, however, though they acknowledged Carey's popular front strategy, testified that he was surely not a Communist.[116]

As a leading GOP officeholder in Chicago, Carey conspicuously supported the successful presidential candidacies of Dwight D. Eisenhower, which won him appointments during each of Ike's two terms. Initially, he served as an alternate delegate to the United Nations and then headed the President's Committee on Government Employment Policy. In the latter position, which investigated black hiring and promotions across the federal government, Carey interacted with Hoover, whose FBI had a better record in the employment of African Americans than many other agencies. For this reason, he featured Hoover in 1960 as a dinner speaker for Quinn Chapel's anniversary.[117]

Because of his amiable dealings with Hoover and his corresponding fiscal support of Martin Luther King Jr.'s Southern Christian Leadership Conference, Carey offered himself as a mediator between Hoover and King, despite the former's "dirty tricks" aimed at harassing the civil rights leader. Though Carey's appearance at FBI headquarters to intervene for King had the sanction of SCLC, the visit yielded neither an audience with Hoover nor any commitment to end the agency's hounding of King. Instead, Carey, who met with a Hoover underling, heeded admonitions that King should start to speak more favorably about the FBI, and fulfilled his promise to deliver this

[116] Lerone A. Martin of Washington University has chronicled the extensive enlistment of black clergy against Martin Luther King, Jr. See Martin's "Bureau Clergymen: How the FBI Colluded with an African American Televangelist to Destroy Martin Luther King, Jr.," *Religion and American Culture: A Journal of Interpretation*, Vol. 28, No. 1, 1–51. For a detailed narrative about J. Edgar Hoover's harassment of Martin Luther King, Jr., see David Garrow, *The FBI and Martin Luther King, Jr.* (New York, W. W. Norton and Company, 1981); Maurine Schiller to SAC, Chicago, August 13, 1954, *Archibald J. Carey Domestic Security Investigation File*—100—CG-20875. PDF (courtesy of Lerone A. Martin, Washington University).

[117] Dickerson, *African American Preachers and Politics*, 131–132, 174.

message to the SCLC leader. Despite Carey's inability to rescue King from Hoover's harassment, he used the occasion to lobby for a recommendation from Hoover for a position in the presidential administration of Lyndon B. Johnson. Though it is unclear whether Carey told King about his self-promotion, Carey remained committed to King. In 1965 an FBI surveillance report reprinted a *Chicago Sun-Times* article that noted "Dr. Martin Luther King, Jr. will occupy the pulpit of Quinn Chapel Sunday morning, at the invitation of his long-time friend, the Reverend Arch Carey."[118]

A blunder similar to Carey's faux pas at the FBI headquarters roiled the 1972 General Conference. The reelection campaign of President Richard M. Nixon had hovering over it a denunciation from Bishop Stephen G. Spottswood of the AME Zion Church. Spottswood, the chairman of the NAACP Board of Directors, said in 1970 that the Nixon administration was antiblack because of its "southern strategy" to attract to the GOP white segregationists, formerly in the Democratic Party, and to mollify them with attacks on the Voting Rights Act that newly empowered southern blacks. Spottswood's episcopal colleague, Bishop Charles Ewbank Tucker, a staunch Republican who delivered a prayer at Nixon's 1969 presidential inauguration, condemned Spottswood, saying that his criticism "was both unjustified and unwarranted" given Nixon's previous record in Congress and as Eisenhower's vice president. When the AMEs convened in Dallas, Texas, Bishop Decatur Ward Nichols, a veteran Republican, like Bishop Tucker, "announced" an interruption in the opening worship service because of "the late arrival of Mr. Edward Nixon, brother of the President of the United States." After a choir selection, "Bishop Jordan and Bishop Primm came to the podium to protest against the interruption of the General Conference's Religious Service by the interpolation of secular matters."[119]

After Edward Nixon entered the Memorial Auditorium, "a group of laymen and ministers rushed to the front of the pulpit protesting the change in the preliminaries of [the] Worship Service [with] some saying that the motive was political." The conference scribe reported that "attempts were made to restore order and to continue [the] service, but the Conference

---

[118] Ibid., 175–176; "*Chicago Sun-Times*," 100-35356-343, *Carey Domestic Security Investigation File* (courtesy of Lerone A. Martin, Washington University).

[119] *Minutes of the General Conference of the Thirty-Ninth Quadrennium of the African Methodist Episcopal Church* held in Dallas, TX, June 21–July 3, 1972 (Nashville, TN, AME Sunday School 1971), 86–87; *New York Times*, July 2, 1970; Telegram: C. Ewbank Tucker to Stephen G. Spottswood, July 3, 1970, *Records of the NAACP*, Administrative File, Board of Directors, Part VI, Box 18, Folder 3, Members: Stephen G. Spottswood, 1970: February–July, Manuscript Division, Library of Congress, Washington, DC.

became more restive." Obviously, Nixon recognized the ruckus that his presence was causing and that the 1,800 AMEs assembled in the auditorium had no desire to hear anything about his brother's reelection as president. Hence, he left the facility, leaving Bishop Nichols to explain how this unwanted speaker happened to come to the AME meeting. The "Committee responsible for the arrangements," Nichols defensively declared, "had merely used the only time available to present the honored guest." Apologetically, the bishop noted that he meant no "irreverence toward the traditions and customs of our Church."[120]

Carey's involvement with the Eisenhower administration, where he was empowered to investigate black federal employment, framed his overly benign perspective of J. Edgar Hoover. Hoover's FBI seemed more receptive to overtures from the Carey-led Government Employment Policy Committee than other federal agencies. Moreover, Carey, like Nichols and Tucker of the AME Zion Church, was exposed to Richard Nixon in the 1950s when he exhibited racially liberal views as Ike's vice president. Racial realities, which starkly contrasted with nonviolent civil rights marches, led Nixon in the late 1960s to exploit white backlash against widespread urban riots in which blacks protested the egregious ghetto conditions in which they lived. Hence, AMEs at the 1972 General Conference and Bishop Spottswood of the AME Zion Church negatively responded to this "new" Nixon who had already nominated to the Supreme Court two white southerners known for their open hostility to black civil rights. Whatever naivete Carey demonstrated at Hoover's FBI headquarters and Nichols showed as a host to Nixon's brother, fellow AMEs loudly reasserted their fealty to their church's liberationist legacy.[121]

ANTI-COLONIALISM, AFRICAN INDEPENDENCE, AND AFRICAN METHODISM

The political awakening in Africa after World War II paralleled the civil rights movement in the United States. Africans demanded independence from European colonial powers and opposed white minority rule in Rhodesia, South Africa, and Southwest Africa. AMEs operated in several territories on the "mother" continent and indigenous ministers and members helped to spearhead and participate in various anti-colonial campaigns. Their counterparts in the United States, either the bishops who were

[120] *Minutes of the General Conference ... 1972*, 87.
[121] Dickerson, *African American Preachers and Politics*, 150–151, 167.

assigned to supervise African districts or rank-and-file clergy and laity, facilitated, endorsed, but sometimes demurred on the aims of self-determination in Africa.

AME leaders recognized the significance of African independence and movements to end white supremacist governments on the continent. Bishop Frederick D. Jordan observed that "a determined assault has been made by the leaders in many countries upon imperialism and colonialism." He added that "the cry of 'freedom' may be heard on every hand." Moreover, he said, "tribal and other national and geographical differences are forgotten, language barriers no longer exist, for the African speaks the same language of freedom."[122]

Jordan's excitement about the prospects of African independence was tempered by the relentless grip of white minority governments in South Africa and Rhodesia. After his election to the episcopacy in 1952, Jordan, who had been sent to Central Africa, also replaced the reassigned Bishop Howard T. Primm in South Africa. Jordan's two episcopal districts included territories under the rule of white settler regimes. Jordan was aware that the Nationalist Party "had just come into power and was faced with riots and forceful resistance by the African people." Artishia Jordan, the bishop's wife, believed that officials in the South African government exerted influence in both northern and southern Rhodesia where colonial British administrators, like South African whites, "did not desire to have an American Negro representing a church whose policy and philosophy of brotherhood and equality were directly at variance with the apartheid advocated by the government."[123]

Additionally, in mineral-rich Northern Rhodesia, Jordan's original assignment, indigenous Africans encountered mandated pay inequities between themselves and settler whites. There was a "general policy," Artishia Jordan observed, "of keeping the African from experiencing equality with the white at any point and is implemented by agreement between white labor unions and the [mine] employers." Similarly, in Southern Rhodesia there were "strict limitations [on] land which the Native Africans are permitted to own." The Jordans concluded that the unusual amount of "red tape" they encountered at British embassies in Rome, Italy, Livingstone, Northern Rhodesia, and elsewhere showed raw opposition to their presence in these colonial territories and their delayed entry into South Africa itself.[124]

---

[122] Artishia Wilkerson Jordan, *The African Methodist Episcopal Church in Africa* (n.p., c. 1960), 8.
[123] Ibid., 109.   [124] Ibid., 65, 101–102, 108.

Besides the Jordans, other AME leaders supported African demands for independence from European rule and encouraged opposition to white settler governments that denied to blacks an equitable share in national governance and in the economic benefits derived from natural resource development in their native lands. When leaders in the colonized countries of Africa and Asia met in 1955 in Indonesia at the Bandung Conference, to declare their alignment against European imperialism, the bishops in their 1956 episcopal address endorsed this objective. They said the meeting would "let the world know that the darker peoples are determined to free themselves from the yoke of colonization by imperial powers." Toward that end the bishops delegated Bishop Richard R. Wright, Jr. and Secretary of Missions A. Chester Clark to represent the denomination in Ghana on March 6, 1957 at ceremonies marking its independence from Great Britain. Moreover, George A. Singleton, the editor of the *AME Church Review*, emblazoned a picture of Kwame Nkrumah on the cover of the April–June 1957 issue. Singleton said "the name KWAME NKRUMAH is a symbol of inspiration to millions of BLACKS the world over and GHANA is prophetic of what the peoples of Africa might become." Furthermore, in keeping the church's focus on African freedom movements, at the 1960 General Conference Frederick C. James proposed a resolution that denounced the recent police killing of sixty-nine black demonstrators in Sharpeville in the Transvaal who had protested South Africa's hated "pass laws." James declared that the "AME Church reaffirm[s] its position and denounce[s] the brutality inflicted upon the people of Africa."[125]

African Methodism in Africa operated in three interrelated spheres. First, establishing and maintaining churches and schools, despite hostility from European colonial and white settler officials, preoccupied AME leaders from the United States and from within affected African areas. Secondly, indigenous ministers and members, in supporting a stubborn AME presence in their colonial regions and embracing African Methodism because of its black institutional autonomy, positioned the denomination to become conspicuously involved in fighting colonialism and white supremacy. Thirdly, the

---

[125] *The Official Minutes of the Thirty-Fifth Session of the General Conference of the African Methodist Episcopal Church which convened in Miami, Florida, May 1956 at the Dinner Key Auditorium,* 346; Jordan, *The African Methodist Episcopal Church in Africa,* 20–21; Alexander Joseph Allen, *The Episcopal Address to the Thirty-Fifth Quadrennial Session of the General Conference of the African Methodist Episcopal Church convening in Miami, Florida, May 2–16, 1956* (n.p., 1956), 33; *AME Church Review,* Vol. 73, No. 192, April–June 1957, cover, 1; *Official Minutes of the Thirty-Sixth Session of the General Conference, AME Church, May 1960, Los Angeles, CA,* 231.

convergence of the liberationist objectives of diasporic blacks and their militant call for African self-determination motivated intellectuals of AME heritage, including an influential cadre of expatriates, to forge consensus with denominational officials in blending the civil rights struggle in the United States with the battle against European colonialism and white supremacy in Africa into a seamless freedom initiative within the black Atlantic.

The late nineteenth-century origins of African Methodism in Sierra Leone and Liberia provided these Creole-ruled nations with mature congregations and schools and energized missionaries to expand the denomination to other territories in West Africa. Europa Randall of Sierra Leone, for example, arrived in the Gold Coast in the late 1930s to organize and build Bethel AME Church at Essa Kado. In the early 1940s over a dozen other congregations with affiliated elementary schools derived from Randall's initiative. Additionally, I. C. Steady of Liberia assisted Randall in her early educational activities. Though a school started at Essa Kado and Payne Collegiate Institute began in Accra, neither operated in a facility of its own. A network of AME schools also functioned in the 1940s and 1950s in the colonial Gold Coast and in independent Ghana, but they usually occupied rental properties with funds that Randall, the general superintendent, received from the Women's Missionary Society.[126]

The initial years of Ghanaian independence coincided with the incumbency of Bishop Samuel R. Higgins in West Africa. His supervision in the Ghana Annual Conference included thirty-five preaching sites organized within ten circuits and five schools, the most important of which was Clayborn College. Higgins, who recognized the urgent condition of Clayborn, planned in 1959 to move it to a better location. The Women's Missionary Society promised to support the Higgins initiative. The bishop's cardiac disease, however, compelled his return to the United States, thus ending his on-site presence in his episcopal district. Nonetheless, the committee that compiled the 1960 AME Discipline met and responded to a recommendation from I. C. Steady of Liberia that Ghana's Clayborn College and the AME Boy's Academy in Kumasi should be eligible for denominational funding.[127]

---

[126] L. L. Berry, *A Century of Missions of the African Methodist Episcopal Church, 1840–1940* (New York, Gutenberg Printing Co., Inc., 1942), 133, 135; Jordan, *The African Methodist Episcopal Church in Africa*, 25.

[127] Jordan, *The African Methodist Episcopal Church in Africa*, 24–25; Wright, *The Bishops of the African Methodist Episcopal Church*, 230; *Official Minutes . . . General Conference, 1960*, 17.

Notwithstanding promised denominational allocations, Higgins and Artishia Jordan, whose husband was later assigned as the bishop in West Africa, believed that AME schools in Ghana were best served by harnessing them to new educational initiatives unfolding in the newly independent nation. Though Higgins had articulated plans to rehabilitate Clayborn College, the government insisted that AME schools should "do an accredited grade of work." Jordan welcomed the admonition because "Ghana, the new and exuberant country [and] a vigorous nation, [is] taking great strides in developing its natural and its human resources. Let us as a great church stride along with them."[128]

Nigeria, which gained its independence from Great Britain in 1960, had a minimal AME presence. Though African Americans from the United States represented the Nigeria Annual Conference at the 1956 General Conference, none were named for the subsequent three quadrennial sessions until 1972 when Nigerians officially participated in the AME meeting. Nonetheless, the 1960 General Conference, which met months before Nigeria's formal independence, impaneled a Committee to Study Nigeria and celebrated its independence and that of other new African nations. "This inescapable challenge," delegates declared, required the AME Church to recognize the "dire need of schools, as well as churches" in Nigeria and other emergent nations on the "mother" continent. As in Ghana, AMEs, though they were "playing catch up," linked their denomination's development to a decolonized Africa.[129]

While successful struggles for independence in Ghana and Nigeria buoyed AMEs, the denomination's dense presence in Africa's other colonial and white settler territories also required daring fights for black empowerment. Blacks in Northern Rhodesia, for example, wrestled their autonomy from the British in 1964 to become an independent Zambia. Decades before this accomplishment, a congruence between the entry of African Methodism and the rise of anticolonialism coalesced by 1953. Both developments drew from indigenous clergy and laity, including some who believed that the proud institutional independence of the AME Church could energize movements to end British colonialism.[130]

African Methodism, through the efforts of native ministers, spread the denomination from strongholds in South Africa. Briefly between 1903 and

[128] Wright, *The Bishops of the African Methodist Episcopal Church*, 247; Jordan, *The African Methodist Episcopal Church in Africa*, 25, 27.
[129] *Official Minutes ... General Conference, 1960*, 26, 94, 228–229.
[130] Walton R. Johnson, *Worship and Freedom: A Black American Church in Zambia* (New York, Africana Publishing Company, 1977), 20.

1906, the AME Church penetrated Northern Rhodesia, and reentered the territory in 1925. Because of clergy with a knowledge of tribal languages and cultural idioms, impressive growth occurred between 1932 and 1945. The denomination had its greatest success where AME congregations established locally funded schools. Despite a dearth of trained ministers, irregular denominational allocations for education, and a poorly equipped clinic, the AME Church sustained its appeal in North Rhodesia. Indigenous ministers and members promoted the idea of African Methodism as an autonomous religious body that was unlike European missionary societies, which often treated Africans as inferior and incapable of self-government within their own churches.[131]

As African Methodism grew, European missionaries accused the denomination of an "active propaganda" that emphasized "all-African-controlled churches." Moreover, African nationalists made common cause with AMEs because the indigenous members were becoming practiced in religious autonomy. One scholar, Walton R. Johnson, said "the AME Church attracted patriots because it was a symbol of the nationalist ideal and because its existence was in fact partial realization of nationalist goals."[132]

AMEs who aligned themselves with Black Nationalist objectives at the 1953 Northern Rhodesia Annual Conference denounced white rule because "racial discrimination is robbing our country of the freedom enjoyed by other countries." At the 1955 session AMEs supported black labor strikes aimed against racially discriminatory practices, and backed the Northern Rhodesia African Congress in its boycott of slaughterhouses where a "colour bar" was being imposed. These and other related issues compelled these indigenous AMEs to declare themselves a church "that should join in condemning injustice and oppression."[133]

The AME Church, alone among religious bodies in Northern Rhodesia, wanted "to have Christian justice put into practical effect." Moreover, the "multi-national and multi-ethnic" identity of AMEs, Johnson observed, showed that the denomination transcended tribalism and thus modeled nationalist goals of uniting the diverse peoples in Northern Rhodesia. As a result, nationalists increasingly identified with the AMEs. Kenneth Kaunda, for example, the future leader of an independent Zambia, belonged to Ebenezer AME Church in Lusaka. He and a few others, however, abandoned African Methodism in 1957 because of an apolitical presiding elder who objected to the denominational involvement in anticolonial causes.

---

[131] Ibid., 6–8, 17–19.   [132] Ibid., 14–15, 20, 29.   [133] Ibid., 30.

Nonetheless, there were innumerable others who ignored the perspectives of conservative clergy and openly blended their AME and nationalist activities. Isaac Mumpansha, who had been a presiding elder, was present at the founding of the Northern Rhodesia African Congress, later served as an ambassador for Zambia to Nigeria and West Germany, and was elected to parliament.[134]

Though individual African Methodists participated in Northern Rhodesia's nationalist movement, there was scarcely any institutional involvement in various political organizations. Church officials, in most instances, feared government decertification of the AME presence in the country if any official denominational insurgencies were detected. Moreover, there were partisan cleavages between competing nationalist groups that gained footholds in one or another AME congregation. In some churches the African National Congress (ANC) was dominant and in others the United National Independence Party was ascendant. Nonetheless, a broader coalition of nationalists, inclusive of some AMEs, created an independent Zambia out of colonial Northern Rhodesia.[135]

The strenuous effort to found a black-ruled Zimbabwe started in 1923 against a blended colonial government and white settler rule in Southern Rhodesia. Black opposition shifted in 1965, however, to political and guerrilla insurgency against a renegade white regime that declared independence from Great Britain. Led by Ian Smith, the white minority faction defied the British and barred blacks from any meaningful say in Rhodesian government. Whether against British colonial hegemony or minority white governance, alignments developed between black nationalists and indigenous African Methodists.

From its origins in South Africa, the denomination initially spread in 1903 to Bulawayo, a newly founded city in Southern Rhodesia. As African Methodism moved into Matabeleland and Mashonaland in the 1920s and into other territories in the 1930s, colonial whites increasingly described AMEs as "political agitators" who regularly chanted "Africa arise; Seek for the Lord and do not be left by other nations." As membership rose from 900 in 1952 to 5,700 in 1961, AMEs became recognizable nationalists whom "some of the African leaders and chiefs had welcomed ... to preach the Gospel ... to mobilize them against the colonial system."[136]

---

[134] Ibid., 31–33.   [135] Ibid., 34–35, 37.
[136] Clement N. Mkwanazi, *The History of the African Methodist Episcopal Church in Zimbabwe* (n.p., 1992), 9, 12–13; Clement N. Mkwanazi, *The History and Expansion of the African Methodist Episcopal Church in Central Africa* (n.p., n.d.), 19.

As white minority rule was hardening, Bishop Harold I. Bearden, assigned in 1964, was denied permission to enter Rhodesia. In fact no AME bishop was allowed in the country between 1964 and 1972. These roadblocks, which cut off denominational support to economically vulnerable congregations and clergy, prevented AME growth beyond the few thousand reported in the early 1960s. These developments, though they undermined AME insurgency against the Smith regime, increased defiance from guerrilla fighters and from a new bishop assigned to Rhodesia in 1972. Bishop H. Hartford Brookins, though permitted to hold an annual conference in Bulawayo in 1974, criticized the Smith government and endorsed a resolution that urged AME participation in "the struggle for freedom." In Rhodesia the indigenous population endured "indignities, deprivations and humiliations at the hands of unchristian government leaders, white racists, and exploiters." Though Brookins later was banned from the country, he addressed the African National Council in 1975 and donated $2,000 to support opposition to the Smith regime. He also funded an African National Council official to attend the Women's Missionary Society convention in the United States, where another $10,000 was allocated to the liberation effort. The ousting of Smith in 1980 and the creation of a black ruled Zimbabwe was mainly thanks to the guerrilla war and a heritage of nationalism drawn in part from the AME presence.[137]

The longevity of the AME Church in South Africa led to a combination of both insurgent and vacillating responses to the nation's apartheid regime. Because of so much institutional infrastructure to protect and maintain, AME leadership accommodated to demands from the white minority government. The General Conference of 1952 assigned Bishop Howard Thomas Primm to South Africa, but he was refused permission to enter the country. When Primm's appointment shifted to another jurisdiction because of a bishop's death, Frederick D. Jordan, his replacement, tried twice without success to enter the country. He succeeded on the third try, and was allowed in on condition that he would "train indigenous leadership" to take the place of African American bishops.[138]

The practical effect of this demand lay in shifting AME leadership from mainly absentee and potentially insurgent African American bishops to colored clergy who enjoyed a higher status in South Africa's racial ranking than that of the majority black population. There existed a tiered structure of

[137] Mkwanazi, *The History of the African Methodist Episcopal Church in Zimbabwe*, 27–28, 30–32.
[138] Jordan, *The African Methodist Episcopal Church in Africa*, 64–65.

rights and privileges, with whites, especially the Afrikaner elite, at the top, the colored or mixed race and Indian peoples in the middle, and indigenous blacks at the bottom. The AME Church, because of its strength within colored communities in the Cape Province, drew leadership disproportionately from within this group. The Jamaica-born Francis McDonald Gow, who identified with the colored population, for example, until his death in 1931 served for about two decades as South Africa's AME superintendent, as a fill-in for the part-time presence of African American bishops.[139]

Like Gow, Josephus R. Coan, an African American based in the Transvaal, served as the AME superintendent during most of the 1940s. His jurisdiction included South Africa's Fifteenth Episcopal District and southern and central Africa's Seventeenth Episcopal District. Because World War II hostilities prevented the travel of the assigned prelate, Bishop Frank Madison Reid, Sr. Coan, who had lived in South Africa since 1938, supervised a membership, inclusive of adjoining territories, that rose from 43,000 to 70,000 and enrollments at Wilberforce Institute that increased from 450 to 1,026. Far from adopting an oppositional posture to South Africa's white government, Coan drew regular aid for AME primary schools from the Provincial Education Department and annual government grants to Crogman Community Clinic. Moreover, in 1941 and 1943 the Native Affairs Department allocated infrastructure funds to Wilberforce Institute that Coan hoped would develop the school as "a young Tuskegee."[140]

Notwithstanding, these achievements, Coan, representing the Seventeenth Episcopal District, failed at the General Conference of 1948 to be elected a bishop for South Africa. His competitor, Fifteenth Episcopal District candidate Francis Herman Gow, the son of Coan's predecessor as superintendent, was the pastor, like his father, at Cape Town's Bethel Memorial Church. Though born in South Africa, Gow had become a United States citizen, a first lieutenant who fought in World War I, a pastor in Ohio and West Virginia, and an instructor at Tuskegee Institute. Despite their loss in the race to fill eight episcopal vacancies, Coan and Gow on the first ballot respectively tallied 360 and 310 votes out of 924. Though Coan abandoned

---

[139] James T. Campbell, *Songs of Zion: The African Methodist Episcopal Church in the United States and South Africa* (New York, Oxford University Press, 1998), 127; Wright, *The Bishops of the African Methodist Episcopal Church*, 188.

[140] Wright, *Encyclopedia of African Methodism*, 68; Campaign Flyer: "Vote for J. R. Coan for Bishop of South Africa" (Private Collection of the Author); Josephus R. Coan, "A Report of the Missionary Activities of the African Methodist Episcopal Church," in *The Seventeenth Episcopal District, African Methodist Episcopal District, Embracing the Transvaal, Orangia, Cape, Natal & Zambesi Annual Conferences, 1940–1944*, (n.p., 1948), 8–9.

his aspiration to the bishopric, Gow, the only candidate from the "mother" continent at the 1952 General Conference, failed a second time to become a bishop.[141]

Gow benefited, however, from the requirement of the Nationalist government that no more African American bishops would be allowed into South Africa and that only an indigenous prelate would be allowed to function in the Fifteenth Episcopal District. In response, the General Conference of 1956 elected Gow to the episcopacy. He was reassigned to South Africa at the 1960 General Conference, and served until 1964. Gow, born in 1887, was nearing seventy years old when he and his African American wife, Louise Ballou of Richmond, Virginia, returned to Cape Town. Gow, who only technically qualified as an indigenous African, left to Easter M. Gordon, a minister in Worcester, the administration of brutish apartheid policies upon South Africa's AME churches.[142]

Gordon, ordained in 1949, was the son of an AME pioneer, Daniel P. Gordon. Bishop Bonner appointed him as a presiding elder and pastor at Zion AME Church in Worcester as his father's replacement. The 1,500-member Zion Church was known for championing "the upliftment of the coloured people in the Worcester District." After the 1964 General Conference reassigned Gow to West Africa, Gordon became the liaison between four succeeding African American bishops and the apartheid government.[143]

The passage of the Group Areas Act in 1950, which upended innumerable colored and black communities, directly affected their local AME congregations. The apartheid legislation declared areas as white and forced the resettlement of nonwhite populations. Hence, AMEs lost their churches in return for other sites in newly designated townships. In Cape Town, for example, parishioners of District 6 who worshipped at the cathedral edifice of Bethel Memorial Church witnessed its demolition. With respect to the Umzimkulu congregation, Gow and Gordon had only a month to accept a new location and merely six months to construct a building. In the Transvaal,

[141] Wright, *The Bishops of the African Methodist Episcopal Church*, 188–189; Campbell, *Songs of Zion*, 245; Official Minutes of the Thirty-Third Session of the General Conference of the African Methodist Episcopal Church held in Kansas City, KS, May 1948, 33–34, in *Combined Minutes of the General Conferences*, 104; *Official Minutes ... General Conference, 1952*, 246–248.

[142] Wright, *The Bishops of the African Methodist Episcopal Church*, 189. Wright incorrectly cites Gow's birthdate as September 29, 1896 when in fact it was September 29, 1887.

[143] Dennis C. Dickerson, *Religion, Race, and Region: Research Notes on AME Church History* (Nashville, TN, AME Sunday School Union, 1995), 131-134.

because the time to approve the relocated site of the congregation of the R. R. Wright Church in Benoni expired owing to government inaction, Gordon had to intervene with white municipal officials to get an extension.[144]

Getting African American bishops into South Africa also preoccupied Gordon. Between 1964 and 1976 Bishops Harrison J. Bryant, G. Dewey Robinson, and Frederick C. James relied on Gordon to negotiate with white authorities for visas to permit their entry. Each was compelled to agree with particular conditions that satisfied the apartheid government. Bryant agreed to establish an executive committee in all annual conferences to explore plans for AME autonomy in South Africa. Similarly, Robinson promised to finish plans for indigenous leadership. Moreover, James was admonished that no more "foreign bishops" would be allowed into the country. Gordon, mindful that government maintained a watchful eye over African American governance in South Africa, inaugurated his own run for the bishopric. With initial support from Gow and others in the Fifteenth Episcopal District, Gordon was an unsuccessful candidate at the 1964, 1968, and 1972 General Conferences.[145]

While AMEs bargained with white officials about routine denominational operations, mounting militancy seethed within South Africa against apartheid. As grassroots demonstrations and riots, especially in the school protests in 1976 in Soweto, drew international attention, AMEs, on both sides of the Atlantic, intensified their support for the anti-apartheid movement. AME involvement in the ANC, dating from the 1920s through such ministers as Nimrod Tantsi and Edward Khalie, connected to a subsequent generation of insurgents in the 1970s and 1980s. Wilfred J. Messiah, a future bishop, for example, eschewed comments of his professor who declared nonwhite students as "only good enough to sweep the floors." Moreover, Messiah's opposition to apartheid caused police to pursue him and force his exit from South Africa in 1979.[146]

Nonetheless, Bishop Donald G. K. Ming, newly assigned to South Africa in 1976, promised the apartheid government a nonpolitical posture and a focus on church development. JET reported that one minister in the Cape Annual Conference said that Ming was not "a politician" and was "a visitor to the country by courtesy of the government." Militant black South

[144] Ibid., 136–137.
[145] *Official Minutes ... General Conference 1964*, 204, 206; Dickerson, *Religion, Race, and Region*, 135–136.
[146] Campbell, *Songs of Zion*, 319–320; *Profile of a Candidate: The Rev Dr. Wilfred J. Messiah*, 2004), private collection of the Author.

Africans, however, believed that the AME Church should abandon its "low profile" in the anti-apartheid struggle. Nonetheless, with a $153,000 quadrennial denominational allocation from the Overseas Development Fund and additional monies that he and his wife, Edith W. Ming, raised, the bishop led in building forty-five new churches. Ming's accomplishments and those of his successor, Bishop John E. Hunter, laid foundations for the 1984 General Conference to spin off another episcopal district in South Africa and to elect a South African, Harold B. Senatle, to preside over it.[147]

AMEs throughout the black Atlantic, however, recognized that institutional advancement required parallel support for insurgencies against apartheid. Hence, the 1984 General Conference realized that black South Africans could be described "as the most oppressed people on the face of the earth." Among the "atrocities" that they endured was a paltry weekly wage of $12 for those who mined for diamonds to make rich whites in South Africa and abroad. Therefore, the social action committees at every level within the AME infrastructure should press the US Congress "to divest" from South Africa, businesses should cease doing business with the apartheid regime, and the public should boycott South African diamonds. Additionally, the Overseas Social Action Committee at the 1988 General Conference, consisting mainly of delegates from South Africa, pressed fellow conferees to ending apartheid "by lobbying, writing letters to the United States Congress and to the South African State President P. W. Botha." Moreover, the General Conference was asked "as a matter of urgency" to help prevent the execution of the Sharpeville Six, "twenty-six other patriots," and other political prisoners "being tried in court cases."[148]

International pressures, expressed in divestment campaigns and indigenous unrest, intensified in the 1970s and 1980s and helped to upend apartheid. The release of Nelson Mandela, the imprisoned leader of the ANC, became the focus of global anti-apartheid initiatives. Mandela, a veteran fighter

[147] *The Combined Minutes of the Forty-First Session of the General Conference of the African Methodist Episcopal Church* held in New Orleans, LA, June 18-28, 1980 (Nashville, TN, AME Sunday School Union, 1980), 248-249; "Donald George Kenneth Ming" in Frank C. Cummings, John H. Dixon, Thelma Singleton-Scott, and Patricia A. P. Green (compilers), *The First Episcopal District's Historical Review of 200 Years of African Methodism* (Philadelphia, PA, First Episcopal District, African Methodist Episcopal District, 1987), 93' JET, February 14, 1980.

[148] *The Combined Minutes of the Forty-Second Session of the General Conference of the African Methodist Episcopal Church* held in Kansas City, MI, July 7-15, 1984 (Nashville, TN, AME Sunday School Union, 1984), 266; *The Combined Minutes of the Forty-Third Session of the General Conference of the African Methodist Episcopal Church* held in Fort Worth, TX, July 6-14, 1988 (Nashville, TN, AME Sunday School Union, 1988), 914-915.

Figure 6.5 AME Church of South Africa Voter Training Manual, 1994 (used with permission from Bishop Paul Kawimbe, Nineteenth Episcopal District, African Methodist Episcopal Church)

against white minority rule, was arrested, tried, and sentenced in 1962 to life in prison for violent opposition to the government. When South Africa's State President F. W. De Klerk released Mandela from twenty-seven years of imprisonment in 1990, the process of apartheid's demise and the genesis of multiracial democracy accelerated.

AMEs moved rapidly to identify with this transformation in South Africa. Mandela's 1990 visit to the United States included a stop in Atlanta at Big Bethel AME Church, where the ANC leader appeared in the pulpit with Bishop Harold B. Senatle, a fellow South African and President of the AME Council of Bishops. Two years later, Big Bethel's pastor, McKinley Young, was elected to the episcopacy and assigned to one of the two jurisdictions in South Africa. In preparation for the 1994 election that would bring Mandela to the presidency, Bishop Senatle and Bishop Young mobilized AME officialdom in South Africa to register blacks to vote and to publish, with funds from the Bishops Council, the *AME Church of South Africa Voters Training Manual* to facilitate the nation's political transition. Fred C. Harrison, formerly the AME Secretary of Missions and now a pastor in South Africa, compiled the thickly detailed pamphlet for "activists and volunteers who will be involved in voter education." An explanation of voters' rights for over 18 million people who had never exercised the franchise was presented. Pictures of sample ballots, "mock election role play" procedures, and scripts for voter education workshops were also included. The ANC especially used the AME Manual in the Western Cape. Additionally, Bishops Senatle, John R. Bryant, and Richard Allen Chappelle joined Bishop Young as election observers. Floyd H. Flake, the pastor at Allen AME Church in Jamaica, New York, and the United States representative from New York's sixth congressional district, visited South Africa a few months before the election. He admonished Mandela and the ANC "to build infrastructure in black regions that were neglected under apartheid."[149]

INTELLECTUALS OF AME PEDIGREE ON FREEDOM IN THE BLACK ATLANTIC

AME involvement in the civil rights movement in the United States and opposition to colonial and white settler rule in Africa identified the denomination with a broad range of insurgent initiatives throughout the Atlantic World. These activities exposed the historic tensions between the dual pursuit of black ecclesiastical autonomy and traditional commitments to liberationist objectives. Those who believed that African Methodism should emphasize its emancipationist ethos rather than ecclesiastical preservation included intellectuals of AME background who envisaged themselves as pan-Africanists and their denomination, at least historically, as an institutional expression of black Atlantic identity. Though they may have been invisible to most ministers and members, these thinkers, as they pursued the life of the mind and engaged in broader intellectual and insurgent activities, envisaged themselves as no less AME than others who regularly populated the church's pulpits and pews.

Beyond formal membership in a congregation and participation in denominational affairs, a cadre of mostly expatriate intellectuals in the 1950s and 1960s expanded the meaning of being AME. Adherence to the AME ethos of insurgency against racial and colonial hegemony defined their allegiance to African Methodism. Moreover, the influence of family lineage

---

[149] Jamye Coleman Williams, "Harold Ben Senatle and Nelson Mandela: A Moment in Time," *AME Church Review*, Vol. 109, No. 354, April–June 1994, 18-19; *AME Church of South Africa Voters Training Manual* (Johannesburg, South Africa, African Methodist Episcopal Church, 1994), 1, 7, 13–21; "Birth of a Nation" pictorial, *AME Church Review*, No. 109, No. 354, April–June 1994, 10; Floyd H. Flake, "Elections of South Africa," *AME Church Review*, Vol. 109, No. 354, April–June 1994, 41–42.

and the effects of Afrocentricism anchored in the AME heritage sustained their identity as African Methodists. Through their scholarship, their advocacy of African independence movements, and their cosmopolitan and continental experiences and interactions in Europe and Africa connected them to other thinkers and activists associated with the resurgence of Africa. They helped to constitute an influential aggregation of modern diasporic thinkers, who in interaction with their AME background, created intellectual scaffolding for a new generation of empowered blacks in the Atlantic World. Hence, African Methodism was expressed through the intellectual tributary of several scholars bred in its proud transatlantic legacy.

Shirley Graham Du Bois, the second wife to the iconic W. E. B. Du Bois, an anticolonialist and a political leftist, drew her militancy and pan-African perspectives, at least foundationally, from her AME family heritage. Though later baptized as a Baptist and scornful of the "narcotizing effect" of accommodationist black churches, Graham Du Bois admired her father, AME pastor David A. Graham, and respected the denomination that he served across several assignments in various states. From the elder Graham she imbibed "the history of our church-founded before the Civil War by free black men in Philadelphia who refused to be discriminated against 'in the house of the Lord.'" In her memoir about her future spouse, she reminded readers that Du Bois' view of the AME Church, "the greatest Negro organization in the world," was aligned with the opinion of her father. As someone who lived as a toddler at Wilberforce University, Graham Du Bois, whose husband had taught on this same campus, had dense exposure to the clergy and congregations among whom her father served in the Midwest, the South, and West until his death in 1936. In 1901 Graham received the honorary D.D. degree from the AME-supported Paul Quinn College in Texas, and in 1916 biographies of him and wife Lizzie Etta Graham appeared in the *Centennial Encyclopedia of the African Methodist Episcopal Church*.[150]

From Indianapolis, where she was born in 1896, to Accra, Ghana, and Cairo, Egypt, several decades later, Graham Du Bois' pan-Africanist

[150] Gerald Horne, *Race Woman: The Lives of Shirley Graham Du Bois* (New York, New York University Press, 2002), 48, 98; Shirley Graham Du Bois, *His Day is Marching On: A Memoir of W. E. B. Du Bois* (Philadelphia, PA, J. B. Lippencott Company, 1971), 12; Richard R. Wright, Jr. (ed.), *Centennial Encyclopedia of the African Methodist Episcopal Church* (Philadelphia, PA, AME Book Concern, 1916), 96–97; David A. Graham in the 1900 United States Federal Census, http://search.ancestry.com/collections/1900usfedcen/40129; Rev David A. Graham in the Indiana Death Certificates, 1899–2011, Indiana State Board of Health, Death Certificates, 1900–2011, microfilm, Indiana Archives and Records Administration, Indianapolis, Indiana.

trajectory grew from her AME beginnings. Her father's black Atlantic sensibilities had been stirred during his childhood in Indiana when Frederick Douglass "allowed him to hold the sword of Toussaint L'Ouverture," the Haitian liberator. Graham Du Bois also recalled when Du Bois visited Colorado Springs, Graham had asked him about his "presentation at [the] Versailles [peace conference] of plans for the decolonization of Africa." Perhaps, more importantly, the Graham family lived in the Atlantic reality of African Methodism. William Sampson Brooks, an uncle by marriage, was elected in 1920 to the AME episcopacy. Accompanying him to his assignment in West Africa was his wife Susan, sister to Lizzie Etta Graham. Because Bishop Brooks's responsibilities included an ill-equipped school in Monrovia, Liberia, he appointed Graham as principal of the Monrovia Boy's College. Though Graham eschewed the emphasis on industrial education rather than the academic emphasis at the AME-operated Wilberforce University, he committed to aid his brother-in-law's educational mission. He disdained, however, haughty Americo-Liberians who ruled Liberia and the derision they expressed toward indigenous African culture. Nonetheless, Bishop Brooks purchased 20 acres of land for the AME school and bought property for the AMEs in downtown Monrovia. Also in Monrovia, the Susan Brooks Memorial AME Church was built to mark the contributions of the aunt of Graham Du Bois.[151]

The family's lived legacy of pan-Africanism blended with Graham Du Bois' inheritance of black insurgency. Throughout his sundry pastorates he supported the NAACP, and while serving in New Orleans called a meeting to denounce the mob burning of a black man. Despite warning that he would also be lynched, Graham persisted in holding the meeting, though he placed a gun next his Bible. Hence, his daughter's lifelong activism and routine radicalism culminated through her second marriage in 1951 to the widowed W. E. B. Du Bois. In 1961 the couple arrived in Ghana at the invitation of Kwame Nkrumah, the nation's first postcolonial president. He wanted Dr. Du Bois to assemble scholarly contributors to develop an *Encyclopedia Africana*. With a house identified, renovations finished, and travel related to Du Bois' medical treatment completed, Graham Du Bois declared "our home was now really Africa."[152]

---

[151] Graham Du Bois, *His Day is Marching On*, 18, 84; Wright, *The Bishops of the African Methodist Episcopal Church*, 108–109.

[152] Horne, *Race Woman*, 40; Graham Du Bois, *His Day is Marching On*, 321–341; David Graham Du Bois, "Mission and Ministry in America and Africa: Reflections on David and Etta Graham," *AME Church Review*, Vol. 117, No. 384, October–December 2001, 41–42.

Just as the Reverend David and Lizzie Etta Graham lived in Liberia along with Bishop William and Susan Brooks, Graham Du Bois, after her husband's death in Ghana in 1963, joined her son, David, in Cairo, Egypt. While her family's presence in Africa focused on the religious dimensions of pan-Africanism, Graham Du Bois pursued anticolonialism as her emphasis. In this objective she found a champion in Egypt's president Gamal Abdul Nasser. Her alliance with the Black Studies movement in the United States provided her with a forum to articulate her views. Nathan Hare, the fired professor and founder of Black Studies at San Francisco State College, and Robert Christman, a poet, launched the *Black Scholar*, a journal dedicated to black and Third World anticolonialism. In the periodical Graham Du Bois explained her perspectives about Egypt as a bulwark against the reentry of western imperialism into Africa.[153]

In two serialized articles in the *Black Scholar*, entitled "Egypt is Africa," Graham Du Bois examined "why the modern white Christian world has so persistently and resolutely ignored and even denied that Egypt is Africa." Egypt's kinship to black Africa, she wrote, was evidenced, for example, in a thirteenth-century BC mask of King Tutankhamen, which was a "portrait," she observed, "of a sensitive young black man." This history was relevant to 1970, the year the articles appeared, because Egypt "is defending Africa's most important gates against imperialist aggression." President Nasser, "the first indigenous Egyptian to be Head of Egypt in two thousand years," she noted, was "hated" by the western powers "because he has broken the chain of their power over Egypt." She added that "Egypt defends Africa" and would prevent "the subjugation not only [of] this continent, but the entire colored world." In this land that protected the boy Jesus from Herod and to where his disciples traveled to spread the Gospel to a receptive population, Christianity and the ancient greatness of Africa were incubated. The pan-Africanism of Graham Du Bois emerged out of her beginnings in a black Atlantic Methodism and was converted into residency and advocacy for Africa in a newly independent Ghana and in a strategically powerful Egypt. In this she was truly an heir to the transatlantic legacy of African Methodism.[154]

[153] Fabio Rojas, *From Black Power to Black Studies: How a Radical Social Movement Became an Academic Discipline* (Baltimore, MD, Johns Hopkins University Press, 2007), 84–85.
[154] Shirley Graham Du Bois, "Egypt is Africa," *The Black Scholar*, Part I, Vol. 1, No. 7, May 1970, 22, 26; Shirley Graham Du Bois, "Egypt is Africa," *The Black Scholar* (Conclusion), Vol. 2, No. 1, September 1970, 33.

Not unlike Graham-Du Bois, the indiscernible link between African Americans and ancient and medieval Egypt and Ethiopia that animated the scholarship of Asa J. Davis seemed energized by an AME background that consciously forged connections to Africa. That early Christianity was tied to the "mother" continent and became in Ethiopia a bulwark against the spread of Islam stirred the intellectual "juices" of Asa J. Davis, a distinguished religious historian and longtime professor at Amherst College. Davis's deep exploration of Christianity's African past focused his scholarly energies upon the study of the Church of Ethiopia, among the oldest of Christian bodies. Perhaps Davis's intimate connection to African Methodism, a venerable black denomination of historic longevity, may have influenced his selection of this project.[155]

Davis, though born in Nashville in 1922 and reared in New York City, derived his family's AME pedigree from South Carolina, a state populous with African Methodists. Moreover, his uncle, Monroe H. Davis, educated at Howard University and seminary trained at Drew University, became a powerhouse among Baltimore AMEs. Married to the daughter of Bishop William W. Beckett, Davis was himself elected to the episcopacy in 1928 and within a few years assigned to the Second Episcopal District, which included his home city. Davis also mentored Charles H. Wesley, a Baltimore Conference presiding elder and a Howard dean, and helped him to navigate the intricacies of AME politics. During Wesley's Wilberforce presidency, Asa Davis, as an undergraduate, was exposed to his productivity as a historian.[156]

Military service in World War II delayed Davis's graduation from Wilberforce until 1948. In the prior two years both Bishop Davis and President Wesley lost out in high stakes AME politics. The bishop had been suspended from the episcopacy at the special General Conference session in 1946 and Wesley, fired from the Wilberforce presidency in 1947, launched a rival school on adjacent state property. Though Bishop Davis was restored and Wesley "landed on his feet" as president of Central State College, Davis, perhaps sobered by these factional fights, though he pursued a divinity degree, chose academia over the AME ministry or the denomination's affiliated schools. Like Wesley, Davis enrolled at Harvard University and earned in 1951 the Bachelor of Sacred Theology. Attaining a Ph.D.

---

[155] Rowland Abiodun, David W. Blight, Rhonda Cobham-Sander, and David W. Wills, "Asa J. Davis, 1922–1999: A Memorial Minute," *AME Church Review*, Vol. 118, No. 388, October–December 2002, 80.

[156] Ibid., 79–80.

in religious history, however, was his ultimate objective. Graduate study in religion at Harvard drew upon scholarly strengths in "classical church history" and its related languages. Davis embraced these fields and applied them to Africa.[157]

Davis's Ph.D. dissertation drew upon his facility with Arabic, Amharic, and Portuguese, and his historical mastery of medieval Ethiopian history and the encounter with Portuguese imperial expansion. "The Mazagaba Haymanot, An Ethiopic Monophysite Text," an explication of a sixteenth-century treatise, earned Davis the doctorate at Harvard in 1960. Davis noted that the Ethiopians, despite an earlier alliance with the Portuguese against Muslim invaders, developed a discourse of resistance to Iberian incursions into Northeast Africa.[158]

The Davis thesis mirrored his AME heritage and the denomination's historic presence in Africa. That his uncle, albeit briefly, served as bishop in West Africa, showed that the "mother" continent was in the Davis family consciousness. Perhaps some combination of family and academic influences convinced Davis to settle in Africa to witness decolonization and help to chart a postcolonial future through his career as a history professor at the University of Ibadan in newly independent Nigeria.[159]

An opportunity to participate in the Ibadan School of Historiography seemed decisive in persuading Davis to launch his academic career in Africa. Accompanying decolonization and independence in the 1950s and 1960s came a different emphasis in African history that reflected growing nationalist perspectives among indigenous scholars. They stressed energized African responses to European commercial and missionary incursions onto the continent. These themes were explicated in major monographs that Kenneth O. Dike and E. A. Ayandele published during this period. These and other scholars, in their emphasis upon political history, wanted to provide Nigeria with a history that would help in state construction. One scholar described the Ibadan School as engaged in undermining "'the dangerous lies Europeans had systematized and institutionalized about the African past'" and to "make that history usable and relevant to promote nation-building." Beyond their books, the Ibadan School, to disseminate their perspectives, established the Historical Society

---

[157] Ibid., 80–81; Wright, *The Bishops of the African Methodist Episcopal Church*, 153–154.
[158] Abiodun et al., "Asa J. Davis, 1922–1999," 80; Asa J. Davis, "The Mazagaba Haymanot, An Ethiopic Monophysite Text," Ph.D. dissertation, Harvard University, 1960, 1.
[159] Abiodun et al., "Asa J. Davis, 1922–1999," 80; Wright, *The Bishops of the African Methodist Episcopal Church*, 153.

of Nigeria, the *Journal of the Historical Society of Nigeria*, and *Tarikh*, a publication for a secondary school audience.[160]

Davis believed in building a sovereign postcolonial Africa through the University of Ibadan. Located in the largest city in the Yoruba majority Oyo State, Davis belonged to the Ibadan history faculty from 1962 to 1969. His tenure coincided with the role of Dike, his mentor, as vice chancellor. Hence, Davis became assistant editor of the *Journal of the Historical Society of Nigeria* to which he contributed essays derived from his research on sixteenth-century Ethiopia. He published "The Sixteenth Century Jihad in Ethiopia and the Impact on its Culture" in two installments in 1963 and 1964. In the first essay he argued that the intervention of a Muslim jihad spearheaded a cultural transformation, forcing a political crisis that compelled Ethiopia to return to the "foundations of the quasi-sacramental union between the Church and State as a weapon with which to repel its enemies." Though Monophysite Ethiopians differed from the Catholic Portuguese and resented their imperial presence, both viewed Muslims as inimical to their respective political and religious interests. Davis showed in the follow-up essay that some Muslim territories failed in ending all Ethiopian sovereignty, with some paying tribute to various Ethiopian rulers.[161]

Though hardly a specialist in Nigerian history, Davis fully participated in the Ibadan School. In his writings he portrayed Africans as parties to foundational doctrinal debates that shaped the theological trajectory of Christianity. Beyond his editorial position with the *Journal of the Historical Society of Nigeria*, Davis also published in *Tarikh* a popular publication that the Ibadan School deployed to expose non-academic audiences to the best scholarship in African history. Hence, Davis, in a special issue on early Christianity, contributed articles on "Coptic Christianity" and "The Orthodoxy of the Church of Ethiopia."

Davis's essays on religion in Egypt and Ethiopia, like AME Bishop Benjamin W. Arnett's 1893 address "The Negro and Christianity," showed Africans as major players in early Christian development. Concerning

---

[160] Paul E. Lovejoy, "The Ibadan School of Historiography and its Critics," in Toyin Falola (ed.), *African Historiography: Essays in Honor of Jacob Ade Ajayi* (London, Longman, 1993), 195–198; A. O. Adeoye, "Understanding the Crisis in Modern Nigerian Historiography," *History in Africa*, Vol. 19, 1992, 2; Kenneth O. Dike, *Trade and Politics in the Niger Delta, 1830–1855* (Oxford, England, Clarendon Press, 1956); E. A. Ayandele, *The Missionary Impact on Modern Nigeria, 1842–1914* (London, Longmans, 1966).

[161] Asa J. Davis, "The Sixteenth Century Jihad in Ethiopia and the Impact on its Culture: Part One," *Journal of Historical Society of Nigeria*, Vol. 2, No. 4, December 1963, 568–569, 592; Asa J. Davis, "The 16th Century Jihad in Ethiopia and the Impact on its Culture: Part Two," *Journal of Historical Society of Nigeria*, Vol. 3, No. 1, December 1964, 113–114, 124–126.

Coptic Christianity, Davis traced its origins in Egypt and how "Old Egyptian beliefs" informed their understanding of a fluid and increasingly contested Christianity. Whether Jesus was fully divine or simultaneously divine and human was debated at Alexandria, Egypt, the center of Coptic Christianity. This discussion led to the Council of Nicaea in 325, when the doctrine of Jesus as "fully man" and "fully God" was pronounced. When in 451 the Council of Chalcedon affirmed the Nicene Creed, Coptic Christians dissented and held to their Monophysite belief in Jesus as singularly divine.[162]

Davis, in a second *Tarikh* article, said that while Coptic influence was present in the Ethiopian church, two Syrian missionaries who evangelized in the region spread the Nicene/Chalcedon doctrine. Hence, the Ethiopian Christianity, an Orthodox body, believed that in Jesus was a "coming together of [the] Godhead and Manhood in the one person of Christ." This formulation, Davis declared, differed subtly from the Chalcedon contention that Jesus functioned in distinct ways through his divine and human natures.[163]

Though no direct reference to African Methodism is evident in Davis's scholarship, one can plausibly surmise that the AME heritage and ethos informed his intellectual perspectives. While the distance of time and variations in theology separated Egyptian and Ethiopian churches from African Methodism, their autonomy and historic authenticity of these religious bodies blended in Davis's scholarly investigations of black Christianity. Though his scholarship related to the objectives of the Ibadan School, it also drew from his black religious background and his Afrocentric writings about early Christianity.

Just as the Ibadan School in Nigeria developed a decolonized historiography, a similar intellectual insurgency that identified with the Third World and protested the exclusion of the black experience in relevant disciplines stirred in the United States. Starting in November 1968 and lasting to March 1969 at San Francisco State University, the Black Student Union, through rallies, encounters with the police, and strikes, demanded a Black Studies Department. The actions of SFSU students reflected other Black Studies movements in this same period at the University of Chicago, the University of Illinois, Chicago Circle, and Harvard University.[164]

[162] Asa J. Davis, "Coptic Christianity," *Tarikh*, Vol. 2, No. 1, (1967), 46–49.
[163] Asa J. Davis, "The Orthodoxy of the Ethiopian Church," *Tarikh*, Vol. 2, No. 1 (1967), 63–65, 67–69.
[164] Fabio Rojas, *From Black Power to Black Studies*, 45, 96, 98–99.

Figure 6.6 Asa Davis, scholar of African History at the University of Ibadan and
Amherst College (Asa Davis on the left standing with Amherst College President John
William Ward at the September 1972 Amherst Convocation) (used with permission
from the Amherst College Archives and Special Collections)

Davis was already connected to Charles H. Wesley, a Carter G. Woodson
protégé and pioneer in the professional study of black history. His link to this
earlier Negro History movement in interaction with his later Ibadan associations prefaced Davis's pull into the Black Studies upheaval. Hence, in 1969,
because of a paucity of professors who studied the African and African
American experience, Davis was attracted to San Francisco State University,
and then in 1971 to Amherst College as chair of its newly established Black
Studies Department. Echoes of this black identity movement resonated
among some AMEs at the 1972 General Conference during discussions of
the budget for the historiographer. In a vain effort, one delegate said "$40,000
was insufficient at a time when Black History is of great demand."[165]

Davis's scholarship provided intellectual scaffolding to the Amherst program and demonstrated the breadth of this area of academic inquiry. His
research on the intersections between Ethiopia and Portugal and between
Christianity and Islam showed a span across time and geography that argued

---

[165] Abiodun et al., "Asa J. Davis, 1922–1999," 81; Harold Wade, Jr., *Black Men of Amherst* (1976),
87; *Minutes of the General Conference of the Thirty-Ninth Quadrennium of the African
Methodist Episcopal Church* held in Dallas, TX, June 21–July 3, 1972, 174.

for the authenticity of the Black Studies enterprise. In an article he published in the same year he arrived at Amherst, for example, Davis discussed a sixteenth-century Ethiopian Zaga Zaab mission to Portugal. Plagued with Muslim incursions into Ethiopia, an empress sent ambassadors to Portugal to forge an alliance between the two Christian countries to repel the Muslims. Furthermore, Davis had just finished a manuscript entitled *The King's One Body: Symbol of Ethiopian Nationality.* His AME background, though hardly salient in his writings, was reflected in his blended focus on Africa and the longevity of black involvement in Christianity.[166]

Like Davis, Samuel W. Allen lived as an expatriate, but in Europe instead of Africa. He shared with Davis, however, a consciousness about the reality of Africa as central to black identity. In his poem, "Africa to Me," Allen declared:

> I listen for the clear song of your sweet voice,
> O matchless one, who will sing an old song
> and tell in a far country of the foothills of an
> unremembered home.

Moreover, Davis and Allen drew intellectual energy from an AME background informed by a heritage of transatlantic exchange between African Americans and the "mother" continent.[167]

Allen possessed an impeccable AME pedigree. His father, Alexander J. Allen, was elected to the episcopacy in 1940 after various pastorates in four states, and as an executive in the American Bible Society with the status of an AME general officer. The bishop's father, George Wesley Allen, served as editor of the *Southern Christian Recorder.* His mother, Jewett Washington Allen, was the granddaughter of Nevis native the Reverend Samuel W. Washington, who was a South Carolina pastor and presiding elder. When her husband was assigned as bishop in the Caribbean and South America, she wrote an Oberlin College masters thesis about AME development in Haiti and published it serially in the 1950s in the *AME Church Review.*[168]

[166] Asa J. Davis, "Background of the Zaga Zaab Embassy: An Ethiopian Diplomatic Mission, 1529–1539," *Studia,* Vol. 32, 1971, 211–212.
[167] Samuel Allen, *Every Round and Other Poems* (Detroit, MI, Lotus Press, 1987), 16.
[168] Wright, *The Bishops of the African Methodist Episcopal Church,* 41–45; Wright, *Encyclopedia of African Methodism,* 27; "Reverend Samuel Washington, D.D.," in *Journal of the Twenty-First Quadrennial Session of the General Conference of the African M.E. Church* held in the Auditorium, Columbus, OH, May 7–25, 1900, 379; Jewett Washington Allen, "Haiti Today," *AME Church Review,* Vol. 70, No. 182, October–December 1954, 17–25; Jewett Washington Allen, "Haiti Today," *AME Church Review,* Vol. 70, Vol. 184, April–June 1955, 36–45, 47–48.

Allen, with pride in his AME kinship, paid tribute to family members and denominational leaders. In one of his books of poems he praised his parents and commended Richard Allen for acting "on the principle of the need to take charge of one's own destiny." These expressions affirmed his daughter's recollection about Allen's "deep attachment to the AME Church" and that "he was only one of the four brothers who would return to church on Sunday evenings to hear his father preach a second time." Literary scholar, Joanne V. Gabbin, said "his voice which rang with sermonic tones from his African Methodist Episcopal upbringing-modulated, measured, and rhythmic-performed the communal rituals of call and response and speaking in tongues that were prophetic, haunting, and uplifting." Allen also published in the *AME Church Review* a poem that he dedicated to his great-grandfather Samuel Washington, his namesake who lived for a time in New York City. Allen had also resided in Gotham and recalled in "Sidewalks of New York" an incident that spurred a reflection about his AME forebear. Part of the poem described:

> The tattered black man wandered down the crowded street
> Addressing everyone he met
> with a passion stripped of any flailing doubt
> to him the awful truth was bared
> The women frowned and hurried on, til safety gained
> they turned and looked behind
> with mixed grimace and rueful smile.[169]

Allen, born in 1917 in Columbus, Ohio and educated at Fisk University and Harvard Law School, was drafted into the US Army in 1942. He served in the Adjutant General's Corp and was honorably discharged in 1946. His education continued in New York City at the New School for Social Research and in Paris in 1949 and 1950 at the Sorbonne. While in France intellectual movements grounded in Afrocentricism absorbed Allen into black Francophone associations tied to negritude and to the avant-garde journal *Presence Africaine*. These interactions reinforced Allen's formative black experiences as a scion of African Methodism and as a product of a creative writing course at Fisk with the well-known James Weldon Johnson.[170]

---

[169] Allen, *Every Round and Other Poems*, Dedication page, Foreword; Catherine Allen to Dennis C. Dickerson, January 30, 2017, private collection of the Author; Joanne Gabbin, "Sam Allen's Memorial Tribute" (courtesy of Catherine Allen), Samuel W. Allen, "Reverend Samuel W. Washington: A Tribute-Sidewalks of New York," *AME Church Review*, Vol. 119, No. 389, January–March 2003, 21–22.

[170] "Samuel Allen" in Samuel Allen, *Paul Vesey's Ledger* (London, Paul Bremen London, 1975), back cover.

Allen met Richard Wright, who was enjoying transatlantic fame for his 1940 novel *Native Son*. The other black expatriates with whom Allen interacted included Langston Hughes, James Baldwin, and Leopold Senghor, the Senegalese poet and intellectual architect of negritude. Allen was a part of "lively and engaging soirees at the Wrights' apartment with Mrs. [Ellen] Wright and their young daughter in attendance." When Wright took a year's sabbatical to make a film, he asked Allen to edit *Presence Africaine* in his absence. Moreover, Wright arranged for Allen to publish three poems in two issues of the journal in 1949.[171]

In "A Moment Please," Allen affirmed his blackness despite doubts that because of his bright brown skin he could be mistaken for an "Arabian." Allen, while pondering an ancient black humanity to which he belonged, bemoaned that in America he was only a "nigger." He wrote:

> What is it that to fury I am roused?
> For still it takes a moment
> What meaning for me
> And now
> In this homeless clan
> I'll turn
> The dupe of space
> And smile
> The tag of time
> And nod my head.[172]

In another poem, "Little Lamb, Who Made Thee?," Allen, the son of an African Methodist bishop, explored the blackness that lay within the same family faith that generated Bishop Henry M. Turner's "God is a Negro" pronouncement. Allen queried what this Afrocentric religion signified in a post-World War II world where a moribund colonialism was losing its grip on its subject peoples. Hence, Allen declared:

> God raised His woolly head and braced His big
> Black fist for silence; and they were humble
> In the heavier presence, no faint mumble
> Dared that enlightened throng, what pale intrigue
> Might hope prevail against omnipotence
> In that dark frame. The Twelve themselves had done
> The parable abandoned by the Son
> As gentle Mary's golden head in reverence

---

[171] Allen to Dickerson, January 30, 2017 (private collection of the Author).
[172] Samuel W. Allen, "A Moment, Please," *Presence Africaine*, No. 6 (1949), 76.

Was bowed; whereon that smoldering continent!
Of God's black face in red convulsions heaved,
The great gums flashed, and His eyes flashed, deceived
Not, He cried, "come on, My Lambs, to judgment."
The high gate swung, there for his last award
Strode lordly, Churchill, a hungry for the Lord.[173]

Edward A. Scott, a philosophy professor and AME pastor, characterized Allen's poetry as "a rich attestation of the power of witness to recover and transform the sense of self and alterity." Allen's African Methodism, a connector to the black past, showed how otherness was mobilized to resist white hegemony. Talking to God and reflecting on Moses-like deliverers such as Harriet Tubman in historic and "mythic" engagement pervaded Allen's poetry. In this way Scott identified Allen as a Biblical narrator and his writings as Biblical narration that addressed the black experience. Allen, "the preaching poet begets [the] remembering poet who begets a ceaseless return of transposition-recollection and regeneration." Like Henry O. Tanner, whose AME interactions with Benjamin and Sarah Tanner laid foundations for his internationally acclaimed religious art, Allen's background in the household of Alexander and Jewett Allen grounded his poetry with a black Atlantic consciousness and an advocacy against black subjugation.[174]

When Allen, after seven years in Europe, returned to the United States in 1955 both to practice and to teach law, he also became a major interlocutor between African American writers and their Caribbean and African counterparts on both sides of the Atlantic. At the First Conference of Negro Writers in 1959, sponsored by the American Society of African Culture, Allen presented "Negritude and Its Relevance to the American Negro Writer." He declared that "the Negro is denied an acceptable identity in Western culture, and the term negritude focuses and carries with it the pejorative implications of that denial." Through this intellectual interpolation, Allen describes negritude as "serving to cast off the cultural imprint of colonial Europe." It "is a type of reconnaissance," he said, "in the formation of a new imaginative world free from the proscriptions of a racist West." He added that "the African finds himself bound fast in the culture prison of the Western world, which has held him for centuries in derision and contempt; his poetic concern has been with his liberation from this prison, with the

[173] S. W. Allen, "Little Lamb, Who Made Thee?," *Presence Africaine*, No. 7 (1949), 300.
[174] Edward A. Scott, "Bardic Memory and Witness in the Poetry of Samuel Allen" in Joanne V. Gabbin (ed.), *The Furious Flowering of African American Poetry* (Charlottesville, University of Virginia Press, 1999), 47–51.

creation of a truer sense of identity, and with the establishment of his dignity as a man."[175]

In the early 1960s Allen elaborated on his consciousness about African writers in "The Black Poet's Search for Identity." He commended them for shedding "the cultural imprint of colonial Europe" before actual independence on the "mother" continent had been achieved. The task of the African writer, he said in citing Leopold Senghor, lay in "the double process of destruction and creation implicit in the formation of a new imaginative world free of the proscriptions of a colonial West." This intellectual enterprise and "preoccupation with the situation of the Negro in a culturally alien world common to the vast majority of Negro African poets" generated the idea of negritude. Through this concept the African writer could revive "a normal self-pride, a lost confidence in himself, a world in which he again has a sense of identity."[176]

Allen disagreed with some black intellectuals, especially in the United States, who shunned negritude because it suggested that African Americans possessed "a specific quality or a complex of traits or attitudes [viewed] as peculiarly Negro." Instead, Allen believed that the rise of negritude was a "necessity" and a "reaction to centuries of humiliation and contempt." From a dialectical perspective, negritude was "an anti-racist racism" and "a moment of negativity as reaction to the thesis of white supremacy."[177]

Negritude, while grounded in a black Francophone community in Paris, reached out to other intellectuals of African descent throughout the diaspora. Its broad appeal lay in its challenge to forge black identities in the inhospitable settings of white cultural hegemony. This was the issue that Allen tackled in his presentation. How could negritude spur the development of an authentic black humanity free from the denigrating labels fixed upon them by supremacist whites. He also rejected the idea "that the Negro's identity as an American precluded him from a substantial participation in that rich (African) heritage that negritude aimed to recover. Moreover, negritude was for Allen "an affirmation of self, of that dwarfed self, [and that] denied realization" derived from slavery and colonialism. Because "the American Negro, like the African has an imposing interest ... in the

---

[175] Samuel W. Allen, "Negritude and Its Relevance to the American Negro Writer," in John A. Davis (compiler), *The American Negro Writer and His Roots: Selected Papers from the First Conference of Negro Writers*, March 1959 (New York, American Society of African Culture, 1960), 9–10.

[176] Samuel W. Allen, "The Black Poet's Search for Identity," in Jacob Drachler (ed.), *African Heritage: An Anthology of Black African Personality and Culture* (1963), 190, 197.

[177] Ibid., 199.

correction of the distorted image of himself," negritude provided an intellectual foundation for this urgent pursuit. Harold Cruse, the black cultural critic and historian, credited Allen for his consistent allegiance to transatlantic interactions between African and African American writers. When some black authors in the American Society of African Culture split and formed the American Festival of Negro Arts (AFNA) in the early 1960s, Allen shifted his affiliation to the latter group. Through AFNA Allen helped to maintain the same black Atlantic project that originally brought him to *Presence Africaine* in an earlier decade. AFNA, like Allen, believed in the intellectual vitality of Negritude and the importance of an ongoing cultural exchange between African and African American writers. The same indivisible linkage across the Atlantic that bound together the AMEs seemed similarly necessary for black authors and artists.[178]

Allen's black self comprised a core of his literary being as a poet and writer. The same tensions between the African heritage and the black experience in the United States that vexed other African American intellectuals also appeared in his own writings. The twoness in Allen's African American and Caribbean lineage in interaction with the African heritage were, in part, reconciled through a pan-African AME presence in his family dynamic. These cultural strands, which lay embedded in his essay on negritude, were cast in contemporary civil rights insurgencies in the United States and heightening anticolonialism in Africa.

Another scion of African Methodism, David Levering Lewis, actually experienced the buoyant days of a newly independent Ghana. He and other expatriate blacks and allied Europeans committed their energies to build what Lewis hoped would be "a lodestar of Black Africa." Despite his civil rights advocacy, Lewis lamented that the constitutional rights of African Americans required protests for service at lunch counters and for empty seats on municipal buses. He viewed these civil rights activities "as a phase of mandated absurdity." In comparison, African decolonization stirred in him "far more revolutionary conceits" that drew from "Marx and Mao, Che Guevara and Robert Williams, a now-forgotten renegade NAACP official" who advocated armed self-defense. "As one of Americas oldest peoples," Lewis declared, "we were demeaned by having to petition for our constitutionally guaranteed rights." Being in Ghana, however, spurred "a hypnotic conception that black people were building a militant black republic destined, it seemed, to jump-start the liberation of Azania [South Africa] and to

---

[178] Ibid., 19–20; Harold Cruse, *The Crisis of the Negro Intellectual* (New York, William Morrow & Company, 1967), 499–500; 503–504.

spearhead the unification of the continent." Hence, residency in Africa was "a considerably more interesting prospect than civil rights duty in Alabama or Mississippi."[179]

As much as Samuel W. Allen, Lewis, as the son of a high-profile denominational leader, interacted with church dignitaries and distinguished visitors to the AME campuses where John H. Lewis served as dean and president. The elder Lewis, a veteran AME pastor with graduate degrees from Yale Divinity School and the University of Chicago, headed Morris Brown College, his undergraduate alma mater in the 1920s and again in the 1950s, and in between led Payne Theological Seminary adjacent to Wilberforce University. Out of these enviable academic environments, Lewis, born in 1936, graduated from Fisk University, received an M.A. from Columbia University, and earned a Ph.D. in European History at the London School of Economics. With exposure to Bishop John A. Gregg, his godfather and a productive prelate in South Africa, Lewis prepared for pan-African interactions in the metropole of a waning British Empire. "Because London had been a crossroads for anti-colonial thinkers and radical students from the British colonies," observed a Lewis chronicler, he connected with Africans preparing at neighboring institutions to lead the decolonization of their native continent. These contacts led Lewis to teach in Ghana and help in resurrecting a once autonomous Africa.[180]

A series of converging events between 1960 and 1963 spurred Lewis's move to Ghana. Two friends with academic connections at the University of Ghana landed him a lectureship in history. Going to Ghana also built on cosmopolitan European and African experiences that drew from his dissertation research in Paris, where he witnessed Algerian resistance to French colonial rule. At the time that he finished his Ph.D. thesis, his draft board in Atlanta inducted him into the US military. Lewis was assigned to a medical battalion in Europe and was stationed eventually at an army hospital in Landstuhl, Germany, as a psychiatric technician. A fortunate proviso in military regulations permitted an early release for college teaching. This technicality allowed Lewis's exit to Africa to teach medieval British and European history at the University of Ghana.[181]

---

[179] David Levering Lewis, "Ghana, 1963: A Memoir," *The American Scholar*, Vol. 68, No. 1, Winter 1999, 41–42.
[180] Wright, *Encyclopedia of African Methodism*, 183; George A. Sewell and Cornelius V. Troup, *Morris Brown College: The First Hundred Years* (Atlanta, GA, Morris Brown College, 1981), 63–68, 89–93; William Jelani Cobb, "David Levering Lewis: Scholar and Teacher," *AME Church Review*, Vol. 118, No. 388, October–December 2002, 88.
[181] Lewis, "Ghana, 1963," 39–40.

Lewis arrived in Ghana at a time when the charismatic President Kwame Nkrumah beckoned African Americans to help construct a propitious postcolonial Africa. "I was one of many pilgrims in a cultural hegira," Lewis recalled, "that brought scores of serenely ill-informed enthusiasts to Accra, the Pan African Mecca." Lewis endorsed Nkrumah's vision because of his seriousness about Ghanaian education. The government, for example, disbursed a greater percentage of its gross national product on education than any other nation on earth and made available tuition-free access to the nation's three universities. The undergraduates he encountered "radiated [a] zeal for learning," a promising omen for Africa's future.[182]

These heady hopes for an African resurgence in a postcolonial era, however, yielded to the unpleasant reality of early disappointment in Nkrumah, culminating in an attempted assassination in 1962. Lewis and his colleagues, he remembered, "were becoming increasingly and uncomfortably conscious" of Nkrumah's "rash of emerging decrees, preventive detention of suspects [and] a ratcheting up of anti-Western rhetoric in the press and on the radio." Additionally, Ghana became a one party state that descended into corruption and declining democracy. The nation's political unraveling was also revealed in curbs on civil liberties, a second assassination attempt against Nkrumah, a rumored CIA intervention, and opposition to the Ghana president. Lewis, seeing the "handwriting on the wall," resigned from the University of Ghana in 1964 to take a faculty position at Howard University. In 1966 a successful coup ended Nkrumah's rule in Ghana.[183]

When Lewis went to Ghana, he believed in self-determination for Africa, a racial ideology that most African American émigrés thought was foundational to a pan-Africanist awakening across the diaspora. The "dystopia" that unfolded in Ghana, however, clarified his "confused self" in showing that the civil rights movement in the United States was a better expression of black libratory objectives than "a shining Africa." Lewis's expectancy about Africa revolved around "educating its young people, modernizing its institutions, implementing an ambitious agenda of political and economic democracy, forming links among its progressive nations, negotiating a dynamic neutrality between the superpowers, and above all, sticking it to Uncle Sam in the United Nations for America's racial hypocrisy." With the end of the Nkrumah era, the fight for African American freedom replaced Africa's

---

[182] Ibid., 41, 44, 48–49.   [183] Ibid., 49–51, 56–58.

postcolonial project as the fulcrum for the emancipation of the black Atlantic. As Ghana was forfeiting its potential as a "frontline" for global black liberation, Lewis awakened to the United States as where he needed to be.[184]

After moving from Howard to Morgan State College in Baltimore, Lewis culminated the 1960s with the first scholarly study of Martin Luther King, Jr. He witnessed the promise and pitfalls of African decolonization and the King assassination as symbolic ends to the civil rights movement. Hence, he chronicled the latter in 1970 with the publication of *King: A Critical Biography*. Lewis acknowledged that "the religious fervor of the black church" had energized King and had provided him with inner strength. Previously, Lewis viewed black religion as a "retrograde force" and nonviolence as a "silly and demeaning prescription for black progress." King, he discovered, corrected his erroneous perspectives, with Lewis declaring that "Martin's message" was embedded "in the language of the prophets and the revivalists."[185]

Part of Lewis's book about King converged around their Ghana experiences. Kwame Nkrumah inspired King and invited him to the 1957 Gold Coast independence celebration. "What most impressed him," Lewis observed about King, "was that Ghana's freedom had been gained nonviolently." Lewis, of course, had viewed Ghana as an indispensable linchpin for a broader black freedom struggle within the black Atlantic, a perspective with which King concurred.[186]

Lewis's lived internationalism in Europe and Africa and King's Nobel Peace Prize and his opposition to the Vietnam War revealed to him linkages between militarism and the residual forces of colonialism. Perhaps Ghana's postcolonial potential and King's anti-war stand lay behind Lewis's admiration of "a black man daring to place the struggle of American blacks on a plane where their authentic victory would contribute to a radical change of not only American relations but also international relations." Lewis's acknowledgement of the AME presence in the civil rights movement evident in sundry sections of the King book and his own denominational beginnings lay embedded in his pan-African internationalism. Perhaps imperceptibly, they probably contributed to his consciousness of Africa and how African Methodism forged transatlantic ties between blacks in the United States and the "mother" continent.[187]

---

[184] Ibid., 60.
[185] David L. Lewis, *King: A Critical Biography* (New York, Praeger Publishers, 1970), x, 394.
[186] Ibid., 90, 96.   [187] Ibid., 73, 267–270, 392, 397.

Less visible than Lewis was Cyril E. Griffith. Through his origins, scholarship, and explicit AME affiliation, Griffith embodied the pan-African character of African Methodism. His Bermuda birth in 1929 and a Wilberforce degree in 1963 cast his intellectual development against a backdrop of civil rights and anti-colonial awakening in the United States and Africa. A Ph.D. in history from Michigan State University prepared him for scholarly explorations in libraries and archives in England, Nigeria, and Canada. His resulting monograph, *The African Dream: Martin Delany and the Emergence of Pan-African Thought*, examined antebellum back-to-Africa movements that Delany pursued, sometimes through his AME interactions. Additionally, he acknowledged in a scholarly essay about Richard Allen that his influence extended throughout the black Atlantic because "local churches in the United States, Canada, the West Indies, and Africa were named for him." Griffith, who became a history professor at Pennsylvania State University, also launched into a major project titled *African Redemption: The Origins of the African Methodist Episcopal Mission in Africa*, 1820–1910, which his death in 1994 left unfinished.[188]

Similarly, Walton R. Johnson, a veteran professor at Rutgers University, leveraged his AME background to study the denomination's African development. Trained in anthropology at the University of London in 1971, Johnson examined the AME presence in colonial Northern Rhodesia and the church's participation in birthing an independent Zambia. Johnson's "family membership in the AME Church," he said, "extend[ed] back several generations." Because of these connections Johnson "was readily welcomed into the congregation of Mount Zion AME Church" in Lusaka, Zambia. From this venue for two and a half years he conducted research within the congregation and in other AME settings in the Central Africa region. Out of this scholarly exploration emerged *Worship and Freedom: A Black American Church in Zambia*.[189]

Johnson, who was deferential to AME longevity and its transatlantic reach, wanted to test whether the denomination's emancipationist ethos embedded within its pan-African identity benefited constituents in Africa.

---

[188] Cyril E. Griffith, *The African Dream: Martin Delany and the Emergence of Pan-African Thought* (University Park, Pennsylvania, PA, Pennsylvania State University Press, 1975), 32, 140–141; Cyril E. Griffith, "Richard Allen: The First Prominent Black Religious Leader in Pennsylvania in Pennsylvania," in John M. Coleman, John B. Frantz, and Robert G. Crist (eds.), *Pennsylvania Religious Leaders*, Pennsylvania Historic Studies, Series 16, Pennsylvania Historical Association, University Park, Pennsylvania (Camp Hill, PA, Plank's Suburban Press, 1986), 20; *Centre Daily Times*, July 24, 1994.

[189] Johnson, *Worship and Freedom*, xiii.

An aborted launch succeeded by subsequent success within the first three decades of the twentieth century tracked the colony's economic and urban development. Failure to sustain medical and educational services, however, checked what should have been a larger AME presence in Northern Rhodesia. Moreover, an uneven involvement in the nationalist movement, despite a general embrace among indigenous Africans of the proud AME heritage, stymied church support for an emergent and independent Zambia. Johnson, far from romanticizing African Methodism as an institutional protector of blacks in America and Africa, examined the difficulties in translating the church's pan-Africanism into concrete anticolonial advocacy.[190]

The pan-Africanism of Graham Du Bois, Davis, Allen, and other intellectuals of AME heritage aligned with colleagues who developed an energetic Black Theology movement. Both pan-Africanists across different disciplines and Black Theology proponents mobilized through their scholarship the emancipationist ethos of African Methodism to resist black subjugation whether perpetrated through segregation and enforced inequality in the United States or through colonialism and white settler rule in Africa. AMEs, especially those who supported black student activism inspired by the rise of Black Power, showed their accommodation to this shift of African American militancy. Black Power, whether envisaged primarily within the American context or expansively as congruent with pan-Africanism, was a contested term. AME youth from the Griffin District at the Macon Georgia Annual Conference during their 1967 Christian education meeting expressed their view of Black Power. "If it means," they said, "to press for those things which are our heritage, we will do so." Moreover, "if it means increase our courage to fearlessly fight for equalization of all services under the control of national, state, and local government, we will do so." They added that "Black Power, we feel, may be understood to mean the purchase of guns, the throwing of Molotov cocktails and 'Burn, Baby, Burn.' This is not the answer." Instead, the same militancy that AME students exhibited in the sit-in movement deserved to be emulated.[191]

Nonetheless, in Memphis, for example, H. Ralph Jackson, who was recently involved in the black sanitation workers strike, backed the demands of the Black Student Association for black faculty and administrators at Memphis State University (MSU) and endorsed their nonviolent protest at

[190] Ibid., 6–14, 17–20.
[191] William D. Johnson, Jr., "Vox Pop Speaks Again: Civil Rights," *AME Church Review*, Vol. 92, No. 234, January–March 1968, 62.

the office of MSU President Cecil C. Humphreys. When Humphreys dispatched police supposedly to keep order, Jackson supported a student rally that denounced this action. Theologians of AME heritage, similarly spurred by militant Black Power advocates, reminded these activists that theological resources were available to deploy against racial hegemonies aimed at black dehumanization.[192]

Perhaps they had in mind such Black Power leaders as James Forman, executive secretary of SNCC, an organization that shifted from integrationism to black nationalism. Forman, reared in Chicago, grew up in Coppin AME Church where Joseph L. Roberts was pastor. Roberts, Forman recalled, "was more of a lecturer on social issues than a preacher. His sermons, unlike any I had heard, did not deal with heaven and hell." Instead, Forman remembered that Roberts "kept raising questions about this world" and "how we must understand our history and what we black people must do to end discrimination." Though Forman read about AME involvement in higher education and its transatlantic ministries, his doubts "about the validity of God began to grow." As a student at Roosevelt University, Forman fully embraced atheism. Though he issued a Black Manifesto in 1969 that demanded white churches should pay reparations to African Americans and convinced the National Committee of Black Churchmen to support the initiative, Forman had no personal use for religion.[193]

Black religious thinkers, who wanted to recover the AME emancipationist legacy and to rally the denomination to the frontline of black liberation, hoped that black nationalists such as Forman would be persuaded that black religion reinforced Black Power. Despite conspicuous AME participation in the civil rights movement, these scholars showed enthusiasm for Black Power and the discursive space that it provided for Black Theology to resurrect a bold AME insurgency against domestic and international systems of racial oppression.

James H. Cone launched the Black Theology movement in 1969 with the publication of his landmark *Black Theology and Black Power*. An AME from

[192] Shirletta J. Kinchen, *Black Power in the Bluff City: African American Youth and Student Activism in Memphis, 1965-1975* (Knoxville, University of Tennessee Press, 2016), 160-162.
[193] *New York Times*, January 12, 2005; James Forman, *The Making of Black Revolutionaries* (Washington, DC, Open Hand Publishing, 1985), 47-48, 82-83; "A Message to the Churches from Oakland, California, Statement by the National Committee of Black Churchmen, Third Annual Convocation, November 11-14, 1969," in Gayraud S. Wilmore and James H. Cone (eds.), *Black Theology: A Documentary History, 1966-1979* (Maryknoll, NY, Orbis Books, 1979), 104-105.

Bearden, Arkansas, his identity was shaped by his local congregation, the heroic founding of the denomination, and such iconic church leaders as Richard Allen and Henry M. Turner. As an adult, however, Cone experienced some of the church's unsavory institutional operations in which bishops and other officials, either jealous or afraid of his Ph.D. in systematic theology from Garrett Seminary/Northwestern University, refused him appointments to pastorates in AME congregations and professorships in AME schools. Superficial pride in the blackness of African Methodism, Cone concluded, seemed articulated by some ministers as a substitute for sustained engagement with serious emancipationist issues, as "the liberation of the poor." Moreover, a pervasive preoccupation with denominational politics and jockeying for election to the episcopacy convinced Cone, who became a professor at Union Theological Seminary in New York City, to leave the AMEs for the United Methodist Church. That denomination's Black Methodists for Church Renewal, Cone believed, appeared more in tune with his Black Theology objectives than the views of most of his AME colleagues. But he returned to African Methodism in the 1970s when the bishops began to wrestle with his scholarship on Black Theology and wanted

Figure 6.7 James H. Cone, "Father of Black Theology" (used with permission from Union Theological Seminary in New York City)

the AME Church to have "a new self-understanding more consistent with its historical origins."[194]

These prelates, many of whom were active in the civil rights movement, including the eight who were elected at the 1972 General Conference as a "talented tenth," were familiar with the National Committee of Negro (renamed Black) Churchmen and their response to Black Power and Black Theology. This interdenominational organization endorsed in statements in 1966 and 1969 the turn to greater black militancy. For them Black Power was a legitimate goal for African Americans and Black Theology as "a theology of liberation" that was "the revelation of God as revealed in the incarnation of Jesus Christ." That AMEs were among the signatories to these statements demonstrated increased institutional consciousness about this shift in black theological thinking. This was affirmed at the 1968 General Conference, which accepted a resolution that solicited an AME response to several urgent issues, including "the cry for 'Black Power.'"[195]

Cone's book clarified the meaning of Black Power and its relationship to Black Theology. Black Power, he declared, paralleled "Christ's central message to twentieth century America," which was "total identification with the suffering poor." Moreover, the core of Black Power, he said, lay in "an attitude [and] an inward affirmation of the essential worth of blackness." Christians needed to acknowledge that Black Theology, the religious alter ego to Black Power, aimed "to apply the freeing power of the gospel to black people under white oppression." He added that "Jesus' work is essentially one of liberation" and shows "the meaning of God's action in history and man's place within it."[196]

The church, Cone contended, "is that people called into being by the power and love of God to share in his revolutionary activity for the liberation of man." In the organizational DNA of Cone's own AME denomination lay the roots of an insurgent tradition that was a "precursor of Black Power." He noted that "Richard Allen and his followers walked out of St. George Methodist Episcopal Church at Philadelphia because they refused to obey the dictates of white superiority." In fact, Cone thought, "that what Richard Allen, the founder of the AME Church, did during the late eighteenth

---

[194] See James H. Cone, *Black Theology and Black Power* (Maryknoll, NY, Orbis Books, 1969); James H. Cone, *My Soul Looks Back* (Nashville, TN, Abingdon, 1982), 64–66, 70–73, 84–86.

[195] *New York Times*, July 3, 1966; Statement by the National Committee of Black Churchmen, June 13, 1969 in Wilmore and Cone, *Black Theology*, 101; *Official Minutes of the Thirty-Eighth Session of the General Conference, 1968*, 263.

[196] Cone, *Black Theology and Black Power*, 1–2, 8, 31, 35.

century and early nineteenth century was as revolutionary as what Martin Luther did in the sixteenth century."[197]

The decline of CORE, SNCC, and the Black Panther Party by the start of the 1970s, due in part to internal sabotage from the FBI's COINTELPRO intrusion, undermined Black Power as an organized force in the African American freedom struggle. Black Theology, however, remained an intellectually vibrant movement that survived secular Black Power advocates and the groups they led. Among AMEs Cone's scholarship grappled with critiques from Cecil W. Cone, his older brother, and Jacquelyn Grant, two scholars who deliberately anchored themselves within denominational institutions and involvements. In *The Identity Crisis in Black Theology*, published in 1975 by the AME Sunday School Union, the older Cone brother viewed black religion as the foundation of Black Theology and the starting point for any black theological discourse. He treated as less important than his brother conversations with white western theologians in arriving at normative ideas and nomenclature for black religious reflection. For example, Henry M. Turner, who declared in 1898 that "God is a Negro," raised in theology a concept never before envisaged and an idea that could upend the entire theological enterprise. This "Africanized God," as a beginning point for black theological conversation, was the intellectual revolution that Black Power required. This illustrated what Cecil Cone meant in asserting that "the only appropriate foundation for Black Theology is black religion." The black religious experience, "forged from African religion and biblical Christianity in the crucible of American slavery" challenged black theologians to ground "their professional identity in the consistent analysis of [t]his tradition and no other."[198]

Cecil Cone, who earned a Ph.D. at Emory University and served in the AME Church as a pastor, seminary dean, and college president, believed that his brother overemphasized his "identification with the Black Power movement" and wrongly "perceived black religion to be primarily political." This focus, he thought, ignored the broader "confessional story of black peoples' relationship with the Almighty Sovereign God." Black religion, though it embraced the political impulse and insurgency of an AME preacher such as Denmark Vesey, capaciously grasped the entirety of black religious experiences. Whether blacks were overt rebels or not, "the ultimate loyalty of black religion must be analyzed in light of the mystery of one's

[197] Ibid., 63, 94–95; Cone, *My Soul Looks Back*, 27.
[198] Cecil W. Cone, *The Identity Crisis in Black Theology* (Nashville, TN, AME Sunday School Union, 1978), 65, 71–72; James H. Cone, *My Soul Looks Back*, 60.

encounter with God" across the immense landscape of African and African American history. In subsequent studies James Cone revised his views along lines that his brother suggested. Both Cones experienced vacillating relationships with their denomination. James Cone remained a trenchant critic of institutional practices that he declared as inimical to vigorous AME insurgency against racial hegemony, and Cecil Cone twice failed to attain the episcopacy in 1980 and 1984. Nonetheless, posthumous encomiums were widely expressed to validate AME identification with their scholarly achievements. After their respective deaths in 2016 and 2018, Bishop Adam J. Richardson, Jr., in asserting a denominational claim upon the theological pair, acknowledged Cecil Cone as his dean at Turner Theological Seminary and James Cone as the "founder of 'Black Liberation Theology.'" He commended these serious thinkers, who "held ordinations in the African Methodist Episcopal Church," because they thought deeply about "what God in Christ means to oppressed people" and they tried "to answer the question 'what is the Gospel to poor people.'"[199]

Jacquelyn Grant, who earned a Ph.D. in theology at Union Theological Seminary with James H. Cone as her advisor, had deep roots in the AME Church in South Carolina. In a volume that Cone coedited with black Presbyterian theologian Gayraud S. Wilmore, Grant presented a critique of Black Theology as a gendered constructed discipline with a glaring absence of black women. "Either Black women have no place in the enterprise," she noted, "or Black men are capable of speaking for us." Since neither was true, black theologians should assert, "if liberation of women is not proclaimed, [then] the church's proclamation cannot be about divine liberation." In the AME Church, for example, "men have monopolized the ministry as a profession" while the ordination of women "has always been controversial." She declared that "until Black women theologians are fully participating in the enterprise," then Black Theology forfeited any claim of being a libratory force for African Americans.[200]

---

[199] Cone, *The Identity Crisis in Black Theology*, 96–97, 100–101; *The Combined Minutes of the Forty-First Session of the General Conference of the African Methodist Episcopal Church* held in New Orleans, LA, June 18–28, 1980 (Nashville, TN, AME Sunday School Union, 1980), 274; *The Combined Minutes of the Forty-Second Session of the General Conference of the African Methodist Episcopal Church* held in Kansas City, MI, July 7–15, 1984 (Nashville, TN, AME Sunday School Union, 1984), 232; Adam J. Richardson, Jr., "The Bishop's Word," in *African Methodist Episcopal Church, Eleventh Episcopal District* [Schedule of Annual Conferences, 2018] (Nashville, TN, AME Sunday School Union, 2018), 5.

[200] Jacquelyn Grant, "Black Theology and the Black Woman" in Wilmore and Cone, *Black Theology*, 420, 423–424, 431.

ON THE FRONTLINES OF BLACK POWER

Black theologians, especially the Cones and Grant, believed in an on-the-ground pursuit of a "grassroots" Black Theology. The National Black United Front in Cairo, Illinois, a case study in AME-inspired activism, fitted this objective. According to a scholar of the Cairo Movement, through the praxis of Black Theology "United Front activists were key agents in its production, consumption, and transmission." Cairo was a troubled racial venue that the local population tried constantly to change. A lynching in 1942 in a nearby Missouri town, for example, stirred the rebirth of the Cairo NAACP. Later, the branch achieved success through a lawsuit in 1944 in favor of equal pay for black teachers and stubbornly pursued the desegregation of Cairo's public schools. Much of this activist history centered around initiatives and leadership from Ward Chapel AME Church, especially through church member Hattie Kendrick, the head of the Cairo NAACP from the early 1940s.[201]

The Cairo Movement shifted gears when Bishop Joseph Gomez assigned Blaine Ramsey, a socially insurgent preacher, as pastor to Ward Chapel. This appointment, greatly pleasing to Hattie Kendrick, induced her to support his election to the local NAACP board. Ramsey's presence in Cairo aligned with Charles Koen, whose family had also affiliated with Ward Chapel. Koen, though a teenager whom Ramsey mentored, possessed a heightened social consciousness about the systemic racial inequalities that victimized Cairo's black population. Additionally, Ramsey and SNCC activists tried to integrate targeted restaurants starting in 1962 and soon extended their protests to the city's other segregated facilities. The cooperating Cairo Nonviolent Freedom Committee selected Koen as president, thus making him a protégé to older AME activists Kendrick and Ramsey, the latter of whom was transferred in 1963 to Bethel AME Church in Champaign, Illinois.[202]

Koen was maturing as a black leader. After he and other marchers demonstrated against a white swimming club, they protested racially exclusionary practices at a skating rink. When whites physically attacked them, including beatings that required hospitalization for Koen and others, the young leader became increasingly receptive to a broader range of strategies to achieve social change. After he returned from college in 1966, Koen, now a Baptist minister, assumed in 1970 leadership of the Cairo United Front.

[201] Kerry Pimblott, *Faith in Black Power: Religion, Race, and Resistance in Cairo, Illinois* (Lexington, University Press of Kentucky, 2017), 64–67, 70–79, 146–147, 225.
[202] Ibid., 79–83, 87–94.

Moreover, his attendance at the Congress of African Peoples exposed Koen to Black Power and black diasporic ideologies. He channeled these ideas, including an ascendant Black Theology perspective, into a united front that built on previous years of activism that Kendrick and Ramsey pioneered in Cairo. This resulted in national support from activist clergy and what one scholar described as an "eclectic bricolage of formal black theologies, radical political ideologies and the organic religious traditions of black Cairoites themselves."[203]

Koen's concept of "grassroots" Black Theology lay in a praxis involving alliances among congregations, national religious bodies, both ecclesiastical and ecumenical, and local communities. Their mission to upend racially discriminatory systems and practices that disfavored vulnerable peoples drew the involvement of a devout layman, Dr. Leonidas H. Berry, a prominent physician in Chicago and head of the AME Church's Health Commission. Berry, whose father had served the denomination as Secretary of Missions, was alarmed at the exclusion of blacks from Cairo's local government and active Ku Klux Klan opposition to United Front marches and boycotts against segregated white businesses. After speaking during a worship service at Ward Chapel and marching in a local demonstration, Berry resolved to mobilize his Chicago connections in the ministry and in medicine to aid the United Front. He learned, for example, that blacks on public assistance were often denied medical care at a local hospital. In response, Berry decided to make available food and medicine through Ward Chapel. He also organized a "flying health service to Cairo."[204]

Berry, upon his return to Chicago, drew support from Bishop Howard Thomas Primm, whose jurisdiction extended into southern Illinois. Bishop Primm and the Fourth Episcopal District provided funds for Berry's food and medicine project. Berry also gathered his physician colleagues into the "Flying Black Doctors," and they paid or the cost for two charter airplanes that flew thirty-two health professionals to Cairo on February 15, 1970. There they set up a clinic at Ward Chapel, where they served about 300 patients. The federal Office of Economic Opportunity committed to continue the initiative after the Berry group departed. The AME Health Commission, the Social Action Commission of Ward Chapel, the United Front, and an intergenerational blend of Cairo residents, both integrationist and advocates of Black Power, realized a "grassroots" Black Theology that black theologians

---

[203] Ibid., 90, 94, 105, 116, 128–149.
[204] Leonidas H. Berry, *I Wouldn't Take Nothin' for My Journey: Two Centuries of an Afro-American Minister's Family* (Chicago, Johnson Publishing Company, 1981), 409–410.

articulated in their scholarly publications and that Koen activated on the ground. A consensus that black religion, as foundationally expressed through Cairo's AME congregation, required insurgencies against the city's structural inequalities. Mobilizing theological perspectives to critique and concretely undermine segregationist systems drew the ideas of black theologians into the on-the-ground activities of Kendrick, Ramsey, and Berry.[205]

Parallel to the transatlantic and Third World landscape that preoccupied pan-Africanist scholars, their theological colleagues connected African Methodism, especially in its unrealized potential, to their counterparts outside the United States. James H. Cone, while acknowledging the AME presence in Africa and the church's imperialist practice of assigning "black American bishops" to the "mother" continent, also wondered about Latin American and Asia. Despite the existence of a jurisdiction in Guyana and Surinam, "why has the black church failed to make itself known" to the 60 million blacks in Latin America. Moreover, in Asia where multiple millions more resided, "the AME Church is unknown to the masses of people." Additionally, Grant, who wrote that black women were intrinsic to black theological discourse, suggested their alignment with their Latin American female counterparts who were raising similar questions about their place in Liberation Theology. Cone and Grant viewed the AME heritage as replete with liberationist possibilities for the Third World and "in liberating the victims [of colonialism] wherever they are found." Starting in the 1940s through the 1980s the civil rights movement, anticolonial insurgencies, and Black Power/Black Theology initiatives drew from AME institutional, intellectual, and activist involvements in resisting and undermining racial hegemonies that had enslaved and colonized peoples within the African diaspora.[206]

[205] Ibid., 410–411.
[206] James H. Cone, *My Soul Looks Back*, 92; Grant, "Black Theology and the Black Woman" in Wilmore and Cone, editors, *Black Theology*, 419.

7

☙

Becoming a Global Church, 1976–2018

EXPANDING TO NEW AREAS

Brazilians in 1996, conscious that African Methodist Episcopal members (AMEs) were attending the World Methodist Conference in Rio de Janeiro, met and entreated them to establish the denomination in this Portuguese speaking country. The 3,647,000 African slaves transported to Brazil during the Atlantic slave trade vastly outnumbered the 399,000 who survived the Middle Passage and landed in what would become the United States. Slavery lasted longer in Brazil, ending in 1888, but dying earlier in the United States, in 1865, because of a civil war. This historical background and a black Brazilian population, estimated at 97 million, framed interactions between Brazilian Methodists and AME Bishops Carolyn Tyler Guidry and Sarah F. Davis who envisaged denominational possibilities in this part of Latin America. Notwithstanding an abortive attempt by the AME Zion Church to spread to Brazil in the 1920s, mainly in black Bahia, several decades passed before some of Brazil's black Methodists could wrest themselves from the foundational influences of the white Methodist Episcopal Church, South.[1]

Hence, in February 2016 the Reverends Paulo and Mirian Mudesto, the pastors of the Communidade Crista Metodista in Rio de Janeiro, visited the AME Church's Dominican Republic Annual Conference. In witnessing the century-old operations of African Methodism in the Spanish-speaking sector of Hispaniola, the Mudestos solidified their interest in this black

---

[1] Philip D. Curtin, *The Atlantic Slave Trade: A Census* (Madison, University of Wisconsin Press, 1969), 87; *Christian Recorder News Break*, June 15, 2016; Dennis C. Dickerson, "Bishop George C. Clement, the AME Zion Church, and Brazil," *AME Church Review*, Vol. 126, No. 420, October–December 2010, 42–45.

Wesleyan body. After they requested admission into the AME Church, a delegation in June 2016, led by Bishop John F. White and General Officer George F. Flowers, traveled to Brazil to meet members of the Rio congregation. From this start, groundwork was laid for their transfer into African Methodism. At the 2017 meeting of the Brazil District Conference, four churches and pastors participated including Communidade Crista in Rio de Janeiro, Covenant Agape Alliance in Bahia, Restauracao in Quelez Sao Paulo, and Colherta in Rio de Janeiro.[2]

In India, despite initiatives starting in the 1950s through the Reverend Henry A. Perry, an Indiana pastor, and in the 2000s with Bishop John and the Reverend Cecelia W. Bryant, the entirety of Asia had received scant attention from the AME Church. In correcting this geographical oversight, the Bryants, in cooperation with the Reverends Abraham and Sarah Pedinny, indigenous Indians, received approval from the 2008 General Conference to organize the India Annual Conference. To encourage this growth into Asia the General Conference accepted the recommendation of the Committee on Boundaries to expand the India jurisdiction to include five congregations in the neighboring nation of Nepal.[3]

These new geographical frontiers reflected the emergence of African Methodism as a global religious body. Beyond ongoing expansion within the Americas and Africa, the arrival of the AME Church in Europe and Asia in the late twentieth and early twenty-first centuries brought the denomination into a more complicated discourse about its racial and ethnic constituencies. This increased demographic diversity drew from a well-established transatlantic heritage and new Indian Ocean identities coming out from fresh growth in East Africa, especially in Kenya, and spreading toward the Asian subcontinent. Concomitant with these developments, other issues pertaining to spirituality and sexuality stirred discourse and division about how African Methodism should be defined. The rise of neo-Pentecostalism, women in ministry, and gay ordination and same-sex marriage, just like the denomination's increased internationalism, required revisions and clarifications in polity and policy in a mutating Methodism. Though discussions and enactments focused on governance and budgetary accountability became foundational to the modernization of the AME Church, they unleashed a broader

[2] *Christian Recorder News Break*, June 15, 2016; *Christian Recorder Online*, October 1, 2017.
[3] Dennis C. Dickerson, "Henry Allen Perry and African Methodism for India: An Historical Note," *AME Church Review*, Vol. 126, No. 419, July–September 2010, 95–99; General Conference Boundaries Committee Final Report, MS, General Conference Minutes, 2016, www.ame-church.com.

discourse about how denominational operations and resources would be mobilized to address transformational changes. Hence, several developments shaped the trajectory of African Methodism as the denomination headed toward the next century. They included increased globalization, structural reformation, women's empowerment, negotiating a complicated discourse surrounding sex and sexuality, and the rise of neo-Pentecostalism.

MODERNIZING THE GLOBAL CHURCH

These modernizing initiatives reached fruition at the 1956 General Conference. Delegates undertook major actions in two seemingly unrelated spheres. The first action pertained to a "budget revolution" that reflected lingering aftershocks from the 1946 special session of the General Conference. At that meeting some bishops were disciplined because of unaccountable behavior with denominational funds. At the 1956 conference new legislation discarded improvised fundraising practices to finance episcopal projects and to supplement shortfalls from an inadequate Dollar Money system. Instead of denominational financing based on one dollar per member along with special fundraising days on an arbitrarily devised ecclesiastical calendar, a regularized budgeting system was enacted. The new budget law provided approved allocations to the episcopacy, to denominational departments, and to other connectional operations. A second but equally compelling issue, related to the election of the first indigenous African bishop for what would be assignments restricted to the "mother" continent. This compelled response to the white minority government in South Africa became urgent because African American bishops were barred from entering the country to oversee AME affairs.

These landmark actions framed the future of African Methodism, first by modernizing the denomination's fiscal infrastructure and enabling it to accommodate important national and international developments requiring an AME reply. Despite some misaligned responses, new structures and programs, derived from the 1956 "budget revolution," were created and folded into a fiscal frame that addressed financial abuse. Moreover, the election of a bishop for Africa foreshadowed increased pressures through the closing decades of the twentieth and early twenty-first centuries for an indigenization of episcopal leadership in areas of AME growth outside the United States.

Only a sound fiscal system for the ample funds collected from AMEs and disbursed for denominational operations would allow African Methodism to function efficiently as a vanguard institution in the black Atlantic. The

General Conference of 1952 recognized this reality when delegates impaneled a Budget Committee "to present a uniform budget for the entire Connection." Despite seeming acceptance from the episcopacy, recalled Budget Committee Chair Bishop Richard R. Wright, Jr., most prelates "preferred the laissez-faire [practices] they had followed for many years." Wright had in mind the bishops' control over funds collected in annual conferences, monies raised in their respective districts for schools, and sundry assessments for special projects. Except for funds earmarked for the connectional treasury for payroll and programmatic expenses, other monies were raised and spent without mandated accountability.[4]

Concurrent with Wright's advocacy of budget reform, two pastors in 1953 organized The Brotherhood, a group of daring clergy committed to this same objective. The Brotherhood founders, H. Ralph Jackson of Tennessee and Ezra M. Johnson of Arkansas, Wright recalled, were "aggressive and uncompromising in their opposition to the [loose] fiscal policies" practiced throughout the denomination. While mobilizing clergy across the United States, Jackson also leveraged his presidency of the Connectional Council to educate them about the urgency for financial reform. "The Brotherhood," Wright observed, "spent over two years" immersing themselves through "their dozen or more committees" in how denominational finances operated and how they should be improved. Moreover, said Wright, "their agitation made the church budget-conscious as never before, and the more information the members got, the more they decided reform was needed."[5]

To enact budget reform at the 1956 General Conference required Brotherhood strategies to neutralize the opposition of bishops, who presided over all of the proceedings, and to navigate through complicated rules and parliamentary procedures. Because few delegates attained their position without the approval of their bishops, it was important to prevent prelates from influencing their votes on the budget proposals. Hence, The Brotherhood advanced a resolution to reassign all bishops to different districts and to vote on it by secret ballot. Moved by an influential Detroit pastor and with Wright as the presiding officer, the resolution overwhelmingly passed. A second strategy pertained to raising the budget legislation when either Wright or Bishop Alexander J. Allen, both supporters of The Brotherhood, would be presiding. This second maneuver became unnecessary because of

[4] Richard R. Wright, Jr., *Eighty-Seven Years Behind the Black Curtain* (Philadelphia, PA, Rare Book Company, 1965), 286.
[5] Ibid., 286–287; Dennis C. Dickerson, *African American Preachers and Politics: The Careys of Chicago* (Jackson, University Press of Mississippi, 2010), 89.

deep delegate support for the bill and because of another episcopal ally, Bishop Joseph Gomez.[6]

Gomez was presiding when the budget bill was presented for its third and final reading. Jackson, whom Gomez recognized to speak, "recounted the efforts of so many to have a Budget for our Church and moved to adopt." Among the three who seconded the motion, one said "it was God's work," another noted "we are on the way to the Promised Land," and a third supporter, A. G. Gaston, a lay delegate from Birmingham, because he was a well-known businessman, lent his stature to the budget bill. "The motion to adopt," wrote the General Conference recorder, "was evidenced by standing which seemed to be so unanimous that it was declared so by [Bishop Gomez], the Chair."[7]

The subsequent celebration dually signified relief shown by pastors tired and troubled by ad hoc demands for assessments for projects not mandated in the denomination's *Doctrine and Discipline* and their release to pursue social holiness ministries absent the demanding distraction to raise funds for bishop initiated programs. Hence, there was "rousing acclaim" which "prevailed for an hour" and "a band [that] marched down the aisles." Moreover, "Brotherhood members followed and hundreds joined the procession" and "banners of Victory were carried and songs of Victory filled the House." Though the grassroots Brotherhood movement achieved budget reform, some bishops made their concurrence clearly known. So, Bishop Allen, in presenting a plaque to H. Ralph Jackson on behalf of The Brotherhood, said that "this is a New Day for African Methodism." Bishop Sherman L. Greene, a budget convert, likened it to the accomplishments of Richard Allen, and Bishop Gomez compared it to reform legislation enacted at the 1928 General Conference that granted equal delegate representation to the laity. Moreover, Gomez told the 1956 Central Tennessee Annual Conference "that the AME Church will never go back to the old system."[8]

[6] Wright, *Eighty-Seven Years Behind the Black Curtain*, 287–288; "The Official Minutes of the Thirty-Fifth Session of the General Conference of the African Methodist Episcopal Church which convened in Miami, Florida, May 1956 at the Dinner Key Auditorium," in *Combined Minutes of the General Conferences*, 347–348; Annetta L. Gomez-Jefferson, *In Darkness With God: The Life of Joseph Gomez, A Bishop in the African Methodist Episcopal Church* (Kent, OH, Kent State University Press, 1998), 273.

[7] "The Official Minutes of the ... General Conference 1956," 392–393.

[8] Ibid., 393; Wright, *Eighty-Seven Years Behind the Black Curtain*, 289; "Minutes of the Eighth Session of the Central Tennessee Annual Conference (of the) African Methodist Episcopal Church held at Quinn Chapel AME Church, Paris, Tennessee, November 7–11, 1956," in *Minutes of the Conferences of the Thirteenth Episcopal District* (African Methodist Episcopal Church), 1956; Rt. Rev. Joseph Gomez (Nashville, AME Sunday School Union, n.d.), 75.

These delegate demonstrations validated what Brotherhood leaders knew about the rank-and-file clergy and laity. The budget law shielded them from unregulated financial requests, however benign, from the episcopacy. Hence, their hunger for fiscal relief burst into celebration when the bill was enacted. The minister, said the *Declaration of Principles of the Brotherhood*, "is the key to the ongoing success of the Kingdom enterprises. His Office warrants becoming dignity and freedom from anything that will not leave him untrammeled to win souls to Christ." Moreover, "he should be encouraged and built up so that the people may revere and respect his leadership." Consonant with Gomez's comments about the laity, Brotherhood principles stated that "Laymen represent the undergirding and are the indispensable compliment to the clergy in the ongoing success of the Kingdom enterprise" meaning that their [counsel] and cooperation are essential to African Methodism." Delegates, both clergy and lay, celebrated the new connectional budget and what it portended for fiscal regularity in the denomination.[9]

The reconstruction of the AME financial system drew from the creation of new fiscal foundations. A central fund and oversight of a General Board became the principal correctives for the denomination's broken funding practices. The General Budget Fund was set annually at $3.2 million based on the collection of $4.00 per member. These sums were allocated to the several departments and programs. An Episcopal Fund was included from which bishops were paid their salaries and expenses, and they were forbidden to receive any other church income. The General Board met annually and was amenable only the General Conference. This fiscal body reviewed department budgets, employed auditors, and ordered "each agency to follow uniform [financial] policies and practices" in their operations. The General Board consisted of equal numbers of clergy and lay from each episcopal district and an equal number of clergy and lay to serve as at-large members. The core of the budget reform lay in its stricture against any bishop or any other official or organizational entity to raise funds "other than stipulated in the General Budget approved by the General Conference." Whenever a special financial appeal was needed, a two-thirds vote of the General Board was necessary to authorize this action.[10]

Bishop David Henry Sims and Bishop Decatur Ward Nichols, former rivals, became political bookends to the Brotherhood Movement. Though

[9] *Declaration of Principles of the Brotherhood of the AME Church*, (n.p., n.d.)
[10] "The Official Minutes of the ... General Conference, 1956," 454–460; Wright, *Eighty-Seven Years Behind the Black Curtain*, 288–289: *Declaration of Principles of the Brotherhood of the AME Church* (n.p., n.d.).

Sims's financial misconduct spurred his suspension from the episcopacy in 1946 and precipitated calls for budget reform, H. Ralph Jackson appealed to the 1956 General Conference to lift Sims's expulsion and "restore" him to the bishopric, though without salary or assignment. The Brotherhood, despite its stand for fiscal accountability, called for "forgiveness, mercy, and brotherly love for our Brother." Jackson's motion was passed after an apology and a promise from Sims to forswear any legal action against the denomination. The 1960 General Conference gave him "full status," a salary, and an assignment to West Africa.[11]

The Sims restoration, in showing that The Brotherhood was pro-budget and not anti-bishop, was unwittingly harnessed to other internal politics that targeted Bishop Nichols as the lone opponent to the new budget system. Bishop Greene and Bishop Wright, while uncomfortable with Nichols's political prominence both within and outside African Methodism, encouraged an investigation of his loan of $56,000 to the denomination to prevent foreclosure on the AME Book Concern building in Philadelphia. Ezra M. Johnson, a Brotherhood founder, also belonged to "Greene's Army," a group of clergy in the bishop's Arkansas diocese that also affiliated with the budget reform movement. At a trial at the Council of Bishops meeting in 1957 in Jacksonville, Florida, Nichols was suspended from the episcopacy, an action that the 1960 General Conference affirmed. Like Sims, who was in ecclesiastical exile for a decade, Nichols was not restored to the episcopacy until the 1968 General Conference. While the Sims restoration closed the chapter on the old financial system, the Nichols disciplinary action demonstrated that the new budget law, despite the crosscurrents of unrelated political matters, would be seriously enforced.[12]

The new budget, however, confronted initial difficulties beyond what the Nichols case presented. Projected revenues assumed an AME membership that exceeded a million with 800,000 annually scheduled to pay $4.00 per member. These numbers were expected to fund an annual budget of $3.2 million, but only $2.6 million was actually collected. "We may have had a

[11] "The Official Minutes of the ... General Conference, 1956," 430–434; *Official Minutes of the Thirty-Sixth Session of the General Conference, AME Church, Shrine Auditorium, Los Angeles, CA, May 1960*, 83–84, 122.
[12] Jeanette T. Johns, *The Upward Journey: A Centenarian's Chronicle: Personal Stories of Bishop Decatur Ward Nichols, Revered Clergyman of the African Methodist Episcopal Church* (Nashville, TN, AME Sunday School Union, 2002), 80–82; Richard R. Wright, Jr., *The Bishops of the African Methodist Episcopal Church* (Nashville, TN, AME Sunday School Union, 1963), 262–263; *The Official Minutes of the ... General Conference 1960*, 111–112; *Official Minutes of the Thirty-Eighth Session of the General Conference, AME Church, The Spectrum, Philadelphia, PA, May 1–14, 1968* (n.p., n.d.),146–148.

million or more members," Bishop Wright observed, "but a large proportion were children and old people and people out of work." Moreover, bloated membership rolls in several reputedly large congregations and ongoing black migration out of the South into the North and West also contributed to miscalculations about AME membership.[13]

The substantial shortfall in revenue motivated some to propose special measures to raise additional funds to meet the budget. Brotherhood stalwarts, however, recoiled and "started a slogan of '$4.00 and no more.'" Instead, the 1960 General Conference authorized "a 20% cut in membership" in relevant episcopal districts in order to develop better budget calculations. Additionally, the $4.00 annual assessment per member remained in place because "a method of Liquidating the Deficit" in the original 1956–1960 quadrennial budget had been developed.[14]

The Brotherhood, in creating the General Board, unleashed reform energies that established other new structures and proposals aimed at modernizing AME operations. H. Ralph Jackson, while advocating for a General Board and a central budget, proposed a new Minimum Salary Department to provide supplemental income for pastors of impecunious congregations. The 1956 General Conference earmarked funds for the minimum salary initiative and the 1960 General Conference formally launched the department. The $250,000 annual allocation merged with the accumulated $1.2 million from the previous quadrennium to fund fully the new department. Jackson, despite his announced candidacy for the episcopacy, was unanimously elected in 1960 as the director.[15]

Other clergy emulated Jackson's advocacy for denominational reconstruction. F. Le Moyne Whitlock, John Hurst Adams, and others, in their own version of "continuing revolution," built on precedents from Jackson's leadership in The Brotherhood. Whitlock, a delegate to the 1956 General Conference from Kansas City, Missouri, was a Brotherhood enthusiast. When the budget law passed, he immediately motioned that the bishops should "meet as soon as possible to make nominations for the New General Board." Later, Whitlock proposed that less partisan delegates at a later General Conference should select General Board members "from a free and open ballot." Like other Brotherhood backers, Whitlock recognized

[13] Wright, *Eighty-Seven Years Behind the Black Curtain*, 289.
[14] Ibid.; *The Official Minutes of the ... General Conference 1960*, 91.
[15] "The Official Minutes of the ... General Conference, 1956," 477, 485; *The Official Minutes of the ... General Conference 1960*, 110, 172–173; "Minutes of the Eighth Session of the Central Tennessee Annual Conference, 1956," in *Minutes of the Conferences of the Thirteenth Episcopal District*, 1956, 75.

"the growing need for an authoritative agency to govern and direct the fiscal administration" of the denomination. In his 1972 book, *The Genius of African Methodism*, he described the creation of the General Board as a step toward addressing AME "imperfections" and its "corrupted 'system.'"[16]

In examining the necessity for ongoing reform, Whitlock articulated his deep commitment to African Methodism as "the visible expression of Black Revolution!" He believed "the destiny of the AME Church is inextricably tied in to the destiny of Black People the world over." Hence, the denomination "must reclaim its role of revolutionary leadership by providing Black People with the spirit of Jesus Christ" else "the black masses" will look to the advocates of violence, such as some in the Black Power movement, for guidance. For Whitlock, institutional reform was the only way to free up AMEs, especially in the clergy, to exert leadership among African Americans.[17]

Ministerial security, for example, needed to be addressed. Since innumerable AME clergy led in their locales insurgent organizations and movements aimed at social reconstruction, their leadership could be upended by the one-year appointment. Though bishops usually reassigned such pastors, these annual uncertainties could bring instability to affected congregations and communities. Moreover, there were "large numbers of our most able and effective pastors" who resisted transfer because of lucrative second jobs, home ownership, and favorable educational opportunities for their children. Moreover, there was the unrealized promise of the Minimum Salary Department whose mission lay in strengthening economically vulnerable clergy in pastoral and community leadership.[18]

Ministerial security was foundational to effective AME involvements in both ecclesiastical and social justice initiatives. Hence, Whitlock called for a reexamination of the appointive powers of the bishops and he showed how a reform achievement of The Brotherhood fell short of its objectives. "The appointive powers of the bishops," he said, "must be modified to the extent that local congregations and pastors will have an authoritative role in the assignment and removal of pastors." He recommended "the tenure of pastors of congregations must be extended to a reasonable length of time in order to remove the yearly anxiety and uncertainty which attends the custom of annual appointments." Whitlock succeeded in one respect. The 1980 General Conference, in response to grassroots ministerial agitation,

---

[16] "Official Minutes of the ... General Conference 1956," 301, 394; F. Le Moyne Whitlock, *The Genius of African Methodism* (n.p., 1972), preface, 33, 101.
[17] Whitlock, *The Genius of African Methodism*, 97.   [18] Ibid., 83.

enacted "A Bill of Rights for African Methodist Episcopal Ministers" that placed a modest curb on the pastoral appointive authority of the episcopacy. The law stipulated that bishops were required in writing to notify pastors "at least ninety days in advance" of an imminent transfer to another congregation."[19]

The Minimum Salary Department, which was established to spur ministerial efficiency among financially vulnerable pastors, drew some of Whitlock's most trenchant criticisms. He lamented that "this noble experiment has never achieved its purpose because the General Conference left too much control of the funds to the direction of one man-the Minimum Salary Director." Only after an accounting of the funds "have been cleared up will the ministers of the AME Church enjoy the full benefit of the economic security which the General Conference [originally] sought to provide." Nonetheless, Whitlock was still convinced that The Brotherhood "made some impact upon the church" by lifting ministerial security as a denominational priority.[20]

Whitlock was amazed that "no religious organization in the world has experienced the demoralizing effects of ecclesiastical corruption, fiscal irresponsibility, exploitation, and Machiavellian politics as has the AME Church, and yet retained the loyalty and devotion of its constituency." That loyalty, Whitlock believed, derived from a common understanding that "the AME Church is truly a Black Man's Church whose doctrines, polity, and organizational structure reflect the spiritual aspirations and ambitions of a people" once enslaved and segregated. Hence, reform was necessary so all could see that "the present day African Methodist Episcopal Church possesses the material resources and the organizational capacity to become the primary base of power for Black People."[21]

As the General Board developed into a crucial component of AME governance, the Minimum Salary Department, another byproduct of The Brotherhood Movement, became administratively controversial. Though H. Ralph Jackson was a "founding father" of the General Board, the management of the Minimum Salary Department, his other "brainchild," drew criticism at the 1968 General Conference. A resolution proposed that the legislative body should elect a Board of Directors for the department "with a Bishop as Chairman." Jackson responded by saying "that a group of

---

[19] Ibid., 85; *The Combined Minutes of the Forty-First Session of the General Conference of the African Methodist Episcopal Church* held in New Orleans, LA, June 18–28, 1980 (Nashville, TN, AME Sunday School Union, 1980), 299.
[20] Whitlock, *The Genius of African Methodism*, 84–85, 93.   [21] Ibid., 6–7, 98, 104.

delegates were seeking to humiliate him, and to do so, they would destroy" the agency. In any case, the department, he noted, was already "owned by the AME Church" and was answerable to the General Board. Though the motion was tabled, the unreadiness showed diminishing support for Jackson as a denominational reformer.[22]

FROM THE BROTHERHOOD TO THE GRASSROOTS FORUM

Brotherhood momentum, however, was already shifting to the Grassroots Forum of John Hurst Adams. Adams, a Seattle pastor and a new member of the General Board, prior to the 1968 General Conference developed a comprehensive blueprint for AME reorganization that broadened the Brotherhood vision. With "a complete overhauling" and "reformation" of the AME Church as objectives, the Grassroots Forum in 1967 met in Pittsburgh with reform-minded clergy and the President of the Connectional Lay Organization to discuss transformative upgrades in the denomination's legal, insurance, budgetary, and programmatic operations. These discussions opened into a broader consideration about "The Mission of the Church" that looked to a "Mission to The World." For Adams that meant "A Radical Reordering of Priorities, Structures, and Investments of African Methodism." These evaluations would eliminate waste in resources and would redirect them to meaningful ministry projects. He cited as ill-advised "spending [of] around a million dollars for a recent] Missionary Convention while not having a single paid Missionary anywhere in the world." Furthermore, it was necessary in a modernized fiscal structure to have "blanket insurance coverage of all Church Property" that could generate premium refunds to provide fresh financing for denominational programs and institutions.[23]

Forum recommendations, however, coincided with the release of the proposed connectional budget to be considered at the 1968 General Conference. What was problematic for Adams and his colleagues was an unwarranted assessment of an additional $1 million from congregations. Forum supporters lamented that the "denomination would abound in wealth, while local churches would be in poverty's vale." Moreover, augmented budget obligations would be levied, they believed, disproportionately on congregations in urban and industrial areas and would benefit departments that

---

[22] *Official Minutes of the ... General Conference 1968*, 150.
[23] *Official Minutes of the ... General Conference 1968*, 144; John H. Adams, "Open Report – "First Grassroots Forum,'" *AME Church Review*, Vol. 91, No. 233, October–December 1967, 32–33.

needed both rigorous review evaluation and probable reform before their allocations swelled with more funds. In the absence of fundamental reorganization in denominational structures this substantive increase seemed imprudent. Before asking rank-and-file AMEs for more money, departments should be required to write job descriptions for their officials and the bishops should "give vision and energy to the interpretation of The Mission of The Church."[24]

The 12.5 percent budget increase that the General Board presented to the 1968 General Conference put Adams in a peculiar position of supporting it over a minority proposal that recommended a 25 percent increase. Though he voted to table the latter recommendation and was in favor of the lesser increase, he remained convinced that whatever the scope of church expenditures, they were misaligned with the "new and emancipated world" in which the denomination had to operate. Already in the *AME Church Review*, Adams outlined how "A Radical Reordering of the AME Church" would look. A transformation of the denomination's infrastructure, he believed, would spur a modernization of African Methodism that was long overdue. He cited "automation and cybernetics," the current buzzwords from the new technologies, and the effects of urbanization that reflected themes from Harvey Cox's recent bestseller, *The Secular City: Secularization and Urbanization in Theological Perspective*. "These forces," Adams observed, "have converged in this decade of the sixties to demand and dictate that the AME Church cease putting fermenting new wine into cracking old bottles." He added that "the methodology, structure and content of our witness to the world be updated and upgraded." This process "requires us to take a bold risk in developing new technique, new organization and new relevance" to achieve reconstruction of African Methodism.[25]

Strengthening connectional departments was the centerpiece of Adams's proposed reform. Their restructuring required "the employment of professionals on the basis of ability, experience, and preparation rather than popularity," adequate staff support, programmatic experimentation, and improved fiscal accountability. The reorganization of these several departments also involved their consolidation into five divisions. The Treasurer's Office, for example, would be transformed into a Division of Finance and

---

[24] Adams, "Open Report," *AME Church Review*, October–December 1967, 34, 36.
[25] *Official Minutes of the ... General Conference 1968*, 121–122; see Harvey Cox, *The Secular City: Secularization and Urbanization in Theological Perspective* (New York, Macmillan, 1965); John Hurst Adams (John Hurst Adams Plugs Away at the Business of Reform), "Preposal: A Radical Reordering of the AME Church," *AME Church Review*, Vol. 92, No. 234, January–March 1968, 64.

Records that would absorb the treasurer, general secretary, and historiographer, General Officers formerly functioning in separate departments. The treasurer, the division head, would work with a combined office of the general secretary/historiographer, legal counsel, comptroller, statistician, and research and planning officer.[26]

Rather than battle the budget increase at the 1968 General Conference, Adams focused on persuading the assembly to enact as legislation the "New Structure of the AME Church." The bill passed and was "placed in the hands of a special committee elected by the General Board and [the] Council of Bishops for study, research, refinement and to plan its implementation" during the ensuing four years. Moreover, the "Proposed New Structure" was inserted in the denomination's *Book of Discipline*, thus presenting restructuring as a priority issue in AME discourse. Hence, the Council of Bishops, in echoing the Adams blueprint, declared in their Episcopal Address at the 1972 General Conference that the denomination's "organizational arrangements are not sacred and can and must be changed 'to serve the present age.'" In addition to the structural realignments suggested in the 1968 legislation, a derivative proposal for a United States census-based rearrangement of episcopal districts was advanced. On all of these matters the bishops repeated "the need for research and study" by a Commission on Reorganization. That Adams was elected a bishop at the 1972 General Conference signaled continued momentum for restructuring the denomination.[27]

Although the episcopal addresses at the 1976 and 1980 General Conferences called for "feasibility studies" about particular proposals related to restructuring and redistricting, Adams adhered to a comprehensive design for denominational reorganization. "Our church," he said in 1984, "is suffering from an internal paralysis which greatly inhibits its effectiveness in the world and which has begun its decline and could indeed lead to its eventual death." He added, "Richard Allen's vision for the African Methodist Episcopal Church as a vehicle of liberation, self-determination and self-help is now being eroded by the church's present confusion over mission and by its disunity of command." Hence, with authorization from the 1980 General Conference that established a Committee on Restructuring of the

[26] Adams, "A Radical Reordering of the AME Church," 65.
[27] *Official Minutes of the ... General Conference 1968*, 154, 270; *The Book of Discipline of the African Methodist Episcopal Church* (Nashville, TN, AME Sunday School Union, 1969), 357–360; *The Episcopal Address to the Thirty-Ninth Quadrennial Session of the General Conference of the African Methodist Episcopal Church Meeting in Dallas, TX, June 21–July 2, 1972* (n.p., n.d.), 26–28.

African Methodist Episcopal Church (COR), Adams approached the Lilly Endowment to fund a systematic study of the denomination's infrastructure. With collaboration from Coopers & Lybrand, the prominent accounting and management firm, Adams envisaged and executed an expert examination of the church's mission, goals, and objectives, its organizational structure, and of a realignment of episcopal districts.[28]

While the rise of large neo-Pentecostal congregations in the United States and a steady spread of the denomination outside North America showed that a rhetoric of AME demise was exaggerated, the institutional inefficiencies that Adams identified were authenticated in the Lilly and Coopers & Lybrand recommendations. The report focused on mission, goals and objectives, organizational structures, and redistricting possibilities. The AME mission statement needed a clear declaration of purpose that said African Methodism aimed "to minister to the spiritual, intellectual, physical, and emotional needs of all people by spreading Christ's liberating gospel through word and deed." To energize this mission a detailed roster of goals, reinforced by specific objectives, should be pursued. For example, the goal "to combat racism in all forms and to enable liberation for the poor and oppressed, especially Blacks," called for a reaffirmation of the 1856 AME creedal statement, "God Our Father, Christ Our Redeemer, Man Our Brother." With this doctrinal grounding AMEs could consciously link their theology to "seeking reconciliation" through various religious and interracial partnerships and to their church's emancipationist ethos in such protest actions as selective buying campaigns against racist vendors. Regular dissemination of the AME creed through church media and at every level of denominational assemblies would "serve as the foundation on which all Church work is based."[29]

With respect to organizational structure, said the report, "there is no clearly established entity with the authority to provide and exert executive coordination over all of the organizational components and officials of the Church." Hence, there was too little "unity of command," "accountability and evaluation," and "delineation of authority and responsibility." Solutions were proposed for each. To remedy the absence of executive authority

---

[28] *The Episcopal Address to the Fortieth Quadrennial Session of the General Conference of the African Methodist Episcopal Church, Atlanta, GA, June 16th–17th, 1976* (n.p., Wamber Press, 1976), 56; *The Combined Minutes of the Forty-First Session of the General Conference 1980*, 102; John Hurst Adams (compiler), [Introduction], *Toward a More Effective AME Church: A Summary of the Results of the Committee on Restructure* [COR-AMEC]: Final Report to the General Board and the 1984 General Conference (n.p., 1984), 2.

[29] Adams, *Toward a More Effective AME Church*, 3, 7.

between meetings of the General Conference and General Board, for example, there could be "a small Executive-Administrative Committee" that could be empowered to oversee denominational affairs.[30]

The denomination's thirteen episcopal districts based in the United States, one that covered the Caribbean and South America, and four located in Africa were not configured for maximum geographical and fiscal efficiency. Some were too large for effective administration and others were too small to underwrite required denominational and district programs. They needed to be realigned to provide "greater equity among districts in terms of member-ship, Black population, and number of churches." Moreover, "state bound-aries where possible" should provide templates for redistricting and to "equalize fund-raising ability." Five plans were presented that ranged from adding an episcopal district in the United States, decreasing districts outside the United States mainly by attaching particular Caribbean and South American areas to particular US jurisdictions, or adding a district in Africa.[31]

Adams presented the COR findings to the 1984 General Conference. The report was received and referred to such relevant bodies as the legislative or revisions committee and the committee on annual conference boundaries. Later, Adams queried whether the proposals would return to the delegates for consideration. A proposal was advanced to divide South Africa into two episcopal districts. The legislation, though separate from the COR report, had its endorsement. Beyond the passage of this measure, there was no substantive action on the comprehensive reorganization plan.[32]

COR initiatives, diffused through sundry reform proposals, did not attain the level of comprehensive restructuring that the 1984 study envisaged. Instead, Adams, as a bishop, pursued change by strengthening AME infra-structure in his areas of episcopal authority. Concurrent with his COR involvements in the 1980s and 1990s, for example, he presided in the Second and Seventh Episcopal Districts, two robust jurisdictions along the Atlantic seaboard. In the Second District he spearheaded over three dozen church starts including areas of northern Virginia and suburban communities in Maryland where no AME congregations had ever existed. Also, additional congregations started in Baltimore, Washington DC, and Charlotte, North Carolina. In the Seventh District in South Carolina Adams targeted the

---

[30] Ibid., 10.   [31] Ibid., 14–15.
[32] *The Combined Minutes of the 42ⁿᵈ Quadrennial Session of the General Conference [of the] African Methodist Episcopal Church* held in Kansas City, MO, July 7–15, 1984, 134–135, 173, 175–176.

state's northern tier, especially Rock Hill and new churches in the Charleston and Columbia vicinities. Adams's COR framework also influenced action at the 2000 General Conference that reduced the denomination's twelve departments headed by general officers and consolidated them into nine departments. One of the affected departments, Minimum Salary, merged with Pensions to become the Department of Ministerial Annuities. The respective offices of the editor of the *AME Church Review* and the historiographer were combined with the latter general officer elected to administer the new Department of Research and Scholarship. Though the *Review* editor, the only female general officer, retired, Teresa L. Fry Brown, a seminary professor at Emory University, was elected in 2012 to succeed the male head of the merged departments as the denomination's third female general officer. Another COR proposal for an AME Church administrator was resurrected in a 2004 General Conference bill to create an ecumenical/ administrative officer. The delegates, however, took no action on the measure. The fate of Jackson's Minimum Salary Department and the diffusion of Adams's Committee on Reorganization recommendations showed an AME system resistant to comprehensive restructuring, but susceptible to reform only in small pieces and through targeted initiatives.[33]

Despite this seeming dissipation of reformist energies, a Strategic Planning Core Team commenced work in 2002 "to reform, reorganize, and restructure the AME Church of the 21st century" with goals similar to the earlier COR study. Two surveys of AME members that drew respective responses numbering 10,500 and 15,058 examined the strengths, weaknesses, opportunities, and threats on how the denomination functioned. These were categorized within thirteen issues that constituted "wake-up calls" for African Methodism. Familiar to COR proponents were proposals to "reconfigure Episcopal Districts" and to "create an Office of the Chief Administrator." Several other recommendations identified needed administrative changes aimed at better reporting of financial and membership

---

[33] *200 Years: Bicentennial History [of the] Second Episcopal District* (Tappan, NY, Custombook, Inc., 1987), 13; John Hurst Adams, *Seventh Episcopal District, African Methodist Episcopal Church, 2000 Report about the Work of Ministry in the District-Adams Years, 1992–2000*; Episcopal District Report to the General Conference, 1992–2000, (n.p., 2000), 5; *The Combined Minutes of the Forty-Sixth Session of the General Conference of the African Methodist Episcopal Church* held in Cincinnati, OH, July 5–11, 2000 (Nashville, TN, AME Sunday School Union, 2000), 313, 359–360, 364; *Minutes [of the] Forty-Seventh Quadrennial Session of the General Conference [of the] African Methodist Episcopal Church* [held in] Indianapolis, IN, June 30–July 7, 2004, 164.

statistics, "clear job descriptions and definitions for all positions and agencies," and the revival of a "Department of Educational Institutions."[34]

African Methodism, notwithstanding inefficiencies in the denominational infrastructure and in the implementation of the creedal statement, continued to spread outside the United States. Mobile ministers and members migrating from the Caribbean and Africa to Europe, indigenous evangelization in virgin areas of the "mother" continent, and the ongoing influence of the Allen legacy that emphasized the church's proud history of black institutional independence energized expansion beyond the Americas. These developments pressed AMEs to broaden episcopal leadership to include Africans and to establish new structures to sustain growth beyond the western hemisphere. While support for these initiatives benefited from Brotherhood and COR reform efforts, they mainly derived from the denomination's expanded visibility among decolonized peoples.

A GLOBAL CONSCIOUSNESS

From the post-World War II era through the late twentieth and early twenty-first centuries, despite debates about fiscal policies and structural reforms, African Methodism expanded globally into territories where it had never existed before. Historically mobile, whether in the United States or within the broader Atlantic World, AMEs routinely emigrated and reestablished in new settings their black-led religious body whose celebrated origins lay in insurgency against slavery and other subsequent systems of racial subjugation. In addition to immigration and the historic appeal of African Methodism, global growth drew from an association between an independent black church and rising nationalism in colonial Africa.

Europe was familiar terrain to several generations of AMEs. Bishops and other AME leaders, starting in 1881, were speakers in England at decennial world Methodist conferences. Moreover, such scholars as Richard R. Wright, Jr., Charles H. Wesley, Samuel Hopkins Giles, Milton S. J. Wright, Charles Leander Hill, and others studied at leading institutions in Germany, Scotland, and France. Moreover, chaplains and other military veterans of AME affiliation served in England and elsewhere in continental Europe during the two world wars. In the aftermath of World War II Caribbean and African immigration anchored African Methodism in Europe. This development

---

[34] *Combined Minutes of the Forty-Seventh Quadrennial Session of the General Conference, 2004* (Nashville, TN, AME Sunday School Union, 2004), 340–344.

grew from a small group of recently arrived Jamaican immigrants who began meeting as an AME body early in the 1950s. Reverend Edgar B. Hinds in Jamaica, their long-distance advisor, and Presiding Elder T. L. M. Spencer, both delegates from the Jamaica Annual Conference to the 1952 General Conference, informed newly assigned Bishop Richard R. Wright, Jr. about the London AMEs. After Wright placed the assembly in the Jamaica jurisdiction, Donald Tony Witter, an AME minister who immigrated to London from Jamaica in the early 1960s, and fellow missionaries and evangelists from the island homeland, nurtured the England AMEs. Additionally, Moses Sephula, an AME minister from South Africa, settled in England in 1964 and committed to expand African Methodism to the Midlands, especially in the Nottingham area.[35]

Witter's oversight of the London mission warranted an invitation in 1966 to Bishop G. Wayman Blakely. The bishop, who was sent to the Caribbean area by the 1964 General Conference, was attending the World Methodist Conference in London. The London AMEs brought Blakely and other visiting AMEs to their worship site, where the bishop officially organized them as a congregation with Witter appointed as the pastor. Sephula and another AME clergyman living in England learned of Blakely's action and received his endorsement to spread the denomination to other areas of the United Kingdom. Moreover, Blakely received the Reverend H. N. Morally and his independent congregation into the London Mission. The 1972 General Conference formally approved the establishment of the London Annual Conference, and this action was affirmed at the 1976 meeting. Other congregations began in England, but only Richard Allen Church, led by its founder, Rudolph U. Aaron, an immigrant from Guyana, survived into the twenty-first century.[36]

The London Annual Conference stretched to both Holland and France because of the same immigration patterns that populated African Methodism in England. An African émigré, the Reverend J. B. Ngubane of South Africa, and others living in Amsterdam, Holland, started to worship in My Father's House Church. In 1993 they petitioned Bishop Zedekiah L. Grady

[35] Rudolph U. Aaron, "History of the AME Church in Europe," *AME Church Review*, Vol. 124, No. 409, January–March 2008, 50; Frederick H. Talbot, "AME Church Organized in London, England," *AME Church Review*, Vol. 89, No. 230, October–December 1966, 18.
[36] Talbot, "AME Church Organized in London, England," *AME Church Review*, 19; *Minutes of the General Conference of the Thirty-Ninth Quadrennium of the African Methodist Episcopal Church* held in Dallas, TX, June 21–July 3, 1972, 201; *Combined Minutes of the Fortieth Session of the General Conference of the African Methodist Episcopal Church* held in Atlanta, GA, June 16–26, 1976 (Nashville, TN, AME Sunday School Union, 1976), 125.

for admission into the AME Church. The official organization happened in Amsterdam in 1995 as Grady AME Church, with local preacher Msizi Dube, another South African, in charge. Later, Bishop William P. De Veaux in 2000 advanced Dube to full ordination. The organization of the Amsterdam body required the jurisdiction to be renamed in 2004 the London-Holland Annual Conference. The Reverend Jonathan Weaver, the pastor at Mt. Nebo AME Church in Bowie, Maryland, through his travels in the Congo, was connected to émigrés at the Nouvelle Alliance Church in Lyon, France. After an introduction to Bishop Carolyn Tyler Guidry, she began to plan for their admission into the London-Holland diocese in 2007. Her successor, Bishop Sarah F. Davis, admitted the church into the annual conference in 2009. This move into France necessitated another name change for the jurisdiction in 2012, to the European Annual Conference.[37]

The greatest growth in African Methodism occurred in Africa, where its presence over several decades provided a foundation for steady expansion. South Africa, where the AME Church had been established since 1896, supplied clergy and structural grounding to spearhead and sustain development in both neighboring and distant territories. Adjacent to South Africa was Southwest Africa, a former German colony whose indigenous population discovered African Methodism from their neighbors in South Africa.

Concomitant with colonial rule by Germany and a later League of Nations mandate conveyed to South Africa, the German-based Rhenish Missionary Society gained religious ascendancy in Southwest Africa. Though the group started numerous schools, a curriculum for Africans that was intentionally restricted stirred long-seething discontent. While AMEs in the 1920s and 1930s, either within Southwest Africa or from nearby South Africa, ceded the territory to Rhenish missionaries, they positioned themselves as a possible alternative to the German group. Mounting impatience toward Rhenish discriminatory practices and increased educational collaboration with the white supremacist Dutch Reformed Church in South Africa precipitated a black secessionist movement. Six black Rhenish evangelists led the withdrawal on May 27, 1946 and they soon joined the AME Church. At a July 6, 1946 meeting Francis H. Gow and two other AME clergy from South Africa received the former Rhenish preachers into their denomination, and in 1947 several were ordained. Numerous churches and schools were either

---

[37] Aaron, "The History of the AME Church in Europe," *AME Church Review*, 53–54; *The Christian Recorder Online*, April 22, 2011.

"established and/or strengthened" in such crucial cities as Keetmanshoop, Gibeon, Windhoek, and Walvisbay.[38]

An alignment between the arrival of African Methodism and the rise of African nationalist movements characterized interactive religious and political developments in Africa in the post-World War II period. Southwest Africa functioned within a United Nations trusteeship that linked it as a vassal state to South Africa. A heritage of black self-determination intrinsic to AME identity and contemporary African nationalism aimed at freeing indigenous populations from colonial and white settler rule, however, converged in Southwest Africa and Mozambique where the emergence of African Methodism reinforced these objectives.

The discontent that AME founders in Southwest Africa experienced toward the Rhenish Missionary Society was similarly stirred against white supremacy in South Africa and its derivative effects in its neighboring subservient state. In traveling to South Africa for AME conferences, Southwest Africa ministers learned in 1952 about the Defiance Campaign to protest newly enacted apartheid laws and their impact in both countries. Southwest Africans supported the campaigns and initiatives at the United Nations to achieve independence from South Africa. The dual tasks of church and nation building engaged several AME clergy. The Witbooi family, whose insurgency coincided with German colonization in the late nineteenth century, became major figures in the establishment of African Methodism in Southwest Africa and in the movement for an independent Namibia.[39]

The Witbooi family, whose origins lay in South Africa, migrated in 1863 to Khaxatsus in Southwest Africa. Kido Witbooi, who renamed the place as Gibeon, was a forebear of the anticolonialist Captain Hendrik Witbooi who attempted to mobilize the region's disparate tribes against German colonizers. Another descendant, Markus Witbooi, was among the dissident black Rhenish evangelists who left the organization and joined the AME Church in 1947. A namesake of Hendrik Witbooi became heir to the family tradition of black autonomy in the religious and political spheres. Combining the roles as an AME minister and as political activist, the second Hendrik Witbooi participated in the transition from a colonized Southwest Africa into an

[38] Willem Simon Hanse, "A History of the African Methodist Episcopal Church in the Republic of Namibia, 1946–2007," *AME Church Review*, Vol. 124, No. 409, January–March 2008, 42–45.
[39] Ibid., 46; Willem Simon Hanse, "Hendrik Witbooi: Marriage of Faith and Politics in Namibia," *AME Church Review*, Vol. 119, No. 396, October–December 2004, 43.

independent Namibia. Educated in Rhenish and Wesleyan schools and at the AME-sponsored Wilberforce Institute in South Africa, Witbooi started in 1958 as a teacher in Southwest Africa and was subsequently ordained into the AME ministry. He served as pastor at St. Mark AME Church in Gibeon, became the presiding elder first on the Gibeon District, and then on the Windhoek District.[40]

Through his role as an official in the Witbooi Traditional Authority, Witbooi became politically involved in defiance and independence movements against white South African rule. His participation in a teachers' strike in 1976 and 1977 drew from his unwarranted transfer out of Gibeon where he was locally influential in calls for separation from South Africa. These activities, including his membership in the insurgent South West Africa People's Organization (SWAPO), landed him in jail in solitary confinement in 1978. Namibia, because of overwhelming international pressure, compelled South Africa to grant independence to Namibia in 1990. The 1992 General Conference awarded Witbooi with a "Richard Allen Plaque for excellent service in his country and organizing an AME Church School in Namibia." Introduced as a vice chairman of SWAPO and Minister of Labor in Namibia, Witbooi presented a flag of Namibia to the assembly and invited fellow delegates to sing with him Namibia's national anthem. Later, Witbooi became Namibia's deputy prime minister.[41]

Witbooi's involvement in the Namibian independence struggle as an AME minister mirrored developments elsewhere in Africa. At the 1976 General Conference, for example, Maros Prameleno, a delegate from the Mozambique, likened the AME Church to his newly independent nation freed in 1975 from Portuguese rule. The founder of the guerrilla group Frente de Libertacaco Mocambique (FRELIMO), Eduardo Mondlane, had been educated in the United States and "was the first delegate to come to the General Conference from Mozambique East Africa." Though he was assassinated in 1969, FRELIMO ousted the Portuguese after his death. Mozambique, Prameleno said, "is like the African Methodist Episcopal Church" because both were "solely governed by Black People."[42]

While AMEs in Namibia and Mozambique aligned their nationalist objectives with their denominational heritage of black autonomy, the

[40] Hanse, "Hendrik Witbooi," *AME Church Review*, 43–44.
[41] Ibid., 44–45; *Combined Minutes of the Forty-Fourth Quadrennial Session of the General Conference of the African Methodist Episcopal Church* held in Orlando, FL, July 8–15, 1992, 48, 144.
[42] *Combined Minutes ... of the General Conference, 1976*, 321.

Figure 7.1 Hendrik Witbooi, Independence Leader and AME minister in Namibia (with Permission from the Khoi & Active Awareness Group, Namibia)

reputation of African Methodism as an independent religious organization was sufficient reason for a dissident Wesleyan body in Angola to seek membership. Zacarias Cardozo, a former United Methodist minister, contacted the AME Council of Bishops in 1992 to initiate a merger with the Independent Methodist Church in Angola. Bishop Donald G. K. Ming and Reverend Frederick C. Harrison, the Secretary of Missions, were dispatched to Angola to meet Cardozo and the 4,000 persons who greeted the AME officials in Luanda. Bishop Harold B. Senatle of South Africa brought from the 33,000 Angolan parishioners and 127 pastors a formal letter of request to unite with the AME Church. They were received as observers at the 1992 General Conference and officially established as the Angola Annual Conference at the 1996 General Conference.[43]

Similarly, an indigenous initiative from Uganda, communicated through James C. Wade, a pastor in Evanston, Illinois, and Daniel Wadabula, a Ugandan studying at Garrett Evangelical Theological Seminary, introduced the Beroya Gospel Fellowship to Bishop Robert V. Webster. Fifteen congregations and pastors and 865 members in 1996 formally transferred into the

[43] Dennis Clark Dickerson, "The Worldwide Mission of the African Methodist Episcopal Church" in *The Doctrine and Discipline of the African Methodist Episcopal Church* (Nashville, TN, AME Sunday School Union, 2102), 12.

AME Church. Elsewhere in Central Africa, Bishop Preston W. Williams reestablished the denomination in the Democratic Republic of the Congo (DRC). On April 22, 2004 Williams came to Kinshasa and participated in celebratory events marking the revival of African Methodism in the region. Though districts were already established in such areas as Tshikapa, Lumbumbashi, and Mbuji Mayi, Williams recommended two additional presiding elder districts in the respective North and South regions. At the 2004 General Conference Williams sought permission to ordain 150 lay preachers for a hurried addition to ministerial personnel in the DRC. In Kenya, however, the start of African Methodism was owed to the initiative of a Texas minister, William M. Campbell, Jr., the pastor of Anderson Chapel AME Church in Killeen. After several mission trips to Kenya, Campbell, in December 2007, started the nation's first AME congregation, Bethel in Nakuru. Bishop Paul Kawimbe, whose jurisdiction extended as far as Tanzania, gave his endorsement to the initiative. An indigenous pastor, Moses Achola, a Luo in the majority Kikuyu nation, became the pastor, and a building to seat 250 people was planned. Within a decade, at Achola's direction, another dozen congregations, including one in Nairobi, Kenya's capital city, were established. They became a part of the new East Africa Annual Conference.[44]

Historically, the Department of Missions and the two women's missionary societies, beginning in the late nineteenth century, became embedded in the AME infrastructure and targeted their support to Liberia, Sierra Leone, South Africa, and Haiti. Expansion both within and beyond these sectors, especially in the closing decades of the twentieth century, necessitated new policies and structures to service the denomination's increased international presence. Among these developments were dual pressures to elevate trans-national leadership into the episcopacy. The self-interested white settler government of South Africa and the legitimate demands of indigenous Africans initially pushed AMEs to elect a prelate from the "mother" continent. Moreover, the press for expanded expenditures and broader programs in health, education, and other projects led to new initiatives to sustain global ministries. These developments in requiring refinements in denominational polity and policies benefited from concurrent conversations about

[44] Robert V. Webster, "A New Image for a New Age in the 17th Episcopal District of the African Methodist Episcopal Church (1992–1996)," *AME Church Review*, Vol. 113, No. 369, January–March 1998, 25–26; Preston W. Williams, II, "African Methodism Awakens in the Democratic Republic of the Congo," *AME Church Review*, Vol. 120, No. 395, July–September 2004, 23–24; *Minutes of the Forty-Seventh General Conference, 2004*, 634; *Killeen Daily Herald*, January 19, 2008; *Christian Recorder Online*, November 12, 2018.

reform and drew support from The Brotherhood and from the proponents of COR.

Mandated responses from the General Conferences of 1956, 1984, and 2004 pertained to internationalizing the AME episcopacy. Despite an historical roster of prelates native either to Canada or the Caribbean, these bishops had served as pastors and in other denominational offices based in the United States. Moreover, they were well integrated among African Americans and often married spouses who were American born. The election of bishops at the 1948 General Conference, however, presaged a diasporic breakthrough that would lead to the selection of an African bishop.

At the meeting D. Ormonde Walker, former president of Wilberforce University and pastor of Bethel in Buffalo, New York, and Joseph Gomez, the pastor of St. James in Cleveland, Ohio, were leading candidates for the episcopacy. Walker and Gomez, born in the West Indies in St. Vincent and

Figure 7.2 AME delegation to the World Council of Churches, Amsterdam, Holland, 1948. Standing, left to right: Bishops A. J. Allen, S. L. Greene, John A. Gregg, Decatur Ward Nichols, Reverend (later Bishop) G. Wayman Blakely; seated, left to right: Alma A. Polk, Charlotte C. Wright, Jewett W. Allen, Kay Bailey Nichols, Anne E. Heath (Used with Permission from Sioux Nichols Taylor, West Columbia, SC)

Antigua respectively, "for years" had endured "a whispering campaign against aspirants who were born in the Islands." In denouncing these nativist sentiments, George A. Singleton, formerly editor of the *AME Church Review*, declared "the Church showed its growing spirit of progressive liberalism by electing these fine clergymen on the same ballot." Gomez's daughter corroborated Singleton's observations. It was "rumored" she wrote, "that the conference would never elect two West Indians." If elected at all, delegates would elevate only one, not both. Because Walker led in an early tally, Gomez supporters believed that the Buffalo pastor would get the nod. In the end Walker and Gomez polled more votes than were needed and with Lawrence H. Hemingway, a general officer, decisively led the field of candidates. The other contenders were left to compete on subsequent ballots for the remaining three vacancies.[45]

Though Gomez was assigned to South Africa, the sudden death of Bishop Henry Y. Tookes shifted him to Texas to replace the deceased prelate. Because Gomez, despite a newly enacted rule that barred bishops appointed to a "foreign district" from filling a vacancy in a "Home District," needed someone to substitute for him in South Africa. Some wanted to name Francis H. Gow, a Cape Town pastor, as a concocted bishop coadjutor, but the assignment of Isaiah H. Bonner, who was elected right after Gomez, provided the district with another non-African bishop. Nonetheless, Gomez maintained transatlantic collegiality with Gow. When Gomez thought that he was going to South Africa, he looked forward to interactions with Gow. Since Gomez would not see Gow in South Africa, he invited him instead to Texas in 1948 to address a missionary meeting at the district Christian education conference.[46]

Though Gomez's West Indian nativity may have troubled his tumultuous tenure as the bishop of Texas in the 1950s, his election and that of Walker's compelled AMEs to reckon with the historic transnational character of their church's episcopal leadership. As African indigenization became palpable during the 1956 General Conference, the 1948 election of two bishops of Caribbean origin became at least tangentially relevant to this important deliberation. Africa, however, became the central focus of this discourse. As a result, AMEs responded to pressures from white South Africans who were suspicious of autonomous African American bishops and barred their

---

[45] George A. Singleton, *The Romance of African Methodism: A Study of the African Methodist Episcopal Church* (New York, Exposition Press, 1952), 181; Gomez-Jefferson, *In Darkness With God*, 197–198.

[46] Gomez-Jefferson, *In Darkness With God*, 199–201, 208.

entry, and from aboriginal Africans increasingly demanded indigenous leadership. Hence, the 1956 General Conference, faced with ongoing difficulties of getting bishops into South Africa, was pushed to elect an African to the episcopacy.

Francis H. Gow, a colored with more privileges in the apartheid system than a full blooded black and already known to several bishops, seemed easiest to elect to the episcopacy and more likely to be accepted by white South African authorities. Though native to South Africa, Gow was married to an African American wife, and had been a pastor, professor, and a World War I army veteran during his twenty years in the United States. Gow, like Walker and Gomez, was well integrated among African Americans and became a naturalized United States citizen. When he returned to South Africa, he was elected president of the African People's Organization and was selected as chairman of the Coloured Advisory Council. Though Gomez admired him as an apartheid opponent, whites seemed reassured because he renewed his citizenship in South Africa and could bypass the bureaucratic hassles that African American bishops encountered.[47]

Gow was already familiar with the electoral process for the bishopric. At the 1952 General Conference he tallied on the first ballot a respectable 112 votes, though he fell short of the 529 votes required for election. The 1956 General Conference, however, would be different. Gow would be spared the usual rigors of intense and marathon campaigning and the possibility of having to run yet again at a subsequent General Conference. Instead, an election outcome was approved that insured Gow would be elected to the bishopric.[48]

The scenario that landed Gow in the episcopacy began with a report from the Episcopal Committee. The creation of a new district in South Africa and the election of five bishops with three designated for several territories in southern Africa were recommended. A delegate who queried whether "the bishop for Africa would be elected from [the] foreign fields" was answered affirmatively. Bishop Frederick D. Jordan, recently assigned and detained from entering South Africa, explained why Africa needed a jurisdiction separate from other adjacent provinces. The greatest number of congregations in the region, he observed, were located in South Africa and they

---

[47] Wright, *The Bishops of the African Methodist Episcopal Church*, 188–190; Gomez-Jefferson, *In Darkness with God*, 199.

[48] "Official Minutes of the Thirty-Fourth Session of the General Conference of the African Methodist Episcopal Church held at Chicago, IL, May, 1952," in *The Combined Minutes of the General Conferences*, 245–246.

required their own bishop. The other two areas in southern Africa could function independently. Jordan added "that the government of South Africa will not admit a Bishop unless he is a citizen of Africa." Bishop Bonner, Jordan's predecessor, affirmed that AMEs were numerous in the country and "suggested that we ought to elect someone who can get into the Union of South Africa." Ezra Johnson and H. Ralph Jackson, leaders of The Brotherhood movement, endorsed what Jordan and Bonner had expressed and supported motions to ratify the recommendations of the Episcopal Committee concerning Africa. Moreover, a delegate from the Ohio Annual Conference "stated that the world was watching the AMEs and he thought it was time to elect an African."[49]

On the day of the election Bishop Alexander J. Allen "asked that one person for Bishop would be considered from Africa." A delegate from the Southern California Annual Conference "moved that the General Conference go on record sharing this thought." After a second to the motion, the delegates approved. Procedurally, Bishop Bonner stated "that only four American Bishops would be voted for, and one from Africa." The Chief Secretary reported on the first ballot that 1,625 votes had been cast, with 813 needed for election to the bishopric. The long roster of candidates including Gow of South Africa and I. C. Steady of Liberia polled 1,355 votes and 50 votes respectively. Though the leading African American candidates received votes ranging from 630 to 471 votes, only Gow polled a sufficient tally to be elected on the first ballot. The other top vote-getters were elected on subsequent ballots. After Bishop Bonner introduced him, Bishop Gow recounted "the intense struggle in South Africa" and declared, "that the loyalty of those in Africa [to the AME Church] would now be stronger than ever."[50]

Gow served in South Africa and Southwest Africa for eight years. Because of episcopal term limits for all bishops, the General Conference of 1964 assigned Gow to West Africa. The difference between Gow and his episcopal colleagues, however, lay in his restricted service to Africa. Though AMEs returned to the familiar pattern of assigning African American bishops to South Africa after Gow's death on March 20, 1968, the issue of indigenization remained. The bishop's heir apparent was Easter M. Gordon, long-time presiding elder and surrogate for Gow and his African American successors in South Africa and Southwest Africa. Gordon, a regular delegate

---

[49] "Official Minutes of the General Conference, 1956," in *The Combined Minutes of the General Conferences*, 293, 383–385; 389.
[50] Ibid., 394–397.

to several General Conferences, like Gow, was classified as colored in their country's racially stratified system, and was well known to AMEs in the United States. At the 1968 General Conference, meeting within weeks of the bishop's death, Gow's mantle as an indigenous bishop for non-American AMEs was contested.[51]

Liberia's J. Benedict Mason, the president of the AME- supported Monrovia College, not Gordon, though not elected, outpolled the South African candidate at the 1968 General Conference. Mason's 261 votes dwarfed Gordon's tally of sixty-one and the thirty received by Frederick H. Talbot of Guyana. At the 1972 General Conference Mason and Gordon polled on the first ballot 132 votes and 117 votes respectively. Talbot, the nephew of D. P. Talbot, a pioneer AME preacher in the former British Guiana, drew an impressive 622 votes and was elected to the episcopacy with 723 votes on a subsequent ballot. "All the delegates joined in the demonstration in the Overseas Areas," reported the General Conference scribe, "over the election of the deserving Bishop-Elect, Frederick Talbot, the first to be elected Bishop from the 16th District" which covered the Caribbean, South America, and England.[52]

Talbot, who served for eight years in the jurisdiction, delivered a valedictory at the 1980 General Conference that celebrated the provisional indigenization of episcopal leadership in the Sixteenth Episcopal District. On a point of personal privilege, he presented the Reverend Philip Van Putten, a nonagenarian and presiding elder in the Haiti Annual Conference, who affirmed AME ties connecting the Americas and Africa. Putten, a veteran delegate to the General Conference starting in 1928, observed that "two of the greatest men coming out of Africa to the New World were Toussaint L'Ouverture of Haiti and Richard Allen of the USA." Moreover, "both started movements of liberation and personhood in 1804 and 1816" respectively. Van Putten also believed "the keys to the Kingdom of Africa are in the hands of the African Methodist Episcopal Church."[53]

Like Gow, Talbot was acculturated in the United States through earning degrees at the AME-supported Allen University in South Carolina, Yale Divinity School, the Pacific School of Religion, and later a D. Min. at Columbia Theological Seminary in Georgia. He was also a pastor in South

---

[51] Dennis C. Dickerson, *Religion, Race, and Region: Research Notes on AME Church History* (Nashville, TN, AME Sunday School Union, 1995), 131–142.

[52] *Combined Minutes . . . of the General Conference, 1968,* 170; *Minutes of the General Conference of the Thirty-Ninth Quadrennium of the African Methodist Episcopal Church* held in Dallas, TX, June 21–July 3, 1972, 113, 176, 178.

[53] *Combined Minutes . . . of the General Conference, 1980,* 211.

Carolina and California and a professor at AME schools in Arkansas and Ohio before returning to his native Guyana to become pastor at St. Peter in Georgetown. Talbot, elected in open competition at the 1972 General Conference, though committing to serve in the Sixteenth Episcopal District for the maximum two four-year terms, presided during the remainder of his episcopacy in the United States.[54]

Gordon, however, persisted in his quest for the episcopacy. At the 1976 General Conference he polled a respectable, but inadequate 115 votes on the first ballot. His tragic death in an automobile accident in 1979 removed Africa's strongest candidate for the bishopric. At the 1980 General Conference four other Africans, vying to replace Gordon, polled votes only in the single digits. At the 1984 General Conference, however, a compelling candidate from South Africa, a Gordon mentee, Harold B. Senate, who had run in 1980, emerged as a potential Gow successor. These South African delegates coalesced around two issues that their populous Fifteenth Episcopal District strongly advocated. They supported the Senate candidacy for the bishopric and they requested the creation of a Nineteenth Episcopal District headquartered in Johannesburg from the parent Fifteenth Episcopal District based in Cape Town.[55]

Three issues pertaining to South Africa lay before the 1984 General Conference. They included the fight against apartheid, jurisdictional reorganization, and the election of an indigenous bishop. The bishops in their Episcopal Address supported AMEs in South Africa and their global allies in "efforts to eradicate the oppressive system of apartheid" and called on the government of the United States "to withhold its support of that regime." They also recognized that the Fifteenth Episcopal District, with 696 churches and 67,477 members in seven annual conferences including one in Namibia, had "more than the total of all the members in the other 4 overseas Episcopal Districts." Therefore, they concluded that "additional supervision is not only desirable," but "imperative" for this sprawling diocese. The bishops, in advocating a division of the Fifteenth Episcopal District, were responding to a 1981 special delegation from South Africa that requested reorganization to reckon with "the vastness of the area" and to assure "development and growth in the future." In the only observation about episcopal supervision outside the United States, the bishops recommended that one's "ability to

---

[54] "Frederick Hilborn Talbot," in A. Lee Henderson (ed.), *The African Methodist Episcopal Church Registry Select* (Nashville, TN, AME Sunday School Union, 1994), 362–363.
[55] *Combined Minutes ... of the General Conference, 1976*, 175; *Combined Minutes ... of the General Conference, 1980*, 73, 75, 274, 276.

serve in special situations" should be the single criterion for an assignment to "overseas areas." Because this oblique statement scarcely satisfied advocates of indigenization, an additional recommendation was attached to the Episcopal Address that asked delegates to vote "in such a way as to elect one of our brothers and sisters of our overseas districts to the Office of Bishop."[56]

Hence, delegates to the General Conference dealt first with a division of AME territory in South Africa and then debated the issue of an African bishop. The reorganization of AME geography belonged to the General Conference Committee on Annual Conference Boundaries. In the proposed creation of two dioceses the Fifteenth Episcopal District retained the Cape and its adjacent areas including Namibia, while the Nineteenth Episcopal District stretched across the Transvaal, Natal, and the former Orange Free State. In response to some delegates who raised various procedural issues including a competing proposal to involve neighboring nations' countries in the Eighteenth Episcopal District realignment, Bishop Frederick C. James, who had served in South Africa, objected. "The people there," he said, "know more about what they need than we do. We shouldn't recommend that we merge independent nations with South Africa." Ultimately, a Nineteenth Episcopal District was approved and it provided the jurisdictional space to accommodate an African indigenous bishop.[57]

After legislation was enacted to establish another jurisdiction in Africa, the Episcopal Committee reinforced the recommendations of the bishops and proposed the election of four bishops, one of whom would be assigned "for the newly created district." John E. Hunter and Donald G. K. Ming, two bishops who presided in South Africa, argued that "a special ballot be made for the Overseas Bishop" and that the Episcopal Committee report should be amended "to include the election of a Bishop from Overseas." Though some bishops objected to geographical origin as a basis for elevation to the episcopacy, delegates voted for the election of an African bishop.[58]

Five Africans qualified for the first ballot. The leading candidates, Daniel M. Mkwanazi, a Zimbabwe minister and administrative assistant to bishops assigned to Central Africa, drew 113 votes, and Senatle attracted 659 votes, more than any contender either from the United States or Africa. Though he missed the 727-vote threshold needed for election, Senatle was well positioned for a victory on a subsequent ballot. His lead drew from the push for

---

[56] *The Episcopal Address to the 42nd Session of the General Conference [of the] African Methodist Episcopal Church, Kansas City, Missouri, July 8–15, 1984* (n.p., 1984), 8–10, 40; *Combined Minutes . . . of the General Conference, 1984,* 125–126.

[57] *Combined Minutes . . . of the General Conference, 1985,* 174–175, 245.   [58] Ibid., 178.

indigenization, his established familiarity with AME leaders in the United States, and through his visibility in denominational media.[59]

Born in 1926 in Christiana in northwest South Africa, Senatle, whose mother was AME, was nurtured among the Anglicans. He answered the call to minister, however, in the AME Church and trained at the denomination's R. R. Wright School of Religion at Wilberforce Institute. Several pastorates in the former Orange Free State and in the Transvaal culminated at St. Peter Church in Vereeniging in East Transvaal, where he grew the membership to 1,400. He also served as a presiding elder and, like Easter M. Gordon, as an administrative assistant to a succession of African American bishops who succeeded Bishop Gow.[60]

Though several bishops knew Senatle, rank and file AMEs became familiar with him through the *Christian Recorder*. In a 1979 article, under the heading, "African Candidate," a ministerial colleague in Vanderbijlpark, South Africa presented him a candidate for the episcopacy. He referred to Gow's election, saying that "what the church did at Miami in 1956, could be done exactly the same way in New Orleans in 1980." Though Senatle polled only nine votes, AME media helped to increase his visibility for another election four years later. On the eve of the 1984 General Conference, the *Christian Recorder* featured Senatle in an article entitled "Flag Bearer" that was written by the president of the Fifteenth Episcopal District Lay Organization. Because the AME Church had "a singular charisma of its own amongst the African masses" and possessed "immense growth potential," indigenous leadership was needed. "Dr. Senatle," he wrote, "is the foremost leadership material with proven ability to have emerged on the African Church scene."[61]

These endorsements generated Senatle's first ballot lead and sustained him on the second ballot. With 648 votes he outpolled all his competitors. Each of the other African candidates drew less than twenty votes, but Henry A. Belin, Jr., a general officer, and Robert L. Pruitt, the pastor of Metropolitan AME Church in Washington DC, drew impressive tallies behind Senatle. Hence, all three were elected on the third ballot with Senatle

---

[59] Ibid., 216–217; Clement N. Mkwanazi, *The History of the African Methodist Episcopal Church in Zimbabwe* (n.p., n.d.), 47.

[60] Abraham Mojalefa, "Harold Benjamin Senatle," www.dach.org/stories/southafrica/senatle_harold.html; Frank C. Cummings, John H. Dixon, Henry A. Wynn, Thelma Singleton-Scott, and Patricia A. P. Green, *The First Episcopal District's Historical Review of 200 Years of African Methodism (1987)*, 98; *AME Christian Recorder*, June 11, 1984.

[61] *AME Christian Recorder*, May 28, 1979; May 11, 1984; *Combined Minutes . . . of the General Conference, 1980*, 276.

leading with 913 votes. Predictably, Senatle was assigned to South Africa's brand new Nineteenth Episcopal District, where he would preside in the same region of his birth and ministry.[62]

That a fourth bishop, Vernon R. Byrd, a Philadelphia pastor, was chosen on a final ballot reflected the consensus that Senatle, like Gow, would be elected first in his episcopal class to validate African indigenization. This development, however, did not mean that transnational tensions entirely disappeared within the AME assembly. When the Episcopal Committee assigned Vinton R. Anderson to Texas, the delegation strongly objected shouting that no "foreigner" should be their bishop. Therefore, Anderson, born in Bermuda and a successful pastor in Kansas and Missouri before his election to the episcopacy in 1972, was reaping a backlash from Gomez's turbulent tenure in Texas. In response, Anderson was reassigned to ecumenical affairs. Texans resented the Episcopal Committee for ignoring their request for Bishop Rembert E. Stokes, who had just completed eight years in two African districts and had been returned to supervise the Eighteenth Episcopal District. Because Texas wanted him, Stokes stated "that for the Episcopal Committee to send him to the foreign field for the third time is an act of hostility."[63]

Stokes's displeasure about a third African assignment echoed comments from Bishop C. E. Thomas, who said in an earlier session during the indigenization debate that "no Bishop should be elected and sent to any district he doesn't want to serve." Thomas, sent to Central Africa by the 1976 and 1980 General Conferences, achieved much, especially in Zimbabwe. Churches were built in Bulawayo and Bembesi and another congregation in Gumtree was revived and an edifice was constructed. He also received the Sizane Secondary School in Bulawayo as an AME institution. Yet, for Thomas and Stokes, the rigors of travel within Africa and the necessity of appointing indigenous surrogates to function in their absence exhausted both of them. In saying that as American-based bishops they had served in Africa long enough, their comments inadvertently strengthened the arguments for indigenization.[64]

The contretemps over episcopal assignments shifted Senatle from the Nineteenth Episcopal District to the Eighteenth Episcopal District that

[62] Combined Minutes ... of the General Conference, 1984, 222, 226–228, 255.
[63] Ibid., 255; Henderson, "Vinton R. Anderson," in The African Methodist Episcopal Church Registry Select, 20–21; Author's recollection and witness to the response of the Texas delegation at the 1984 General Conference in Kansas City, MO.
[64] Combined Minutes ... of the General Conference, 1984, 178; Mkwanazi, History of the African Methodist Episcopal Church in Zimbabwe, 33–34.

covered Lesotho, Swaziland, Botswana, and Mozambique. At General Conferences in 1988 and 1992 the Nineteenth District finally received a bishop. In 1990 he dedicated a four-story headquarters for the jurisdiction and it became the only black-owned property in downtown Johannesburg. He spent his final four years, however, in the Fifteenth Episcopal District, from which he retired in 2000.[65]

Senatle's episcopal tenure resembled what Gow experienced. Elected in 1956 and 1984 respectively as "overseas bishops," the Episcopal Committee at both General Conferences gave them assignments that restricted them to districts in Africa. That is how AMEs defined indigenization in the episcopacy. Though Senatle served a year-long term as President of the Council of Bishops, a position that made him the titular head of the AME Church, his bishopric, at least operationally, was regional rather than connectional.

At least six African candidates vied for the bishopric at the 2000 General Conference to replace Senatle. Though delegates were focused on electing a female bishop, the choice of an African remained a priority. Delegates from the five African districts and the one based in the Caribbean offered a resolution that reminded the General Conference only two of the denomination's 115 bishops came from Africa. To enhance these minuscule numbers, they requested fellow delegates to "elect at least one (1) Bishop from outside the U.S.A." Perhaps, Clement N. Mkwanazi, a previous candidate for the episcopacy from the Seventeenth Episcopal District, was buoyed by this declaration. A longtime AME leader in Zimbabwe and a participant in "the Liberation struggle" against white minority rule in the former Rhodesia, Mkwanazi had been a pastor and presiding elder since 1953 and an administrative assistant to African American bishops assigned to his episcopal district between 1968 and 1976. Trained in theology and social work, he earned degrees at the R. R. Wright School of Religion in South Africa, the University of Zimbabwe, and in the United States at Morris Brown College and Atlanta University. He must have been disappointed with his tally of seventy-nine votes. The veteran African leader dropped out after the first ballot and symbolically yielded to a younger contender from South Africa.[66]

---

[65] *AME Christian Recorder*, August 21, 1989.
[66] *Combined Minutes of the Forty-Sixth Session of the General Conference of the African Methodist Episcopal Church* held in Cincinnati, OH, July 5–11, 2000 (Nashville, TN, AME Sunday School Union, 200), 284, 602; (Campaign Pamphlet) "Central Africa Presents Dr. Clement N. Mkwanazi for Bishopric 1992" (1992).

Wilfred J. Messiah, the president of the renamed Richard Robert Wright Theological Seminary, emerged as a formidable candidate. The son of a veteran pastor in South Africa, Messiah, an apartheid opponent, sought his education in the United States. He earned his undergraduate and seminary degrees at Wilberforce University and Payne Theological Seminary and a D. Min. at Pittsburgh Theological Seminary. Like Gow, he served as a pastor in the United States in Ohio and Pennsylvania before returning to South Africa in 1997 to head the AME Seminary. He also became the pastor at Mokone Memorial Church near the campus, where he developed a membership of over 1,000. Though four bishops, including a woman, were elected and assigned to African districts, Messiah attracted impressive tallies on two ballots that well positioned him for another run in 2004.[67]

The coming of the 2004 General Conference cheered aspirants to the episcopacy. The retirement of eight bishops whetted the ambitions of clergy on both sides of the Atlantic. These vacancies created opportunities for African Americans to attain the bishopric and accommodate the indigenization goals of African candidates. Moreover, a rhetoric of parity between episcopal districts in the Americas and Africa led delegates officially to discard the term "overseas" districts. Instead, jurisdictions outside the United States became known as Districts 14–19 and dioceses in the United States were referenced as Districts 1–13.[68]

In their Episcopal Address the bishops recommended the election of five bishops from the United States and three bishops from outside the United States. Bishop McKinley Young put the motion and the delegates approved. The African Jurisdictional Council (AJC), a body that had been created to voice the perspectives of AMEs in Africa, detailed how indigenization would actually operate. Based on previous assignment practices with Bishop Gow and Bishop Senatle, the AJC proposed that three African bishops would sign "a covenant commitment" that would restrict their service and rotation within Districts 14–19. These jurisdictions included five districts in Africa and one that was Caribbean-based but stretching to both South America and Europe.[69]

Additionally, the three indigenous bishops "would agree to a lesser salary, approximately 43 percent of their American counterparts." The rationale lay

---

[67] *Combined Minutes . . . of the General Conference, 2000*, 602; *A Profile of a Candidate: The Rev. Dr. Wilfred J. Messiah* (n.p., n.d.).

[68] *Combined Minutes of the Forty-Seventh Quadrennial Session of the General Conference (of the) African Methodist Episcopal Church* held in Indianapolis, IN, June 30–July 7, 2004 (Nashville, TN, AME Sunday School Union, 2004), 670.

[69] Ibid., 154, 636.

in "the difference in the cost of living in Africa versus America, and the exchange rate on American currency on the Continent of Africa." Delegates were assured that "even with this adjustment, African Methodist Episcopal bishops would receive a much higher salary than comparable professionals living in Africa." With support from bishops in their Episcopal Address and the AJC presentation from Bishop Adam J. Richardson, Jr., the delegates approved the proposal.[70]

When the balloting for the bishopric began, a separate election also started for the fourteen candidates from outside the United States. Wilfred J. Messiah of South Africa transferred his strong showing in 2000 to a first ballot win with 953 votes. Following him with totals over 600 in descending order were Paul Kawimbe of Zambia, Andrew Lewin of South Africa, and David R. Daniels of Liberia. Since Kawimbe attained his vote threshold on the second ballot, Lewin and Daniels were left in contention for the third indigenous slot. Because of a desire for diverse regional representation, Daniels, who trailed Lewin on the first ballot, took the lead on the second ballot and won election on the third ballot. N. Jordan Mkwanazi, a Texas pastor and the nephew and son of previous candidates from Central Africa, garnered impressive votes on two ballots, but not enough for election. The other election for the remaining five vacancies brought two women, Carolyn Tyler Guidry and Sarah F. Davis, to the bishopric.[71]

Like Senatle in 1984, the 2004 General Conference sent Messiah to a newly created episcopal district, a coincidental development that expanded jurisdictional opportunities for the new indigenous bishops. To accomplish this objective the delegates approved a split of the Seventeenth Episcopal District that yielded a Twentieth Episcopal District, which included Uganda, Tanzania, Malawi, and Zimbabwe. Kawimbe presided in the remainder of the diocese, which covered the Congo Brazzaville, the DRC, Rwanda, Burundi, and Zambia. Daniels went to West Africa with established annual conferences in Sierra Leone, Liberia, Ghana, and Nigeria, and recently founded jurisdictions in Côte d'Ivoire and Togo-Benin. Both Kawimbe and Daniels were appointed to their indigenous districts.[72]

Though the AJC claimed that no harm had been done to "the principle of the General Superintendency" in the AME bishopric and that indigenous bishops were equal in every respect to their African American colleagues, an

---

[70] Ibid., 178; *Episcopal Address, 47th Quadrennial Session of the General Conference, African Methodist Episcopal Church, Indianapolis, IN, June 30–July 7, 2004* (Nashville, TN, AME Sunday School Union, 2004), 76.

[71] *Combined Minutes . . . of the General Conference, 2004*, 169, 217.   [72] Ibid., 190–191, 704.

operational inequality was still embedded in the covenant commitment that Messiah, Kawimbe, and Daniels signed. While their African American counterparts appointed to the remaining districts outside the United States were eligible at a future General Conference for assignments in the United States, the indigenous bishops were not. The Gow and Senatle pattern established at the time of their respective elections in earlier decades remained operative for their indigenous successors.[73]

An irony, however, developed with indigenization. Though energized through the reform initiatives of The Brotherhood and COR, the mixed results of these movements proved injurious to the implementation of indigenization. Without the institutional safeguards that The Brotherhood and COR envisaged, indigenization became vulnerable to the same structural weaknesses that these movements tried to correct. In July 2017, for example, a committee of three bishops, all of them former prelates in Africa, heard the grievances of the Concerned Pastors (Lekgotha) and Laity in the Nineteenth Episcopal District assembled in Johannesburg at the H. B. Senatle Centre. The bishops came from the United States in response to a planned march to the Senatle building to protest irregularities in disbursements from an AME ministers' pension fund and unsatisfactory explanations from their bishop who had been one of those elected as an indigenous prelate. The President of the Council of Bishops, Clement W. Fugh, requested a suspension of the march until AME judicial procedures dealt with the issue. The Council of Bishops also put the prelate of the Johannesburg diocese "in a supervised relationship" in which his colleagues would "monitor the Bishop's actions." Moreover, they mandated "a significant restructuring of the 19th Episcopal District Office." Despite dependable adjudication processes and episcopal intervention, deficient fiscal practices threatened ministers and members whether in America or Africa. They exposed what earlier Brotherhood and COR reformers had addressed in previous decades. Episcopal District operations in Africa, where indigenization had occurred provided no immunity from what Brotherhood and COR advocates had identified as structural weaknesses in AME governance.[74]

---

[73] Ibid., 636.
[74] *Christian Recorder Breaking News*, July 29, 2017; SOWETAN, July 14, 2017, "Open Letter to the 19th Episcopal District from the President of the Council of Bishops, *Christian Recorder Breaking News*, July 23, 2017; *Christian Recorder Breaking News*, August 9, 2017; *Christian Recorder Breaking News*, December 13, 2017.

FROM MISSIONS TO DEVELOPMENT

Prescient legislation at the 1968 General Conference proposed that "the Overseas Districts of the AME Church [should] be included in both the responsibilities and every activity of the Church." Jurisdictions outside the United States should not be "treated separately or differently in any way" with regard to "finance and participation in decisions." This legislation, which John Hurst Adams proposed and was endorsed by a delegate from South Africa, pertained to expected payments of districts in the Caribbean and Africa into the denominational budget and operating the fiscal affairs of annual conferences just like those in the United States. Indigenization, a component of development initiatives for districts outside the United States, scarcely outweighed the corresponding responsibilities of AMEs outside the United States to fund denominational operations.[75]

To attain these objectives AME infrastructure was enhanced with programs and agencies aimed at the institutional and programmatic development of Caribbean-based and African districts. Beginning in the 1970s, denominational budgets targeted these jurisdictions with funds to sustain service centers, underwrite district projects, and finance special initiatives in health and other social programs: the founding of the F. C. James Center, the evolution of the Overseas Partnership into the Overseas Development Fund, and the launch of the Service and Development Agency.

Frederick C. James, the social activist who was elected as bishop in 1972, was assigned to the Eighteenth Episcopal District. Weeks after the General Conference, the death of Bishop G. Dewey Robinson on July 30, 1972 required a reshuffling of episcopal assignments. This realignment added South Africa and Southwest Africa to James's original assignment. Determined that southern Africa should have publishing and programmatic entities located in the region, he established AME organizations to serve his ministers and members. In front of a crowd of 5,000, in 1973 James dedicated an AME Church Publishing House at Bellville in the Western Cape, South Africa. The purpose was to publish religious literature "in the languages of [the] many people of Southern Africa and Central Africa." The target languages were Xhosa, Sesuto, and the dialects spoken in the region. James announced that "the AME Church has bought the highly regarded and reliable printing firm of Erentzen Printers and incorporated it within the AME Church Publishing House program." James declared that the publishing initiative together with Operation Education, a second program to be

---

[75] *Official Minutes ... of the General Conference 1968*, 77, 167, 273–274.

housed at the printing plant, represented "a new AME witness in Southern Africa and the world."[76]

Though James envisaged the publishing house as a self-help and self-sustaining enterprise, he structured the F. C. James Centre of AME Service in Maseru, Lesotho, as a denominational project. Operational funds would be allocated within the overseas development budget, but other monies could also be raised. Because James presided simultaneously in the Fifteenth and Eighteenth Episcopal Districts, jurisdictions that were geographically contiguous, the advisory board, through episcopal appointment, would be drawn from both dioceses. A building was constructed and a variety of social services were to be made available "to the members and neighbors of the AME Church in Southern Africa." Beginning with the 1976 *Book of Discipline*, the James Centre was officially designated as part of the denominational infrastructure.[77]

Backing of the James Centre derived from a broader denominational discourse that formalized church policies beyond the routine charitable activities of AME missionary agencies. Church funds, in addition to what the Secretary of Missions and the Women's Missionary Society (WMS) disbursed for schools, scholarships, and general benevolence, shifted to episcopal budgets focused on district operations, development, and special programs. Starting in 1976, there was an annual line item of $250,000 for overseas development in the Caribbean-based and African districts. During its first quadrennium in operation, Bishop Talbot, for example, reported expenditures in his Caribbean-based district at the 1980 General Conference. He described initiatives in social and economic development, education and health services, hiring and training of agricultural specialists, and enhancements in church facilities and programs. He described projects in agriculture, refugee relief and housing and support for clinics with programs in prenatal care and nutrition. Additionally, a church in the Dominican Republic "ravaged by [a] hurricane" received $3,000. Funds were also allocated to purchase the first AME property in the London Annual Conference at Gloucester, England. The bishops in the African districts reported similar expenditures in their dioceses.[78]

Concomitant with this budgetary initiative was Operation Partnership. The program acknowledged that the AME Church was "a denomination with a strong international base" that should forge "a partnership

[76] *AME Christian Recorder*, August 27, 1973.   [77] *The Book of Discipline*, 301–302.
[78] *Combined Minutes ... of the General Conference, 1976*, 207; *Combined Minutes ... of the General Conference, 1980*, 247, 250–266.

relationship" between United States jurisdictions and overseas episcopal districts. The program aimed to "facilitate through careful coordination, supervision, and monitoring the implementation of a variety of projects needful for, and crucial to the economic and social development of some of our overseas territories." Moreover, the partnership would "concretize the opportunities for a black denomination to relate more meaningfully and maturely with blacks in developing countries at several levels." The partnership gained some traction in the redistricting possibilities cited in Adams's 1984 Committee on Reorganization report. In two of the five plans Caribbean countries were "made part of several U. S. districts" to aid their growth and development. That Bermuda had long been attached to the First Episcopal District in the Northeastern states and that the Bahama Islands had been connected to the Florida jurisdiction since 1960 showed the relevance of this proposal.[79]

Operation Partnership functioned interactively with the Consultation on the Development of Overseas Districts inclusive of Africa, the Caribbean Islands, South America, and England Districts. Among its several responsibilities, "this consultation shall determine the potential, resources, programs, and target dates for the election of nationals as Bishops, General Superintendents, and other administrative officers to serve the Overseas Episcopal Districts." Most substantively, the African Jurisdictional Council evolved out of these organizational initiatives and became a fulcrum to elect three indigenous bishops in 2004. It was charged to "address the needs, aspirations, beliefs, and cultures of the members of the AME Church" on the three continents outside the United States.[80]

Momentum from the denomination's Overseas Development Fund and other global initiatives showed a determination to tackle the complicated issues of Third World development. Some of the same AME leaders who reckoned first hand with the denomination's international structures and programs launched in 1980 an additional unit to deepen the church's global outreach. Three bishops and a missionary supervisor, John Hurst Adams, Frederick C. James, Donald G. K. Ming, and Edith W. Ming, who had involvements either in institutional reform or in leading AMEs in southern Africa, joined with two members of Ward Memorial AME Church in Washington DC, General Officer Joseph C. McKinney, the AME treasurer,

---

[79] *The Book of Discipline*, 300 Adams, *Toward a More Effective AME Church*, 15.
[80] *Combined Minutes . . . of the General Conference, 1980*, 305; *The Doctrine and Discipline of the African Methodist Episcopal Church* (Nashville, TN, AME Sunday School Union, 2000), 301–302.

and Wilburn L. Boddie, a veteran official in the United States Agency for International Development, and an Oklahoma presiding elder, Lonnie Johnson, in founding the Service and Development Agency (SADA). This 501 (C) (3) agency, a tax-exempt organization engaged in charity, became "the humanitarian relief and development entity of the AME Church." From the start of its on the ground operations in the 1980s to 2004, SADA, in demonstrating an appeal to non-AME donors, raised in excess of $7 million for various Caribbean and African project and partnership initiatives."[81]

When SADA officials asked the 1988 General Conference to endorse the agency as an AME-affiliated organization, an executive director was already in place. Jonathan L. Weaver appeared at the assembly a few months after his assignment as pastor at Mt. Nebo AME Church in Upper Marlboro, Maryland. In addition to his M.Div. degree, Weaver had earned an MBA at Harvard University and had extensive experience working with Operations Crossroads Africa. In a report for the delegates Weaver introduced SADA's Haitian Project, which designed to bring to "targeted populations complete health coverage both preventive and curative." Through an on-site project manager, Weaver planned for professional, missionary, and student volunteers to facilitate programs at the Richard Allen Hildebrand Clinic at St. Paul AME Church in Port-au-Prince and at selected rural churches that housed SADA health and agricultural projects. Weaver recruited two Haitian physicians and two mobile health units to focus on infant immunization at AME churches where infant baptisms were taking place.[82]

In their 1992 Episcopal Address the bishops reflected the increased sophistication of the denomination in international affairs. They commended the WMS for gaining non-governmental organization status in the United Nations: "This relationship of advocacy can be of significant benefit in elevating human rights and human needs issues." The bishops viewed SADA as a "second vehicle, which provides AME intervention on an international scale." Bishop Vinton R. Anderson, who wrote the address, described SADA as "a bona fide private voluntary organization" that operated "in partnership with the United States government and private foundations as a delivery

---

[81] *Combined Minutes ... of the General Conference, 2004,* 145; *The African Methodist Episcopal Church: Service and Development Agency, Inc.,* AME-SADA, *2015 Annual Report,* ame. streampoint.com/wp-content/uploads. . ./SADA-Report-AMEC-GC-2016-1.pdf (n.p.).

[82] *Combined Minutes of the Forty-Third Session of the General Conference of the African Methodist Episcopal Church* held in Fort Worth, TX, July 6–14, 1988, 545–550; *Baltimore Sun,* May 29, 1988; "Jonathan Leslie Weaver," Pastor's Corner-Greater Mt. Nebo Church, Bowie, MD, www.gmnebo.org/pastors-corner.

system [in] funding educational enterprises, child-care, health, agricultural and economic development programs." SADA, the address emphasized, "could greatly enhance [the] AME presence in our episcopal districts both in Africa and the Caribbean." For these reasons the bishops recommended "denominational ownership of SADA."[83]

Cherie F. Bellamy, who replaced Weaver, updated delegates at the 1996 General Conference about a $2.3 million grant from the United States Agency for International Development. The funds were earmarked "for construction of the Wilberforce Community College in Evaton, South Africa," a successor school to the defunct Wilberforce Institute. She also joined the AME treasurer and four bishops in meeting selected members of Congress, including the chair of the Congressional Black Caucus, to press for more foreign aid to Africa. As a result, two bishops, Richard Allen Chappelle and C. Garnett Henning, prelates in Africa, testified to a House of Representatives Sub-Committee on Africa about AME involvements on the continent.[84]

Robert Nicolas, who followed Bellamy, brought unusually broad international experiences to SADA. An attorney by training, Nicolas had directed the International Division of a Washington DC law firm and had worked for the Peace Corps, the Phelps Stokes Fund, and other organizations that interacted with the World Bank, the African Development Bank, the United States Agency for International Development (USAID), and various private and federal agencies. Like his predecessor, he also drew substantial AME support from theWMS, the Connectional Lay Organization, and sundry episcopal districts based in the United States.[85]

USAID, however, remained a major benefactor of SADA. In his report to the 2004 General Conference, Nicolas discussed impressive USAID funding for SADA projects in Haiti. These initiatives focused on education, microcredit, and health with special attention to the scourge of HIV/AIDS. Additionally, there were vaccinations for young children, pre/postnatal health services, family planning, and nutrition programs. These and other programs were delivered to four venues and six mobile clinics in the

---

[83] *Episcopal Address [to the] 44th Session of the General Conference of the African Methodist Episcopal Church*, July 8, 1992, Orlando, FL (Nashville, TN, AME Sunday School Union, 1992), 11, 18.

[84] *Combined Minutes of the Forty-Fifth Session of the General Conference of the African Methodist Episcopal Church* held in Louisville, KY, June 26–July 3, 1996 (Nashville, TN, AME Sunday School Union, 1996), 142, 412–413.

[85] "Resume of Robert Nicolas," www.dwatch.com/archives/council14/14-228.htm; *Combined Minutes ... of the General Conference, 2004*, 694.

Archahise and Cabaret areas of Haiti. Moreover, at respective sites in Port-au-Prince and in Port Matheux the AME-sponsored Hildebrand Clinic and the Donald K. Ming Clinic served 45,000 patients.[86]

During the ensuing decade Nicolas deepened SADA's Caribbean and African operations. In addition to existing clinic facilities and mobile units in Haiti, he proposed new clinic sites at Bercy and Delice in the Nan Michel region. Moreover, school health sites were established to focus on curving malnutrition. SADA also trained birth attendants for rural locations to help with pregnancies and childbirth and provided health agents to assist with general medical services. In South Africa more investment was mobilized for additional construction at Wilberforce Community College. USAID, AME, and other donors funded a range of proposed facilities including dormitories, a dining hall, venues for instructional and administrative personnel, and a community center.[87]

Though SADA functioned as an autonomous humanitarian organization, the agency aligned closely with AME development within the Atlantic World. In Ghana, for example, at Bethel AME Church in Accra SADA established a site adjacent to the edifice that operated programs in health, education, agriculture, and microfinance. Bishop Clement W. Fugh, the prelate in West Africa, helped to underwrite the SADA office and enabled the agency to inaugurate these programs, beginning in March 2016.[88]

In his 2015 report, Nicolas noted plans for new facilities for Haiti's Delice Clinic. SADA already had a corps of sixty-four health care providers attached to the project. A new health complex, renamed the Bishop Sarah Frances Davis Outpatient Delice Health Center, was dedicated in 2017. The project was a joint venture between SADA and theWMS with support from the Department of Global Witness and Ministry, the successor organization to the Department of Missions. In building on this initiative Bishop E. Anne Henning-Byfield, prelate for the Caribbean-based episcopal district, received into the 2017 Haiti Annual Conference the fifty-three members in the Eben Ezer congregation in Delice. Hence, a denominational alignment with SADA enabled AMEs to strengthen Caribbean and African episcopal districts and congregations in their provision of vital services to their vulnerable populations.[89]

[86] *Combined Minutes . . . of the General Conference, 2004*, 694–695.
[87] *AME-SADA*, 2015 Annual Report, n.p.   [88] Ibid.
[89] Ibid.: Rev. Raymond Rodelet, "From the Haitian Annual Conference," *Voice of Missions*, Vol. 151, No. 1, June–August 2017, 16.

WOMEN'S EMPOWERMENT

Concurrent with these global developments, issues pertaining to women's empowerment, sex, and sexuality pervaded AME discourse from the last quarter of the twentieth century. The analytic category of intersectionality seems best to explain these phenomena. Intersectionality is the idea that marginalized groups, sometimes with multiple identities, struggled to upend interconnected structures that maintained the dominance of self-perpetuating elites. Interrelated systems and practices of racial, ethnic, and gender subordination distilled and enforced through the polity and institutional culture of African Methodism, despite a subaltern constituency, compelled an energetic discourse and corrective actions surrounding women's empowerment within the denomination. Similarly, issues of intersectionality stimulated debates about the multiple facets of sexuality pertaining to abortion, same-sex relationships, and the stigmatization of victims of HIV/AIDS. Though these developments were distinct, they unfolded in parallel chronological streams. This discourse also led to a growing body of teaching and scholarship on womanism and intersectionality in leading theological seminaries. Black female scholars, some of them AME such as Teresa L. Fry Brown of Candler School of Theology at Emory University, Monica Coleman of Claremont School of Theology, and Jennifer S. Leath of the Iliff School of Theology, produced scholarly works on this intellectual "cutting edge."[90]

The push for the ordination of women, rooted in the nineteenth century, advanced with the 1885 ordination of Sarah Ann Hughes as an itinerant deacon in the North Carolina Annual Conference. At a subsequent annual conference in 1887, her ordination was nullified, and thereafter AMEs restricted women to the office of evangelist through several decades into the twentieth century. Nonetheless, they functioned as ministers in every activity except in the sacramental sphere of baptism and the Eucharist and in the priestly domain of performing marriages and burying the dead. Male

---

[90] Kimberle Williams Crenshaw, "Toward a Field of Intersectionality Studies: Theory, Application, and Praxis," SIGNS, Vol. 38, No. 4, Summer 2003, 785–810; Patricia H. Collins, "Intersectionality's Definitional Dilemmas," *Annual Review of Sociology*, Vol. 41, 2015, 1–20. Also see Teresa L. Fry Brown, *God Don't Like Ugly: African American Women Handing on Spiritual Values* (Nashville, TN, Abingdon Press, 2000) and *Weary Throats and New Songs: Black Women Proclaiming God's Word* (Nashville, TN, Abingdon Press, 2003); Monica Coleman, *Making a Way Out of No Way: A Womanist Theology* (Minneapolis, MN, Fortress Press, 2008); and Jennifer S. Leath, "Revising Jezebel Politics: Toward a New Sexual Ethic," in Monica Michlin and Jean Paul Rocchi (eds.), *Black Intersectionalities: A Critique for the 21st Century* (Liverpool, Liverpool University Press, 2013), 195–210.

bishops, presiding elders, and pastors, however, facilitated female evangelists in enlarging their ministerial presence as preachers and revivalists, as pastors at small and distant parishes, and as missionaries to the poor, the sick, and the homeless. Writing in 1916, Richard R. Wright, Jr. noted that "a large number of women who are unordained but who have success in revival meetings are termed evangelists for want of a better designation."[91]

Wright, a prolific compiler of AME biographies, in both the *Centennial Encyclopedia of the African Methodist Episcopal Church* in 1916 and in *Who's Who in the General Conference [of] 1924* respectively included Mary G. Evans and Martha Jayne Keys. Though their entries read like the male ministerial profiles these women, though they were seminary trained pastors, lacked full clerical standing. Evans, born in Maryland in 1891, was licensed to preach at Quinn Chapel in Chicago and received an evangelist's license in the Indiana Annual Conference where she served as pastor to two congregations. Educated at Payne Theological Seminary at Wilberforce, Evans, according to Wright, "has won thousands of souls to Christ." During her pastorate at St. John AME Church in Indianapolis, she was invited in 1926 to conduct a revival in New York's Harlem at St. Mark Methodist Episcopal Church. The *New York Age* noted her "reputation as an evangelist is the product of an unusual passion for souls," and that Evans was a "forceful and eloquent preacher." Keys was born in 1892 in Kentucky, licensed to preach as an adolescent, and was educated at Lane College and Payne Theological Seminary. Like Evans, Keys, Wright declared, "has traveled extensively and has held revival campaigns" in AME churches both large and small, and because of her preaching "thousands of persons have been converted." Keys, "always in demand as an evangelist," was appointed in 1920 as pastor to a congregation in Clinton, Kentucky.[92]

Evans and Keys, however, chose diverging paths in relation to the AME Church. In 1932 Evans became the second pastor to the Cosmopolitan Community Church in Chicago. After the death of the founding minister, a dissident AME, some parishioners heard Evans preach and decided to call her as their next leader. In subsequent years, she upgraded the debt-ridden and faltering structure with a renovated edifice and community center.

---

[91] Edward W. Lampton, *Digest of Rulings and Decisions of the Bishops of the African Methodist Episcopal Church From 1847 to 1907* (Washington, DC, Record Publishing Company, 1907), 189; Richard R. Wright, Jr. (ed.), *Centennial Encyclopedia of the African Methodist Episcopal Church* (Philadelphia, PA, AME Book Concern, 1916), 306.

[92] Wright, *Centennial Encyclopedia*, 88–89; *New York Age*, July 31, 1926; *Chicago Tribune*, April 13, 1966; JET, April 28, 1966; Richard R. Wright, Jr. (compiler), *Who's Who in the General Conference [of] 1924*, 151–152.

Evans, who never married, had two female companions, which fueled rumors that she was in lesbian relationships. Whatever the truth about her sexuality, Evans's shift to a non-denominational ministry, which saved her from gender discrimination within the AME clergy, also shielded her from any possible scrutiny about her living arrangements from an annual conference. Keys, a lifelong AME, married a fellow AME minister, Willie K. Marshall, in New Orleans in June 1930. Though they later divorced, Marshall remained a stalwart supporter of her ministry. Keys's visibility as an officer in the Women's Parent Mite Missionary Society and her successful pastorates at four churches in Louisville strengthened her stubborn and strategic push over three decades for full female ordination.[93]

Through her activities as a worship leader, soloist, and preacher in annual conferences in Kentucky and Tennessee, Keys leveraged these roles into beneficial interactions with several male bishops, presiding elders, and pastors who could support her quest for women's ordination. Concurrent with Keys's involvements, scores of other evangelists became a crucial presence in their regional jurisdictions. Because of pent-up aspirations for full ordination, Keys and other female preachers energized the office of evangelist as a subtle but insurgent force against gender barriers in the AME ministry. Their names appeared on annual conference rosters, their yearly reports were published in diocesan minutes, and they accepted appointments to serve as pastors. In the Michigan Annual Conference, for example, in 1928 female evangelists organized an Evangelist Bureau. A presiding elder installed the officers at a ceremony at Detroit's Ebenezer AME Church and gave them official standing in the diocese. Their purpose lay in doing revivals, "in ministering to those shut-in, visiting hospitals and prisons, conducting ... prayer meetings, welcoming strangers and new-comers and inviting them to church, and canvassing neighborhoods seeking the lost ones."[94]

Some twenty female evangelists appeared on a roster in the minutes of the 1943 Michigan Annual Conference. Ten of them submitted written reports that outlined their activities during the previous year. Like Evans and Keys, Josie L. Brown took courses from Payne Theological Seminary. Brown, who

---

[93] *Chicago Tribune*, April 13,1966; *Jet*, April 28, 1966; Best, *Passionately Human, No Less Divine: Religion and Culture in Black Chicago, 1915–1952*, 156–157, 166; "Martha J. Keys in the New Orleans, Louisiana Marriage Records Index, 1831–1964," database online; Dennis C. Dickerson, *A Liberated Past: Explorations in AME Church History* (Nashville, TN, AME Sunday School Union, 2003), 147, 150, 155.

[94] Dickerson, *A Liberated Past*, 148–151; Richard R. Wright, Jr. (compiler), *Encyclopedia of African Methodism* (Philadelphia, PA, AME Book Concern, 1947), 375.

was "seeking for more knowledge of God's word," commended the instructor at the seminary extension school, Dean Charles S. Spivey, Sr., for being "very helpful to me." Because of Brown's "city missionary work" in Detroit at local hospitals, the county prison, and at the Goodwill Industry, "many souls have been brought to Christ." Similarly, scores of patients in shut-in homes, the bereaved, and needy families benefited from Brown's ministry. Thanks to Bishop John A. Gregg she was appointed as supervisor of the Fourth Episcopal District committee on evangelism. In Detroit, at the group's first annual session, she boasted, was unlike any "in the history of the AME Church." Elizabeth Crews did two revivals in Chatham, Ontario, "where we had three conversions" and "several were reclaimed." She also participated in revivals in Windsor, Ontario, and at her home congregation, Oak Grove AME Church in Detroit. "We were blessed with three converts" at her home congregation. Moreover, Crews was reelected as president of the Evangelist Bureau of the Michigan Annual Conference and planned "a definite program for youth." This critical corps of female evangelists, like those in Michigan, invigorated Keys's push for full ordination.[95]

The vocations of female evangelists in the Caribbean paralleled their counterparts in the United States. Clara Kathleen Hanson, for example, born in 1893 in Jamaica, received her evangelist license in 1932 right after her husband, Reverend J. Dailey Hanson, was ordained as an itinerant deacon. Previously, in the early 1920s, the couple had belonged to the Salvation Army and worked as missionaries in West Africa. After Bishop Monroe H. Davis appointed her husband as the missionary supervisor in Jamaica, she joined him "in this phase" of his work. He also became pastor of Allen's Mount AME Church in Spring Garden, St. Thomas, Jamaica, where his wife founded a school. After her husband's death, Hanson succeeded him in 1948 as pastor. After a destructive hurricane in the early 1950s destroyed the school, church, and parsonage, Hanson implemented plans to rebuild the church and manse. Like Keys, Hanson had been active as an evangelist in the women's missionary society both in Jamaica and at international meetings.[96]

Peer acceptance from male pastors in the West Kentucky Annual Conference facilitated Keys's election to represent the jurisdiction at the General Conference. Her lack of clerical credentials, however, placed her on the

[95] *Journal of the Fifty-Seventh Annual Session of the Michigan Conference of the African Methodist Episcopal Church* held in St. Stephen AME Church, Detroit, MI, August 24, 1943 (n.p., n.d.), 67–68; 74.
[96] Richard R. Wright, Jr. (compiler), *Sixteenth Episcopal District of the African Methodist Episcopal Church* (n.p., n.d.), 1964, 96–97.

roster of lay delegates. Though the title "Mrs." or "Dr." rather than "Rev." was affixed to her name, Keys had the right to submit legislation and was eligible to speak during General Conference proceedings. Starting at the 1936 General Conference, Keys filed a bill for women's ordination. Though tabled, her efforts at the 1940 and 1944 assemblies bore fruit at the 1948 General Conference, when the ordination of women as local deacons was approved. While this legislation only achieved the first step for full ministerial standing, JET reported in 1954 that nearly 200 AME women had been ordained.[97]

JET affirmed the observations of Vince Monroe Townsend, a presiding elder in Arkansas, who said in *Fifty-Four Years of African Methodism* that "the number of women coming into the ministry is increasing almost daily." He also recalled that across thirty-five years as a presiding elder he had licensed "a large number of women to preach." Townsend lamented persistent male opposition to women preachers, noting "it is peculiar how strong many of our leaders are against women being licensed to preach," often citing St Paul's advice to "let your women keep silence in church." Since a "man's testimony "that he is called to preach" was accepted as valid, then why "deny that [same claim] by the woman?" He singled out several women preachers, including Mary G. Evans and Martha Jayne Keys, "who have been regarded as great preachers," and added that "teeming thousands have been brought into the church through their ministry." Townsend also predicted "all of this indicates that their ambition for leadership will finally lead to women presiding elders and to the bishopric of the church."[98]

Townsend, while he celebrated the passage of the 1948 law, viewed it as too weak to advance women in the ministry. He described it as "so bunglesome and discriminatory that it humiliates the women instead of elevating them." He advised observers to "think of the inconsistency of denying an ordained deacon membership in the Annual Conference, when in fact the ordination of deacons entitles one to membership after two years in the traveling membership." Townsend recognized that women's ordination as local deacons, rather than traveling or itinerant deacons, represented only scarce progress toward full ordination. The 1948 law, he noted, only established

---

[97] *Journal of the Thirtieth Quadrennial Session of the General Conference of the African Methodist Episcopal Church* held in The Rockland Palace [in] New York City, May 6–18, 1936, 19; *Official Minutes . . . of the General Conference 1956*, in *The Combined Minutes of the General Conference*, 329; Dickerson, *A Liberated Past*, 151–154; JET, February 18, 1954.

[98] Vince M. Townsend, *Fifty-Four Years of African Methodism* (New York, Exposition Press, 1953), 37–38.

women preachers as "lay workers, ordained by request of the local church to which they belong."[99]

The office of local deacon prescribed a restricted sphere of ministerial activity within a congregation. In the Indiana Annual Conference, for example, males and females in this ministerial office were described unambiguously as "Deacons for Local Purposes." This seeming advancement toward ordination actually reduced the territorial breadth in which female evangelists usually operated. Female local deacons, while focused on local church involvements, intentionally retained the extramural pursuits embedded in their former status as evangelists and tried for a synthesis between the two ministries. Those in the Indiana Annual Conference, however, tended toward local activities and validated Townsend's doubts about whether the office of local deacon advanced women in ministry. The experiences of Eddy L. Hutchins and Ethel Mae Buckner were illustrative.[100]

The 1952 Indiana Annual Conference included four women in the ranks of local deacons. One of them, Eddy L. Hutchins, in her annual conference report, recorded twelve preaching assignments and several hospital and prison visits. Her principal activities, however, lay within the sphere of St. Paul AME Church in Indianapolis where she was a member. "I have striven," she said, "to serve my church as Sup[erintenden]t of the Sunday School, a worker in the junior church, [the] sponsor of the youth singing group, a member of the steward board and the Missionary Society." Hutchins, in her 1953 report, noted a revival she conducted for congregations on the Frankfort and Lebanon Circuit and that she had twice preached for the pastor at another Indianapolis church during his absence. Still, she emphasized that her duties lay in whatever area her pastor "has seen fit to place me." Hence, she continued in the same roles that she outlined in her 1952 report. Ethel Mae Butler was also a local deacon and a member of St. Paul in Indianapolis. Because she was similarly limited to congregational obligations, Butler led the "Wednesday night service for my pastor" and "I have two classes of children I teach twice a week."[101]

Townsend, Keys, and other advocates of full ordination for women understood that going beyond the level of local deacon was imperative for

[99] Ibid., 37, 76.
[100] *Official Minutes of the 114th Annual Session of the Indiana Conference of the African Methodist Episcopal Church* held in Allen Temple AME Church, Marion, IN, September 24–28, 1952 (n.p., n.d.), 6.
[101] Ibid., 6, 71; *Official Minutes of the 115th Annual Session of the Indiana Conference of the African Methodist Episcopal Church* held in Allen Chapel AME Church, Terre Haute, IN, September 23–27, 1953 (n.p., n.d.), 6, 31, 78–79.

females aspiring to broader opportunities in ministry. Townsend also reported that women at the 1952 General Conference "demanded elder orders." Though Keys, despite a plea on the floor of the AME assembly, elicited no action from the delegates, she harnessed the women's momentum to reintroduce the issue at the 1956 General Conference. At this meeting Keys challenged delegates "to improve on its laws." Strong support came from Bishop Frederick D. Jordan, General Officer Russell S. Brown, and the Reverend Joseph L. Roberts, Chair of the Revisions Committee, the body in charge of General Conference legislation. With a decisive vote of 757 to 139 to authorize women's ordination as local elders, Keys and others treated this advancement as a major moment in achieving their ultimate objective.[102]

Polly Bland, an Afro-Indian evangelist in the Great Plains, through her longevity in ministry, showed how the lowly status of female preachers demanded denominational attention. Born in around 1885 in Kansas, Bland who completed three years of high school, was married to a laborer, and worked herself as a servant for private families. At the 1956 Kansas Annual Conference, Bland delivered her fiftieth report as an evangelist. She also noted that while the pastor at Hutchinson, Kansas, traveled to the 1956 General Conference, she stayed behind to occupy his pulpit. How much Bland, an unordained preacher since the early 1900s, knew about AME approval of women's ordination as local elders and whether she planned to benefit from the development are unknown. Nonetheless, her half-century as an evangelist symbolized for Keys and others that the fight to elevate the status of female preachers had lasted long enough.[103]

The experiences of Keys and her female colleagues in the West Kentucky Annual Conference, the advancement of women preachers in the Philadelphia Annual Conference, and the ordeal of Geneva Josephine Johnson Crawford in the Texas Annual Conference showed how the push for the full ordination of women became an unavoidable issue at the forthcoming 1960 General Conference. At most annual conferences women pressed for the ordinations available to them at the level of local ministry. At the

---

[102] Townsend, *Fifty-Four Years of African Methodism*, 37; Dickerson, *A Liberated Past*, 152–153.
[103] "Minutes of the Eighty-First Session of the Kansas Annual Conference of the African Methodist Episcopal Church held in St. Paul AME Church, Wichita, KS, September 26–30, 1956," in *African Methodist Episcopal Church, Fifth Episcopal District*, 1956 (Nashville, AME Sunday School Union, 1956), 235; Polly Bland in the Kansas State Census Collection, 1855–1925 (database online); Polly Bland in the 1930 United States Census, Ancestry.com. 1930 United States Federal Census (database online); Polly Bland in the 1940 United States Federal Census, Ancestry.com. United States Federal Census (database online), Provo, Utah.

1956 West Kentucky Annual Conference three women were presented for ordination as local deacons. Keys, already a local deacon and pastor of Greater St. James AME Church in Louisville, was host to the annual juris-dictional meeting. She lost no time after the 1956 General Conference to secure ordination as a local elder. Additionally, three other women appeared before the West Kentucky Conference Committee of Examiners "seeking further study" to qualify for ministerial orders. At the 1957 Philadelphia Annual Conference six women were ordained as local deacons and four became local elders, including Olivia S. Henry, the pastor to Tyree AME Church in Philadelphia. Another dozen women were ordained as local deacons at the 1958 session and four became local elders.[104]

The ambiguous effects of the 1948 and 1956 legislation unfolded in Texas in the experiences of Geneva Josephine Johnson Crawford. Born in Brazoria, Texas, in 1914, she married in 1941, and with her husband and other AMEs established a congregation in La Marque. She accepted her call to preach in 1950 and received in 1953 an appointment from Bishop Joseph Gomez to plant a congregation in Hitchcock, Texas. She served as pastor to this church for the ensuing sixteen years. When an opportunity came to relocate the small congregation to a larger facility, her presiding elder intervened to secure the edifice for another parish. Without full ordination, Crawford, more than most male pastors, was vulnerable to such high-handed behavior.[105]

Though Crawford in 1956 finished the requirements for a restricted ordination as a local deacon, Bishop Gomez asked her to wait until after the General Conference. The bishop arranged with his successor, Bishop Howard Thomas Primm, to ordain Crawford as an itinerant elder. "To keep down the fighting from the male preachers," Crawford recalled, "it was not announced that I was being ordained as an itinerant elder so the female preacher fighters thought I was ordained a local elder like the other two

---

[104] "Minutes of the Seventy-Sixth Session of the West Kentucky Annual Conference held in Greater St. James AME Church, Louisville, KY, October 17–21, 1956," in *Minutes of the Conferences of the Thirteenth Episcopal District*, 1956, 27–31; *Official Journal of Proceedings of the Philadelphia Annual Conference of the African Methodist Episcopal Church, One Hundred Forty-First Session* held in Allen AME Church, Philadelphia, PA, May 21–26, 1957, in *Official Journal of Proceedings of the Philadelphia Annual Conference of the African Methodist Episcopal Church, One Hundred Forty-Second Session* held in St. Matthew AME Church, Philadelphia, PA, May 14–18, 1958, in *Combined Minutes of the Annual Conferences of the First Episcopal District, African Methodist Episcopal Church, 1957–1958*, Right Rever-end George W. Baber (Nashville, TN, AME Sunday School Union, 1958), 57, 62, 125.

[105] Geneva Josephine Johnson Crawford, "This is My Story," *AME Church Review*, Vol. 124, No. 410, April–June 2008, 89–90.

women ordained with me." Bishop Primm told her not to divulge her actual status until the "Holy Spirit said to step out and take your rightful place as an itinerant elder." After Bishop William F. Ball succeeded Bishop Primm in Texas in 1960, Crawford was acknowledged as a fully ordained minister.[106]

The compact among the bishops who presided consecutively in Texas expanded the meaning of the 1948 and 1956 legislation on women's ordination and anticipated their full ordination at the 1960 General Conference. One of the bishops, Joseph Gomez, read the 1960 Episcopal Address and urged "that all restrictions on women relative to their status as itinerant ministers of the Church be removed." The Revisions Committee endorsed the recommendation from the bishops and the delegates and adopted the proposal as AME law.[107]

An immediate consequence of the 1960 legislation was the candidacy of Carrie T. Hooper for bishop at the 1964 General Conference. Hooper, born in 1894 in Lake City, Florida, and the founder and pastor of True Vine AME Church in New York City, ran on the platform of "My Bible, My Guide, is a Friend, Always By My Side. It Lightens and Brightens My Pathway Each Day as I Read It and Heed It Today." Hooper, a widow, tallied only eleven votes, but ran again at four subsequent General Conferences in 1968, 1972, 1976, and 1980.[108]

Other female pastors succeeded her as episcopal candidates, including Elizabeth Scott of the Pittsburgh Annual Conference in 1984 and 1988, Louise Harris of the Ohio Annual Conference in 1988, and Gloria J. Barrett of the West Virginia Annual Conference and Dolores Jacobs of the New York Annual Conference in 1992. At times more than one woman presented herself as a candidate. In 1988 Scott and Harris were running and in 1992 they were joined on ballots with Barrett and Jacobs. Scott and Barrett returned in 1996, but Carolyn Tyler Guidry, a presiding elder in the Southern California Annual Conference, became in that year the sixth woman to seek the episcopacy. Her five predecessors always polled in double digits, but Tyler-Guidry, though losing, tallied an impressive 190 votes on the first ballot and a respectable 153 votes on the second ballot.[109]

Concurrent with these campaigns were significant attainments for women in other areas of AME governance starting in South America. In 1973 Bishop Frederick H. Talbot appointed Dorothy Millicent Stephens Morris as an acting presiding elder in the Guyana Annual Conference. Her marriage in

---

[106] Ibid., 91.   [107] Dickerson, *A Liberated Past*, 155.
[108] Dennis C. Dickerson, "The Making of a Female Bishop: From Jarena Lee to Vashti Murphy McKenzie," *AME Church Review*, Vol. 116, No. 278, Summer 2000, 15.
[109] Ibid.

1956 to Reverend Alphonso Morris brought her to Ebenezer AME Church in Georgetown where she functioned as a missionary. After her husband died in 1962, Morris remembered that "Ebenezer's members said they wanted nobody but me" as their pastor. Her ordination as a local deacon in 1964 preceded full ordination as an itinerant elder in 1969. Bishop Talbot made her a full-fledged presiding elder at the 1974 annual conference. Additionally, Bishop Talbot in 1976 appointed Helen C. Patrick, the pastor of Bethel AME Church in Neiuw Nickerie, Suriname, as the presiding elder in the Suriname Annual Conference.[110]

Robert H. Reid, Jr., the editor of the *Christian Recorder*, reminded AMEs about the election of Marjorie Matthews in 1980 as the first female bishop in the United Methodist Church. Concurrent with this development was the appointment in 1983 by Bishop Vinton R. Anderson of Cornelia M. Wright as a presiding elder in the West Virginia Annual Conference and the election in 1984 of Yvonne Walker Taylor as the first female president of Wilberforce University. Wright, born in North Carolina, was ordained as an itinerant elder in 1973 and served several West Virginia congregations. Following her appointment, in 2000 another fifteen women were named as presiding elders, including three in southern Africa. One of them, Alina K. Masehela, was appointed in 1994 by Bishop C. Garnett Henning, Sr. to supervise the Venda District in the North Transvaal Annual Conference in South Africa. Taylor, the daughter of a previous Wilberforce president and bishop, D. O. Walker, had been a professor of French and an administrator at the AME school.[111]

At the 1984 General Conference Jamye Coleman Williams, a Ph.D. and daughter and sister of AME clergy, was elected as a general officer and editor of the *AME Church Review*. This denominational first drew strong support from Joseph C. McKinney, the AME church treasurer, and from the Connectional Lay Organization in which McKinney and Williams had been major officers. Williams served for eight years until retirement in 1992. In drawing from the same sources of support, Paulette Coleman, Ph.D. defeated two contenders, including another female candidate, a pastor, to succeed Williams.[112]

The confluence of all of these developments in female empowerment laid foundations for a successful agitation to elect a woman bishop. Initially, the

[110] Dennis C. Dickerson, "The Female Presiding Elders of the African Methodist Episcopal Church," *AME Church Review*, Vol. 118, No. 385, January–March 2002, 13.
[111] Ibid., 12, 14, 19; Robert H. Reid, Jr., *Irony of Afro-American History: An Overview Of AME History and Related Developments* (Nashville, TN, AME Sunday School Union, 1984), 38–41.
[112] Dickerson, *A Liberated Past*, 81–82.

original five, Jacquelyn Grant, Lillian Frier Webb, Alyson B. Johnson, Jeanne Williams, and Nurjhan Govan, were solicited from the 1976 Bishops Council authorization for an ad hoc committee on women in the ministry. Moreover, Grant, a Ph.D. student at Union Theological Seminary and the daughter of an AME minister in South Carolina, articulated in a position paper at the 1976 General Conference the urgency of integrating women into denominational leadership. Out of this declaration, a formalized ad hoc committee, headed successively by Jeanne Williams and Carolyn Tyler (Guidry), preceded Women in Ministry, a new agency that elected Webb as the first president.[113]

Bishop Frank Madison Reid, Jr. and Bishop H. Hartford Brookins served as chair and co-chair of a Council of Bishops special committee on AME position papers. They commissioned a panel of AME scholars to prepare reports on several pressing issues facing the denomination. Grant's paper pertained to "The Status of Women in the African Methodist Episcopal Church." Two fundamental principles framed the report. Women should be "recognized and treated as human beings equal to men." Furthermore, they should be represented "in proportion to their membership" in every facet of leadership at the local and denominational levels. With respect to the clergy, women should be "encouraged to enter the itinerant ministry and not just to the local ministry and evangelism" and have opportunities for pastorates "on [the] basis of talents and abilities and not rejected on [the] basis of sex." Moreover, women should be appointed as presiding elder and "be given the opportunity to serve in the highest office of this church, the office of bishop."[114]

To attain these objectives, the General Conference should create a Committee for Affirmative Action on the Status of Women in the African Methodist Episcopal Church and to fund the agency with an annual budget. Sixteen years later the General Conference of 1992 created African Methodist Episcopal Women in Ministry (WIM) to "address the issue of sexism in the church" and "address issues of opportunities" for AME women. Additionally, WIM would be organized at all denominational levels. The first

---

[113] Lillian Frier Webb, "Quadrennial Report of the Commission of the Commission on Women in Ministry," *AME Church Review*, Vol. 108, No. 348, October–December 1992, 41; Kenneth H. Hill, *The Romance of Teaching in the Wesleyan African Methodist Tradition* (Nashville, TN, AME Sunday School Union, 2016), 149–151.

[114] *Combined Minutes . . . of the General Conference, 1976*, 223, 225; Also, see Jacquelyn Grant, "Black Theology and the Black Woman," in James H. Cone and Gayraud S. Wilmore (eds.), *Black Theology: A Documentary History*, Vol. 1 (Maryknoll, NY, Orbis Books, 1979), 323–338.

president, Lillian Frier Webb, the daughter of the Reverend Richard Frier, the founder and pastor of Mt. Zion AME Church in New York City, belonged to the first generation of women fully ordained in the New York Annual Conference. She was licensed to preach in 1960 and ordained as an itinerant deacon and itinerant elder in 1964 and 1966 respectively.[115]

The launch of WIM and ongoing momentum derived from the increase of women presiding elders, the election of two female general officers, and a succession of women candidates for the episcopacy accelerated in the 1990s the movement to elect a woman to the bishopric. During this period two bishops positioned two women in leading pastorates and conferred on them compelling pastoral and administrative credentials that made them competitive with male contenders for the bishopric. Bishop Brookins sent Carolyn Tyler Guidry to serve as pastor of Cain Memorial AME Church in Bakersfield, California, in 1983. Then, in 1989, Bishop Anderson assigned her to Walker Temple AME Church, a sizeable congregation in Los Angeles, and next appointed her in 1994 as a presiding elder of the Los Angeles-Pasadena District in the Southern California Annual Conference. Similarly, Bishop Brookins sent Vashti Murphy McKenzie in 1990 to the newly constructed Payne Memorial AME Church in Baltimore, where her preaching talents spearheaded growth within the decade from a few hundred to over 1,700 members.[116]

Beyond these developments, other influential bodies within the AME Church pushed for women bishops. At a 1995 General Board meeting a resolution was passed saying "that a woman [should] be elected to the bishopric in 2000." The bishops in their Episcopal Address to the 1996 General Conference urged "a plan of action to elect women to the office of bishop some time in the future." The Connectional Lay Organization's executive board in 1998, like the General Board, targeted the 2000 General Conference as the designated time to elect a female bishop. Additionally, delegates at the 1999 lay organization convention endorsed the resolution of its leadership council that backed a woman for the episcopacy.[117]

[115] Ibid., 225; *Combined Minutes [of the] 44th Quadrennial Session [of the] General Conference [of the] African Methodist Episcopal Church held on Orlando, FL, July 8–15, 1992* (Nashville, TN, AME Sunday School Union, 1992), 254–255; *Combined Minutes of the One Hundred Forty-Third and Forty-Fourth Session[s] of the New York Annual Conference [of the] African Methodist Episcopal Church, 1965–1966* (n.p., n.d.), 49, 120.

[116] Dickerson, "The Female Presiding Elders," *AME Church Review*, January-March 2002, 17–19; Henderson, *AME Registry Select*, 269–270.

[117] *Combined Minutes of the Forty-Sixth Session of the General Conference of the African Methodist Episcopal Church held in Cincinnati, OH, July 5–11, 2000*, 281; *Episcopal Address, 45th Session of the General Conference of the African Methodist Episcopal Church, [Presented*

The bishops in their Episcopal Address to the 2000 General Conference acknowledged that AME women clergy numbered over 2,500 and were "well prepared" with "academic degrees" and "previous careers." Nonetheless, "there are still roadblocks to ordination, pastoral assignment, and leadership promotion." Despite the long history of female preachers in the denomination, "we must seriously consider the 'place' of women in ministry. Though the bishops cited an emerging consensus about the "election of a woman bishop by the year 2000," they did not recommend that General Conference delegates should act on this objective. Similar equivocation came from the Episcopal Committee, which rejected a request for a "'set aside' to elect a female bishop" because the committee lacked "jurisdiction" in the matter and that General Conference delegates should make the decision. When put to a vote on the General Conference floor, the proposal failed with 667 delegates voting yes, but 716 voting no.[118]

During these proceedings Jamye Coleman William, the first female general officer, with co-signatories, J. L. Williams, former president of the Connectional Lay Organization, and Sandra Smith Blair, the president of WIM, offered their own resolution to the delegates. As heirs to a tradition of "protest against injustice," the resolution advocated "an end to gender bias in the hierarchy of our Church. We call for the full inclusion of women as decision and policy makers at the highest level of our Church, [in] the bishopric." They cited Jarena Lee and Martha Jayne Keys and their push for "inclusion, parity, and equity" for AME women clergy. Because the United Methodist Church in 1984 and the Episcopal Church in 1989 had elected African American women to the episcopacy and Louis Farrakhan, head of the Nation of Islam, selected a woman to lead the group's Southern Region in 1999, "we in African Methodism, who profess to be a liberating and reconciling Church, can no longer engage in gender bias." Therefore, the General Conference should "instruct the Episcopal Committee that in its recommendation of the number of bishops to be elected one shall be a woman."[119]

Despite the inaction of the Episcopal Committee and the delegates on the female "set aside," Carolyn Tyler Guidry and Vashti Murphy McKenzie were already certified candidates and eligible for two of the four vacancies in the

by) *Bishop Frank Curtis Cummings*, Louisville, KY, June 26–July 3, 1996 (Nashville, TN, AME Sunday School Union, 1996), 17.
[118] *The African Methodist Episcopal Church Episcopal Address, 2000, 46th Session of the General Conference Presented by Bishop Donald George Kenneth Ming, July 5, 2000, Cincinnati, OH, 44–46, 72–73, Combined Minutes ... of the General Conference, 2000, 185–186.*
[119] *Combined Minutes ... of the General Conference, 2000, 281–282.*

episcopacy. Both were formidable candidates, with each tallying strongly on the first ballot and McKenzie outpolling Guidry. The strength of their male competitors, however, narrowed the opportunity for both women to be elected. McKenzie drew 847 votes on the second ballot, which placed her a close second to her leading male contender, Richard F. Norris. Each won the bishopric, with McKenzie becoming the denomination's 117th elected and consecrated bishop. Guidry's impressive 614 votes on the second ballot and her 591 votes on the third ballot were not enough to outpoll the two winning candidates, Gregory G. M. Ingram and Preston W. Williams.[120]

In a front-page article the *New York Times* declared "After 213 Years, AME Church Elects First Woman as a Bishop." With her husband, children, and members of Payne Memorial Church in Baltimore, McKenzie said, "The stained glass ceiling has been pierced." She added, "I stand here tonight on the shoulders of the unordained women who serve[d] without affirmation or appointment." In the *AME Church Review* Jacquelyn Grant reflected on "A Crack, A Break, A Shattering: State of the Glass: A Theological Interpretation of the Election of Bishop Vashti Murphy McKenzie." The election affirmed, Grant wrote, that "the liberation agenda of God is enhanced by this historic happening," that God, "no respecter of gender" shows that the Lord is an "equal opportunity employer," and that God "advocate[s] justice for women and liberation for all in the church and beyond." Additionally, the election meant that "God Likes Ear Rings: A New Model for Ministry." Grant said that "the presence of a woman bishop in an historic black church broadens possibilities for women."[121]

McKenzie was assigned to the Eighteenth Episcopal District, which covered Botswana, Swaziland, Lesotho, and Mozambique. She remained the denomination's sole female bishop, however, for only four years. At the 2004 General Conference, with eight vacancies to be filled, AMEs, in addition to electing three African bishops, also elevated two women to the episcopacy. Carolyn Tyler Guidry became the 122nd bishop and was assigned to the Caribbean-based Sixteenth Episcopal District. The 126th bishop was Sarah Frances Davis, a pastor in San Antonio, Texas, who replaced McKenzie in her diocese in southern Africa. McKenzie went to preside in Kentucky and Tennessee while Guidry was assigned in 2008 to Mississippi and Louisiana, with Davis following her in the Caribbean. In

---

[120] Ibid., 601–602.
[121] *New York Times*, July 12, 2000; Jacquelyn Grant-Collier, "A Crack, A Break, A Shattering: State of the Glass: A Theological Interpretation of the Election of Bishop Vashti Murphy McKenzie," *AME Church Review*, Vol. 116, No. 378, Summer 2000, 18–19.

2012 McKenzie was shifted to Texas, Guidry was retired, and Davis died in 2013. A fourth female bishop, E. Anne Henning-Byfield, a presiding elder in the Indiana Annual Conference, was elected in 2016 and assigned to the Sixteenth Episcopal District where both Guidry and Davis had served. The AME Zion Church followed the AMEs and elected a female bishop, Mildred B. Hines, in 2008, while the CMEs elected Teresa E. Snorton in 2010. The United Methodist Church outdistanced all three black Methodist bodies in their lengthy roster of African American women bishops, including four who were elevated in 2016.[122]

SEX AND SEXUALITY

Other sex and sexuality issues compelled AMEs to extend their emancipationist ethos to areas beyond women's empowerment and racial and colonial subjugation. Their traditional focus on systemic suppression on the basis of racial identity reckoned with controversial sensual and interpersonal practices within the AME and black Atlantic populations served by this liberationist religious body. When the Equal Rights Amendment campaign, reproductive health and HIV/AIDS challenges, and same-sex relationships were thrust into thunderous public discourse, AMEs initially relied on their traditional heteronormative and patriarchal attitudes and structures grounded in familiar recitations of Old Testament and Pauline scriptures that seemingly opposed these developments. These AME responses intersected uncomfortably with the perspectives of conservative white religious communities that African Methodists usually eschewed.

Four landmark events that coalesced during the decades following the late 1960s framed public discourse about sex and sexuality issues and elicited religious responses. First, a police raid on a gay meeting place at Stonewall in 1969 in New York City's Greenwich Village energized an uprising that inaugurated the Lesbian, Gay, Bisexual, Transgender (LGBT) liberation movement. Secondly, the US Supreme Court in 1973 in *Roe* v. *Wade* legalized

[122] *Combined Minutes ... of the General Conference, 2000*, 280; *Combined Minutes ... of the General Conference, 2004*, 674; *Combined Minutes of the 48th Quadrennial Session of the General Conference, [of the] African Methodist Episcopal Church* [held in] St. Louis, MO, July 4–11, 2008 (Nashville, TN, AME Sunday School Union, 2008), 177; *The Doctrine and Discipline of the African Methodist Episcopal Church, 2012* (Nashville, TN, AME Sunday School Union, 2012), 596, 599, 600; *Combined Minutes [of the] 50th Quadrennial Session [of the] General Conference, [of the] African Methodist Episcopal Church* [held in] Philadelphia, PA, July 6–13, 2016 (Nashville, TN, AME Sunday School Union, 2018), 64; *Los Angeles Sentinel*, July 24, 2008; Bishop Teresa E. Snorton, www.teresasnorton.com; "United Methodist Church Elects 4 Black Women Bishops," Afro.com, July 16, 2016.

first trimester abortions. Thirdly, the approval of an Equal Rights Amendment to the US Constitution in behalf of women passed both houses of the US Congress in 1971 and 1972 respectively. Despite ratification by thirty-five states and a deadline extension from 1979 to 1982, the three additional states needed to finish the process failed to materialize. Fourthly, the federally operated Centers for Disease Control and Prevention discovered HIV/AIDS in five gay men. The incurable disease, primarily transmitted through male on male intercourse and also through intravenous drug use, became mostly associated with the gay population. All of these developments, along with an increased acknowledgment and litigation surrounding sexual harassment in the workplace and principally perpetrated by male superiors against female subordinates, added another dimension to sex and sexuality issues.[123]

Energetic opposition to these changes in the social order came mostly from conservative white religious leaders. White evangelicals who were especially upset about the seeming advance of "secular humanism" and "moral decay," established the Moral Majority in 1979. The founder, Jerry Falwell, a fundamentalist Baptist pastor in Lynchburg, Virginia, and an influential television preacher, prepared to fight a "holy war" that would enlist Republican Party officeholders and candidates to promote government policies to uphold traditional values. With respect to LGBT activism, historian E. Marie Griffith noted that as this movement "came to be more visible to those outside those communities, many prominent conservative religious leaders began speaking about homosexuality and its potential to destroy the United States." She added that "to them, it seemed clear that the movement was one more arm of the secular humanist campaign to destabilize the nuclear family, weaken male authority, and de-Christianize the nation."[124]

Some mainline religious bodies, such as the Episcopal Church, were directly affected by the LGBT rights movement. The election of V. Gene Robinson as bishop coadjutor and bishop of New Hampshire in 2003 and 2004 respectively, split the venerable denomination. These actions involving Robinson, divorced from his heterosexual marriage and living in a same sex relationship, precipitated the founding of a dissident denomination, the Anglican Church of North America, in 2010. Griffith observed that in several denominations in which these issues brewed "the persistence of stalwart

[123] Frances Fitzgerald, *The Evangelicals: The Struggle to Shape America* (New York, Simon & Schuster Paperbacks, 2017), 235, 291, 294–295, 327, 366; E. Marie Griffith, *Mortal Combat: How Sex Divided American Christians and Fractured American Politics* (New York, Basic Books, 2017), 201–206, 241–272, 282.
[124] Fitzgerald, *The Evangelicals*, 291, 299–300; Griffith, *Mortal Combat*, 282, 288.

activists on all sides confirms the high stakes for those wanting to conserve a particular model of the status quo that maintains an older notion of traditional order, gender hierarchy, and obedience to strict sexual limits." She further argued that "those fearing change have instilled that dread in others through warnings of moral ruin" while their opponents in "welcoming" the change "have offered visions of a healthy society freed from archaic constraints."[125]

Though sex and sexuality issues were scarcely nonexistent in the AME Church, the topics of abortion and homosexuality, however, emerged as subjects that African Methodists needed to address at the 1976 General Conference. Moreover, the denomination in subsequent decades vacillated between an articulation of conservative religious views to perspectives that emphasized tolerance and compassion especially for victims of HIV/AIDS. While no fissure, as occurred in the Episcopal Church, happened among AMEs, dissident voices calling for an expansive discursive reckoning with newer understandings of the biological and psychological constructions of gender showed that sex and sexuality issues were hardly resolved.

At the 1976 General Conference commissioned AME position papers about abortion and homosexuality were presented to the assembly and were adopted at the 1980 General Conference. "The Church can in no wise sanction abortion," said the statement, because life starts when pregnancy begins. Since "we cannot make life, so we must not take life," no woman has "the sole right to do with her body as she wills." Though the United States Supreme Court in *Roe* v. *Wade* (1973) legalized abortion within the first trimester of pregnancy, this choice for women, said the position paper, did not "erase the sin and guilt attached." At the same time AMEs acknowledged "extenuating circumstances" where "pregnancy endangers the life of the mother," and that could be a moral exception to the denomination's anti-abortion posture.[126]

This General Conference pronouncement resonated in the subordinate jurisdictions within the denomination. Bishop Adams, during his tenure in the 1990s in South Carolina, for example, impaneled district clergy and laity to produce a book, published in 2000, entitled *What AMEs Believe*. On abortion five collaborators, three male, one a future bishop, and two females,

[125] Griffith, *Mortal Combat*, xx, 274–276.
[126] *Combined Minutes ... of the General Conference, 1976*, 224; *Combined Minutes of the Forty-First Session of the General Conference of the African Methodist Episcopal Church* held in New Orleans, LA, June 18–28, 1980 (Nashville, TN, AME Sunday School Union, 1980), 142–143.

drew upon scriptures that affirmed "the existence of life before birth and speak of no circumstance that justifies the taking of an unborn life." Therefore, "abortion is the taking of a life and is contrary to the word and will of God" position. Within Luke 1:39–45, the South Carolinians noted, "how John the Baptist, still in his mother Elizabeth's womb leaped with joy when Mary greeted Elizabeth. Where would we be if Joseph and Mary had done the 'prudent' thing and chosen to abort the baby that threatened their relationship and their marriage?"[127]

AMEs articulated a stance on abortion that was awkwardly congruent with the thinking of conservative white Christians. Falwell of the Moral Majority, who opposed black civil rights and promoted the so-called seg academies to circumvent school integration, was surely no liberationist ally. Nonetheless, AMEs, who traditionally opposed drinking, dancing, gambling, and other examples of lax lifestyles, like the Virginia preacher, may have defined abortion as another example of moral decay. Just as AMEs allied with white religious leaders in their support of temperance in the late nineteenth and early twentieth centuries, their posture on abortion put them in the company of white Christians who were comfortable with the subordination of blacks. For these reasons, the South Carolina AMEs acknowledged their problematic posture on abortion. "It should be noted," they said "that abortion has become a political issue and the wider community has sought the support of the historically black church in their protests."[128]

Though AMEs denounced "abortion as the taking of a life," the Church of Richard Allen needed to be "circumspect in the protests" of anti-abortion advocates who at the same time lent little support to the black civil rights movement. These same white conservative Christians "who most stridently march and resort to confrontation for the rights of the unborn also support political positions-such as welfare reform, the abolition of public education, and cruel prison reform that trample on the rights of those already born." Therefore, "the AME Church does not stand with those who make abortion a political issue, unless they in turn embrace a wider political agenda that affirms and secures the well-being of the living, as well as that of the yet unborn."[129]

---

[127] John Hurst Adams (compiler), *What AMEs Believe, Developed for the African Methodist Episcopal Church by the Seventh Episcopal District* (Nashville, TN, AME Sunday School Union, 2000), 43, 79.

[128] See, for example, *Book of Discipline of the AME Church* (Nashville, TN, AME Sunday School Union, 1916), 264–265; Adams, *What AMEs Believe*, 44.

[129] Adams, *What AMEs Believe*, 44.

The matter of abortion for AMEs also intersected with issues of women's ecclesiastical empowerment. What could be construed as official opposition to female reproductive freedom coincided with male responses to women in ministry that ranged from resistance to ambivalence to grudging acceptance. AME attitudes toward homosexuality generated the same official reply as did the issue of abortion. The 1976 AME position papers recognized that homosexuality was not a modern "phenomenon." There was, however, "increased openness by those who are practicing homosexuals and increased tolerance, if not acceptance, by the American culture." Moreover, "as a Christian church we are alarmed by the notoriety and legal acceptance of a lifestyle which has so much potential for cultural decadence." Hence, a statement was presented for General Conference consideration about same sex marriage, the homosexual lifestyle, and how homosexuality threatened black families.[130]

With respect to homosexual marriage, "as a church we categorically, unreservedly, and unequivocally reject the concept," the statement said, because it is "totally inconsistent with the biblical and theological conceptualization of marriage" as AMEs understood it. Marriage, according to denominational teachings, is "a divine and sacred institution created by God as a union between man and woman." Hence, "we therefore, expect our ordained ministry to reserve the rite of marriage for those who are of different sexes. We expressly forbid our ministers to extend the marriage rites to homosexuals of two persons of the same sex." Furthermore, the homosexual lifestyle, the statement added, had no place among AMEs: "we believe that the normative sexual relationship is between man and woman." Any other sexual relationship is "an abrogation and perversion of the God ordained process for the procreation and continued life of the species."[131]

Additionally, the black family was already assaulted by "institutional racism," which resulted in "emasculating black males, dehumanizing black females, and psychologically enslaving black children." Homosexuality, the statement said, is "still another force which mitigates against the strength of black people." Neither black males, black females, nor black children can "actualize their potential" if they choose "homosexual lifestyles." As with abortion, the General Conference of 1980 adopted the statement on homosexuality as an official AME position. A subsequent position paper prepared for the General Conference of 1996 affirmed the condemnatory view of homosexuality. Though other sexual sins deserved censure, said the female

---

[130] *Combined Minutes . . . of the General Conference, 1976*, 226–227.   [131] Ibid.

physician and AME organist who wrote the paper, homosexuality violated God's "biological design."[132]

In *What AMEs Believe*, South Carolina AMEs addressed homosexuality in ways similar to their treatment of abortion. In a chapter on "Alternate Lifestyles" the same coauthors who wrote the section on abortion also bemoaned the rise of a "more permissive" society that tolerated "same-sex marriage, homosexuality, [and] heterosexual cohabitation without the benefit of marriage." Those engaged in these "lifestyle choices" have in many cases been granted benefits and legal status once reserved for married heterosexual couples." These activities, the coauthors contended, led to "a 'more open' attitude towards such behaviors as fornication, transsexuality and pedophilia." Moreover, "the AME Church, through the Word of God," the coauthors observed, "strongly disagrees with any theory or idea of homosexual, bisexual, and transsexual practice." The scripture in Genesis 2:24 declared "the divine union between a man and a woman." Sodom and Gomorrah, AMEs were reminded, were destroyed because of sexual perversions.[133]

Official AME responses to issues of homosexuality as they pertained to the clergy strongly validated views articulated in General Conference-approved position papers. In 2003, for example, *USA Today*, in an article about the policies of major religious bodies toward openly gay candidates for ordination, listed the AME Church as sanctioning their admission to the ministry. "With indignation and great offense" the Council of Bishops, in a special meeting in Dallas, Texas, declared that *USA Today* was wrong about the AME Church. The bishops noted that they "ruled and affirmed on several occasions-and the AME Church through position papers and public statements-that the Church does not support the ordination of openly gay clergy. To do so is to take action contrary to our theological interpretation of the scriptures."[134]

On the matter of same-sex marriage, a position paper prepared for the 1996 General Conference opposed "the union of two persons of the same sex as constituting a marriage. This 'arrangement' is not biblical and does great violence to the understanding of family and marriage." The General

---

[132] Ibid.; *Combined Minutes . . . of the General Conference, 1980*, 142–143; Cornelia R. Graves , "Sexuality and Spirituality," *AME Church Review*, Vol. 114, No. 372, October–December 1998, 18–19.

[133] Adams, *What AMEs Believe*, 7, 19, 79.

[134] "African Methodist Episcopal Church Does Not Ordain Openly Gay Clergy-Contrary to the *USA Today* (August 7, 2003) Article, 'God Have Mercy on His Church,'" The Council of Bishops, *AME Church Review*, Vol. 119, No. 391, July–September 2003, 13.

Conference of 2004 was similarly adamant, saying that AME legislation was necessary because "some court rulings have been in favor of same sex marriage" and that "has given it credibility." Therefore, the AME Church prohibited any of its clergy "from performing or participating in or giving any blessing to any ceremony designed to result in any pairing between persons of the same sex gender, including, but not limited to, marriage or civil unions." Moreover, no AME properties could be sites for any same sex marriages or blessings. Clergy who violated these rules would be tried, and if found guilty "such person's ordination shall be revoked."[135]

Despite official condemnation of homosexuality, a broader discourse about the larger issues of sex and sexuality spread among the AME clergy and laity. For them, homosexuality was only one facet of a wide range of concerns requiring the sober reflection of church leaders. They addressed such urgent matters as the AME response to the HIV/AIDS health crisis and the scourge of sexual misconduct within the denomination. Because the first cases of HIV/AIDS were identified among gay men in the United States in 1981, the disease, despite its spread among heroin drug users and hemophiliacs, became associated with male-on-male sex.

Because HIV/AIDS was viewed as judgment visited upon same-sex male intercourse, few AMEs, like those in other denominations, addressed this emerging epidemic, except to denounce the now diseased sinners. Into this context of silence and denunciation appeared M. Joan Cousin, a former North Carolina teacher and the wife of the bishop of Florida and the Bahamas, who became first within the AME hierarchy to pursue a frontline response to the HIV/AIDS crisis. Available to her, as titular leader of the missionary society in the Eleventh Episcopal District, were thousands of women to support her health initiatives. Hence, at Greater Bethel AME Church in Miami in 1985 she launched the Sarah Allen House. She provided clothes and medical services to the needy, including Haitian immigrants who had been housed in prisons, and also started workshops on HIV/AIDS and drug abuse. When her husband was assigned to the Northeast and Bermuda she was involved with a Health Awareness Center connected to the New Jersey Housing Authority. HIV/AIDS programs became a part of this project. The facility was named in honor of Cousin, and with her input produced a publication on *AIDS Prevention Through Education*. Her widespread lecturing about HIV/AIDS awareness helped in the establishment

---

[135] *Combined Minutes of the Forty-Fifth Session of the General Conference of the African Methodist Episcopal Church* held in Louisville, KY, June 26–July 3, 1996, 427; *Combined Minutes . . . of the General Conference, 2004,* 362.

among AMEs in Botswana the M. Joan Cousin Women and Youth Development Center, which focused on education and services for women and children infected with HIV/AIDS. In South Africa two AMEs started the Joan Cousin HIV/Aids Mission in the Cape Town area. Similarly, Bishop Vashti Murphy McKenzie, while presiding in Swaziland, established the Selulasandla Vashti Children Village to serve orphans whose parents had succumbed to HIV/AIDS. Constructed in 2002 with funding from the Delta Sigma Theta Sorority, the facility housed two dozen residents and provided them with educational and health services.[136]

While M. Joan Cousin stoked awareness of HIV/AIDS, its impact within the black population also raised recognition of the disease. Chiquita A. Fye, a Georgia physician and medical director of the AME Health Commission, presented a position paper at the General Conference of 1996 on "The AIDS Epidemic: A Threat to Black Survival." She recounted that out of an infected population of 510,310, blacks, who were 12 percent of all Americans, represented 38 percent of those afflicted with AIDS. An astonishing 51 percent of females with the disease were African American and 52 percent of pediatric cases of AIDS occurred among black infants and children. "Because of the nature of this disease and the stigma associated with it," the doctor declared," the church must move beyond all 'isms' and make the church a place where all those who are affected by AIDS, victims, families, [and] friends, will have a refuge where full acceptance is present." Fye also recommended that congregations should teach prevention and provide "explicit and very clear information describing HIV and its transmission."[137]

The Cousin and Fye admonitions about HIV/AIDS resonated with some ministers who surveyed the on-the-ground impact of the pandemic within the communities where they served. Two pastors, later elected as bishops, respectively wrote D.Min. and Ed.D. theses in 1997 and 2002 that examined the diverse population of blacks afflicted with the disease. Stafford J. Wicker, pastor at the burgeoning Antioch AME Church in suburban Atlanta, submitted a dissertation to the Interdenominational Theological Center on "An AIDS Ministry with a Black Church in Decatur, Georgia." In it he explored

[136] *African Methodism: Fulfilling the Mission in Florida and the Bahamas, 1865–1987, Compiled under the Administration of Bishop Philip R. Cousin* (Hempstead, NY, JAE Associates, 1988), 41; Ethel H. Russaw, *Call the Roll: Laity in the African Methodist Episcopal Church* (Bloomington, IN, AuthorHouse, 2011), 66–68; *The Christian Recorder Online*, February 8, 2008; http://ame18.org/selulasandla-vashti-children-village.

[137] *Combined Minutes ... of the General Conference, 1996*, 149; (Chiquita Fye), "The AIDS Epidemic: A Threat to Black Survival," in "Summaries of Selected Position Papers," *AME Church Review*, Vol. 112, No. 363, July–September 1996, 19–20.

how "to institute an educational awareness model which emphasizes prevention of the HIV virus." His consciousness about the issue drew from a summer experience in 1991 as chaplain at Atlanta's Grady Memorial Hospital. There he interacted with two HIV/AIDS patients. One was a black man who was twenty-seven years old, and the other was a baby whose parents contracted the HIV virus. All of these persons died because of the disease.[138]

What could an AME congregation do? At Wicker's Antioch Church, he developed partner/teams consisting of "members of the congregation who had been touched by AIDS" in their families. In addition to "individual pastoral care sessions," Wicker chose ten trainers who would work in a HIV/AIDS ministry and devote four to six weeks of training about the disease at various educational sites in the Atlanta area. Another initiative involved a volunteer group of members "to foster HIV/AIDS awareness." There was also a door-to-door campaign, with six adult volunteers who would train nine teenagers to place brochures about HIV/AIDS at the homes of Decatur area residents. "The lasting effects of the project," Wicker wrote, "are evidences in the congregation's receptivity to high risk persons (e.g. homosexuals and drug users) who attend public worship" at Antioch Church.[139]

John F. White, who successively served as pastor in Florida at Greater Bethel AME Church in Miami and Mount Hermon AME Church in Fort Lauderdale, noted in his dissertation that HIV/AIDS disproportionately afflicted the black population in neighboring Miami-Dade and Broward Counties. In Miami-Dade in 2000, for example, there were 27,551 cases of HIV/AIDS, but 54 percent of the number was African Americans. White explored how AME congregations in the two counties "can significantly affect persons with HIV/AIDS and provide preventive education for those with the potential of becoming infected by the disease." From his survey of AME members in twenty-four congregations in the counties White discovered that the disease was not viewed as restricted to the gay population but afflicted the family members of some of the interviewees. They and their pastors committed to attending workshops to learn more about HIV/AIDS. White recommended that AME congregations should "form collaborative partnerships with other churches to address the HIV/AIDS issue."[140]

[138] Stafford J. Wicker, "A Local Faith Community Responds to HIV/AIDS Epidemic: An Effective AIDS Witness in Decatur, Georgia," D.Min. dissertation, The Atlanta Theological Association and The Interdenominational Theological Center, April 1997, iii, 10.
[139] Ibid., 60–62, 67, 71, 94.
[140] John F. White, "The Impact of the Black Church on the HIV/AIDS Epidemic in the Black Community of Broward and Miami-Dade Counties," AME Church Review, Vol. 119, No. 392, October–December 2003, 13, 33–34, 36.

Notwithstanding these efforts, the editor of the *Christian Recorder*, Calvin
H. Sydnor III, observed that HIV/AIDS testing happened at the 2007 General
Board/Bishops Council meeting in Columbus, Ohio. Yet he lamented that "it
was a start, and it made a big splash in several outlets, but only a relatively
few persons got tested." He added, "we should have had long lines, but we
didn't." AME congregations, he said, should inaugurate screening initiatives
for HIV/AIDS because "testing and education are keys to attacking this
problem." Through the AME infrastructure, mainly through the episcopal
districts and the denomination's Health Commission, had an uneven impact
in both the Americas and Africa, Cousin's crusade was acknowledged at the
General Conference of 2012, where she received the Bishops' Quadrennial
Award for three decades of advocacy against "the suffering and stigma
imposed by HIV and AIDS." In response, she said, "we have been able to
dispel myths surrounding it and we have been able to let the world know
that HIV/AIDS is a preventable disease of behaviors and not a gay
disease."[141]

Cousin's comprehensive construction of HIV/AIDS as a disease with a
capacious impact on diverse populations in the Americas and Africa resonated at the General Conference of 2016. Delegates enacted two bills that
integrated the fight against HIV/AIDS as a health priority for the denomination. The first proposal aimed "to institutionalize across the global AME
Church" an urgent effort to stop "the advance of HIV/AIDS that is disproportionately affecting African, African Americans, and others served by the
global AME Church." Toward that end ministers were mandated to say in
their annual pastoral reports whether their churches had a Health Ministry
and how they were "eliminating or addressing" the scourge of HIV/AIDS.
Other legislation instructed either bishops or presiding elders to establish
within their jurisdictions training programs for clergy. These sessions would
provide ministers with "a basic scientific foundation to understand HIV/
AIDS."[142]

As Cousin was asserting that HIV/AIDS could not be typecast as an
exclusively homosexual disease, but a broader matter of sexual practice,
the behavior of mostly heterosexual clergy highlighted egregious misconduct
that required institutional intervention. The sexual harassment of women by
male ministers, though hardly unknown, emerged as a major issue at the

[141] *Christian Recorder Online*, February 8, 2008; September 21, 2012.
[142] *Combined Minutes of the Fiftieth Quadrennial Session of the General Conference of the African Methodist Episcopal Church*, Vol. I held in Philadelphia, PA, July 6–13, 2016, 576, 578.

General Conference of 1996. Delegates enacted legislation that punished sexual harassment and sexual exploitation by compelling clergy to surrender their ministerial office for varying lengths of time for the first and second offenses and to be ousted from the ministry after a third offense. Appearing in the 1996 *Doctrine and Discipline of the African Methodist Episcopal Church* was a skeletal outline of the punitive measures mandated for clergy sexual misconduct. One bishop noted that "we should not leave this conference without a bill of harassment," but he did not believe "that these graphic descriptions should be in our discipline." Hence, the detailed content of the several categories of sexual misbehavior and harassment and the compulsory responses required of those in supervision of AME clergy at all levels of the denomination were published separately in an *AME Manual on Sexual Misconduct*. Printed at the AME Sunday School Union, the book became "required reading by AME clergy."[143]

Heightened awareness of sexual harassment permeated a special edition of the *AME Church Review* in 1998. Editor Paulette Coleman, in a lead editorial entitled "Sex, Sexuality, and Sexual Misconduct Among the Faithful," observed "that there is a perception within the denomination that accusations of sexual misconduct, particularly sexual harassment are increasing." Hence, "as a faith community, the African Methodist Episcopal Church must create an environment where sexual misconduct is not tolerated and where every possible precaution is taken to prevent such acts." She admonished that "litigious times" made it "imperative that Church officials investigate thoroughly and remedy alleged misconduct as quickly as possible for the sake of the Church." She added that child molestation was "the new frontier for litigation" and warned that "several denominations had to pay multimillion dollar settlements in response to jury verdicts and out of court settlements of clergy misconduct cases involving the abuse of children."[144]

Monica Coleman, a recent seminary graduate, challenged AME congregations to find "ways to talk about sexual health, sexual promiscuity, sexual abstinence, sexual orientation, sexual harassment, [and] sexually transmitted diseases." She repeated that the church "has had numerous cases of clergy sexual misconduct that have been settled out of court with significant financial cost to the denomination." Moreover, "our silence" about ministerial

---

[143] *The Doctrine and Discipline of the African Methodist Episcopal Church*, 1996 (Nashville, TN, AME Sunday School Union, 1996), 333; *Combined Minutes . . . of the General Conference, 1996*, 188, 472–474; *Combined Minutes . . . of the General Conference, 2004*, 558–563.

[144] Paulette Coleman, "Sex, Sexuality, and Sexual Misconduct among the Faithful," *AME Church Review*, Vol. 114, No. 372, October–December 1998, 5–7.

misbehavior permeated the denomination because "none of these cases could be found in legal records, nor would high officers of the denomination reveal the information they knew about these cases." She warned that "as long as we continue to be silent, and move offending clergy from one assignment to another, we fail to address the root of the problem and we send the message that this behavior is indeed acceptable in our churches."[145]

The prescient perspectives of both Colemans anticipated a case in the episcopal district that included Missouri became a denominational cause célèbre. The female pastor of a congregation in Kansas City charged a male pastor with sexual harassment and her presiding elder with sexual assault and demands for sexual favors. She also alleged that her bishop refused to investigate and to prevent the presiding elder from removing the woman from her pastorate. A local court in 1999 heard the complaint against the two church officials and the bishop, who stood in the place of the AME Church as the institutional defendant. A jury found as liable the presiding elder and the denomination whose episcopal representative failed to exercise proper oversight and discipline over the woman's predatory superior. A judgment of $6 million was the verdict in favor of the harassed female pastor. As denominational officials pursued an appeal, a required bond of $4.5 million was posted. The Missouri Court of Appeals, Western District in *Weaver v. African Methodist Episcopal Church, Inc. Board of Incorporators* in 2001 upheld the lower court in backing the claims of the female minister. The high court affirmed that there was sexual harassment, a retaliatory discharge of the woman from her church, and a failure by the bishop properly to supervise and discipline the harassers. Although the denomination escaped, on technicalities, the millions in judgment levied against it in the lower court, the case showed the church's ongoing vulnerabilities if its own rules and regulation, already enacted, were not followed.[146]

The Missouri case spurred enabling legislation at the General Conference of 2004 that emphasized more effective dissemination about the denominational policy on sexual misconduct and greater attention to liability protections for the church. Delegates agreed that the *AME Manual*, because it was generally purchased as a companion volume to the *Doctrine and Discipline*, left most AMEs "unaware of the existence of the policy" on sexual

---

[145] Monica Coleman, "Clergy Sexual Misconduct in the AME Church: An Open Letter to My Brothers and Sisters in the Clergy," *AME Church Review*, October–December 1998, 25, 30.

[146] *Kansas City Star*, December 3, 1999; *Weaver v. African Methodist Episcopal Church, Inc.* http://caselaw.findlaw.com/mo-court-of-appeals/1257637.html; "AME Fighting Multi-Million Dollar Harassment Suit," beliefnet.com/news/2000/06.

misconduct. Therefore, the content of the *AME Manual* would now be printed in the new *Doctrine and Discipline*. Moreover, "all clergy and candidates for ministerial orders, employees, appointed or elected officials, and volunteers of the AME Church shall be required to attend a seminar by professional subject matter experts on the issues of sexual misconduct." Additionally, congregations were mandated to insert in their liability insurance policies for sexual abuse.[147]

Despite stands against abortion and homosexuality, AMEs discovered that not all issues of human sexuality had been addressed. Bans on same-sex marriage, opposition to ordaining openly gay clergy, and punitive measures against sexual misconduct, though amendable by church regulations, still left lingering issues of human sexuality to be discussed. Notwithstanding the clarion admonitions of M. Joan Cousin and Chiquita A. Fye about the complexities of the HIV/AIDS crisis, too few AMEs understood that the transmission of the disease had a far-reaching impact affecting cross-sections of gender and age cohorts. Transsexual identities and diverse intimacy practices also emerged within these broadened spheres of human sexuality, requiring denominational discourse and a potential reordering of church statues.

Jennifer S. Leath, a Denver pastor and seminary professor, in 2017 surmised "that there is [no] agreement within the AME Church when it comes to matters of sexual orientation and gender identity." She outlined three areas to guide AME discourse about these issues. Sexual orientation and gender identity, she said, are "sacred" and if these persons stand "outside of heterosexual, cisgender categorization" they "will neither hide and lie nor leave and disappear." These issues challenge church leaders to develop "consistent interpretive methods" to explicate scripture and engagement with the science and biological research that affirms sexual and gender diversities." Leath also proposed that AME polity should "catch up" with enhanced understandings of what constitutes human sexuality. "Our legislation and position papers on sexual orientation and gender identities," she declared, "are dated, inconsistent, incomplete, prejudiced, contradictory, and unholy." An "updated polity," she concluded, "is right" and badly needed.[148]

Teboho G. Klaas, a self-described "heterosexual man, Christian, and pastor in the AME Church in South Africa," endorsed the Leath perspective. In the *Christian Recorder* he wrote that he was "motivated by my hate for hatred, injustice, and inequality" and was thus "an ally of sexual and gender

---

[147] *Combined Minutes . . . of the General Conference, 2004,* 558, 563.
[148] *Christian Recorder,* April 24, 2017.

non-conforming people." The liberationist heritage of African Methodism, he declared, informed his "conscientious objection to homophobia." He queried "why is our denomination silent to the lived reality of people whose sexual and gender non-conformity is not heteronormative?" Is there any justification for their exclusion from the human race other than they are simply not categorized as cisgender people?" He celebrated the expansion of the denominational motto, originally written in 1856 by Daniel A. Payne and revised in 2009 to say "God Our Father, Christ Our Redeemer, the Holy Ghost Our Comforter, and Humankind Our Family." The addition, "Humankind Our Family," by including all, regardless of sexual orientation, circumvented "the limitations of General Conferences" in legislating on "doctrinal decisions." Leath, a fourth-generation AME minister and the daughter of a bishop who had previously pastored Richard Allen's Mother Bethel Church, and Klaas, an activist pastor keenly affected by his nation's apartheid past, harnessed their capacious perspectives about human sexuality to their denomination's emancipationist ethos. In this respect, both ministers viewed themselves in alignment with the liberationist legacy of AME pioneers.[149]

NEO-PENTECOSTALISM

Facilities for victims of HIV/AIDS at AME sites in the Americas and Africa and transatlantic discourse about human sexuality tracked the denomination's global reach. Concurrently, Pentecostalism, launched at a former AME edifice in Los Angeles in 1906, emerged as a worldwide religious phenomenon just as African Methodism became increasingly globalized. The presence of 279 million Pentecostals in the early twenty-first century, mainly in the global South, has populated both mainline and charismatic religious bodies including the AME Church. Characterized by exuberant, emotional worship, glossolalia, and popular gospel music, AMEs in sundry settings have adopted this worship motif. Hence, neo-Pentecostalism, a derivative religious practice borrowed by historic black denominations, has upended, in some congregations, the formality of traditional worship grounded in hymnody, expository preaching, and a dignified, but uplifting order of service. Though neo-Pentecostalism maintained the evangelical objectives of AME worship and preaching, its intense, unconstrained and energetic displays of ceremonial praise especially appealed to young adult blacks coming of age in the post-civil rights, Black Power, anticolonial eras.

[149] *Christian Recorder*, September 16, 2017.

Although neo-Pentecostalism sometimes introduced an awkward blending with AME rituals and worship practices, it spearheaded exponential growth in selective congregations and developed them into megachurches. John R. Bryant, an architect of neo-Pentecostalism in the AME Church, attracted apprentice clergy to his successive pastorates in Massachusetts and Maryland, and later they grew their own large congregations. Frank M. Reid III, a beneficiary of Bryant's model of ministry, wrote that he "pioneered an important reform movement that spawned a new generation of AME leaders." Bryant, he said, spurred "a paradigm shift in North American Christianity" not unlike what the Allens, Jarena Lee, Henry M. Turner, and others spearheaded in previous centuries. Bryant, the son of Harrison J. Bryant, an AME pastor and later a bishop, was born in Baltimore in 1943. A graduate of Morgan State College in 1965, Bryant volunteered for the Peace Corps and was assigned for two years in Liberia. Thereafter, he earned his divinity degree at the School of Theology at Boston University. As a licensed minister since the age of eighteen, known in Liberia as the Peace Corps preacher and assistant pastor at Eliza Ann Turner Memorial AME Church in Monrovia, and later pastor at Bethel AME Church in Fall River, Massachusetts, Bryant, when transferred in 1970 to St. Paul AME Church in Cambridge, Massachusetts, was already a skilled pulpiteer. Bryant's high-spirited preaching and social Gospel ministries grew St. Paul in 1971 from sixty-eight members to 902 members in 1975. Within the congregation was a noticeable pan-African following and high-achieving students from prestigious campuses across the Boston–Cambridge area. All responded to the energetic and emergent neo-Pentecostalism of this preacher still in his early thirties. Bryant shifted to Bethel AME Church in inner city Baltimore where his father formerly served. At his third pastorate Bryant's preaching and the deployment of drums, the electric guitar, and contemporary gospel music, as at St. Paul, spearheaded growth in the congregation from 600 members in 1975 to 7,000 in 1988, the year that he was elected a bishop.[150]

Bryant identified neo-Pentecostalism as a vehicle to recover a lost AME recognition of the power of the Holy Spirit. Though unaware that the

---

[150] C. Eric Lincoln and Lawrence H. Mamiya, *The Black Church in the African American Experience* (Durham, NC, Duke University Press, 1990), 385–386; Mankekolo Mahlangu-Ngcobo, *The Preaching of Bishop John Bryant* (Baltimore, MD, Victory Press, 1992), 26, 28, 73, 76–77, 95; Frank M. Reid III, *Up from Slavery: A Wake Up Call for the African Methodist Episcopal Church*, (n.p., Frank M. Reid Ministries, 2004), 12–13; John R. Bryant, "The Peace Corps: Gateway to a New Life," *AME Church Review*, Vol. 128, No. 421, January–March 2011, 11, 13.

1908 General Conference declared "God Our Father, Christ Our Redeemer, the Holy Ghost Our Comforter, Man Our Brother," Bryant unwittingly endorsed this revision of Daniel A. Payne's 1856 motto, which omitted the third person in the Trinity. Stress on the Father and the Son without a corresponding emphasis on the Holy Ghost, Bryant believed, discouraged a flourishing spirituality among AMEs. Traditionally, AMEs, though assertive and unashamed of ecstatic worship services, held these practices in tension with their promotion of higher education and a dignified demeanor for both the clergy and the laity. Bryant pondered these issues while matriculating in the seminary in Boston and at his first pastorate in Fall River. At the latter location he deepened his exploration of pneumatology, learned how the Church of God in Christ (COGIC) interpreted this doctrine, and consulted with a local COGIC bishop about glossolalia. What fueled membership growth at Bryant's Cambridge and Baltimore congregations was preaching that put the Holy Spirit at the center of the sermons and worship.[151]

Bryant's restoration initiative on AME spirituality did not mean an abandonment of the denominational ethos of Allenite activism and pan-Africanist ideology. African American Pentecostals, whose institutional histories commenced more than a century after the founding of African Methodism, were less identified with the long trajectory of transatlantic insurgency against slavery, segregation, and colonialism. Bryant, though committed to preaching about the baptism of the Holy Spirit, believed this doctrine also invigorated AME social holiness. Hence, at St. Paul in Cambridge he gained city approval to change the church's street name to Bishop Allen Drive. Furthermore, he established the Henry Buckner School that extended from pre-kindergarten to the fourth grade. Funds were raised to help to fight a drought in Africa's Sahel region, and the Artisha Jordan Pan African Missionary Unit was organized. St. Paul's unmistakable black identity was reinforced in a mural that Bryant commissioned for the sanctuary to depict everyday African Americans.[152]

[151] Lincoln and Mamiya, *The Black Church in the African American Experience*, 387–388; *Journal of the Twenty-Third Quadrennial Session of the General Conference of the African Methodist Episcopal Church* held in St. John AME Church, Norfolk, VA, May 4–21, 1908, 1; Lawrence H. Mamiya, "A Social History of the Bethel African Methodist Episcopal Church in Baltimore: The House of God and the Struggle for Freedom," in James P. Wind and James W. Lewis (eds.), *American Congregations: Portraits of Twelve Religious Communities*, Vol. 1 (Chicago, University of Chicago Press, 1994), 265–266.
[152] Lincoln and Mamiya, *The Black Church in the African American Experience*, 386–387; Mahlangu-Ngcobo, *The Preaching of Bishop John Bryant*, 77–79; Mamiya, "A Social History of the Bethel AME Church," 266.

Similarly, Bryant, at Bethel in Baltimore, inaugurated a prison ministry, the Bethel Christian School, and an Early Childhood Development Ministry. There was also a Spirit of Wisdom program to address illiteracy, an Unemployed Discount Coupon initiative that operated cooperatively with the American Federation of Labor-Congress of Industrial Organizations (AFL-CIO), and the establishment of a hosting site for Alcoholics Anonymous. Politically, the 1984 Jesse Jackson presidential campaign was celebrated as a milestone for African Americans, and opposition to apartheid in South Africa was pursued through agitation for divestment in corporations doing business in the white supremacist regime. When the popular COGIC singer and songwriter, Andre Crouch, did a concert in South Africa, Bethel members were discouraged from attending his Baltimore performance. Never did neo-Pentecostalism in the Bryant ministry attenuate generic AME activism.[153]

Bryant's pastorates became venues where aspiring clergy were exposed to neo-Pentecostalism and its deft blending with the Allenite activism that was deeply embedded in the AME heritage. In the congregations that Bryant mentees subsequently served, there was a palpable revitalization of spiritual and social consciousness. Some energized existing congregations while others established new churches and branded them with a neo-Pentecostal imprint. Over a dozen clergy and clergy aspirants pursuing seminary and other advanced degrees at universities in the Boston-Cambridge area imbibed neo-Pentecostal practice at St. Paul. Dozens more interacted with Bryant at Bethel in Baltimore where, according to one scholar, "the Holy Spirit has been emphasized in all of its activities, from prayer, Bible study, sermons, and music." At both St. Paul and Bethel neo-Pentecostalism showed the "potent combination of an enthusiastic black evangelical tradition and socially progressive lay ministries."[154]

Bryant's successor at Bethel, Frank Madison Reid III, while a student at Harvard Divinity School, absorbed neo-Pentecostal practice and brought it to his pastorates at Greater Bethel in Charlotte, North Carolina, and at Ward in Los Angeles. At the California church the "enthusiastic, spirit-filled worship and its activist community outreach" grew the membership from 500 to 5,000. This track record convinced Bishop John Hurst Adams to assign Reid to Bethel in Baltimore, a congregation where his father and namesake had also pastored and mentored John R. Bryant. Hence, Bethel's exuberant worship continued with Reid as pastor and so did the

---

[153] Mahlangu-Ngcobo, *The Preaching of Bishop John Bryant*, 96, 98–99, 103–104.
[154] Ibid., 107–111; Mamiya, "A Social History of the Bethel AME Church," 282.

congregation's social Gospel ministries. The Teen Prep Program, for example, involved teen fathers in addressing the high incidence of teen pregnancy in neighborhoods surrounding Bethel. Another focus on black men included a sixty-member Black Men's Chorus and a Manhood Rites of Initiation program. These and other initiatives after 1988 spurred a substantial increase in Bethel's male membership.[155]

Fred A. Lucas, Jr. was another student at Harvard Divinity School who connected with Bryant at St. Paul. After graduation, Bishop Richard Allen Hildebrand steered his ministerial career, raising him from a small Philadelphia parish to Agape AME Church in Buffalo, New York. Originally an independent congregation that began in 1969, the group affiliated with the AMEs in 1973. Hildebrand, who mobilized funds from the First Episcopal District to purchase in 1980 a stunning edifice, assigned Lucas to develop the congregation. Lucas's record of lively worship services, community engagement, and impressive membership growth persuaded Hildebrand to transfer him to the populous Bridge Street Church in Brooklyn. Lucas applied the same neo-Pentecostal template that worked for him in Buffalo to the historic Brooklyn parish. Among several programs he planned a Bridge Street Preparatory Academy for the church's Bedford-Stuyvesant community.[156]

Floyd H. Flake leveraged the neo-Pentecostalism that he observed at St. Paul in Cambridge into an ecclesiastical paradigm that other Bryant associates emulated. Flake, raised in Texas and nurtured at Wesley Chapel AME Church in Houston, graduated from Wilberforce University and attended Payne Theological Seminary for two years. He served two AME congregations in Ohio and a black Presbyterian church close to Lincoln University in Pennsylvania, where he was a dean in student activities. When a similar position in student affairs landed him at Boston University, he met John R. Bryant "whose support, encouragement, and model of worship opened my eyes to new ways of defining the ministry." Flake described the Cambridge church as "alive with vitality, vibrance, and community outreach that involved many of the students who gathered there from the surrounding colleges and universities." He credited "the power and spiritual dynamism of that ministry" with equipping him for an appointment in 1976 from Bishop Hildebrand to Allen AME Church in Jamaica, New York.[157]

[155] Mamiya, "A Social History of the Bethel AME Church," 279–280.
[156] Frank C. Cummings, John H. Dixon, Henry A. Wynn, Thelma Singleton-Scott, and Patricia A. P. Green (compilers), *The First Episcopal District's Historical Review of 200 Years of African Methodism*, (n.p., 1987), 295; *Our Press Time*, January 1, 2005.
[157] Floyd H. Flake, *The Way of the Bootstrapper: Nine Action Steps for Achieving Your Dreams* (New York, Harper San Francisco, 1999), 18–20.

Donald G. K. Ming, recently elected a bishop, had relocated the congregation of 1,400 and led them in building a new and modern edifice. Immediately, Flake put his imprint upon an already strong congregation by establishing in 1976 the Allen AME Housing Corporation, Neighborhood Preservation, and Development Division to spearhead a housing ministry in South Jamaica. Through this initiative 225 two family housing units were constructed and 300 units were rehabilitated. Moreover, in 1981 the Allen Senior Citizens Complex, a building that cost $11.2 million, accommodated 300 residents. The Allen Multi-Service Center was built, including a community health center and programs in women's and infant care, teen pregnancy, Head Start for preschool children, and other services. In 1982 the Allen Christian School was founded and housed in a $3.7 million facility with eighteen classrooms. In 1997 Flake led the congregation in building the Cathedral of Allen AME Church that seated 2,300 people. The original worship space, constructed during the Ming era, became the Shekinah Youth Chapel for youth ministry. In 2001 Allen Cathedral had 20,000 members. The strength of the church's spiritual and ministry engagement evident in Queens Borough spurred Flake's election to the United States House of Representatives from 1987 to 1997 from New York's Sixth Congressional District.[158]

NEW MODELS OF MINISTRY

As neo-Pentecostalism blended within African Methodism a revitalized spirituality and a reinvigorated social witness, these developments drew from a ministerial model that reflected recent advancements for women clergy. The emergence of heterosexual clergy couples went beyond what Dolly Desselle Adams outlined in her 1990 publication, *She in the Glass House: A Handbook for African Methodist Episcopal Church Wives and Widows*, as a primer for "a Christian lay woman who is married to a Christian minister. Though she advised women to "be your own best self," Adams enumerated several duties that were congruent with being "a layperson." She said "be careful to remember you are not the assistant pastor nor the pastor." Adams recognized, however, that this admonition did not apply to situations "where she too is an ordained minister." She observed "that

---

[158] Gregory G. M. Ingram (ed.), *Extraordinary History: Bicentennial Commemorative Journal, First Episcopal District, African Methodist Episcopal Church* (Ann Arbor, MI, University Lithoprinters, 2016), 165; Cummings et al., *The First Episcopal District's Historical Review*, 245–247; Flake, *Way of the Bootstrapper*, 20–21.

presents an entirely different set of circumstances." The neo-Pentecostal congregations associated with Bryant and several of his former colleagues, however, featured clergy couples that included female spouses who served as copastors, and this new phenomenon represented a paradigm shift that diversified the gender makeup of the AME ministry and broadened how women served in the denomination.[159]

Adams exemplified a traditional paradigm for clergy wives. Most spouses, in addition to parish and denominational activities, like earlier generations of AME women, extended their involvements to leadership and participation in various social service and political organizations. Adams, spouse of Bishop John Hurst Adams, while she served as the episcopal supervisor of missionary societies in her husband's district headquartered in Washington DC, became from 1982 to 1986 the president of the Links, an elite service organization. Her immediate predecessor was Julia Brogdon Purnell of the influential AME Brogdon-Hildebrand family, originally from South Carolina. One of Adams' successors was Attorney Patricia Russell McCloud, a committed supporter of theWMS, who served as president of the Links from 1994 to 1998. Her husband, E. Earl McCloud, was an Atlanta pastor who was elected a bishop in 2004.[160]

Since the1970s theWMS had been affiliated with the national Research and Status of Black Women that "focus[ed] on the progress and plight of black women" and was established as a WMS standing committee. In 1973, for example, AME women, a mixture of clergy and non-clergy spouses, comprised a WMS delegation that was the third largest group attending in Louisville, Kentucky a Research and Status of Black Women workshop. In 1985 President Wilhelmina Lawrence announced that the WMS received non-governmental organization status from the United Nations Committee for Non-Governmental Organizations. This "consultative" assignment from the UN's Economic and Social Council entitled the WMS to space at the United Nations Church Center in New York City to aid in "the implementation of the goals" of the international organization.[161]

---

[159] Dolly Desselle Adams, *She in the Glass House: A Handbook for African Methodist Episcopal Church Ministers' Wives and Widows* (Nashville, TN, AME Sunday School Union, 1990), 5, 9, 14.

[160] "Mrs. Dolly Desselle Adams," In *Directory/History Book of the Bishop' Wives Council: African Methodist Episcopal Church, 1955–1989*, 12; "Dolly Desselle Adams," Julia Brogdon Purnell," "Patricia Russell McCloud," www.linksinc.org/portfolio-item.

[161] Verdelle Jennings Johnston, *One Hundred Years of Service: A History of the Woman's Missionary Society of the African Methodist Episcopal Church*, (n.p., 1975), 94; Octavia Dandridge, *A History of the Women's Missionary Society of the African Methodist Episcopal Church, 1874–1987* (n.p., 1987), 20–21, 168.

These significant, but time-honored female ministries were juxtaposed to the expanded space that women in clergy couples established. John Bryant's wife, Cecelia, a native of Yonkers, New York, presented a model of the clergy couple after they met at Boston University. During her husband's pastorate at Bethel in Baltimore, she earned a divinity degree at the School of Religion at Howard University. She also started the Kingdom Women Broadcast Ministries, a daily radio program of Biblical teaching, and the Women's Resource and Development Center. The Flakes mirrored the ministerial partnership that the Bryants exhibited. M. Elaine Flake, a Memphis native, matriculated at Boston University, sang in the St. Paul, Cambridge, choir, and met her husband at the Bryant home. In 1982 she joined Flake in ministry as the educational director of the Allen Christian School. She also graduated from Union Theological Seminary in New York City and, like her husband, earned a D.Min. from United Theological Seminary. As copastor of Greater Allen Cathedral she was a cofounder of Allen's Women's Resource Center for victims of domestic violence and published in 2007 *God in Her Midst: Preaching Healing to Hurting Women.*[162]

Two bishops, Richard Allen Hildebrand and John Hurst Adams, both graduates of the School of Theology at Boston University and traditionalists in AME worship, facilitated the rise of neo-Pentecostalism. They extended to the Bryants, the Flakes, and Fred A. Lucas, whose wife, Barbara, became his ministerial partner at Bridge Street in Brooklyn, among the best of AME pastoral appointments. The Brownings and the Hammonds, however, all Bryant associates at St. Paul, Cambridge, launched ministries in start-up circumstances. Grainger Browning, Jr. entered the ministry in 1979 at St. Paul in Cambridge. After he received a divinity degree at Howard University in 1982, Bishop Adams appointed him in 1983 to Ebenezer AME Church in Washington DC. The venerable congregation, where the distinguished scholar, Charles H. Wesley, once had served, had dwindled to seventeen members in a deteriorating inner city neighborhood. With strong backing from Bishop Adams and his energetic neo-Pentecostal preaching, Browning relocated the congregation to a burgeoning black bourgeois community in Fort Washington in Prince George's County, Maryland. The church, which eventually grew to 8,000 members, funded an array of socially conscious ministries, including impressive expenditures for student scholarships. His spouse and copastor, Jo Ann Browning, though she started preaching in 1982 at Hemingway Memorial AME Church in Chapel Oaks, Maryland,

---

[162] Henderson, *The African Methodist Episcopal Church Registry Select*, 69–70; Flake, *Way of the Bootstrapper*, 21; www.allencathedral.org/allen-ame-flake.

spent nine months as an assistant minister at St. Paul in Cambridge. She conducted several spiritual retreats for women and published two books, one of which was *Our Savior, Our Sisters, Ourselves: Biblical Teachings and Reflections on Women's Relationships.*[163]

Ray A. and Gloria E. White- Hammond were another clergy couple that the Bryants influenced at St. Paul in Cambridge. Each trained as physicians who received MD degrees at Harvard and Tufts respectively. While practicing emergency medicine and pediatrics in the Boston area, both pursued ministerial studies at Harvard where Ray Hammond earned an MA in Christian and Medical Ethics and Gloria Hammond received an M.Div. In 1988 they founded Bethel AME Church in Jamaica Plain, Massachusetts. Along with their rapidly growing, socially conscious congregation, the Hammonds enlarged their ministries in both local and global settings. He cofounded and chaired the Ten Point Coalition that focused on high-risk youth and he directed Bethel Church's Generation Excel program. She became internationally influential in combating slavery and genocide in Sudan as the founder of the Massachusetts Coalition to Save Darfur and as head of the Million Voices for Darfur campaign. Starting in 2001, she traveled to Sudan at least nine times as an "abolitionist" to rescue 10,000 women and children victimized in the Sudan civil war.[164]

Despite tensions between neo-Pentecostalism and partisans of dignified AME worship, the surge in pursuits of the gifts of the Holy Spirit reinforced rather than distracted from traditional African Methodism. The recovery of AME spirituality that John R. Bryant emphasized and that energized social holiness ministries across broad spectrums of local and global outreach defined the content of AME neo-Pentecostalism. That its most visible proponents merged themselves into the AME ecclesia showed their compatibility and celebration of a proud and black denominational heritage. Just as John R. Bryant became a bishop in 1988, two mentees at St. Paul and Bethel followed him into the bishopric. Elected in 2000 and 2016 were Vashti Murphy McKenzie, a Bethel associate, and Frank Madison Reid III, who knew him at Bethel where his father served, and benefited from Bryant's tutelage at St. Paul.

Floyd H. Flake, who eschewed any episcopal aspirations, while retaining his pastorate in Jamaica, New York, also served as president of Wilberforce

[163] www.ebenezerame.org/about-us/meet-the-pastors/.
[164] www.bethelame.org/meet-pastor-ray/; "About the Cover-Reverend Gloria White Hammond, M.Div., M.D.: Modern Abolitionist and Angel for the Victims at Darfur," *AME Church Review*, Vol. 124, No. 410, April–June 2008, 4–5.

University from 2002 to 2008. He credited the influence of John Hurst Adams and Philip R. Cousin, both of whom became bishops, for steering him toward a position in AME higher education. During Flake's adolescence in Texas, he was impressed with Adams, then the president of Paul Quinn College in Waco, Texas. Flake found it "unbelievable that someone at that [young] age could be so intelligent and powerful." Similarly, on a trip to a youth conference at Kittrell College in North Carolina, Flake recalled "I met Philip R. Cousin, who was also in his twenties and president of that college." Observing them persuaded Flake that he would be "a preacher and college president." From the perspective of Bryant, Flake, and Browning, who became a Wilberforce trustee, neo-Pentecostalism was no separate phenomenon distinct from what they understood as generic African Methodism.[165]

Out of neo-Pentecostalism several AME congregations morphed into the megachurch movement. Fueled by popular media, contemporary gospel music, and spiritually intense preaching and worship, some expanded to serve followers in satellite locations. Those that were AME fitted the pattern of most other megachurches as shown in a 2006 Hartford Seminary survey. In "Eleven Myths About Mega Churches" one myth said, "mega churches are not deeply involved in social ministry." Actually, "considerable ministry is taking place at and through these churches." Another myth declared that "all mega churches" as "nondenominational." The reality was that "the vast majority belongs to some denomination." The growth of Reid Temple AME Church in Glen Dale, Maryland, and Union Bethel AME Church in Brandywine, Maryland, substantiated another Hartford Seminary finding that megachurches, far from reaching their peak, would continue to thrive and that "more are on the way."[166]

In 1989 Lee P. Washington, the pastor of Reid Temple in Washington DC, moved the 300-member congregation to suburban Lanham in Prince George's County, Maryland. In three years Washington's neo-Pentecostal preaching grew the church to 1,500 members and in 2004 moved them again to a 32-acre campus in nearby Glenn Dale, Maryland. Included on the grounds was the Reid Temple Christian Academy, educating youth from pre-K through the eighth grade. Continued membership growth, however, necessitated a second location, Reid Temple North in Silver Springs, Montgomery County, Maryland. Reid, with earned degrees in divinity and ministry from Howard University and formal training in business, has produced

---

[165] Flake, *The Way of the Bootstrapper*, 18.
[166] "Eleven Myths About Mega Churches," reprinted in *AME Church Review*, Vol. 122, No. 402, July–September 2008, 82–83.

publications on discipleship, stewardship, and development for corporately structured churches. Washington tutored Harry L. Seawright, who served on his ministerial staff at Reid Temple while still located in the District of Columbia and before he transferred to a similar position at Pilgrim AME Church in Washington DC. Seawright was then assigned to pastorates at Jessup, Maryland, and in Washington DC prior to an appointment to Union Bethel in Brandywine, Maryland. In 1991 he led the congregation in building a $1.6 million edifice that housed fifty different ministries. When two students in the before-and-after-school program relocated to Temple Hills, Maryland, Seawright extended the educational ministry to this municipality. Out of this initiative also came satellite worship. Now Union Bethel, Seawright said, "was operating as one church in two locations." Seawright, whose wife, the former Sherita Moon, joined him in the ordained ministry, was elected in 2016 to the episcopacy.[167]

The rise of neo-Pentecostalism hardly inverted AME identity as a mainline denomination. Alignment with majority white ecumenical organizations, characterized by what scholar David W. Wills described as "an enduring distance" and AME leadership in successive groups of national black denominations, brought them to the forefront of interdenominational affiliations and mainline visibility. The AME Church, an independent ecclesial body that emerged out of a transatlantic movement of evangelical renewal, was leavened with formative influences from the African religious background and African American enslavement. The institutional longevity of African Methodism, among the oldest of Protestant denominations founded in the United States, established it as a mainline religious organization of national and international standing.[168]

Together with the AME Zion and CME denominations, AMEs, beginning in 1881, participated in the global decennial meetings of Methodists held in both Europe and the Americas. Moreover, the AME Church was the only black religious body represented at the 1893 World's Parliament of Religions held in Chicago. The long affiliation of the denomination in the Federal Council of Churches, founded in 1908, its successor federation, National Council of Churches (NCC), established in 1950, and the World Council of Churches (WCC), launched in 1948, led to AME leadership in all three

[167] www.reidtemple.org/locations/glenn-dale/about;   ninthamechurch.org/bishop-seawright; Harry L. Seawright, *Don't Faint: Help for Hurting Pastors and Their Families* (Bloomington, IN, XLibris Corporation, 2012), 51, 71.
[168] David W. Wills, "An Enduring Distance: Black Americans and the Establishment," in William R. Hutchison (ed.), *Between the Times: The Travail of the Protestant Establishment in America, 1900–1960* (New York, Cambridge University Press, 1989), 168–171.

ecumenical bodies. Bishop Philip R. Cousin became the NCC president in 1983 and Bishop Vinton R. Anderson was elected president of the WCC in 1991. Despite this long trajectory of AME ecumenism, leaders of the denomination viewed it as no substitute for the coalescence of the black religious establishment to focus on the special plight of African Americans. Hence, Bishop Reverdy C. Ransom started the Fraternal Council of Negro Churches in 1934, on the heels of failed merger talks among the three large black Methodist denominations. Following in these precedents of black ecumenism, Bishop John Hurst Adams organized the Congress of National Black Churches in 1978.[169]

At the start of the twenty-first century African Methodism, beginning as a religious movement in the Atlantic World, increasingly realized a global posture as foundationally pan-Africanist, but proactively internationalist in its expansionist trajectory into Latin America and Asia. These ambitious externalities coexisted with internal developments focused on structural reformation, women's empowerment, and the multiple facets of sex and sexuality both in their affirming and problematic practices. These external and internal forces, inexorable in their AME impact, pushed African Methodism into modernizing discourses and transformations crucial to becoming a global church. An uneven maintenance of the denomination's emancipationist ethos in its encounter with racial, colonial, and sexual oppression tested its historic identity as an Atlantic World religious body born to battle slavery and to end the subjugation of vulnerable peoples.

---

[169] Mary R. Sawyer, *Black Ecumenism: Implementing the Demands of Justice* (Valley Forge, PA, Trinity Press International, 1994); also see Dennis C. Dickerson, "Black Ecumenism: Efforts to Establish a United Methodist Episcopal Church, 1918–1932," *Church History*, Vol. 52, December 1983, 479–491.

Epilogue

Though the genesis of African Methodism lay in the founding of the Free African Society in 1787, the denomination, organized in 1816, maintained an historical consciousness about its significance as a religious body for the black Atlantic. Since 1848, when Daniel A. Payne was elected as the first historiographer, AMEs have sustained this office as the official guardian of the church's institutional memory. Additionally, regular commemorations of the birth of Richard Allen, the marking of the chronological milestones of annual and General Conferences, and special ceremonies for succeeding cohorts of centennial congregations routinely highlighted the AME ecclesiastical calendar.

The longevity of African Methodism also meant that its emancipationist ethos influenced both affiliated families as well as those without formal membership in the denomination. This Allenite legacy, though often understood apart from its origins in Wesleyan salvific and social holiness, still exercised a powerful sway among AME descendants. On February 3, 2017, for example, David Khari Webber Chappelle, the comedian/actor familiarly known as Dave Chappelle, visited Allen University. In his widely publicized appearance, Chappelle, a comedic icon in both American and African American popular culture, connected to his family legacy in the AME Church. His great-grandfather, William David Chappelle, a South Carolina pastor, secretary-treasurer of the AME Sunday School Union, and a bishop elected in 1912, had a lifelong relationship with Allen University. He served as a trustee, twice as president, and chairman of the board during his tenure as South Carolina's bishop from 1916 to 1925. The Chappelle Auditorium was constructed during his long association with the school. Similarly, the bishop's son, William David Chappelle, Jr., MD, aside from his medical

546

practice in Columbia, South Carolina, taught chemistry and biology at Allen and helped to fund local civil rights litigation.[1]

Standing in the newly renovated Chappelle Auditorium, Dave Chappelle declared that other comedians, notwithstanding their greater fame, could not claim a great-grandfather whose contributions matched those of Bishop Chappelle. He recalled that his father, William David Chappelle III, a statistician, ended his employment with a company because it did business in apartheid-era South Africa. Similarly, Dave Chappelle rejected a $50 million Comedy Central deal in order to affirm his autonomy as a black performer. His father's opposition to South African apartheid and his mother's enthusiasm for the newly independent Ghana in 1957 and the leadership of Patrice Lumumba in the former Belgian Congo in 1960, intersected with an AME heritage grounded in a black Atlantic consciousness. Though Islam and Unitarianism claimed adherents among immediate relatives, Chappelle, through Allen University, discovered in his genealogy an emancipationist ethos that had been an formative influence in shaping his family heritage. Moreover, Chappelle, like Harold Cruse, the black cultural critic, believed that "the artists and intellectuals of each generation" had a responsibility to "create the new ideas and the new images of life and man" for the African American population. This template became for Chappelle, already an edgy, uncensored, and socially conscious comedian, a defining feature of an insurgent identity in which African Methodism was an integral component.[2]

According to the *Christian Recorder*, contemporaries of Chappelle also personified the denomination's liberationist heritage and deployed it as a signature vocational trait. The newspaper announced in 2018, for example, that Cornell William Brooks, an AME minister and attorney, who from 2014 to 2017 led the National Association for the Advancement of Colored People (NAACP) as president and chief executive officer, was named as a Professor of the Practice of Public Leadership and Social Justice at the John F. Kennedy School of Government at Harvard University. Additionally, the

---

[1] *Allen University Newsletter, The Buzz*, No. 2, Spring 2017; Richard R. Wright, Jr. (compiler), *Who's Who in the General Conference 1924* (Philadelphia, PA, AME Book Concern, 1924), 10; "Dave Chappelle at Allen University," www.youtube.com/watch?v=NN-KWdZB14; E. H. Beardsley, "William D. Chappelle, Jr., M.D.: A Physician and Churchman in South Carolina," *AME Church Review*, Vol. 117, No. 382, April–June 2001, 57, 59–61.

[2] George Kibala Bauer, "How Many of You Know Dave Chappelle's Mother Worked for Patrice Lumumba," May 19, 2015, https://africasacountry.com/2015/05/how-many-of-you-know-dave–chappelles-mother-worked-for-patrice-lumumba; https://me/i/wtcare-regrann-from-wtficare-dave-chappelles-mother-yvonne-seon-7257827; Harold Cruse, *The Crisis of the Negro Intellectual* (New York, William Morrow & Company, 1967), 96.

Recorder reported that Florida AMEs, whose district history was grounded in nineteenth-century Reconstruction politics and extensive office-holding aimed at protecting the freedom gains of newly emancipated African Americans, celebrated the Democratic primary election victory of Andrew Gillum for Governor of Florida. Gillum, the Mayor of Tallahassee and a member of the city's Bethel AME Church, reflected recent successes among other Florida AMEs either nominated or elected to influential offices at other levels of governments. Gillum, who narrowly lost a gubernatorial race to become the state's first black governor, shared political firsts with fellow AMEs Alcee Hastings of Fort Lauderdale and Valdez Demings of Orlando, two candidates for reelection to the United States House of Representatives. Gillum, running on a platform that backed federally funded Medicaid expansion that Florida's Republicans-led, legislature previously rejected, aligned this objective to the historic tenets of AME social holiness.[3]

At the same time the denomination's liberationist heritage stood alongside ongoing institutional abuses mainly related to elections for high office. Frank Madison Reid III, the son, grandson, and namesake of these two bishops, chronicled in his 2004 publication *Up from Slavery: A Wake Up Call for the African Methodist Episcopal Church* unsavory activities in the church's ecclesiastical operations. Reid, eventually elected a bishop himself and possessed of the same reform sensibilities as Charles Leander Hill, H. Ralph Jackson, and John Hurst Adams, believed "the AME Church had a revolutionary tradition" that had been diluted during the second half of the twentieth century. "From 1952 to the present," he said that "the AME Church has lost its global revolutionary influence." To recover its heritage of insurgency, he argued for a twelve-point program including a focus on a revamped ecclesiastical structure that would unleash "maximum growth in membership, new church creation, and community outreach." What Chappelle discovered in his family lineage and what Reid problematized through his lived institutional experiences showed the historic tensions between a palpable liberationist legacy embodied in Cornell William Brooks and Andrew Gillum and the distractions of institutional self-absorption that at times dulled the cutting edge of emancipationist insurgency that lay in the origin of African Methodism.[4]

[3] *Christian Recorder Breaking News*, August 29, 2018; Rivers and Brown, *Laborers in the Vineyard of the Lord*, 43–61, 101–121; https://andrewgillum.com/issue/healthcare/.

[4] Frank M. Reid, *Up from Slavery: A Wake Up Call for the African Methodist Episcopal Church*, (n.p., Frank M. Reid Ministries, 2004), 4, 7, 20–21.

At the start of the twenty-first century AMEs resolved that intramural celebrations of their historicity should transfer to public acknowledgments of African Methodism as a foundational force for inclusive freedom in American society and within the broader Atlantic world. Hence, a marathon campaign was inaugurated to place the image of Richard Allen on a United States postage stamp. Though this initiative seemed to be an innocent church and state entanglement, Allen's civic leadership boldly affirmed the high-powered descriptions that his biographers assigned to him. For Charles H. Wesley, Allen, a former slave, was an apostle of freedom "who was willing to demand his manhood rights in America," and for Richard S. Newman, he was a black founding father with as much civic standing as George Washington and Thomas Jefferson.[5]

The longevity and civic engagement of African Methodism were continuously recognized through successive interactions between bishops and other AME leaders with several United States presidents. In 1862 Bishop Payne met Abraham Lincoln to speak about slave emancipation in the District of Columbia. In a well-publicized White House meeting in 1963 President John F. Kennedy, in response to remarks from Bishop Eugene C. Hatcher, said that AMEs "are not only a force for spiritual enlightenment throughout this nation, but for years you have been well known as a force for better social conditions." Kennedy also noted that in the civil rights movement "headquarters for the battle in almost every community have always been a church and often an AME Church."[6]

President William Jefferson (Bill) Clinton, owing in part to associations with Bishop Frederick C. James, who presided in the president's native Arkansas, recognized the same civic consciousness among AMEs that Lincoln and Kennedy experienced. Hence, he selected Metropolitan AME Church in Washington DC as the site for both of his televised inaugural prayers services in 1993 and in 1997. Though the Washington National Cathedral, a part of the Episcopal Diocese of Washington DC, was the usual venue for this special service since the first inauguration of President Franklin D. Roosevelt in 1933, Clinton interrupted this practice and relocated the service to the church where abolitionist Frederick Douglass and the Little Rock Nine's Ernest Green worshipped, and where Clinton confidante Vernon Jordan and his second-term Secretary of Transportation, Rodney E. Slater, were members.[7]

[5] Wesley, *Richard Allen: Apostle of Freedom*, 1, 47; Newman, *Freedom's Prophet*, 21–26.
[6] Gregg, *The AME Church the Current Negro Revolt*, 48–49.
[7] *Episcopal News Service*, December 22, 2016.

Because of the historic presidential candidacy of Illinois Senator Barack Obama, he addressed the 2008 General Conference at which the bishops laid on hands and prayed for the Democratic Party nominee. On the night of Obama's landmark election as the first black President of the United States, before a crowd of 250,000 in Chicago's Grant Park, the resident AME prelate, Bishop Philip R. Cousin, launched the celebration with a prayer. Obama later appointed Bishop Vashti Murphy McKenzie to the President's Advisory Council of White House Faith-Based and Neighborhood Partnerships. All of these historic interactions validated AME initiatives to seek an explicit recognition of Richard Allen as a "black founding father" and to gain a derivative acknowledgment of the denomination that he established.[8]

Numerous ministers and members who envisaged a Richard Allen stamp believed that denominational celebrations did too little to elicit a public recognition of AME historicity. More than a religious milestone in black history, the AME heritage, they argued, rivaled in sacred and secular significance that of other white and black ecclesiastical bodies, and it reflected the large contributions of the denomination to national and international developments. To honor Richard Allen mirrored in reflective glory the roster of AME greats whom Reverend J. Curtis Foster, Jr., a California pastor, celebrated in his 1976 volume *The African Methodist Episcopal Church Makes Its Mark in America*. Foster noted that "as the Nation grew, the demand for leadership increased. With the organization of the African Methodist Episcopal Church in 1816, a rich and rewarding source of leadership became available." Foster cited an impressive roster of AMEs who, in service to church and state, advanced the freedom objectives of their denomination and their nation. They included Henry M. Turner, commissioned in 1863 as the first black military chaplain, followed by his "spiritual granddaughter," Alice Henderson, who in 1974 became the first female chaplain in the US Army. Hiram R. Revels, a black US Senator from Mississippi in 1870, William T. Vernon, whom President Theodore Roosevelt appointed as registrar of the Treasury in 1906, and Thomas Bradley, the first black mayor of Los Angeles in 1973 also qualified as making a mark in America for African Methodism.[9]

The civic engagement of the AME Church that Foster described was foundational to seeking a public recognition of Richard Allen and significant

[8] *Chicago Defender*, November 18, 2008.
[9] J. Curtis Foster, *The African Methodist Episcopal Church Makes Its Mark in America* (Nashville, TN, AME Sunday School Union, 1976), 57, 7–71, 81, 121–123, 151.

to the church's Atlantic reach. Bishop Vinton R. Anderson, a Bermuda native, on the eve of his retirement from the episcopacy in 2004, recommended denominational action on the Allen stamp and to affirm his national and pan-Africanist importance. He admired Allen for establishing Mother Bethel as "the foundation of black institutional life in the Western hemisphere and pointed to untold possibilities for the black diaspora." Moreover, Allen made the church "the seat of black constitutionalism where free Africans hammered out their bill of rights on the anvil of justice, liberation and reconciliation." He, like stamp advocate Bishop Frederick H. Talbot, a Guyana native and former ambassador from his country to the United Nations and to the United States, also validated the international influence of the AME founder in the black Atlantic. In his own book about Allen, Talbot recalled that "as a teenager" in colonized British Guiana, he read *The Life Experience and Gospel Labors of the Rt. Rev. Richard Allen* "and was fascinated by his journey." Allen's compelling biography was also a proxy for the denomination's global presence and unsung history that the stamp, with the imprimatur of the United States government, would make official.[10]

Anderson's stamp proposal drew support from Jacqueline DuPont Walker, the daughter of the Reverend King Solomon DuPont, a Tallahassee bus boycott leader. Walker, the director of the AME Social Action Department, together with a Mother Bethel member who served on the US Postal Commission, helped to operationize the AME initiative. Rather than emphasize Allen as a religious leader, AMEs were instructed to stress his patriotic participation in the Revolutionary War by driving a salt wagon for the Continental Army and for his humanitarian relief in Philadelphia for victims of the 1793 yellow fever epidemic.[11]

Walker, with her Social Action chair, Bishop Carolyn Tyler Guidry, formerly an administrative assistant to the martyred Mississippi NAACP leader, Medgar Evers, shifted the stamp campaign into high gear. A petition with 40,000 signatures, with support from several denominations, including the AME Zion and Christian Methodist Episcopal Churches, was delivered to the U. S. Postal Commission. After several years, the request for the Allen stamp was granted and unveiled at Mother Bethel on February 2, 2016. In the

[10]   Vinton R. Anderson, *An Ecumenical Hermeneutic: Rhyme, Reason, and Urgency* (n.p., 2010), 221; Frederick H. Talbot, *God's Fearless Prophet: The Story of Richard Allen* (Nashville, TN, AME Sunday School Union, 2007), 14; Official Announcement, Richard Allen Forever Stamp, ame-church.com/news/bishop-richard-allen-stamp.
[11]   Official Announcement, Richard Allen Forever Stamp, ame-church.com/news/bishop-rich-ard-allen-stamp.

edifice where Allen was entombed, the program included civil rights veteran Vernon Jordan as master of ceremonies, comments from four bishops, and a response from Richard Lawrence, an Atlanta physician and Richard Allen descendant. This wide and public dissemination of Allen's likeness spurred an increased awareness of African Methodism as a major, mainline denomination with crucial civic significance.[12]

Allen's emancipationist persona complemented his enduring reputation as "the 'Father of self-help among Negroes.'" Howard D. Gregg, a scholar of African Methodism who served as historiographer, described Allen's early involvement with the Free African Society, "the first Insurance Company in America to be owned and operated by Negroes." This Allenite tradition informed the ministry and leadership of Frank C. Cummings, a bishop elected in 1976 who presided in four jurisdictions within the United States. In a celebratory volume that he coedited, Cummings was described "as an astute businessman and a skilled administrator who has contributed much to the economic development of the black community and the African Methodist Episcopal Church. When he served as a general officer in charge of the Department of Church Extension, for example, Cummings "founded the Allen Travel Service" and "single-handedly turned it into a successful business enterprise." Similarly, as a bishop, in two of his episcopal assignments Cummings, who consciously personified Allen's self-help philosophy, built profit-making headquarters facilities. He and other AMEs in the clergy and laity interpreted Allen's emancipationist ethos as a warrant for black economic autonomy.[13]

African Methodism, though defined by its socially insurgent origins, possessed an historic Christian orthodoxy that was codified in the denomination's 25 *Articles of Religion*. They included "Faith in the Holy Trinity," belief in the "sufficiency of the Holy Scriptures for Salvation," observance of the sacraments of baptism and the Lord's Supper, and other doctrinal verities and practices. Though dissenters of AME background eschewed these foundational precepts, they affirmed the church's witness to its historic ethos of emancipationist ministry. The compelling influence of this AME

[12] Ibid.; *Christian Recorder Online*, February 5, 2016.
[13] Howard D. Gregg, *Richard Allen and Present Day Social Problems*, Nashville, TN, AME Sunday School Union, c. 1959/1960, 95; Frank C. Cummings, John H. Dixon, Thelma Singleton-Scott, and Patricia A. P. Green (compilers), *The First Episcopal District's Historical Review of 200 Years of African Methodism* (Philadelphia, PA, First Episcopal District, African Methodist Episcopal District, 1987), 75; Frank C. Cummings, *To Whom Much Is Given, Much Is Required* (Nashville, TN, AME Sunday School Union, 2008), 104–106.

Figure E.1 Richard Allen, on United States Postal Services stamp, 2016 (used with Permission)

legacy, notwithstanding doubts about the salvific basis of Allenite social holiness, transcended the disbelief of lapsed African Methodists.[14]

Lewis A. McGee, the son of an AME minister who had been a slave, was educated at Wilberforce University and Payne Theological Seminary. McGee appreciated the denomination's emphasis on higher education, itself a libratory activity, as complementary to black spirituality. During his service as a chaplain in both world wars and pastor to AME congregations mainly in the Midwest, McGee's encounters with the Unitarian Universalists showed him that he was actually a humanist and not tethered to orthodox Christian dogma. Though liberal religion won his allegiance, his social consciousness drew, at least in part, from his grounding in African Methodism.[15]

Other doctrinal dissenters similarly retained an allegiance to the liberationist legacy of their former denomination. Anthony B. Pinn, McGee's

---

[14] *The Doctrine and Discipline of the African Methodist Episcopal Church 2016, Bicentennial Edition* (Nashville, TN, AME Sunday School Union, 2017), 25–31.
[15] Mark Morrison-Reed, *Black Pioneers in a White Denomination* (Boston, MA, Beacon Press, 1980), 115–119.

intellectual heir, was born in Buffalo, New York, in 1964 and nurtured in Agape AME Church, previously a nondenominational congregation. Pastor Fred A. Lucas steered Pinn through his call to ministry and exposed him to a blend of energetic preaching and social Gospel outreach. At the same time, Pinn's ongoing doubts about Christian orthodoxy climaxed during his matriculation at Harvard University where he received the M.Div. and Ph. D. degrees. "God," he later declared, "created problems and then punished humans for falling prey to those problems." He asserted that "my new God was still loving and just, but without power to make anything happen." He rejected the traditional Christianity that African Methodism espoused in favor of exploring "how humanism and atheism developed in African American communities." Humanists and atheists, he concluded, believed in "cooperation and collaboration on a shared concern with the integrity of life," and these common values provided a connection to historic black Christianity.[16]

The praxis of self-help that Richard Allen pioneered, Pinn acknowledged, was realized in the wide-ranging social Gospel initiatives of Floyd H. Flake at Allen Church in Jamaica, New York, First Church in Los Angeles, Bethel Church in Baltimore, and Bridge Street Church in Brooklyn. These ministries, including the Brooklyn parish where Pinn himself was involved, affirmed the "integrity of life" that he articulated. Moreover, with coeditor, Stephen W. Angell, a biographer of Henry M. Turner, Pinn produced a voluminous chronicle entitled *Social Protest Thought in the African Methodist Episcopal Church, 1862–1939*. This detailed documentary record of AME perspectives on education, civil rights, theology, missions and emigration, and women's identities highlighted the denomination's "critical reflection" on these cutting edge issues and how they "informed the church's practice." The documents showed "the quality, depth and passionate character of the thought that AME Church members devoted to sorting out the implications of the social issues of the time, and to designing action agendas." Pinn's unorthodox views, while concurrent with the small but significant presence of "nones" within the African American population, precluded neither him nor McGee, who died in 1979, from recognizing the resilient ethos of emancipationist engagement embedded in the AME tradition.[17]

---

[16] Anthony B. Pinn, *Writing God's Obituary: How a Good Methodist Became a Better Atheist* (Amherst, NY, Prometheus Books, 2014), 21, 47, 67, 72–75, 159–160, 169, 196.

[17] Anthony B. Pinn, *The Black Church in the Post-Civil Rights Era* (Maryknoll, NY, Orbis Books, 2002), 77–79, 82; Stephen W. Angell and Anthony B. Pinn (eds.), *Social Protest Thought in the African Methodist Episcopal Church, 1862–1939* (Knoxville, University of Tennessee Press, 2000), xxiii, xxvii; *New York Times*, October 13, 1979; David Masci, "Black

Despite Pinn's recognition of the AME liberationist legacy, he joined a vocal minority of contemporaries in pressing African Methodism and other black religious bodies to apply their emancipationist ethos to issues of sexuality. "Few issues across denominations," he noted, "have been handled as badly as that of sexuality." He referred to "a ministry for gays and lesbians" at a AME church in Florida where the area bishop refused ordination to the otherwise qualified sponsor of the program because of that person's sexual orientation. Pinn said that "not all AME ministers agree with this position, but until the church hierarchy in this denomination and others like it change its attitude, the heterosexist perspective will continue and gay and lesbian ministers will need to hide their sexuality in order to pursue ordained ministry" and openly operate as members.[18]

Two landmark events also spotlighted how much the AME Church was still defined by an emancipationist ethos and by ongoing evangelism in new areas within the African diaspora. On June 17, 2015 white supremacist Dylann Roof invaded Emanuel AME Church in Charleston, South Carolina, and murdered the pastor and eight others at a Wednesday night Bible Study. The Emanuel Nine were Pastor Clementa Pinckney, Myra Thompson, DePayne Middleton Doctor, Cynthia Hurd, Sharonda Coleman-Singleton, Ethel Lance, Susie Jackson, Tywanza Sanders, and Daniel L. Simmons, Sr., formerly a pastor in the Columbia and Charleston areas. That this mass killing happened at the site of a church with a storied history of black liberationist contributions provided public instruction about Emanuel's emancipationist heritage and how this legacy reflected the core character of African Methodism.[19]

The insurgent legacy of Emanuel Church, anchored in the Vesey slave conspiracy of 1822, continued through Reconstruction pastor Richard H. Cain, who served in the state Senate and in the US House of Representatives. The martyred Clementa Pinckney became Emanuel's minister in 2010, having already been elected to the South Carolina House of Representatives in 1996 and to the state Senate in 2000. As a successor to Cain in both the pastorate and in politics, Pinckney viewed public office as an extension of his ministry to the broader black community. President Barack Obama, the eulogist at the funeral for Pastor Pinckney, observed that "his ministry,

Americans are more likely than overall public to be Christian, Protestant," *Pew Research Center*, April 23, 2018, www.pewresearch.org/...black-americans-are-more–likely-than-over all-public-to-be–christian-protestant.

[18] Pinn, *The Black Church in the Post-Civil Rights Era*, 105, 109.

[19] Herb Frazier, Bernard Edward Powers, Jr., and Marjory Wentworth, *We are Charleston; Tragedy and Triumph at Mother Emanuel* (Nashville, TN, W Publishing Group, 2016), 1–9.

which is intrinsic to the AME Church" showed that "our calling ... is not just within the walls of the congregation but ... the life of the community in which your congregation resides." AMEs, anxious that no one would over-look its emancipationist ethos, enacted at the 2016 General Conference a law that mandated an annual observance of the "Emanuel Martyrs and Sur-vivors" on the Sunday immediately following June 17, the date that Dylann Roof attacked, but did not extinguish the liberationist legacy of an historic congregation.[20]

The emancipationist ethos of African Methodism in the later twentieth and early twenty-first centuries interacted with the neo-Pentecostalism of an influential cadre of congregations that emphasized ecstatic worship and explored the gifts of the Holy Spirit. This religious phenomenon emerged as a lasting feature in AME worship and ritual. The prominent presence of the mega-member Empowerment Temple in Baltimore, which the colorful and controversial Jamal H. Bryant founded in 2000, for example, blended popular neo-Pentecostal worship with an energetic engagement with issues pertaining to urban poverty, police brutality toward African Americans, and political indifference to black concerns. Bryant, the son and grandson of AME bishops, merged into his ministries a consciousness about his denom-ination's tradition of Allenite activism. This impulse, at least in part, explained his announcement in 2015 to challenge incumbent US Represen-tative Elijah Cummings on the pretext of offering new generational leader-ship to their majority black Seventh Congressional District in Maryland. Though he later withdrew, Bryant, the high-profile media preacher, as a possible office seeker, gestured to his AME heritage of Wesleyan social holiness. Through this flirtation with running for Congress, like Richard H. Cain in the nineteenth century and Floyd H. Flake in the twentieth century, Bryant in the twenty-first century viewed involvement in the public square as an extension of pastoral ministry to the inner city community to which his congregation belonged. Additionally, in 2015 he eulogized Freddie Gray who died while in the custody of Baltimore police and the demonstra-tions during this same time period against the criminal justice system when no convictions occurred after the wrongful deaths of three other black men, Trayvon Martin, Michael Brown, and Eric Garner. In 2016 Bryant was one of

[20] Ibid., 68–72, 86–90, 182; Reginald F. Hildebrand, "Richard Harvey Cain, African Methodism, & the Gospel of Freedom in South Carolina," *AME Church Review*, Vol. 117, No. 381, January–March 2001, 39–45; *Combined Minutes of the Fiftieth Quadrennial Session of the General Conference of the African Methodist Episcopal Church*, Vol. I held in Philadelphia, PA, July 6–13, 2016 (Nashville, TN, AME Sunday School Union, 2016), 384–385.

six inductees selected for the International Civil Rights Walk of Fame, located in Atlanta near the Martin Luther King, Jr. Center for Nonviolent Social Change. Despite visible associations with leading nondenominational and evangelical preachers such as the apolitical T. D. Jakes of Dallas's Potter's House and a shift to serve as pastor of New Birth Missionary Baptist Church in Atlanta, Bryant, while he sustained his AME ministerial orders, continuously affirmed that his neo-Pentecostalism, inherited from his father, Bishop John R. Bryant, harmonized with the insurgent traits of African Methodism.[21]

The other facet of AME identity lay in an historic commitment of African Methodism as a religious body for the black Atlantic. In early December 2016, Bishop E. Anne Henning-Byfield led a delegation to Central America to Belize, the former British Honduras. This initiative lay with media figure Virginia Echols, a Detroit native and a licensed AME missionary who had lived in Belize since 1993. The AME Belize Connection meeting in Belize City aimed to extend African Methodism into this multiethnic population. This initiative yielded the establishment of the Kingdom Covenant congregation. Together with Henning-Byfield's energetic development of African Methodism in Brazil, and plans to revive the church in Cuba and introduce African Methodism to Panama, the Belize initiative continued a Pan Africanist push into areas that AMEs had previously neglected.[22]

Concomitant with continued AME expansion within the black Atlantic and to the Indian Ocean areas of India and Nepal was the launch of the denomination in the Pacific. An AME military chaplain, David R. Brown, while stationed at the Marine Corps base in Hawaii, founded the Hale Ho'onani Fellowship. With approval from Bishop Clement W. Fugh and the Southern California Annual Conference, an inaugural worship service was held on October 9, 2016 about 12 miles from Honolulu in Kailua, Hawaii. With a focus on a Hawaiian population of "multi-cultural Millenials," an expanded global identity stretched to include peoples of both African and Asian descent.[23]

Growth as a global church hardly spared the denomination from lagging in preparations in policies and practices for this unfolding institutional reality. At the 2017 biennial convention of the Connectional Lay Organization, for example, the president of the branch in the Dominican Republic Annual Conference, Dr. Isabel Medina Dishmey, complained that AMEs failed in comprehending "what it truly means to be a 'global' church."

---

[21] *Baltimore Sun*, September 14, 2015, September 22, 2015; atlanta.cbslocal.com/2016.../who-will-be-inducted-into-the-civil-rights-walk-of-fame.
[22] *Christian Recorder*, February 5, 2018, July 2, 2018.   [23] *Christian Recorder*, May 22, 2017.

Throughout the proceedings none of the reports were available in Spanish. In response to some delegates who insisted that she speak English, Dishmey went to the conference floor to condemn this discriminatory treatment. Embarrassed attendees from the United States, some of whom spoke Spanish, and others from outside the United States, endorsed Dishmey's protest. The editor of the *Christian Recorder*, John Thomas III, a fluent Spanish speaker, in "New Eyes for the Global Church" denounced the "xenophobic, American-centric attitude" of the denomination and admonished ministers and members that "we still have a long way to go before" African Methodists actually recognized the global reach of their church.[24]

African Methodism, notwithstanding roots and identity tied to the African diaspora, extended deeper among related peoples in the Americas and in the Asian subcontinent. The denomination had 2.5 million members in 2016, a fraction of the multiple millions that the church targeted on five continents in North and South America, Africa, Europe, and Asia. Nonetheless, AMEs remained committed to their historic mission as a protector of these same peoples and their descendants who had launched the religious body over two centuries earlier. Because Richard Allen and Daniel Coker established African Methodism as an institutional aegis for the black Atlantic and because succeeding generations of diasporic AMEs such as Henry M. Turner and Charlotte Manye Maxeke sustained that tradition, this transnational vision became firmly implanted into the DNA of the denomination. In the makeup of the AME ministry and membership, a pan-African demography showed the transatlantic reach of African Methodism.

A mixed record that included a weakening of the church's liberationist thrust, however, sprang from tensions between the demands of institutional maintenance and expansion and a risky mandate to spur insurgency against hegemonic structures and practices. Examples of transformative social holiness pushed by such rank-and-file preachers and parishioners such as the nineteenth- and twentieth-century abolitionists J. J. G. Bias and Gloria W. Hammond and nineteenth- and twentieth century civil rights advocates Ezekiel Gillespie and King Solomon DuPont coexisted with counterparts whose institutional activities led to debates at the 1856 General Conference about the membership of black slaveholders and accommodations to South Africa's apartheid government after the Nationalist Party victory in 1948. Nonetheless, an emancipationist ethos stubbornly persisted as a primary driver of AME theology and praxis and energized its transatlantic reach.

---

[24] *Christian Recorder*, August 28, 2017.

This same emancipationist ethos, palpable at times in rhetorical gestures, and at other times in concrete acts of insurgency against racially oppressive structures was viewed with skepticism both from commentators with formal AME affiliations and others with claims to past or familial connections. They wondered whether the church's historic opposition to slavery, segregation, and colonialism included condemnations of male dominance in the denominational hierarchy, policies that favored heteronormality both in ministry and membership, and token indigenization of church leadership in the Caribbean and Africa. The transatlantic identity of African Methodism and its corresponding commitment to fight racial oppression, despite their uneven and inconsistent implementation, had driven denominational thought and action since its origins in the eighteenth century. AMEs, at times imperfectly, sustained an unbroken memory of their insurgent beginnings and their mission to be an ecclesiastical organization for the African diaspora and in the twenty-first century to formerly colonized peoples on five continents.

APPENDIX

The Bishops of the African Methodist Episcopal Church, 1816–2018

	Bishop	Elected & Consecrated	Birthplace
1.	Richard Allen	1816	Pennsylvania
2.	Morris Brown	1828	South Carolina
3.	Edward Waters	1836	Maryland
4.	William Paul Quinn	1844	Caribbean?
5.	Willis Nazrey	1852	Virginia
	Presided simultaneously until 1864 as the Bishop of the British Methodist Episcopal (BME) Church		
6.	Daniel A. Payne	1852	South Carolina
7.	Alexander W. Wayman	1864	Maryland
8.	Jabaz P. Campbell	1864	Delaware
9.	James A. Shorter	1868	District of Columbia
10.	Thomas Myers Decatur Ward	1868	Pennsylvania
11.	John M. Brown	1868	Delaware
12.	Henry M. Turner	1880	South Carolina
13.	William F. Dickerson	1880	New Jersey
14.	Richard H. Cain	1880	West Virginia
15.	Richard R. Disney	1884	Maryland
	Presided from 1872 to 1884 as the Bishop of the BME Church		
16.	Wesley J. Gaines	1888	Georgia
17.	Benjamin W. Arnett	1888	Pennsylvania
18.	Benjamin T. Tanner	1888	Pennsylvania
19.	Abram Grant	1888	Florida
20.	Benjamin F. Lee	1892	New Jersey
21.	Moses B. Salter	1892	South Carolina

(*cont.*)

	Bishop	Elected & Consecrated	Birthplace
22.	James A. Handy	1892	Maryland
23.	William B. Derrick	1896	Antigua
24.	Josiah H. Armstrong	1896	Pennsylvania
25.	James C. Embry	1896	Indiana
26.	Evans Tyree	1900	Tennessee
27.	Morris M. Moore	1900	Florida
28.	Charles S. Smith	1900	Canada
29.	Cornelius T. Shaffer	1900	Ohio
30.	Levi J. Coppin	1900	Maryland
31.	Edward W. Lampton	1908	Kentucky
32.	Henry B. Parks	1908	Georgia
33.	Joseph S. Flipper	1908	Georgia
34.	J. Albert Johnson	1908	Canada
35.	William H. Heard	1908	Georgia
36.	John Hurst	1912	Haiti
37.	William D. Chappelle, Sr.	1912	South Carolina
38.	Joshua H. Jones, Sr.	1912	South Carolina
39.	James M. Conner	1912	Mississippi
40.	William W. Beckett	1916	South Carolina
41.	Isaac N. Ross	1916	Tennessee
42.	William D. Johnson, Sr.	1920	Georgia
43.	Archibald J. Carey, Sr.	1920	Georgia
44.	William S. Brooks	1920	Maryland
45.	William T. Vernon	1920	Missouri
46.	William A. Fountain, Sr.	1920	Georgia
47.	Abraham L. Gaines	1924	Georgia
48.	Reverdy C. Ransom	1924	Ohio
49.	John A. Gregg	1924	Kansas
50.	Robert A. Grant	1928	Florida
51.	Sherman L. Greene, Sr.	1928	Mississippi
52.	George B. Young	1928	Texas
53.	Monroe H. Davis	1928	South Carolina
54.	Noah W. Williams	1932	Illinois
55.	David H. Sims	1932	Alabama
56.	Henry Y. Tookes	1932	Florida
57.	Richard R. Wright, Jr.	1936	Georgia
58.	Edward J. Howard	1936	Missouri
59.	Decatur Ward Nichols	1940	South Carolina

(*cont.*)

	Bishop	Elected & Consecrated	Birthplace
60.	George E. Curry	1940	South Carolina
61.	Frank Madison Reid, Sr.	1940	Tennessee
62.	Alexander J. Allen, Sr.	1940	Georgia
63.	George W. Baber	1944	Ohio
64.	John H. Clayborn	1944	Arkansas
65.	Lawrence H. Hemmingway	1948	South Carolina
66.	Dougal O. B. Walker	1948	St. Vincent
67.	Joseph Gomez	1948	Antigua
68.	Isaiah H. Bonner	1948	Alabama
69.	William R. Wilkes, Sr.	1948	Georgia
70.	Carey A. Gibbs	1948	Florida
71.	Howard T. Primm	1952	Tennessee
72.	Frederick D. Jordan	1952	Georgia
73.	Eugene C. Hatcher	1952	Alabama
74.	Francis H. Gow	1956	South Africa
75.	Ernest L. Hickman	1956	Tennessee
76.	Samuel R. Higgins	1956	South Carolina
77.	William F. Ball, Sr.	1956	South Carolina
78.	Odie L. Sherman	1956	Texas
79.	John D. Bright, Sr.	1960	Georgia
80.	George N. Collins	1960	Florida
81.	G. Wayman Blakely, Sr.	1964	Arkansas
82.	Harrison J. Bryant	1964	South Carolina
83.	Harold I. Bearden	1964	Georgia
84.	Hubert N. Robinson	1964	Ohio
85.	G. Dewey Robinson	1968	South Carolina
86.	Henry W. Murph	1968	South Carolina
87.	John Hurst Adams	1972	South Carolina
88.	Richard Allen Hildebrand	1972	South Carolina
89.	Samuel S. Morris, Jr.	1972	Virginia
90.	Frederick H. Talbot	1972	Guyana
91.	H. Hartford Brookins	1972	Mississippi
92.	Vinton R. Anderson	1972	Bermuda
93.	Frederick C. James	1972	South Carolina
94.	Frank Madison Reid, Jr.	1972	Kentucky
95.	Frank C. Cummings	1976	Alabama
96.	Philip R. Cousin, Sr.	1976	Pennsylvania
97.	Donal G. K. Ming	1976	Bermuda

(cont.)

	Bishop	Elected & Consecrated	Birthplace
98.	Rembert E. Stokes	1976	Ohio
99.	Cornelius E. Thomas	1976	Alabama
100.	J. Haskell Mayo	1980	Ohio
101.	John E. Hunter	1980	Ohio
102.	Harold B. Senatle	1984	South Africa
103.	Robert L. Pruitt	1984	South Carolina
104.	Henry A. Belin, Jr.	1984	Louisiana
105.	Vernon R. Byrd, Sr.	1984	South Carolina
106.	John R. Bryant	1988	Maryland
107.	Robert Thomas, Jr.	1988	Illinois
108.	Richard Allen Chappelle, Sr.	1988	Florida
109.	McKinley Young	1992	Georgia
110.	Robert V. Webster	1992	Arkansas
111.	Zedekiah L. Grady	1992	Florida
112.	C. Garnett Henning, Sr.	1992	Tennessee
113.	William P. DeVeaux	1996	Arizona
114.	Theodore L. Kirkland	1996	Alabama
115.	Adam J. Richardson, Jr.	1996	Florida
116.	Richard F. Norris	2000	Georgia
117.	Vashti Murphy McKenzie	2000	Maryland
118.	Gregory G.M. Ingram	2000	Michigan
119.	Preston W. Williams II	2000	Georgia
120.	Wilfred J. Messiah	2004	South Africa
121.	Paul J. M. Kawimbe	2004	Zambia
122.	Carolyn Tyler Guidry	2004	Mississippi
123.	James L. Davis	2004	Alabama
124.	Daniel R. Daniels	2004	Liberia
125.	Samuel L. Green, Sr.	2004	Florida
126.	Sarah F. Davis	2004	Texas
127.	E. Earl McCloud, Jr.	2004	Alabama
128.	Jeffrey N. Leath	2008	New York
129.	Julius H. McAllister, Sr.	2008	South Carolina
130.	John F. White	2008	Florida
131.	Clement W. Fugh	2012	Tennessee
132.	Reginald T. Jackson	2012	Delaware
133.	Harry L. Seawright	2016	South Carolina
134.	Michael L. Mitchell	2016	Florida
135.	E. Anne Henning Byfield	2016	Tennessee

(*cont.*)

Bishop	Elected & Consecrated	Birthplace
136. Ronnie E. Brailsford, Sr.	2016	South Carolina
137. Stafford J.N. Wicker	2016	Louisiana
138 Frank Madison Reid III	2016	Illinois

Source: THE DOCTRINE AND DISCIPLINE OF THE AFRICAN METHODIST EPISCOPAL CHURCH 2016, THE BICENTENNIAL EDITION, (Nashville, AME Sunday School Union, 2017), 3–6.

Bibliography

PRIMARY SOURCES

Manuscript Collections

Easter M. Gordon Collection, Institute for Historical Research, University of the Western Cape, Bellville, Cape Province, Republic of South Africa.
Sadie Tanner Mossell Alexander Papers, University Archives & Records Center, University of Pennsylvania, Philadelphia, Pennsylvania.

Unpublished Manuscripts

Harris, Janette H. "Charles Harris Wesley, Educator and Historian, 1891–1947," Ph.D. dissertation, Howard University, 1975.
Wesley, Charles H. "Stranger in One's Own Land: Autobiography of Charles H. Wesley," unpublished MS (compiled and edited by Constance Porter Uzelac, Fort Lauderdale, FL, 2011).
Wills, David W. "Aspects of Social Thought in the African Methodist Episcopal Church," Ph.D. dissertation, Harvard University, 1975.
Winford, Brandon K. L. "'The Battle for Freedom Begins Every Morning': John Hervey Wheeler, Civil Rights, and New South Prosperity," Ph.D. dissertation, University of North Carolina, Chapel Hill, 2014.

African Methodist Episcopal General and Annual Conference Minutes

General Conference Minutes

Minutes of the General and Annual Conferences of the African Methodist Episcopal Church, Comprising Four Districts for A.D. 1836–1840. Brooklyn, NY, George Hogarth, 1840.

Eighth General Conference of the African M. E. Church held in the City of Philadelphia, May 1, 1848, and continued in session twenty-one days. Pittsburgh, PA, *Christian Herald* Office, 1848.

Minutes of the Tenth General Conference of the African Methodist Episcopal Church held in the City of New York, from May 3–20, 1852. Inclusive. Philadelphia, PA, Wm. S. Young, Printer, 1852.

Twelfth General Conference of the African M. E. Church held in Pittsburgh, PA, May 7, 1860. Philadelphia, PA, Wm. S. Young, Printer, 1860.

Thirteenth General Conference of the African M. E. Church held in Philadelphia, PA, May 2, 1864. Philadelphia, PA, William S. Young, Printer, 1864.

Fifteenth Quadrennial Session of the General Conference of the African Methodist Episcopal Church. Place of Session, Nashville, TN, May 6, 1872. Philadelphia, PA, Publishing Department of the African Methodist Episcopal Church, 1872.

Sixteenth Session and the Fifteenth Quadrennial Session of the General Conference of the African Methodist Episcopal Church. Place of Session, Atlanta, Georgia, from May 1–18, 1876. Philadelphia, PA, Publishing Department of the African Methodist Episcopal Church, 1876.

Journal of the 17th Session and the 16th Quadrennial Session of the General Conference of the African Methodist Episcopal Church in the United States held at St. Louis, Missouri. May 3–25, 1880. Xenia, OH, Torchlight Printing Company, 1882.

Journal of the 18th Session and the 17th Quadrennial Session of the General Conference of the African Methodist Episcopal Church held in Bethel Church, Baltimore, MD, May 5–26, 1884. Philadelphia, PA, Rev. James C. Embry, General Business Manager, 1884.

Journal of the 19th Session and the 18th Quadrennial Session of the General Conference of the African Methodist Episcopal Church in the World held in Bethel Church, Indianapolis, Ind., May 7, 1888. (Philadelphia, PA, Rev. James C. Embry, 1888.

Journal of the 20th Session and the 19th Quadrennial Session of the General Conference of the African Methodist Episcopal Church in the World held in Bethel Church, Philadelphia, Pennsylvania, May 2, 1892. Philadelphia, PA, Rev. James C. Embry, General Business Manager, 1892.

Journal of the Twentieth Quadrennial Session of the General Conference of the African Methodist Episcopal Church held in St. Stephen AME Church, Wilmington, NC, May 4–22, 1896. Philadelphia, PA, AME Publishing House, 1896.

Journal of the Twenty-First Quadrennial Session of the General Conference of the African M. E. Church, held in the Auditorium, Columbus, Ohio, May 7–25, 1900. Philadelphia, PA, AME Book Concern, 1900.

Journal of the Twenty-Second Quadrennial Session of the General Conference of the African M. E. Church held in the Quinn Chapel AME Church,

Chicago, Illinois. May 2–27, 1904. Nashville, TN, AME Sunday School Union, 1905.

Journal of the Twenty-Third Quadrennial Session of the General Conference of the African Methodist Episcopal Church held in St. John AME Church, Norfolk, Virginia, May 4–21, 1908. Nashville, TN, AME Sunday School Union, 1908.

Journal of the Twenty-Fourth Quadrennial Session of the General Conference of the African Methodist Episcopal Church held in Allen Chapel, African M. E. Church, Kansas City, Missouri, May 6–23, 1912. Nashville, TN, AME Sunday School Union, 1912.

Journal of the Twenty-Fifth Quadrennial Session of the General Conference of the African Methodist Episcopal Church, Philadelphia, Pennsylvania, May 3–23, 1916. Nashville, TN, AME Sunday School Union, 1916.

Journal of the Twenty-Sixth Quadrennial Session of the General Conference of the African Methodist Episcopal Church held in St. Louis, Missouri, May 3–18, 1920. Nashville, TN, AME Sunday School Union, 1922.

Journal of the Twenty-Seventh Quadrennial Session of the General Conference of the African Methodist Episcopal Church held in Louisville, Kentucky, May 5–21, 1924. Philadelphia, PA, AME Book Concern, 1924.

Journal of the Twenty-Eighth Quadrennial Session, General Conference of the AME Church, Chicago, Illinois, May 27–23, 1928. Nashville, TN, AME Sunday School Union, 1928.

Journal of the Twenty-Ninth Quadrennial Session, General Conference of the AME Church, Cleveland, Ohio, May 2–16, 1932. Philadelphia, PA, AME Book Concern, 1932.

Journal of the Thirtieth Quadrennial Session of the African Methodist Episcopal Church held in The Rockland Palace, New York City, May 6–18, 1936. Philadelphia, PA, AME Book Concern, 1936.

Journal of Proceedings of the Thirty-First Quadrennial Session of the General Conference of the African Methodist Episcopal Church held in Ebenezer AME Church, Detroit, Michigan, May 1–15, 1940. Philadelphia, PA, AME Book Concern, 1940.

Journal of Proceedings of the Thirty-Second Quadrennial Session of the General Conference of the African Methodist Episcopal Church held in The Arena, Philadelphia, Pennsylvania, May 3–14, 1944. n.p., Dr. George T. Sims, Chief Secretary, AME General Conference, 1944.

Combined Minutes of the General Conference, African Methodist Episcopal Church, 1948 (Kansas City, Kansas) – 1952 (Chicago, Illinois) – 1956 (Miami, Florida). Nashville, TN, AME Sunday School Union, 1956.

Official Minutes of the Thirty-Sixth Session of the General Conference, AME Church, Shrine Auditorium, Los Angeles, California, May 1960. Nashville, TN, AME Sunday School Union, 1960.

Official Minutes of the Thirty-Seventh Session of the General Conference, AME Church, held at The Cincinnati Gardens, Cincinnati, Ohio, Beginning May 6, 1964. n.p., n.d.

Official Minutes of the Thirty-Eighth Session of the General Conference, AME Church, The Spectrum, Philadelphia, Pennsylvania, May 1–14, 1968. n.p., n.d.

The Minutes of the General Conference of the Thirty-Ninth Quadrennium of the African Methodist Episcopal Church held in Dallas, Texas, June 21–July 3, 1972. Nashville, TN, AME Sunday School Union, 1972.

The Combined Minutes of the Fortieth Session of the General Conference of the African Methodist Episcopal Church, held in Atlanta, Georgia, June 16–26, 1976. Nashville, TN, AME Sunday School Union, 1976.

The Combined Minutes of the Forty-First Session of the General Conference of the African Methodist Episcopal Church held in New Orleans, Louisiana, June 18–28, 1980. Nashville, TN, AME Sunday School Union, 1980.

The Combined Minutes of the 42nd Quadrennial Session, General Conference, African Methodist Episcopal Church held in Kansas City, Missouri, July 7–15, 1984. Nashville, TN, AME Sunday School Union, 1984.

The Combined Minutes of the 43rd Quadrennial Session, General Conference, African Methodist Episcopal Church held in Fort Worth, Texas, Tarrant County Convention Center, July 6–14, 1988. Nashville, TN, AME Sunday School Union, 1988.

The Combined Minutes, of the 44th Quadrennial Session, General Conference, African Methodist Episcopal Church held in Orange County Convention/ Civic Center, Orlando, Florida, July 8–15, 1992. Nashville, TN, AME Sunday School Union, 1992.

The Combined Minutes, of the 45th Quadrennial Session, General Conference, African Methodist Episcopal Church held in Commonwealth Convention Center, Louisville, Kentucky, June 26–July 3, 1996. Nashville, TN, AME Sunday School Union, 1996.

Minutes of the Forty-Sixth Quadrennial Session, General Conference, African Methodist Episcopal Church, Cincinnati, Ohio, July 5–11, 2000. Nashville, TN, AME Sunday School Union, 2000.

Minutes (of the) Forty-Seventh Quadrennial Session of the General Conference, African Methodist Episcopal Church, The Indianapolis Convention Center & RCA DOME, Indianapolis, Indiana, June 30–July 7, 2004. Nashville, TN, AME Sunday School Union, 2004.

Combined Minutes, 48th Quadrennial Session of the General Conference, African Methodist Episcopal Church, St. Louis, Missouri, July 4–11, 2008. Nashville, TN, AME Sunday School Union, 2008.

Combined Minutes, 49th Quadrennial Session of the General Conference, African Methodist Episcopal Church, Gaylord Opryland Resort and Convention Center, Nashville, Tennessee, June 27–July 4, 2012, Vols. 1 & 2. Nashville, TN, AME Sunday School Union, 2012.

Combined Minutes, 50th Quadrennial Session of the General Conference, African Methodist Episcopal Church, Philadelphia, Pennsylvania, July 6–13, 2016, Vols. 1 & 2. Nashville, TN, AME Sunday School Union, 2018.

Episcopal Addresses

Episcopal Address by Bishop W. Sampson Brooks to the Bishops, General Officers and Members of the Twenty-Ninth Quadrennial Session of the General Conference of the African Methodist Episcopal Church, 1932, Cleveland, Ohio, May 2–16, 1932. Philadelphia, PA, AME Book Concern, 1932.

The Episcopal Address Presented by Bishop William Alfred Fountain, Sr., A.M., D.D., LL.D. to the Thirtieth General Conference of the African Methodist Episcopal Church, New York City, N.Y., May 6, 1936. Philadelphia, PA, AME Book Concern, 1936.

The Episcopal Address Presented by Bishop John Andrew Gregg, A.M., D.D., LL.D. to the Thirty-First Quadrennial Session of the General Conference of the African Methodist Episcopal Church at Detroit, Michigan, May 1940. n.p., 1940.

The Episcopal Address Presented by Bishop M. H. Davis to the General Conference of the African Methodist Episcopal Church at Philadelphia, Pennsylvania, May 1944. Nashville, AME Sunday School Union, 1944.

The Episcopal Address to the Thirty-Fifth Quadrennial Session of the General Conference of the African Methodist Episcopal Church convening in Miami, Florida, May 2–16, 1956, Prepared by Bishop Alexander Joseph Allen. n.p., 1956.

The Episcopal Address to the Thirty-Sixth Quadrennial Session of the General Conference of the African Methodist Episcopal Church meeting in Los Angeles, California, May 6–14, 1960, Prepared by Bishop Joseph Gomez. Nashville, TN, AME Sunday School Union, 1960.

The Episcopal Address of the Bishops of the African Methodist Episcopal Church to the General Conference by (Bishop) Ernest Lawrence Hickman, meeting in Dallas Civic Center Auditorium, Dallas, Texas, June 21–July 2, 1972. n.p., 1972.

The Episcopal Address to the Fortieth-Quadrennial Session of the General Conference of the African Methodist Episcopal Church, Atlanta, Georgia, June 16–27, 1976, Prepared by Bishop Harold Irvin Bearden. n.p., Wamber Press, 1976.

The Episcopal Address to the 42nd Session of the General Conference 1984, Kansas City Municipal Auditorium and Convention Center, Kansas City, Missouri, July 8–15, 1984, Bishop Richard Allen Hildebrand. n.p., 1984.

[The] Episcopal Address, 44th Session of the General Conference of the African Methodist Episcopal Church, July 8, 1992, Orlando, Florida, Bishop Vinton R. Anderson. n.p., 1992.

[The] Episcopal Address to the 45th Session of the General Conference of the
  African Methodist Episcopal Church, Commonwealth Convention
  Center, Louisville, Kentucky, June 26–July 3, 1996. Bishop Frank Curtis
  Cummings. Nashville, AME Sunday School Union, 1996.
[The] Episcopal Address, 47th Quadrennial Session of the General Confer-
  ence [of the] African Methodist Episcopal Church, The Indiana Con-
  vention Center, Indianapolis, Indiana, June 30–July 7, 2004, Presented
  by Bishop Vernon Randolph Byrd. Nashville, AME Sunday School
  Union, 2004.

Annual Conference Minutes

*Proceedings of the Seventeenth (Ohio) Annual Conference of the African M. E.
  Church* held in the City of Zanesville, October 16, 1847, and continued in
  Session eleven days, 1847. Cincinnati, OH, *Herald of Truth*, 1847.
Minutes of the Baltimore Annual Conference of the African M. E. Church held
  in Baltimore, From April 21–30, 1849. Pittsburgh, PA, *Christian Herald*,
  1849.
*Minutes of the Twentieth Ohio Annual Conference of the African Methodist
  E. Church* held at Bethel Church, Columbus, Ohio, August 1, 1850.
  Pittsburgh, PA, Christian Herald, 1850.
*Minutes of the Thirty-Fourth Annual Conference of the African Methodist
  E. Church for the Baltimore District*, April 18, 1851. Baltimore, MD, Sher-
  wood & Co., 1851.
*Minutes of the Philadelphia District Annual Conference of the African Meth-
  odist Episcopal Church, 1851*. Philadelphia, PA, William S. Young, 1851.
*Minutes of the New England Annual Conference of the African Methodist
  Episcopal Church* held in the City of New Bedford, Massachusetts from
  June 10–21, 1852. New Bedford, MA, Press of Benjamin Lindsey, 1852.
*Minutes of the Annual Conference for the New York District of the African
  Methodist Episcopal Church* held in Vine Street Church, Buffalo. New
  York, William S. Dorr, 1852.
Minutes of the Ohio Annual Conference of the African M. E. Church held in
  Cincinnati, Ohio from August 6–18, 1852. Pittsburgh, PA, *Christian
  Herald*, [A. R. Green], 1852.
*Minutes of the Annual Conference for the New York District, African Methodist
  Epis. Church*, held in Bethel Church, Second Street, New York, 1853. New
  York, D. Mitchell, 1853.
Minutes of the Philadelphia District Annual Conference, 1853. [African Meth-
  odist Episcopal Church]. n.p., n.d.
*Journal of Proceedings of the Fifteenth Annual Conference of the African
  Methodist Episcopal Church for the District of Indiana* held at Indianapo-
  lis, September 6, 1854. Indianapolis, IN, Rawson Vaile, 1854.

Minutes of the Fourth Annual Conference of the New England District of the African Methodist Episcopal Church held in Plymouth Hall, Boston, From June 21–30, 1856. Providence, MA, Knowles, Anthony, & Co., 1856.

Journal of Proceedings of the Third Annual Conference of the African M. E. Church for the District of Missouri, 1857. Louisville, MO Rev. John M. Brown, 1857.

Minutes of the Baltimore Conference of the African M. E. Church held in Washington City, D. C. From April 17–May 2, 1862. Bull & Tuttle, Clipper, 1862.

Minutes of the Thirty-Second Session of the Ohio Annual Conference of the African M. E. Church held in Zanesville, Ohio, From April 15–23, 1862. n. p., 1862.

Minutes of the Thirty-Fourth Session of the Ohio Annual Conference of the African M. E. Church held in Pittsburgh, Pennsylvania, From April 16–27, 1864. Philadelphia, PA, Samuel Loag, Book and Fancy Job Printer, 1864.

Minutes of the Forty-Eighth Session of the Philadelphia District Annual Conference of the African Methodist Episcopal Church. Philadelphia, PA, James B. Rodgers, Printer, 1864.

Proceedings of the Forty-Eighth Session of the Baltimore Conference of the African Methodist Episcopal Church, held at Bethel Church, Baltimore, Md, April 13, 1865. Baltimore, MD, James Young, 1865.

Minutes of the Thirty-Fifth Session of the Ohio Annual Conference of the African M. E. Church held in Delaware, Ohio From April 15–24, 1865. Pittsburgh, PA, Publishing Committee: Samuel Watts, G. H. Graham and E. D. Davis, 1865.

Minutes of the Ninth Session of the Arkansas Annual Conference of the African Methodist Episcopal Church held in Little Rock, Arkansas, November 9-13, 1876. Little Rock, AR, W. H. Windsor, 1876.

Minutes of the Eleventh Session of the Arkansas Annual Conference of the African Methodist Episcopal Church held in Bethel Church, Little Rock, Arkansas, March 10, 1879. Atlanta, GA, Jas. P. Harrison & Co., Publishers, 1879.

Minutes (of the) Twelfth Session [of the] Pittsburgh Conference of the AME Church held at Erie, PA, Sept. 11–17, 1879. Pittsburgh, PA, Hagan & Co. Book and Job Printers, 1879.

Proceedings of the Fourth Annual Session of the Kansas Conference of the African Methodist Episcopal Church held at Leavenworth, Kansas, Commencing Wednesday, October 1 and Closing October 7, 1879. Kansas City, MO, Press of Chas. Baker & Co., 1879.

Minutes of the Fifty-First Session of the Ohio Annual Conference of the African Methodist Episcopal Church held in Asbury AME Church, Middleport, Ohio, from September 29–October 6, 1881. Columbus, OH, J. F. Earhart, Book and Job Printer, 1881.

Minutes of the Fifty-Second Session of the Ohio Annual Conference of the African Methodist Episcopal Church held in Quinn Chapel, Chillicothe, From September 20–25, 1882. Zanesville, OH, Visitor Power Press Print, 1882.

Minutes of the Fifty-Third Session of the Ohio Annual Conference of the African Methodist Episcopal Church held in Wayman Chapel, Hillsboro, From September 19–24, 1883. Zanesville, OH, Visitor Power Press Print, 1883.

Minutes of the Sixty-Ninth Session of the Baltimore Annual Conference of the African Methodist Episcopal Church in the United States of America, held in Mt. Moriah AME Church, Annapolis, MD, April 28 to May 5, 1886. Baltimore, MD, Hoffman & Co., 1886.

Minutes of the First and Second Session of the Ontario Annual Conference of the African Methodist Episcopal Church convened at John Street AME Church, Hamilton, Ontario June 30, 1885 [&] King St. AME Church, Amherstburg, July 1, 1886, complied by Rev. J. A. Johnson. Hamilton, Ontario, H. A. Martin, Fine Book and Job Printer, 1886.

Minutes of the Twenty-Seventh Session of the Pittsburg[h] Annual Conference of the African Methodist Episcopal Church held in Wayman's Chapel AME Church, Wheeling, West Virginia, October 3–7, 1894. Altoona, PA, H. & W. H. Slep, 1894.

Minutes of the Twenty-Eighth Session of the Pittsburg[h] Conference of the African Methodist Episcopal Church held at Bethel AME Church, Wilkes Barre, Penna., October 10–14, 1895. Altoona, PA, H. & W. Slep, 1895.

Minutes of the Sixty-Sixth Session of the Ohio Annual Conference of the African Methodist Episcopal Church held in Wayman Chapel AME Church, Hillsboro, Ohio, September 10–16, 1896. Xenia, OH, Chew (Pub.?), 1896.

Minutes of the Twenty-Ninth Session of the Pittsburgh Annual Conference of the African Methodist Episcopal Church held in St. Paul AME Church, Washington, PA., October 8–14, 1896. n.p., Publishing Committee: David F. Caliman, William H. Palmer & Price A. Scott, 1896.

Minutes of the Thirteenth Session of the Nova Scotia Annual Conference of the African Methodist Episcopal Church held in Highlands AME Church, Amherst, N. S., From August 25–29, 1897. Saint John, NB, Geo. A. Knodell, Printer, 1897.

Minutes of the Thirtieth Session of the Pittsburg[h] Annual Conference held in Euclid Ave. AME Church, Pittsburg[h], Pennsylvania, October 7–13, 1897. n.p., Publishing Committee: D. F. Caliman, Price A. Scott & R. H. Bumry, 1897.

Minutes of the Twenty-Sixth Session of the North Georgia Annual Conference of [the] AME Church held in St. Paul AME Church, Madison, GA., November 9–15, 1898, n.p., n.d.

Minutes of the Macon [GA] Seventeenth Annual Session of the African Methodist Episcopal Church held in Brown's AME Church, Dublin, Ga., Nov. 16–22, 1898. Atlanta, GA, Franklin Printing and Publishing Co., 1898.

Minutes of Proceedings of the Thirty-Third Session of the Georgia Annual Conference of the African Methodist Episcopal Church held in St. Andrew's Chapel AME Church, Darien, GA., Dec. 14–19, 1898. Atlanta, GA, Franklin Publishing Co., 1898.

Minutes of the Thirty-Second Session [of the] Pittsburg[h] Annual Conference [of the] African Methodist Episcopal Church, Brownsville, PA., October 12–17, 1899. n.p., Publishing Committee: P. A. Scott, S. P. West, & T. J. Askew, 1899.

Minutes of the Sixth Session of the Demerara Annual Conference of the AME Church held at Bethel Church, Anna Catherina, Demerara, December 7–9, 1899. Barbados, C. P. Cole, Printer, 1900.

A Minute Book of the Orangia District Conference of the African Methodist Episcopal Church held in Bloemfontein, September 3, 1902. Bloemfontein, F. Wienand & Co., 1903.

Journal of Proceedings of the Thirty-Eighth Session of the Pittsburgh Annual Conference of the African Methodist Episcopal Church held in Bethel AME Church, Wilkes Barre, PA, October 4–9, 1905. n.p., Publishing Committee: C. J. Powell, D.S. Bentley, C. M. Tanner, 1905.

Journal of Proceedings of the Forty-Second Session of the Pittsburgh Annual Conference of the African Methodist Episcopal Church held in Brown [Chapel] AME Church, North Side, Pittsburg[h], October 6–11 inclusive, 1909. n.p., Publishing Committee: C. J. Powell, T. J. Askew, P. A. Scott, W. B. Anderson, D. S. Bentley, & W. S. Lowry, 1909.

Minutes of the 29th Session of the Bermuda Annual Conference of the African Methodist Episcopal Church held at Hamilton, Bermuda, from July 29-August 5, 1912. Hamilton, Bermuda, S. S. Todding-Mid-Ocean Press, 1912.

Minutes of the Thirtieth Session of the Bermuda Annual Conference of the African Methodist Episcopal Church held at Richard Allen AME Church, St. George, July 24–28, 1913. n.p., 1913.

Journal of Proceedings of the Joint Session of the Cape and O.F.S. Annual Conferences of the African Methodist Episcopal Church held at Kimberly, on October 21–26, 1913. Cape Town, Citadel Press, 1913.

Journal of Proceedings of the Eighty-Third Session of the Ohio Annual Conference of the African M. E. Church held in St. Paul AME Church, Zanesville, Ohio, September 24–28, 1913. Nashville, TN, AME Sunday School Union, 1913.

Journal of Proceedings of the Forty-Sixth Session of the Pittsburgh Annual Conference of the African Methodist Episcopal Church held in St. Paul AME Church, Uniontown, PA, October 8–12, 1913. Nashville, TN, AME Sunday School Union, 1913.

Minutes of the Thirty-First Session of the Bermuda Annual Conference of the African Methodist Episcopal Church held at Somerset in Allen Temple, July 23–27, 1914. Hamilton, Bermuda, S.S. Todding-Mid-Ocean Press, 1914.

Minutes of the Forty-Seventh Session of the Pittsburgh Annual Conference (of the) African Methodist Episcopal Church held in Bethel AME Church, Williamsport, PA, October 7–11, 1914. Philadelphia, PA, AME Book Concern, 1914.

Minutes of the Thirty-First Session of the Bermuda Annual Conference held at St. Paul's AME Church, Hamilton, July 20–24, 1916. Hamilton, Bermuda, S. S. Todding-Mid Ocean Press, 1916.

Minutes of the Thirty-First Annual AME [Sunday] [School] Convention and Teacher's Institute of the Bermuda Annual Conference held at Warwick AME Church Mission (East) on September 7, 1916. Hamilton, Bermuda, S.S. Todding-Mid-Ocean Press, 1916.

Minutes of the Thirty-Fourth Session of the Bermuda Annual Conference, 1917. Hamilton, Bermuda, S. S. Todding-Mid-Ocean Press, 1917.

Journal of Proceedings and Yearbook of the Fifty-First Annual Session of the Georgia Annual Conference, African Methodist Episcopal Church held in St. Paul AME Church, Brunswick, GA., November 22–26, 1916. Nashville, TN, AME Sunday School Union, 1917.

Journal of Proceedings of the Forty-Fourth Annual Session of the North Georgia Annual Conference of the African Methodist Episcopal Church held in Turner Chapel AME Church, Marietta, GA., October 25–29, 1916. Nashville, TN, AME Sunday School Union, 1917.

Journal of Proceedings of the Thirty-Fifth Annual Session of the Macon Georgia Conference of the African Methodist Episcopal Church held in Wesley Chapel AME Church, Milledgeville, Georgia, November 15–19, 1916. Nashville, TN, AME Sunday School Union, 1917.

Journal of Proceedings of the Joint Session of the Transvaal, Natal, Cape & Orange Free State Annual Conferences of the African Methodist Episcopal Church held at Bloemfontein, (O.F.S.), November 29–December 3, 1916. Cape Town, Citadel Press, 1917.

Minutes of the Thirty-Fourth Session of the Bermuda Annual Conference [of the] African Methodist Episcopal Church held in St. John's AME Church, Bailey's Bay, July 19–23, 1917. Hamilton, Bermuda, S. S. Toddings-Mid-Ocean Press, 1917.

Journal of Proceedings of the Eighty-Seventh Annual Session of the Ohio Annual Conference of the African Methodist Episcopal Church held in St. Paul AME Church, Columbus, Ohio, From September 12–16, 1917. Philadelphia, PA, AME Book Concern, 1917.

Minutes (of the) Thirty-Sixth Session of the North Ohio Annual Conference of the African Methodist Episcopal Church held in North St. AME Church Springfield, Ohio, September 19–23, 1917. Philadelphia, PA, AME Book Concern, 1917.

Journal of Proceedings [of the] Fiftieth Session [of the] Pittsburgh Conference, African Methodist Episcopal Church held in Brown Chapel AME Church,

Pittsburgh, PA., Wednesday, October 3–7, 1917. Philadelphia, PA, AME Book Concern, 1917.

Minutes of the Thirty-Fifth Session of the Bermuda Annual Conference of the African Methodist Episcopal Church held at Allen Temple, Somerset, August 8–11, 1918. Hamilton, Bermuda, S. S. Todding-Mid-Ocean Press, 1918.

Journal of Proceedings of the Emergency Executive Committee of the Fifty-First Annual Session of the Pittsburg[h] Conference of the African Methodist Episcopal Church held in St. Paul AME Church, Washington, PA., Weds., Thurs., October 30–31, 1918. Philadelphia, PA, AME Book Concern, 1918.

Journal of Proceedings of the Thirty-Sixth Annual Session of the Macon Georgia Annual Conference of the African Methodist Episcopal held in St. Peter's AME Church, Fort Valley, GA., November 15–18, 1917. Nashville, TN, AME Sunday School Union, 1918.

Journal of Proceedings of the One Hundred and Second Session of the Philadelphia Annual Conference of the African Methodist Episcopal Church held in Bethel AME Church, Wilmington, DE., From May 16–19, 1918. n. p., 1918.

Journal of Proceedings of the North Georgia Annual Conference of the African Methodist Episcopal Church held in Bethel AME Church, Dalton, GA., Beginning November 7, 1918. n.p., 1918.

Minutes of the Thirty-Sixth Session of the Bermuda Annual Conference of the African Methodist Episcopal Church held at St. Paul's, Hamilton, Bermuda, Beginning Thursday, July 17, 1919. Hamilton, Bermuda, S. S. Todding-Mid-Ocean Press, 1919.

Minutes of the Thirty-Eighth Annual Session of the North Ohio Conference of the African Methodist Episcopal Church held in Payne's Chapel AME Church, Hamilton, Ohio, October 8–12, 1919. Philadelphia, PA, AME Book Concern, 1919.

Journal of Proceedings of the Fifty-Second Annual Conference of the Pittsburg [h] Conference of the African Methodist Episcopal Church held in Washington, Pa., October 22, 1919. Philadelphia, PA, AME Book Concern, 1919.

Journal of Proceedings of the One Hundred and Fourth Session of the Philadelphia Annual Conference of the African Methodist Episcopal Church held in Bethel AME Church, Steelton, PA., June 9–15, 1920. n.p., 1920.

Minutes of the Thirty-Seventh Session of the Bermuda Annual Conference of the African Methodist Episcopal held at Richard Allen AME Church, St. Georges, Beginning Thursday, October 7–9. n.p., 1920.

Journal of Proceedings of the One Hundred and Fifth Session of the Philadelphia Annual Conference of the African Methodist (Episcopal) Church held in Mt. Olive AME Church, Philadelphia, PA., May 18–22, 1921. Philadelphia, PA, AME Book Concern, 1921.

Journal of Proceedings of the Fifty-Fourth Annual Session of the Georgia Annual Conference, African Methodist Episcopal Church held at Bethel

AME Church, Statesboro, Georgia, November 23–27, 1921. Nashville, TN, AME Sunday School Union, 1922.

Minutes of the Thirty-Sixth Session of the Michigan Annual Conference of the African Methodist Episcopal Church held in Quinn Chapel AME Church, Flint, Michigan, September 13–17, 1922. Philadelphia, PA, AME Book Concern, 1922.

Journal of Proceedings of the First Session of the Pennsylvania Annual Conference, Third Episcopal District, AME Church held in Bethel AME Church, Wilkes Barre, Pa., October 25–29, 1922. n.p., 1922.

Journal of Proceedings of the Fifty-First Annual Session of the Pittsburgh Conference of the African Methodist Episcopal Church held in Park Place AME Church, Homestead, Pa., November 1–5, 1922. Philadelphia, PA, AME Book Concern, 1922.

Journal of Proceedings of the Fifty-Seventh Session of the Pittsburgh Annual Conference, Third Episcopal District held in Wayman Chapel AME Church, New Brighton, Pa., November 5–9, 1924. New Castle, PA, Expert Printing Company, 1924.

Journal of Proceedings of the Fifty-Fifth Session of the Georgia Annual Conference of the African Methodist Episcopal Church held at St. Paul AME Church, Brunswick, Georgia, November 22–26, 1922. Nashville, TN, AME Sunday School Union, 1923?.

Journal of Proceedings of the Fifty-Sixth Annual Session of the Pittsburgh Conference of the African Methodist Episcopal Church held in Bethel AME Church, Pittsburgh, Pa., November 7–11, 1923. Philadelphia, PA, AME Book Concern, 1923.

Minutes of the Thirty-Eighth Session of the Michigan Annual Conference of the African Methodist Episcopal held in First Community AME Church, Grand Rapids, Mich., September 10–14, 1924. Nashville, TN, AME Sunday School Union, 1924.

Journal of Proceedings of the Eighty-Sixth Annual Session of the Indiana Conference, African Methodist Episcopal Church held in Bethel AME Church, Indianapolis, Indiana, September 24–28, 1924. n.p., 1924.

Proceedings of the Third Annual Session of the South Ohio Conference of the African Methodist Episcopal Church held in Quinn Chapel AME Church, Wilmington, Ohio, October 22–26, 1924. n.p., Publication Committee: O. W. Childers, J. B. Harewood, M. M. Lewis, n.d.

Journal of Proceedings of the Third Session of the Pennsylvania Annual Conference, Third Episcopal District, AME Church held in St. Paul AME Church, McKeesport, PA, October 29–November 2, 1924. n.p., 1924.

Minutes of the Sixtieth Session of the California Annual Conference of the African Methodist Episcopal Church held in San Francisco, California, September 23–27, 1925. Nashville, TN, AME Sunday School Union, 1925.

Journal of Proceedings of the Eighty-Seventh Annual Session of the Indiana Conference of the African Methodist Episcopal Church held in Allen Chapel AME Church, Terre Haute, Indiana, September 23–27, 1925. Nashville, TN, AME Sunday School Union, 1925.

Journal of Proceedings of the One Hundred and Tenth Annual Session of the Philadelphia Annual Conference of the African Methodist Episcopal Church held in Mt. Pisgah AME Church, Philadelphia, PA. May 12–16, 1926. n.p., 1926.

Minutes of the Bermuda Annual Conference, Forty-Third Session, African Methodist Episcopal Church, Allen Temple AME Church, Somerset, Bermuda, Friday, May 21, 1926. n.p., 1926.

Official Minutes of the Pennsylvania Annual Conference, Third Episcopal District, AME Church, St. Paul AME Church, Uniontown, Penna., November 3-7, 1926. New Castle, PA, Expert Printing Co., 1926.

Official Minutes of the Pittsburgh Annual Conference, Third Episcopal District, AME Church, [held] in Bethel AME Church, Meadville, Penna., November 10–14, 1926. New Castle, PA, Expert Printing Company, 1926.

Minutes of the Bermuda Annual Conference, Forty-Fourth Session, African Methodist Episcopal Church, St. Paul's AME Church, Hamilton, Bermuda, Friday, April 22, 1927, n.p., 1927.

Journal of Proceedings of the Forty-Fifth Annual Session of the Chicago Conference of the African Methodist Episcopal Church held in Ebenezer AME Church, Evanston, Illinois, September 21-25, 1927. Nashville, TN, AME Sunday School Union, 1927.

Minutes [of the] 97th Annual Session [of the] Ohio Annual Conference [of the] African Methodist Episcopal Church held in North Street AME Church, Springfield, Ohio, October 12–16, 1927, n.p., 1932.

Minutes of the Bermuda Annual Conference, Forty-Fifth Session, African Methodist Episcopal Church, Richard Allen AME Church, St. Georges, Bermuda, Thursday, August 16, 1928. n.p., 1928.

Minutes of the Sixth Annual Session of the Nebraska Conference of the Fifth Episcopal District of the African Methodist Episcopal Church held at Bethel AME Church, Leavenworth, Kansas, September 12–16, 1928. Nashville, TN, AME Sunday School Union, 1928.

Official Minutes (of) the Seventh Annual Session of the Pennsylvania Annual Conference of the African Methodist Episcopal Church [held in] Calvary AME Church, Braddock, Pa., October 10–14, 1928. Philadelphia, PA, AME Book Concern, 1928.

Official Minutes of the Pittsburgh Annual Conference, Third Episcopal District, African Methodist Episcopal Church [held in] Bethel AME Church, Wilkes Barre, Pa., October 2–6, 1929. n.p., 1929.

Minutes of the Bermuda Annual Conference, Forty-Sixth Session, African Methodist Episcopal Church, Bethel AME Church, Shelly Bay, Bermuda, Thursday, December 18, 1929. n.p., 1929.

Minutes of the One Hundred and Eighth Session of the New York Annual Conference, African Methodist Episcopal Church held at St. John's AME Church, New York City, May 28–June 1, 1930. n.p., 1930.

Official Minutes of the Pittsburgh Annual Conference, Third Episcopal District, African Methodist Episcopal Church, [held] at Trinity AME Church, Pittsburgh, Pa., September 24–28, 1930. n.p., 1930.

Minutes of the Forty-Ninth Annual Session of the North Ohio Conference of the African Methodist Episcopal Church of the Third Episcopal District held in Quinn Chapel AME Church, Steubenville, Ohio, October 1–5, 1930, n.p., 1930.

Journal of Proceedings of the Forty-Eighth Annual Session of the Macon Georgia Conference of the African Methodist Episcopal Church held in Allen Temple AME Church, Cordele, Georgia, November 19–24, 1930. Nashville, TN, AME Sunday School Union, 1930.

Journal of the Eighty-First Session of the New England Annual Conference of the African Methodist Episcopal Church held in the Loring Street AME Church, Springfield, Mass., June 23–26, 1932. n.p., 1932.

Minutes of the Bermuda Annual Conference, Fiftieth Session, African Methodist Episcopal Church, Bethel AME Church, Shelley Bay, Bermuda, April 1933. n.p., 1933.

Official Journal of the New York Annual Conference of the African Methodist Episcopal Church. Minutes of the One Hundred and Eleventh Session 1933 (Abridged) and of the One Hundred and Twelfth Session held at Macedonia AME Church, Flushing, Long Island, N.Y., May 24–27, 1934. Philadelphia, PA, AME Book Concern, n.d.

Proceedings of the Sixty-Seventh Session of the Georgia Annual Conference of the African Methodist Episcopal Church held in Gaines AME Church, Waycross, Georgia, November 28–December 2, 1934, n.p., 1934.

Minutes of the Fifteenth Annual Session of the Northwestern Conference of the African Methodist Episcopal Church held in St. Paul AME Church, Des Moines, Iowa, September 10–15, 1935. n.p., 1935.

Journal and Yearbook of the Fifty-Third Annual Session of the Chicago Conference of the African Methodist Episcopal Church held in Quinn Chapel AME Church, September 18–22, 1935, n.p., 1935.

Proceedings of the Sixty-Eighth and Sixty-Ninth Sessions of the Georgia Annual Conferences of the African Methodist Episcopal Church, 1935 and 1936. Philadelphia, PA, AME Book Concern, 1936.

Official Journal of the New York Annual Conference of the African Methodist Episcopal Church being Minutes of the One Hundred and Fifteenth

Session, May 19-23, 1937 held in The Israel AME Church, Albany, New York. n.p., n.d.

Journal of the Fifty-First Annual Session of the Michigan Conference of the African Methodist Episcopal Church held in Turner Chapel AME Church, Fort Wayne, Indiana, September 1–5, 1937. Nashville, TN, AME Sunday School Union, 1937.

Minutes of the Fifty-Sixth Annual Session of the North Ohio Conference of the African Methodist Episcopal Church held in Bethel AME Church, Akron, Ohio, September 29–October 3, 1937. Nashville, TN, AME Sunday School Union, 1937.

Minutes of the Eighteenth Annual Session of the Northwestern Conference of the African Methodist Episcopal Church held in Bethel AME Church, Davenport, Iowa, September 7–11, 1938. n.p., 1938.

Journal of the Fifty-Fourth Annual Session of the Michigan Conference [of the] African Methodist Episcopal Church held in Quinn Chapel AME church, Flint, Michigan, August 1940. n.p., 1940.

Official Minutes of the Seventy-Third Annual Session of the Pittsburgh Annual Conference of the African Methodist Episcopal Church of the Third Episcopal District held in Bethel AME Church, Wilkes Barre, PA., September 24–29, 1940. n.p., n.d.

Journal of the Fifty-Fifth Annual Session of the Michigan Conference (of the) African Methodist Episcopal Church held in Community AME Church, Jackson, Michigan, August 27–31, 1941. n.p., 1941.

Journal of Proceedings of the Seventieth Session of the New Jersey Annual Conference of the African Methodist Episcopal Church held in Mt. Zion AME Church, Plainfield, New Jersey, May 1942. n.p., 1942.

Official Journal and Minutes of the Baltimore Annual Conference of the African Methodist Episcopal Church held in Trinity AME Church, Baltimore, Maryland, May 5–9, 1943. Nashville, TN, AME Sunday School Union, 1943.

Journal of the Fifty-Seventh Annual Session of the Michigan Conference (of the) African Methodist Episcopal Church held in St. Stephen AME Church, Detroit, Michigan, August 24, 1943. n.p., 1943.

Minutes of the Twenty-Third Annual Session of the Northwestern Conference of the African Methodist Episcopal Church held in Payne Chapel AME Church, Waterloo, Iowa, September 8–13, 1943. n.p., 1943.

Official Minutes of the Seventy-Sixth Annual Session of the Pittsburgh Annual Conference of the African Methodist Episcopal Church of the Third Episcopal District held in St. James AME Church, Pittsburgh, PA., September 21–26, 1943. Nashville, TN, AME Sunday School Union, 1943.

Official Journal of the Sixty-Second Annual Session of the Macon Georgia Conference of the African Methodist Episcopal Church held in Stewart

Chapel AME Church, Macon, Georgia, November 24–28, 1943. n.p., 1943.

Journal and Yearbook of the Sixty-Second Annual Session of the Chicago Annual Conference of the African Methodist Episcopal Church held at Arnett AME Church, Chicago, Illinois, September 12–17, 1944. Nashville, TN, AME Sunday School Union, 1944.

Minutes of the Seventy-Seventh Annual Session of the Pittsburgh Annual Conference [of the] African Methodist Episcopal Church of the Third Episcopal District held in Brown Chapel AME Church, Pittsburgh, PA., September 19–24, 1944. n.p., 1944.

Minutes of the Sixty-Third Annual Session of the North Ohio Conference [of the] African Methodist Episcopal Church held in Community AME Church, Cleveland, Ohio, September 26–October 1, 1944. Cleveland, OH, Babby's Printing Co., 1944.

Official Minutes of the 114th Session of the Indiana Conference of the African Methodist Episcopal Church held in Allen Temple AME Church, Marion, Indiana, September 24–28, 1952. n.p., n.d.

Minutes of the Conferences of the Thirteenth Episcopal District (African Methodist Episcopal Church), 1954, The Rt. Rev. E. C. Hatcher. Nashville, TN, AME Sunday School Union, n.d.

Combined Minutes of the Conferences of the Fifth Episcopal District, African Methodist Episcopal Church, 1956. (Bishop) Frederick D. Jordan, Presiding Bishop. Nashville, TN, AME Sunday School Union, n.d.

Minutes of the Conferences of the Thirteenth Episcopal District (African Methodist Episcopal Church), 1956, Rt. Rev. Joseph Gomez. Nashville, AME Sunday School Union, n.d.

Combined Minutes of the Annual Conferences of the First Episcopal District, African Methodist Episcopal Church, 1957–1958, Edited by Rev. Edward L. Kinzer. District Secretary to Bishop George W. Baber. Nashville, TN, AME Sunday School Union, n.d.

Combined Minutes of the 1957 Conferences of the Ninth Episcopal District (African Methodist Episcopal Church), Bishop Carey A. Gibbs. Nashville, TN, AME Sunday School Union, n.d.

West Tennessee Annual Conference, African Methodist Episcopal Church, Official Journal, 1959, 1960, 1961, Rt. Rev. E. L. Hickman. n.p., n.d.

Combined Minutes of the One Hundred Forty-Third and [One Hundred] Forty-Fourth Session[s] of the New York Annual Conference [of the] African Methodist Episcopal Church, 1965–1966. n.p., n.d.

Combined Minutes of the First Episcopal District, African Methodist Episcopal District, 1967. Bishop John D. Bright, Sr. n.p., n.d.

Combined Minutes of the 1968 Annual Conference, First Episcopal District, African Methodist Episcopal Church, Bishop John D. Bright, Sr. n.p., n.d.

Women's Parent Mite Missionary Society Minutes

Report of the Board of Managers of the Woman's Mite Missionary Society of the African Methodist Episcopal Church, Philadelphia, From November 1888 to November 1892. Philadelphia, PA, Pastoral Printing House, 1892.

Minutes of the Sixth Annual Convention of the Women's Mite Missionary Society, Pittsburg(h) Conference Branch of the African Methodist Episcopal Church held at AME Church, Brownsville, PA. July 3–6, 1902. n.p., Publishing Committee: Lilian S. Dorkins, M. Levada Carter, and Libbie Skinner, 1902.

Journal of Proceedings of the Third Quadrennial Convention of the Women's Parent Mite Missionary Society of the African Methodist Episcopal Church held in Wylie Avenue AME Church, Pittsburgh, PA., November 5–9, 1903. n.p., M. Levada Carter, Libbie Skinner, and Emma Chambers., 1903.

Minutes of the Fourth Annual Convention of the Woman's Mite Missionary Society, Pittsburgh Conference Branch of the African Methodist Episcopal Church, Allegheny City, PA, held July 5–9, 1904. n.p., Publishing Committee: Lilian S. Dorkins, Libby Skinner, and M. Levada Carter, 1904.

Mrs. I. M. B. Yeocum (compiler), *The Fourth Quadrennial Convention of the Women's Parent Mite Missionary Society of the African Methodist Episcopal Church*, 1907. Philadelphia, PA, AME Book Concern, 1907.

Minutes of the Twelfth Annual Meeting of the Women's Mite Missionary Society, Pittsburg(h) Conference Branch, African Methodist Episcopal Church held at AME Church, New Castle, PA, July 2–July 6, 1908. Pittsburg[h], PA, Nelson J. Miles, Printer, 1908.

The Biennial Convention and Thirty-Fifth Anniversary of the Women's Parent Mite Missionary Society, St. John AME Church, Cleveland, Ohio, November 11–14, 1909. Philadelphia, PA, AME Book Concern, 1909.

Minutes of the Fifteenth Annual Meeting of the Women's Mite Missionary Society, Pittsburgh Conference Branch, African Methodist Episcopal Church held at St. James AME Church, E.E., Pittsburgh, PA, July 13–16, 1911. n.p., Publishing Committee: Fern Hurrington. M. Levada Carter Norris, and Isetta Jefferson, 1911.

Minutes of the 20th Annual Convention (of the) Women's Mite Missionary Society, Pittsburgh Conference Branch, African Methodist Episcopal Church held in Bethel AME Church, Franklin, Pa., July 5–8, 1917. n.p., 1917.

Minutes of the 22nd Annual Convention [of the] Women's Mite Missionary Society, Pittsburgh Conference Branch, African Methodist Episcopal Church held in the Bethel AME Church, Williamsport, Pa., July 4–7, 1918. n.p., 1918.

Dovie King Clarke, Sadie J. Anderson, and Mattie J. Ford (compilers), *The Seventh Quadrennial Convention of the Women's Parent Mite Missionary*

Society of the African Methodist Episcopal Church, 1919. Jacksonville, FL, Edward Waters Press, 1919.

Minutes of the Twenty-Eighth Annual Convention of the Women's Mite Missionary Society, Pittsburgh Conference Branch [of the] African Methodist Episcopal Church held at Park Place AME Church, Homestead, PA., July 10–13, 1924. Franklin, PA, The News Herald Press, 1924.

Doctrine and Discipline

Doctrine and Discipline of the African Methodist Episcopal Church, First Edition, Philadelphia, Published by Richard Allen and Jacob Tapsico for the African Methodist Connection in the United States, 1817.

Doctrine and Discipline of the African Methodist Episcopal Church, 2004–2008. Nashville, TN, AME Sunday School Union, 2005.

SECONDARY SOURCES

Books

Adams, Dolly D. *She in the Glass House: A Handbook for African Methodist Church Ministers' Wives and Widows.* Nashville, TN, AME Sunday School Union, 1990.

Adams, E. A. Sr. (compiler and ed.). *Year Book and Historical Guide to the African Methodist Episcopal Church.* Columbia, SC, Bureau of Research and History, 1955.

Adams, John H. (compiler). *Toward a More Effective AME Church: A Summary of the Results of the Committee on Restructure (COR-AMEC):* A Final Report to the General Board and the 1984 General Conference. n. p., 1984.

(compiler). *What AMEs Believe.* Developed for the African Methodist Episcopal Church by the Seventh Episcopal District. Nashville, TN, AME Sunday School Union, 2000.

Allen, Richard. *The Life Experience and Gospel Labors of the Rt. Rev. Richard Allen.* Nashville, TN, AME Sunday School Union, Reprint 1990.

Andrews, Dale P. *Practical Theology and African American Folk Religion.* Louisville, KY, Westminster John Knox Press, 2002.

Angell, Stephen W. *Bishop Henry McNeal Turner and African American Religion in the South.* Knoxville, University of Tennessee Press, 1992.

Bailey, Julius H. *Around the Family Altar: Domesticity in the African Methodist Episcopal Church, 1865–1900.* Gainesville, University Press of Florida, 2005.

Baldwin, Lewis V. *"Invisible" Strands of African Methodism: A History of the African Union Methodist Protestant and Union American Methodist*

Episcopal Churches, 1805-1980. Metuchen, NJ, Scarecrow Press/American Theological Library Association, 1983.

Bates, Daisy. *The Long Shadow of Little Rock: A Memoir*. New York, David McKay Company, 1962.

Berry, Leonidas H. *I Wouldn't Take Nothin' for My Journey: Two Centuries of an Afro-American Minister's Family*. Chicago, Johnson, 1981.

Berry, L. L. *A Century of Missions of the African Methodist Episcopal Church, 1840–1940*. New York, Gutenberg Printing Co., 1940.

Braithwaite, J. Roland (ed.). *Richard Allen: A Collection of Hymns and Spiritual Songs*. Nashville, TN, AME Sunday School Union, 1987.

Brinkley, Douglas. *Rosa Parks*. New York, A. Lipper/Viking, 2000.

Burkett, Randall. *Garveyism as a Religious Movement: The Institutionalization of a Black Civil Religion*. Metuchen, NJ, Scarecrow Press/American Theological Library Association, 1978.

Butt, Israel L. *History of African Methodism in Virginia or Four Decades in the Old Dominion*. Hampton, VA, Hampton Institute Press, 1908.

Campbell, James T. *Songs of Zion: The African Methodist Episcopal Church in the United States and South Africa*. New York, Oxford University Press, 1998.

Coan, Josephus R. *Daniel Alexander Payne: Christian Educator*. Philadelphia, PA, AME Book Concern, 1935.

Collier-Thomas, Bettye. *Jesus, Jobs, and Justice: African American Women and Religion*. New York, Alfred Knopf, 2010.

Cone, Cecil W. *Identity Crisis in Black Theology* (Revised Edition). Nashville, TN, AME Sunday School Union, 1975, 2003.

Cone, James H. *Black Theology and Black Power*. Maryknoll, NY, Orbis Books, 1969.

My Soul Looks Back. Nashville, TN, Abingdon Press, 1982.

Coppin, Levi J. *In Memoriam: Catherine S. Campbell Beckett*. n.p., 1888.

Unwritten History. Philadelphia, PA, AME Book Concern, 1919.

Cummings, Frank C. *To Whom Much Is Given, Much Is Required*. Nashville, TN, AME Sunday School Union, 2008.

Cummings, Frank C., John H. Dixon, Thelma Singleton-Scott, and Patricia Green(eds.). *The First Episcopal District's Historical Review of 200 Years of African Methodism*. Philadelphia, PA, First Episcopal District, African Methodist Episcopal Church, 1987.

Davis, John A. (ed.). *The American Negro Writer and His Roots, Selected Papers from the First Conference of Negro Writers, March 1959*. New York, American Society of African Culture, 1960.

Dickerson, Dennis C. *African American Preachers and Politics: The Careys of Chicago*. Jackson, University of Mississippi, 2010.

African Methodism and Its Wesleyan Heritage: Reflections on AME Church History. Nashville, TN, AME Sunday School Union, 2009.

A Liberated Past: Explorations in AME Church History. Nashville, TN, AME
Sunday School Union, 2003.
Militant Mediator: Whitney M. Young, Jr. Lexington, University Press of
Kentucky, 1998.
Out of the Crucible: Black Steelworkers in Western Pennsylvania. Albany,
State University of New York Press, 1986.
Religion, Race, and Region: Research Notes on AME Church History. Nash-
ville, TN, AME Sunday School Union, 1995.
Du Bois, W. E. B. *The Souls of Black Folk*. New York, New American Library,
1903, 1969.
Duncan, Sara J. *Progressive Missions in the South and Addresses*. Atlanta, GA,
Franklin Printing and Publishing Company, 1906.
Du Bois, Shirley Graham. *His Day is Marching On: A Memoir of W. E. B. Du
Bois*. Philadelphia, PA, J. B. Lippincott Company, 1971.
Earley, Charity Adams. *One Woman's Army: A Black Officer Remembers the
WAC*. College Station, Texas A & M University Press, 1989.
Early, Sarah J. W. *Life and Labors of Rev. Jordan W. Early: One of the Pioneers
of African Methodism in the West and South*. Nashville, TN, AME Sunday
School Union, 1894.
Embry, James C. *The Digest of Christian Theology*. Philadelphia, PA, AME
Book Concern, 1890.
Flake, Floyd H., and Donna Marie Williams. *The Way of the Bootstrapper:
Nine Action Steps for Achieving Your Dreams*. New York, Harper San
Francisco, 1999.
Foner, Eric. *Freedom's Lawmakers: A Directory of Black Office Holders During
Reconstruction*. New York, Oxford University, 1993.
Frazier, Herb, Bernard E. Powers, Jr., and Majory Wentworth. *We Are
Charleston: Tragedy and Triumph at Mother Emanuel*. Nashville, TN,
W Publishing Group, 2016.
Gaines, Wesley J. *African Methodism in the South: Twenty-Five Years of
Freedom*. Atlanta, GA, Franklin Publishing House, 1890.
Gaston, A. G. *Green Power: The Successful Way of A. G. Gaston*. Troy, AL,
Troy State University Press, 1968.
George, Carol V. R. *Segregated Sabbaths: Richard Allen and the Emergence of
Independent Black Churches, 1760-1840*. New York, Oxford University
Press, 1972.
Glaude, Eddie S., Jr. *Exodus: Religion, Race, and Nation in Early Nineteenth-
Century Black America*. Chicago, University of Chicago Press, 2000.
Gona, Ophelia DeLaine. *Dawn of Desegregation: J. A. Delaine and Briggs
v. Elliott*. Columbia, University of South Carolina Press, 2011.
Gomez, Joseph. *Polity of the AME Church*. Nashville, TN, Division of Chris-
tian Education of the African Methodist Episcopal Church, 1971.

Gregg, Howard D. *The AME Church and the Current Negro Revolt*. AME Sunday School Union, n.d.

History of the African Methodist Episcopal Church. Nashville, TN, AME Sunday School Union, 1976.

Richard Allen and Present-Day Social Problems. Nashville, TN, AME Sunday School Union, c. 1959/1960.

Gregg, John A. *Of Men and Arms*. Nashville, TN, AME Sunday School Union, 1945.

Gregg, Robert. *Sparks from the Anvil of Oppression: Philadelphia's African Methodists and Southern Migrants, 1890–1940*. Philadelphia, PA, Temple University Press, 1993.

Handy, James A. *Scraps of African Methodist Episcopal History*. Philadelphia, PA, AME Book Concern, n.d.

Heard, William H. *The Bright Side of African Life*. Philadelphia, PA, AME Publishing House, 1898.

From Slavery to the Bishopric in the AME Church: An Autobiography. n.p., 1924, 1937.

Hempton, David N. *Methodism: Empire of the Spirit*. New Haven, CT, Yale University Press, 2006.

Hildebrand, Reginald F. *The Times Were Strange and Stirring: Methodist Preachers and the Crisis of Emancipation*. Durham, NC, Duke University Press, 1995.

Hill, Charles Leander. *He Followed His Star: A Pen Portrait of the Life, Personality and Chief Exploits of William Alfred Fountain, Sr*. Nashville, TN, AME Sunday School Union, 1987.

Hill, Kenneth H. *Charles Spencer Smith: A Portrait: Sable Son of God*. Nashville, TN, AME Sunday School Union, 1993.

Horne, Gerald. *Race Woman: The Lives of Shirley Graham Du Bois*. New York, New York University Press, 2002.

Jackson, Hattie E. *65 Dark Days in '68: Reflections: Memphis Sanitation Strike*. Southhaven, MS, The King's Press, 2004.

Jefferson, Annetta L. Gomez. *In Darkness with God: The Life of Joseph Gomez, A Bishop in the African Methodist Episcopal Church*. Kent, OH, Kent State University Press, 1998.

Jenifer, John T. *Centennial Retrospect History of the African Methodist Episcopal Church*. Nashville, TN, AME Sunday School Union, 1916.

Johns, Jeanette T. *The Upward Journey: A Centenarian's Chronicle: Personal Stories of Bishop Decatur Ward Nichols, Revered Clergyman of the African Methodist Episcopal Church*. Nashville, TN, AME Sunday School Union, 2002.

Johnson, Walton R. *Worship and Freedom: A Black American Church in Zambia*. New York, Africana Company, 1977.

Jordan, Artishia W. *The African Methodist Episcopal Church in Africa*. n.p., n.d.

Jordan, Vernon E. Jr., and Annette Gordon-Reed, *Vernon Can Read: A Memoir*. New York, Public Affairs, 2001.

Kealing, Hightower T. *History of African Methodism in Texas*. Waco, TX, C. F. Blanks, 1885.

Killens, John O. *The Trial Record of Denmark Vesey*. Boston, MA, Beacon Press, 1970.

Kinchion, L. Brackett. *The Life and Works of Arthur Smith Jackson*. Nashville, TN, AME Sunday School Union, 1944.

Lampton, Edward W. *Digest of Rulings and Decisions of the Bishops of the African Methodist Episcopal Church From 1847 to 1907*. Washington DC, Record Publishing Company, 1907.

Lee, Jarena. *The Religious Experiences and Journal of Mrs. Jarena Lee*. Nashville, TN, AME Sunday School Union, Reprint 1991.

Little, Lawrence S. *Disciples of Liberty: The African Methodist Episcopal Church in the Age of Imperialism, 1884-1916*. Knoxville, University of Tennessee Press, 2000.

Long, Charles S. *History of the AME Church in Florida*. Philadelphia, PA, AME Book Concern, 1939.

Maddox, Randy L. *Responsible Grace: John Wesley's Practical Theology*. Nashville, TN, Kingswood Books, 1994.

Mahlangu-Ngcobo, Mankekolo. *The Preaching of Bishop John Bryant*. Baltimore, MD, Victory Press, 1992.

To God be the Glory: A Celebration of the Life of Bishop Frederick Calhoun James. Baltimore, MD, Gateway Press. 1996.

Middleton, Merlisse Ross. *Reflections on the Man: John Middleton*. Nashville, TN, AME Sunday School Union, n.d.

Miller, A. G. *Elevating the Race: Theophilus G. Steward, Black Theology, and the Making of an African American Civil Society, 1865-1924*. Knoxville, University of Tennessee Press, 2003.

Mixon, W. H. *History of the African Methodist Episcopal Church in Alabama with Biographical Sketches*. Nashville, TN, AME Church Sunday School Union, 1902.

Mkwanazi, Clement N. *The History of the African Methodist Episcopal Church in Zimbabwe*. n.p., 1992.

The History and Expansion of the African Methodist Episcopal Church in Central Africa. n.p., n.d.

Mokone, J. M. *The Early Life of Our Founder (M. M. Mokone)*. South Africa. n.p., 1935.

Newman, Richard S. *Freedom's Prophet: Bishop Richard Allen, The AME Church, and the Black Founding Fathers*. New York, New York University Press, 2008.

Payne, Daniel A. *Bishop Payne's Address Before the College Aid Society*. Xenia, OH, Torchlight Company, 1868.

History of the African Methodist Episcopal Church. Nashville, TN, AME
   Sunday School Union, 1891.
Recollections of Seventy Years. New York, Arno Press and the *New York
   Times,* 1888, 1969.
A Treatise on Domestic Education. Cincinnati, OH, Cranston & Stowe, 1889.
Primm, Howard T. *Footprints of Service: Paths Made by Howard Thomas
   Primm as Seen and Witnessed by Others.* Nashville, TN, AME Sunday
   School Union, n.d.
Reid, Frank M., III. *Up From Slavery: A Wake Up Call for the African
   Methodist Episcopal Church.* n.p., Frank M. Reid Ministries, 2004.
Reid, Robert H., Jr. *Irony of Afro-American History: An Overview of AME
   History and Related Developments.* Nashville, TN, AME Sunday School
   Union, 1984.
Ridgel, Alfred Lee. *Africa and African Methodism.* Atlanta, GA, Franklin
   Printing and Publishing Company, 1896.
Rivers, Larry E. and Canter Brown, Jr. *Laborers in the Vineyard of the Lord:
   The Beginnings of the AME Church In Florida, 1865-1895.* Gainesville,
   University Press of Florida, 2001.
Seraile, William. *Fire in His Heart: Bishop Benjamin Tucker Tanner and the
   AME Church.* Knoxville, University of Tennessee Press, 1998.
Singleton, George A. *The Autobiography of George A. Singleton.* Boston, MA,
   Forum Publishing Company, 1964.
   *The Romance of African Methodism: A Study of the African Methodist
   Episcopal Church.* Boston, MA, Exposition Press, 1952.
Smith, Amanda. *An Autobiography: The Story of the Lord's Dealings with Mrs.
   Amanda Smith: The Colored Evangelist.* New York, Oxford University
   Press, Publishers, 1893, 1988.
Smith, Charles S. (compiler). *Dedicatory Services at the Publishing House of the
   AME Sunday School Union.* Nashville, TN, AME Sunday School Union,
   1894.
Smith, David. *Biography of David Smith of the AME Church.* Xenia, OH, Xenia
   Gazette Office, 1881.
Smith, Warren T. *Harry Hosier: Circuit Rider.* Nashville, TN, Upper Room, 1981.
Talbot, Frederick H. *Forward in Faith: Bishop Frederick Calhoun James: The
   Story: A Faithful Bishop's Witness & Work.* n.p., 2011.
   God's Fearless Prophet: The Story of Richard Allen. Nashville, TN, AME
   Sunday School Union, 2007.
Tanner, Benjamin T. *Dispensations in the History of the Church and Interreg-
   nums, Vol. I.* n.p., 1898.
Townsend, V. M. *Fifty-Four Years of African Methodism: Reflections of a
   Presiding Elder on the Law and Doctrine of the African Methodist Epis-
   copal Church.* New York, Exposition Press, 1953.

Tudas, Jonathan. *The Sword of Truth: Or a Reply to Facts Relative to the Government of the African Methodist Episcopal Church Called Bethel.* Philadelphia, PA, 1823.

Walker, Clarence E. *A Rock in a Weary Land: The African Methodist Episcopal Church during the Civil War and Reconstruction.* Baton Rouge, Louisiana State University Press, 1982.

Walker, D. Ormonde. *The Struggle for Control of Wilberforce University: An Address Delivered Before the St. James Literary Forum, Cleveland, Ohio, April 27, 1947.* n.p., 1947.

Wesley, Charles H. *Negro Labor in the United States, 1850–1925: A Study in American Economic History.* New York, Vanguard Press, 1927.

   Richard Allen: Apostle of Freedom. Washington DC, Associated Publishers, Inc., 1935.

White, Andrew. *Know Your Church Manual: An Introductory Study of the Local Church for Officers and Members.* Nashville ,TN, AME, Sunday School Union, 1965.

   Lest We Forget: A Brief Review of the Bitter Struggles and Heartaches Suffered by the AME Sunday School Union. Nashville, TN, AME Sunday School Union, n.d.

Whitehead, Ruth H., and Roberta Robertson (eds.). *The Life of Boston King.* Nimbus Publishing & Nova Scotia Museum, 2003.

Whitlock, F. LeMoyne. *The Genius of African Methodism.* n.p., 1972.

Wigger, John H. *American Saint: Francis Asbury and the Methodists* New York, Oxford University Press, 2012.

Wright, Richard R., Jr. *The Bishops of the African Methodist Episcopal Church.* Nashville, TN, AME Sunday School Union, 1963.

   Centennial Encyclopedia of the African Methodist Episcopal Church. Philadelphia, PA, AME Book Concern, 1916.

   Eighty-Seven Years Behind the Black Curtain. Philadelphia, PA, Rare Book Company, 1965.

   Encyclopedia of African Methodism. Philadelphia, PA, AME Book Concern, 1947.

   Who's Who in the General Conference 1924. Philadelphia, PA, AME Book Concern, 1924.

Articles

Angell, Stephen W. "The Controversy over Women's Ministry in the African Methodist Episcopal Church during the 1880s: The Case of Sarah Ann Hughes," in Judith Weisenfeld and Richard Newman (eds.), *This Far by Faith: Readings in African American Women's Religious Biography.* New York, Routledge, 1996.

"'The Shadows of the Evening Stretched Out': Richard Robinson and the Shaping of African Methodist Identity, 1823–1862," *Journal of Africana Religions*, Vol. 3, No. 3, (2015), 227–250.

Cone, James H. "God Our Father, Christ Our Redeemer, Man Our Brother: A Theological Interpretation of the AME Church," *AME Church Review*, Vol. 106, No. 341, January–March 1991, 25–33.

Dickerson-Cousin, Christina M. "'I Call You Cousins': Kinship, Religion, and Black-Indian Relations in Nineteenth Century Michigan." *Ethnohistory*, Vol. 61, No. 1, Winter 2014, 79–98.

"Triangular Integration in a Black Denomination: James Sisson, African Methodism, and the Indian Mission Conference," *Methodist History*, Vol. 53, No. 3, April 2015, 133–151.

Dickerson, Dennis C. "Liberation, Wesleyan Theology, and Early African Methodism, 176–1840," *Wesley and Methodist Studies*, (2011), Vol. 3, 109–120.

Dodson, Jualynne E. "Encounters in the African Atlantic World: The African Methodist Episcopal Church in Cuba," in Lisa Brock and Digna Castaneda Fuertes (eds.), *Between Race and Empire: African Americans and Cubans Before the Cuban Revolution*. Philadelphia, PA, Temple University Press, 1998, 85–103.

Fulop, Timothy E. "'The Future Golden Day of the Race': Millennialism and Black Americans in the Nadir, 1877–1901," *Harvard Theological Review*, Vol. 84, No. 1, January 1991, 75–99.

George, Carol V. R. "Widening the Circle: The Black Church and the Abolitionist Crusade," in Timothy E. Fulop and Albert J. Raboteau (eds.), *African American Religion: Interpretive Essays in History and Culture*. New York, Routledge, 1996., 157–173.

Grant, Jacquelyn. "Black Theology and the Black Woman," in Gayraud S. Wilmore and James H. Cone (eds.), *Black Theology: A Documentary History, 1966–1979*. Maryknoll, New York, Orbis Books, 1979, 418–433.

Hill, Charles Leander. "The Episcopacy-Its Function, Its Authority, Its Limitations," in E. A. Adams (compiler), *Year Book and Historical Guide to the African Methodist Episcopal Church*. Columbia, South Carolina, Bureau of Research and History, 1955, 31–43.

Knight, Frederick. "The Many Names for Jarena Lee," *Pennsylvania Magazine of History and Biography*, Vol. 141, No. 1, January 2017, 59–68.

Lloyd, Gareth. "Scipio Africanus: The First Black Methodist," *Wesley and Methodist Studies*, Vol. 3 (2011), 87–95.

Maffly-Kipp, Laurie. "Denominationalism and the Black Church," in Robert Bruce Mullin and Russell E. Richey (eds.), *Reimagining Denominationalism: Interpretive Essays*. New York, Oxford University Press, 1994, 58–73.

Markwei, Matei. "The Rev. Daniel Coker of Sierra Leone," *Sierra Leone Bulletin of Religion*, Vol. 7, No. 2, 1965, 43–47.

Miller, Edward A., Jr. "Garland H. White: Black Army Chaplain," *Civil War History*, Vol. 43, No. 3., September 1997, 201–218.

Nash, Gary B. "New Light on Richard Allen: The Early Years of Freedom," *William and Mary Quarterly*, Third Series, Vol. 46, No. 2, April 1989, 332–340.

Phillips, Christopher N., "Versifying African Methodism: Or, What Did Early African-American Hymnbooks Do?," *The Papers of the Bibliographical Society of America*, Vol. 107, No. 3 September 2013, 325–333.

Powers, Bernard E. Jr. "'I Go to Set the Captives Free': The Activism of Richard Harvey Cain, Nationalist Churchman and Reconstruction-Era Leader," in Randy Finley and Thomas A. DeBlack (eds.), *The Southern Elite and Social Change*. Fayetteville, University of Arkansas Press, 2002, 34–52, 186–189.

Raboteau, Albert J. "Richard Allen and the African Church Movement," in Leon Litwack and August Meier (eds.), *Black Leaders of the Nineteenth Century*. Urbana, University of Illinois Press, 1988, 1–18, 324–325.

Redkey, Edwin S. "Bishop Turner's African Dream," *Journal of American History*, Vol. 54, No. 2, September 1967, 271–329.

"Black Chaplains in the Union Army," *Civil War History*, Vol. 33, No. 3, December 1987, 331–350.

Scott, Edward A. "Bardic Memory and Witness in the Poetry of Samuel Allen," in Joanne V. Gabbin (ed.), *The Furious Flowering of African American Poetry*. Charlottesville, University of Virginia Press, 1999.

Stokes, Arthur P. "Charles Leander Hill: Profile of a Scholar." An Address Delivered before a Symposium of the Charles Leander Hill Day Memorial, May 9, 1984. n.p., 1984.

Index

Pennington, James W.C., 97
Pennsylvania Abolition Society, 46
Pennsylvania Supreme Court, 39
Perkins, Cato, 20
Philadelphia Annual Conference, 72, 91, 95, 111
Pilmore, Joseph, 18
Pinckney, Clementa, 548–556
Pinn, Anthony B., 553–555
Plessy v. *Ferguson*, 180, 374
political awakening in Africa, 424–437
practical Christianity, 282
practical divinity, 8, 64
practical theology, 3
Practical Theology for Black Churches (Andrews), 8–9
Primm, Howard Thomas, 332, 344–345, 431, 463
Prioleau, George, 214
protest rights, 187

Quinn, William Paul, 50, 67, 84–87, 103
Quinn Chapel AME Church, 276

R. R. Wright Theological Seminary, 433–434, 495, 497
racial accommodationism, 182–189
racial discrimination/inequality, 49–51, 81, 187, 248, 305, 395–396
racial identity, 158
racial ideology of African Americans, 188–189
racial segregation in church, 31
radio broadcast sermons, 280
Randall, Europa, 10–11
Randolph, A. Philip, 327–328, 347–349, 417–418
Randolph, J.W., 148–149
Ransom, Emma, 235, 269
Ransom, Reverdy C., 184–186, 188, 226–227, 241–242, 253, 256–257, 269–270, 308, 545
rational orthodox theology, 173
Ray, Charles B., 60–64
Reconstruction era, 7, 124–135
Reconstruction Finance Corporation (RFC), 312
Reddie, Anthony G., 34
Reed, Harrison, 134–135
Reformed Union Methodist Episcopal Church, 150
Reid, Frank Madison, 337
Reid, Frank Madison, III, 537–538, 548
Reid, Frank Madison, Jr., 517

religious music mediums, 280
Revels, Hiram, 132
Revels, Willis R., 102
Rhenish missionaries, 483–484
Richard Allen: Apostle of Freedom (Wesley), 305–362
Ridgel, Alfred L., 14–15
Roberts, Turner W., 103–104
Robinson, Catherine L., 145
Robinson, James G., 277, 286, 312, 317–318, 324
Robinson, Richard, 70–71
Roe v. *Wade* (1973), 521–522
Roman, Charles V., 237–238
Roosevelt, Eleanor, 343–344
Roosevelt, Franklin D., 312–313, 317–326, 333–334, 342–343, 345–346, 385
Roosevelt, Theodore, 186
Ross, Mamie Robinson Fletcher, 234–235
Rue, George A., 121–122, 126–127, 131
Rush, Christopher, 45–46
Rustin, Baynard, 342

same-sex marriage, 466, 522–523
sanitation workers strike, 413–415
school segregation, 374–375
Scipio Africanus, 17
Scott, Edward A., 449
Sealy, Rueben A., 213, 223
Second Confiscation Act, 112
segregation in education, 374–375
segregation in South Africa, 189–190
self-determinism, 66, 73
Senatle, Harold B., 436, 493–496
Service and Development Agency (SADA), 501, 504–506
sex/sexuality issues, 521–534
sexual harassment issues, 530–533
Shavers, Daniel, 103
Sheppard, Peter, 129
Shorter, James A., 128, 141
Shorter, Julia Ann, 80
Shortridge, W.E., 408
Sierra Leone, 198–200
Simmons, Sallie G., 233
Sims, David Henry, 325, 334–349, 363–364, 470–471
Singleton, George A., 3, 239, 426, 489
Singleton, Richard H., 253–254
Sisson, James F.A., 150–151

Lightning Source UK Ltd.
Milton Keynes UK
UKHW022114260920
370595UK00005B/15